BUSINESS ECONOMICS

N. Gregory Mankiw, Mark P. Taylor
and Andrew Ashwin

CENGAGE
Learning

Australia • Brazil • Japan • Korea • Mexico • Singapore • Spain • United Kingdom • United States

CENGAGE
Learning®

Business Economics, 1st Edition
N. Gregory Mankiw, Mark P. Taylor,
and Andrew Ashwin

Publishing Director: Linden Harris

Publisher: Andrew Ashwin

Editorial Assistant: Lauren Darby

Production Editor: Alison Cooke

Production Controller: Eyvett Davis

Marketing Manager: Anne Renton

Typesetter: MPS Limited

Cover design: Adam Renvoize

For product information and technology assistance,
please contact **emea.info@cengage.com.**

For permission to use material from this text or product,
and for permission queries.
email **emea.permissions@cengage.com.**

This work is adapted from *Economics*, 2nd edition by N. Gregory Mankiw and Mark P. Taylor published by Cengage Learning EMEA © 2011.

British Library Cataloguing-in-Publication Data
A catalogue record for this book is available from the British Library.

ISBN: 978-1-4080-6981-3

Cengage Learning EMEA
Cheriton House, North Way, Andover, Hampshire, SP10 5BE
United Kingdom

Cengage Learning products are represented in Canada by Nelson Education Ltd.

For your lifelong learning solutions, visit **www.cengage.co.uk**

Purchase your next print book, e-book or e-chapter at
www.cengagebrain.com

Printed in China by RR Donnelley
1 2 3 4 5 6 7 8 9 10 – 15 14 13

BRIEF CONTENTS

CONTENTS

PART 1

THE ECONOMIC AND BUSINESS ENVIRONMENT – SETTING THE SCENE   1

PART 2

MICROECONOMICS – THE MARKET SYSTEM   53

PART 3

MICROECONOMICS – THE LIMITATIONS OF MARKETS 119

PART 4

MICROECONOMICS – THE ECONOMICS OF FIRMS IN MARKETS 177

MICROECONOMICS – FACTOR MARKETS   331

INTRODUCTION TO MACROECONOMICS   385

GLOBAL BUSINESS AND ECONOMICS 517

N. GREGORY MANKIW is Professor of Economics at Harvard University. As a student, he studied economics at Princeton University and the Massachusetts Institute of Technology. As a teacher he has taught macroeconomics, microeconomics, statistics and principles of economics. Professor Mankiw is a prolific writer and a regular participant in academic and policy debates. In addition to his teaching, research and writing, Professor Mankiw has been a research associate of the National Bureau of Economic Research, an advisor to the Federal Reserve Bank of Boston and the Congressional Budget Office. From 2003 to 2005, he served as chairman of the US President's Council of Economic Advisors. Professor Mankiw lives in Wellesley, Massachusetts, with his wife Deborah, their three children and their border terrier Tobin.

MARK P. TAYLOR is Dean of Warwick Business School at the University of Warwick and Professor of International Finance. He obtained his first degree in philosophy, politics and economics from Oxford University and his master's degree in economics from London University, from where he also holds a doctorate in economics and international finance. Professor Taylor has taught economics and finance at various universities (including Oxford, Warwick and New York) and at various levels (including principles courses, advanced undergraduate and advanced postgraduate courses). He has also worked as a senior economist at the International Monetary Fund and at the Bank of England and, before becoming Dean of Warwick Business School, was a managing director at Black-Rock, the world's largest financial asset manager, where he worked on international asset allocation based on macroeconomic analysis. His research has been extensively published in scholarly journals and he is today one of the most highly cited economists in the world. Professor Taylor lives with his family in a 15th century farmhouse near Stratford upon Avon, Warwickshire, where he collects clocks and keeps bees.

ANDREW ASHWIN has over 20 years experience as a teacher of economics. He has an MBA and is currently researching for a Ph.D. investigating assessment and the notion of threshold concepts in economics. Andrew is an experienced author writing a number of texts for students at different levels, journal publications related to his Ph.D. research and has a recently published a text on the business environment for undergraduates with Dr Phil Kelly. Andrew was Chair of Examiners for a major awarding body in England and Wales for business and economics and is Editor of the Economics, Business and Enterprise Association (EBEA) journal. Andrew also acts as a consultant to the qualifications regulator in England and Wales and is pursuing Chartered Assessor status with the Chartered Institute of Educational Assessors. Andrew lives in Rutland with his wife Sue and their twin sons Alex and Johnny.

How much of business is economics and how much of economics is business? This is a difficult question to answer but perhaps what is at the heart of both is decision-making. This book is about decision making. Alfred Marshall, the great 19th-century British economist, in his textbook, *Principles of Economics* published in 1890 wrote: 'Economics is a study of mankind in the ordinary business of life.' For many people the ordinary business of life is interwoven with relationships with business. Every single day, billions of people around the world make decisions. When we make decisions we are being economist. A great proportion of these decisions are made by people in the context of their work which in turn is part of business. So Business and Economics are very closely linked. So wrote.

A study of economics in a business context will help you understand the world in which you live. There are many questions about businesses and the economy that might spark your curiosity. Why do airlines charge less for a return ticket if the traveller stays over a Saturday night? Why are movie businesses prepared to pay some actors extremely large sums to star in films whilst others struggle to even get a bit part? Why are living standards so meagre in many African countries? Why do some countries have high rates of inflation while others have stable prices? Why do businesses produce many products that are so similar – surely they succeed only in cannibalising their market? Why is it so important to have a better understanding of how consumers behave? Why have some European countries adopted a common currency? These are just a few of the questions that a course in Business Economics will help you answer.

The second reason to study Business Economics is that it will make you a more astute participant in the economy and in business. As you go about your life, you make many economic decisions. While you are a student, you decide how many years to stay in full-time education. When you have completed your degree you will have to decide on a career path and (which may be difficult despite being highly qualified) find a job. Once you take a job, you decide how much of your income to spend, how much to save and how to invest your savings. In your daily work you will have to make many decisions and respond to an ever-changing environment. One day you may find yourself running your own small business or a large firm, and you will decide what prices to charge for your products and what products to offer for sale. The insights developed in the coming chapters will give you a new perspective on how best to make these decisions.

A study of Business Economics will give you a better understanding of the potential and limits of economic policy and how such policy can influence business behaviour. In your business career you may find yourself asking various questions about economics. What are the burdens associated with alternative forms of taxation? What are the effects of free trade with other countries? To what extent do businesses have a responsibility to protect the environment? How does the government budget deficit affect the economy and thus your business?

A study of Business Economics will go some way towards helping you make more sense of the world, your place in it and how business is affected and behaves as a consequence.

FOR WHOM IS THIS BOOK WRITTEN?

The book has been written with the non-specialist economist in mind but who has to embark on a course of study in economics as part of a degree in Business. Your degree might be Business Economics, it might be Business Management or it might be Sports

Coaching and Management. An increasing number of degree courses will include some coverage of economic principles and this book is designed for just such courses. We have tried to put ourselves in the position of someone seeing economics for the first time and not necessarily looking forward to the prospect. Our goal has been to emphasize the material that *students* should and do find interesting about the study of the economy and business.

One result is that this book is briefer than many books used to introduce students to economics. Throughout this book we have tried to return to applications and policy questions as often as possible. All the chapters include case studies illustrating how the principles of economics are applied. In addition, 'In the News' boxes offer highlights from news events showing how economic ideas shed light on current issues facing business and society along with questions to help you apply your knowledge to new contexts – a vitally important part of learning.

HOW IS THIS BOOK ORGANIZED?

In deciding what topics to include in the book we started with the typical course structures at universities offering some sort of Business Economics modules as part of a degree programme. Some lecturers will choose to study topics is a slightly different order but our thinking was to try and present what we felt was a logical way of presenting an introduction to economics as it applies to a business context.

Introductory Material

Chapter 1, 'What is Business Economics', sets the scene by introducing students to the economists' view of the world through the 'Ten Principles of Economics' and business decision making. It previews some of the big ideas that recur throughout economics, such as opportunity cost, marginal decision making, the role of incentives, the gains from trade, and the efficiency of market allocations. Throughout the book, we refer regularly to the *Ten Principles of Economics* introduced in Chapter 1 to remind students that these ideas are the foundation for all economics. Chapter 2, 'Economics and Business Decision Making', explores decision making in more detail and includes a discussion about a crucial part of any business – recruiting and retaining customers. Chapter 3, 'The Business Environment', presents an overview of what we mean by business activity, how businesses transform inputs into outputs, the meaning of adding value and the internal and external environment within which businesses have to operate. We have looked at this environment through what is called the PESTLE framework – political, economic, social, technological and environmental.

Microeconomics – The Market System

The next two chapters introduce the market system through looking at the basic tools of supply and demand. Chapter 4, 'The Market Forces of Supply and Demand', develops the supply curve, the demand curve and the notion of market equilibrium. Chapter 5, 'Elasticity and Its Application', introduces the concept of elasticity and uses it to analyze events in three different markets.

Microeconomics – The Limitations of the Market System

Whilst many economies work based on market systems, they do, like most things, have their limitations. The next two chapters use the tools developed to look at Market Failure and The Consumer and Consumer Behaviour. You will learn that the costs and benefits of market activity are not always taken into account by decision makers and as a result the allocation of resources is less than efficient. In Chapter 7 you will learn that consumers (both businesses and individuals) do not always behave rationally and this can also lead to a less than efficient resource allocation. An understanding of consumer behaviour is an important aspect of business – after all, if we do not understand how the individuals and businesses we want to sell products to then businesses will suffer and be more likely to fail.

Microeconomics – The Economics of Firms in Markets

Part 4 includes 6 chapters devoted to understanding and analysing the actions and behaviour of firms. Chapter 8 looks at business goals and behaviour to get an understanding of why businesses exist, what they aim to do and how changes to business goals can lead to different behaviour. Chapter 9 builds on some of the concepts introduced in Chapter 8 and covers firms' costs and revenues in the short and long run. Chapter 10 presents a model of the firm in equilibrium and how production decisions are made in competitive conditions. Chapter 11 follows up on this by looking at pricing decisions and an introduction to business strategy before Chapter 12 covers the effect on business behaviour of operating in different market structures such as when a firm has monopoly power. This enables you to understand how degrees of market power influence the way firms behave. Chapter 13 follows on by looking at other forms of market structure including monopolistic competition (not to be confused with monopoly) and oligopoly – competition amongst the few.

Microeconomics – Factor Markets

We complete our look at microeconomics with Part 5 which looks at the markets for labour and capital, two key components of factor inputs for a business. Chapter 14, emphasizes the link between factor prices and marginal productivity and discusses the determinants of equilibrium wages. Chapter 15 introduces important concepts in the theory and practice of financial markets including the time value of money, how asset prices are determined and the supply and demand for loanable funds.

Macroeconomics

The next five chapters cover the macroeconomic environment in which firms have to operate. Our overall approach to teaching macroeconomics is to examine the economy in the long run (when prices are flexible) before examining the economy in the short run (when prices are sticky). We believe that this organization simplifies learning macroeconomics for several reasons. First, the classical assumption of price flexibility is more closely linked to the basic lessons of supply and demand, to which you have already been introduced. Secondly, the classical dichotomy allows the study of the long run to be broken up into several, easily digested pieces. Thirdly, because the business cycle represents a transitory deviation from the economy's long-run growth path, studying the transitory deviations is more natural after the long-run equilibrium is understood. Fourthly, the macroeconomic theory of the short run is more controversial among economists than the macroeconomic theory of the long run. For these reasons, most upper-level courses in macroeconomics now follow this long-run-before-short-run approach; our goal is to offer introductory students the same advantage. There would be nothing to stop lecturers who prefer to approach the short run first from so doing – the book is flexible enough to allow this approach to be adopted.

Chapter 16, introduces some basic macroeconomic concepts including a discussion of the meaning of gross domestic product and related statistics from the national income accounts, the measurement and use of the consumer price indices, real and nominal interest rates, trade and exchange rates. These concepts are developed in the next four chapters which look in more detail at aggregate demand and supply, employment and unemployment, inflation and price stability and macroeconomic policy.

Global Business and Economics

We complete our journey through Business Economics by looking at the impact of doing business globally. Increasingly firms are involved in global trade and having some understanding of emerging markets, different business cultures and the European Union and the single market provides a foundation for what will be likely to be further study as you progress through your degree.

LEARNING TOOLS

The purpose of this book is to help students learn the fundamental lessons of economics and to apply these lessons to a business context. Towards that end, we have used various learning tools that recur throughout the book.

- *Case Studies.* Economic theory is useful and interesting only if it can be applied to understanding actual events and policies. This book, therefore, contains numerous case studies that apply the theory that has just been developed in a business context.
- *'In the News' boxes.* One benefit that students gain from studying economics is a new perspective and greater understanding about news from around the world. To highlight this benefit, we have incorporated discussions of news events including excerpts from newspaper articles from around Europe, the Middle East, Africa and India. These articles, together with our brief introductions, show how basic economic theory can be applied and raise important questions for discussion in business. To help further develop application skills we have included some questions at the end which can either be used as practice for self-study or as the basis for seminar or tutorial discussion.
- *'FYI' Boxes.* These boxes provide additional material 'for your information'. Some of them offer a glimpse into the history of economic thought. Others clarify technical issues. Still others discuss supplementary topics that instructors might choose either to discuss or skip in their lectures but which students should find useful in supplementing their knowledge and understanding.
- *Definitions of key concepts.* When key concepts are introduced in the chapter, they are presented in **bold** typeface. In addition, their definitions are placed in the margins. This treatment should aid students in learning and reviewing the material.
- *Pitfall Preventions.* The authors have used their collective teaching wisdom to outline areas where students make frequent mistakes and which can be a cause of confusion. The Pitfall Prevention boxes alert students to the potential for these mistakes.
- *Jeopardy Problems.* These are problems designed to help you think as an economist. You will be given end- points or solutions and you have to think through the different ways in which the solutions or end-point given might have been arrived at using your knowledge of economics and business.
- *What if...?* Questions designed to get you thinking about different scenarios in business and economics.

- *Quick quizzes.* After most major sections, students are offered a 'quick quiz' to check their comprehension of what they have just learned. If students cannot readily answer these quizzes, they should stop and reread material before continuing.
- *Chapter summaries.* Each chapter ends with a brief summary that reminds you of the most important lessons that you have just learned. Later in your study it offers an efficient way to revise for exams.
- *List of key concepts.* A list of key concepts at the end of each chapter offers you a way to test your understanding of the new terms that have been introduced.
  Page references are included so that you can review the terms you do not understand. All key terms can also be found in the glossary at the end of the book.
- *Questions for review.* At the end of each chapter are questions for review that over the chapter's primary lessons. You can use these questions to check your comprehension and to prepare for exams.
- *Problems and applications.* Each chapter also contains a variety of problems and applications that ask you to apply the material you have learned. Some instructors may use these questions for homework assignments. Others may use them as a starting point for classroom discussions.

WALK THROUGH TOUR

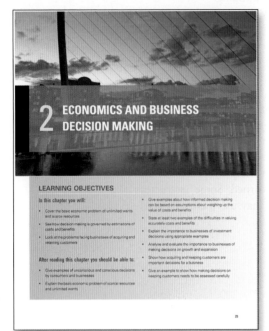

Learning Objectives and 'After reading this chapter you should be able to' Bullet points appear at the start of each chapter in order to highlight to the student chapter's key ideas

Glossary Terms Key terms relevant to Buisness Economics are defined throughout the text and also featured in the glossary at the back of the book.

Case studies are provided throughout the text that apply the theory that has been developed to understanding events and policies.

Pitfall Preventions The authors have used their collective teaching wisdom to outline areas where students make frequent mistakes and which can be a cause of confusion. The Pitfall Prevention boxes alert students to the potential for these mistakes.

Quick quizzes are provided at the end of each section and allow students to check their comprehension of what they have just learned.

FYI provides additional material 'for your information'; the boxes offer a range of supplementary material, such as a glimpse into the history of economic thought, technical issues and current topics that can be discussed in lectures.

'what if' boxes Questions designed to get you thinking about different scenarios in business and economics.

Jeopardy Problems These are problems designed to help you think as an economist. You will be given end-points or solutions and you have to think through the different ways in which the solutions or end-point given might have been arrived at using your knowledge of economics and business.

In the News articles relate key ideas covered in the chapter to topical news events to highlight the application of economic ideas and introduce new angles to consider in topical debates.

Summaries at the end of each chapter remind students of what they have learned so far, offering a useful way to review for exams.

Questions for review cover each chapter's primary lessons. These can be used to check comprehension and to prepare for exams.

Problems and applications allow students to apply the material they have learned within the chapter. These can also be used for classroom discussions or homework assignments.

ACKNOWLEDGEMENTS

The authors would like to thank the following reviewers for their comments:

Andrew Abbott – University of Hull
Dr. Turner Anna – CEU Business School
Emanuele Bracco – Lancaster University
Dr Yu-Fu Chen – Economic Studies, Dundee University
Matthew T. Col – University College Dublin
Gary Cook – University of Liverpool
Dr John Duignan – University of the West of Scotland
Aat van Eeden – Zuyd University of Applied Science
Robert Elliott – University of Birmingham
John Forde – University of Salford
Richard Godfrey – Cardiff School of Management
Marco Gundermann – Cardiff Metropolitan University
Dr. Hala Helmi El Hadidi – British University, Egypt
Juan Garcia Lara – Universidad Carlos III Madrid, Spain
Paul L. Latreille – Swansea University
Dr. Bobby Mackie – University of the West of Scotland
Tim Maxfield – University of Worcester
Natalie Moore – University of Nottingham
Yoko Nagase – Oxford Brookes University
Adel Nemeth – Jacobs University Bremen
Dr Matthew Olczak – Aston University, UK
Quentin Outram – Leeds University Business School
Bruce Philp – Nottingham Business School
Julia Planko – Hogeschool Utrecht
Neil Reaich – Economic, Business and Enterprise Association
Jose R. Sanchez-Fung – Kingston University London, UK
Ulrich Schüle – School of Business FH Mainz-University of Applied sciences
Cemil Selcuk – Cardiff University
Vasilios Sogiakas – University of Glasgow
Nicholas Spearman – University of the Witwatersrand, South Africa
Dr F Steffen – University of Liverpool Management School
Michael Wood – London South Bank University
Dr Michael Wynn-Williams – University of Greenwich
Gaston Yalonetzky – Leeds University Business School

SUPPLEMENTS

Cengage Learning offers various digital resources for instructors and students who use this book. These resources are designed to make teaching the principles of business economics easy for the instructor and learning them easy for the student.

ABOUT THE DIGITAL RESOURCES

More information about the digital support resources accompanying this book can be found on page xix.

For instructors

Teaching the principles of business economics can be a demanding job. The supplements designed for the instructor make the job less difficult.

- **Instructor's Manual** – a detailed outline of each chapter of the text that provides earning objectives, identifies stumbling blocks that students may face, offers helpful teaching tips and provides suggested in-classroom activities for more cooperative learning experience. The Instructor's Manual also includes solutions to all of the end-of-chapter exercises, Quick Quizzes, Questions for Review and Problems and Applications found in the text.
- **PowerPoint™ Lecture Slides and Exhibit Slides** – Instructors can save valuable time as they prepare for classes using these fully adaptable comprehensive lecture presentations with integrated graphs, tables, lists and concepts. A separate exhibit presentation provides instructors with all of the tables and graphs from the main text.

For students

The supplements designed for the student enrich and support the learning experience, providing excellent revision tools and further study opportunities.

- **Learning Objectives** – listed for each chapter, they help the student to monitor their understanding and progress through the book.
- **Exhibit Slides** – provided in PowerPoint™, the exhibit presentations provide students with animated figures from the main text.
- **Glossary** – the full glossary of key terms that appears at the end of the book in downloadable PDF file.
- **Self-test questions** - a wide array of different types of questions, including objective tests, short-answer questions and problems, topical case studies and advance critical thinking questions, providing variety for the student and testing all areas of their knowledge and skills. The student can check their work by revealing the correct answers, where appropriate, providing instant feedback.

OTHER SUPPLEMENTARY RESOURCES

- **Exam View®** The computerized test generator software contains a testbank of questions for each chapter, allowing instructors to create online, paper or local area network (LAN) tests. This product is only available from your Cengage Learning sales representative.
- **Virtual Learning Environment** All of the web material is available in a format that is compatible with virtual learning environments such as Moodle and Blackboard. This version of the product is only available from your Cengage Learning sales representative.

DIGITAL SUPPORT RESOURCES

Dedicated Instructor Resources

To discover the dedicated instructor online support resources accompanying this textbook, instructors should register here for access:
http://login.cengage.com

Resources include:

- Instructor's Manual
- ExamView Testbank
- PowerPoint slides

Online Student Resources

Instructor access

Instructors can access the online student resources by registering at **http://login.cengage.com** or by speaking to their local Cengage Learning EMEA representative.

Instructor resources

Instructors can use the integrated Engagement Tracker in CourseMate to track students' preparation and engagement. The tracking tool can be used to monitor progress of the class as a whole, or for individual students.

Student access

Students can access CourseMate using the unique personal access card included in the front of the book.

Student resources

CourseMate offers a range of interactive learning tools tailored to the 1st edition of *Business Economics*, including:

- Quizzes and self-test questions
- Interactive eBook
- Games
- Photo case studies
- Glossary
- Flashcards
- Links to useful websites

PART 1

THE ECONOMIC AND BUSINESS ENVIRONMENT – SETTING THE SCENE

1 WHAT IS BUSINESS ECONOMICS?

LEARNING OBJECTIVES

In this chapter you will:

- Learn that economics is about the allocation of scarce resources

- Examine some of the trade-offs that people face

- Learn the meaning of opportunity cost

- See how to use marginal reasoning when making decisions

- Discuss how incentives affect people's behaviour

- Consider why trade among people or nations can be good for everyone

- Discuss why markets are a good, but not perfect, way to allocate resources

- Learn what determines some trends in the overall economy

After reading this chapter you should be able to:

- Define scarcity

- Explain the classic trade-off between 'guns and butter'

- Add up your particular opportunity cost of attending university

- Compare the marginal costs and marginal benefits of continuing to attend school indefinitely

- Consider how a quadrupling of your tuition payments would affect your decision to educate yourself

- Explain why specialization and trade improve people's choices

- Give an example of an externality

- Explain the source of large and persistent inflation

THE TEN PRINCIPLES OF ECONOMICS

The word 'economy' comes from the Greek word *oikonomos,* which means for 'one who manages a household'. At first, this origin might seem peculiar. But, in fact, businesses and economies have much in common.

A business faces many decisions. It must decide how many people to employ, what each of those people will do to contribute to the business, how much each employee gets in return, who should receive a bonus scheme and who should not, how to increase output per worker, how best to manage costs, when to invest, how much to invest and where best to get the funds to invest from, what products to produce, what products not to produce, when to stop producing products, when to expand, when to contract, how best to manage the sales process and customer relations, whether to be environmentally friendly or whether to give the impression of being so, how to deal with competitors and whether to charge a high price or a low price (or one in between). In short, business must allocate scarce resources among competing uses, taking into account a range of stakeholder wants and needs. A **stakeholder** is any group or individual with an interest in a business.

stakeholder any group or individual with an interest in a business such as workers, managers, suppliers, the local community, customers and owners

Like businesses, a society faces many decisions. A society must decide what jobs will be done and who will do them. It needs some people to grow food, other people to make clothing and still others to design computer software. Once society has allocated people (as well as land, buildings and machines) to various jobs, it must also allocate the output of goods and services that they produce. It must decide who will eat caviar and who will eat potatoes. It must decide who will drive a Ferrari and who will take the bus.

The management of society's resources is important because resources are scarce. **Scarcity** means that society has limited resources and therefore cannot produce all the goods and services people wish to have. Just as a household cannot give every member everything he or she wants, a society cannot give every individual the highest standard of living to which he or she might aspire.

scarcity the limited nature of society's resources

Economics is the study of how society manages its scarce resources. In most societies, resources are allocated not by a single central planner but through the combined actions of millions of households and firms. Economists therefore study how people make decisions: how much they work, what they buy, how much they save and how they invest their savings. Economists also study how people and people in businesses interact with one another. For instance, they examine how the multitude of buyers and sellers of a good together determine the price at which the good is sold and the quantity that is sold. Economists analyse forces and trends that affect the economy as a whole, including the growth in average income, the fraction of the population that cannot find work and the rate at which prices are rising. Many of the concepts that economists use are also directly applicable and of relevance to businesses. In a sense, economics can be described as the science of decision making and since businesses all around the world have to make millions of decisions every day then having some understanding of the process of decision making and the consequences that might arise from such decision making is important.

economics the study of how society manages its scarce resources

Although the study of economics has many facets, the field is unified by several central ideas, all of which are of direct relevance to business. In the rest of this chapter we look at *Ten Principles of Economics.* Don't worry if you don't understand them all at first, or if you don't find them completely convincing. In the coming chapters we will explore these ideas more fully. The ten principles are introduced here just to give you an overview of what economics is all about. You can think of this chapter as a 'preview of coming attractions'.

HOW PEOPLE AND BUSINESSES MAKE DECISIONS

We use the term 'the economy' on a regular basis but have you ever stopped to think about what the term really means? Whether we are talking about the economy of a group of countries such as the European Union or the Middle East, or the economy of one particular country, such as South Africa or the United Kingdom, or of the whole world, an economy is just a group of people interacting with one another as they go about their lives. This interaction is invariably through a process of exchange. Whether it be an individual buying a morning newspaper, a business buying several hundred tonnes of steel for a construction project or a government funding a higher education institution, the interaction consists of millions of individuals all making decisions and together we describe these interactions as 'the economy'. Because the behaviour of an economy reflects the behaviour of the individuals, both acting on their own and as part of businesses who make up the economy, we start our study of economics with four principles of individual decision making.

CASE STUDY

Coal or Sun – or do you not care provided you have electricity?

For many people in Europe, the Middle East and parts of Africa, the idea of switching on a light, charging a mobile phone with the flick of a switch, plugging in the power cable for a laptop, taking a shower with hot running water, doing the washing and thousands of other daily tasks is taken largely for granted. There are plenty of people and businesses in the region, however, who recognize how fortunate they are to have access to supplies of electricity 24 hours a day, 365 days a year. South Africa is one country which suffers from shortages of electricity and the government is under pressure to increase capacity.

The question is, how should this capacity increase? South Africa is relatively rich in coal supplies. The country is the fourth largest coal exporter in the world and produces around 244 million tonnes of coal a year. Over 90 per cent of the electricity generated in South Africa comes from coal fired power stations. Despite this rich endowment of a valuable resource, the country's people and businesses suffer from regular power shortages. The demand for electricity has risen at a faster rate than the ability of the country to generate it and as a result electricity prices are high and could lead to slower economic growth.

Given the endowment of coal supplies, one way to increase electricity supplies would be to build new coal fired power stations and also upgrade existing older stations. The benefits of such a programme would be an increase in the amount of electricity available to businesses and people in the country, but the downside is that coal fired power stations are alleged to be a major contributor to carbon emissions and climate change. Other options open to South Africa include investing more in solar and wind energy – so called 'clean energy'.

Indeed, the World Bank agreed in October 2011 to help the South African utility company, Eskom, fund the construction of a 100 megawatt wind and solar power plant in Uppington in the Northern Cape province. The funding will amount to $250 million. This sounds like a positive step forward but critics argue that the plant will not increase the supply of electricity sufficiently to have much effect on the power shortage the country experiences.

The World Bank had previously been criticized for helping to fund another power generation project for Eskom, the construction of new coal fired power stations worth around $3.75 billion. Critics argued that this would just exacerbate Eskom's carbon footprint but the company countered by saying it had to adopt a balanced approach to power generation and would have to not only upgrade existing coal fired stations to become more efficient (in terms of reducing carbon emissions and producing more electricity with lower inputs and at lower cost) but to build new stations to meet the growing demand of the country.

WWW.HUDU.CO.ZA

The sun is a natural resource in South Africa which can be utilized to provide energy as in this case of a solar power field designed to capture the energy of the sun and convert it to electricity.

The case here highlights the trade-offs facing businesses in making decisions. In economics, there are rarely 'right answers' – businesses have to make decisions and face trade-offs. On the one hand, demand for electricity in South Africa means it is only 'right' and 'sensible' to exploit its natural resources and provide for the needs of its people. In doing so it has to recognize the negative impact of using coal as a means of generating electricity. Solar and wind may be cleaner sources of energy but can enough investment be generated in these sources, quickly, to meet the more immediate demands of the nation for power which will help to boost economic growth and help it deal with the pockets of chronic poverty that exist? There is no right answer to the predicament that Eskom finds itself in – it has to chart a path to balance out the costs and benefits to try and maximize the benefits but reduce the costs to a minimum and that involves recognizing and accepting the trade-offs that exist.

Principle 1: Decision Making Involves Trade-Offs

The first lesson about making decisions is summarized in an adage popular with economists: 'There is no such thing as a free lunch'. To get the benefits of one thing that we like, we usually have to give up the benefits of another thing that we also like, or accept that we might have to give up something else and incur a cost of some sort (cost here being used in its widest sense not just a monetary one). Making decisions requires trading off one goal or the benefits against another.

Consider a business manager who must decide how to allocate her most valuable resource – her time. She can spend all of her time reflecting on strategy in her office; she can spend all of her time walking around the business premises talking to staff; or she can divide her time between the two fields. For every hour she spends reflecting and strategizing, she gives up an hour she could have used talking to staff. And for every hour she spends doing either, she gives up an hour that she could have spent talking to customers, being out promoting the business, working with suppliers to improve efficiency or networking with colleagues at conferences.

Or consider employees of this business deciding how to spend the income they receive from working at the business. They can buy food, clothing or a family holiday. Or they can save some of the family income for retirement or perhaps to help the children buy a house or a flat when they are grown up. When they choose to spend an extra euro on one of these goods, they have one less euro to spend on some other good.

When people are grouped into societies, they face different kinds of trade-offs. The classic trade-off is between 'guns and butter' – these two products just represent defence and consumer goods in general. The more we spend on national defence (guns) to protect our country from foreign aggressors (the benefit), the less we can spend on consumer goods (butter) which brings the benefit of raising our standard of living at home. Also important in modern society is the trade-off between a clean environment and a high level of income. Laws that require firms to reduce pollution raise the cost of producing goods and services but bring the benefit to society as a whole (and possibly to the firm in the form of good publicity) . Because of the higher costs, these firms end up earning smaller profits, paying lower wages, charging higher prices, or some combination of these three. Thus, while pollution regulations give us the benefit of a cleaner environment and the improved levels of health that come with it, they have the cost of reducing the incomes of the firms' owners, workers and customers.

Another trade-off society faces is between efficiency and equity. **Efficiency** can be looked at in three different ways. In essence, efficiency is about getting the most we can

efficiency the property of society getting the most it can from its scarce resources

from scarce resources. More specifically we can look at it in four ways related to business:

- Technical efficiency – a business can improve its technical efficiency if it could find a way of using its existing resources to produce more. It may be that it could use machinery instead of people that do the same job but do it much faster without having to take a break!
- Productive efficiency – a business can improve productive efficiency by producing output at the lowest cost possible. If it can find a way of producing its products cheaper, for example, by sourcing cheaper raw materials, then it can improve its productive efficiency.
- Allocative efficiency – this looks at efficiency from the perspective of consumers. Are the products being produced by businesses actually wanted and valued by consumers (both individual consumers and business consumers)? Efficiency occurs where the goods and services being produced match the demand by consumers. Allocative efficiency occurs where the cost of resources used to produce the products is equal to the value placed on the product by consumers represented by the price they are willing to pay.
- Social efficiency – when businesses produce products they incur costs – raw materials, wages, rents, interest payments, insurance, plant and equipment and so on – the private costs. However, there are also costs which businesses may not take into account such as the pollution they generate in production. These are costs borne by society as a whole. Social efficiency occurs where the private and social cost of production is equal to the private and social benefits derived from their consumption.

Equity means that the benefits of those resources are distributed fairly among society's members. In other words, efficiency as an overall concept, refers to the size of the economic cake, and equity refers to how the cake is divided. Often, when government policies are being designed, these two goals conflict; in addition, when businesses make decisions conflicts arise between equity and efficiency.

equity the property of distributing economic prosperity fairly among the members of society

> **Pitfall Prevention** If you are writing about efficiency, be careful to distinguish which measure of efficiency you mean – each may have different implications and consequences for businesses.

Consider, for instance, policies aimed at achieving a more equal distribution of economic well-being. Some of these policies, such as the social security system or unemployment insurance, try to help those members of society who are most in need. Others, such as the individual income tax, ask the financially successful to contribute more than others to support the government. Although these policies have the benefit of achieving greater equity, they have a cost in terms of reduced overall efficiency. When the government redistributes income from the rich to the poor, it reduces the reward for working hard; as a result, people work less and produce fewer goods and services. In other words, when the government tries to cut the economic cake into more equal slices, the cake gets smaller.

Equally, when a business decides to outsource some of its production abroad, workers in the domestic economy may find that they lose their jobs. For the business as a whole, the decision may increase productive efficiency but workers would consider the decision unfair and the consequences in terms of morale and motivation could affect productivity elsewhere in the business in a detrimental way.

Recognizing that people and businesses face trade-offs does not by itself tell us what decisions they will or should make. A chief executive officer (CEO) should not abandon time set aside for reflection and thinking just because doing so would increase the time available to talk to workers. Society should not stop protecting the environment just because environmental regulations reduce our material standard of living. The poor should not be ignored just because helping them distorts work incentives. Nevertheless, acknowledging life's trade-offs is important because people and businesses are likely to make good decisions only if they understand the options that they have available and can quantify them in some way to enable them to make informed decisions.

> **Quick Quiz** Does the adage 'there is no such thing as a free lunch' simply refer to the fact that someone has to have paid for the lunch to be provided and served? Or does the recipient of a 'free lunch' also incur a cost?

Principle 2: The Cost of Something Is What You Give Up to Get It

Because people and businesses face trade-offs, making decisions requires comparing the costs and benefits of alternative courses of action. In many cases, however, the cost of some action is not as obvious as it might first appear.

Consider, for example, the decision by a business to cease production of a product that is not selling very well any more. The benefit is that resources can be made available to invest in other parts of the business that are more successful. But what is the cost? To answer this question, you might be tempted to add up the money the business has to pay in redundancy to workers who may no longer be needed, to close down plant, get rid of defunct machinery and equipment. Yet this total does not truly represent what the business gives up when it ceases production of a product.

The first problem with this answer is that it ignores many wider issues that the business might face as a result of its decision. How do competitors view the decision? Will they seek to use it as an example of the decline of the business? What about customers – will they be disappointed that the product has disappeared? A number of businesses have found themselves under pressure to bring back much loved products that may not have been financially viable and have incurred disappointment from customers and possible loss of loyalty as a result. Then there is the attitude amongst workers – is this closure the first of others, does it send negative signals to the rest of the workforce and result in a decline in motivation and increases in staff turnover as workers seek to get out before they are pushed out?

The second problem is that it does not include the lost revenue from sales of the product. It may be that sales were low and not that it was not viable to continue with production. Assuming that sales were not zero there was some revenue being generated and this will now be lost. That has to be taken into consideration.

The decision, therefore, has costs far greater than pure money costs. The cost of loss of goodwill, worker and customer loyalty and bad publicity also has to be taken into consideration in assessing the costs of the decision and these may not be immediately obvious and sometimes not easy to work out.

opportunity cost whatever must be given up to obtain some item – the value of the benefits foregone (sacrificed)

The **opportunity cost** of an item is what you give up to get that item. When making any decision, such as whether to close down production of a product, decision makers should be aware of the opportunity costs that accompany each possible action.

> **Quick Quiz** A bakery is planning to invest €20 000 in a new machine which will increase its production of croissants by 10 per cent. The financial director of the company points out that account needs to be taken of what that €20 000 could earn if invested in another way, such as in an interest-bearing account at a bank, as part of the cost calculations. Why do you think she insisted that this was taken into consideration and why is it classed as a cost?

Principle 3: Rational People and Businesses Think at the Margin

Decisions in life are rarely black and white but usually involve shades of grey. The decision by a company worker of whether to put in the extra hour at the end of the working day is not a case of working all day or not but about that extra time to finish a project before going home. A publisher may have to make a decision about whether to print an extra thousand copies of a textbook when it is not certain that all these extra books will sell. Many workers have to make decisions about whether to spend a bit more time with their families or whether to shut themselves away and get on with the bit of work that needs finishing for a deadline the next week. Economists use the term **marginal changes** to describe small incremental adjustments to an existing plan of action. Keep in mind that 'margin' means 'edge', so marginal changes are adjustments around the edges of what you are doing.

> **marginal changes** small incremental adjustments to a plan of action

In many situations, people make the best decisions by thinking at the margin. Suppose, for instance, that you asked a friend for advice about how many years to stay in education. If he were to compare for you the lifestyle of a person with a PhD to that of someone who finished secondary school with no qualifications, you might complain that this comparison is not helpful for your decision. Perhaps you have already been at university for a few years but you're getting a little tired of studying and not having enough money and so you're deciding whether or not to stay on for that last year. To make this decision, you need to know the additional benefits that an extra year in education would offer (higher wages throughout your life and the sheer joy of learning) and the additional costs that you would incur (another year of tuition fees and another year of foregone wages). By comparing these *marginal benefits* and *marginal costs,* you can evaluate whether the extra year is worthwhile.

As another example, consider an airline company deciding how much to charge passengers who fly standby. Suppose that flying a 200-seat aeroplane from London to Warsaw costs the airline €100 000. In this case, the average cost of each seat is €100 000/200, which is €500. One might be tempted to conclude that the airline should never sell a ticket for less than €500. In fact, however, the airline can raise its profits by thinking at the margin. Imagine that a plane is about to take off with ten empty seats, and a standby passenger is waiting at the gate willing to pay €300 for a seat. Should the airline sell it to him/her? Of course it should. If the plane has empty seats, the cost of adding one more passenger is minuscule. Although the *average* cost of flying a passenger is €500, the *marginal* cost is merely the cost of the airline meal that the extra passenger will consume (which may have gone to waste in any case) and possibly an extremely slight increase in the amount of aircraft fuel used. As long as the standby passenger pays more than the marginal cost, selling him or her a ticket is profitable.

As these examples show, individuals and firms can make better decisions by thinking at the margin. A rational decision maker takes an action if and only if the marginal benefit of the action exceeds the marginal cost. For businesses this principle is extremely important because there are more likely to be attempts to rationalize decision making than individuals do on a day-to-day basis.

Principle 4: People and Businesses Respond to Incentives

Because people and businesses make decisions by comparing costs and benefits, their behaviour may change when the costs or benefits change. That is, people respond to incentives. When the price of an apple rises, for instance, people decide to eat more pears and fewer apples because the cost of buying an apple is higher. At the same time, apple orchards decide to hire more workers and harvest more apples, because the benefit of selling an apple is also higher. As we shall see, the effect of price on the behaviour of buyers and sellers in a market – in this case, the market for apples – is crucial for understanding how the economy works.

Public policy makers should never forget about incentives, because many policies change the costs or benefits that people face and, therefore, alter behaviour. A tax on petrol, for instance, encourages people to drive smaller, more fuel-efficient cars. For vehicle manufacturers this change in demand has to be accommodated and shifts resources into the production of smaller, more fuel efficient cars and away from larger, more fuel expensive cars. It also encourages people to use public transport rather than drive and to live closer to where they work. This in turn has an effect on decisions about provision of public transport and what type of transport and affects businesses in the construction industry. If the tax were large enough, people would start driving electric cars, which requires investment by vehicle manufacturers in this technology and a host of other businesses who may be involved in setting up the infrastructure to facilitate the use of electric cars.

When policy makers fail to consider how their policies affect incentives, they often end up with results they did not intend. For example, consider public policy regarding motor vehicle safety. Today all cars sold in the European Union, South Africa and most countries in the Middle East have to have seat belts fitted by law (although actual seat belt use – especially by rear-seat passengers – varies widely, with official estimates ranging from about 30 per cent of car occupants in some member states of the EU to around 90 per cent in others, notably Sweden).

How does a seat belt law affect car safety? The direct effect is obvious: when a person wears a seat belt, the probability of surviving a major car accident rises. But that's not the end of the story, for the law also affects behaviour by altering incentives. The relevant behaviour here is the speed and care with which drivers operate their cars. Driving slowly and carefully is costly because it uses the driver's time and energy. When deciding how safely to drive, rational people compare the marginal benefit from safer driving to the marginal cost. They drive more slowly and carefully when the benefit of increased safety is high. It is no surprise, for instance, that people drive more slowly and carefully when roads are icy than when roads are clear.

Quick Quiz   The emphasis on road safety throughout Europe has increased over the last 25 years. Not only are cars packed with safety technology and devices but roads are also designed to be safer with the use of safety barriers and better road surfaces, for example. Is there a case, therefore, for believing that if people feel that they are safer in their cars there is an incentive to drive faster because the marginal cost is now outweighed by the marginal benefit?

Consider how a seat belt law alters a motorist's cost–benefit calculation. Seat belts make accidents less costly because they reduce the likelihood of injury or death. In other words, seat belts reduce the benefits to slow and careful driving. People respond to seat belts as they would to an improvement in road conditions – by faster and less careful driving. The end result of a seat belt law, therefore, is a larger number of accidents and so it will affect both motorists and pedestrians. The decline in safe driving has a clear, adverse impact on pedestrians, who are more likely to find themselves in an accident but (unlike the motorists) don't have the benefit of added protection.

At first, this discussion of incentives and seat belts might seem like idle speculation. Yet a 1981 study of seat belt laws in eight European countries commissioned by the UK Department of Transport showed that the laws did appear to have had many of these effects. Similar evidence was also presented in a 1975 study of US seat belt laws by the American economist Sam Peltzman. It does indeed seem that seat belt laws produce both fewer deaths per accident and more accidents. The net result is little change in the number of motorist deaths and an increase in the number of pedestrian deaths.

This is an example of the general principle that people respond to incentives. Many incentives that economists study are more straightforward than those of the car-safety laws. No one is surprised that people drive smaller cars in Europe, where petrol taxes

Music, TV and television producer and executive Simon Cowell understood opportunity cost and incentives. He decided to leave school before completing his post-16 education and is reported to earn in excess of £50 million a year!

S. BUKLEY/SHUTTERSTOCK

are relatively high, than in the United States, where petrol taxes are lower. Yet, as the seat belt example shows, policies can have effects that are not obvious in advance. When analysing any policy, we must consider not only the direct effects but also the indirect effects that work through incentives. If the policy changes incentives, it will cause people to alter their behaviour.

> **Quick Quiz** List and briefly explain the four principles of individual decision making.

HOW PEOPLE INTERACT

The first four principles discussed how individuals and businesses make decisions. As we go about our lives, many of our decisions and the decisions of businesses affect not only ourselves but other people and businesses as well. The next three principles concern how people and businesses interact with one another.

Principle 5: Trade Can Make Everyone Better Off

The Americans, South Africans and the Japanese are often mentioned in the news as being competitors to Europeans in the world economy. In some ways this is true, because American, South African and Japanese firms do produce many of the same goods as European firms. Airbus and Boeing compete for the same customers in the market for aircraft. Toyota and Citroën compete for the same customers in the market for cars. South African and American fruit growers compete in the same market as European fruit growers and South African and American wine producers compete in the same market as French, Spanish and Italian wine makers.

Yet it is easy to be misled when thinking about competition among countries. Trade between Europe and South Africa or the United States, or between Europe and Japan, is not like a sports contest where one side wins and the other side loses (a zero-sum game). In fact, the opposite is true: trade between two economies can make each economy better off.

To see why, consider how trade affects a business. When a business produces a product it competes against other businesses that are also producing similar products. Despite this competition, a business would not be better off isolating itself from all other businesses. If it did, the business would have to supply all its own raw materials and components, find its own staff, arrange its own insurance, do its own banking, arrange its own security and so on. Clearly, businesses gain much from their ability to trade with others. Trade allows each business to specialize in the activities it does best, whether it is farming, making clothes or home building. By trading with others, businesses can buy a greater variety of goods and services at lower cost and therefore (potentially) increase both productive and technical efficiency.

Countries as well as businesses benefit from the ability to trade with one another. Trade allows countries to specialize in what they do best and to enjoy a greater variety of goods and services. The Japanese and the Americans, as well as the Egyptians and the Brazilians, are as much our partners in the world economy as they are our competitors.

Principle 6: Markets are Usually a Good Way to Organize Economic Activity

The collapse of communism in the Soviet Union and Eastern Europe in the 1980s may be the most important change in the world during the past half century (although sorting out the European debt crisis, which arose partly because of market failure, has also been cited as being at least on a par with this and possibly even more significant in the coming 50 years). Communist countries worked on the premise that central planners in the government were in the best position to guide economic activity. These planners decided what goods and services were produced, how much was produced, and who produced and consumed these goods and services. The theory behind central planning was that only the government could organize economic activity in a way that promoted economic well-being for the country as a whole.

market economy an economy that allocates resources through the decentralized decisions of many firms and households as they interact in markets for goods and services

Today, most countries that once had centrally planned economies have abandoned this system and are trying to develop market economies. In a **market economy**, the decisions of a central planner are replaced by the decisions of millions of firms and households. Firms decide whom to hire and what to make. Households decide which firms to work for and what to buy with their incomes. These firms and households interact in the marketplace, where prices and self-interest guide their decisions.

At first glance, the apparent success of market economies in raising standards of living for many of the population in countries is puzzling. After all, in a market economy, no one is considering the economic well-being of society as a whole. Free markets contain many buyers and sellers of numerous goods and services, and all of them are interested primarily in their own well-being. Yet, despite decentralized decision making and self-interested decision makers, market economies have proven remarkably successful in organizing economic activity in a way that promotes overall economic well-being.

In his 1776 book *An Inquiry Into the Nature and Causes of the Wealth of Nations,* the British economist Adam Smith made the most famous observation in all of economics: households and firms interacting in markets act as if they are guided by an 'invisible hand' that leads them to desirable market outcomes. One of our goals in this book is to understand how this invisible hand works its magic. As you study economics, you will learn that prices are the instrument with which the invisible hand directs economic activity. Prices reflect both the value of a good to society and the cost to society of making the good. Because households and firms look at prices when deciding what to buy and sell, they unknowingly take into account the social benefits and costs of their actions. As a result, prices guide these individual decision makers to reach outcomes that, in many cases, maximize the welfare of society as a whole.

However, a caveat has to be put on this principle. It is that markets are *usually* a good way to organize economic activity. We emphasize *usually* because markets are not devoid of problems as we will outline in the next principle. We alluded above to the European debt crisis which has been rumbling on since the financial crisis of 2007–2008 and may well be continuing after this book is published. We will look at the reasons why markets may not work properly all the time in later chapters but we will assume that a market system, which is adopted by the vast majority of countries in the world, is the standard economic system which we will use and analyse.

FYI

Adam Smith and the Invisible Hand

Adam Smith's great work *The Wealth of Nations* is a landmark in economics. In its emphasis on the invisible hand of the market economy, it reflected a point of view that was typical of so-called 'enlightenment' writers at the end of the 18th century – that individuals are usually best left to their own devices, without the heavy hand of government guiding their actions. This political philosophy provides the intellectual basis for the market economy.

Why do decentralized market economies work so well? Is it because people can be counted on to treat one another with love and kindness? Not at all. Here is Adam Smith's description of how people interact in a market economy:

Man has almost constant occasion for the help of his brethren, and it is vain for him to expect it from their benevolence only. He will be more likely to prevail if he can interest their self-love in his favour, and show them that it is for their own advantage to do for him what he requires of them. ... It is not from the benevolence of the butcher, the brewer, or the baker that we expect our dinner, but from their regard to their own interest. ... Every individual ... neither intends to promote the public interest, nor knows how much he is promoting it. ... He intends only his own gain, and he is in this, as in many other cases, led by an invisible hand to promote an end which was no part of his intention. Nor is it always the worse for the society that it was no part of it. By pursuing his own interest he frequently promotes that of the society more effectually than when he really intends to promote it.

Wealth of Nations 1776

Smith is saying that participants in the economy are motivated by self-interest and that the 'invisible hand' of the marketplace guides this self-interest into promoting general economic well-being. Many of Smith's insights remain at the centre of modern economics. Our analysis in the coming chapters will allow us to express Smith's conclusions more precisely and to analyse fully the strengths and weaknesses of the market's invisible hand.

There is an important corollary to the skill of the invisible hand in guiding economic activity: when the government prevents prices from adjusting naturally to supply and demand, it impedes the invisible hand's ability to coordinate the millions of households

Adam Smith, 1723–1790.

WORD HISTORY ARCHIVE

and firms that make up the economy. This corollary explains why taxes adversely affect the allocation of resources: taxes distort prices and thus the decisions of households and businesses. It also explains the even greater harm caused by policies that directly control prices, such as rent control. And it also explains the failure of communism. In communist countries, prices were not determined in the marketplace but were dictated by central planners. These planners lacked the information that gets reflected in prices when prices are free to respond to market forces. Central planners failed because they tried to run the economy with one hand tied behind their backs – the invisible hand of the marketplace.

Principle 7: Governments Can Sometimes Improve Market Outcomes

If the invisible hand of the market is so wonderful, why do we need government? One answer is that the invisible hand needs government to protect it. Markets work only if property rights are enforced. A farmer won't grow food if he expects his crop to be stolen, and a restaurant won't serve meals unless it is assured that customers will pay before they leave. In many countries the idea that a business should have the sole right to exploit its inventions, processes, ideas, brands and trademarks is based in law. In other countries such ideas are viewed with a degree of scepticism and curiosity. We all rely on government-provided police and courts to enforce our rights over the things we produce.

Yet there is another answer to why we need government: although markets are usually a good way to organize economic activity, this rule has some important exceptions. There are two broad reasons for a government to intervene in the economy – to promote efficiency and to promote equity. That is, most policies aim either to enlarge the economic cake or to change the way in which the cake is divided.

> **market failure** a situation in which a market left on its own fails to allocate resources efficiently

Although the invisible hand usually leads markets to allocate resources efficiently, that is not always the case. Economists use the term **market failure** to refer to a situation in which the market on its own fails to produce an efficient allocation of resources. One possible cause of market failure is an **externality**, which is the uncompensated impact of one person's actions on the well-being of a bystander or third party. For instance, the classic example of an external cost is pollution. Another possible cause of market failure is **market power**, which refers to the ability of a single person (or small group) to unduly influence market prices. For example, if everyone in a remote village in the Scottish Highlands needs water but there is only one well, the owner of the well is not subject to the rigorous competition with which the invisible hand normally keeps self-interest in check. In the presence of externalities or market power, well designed public policy can enhance economic efficiency.

> **externality** the uncompensated impact of one person's actions on the well-being of a bystander or third party

> **market power** the ability of a single economic agent (or small group of agents) to have a substantial influence on market prices

> **?** **what if...** The intervention by government actually leads to a worse outcome than if it had not done anything in the first place. Does this mean governments should never interfere in the market?

The invisible hand may also fail to ensure that economic prosperity is distributed equitably. A market economy rewards people according to their ability to produce things for which other people are willing to pay. The world's best footballer earns more than the world's best chess player simply because people are willing to pay more to watch football than chess. The invisible hand does not ensure that everyone has sufficient food, decent clothing and adequate health care. Many public policies, such as income tax and the social security system, aim to achieve a more equitable distribution of economic well-being.

To say that the government *can* improve on market outcomes at times does not mean that it always *will*. Public policy is made not by angels but by a political process that is far from perfect. Sometimes policies are designed simply to reward the politically powerful. Sometimes they are made by well intentioned leaders who are not fully informed or who are unduly swayed by lobbying from businesses with a great deal of influence and power. One goal of the study of economics is to help you judge when a government policy is justifiable to promote efficiency or equity, and when it is not.

> **Quick Quiz** List and briefly explain the three principles concerning economic interactions.

HOW THE ECONOMY AS A WHOLE WORKS

We started by discussing how individuals make decisions and then looked at how people interact with one another. All these decisions and interactions together make up 'the economy'. The last three principles concern the workings of the economy as a whole. A key concept in this section is **economic growth** – the percentage increase in the number of goods and services produced in an economy over a period of time, usually expressed over a quarter and annually.

economic growth the increase in the amount of goods and services in an economy over a period of time

Principle 8: An Economy's Standard of Living Depends on Its Ability to Produce Goods and Services

Table 1.1 shows **gross domestic product (GDP) per head** of the population in a number of selected countries. In 2012 the average annual income per head of population in the Netherlands, Finland, Singapore and Canada was about $52000, while it was a little lower in the UK and Germany at around $41000 and $45000, respectively, somewhat

gross domestic product per head the market value of all final goods and services produced within a country in a given period of time divided by the population of a country to give a per capita figure

TABLE 1.1

Gross domestic product (GDP) per capita, US dollars, 2012 estimate

Country	2012
Australia	69007
Bahrain	23750
Belgium	49630
Brazil	13316
Burkina Faso	705
Canada	52681
Denmark	65250
Egypt	3123
Finland	52568
France	45468
Germany	45619
Greece	27349
India	1646
Italy	37577
Japan	47960
Kenya	965
Lebanon	11197
Luxembourg	126326
Malta	22936
Mozambique	582
Netherlands	52582
Norway	98683
Oman	21652
Saudi Arabia	20214
Singapore	53072
South Africa	8658
Spain	34051
United Arab Emirates	67899
United Kingdom	41289
Republic of Yemen	1517
Zimbabwe	799

Source: International Monetary Fund, World Economic Outlook Database, September 2011.

higher in Norway at around $98 600 and an enviable $126 326 in Luxembourg. By contrast, we can see differences in income and living standards around the world that are quite staggering. For example, in the same year, 2012, average income in South Africa, at around $8600, was about a quarter of the level in Spain, while in Egypt it was around $3100, in India around $1600, in Yemen about $1500 and in Burkina Faso it was only about $700 – around one half of one per cent of the annual income per person in Luxembourg! Not surprisingly, this large variation in average income is reflected in various other measures of the quality of life and **standard of living**. Citizens of high-income countries have better nutrition, better health care and longer life expectancy than citizens of low-income countries, as well as more TV sets, more DVD players and more cars.

standard of living a measure of welfare based on the amount of goods and services a person's income can buy

Changes in the standard of living over time are also large. Over the last 50 years, average incomes in Western Europe and North America have grown at about 2 per cent per year (after adjusting for changes in the cost of living). At this rate, average income doubles every 35 years, and over the last half-century average income in many of these prosperous economies has risen approximately three-fold. On the other hand, average income in Ethiopia rose by only a third over this period – an average annual growth rate of around only 0.5 per cent.

What explains these large differences in living standards among countries and over time? The answer is surprisingly simple. Almost all variation in living standards is attributable to differences in countries' **productivity** – that is, the amount of goods and services produced from each hour of a worker's time. In nations where workers can produce a large quantity of goods and services per unit of time, most people enjoy a high standard of living; in nations where workers are less productive, most people must endure a more meagre existence. Similarly, the growth rate of a nation's productivity determines the growth rate of its average income. Productivity is not only important to a country's well-being but is also vital to that of businesses.

productivity the quantity of goods and services produced from each hour of a worker's time

The fundamental relationship between productivity and living standards is simple, but its implications are far-reaching. If productivity is the primary determinant of living standards, other explanations must be of secondary importance. For example, it might be tempting to credit trade unions or minimum wage laws for the rise in living standards of European workers over the past 50 years. Yet the real hero of European workers is their rising productivity.

The relationship between productivity and living standards also has profound implications for public policy. When thinking about how any policy will affect living standards, the key question is how it will affect our ability to produce goods and services. To boost living standards, policy makers need to raise productivity by ensuring that workers are well educated, have the tools needed to produce goods and services and have access to the best available technology. These policies are important in providing the resource infrastructure that businesses need to be able to thrive. Without well educated workers with high levels of employability skills, business costs would be higher because they would have to pay to train workers in these skills themselves. Without an adequate transport and communications network, business activity is hampered and again costs are higher and productivity lower.

Differences in standards of living not only occur between countries but also within countries.

© ANDREW ASHWIN

Principle 9: Prices Rise When the Government Prints Too Much Money

In Germany in January 1921, a daily newspaper was priced at 0.30 marks. Less than two years later, in November 1922, the same newspaper was priced at 70 000 000 marks. All other prices in the economy rose by similar amounts. This episode is one of history's most spectacular examples of **inflation**, an increase in the overall level of prices in the economy.

inflation an increase in the overall level of prices in the economy

While inflation in Western Europe and North America has been much lower over the last 50 years than that experienced in Germany in the 1920s, inflation has at times been an economic problem. During the 1970s, for instance, the overall level of prices in the UK more than tripled. By contrast, UK inflation from 2000 to 2008 was about 3 per cent per year; at this rate it would take more than 20 years for prices to double. In more recent times, Zimbabwe has experienced German-like hyper inflation. In March 2007 inflation in the African state was reported to be running at 2200 per cent. This means that a good priced at the equivalent of €2.99 in March 2006 would be priced at €65.78 just a year later. In July 2008 the government issued a Z$100 billion note. At that time it was just about enough to buy a loaf of bread. Estimates for inflation in Zimbabwe in July 2008 put the rate of growth of prices at 231 000 000 per cent. In January 2009, the Zimbabwean government issued Z$10, 20, 50 and 100 trillion dollar notes – 100 trillion is 100 followed by 12 zeros. Because high inflation imposes various costs on businesses and society, keeping inflation at a low level is a goal of economic policy makers around the world.

What causes inflation? In almost all cases of high or persistent inflation, the culprit turns out to be the same – growth in the quantity of money. When a government creates large quantities of the nation's money, the value of the money falls. In Germany in the early 1920s, when prices were on average tripling every month, the quantity of money was also tripling every month. Although less dramatic, the economic history of other European and North American countries points to a similar conclusion: the high inflation of the 1970s was associated with rapid growth in the quantity of money and the low inflation of the 2000s was associated with slow growth in the quantity of money.

Principle 10: Society Faces a Short-Run Trade-Off Between Inflation and Unemployment

When the government increases the amount of money in the economy, one result is inflation. Another result, at least in the short run, is a lower level of unemployment. The curve that illustrates this short-run trade-off between inflation and unemployment is called the **Phillips curve**, after the economist who first examined this relationship while working at the London School of Economics.

Phillips curve a curve that shows the short-run trade-off between inflation and unemployment

The Phillips curve remains a controversial topic among economists, but most economists today accept the idea that society faces a short-run trade-off between inflation and unemployment. This simply means that, over a period of a year or two, many economic policies push inflation and unemployment in opposite directions. Policy makers face this trade-off regardless of whether inflation and unemployment both start out at high levels (as they were in the early 1980s), at low levels (as they were in the late 1990s) or somewhere in between.

The trade-off between inflation and unemployment is only temporary, but it can last for several years. The Phillips curve is, therefore, crucial for understanding many developments in the economy. In particular, it is important for understanding the **business cycle** – the irregular and largely unpredictable fluctuations in economic activity, as measured by the number of people employed or the production of goods and services.

business cycle fluctuations in economic activity, such as employment and production

JEOPARDY PROBLEM

A government announces that unemployment has gone up by 75 000 over the last month but employment has risen by 40 000. How can this outcome arise?

Policy makers can exploit the short-run trade-off between inflation and unemployment using various policy instruments. By changing the amount that the government spends, the amount it taxes and the amount of money it prints, policy makers can influence the combination of inflation and unemployment that the economy experiences. Because these instruments of monetary and fiscal policy are potentially so powerful, how policy makers should use these instruments to control the economy, if at all, is a subject of continuing debate.

Quick Quiz List and briefly explain the three principles that describe how the economy as a whole works.

IN THE NEWS

Accepting Principles?

The ten principles of economics presented in this chapter are fundamental to the understanding of economics. However, these principles do not mean that everyone will agree or adhere to them even if research suggests links between some of these principles and improvements in welfare and well-being. This article shows how countries and businesses will choose to ignore some of these principles if they believe it benefits certain sections of society, despite recognizing that their decisions may have adverse effects on other people and businesses.

Cotton Ban Imposed by Egypt

Prices of raw cotton in the 2010/11 season were relatively high. These high prices acted as an incentive for farmers to grow more cotton in Egypt and so reap the benefit of the higher prices. However, a year later, global cotton prices are not as high and so the harvest has seen Egyptian cotton growers facing much lower prices than they anticipated. Cotton traded on global markets is measured in qintirs with one qintir being around 160 kg of cotton.

Cotton growers in Egypt not only supply the local domestic market but also export a major proportion of their output. The cotton crop for 2011/12 was expected to be around 3.7 million qintirs

Incentives to plant cotton are dependent on the price at planting time rather than what price is received at harvest.

and of that amount about 54 per cent will be sold abroad.

Growers had been expecting prices of around 1700 Egyptian pounds per qintir but market prices were nearer to 1500 Egyptian pounds per qintir. As a result, growers put pressure on the Egyptian trade minister to impose a ban on imports of cotton allowing domestic growers to sell their remaining stock of cotton within the country first. Such an idea is of course contrary to the principle that markets are usually the best way of allocating resources (in this case cotton) and that trade can make everyone better off. The initial incentives provided by higher prices acted as a spur to growers to plant more cotton but now they fear being left with stocks of cotton they won't be able to sell at high enough prices to cover their costs.

The ban on imported cotton means that domestic buyers will not be able to access cotton at the cheaper prices and instead they will be forced to pay higher prices to domestic Egyptian growers. The trade-off is clear; Egyptian growers are able to maintain their incomes as a result of the import ban and therefore benefit from the decision, but domestic buyers of cotton will face higher prices than would be the case under 'free trade' and so their costs will rise and possibly damage their competitiveness.

The trade minister noted that the ban on imports was only likely to be

temporary, perhaps for a three-month period until stocks had been sold. This might be of small comfort to the buyers of cotton who know that the 1.7 million qintirs of cotton left for the domestic market after export sales have been met is less than the total domestic demand for cotton. When supply is less than demand the result is that prices will rise and so domestic buyers will have to pay higher prices than they otherwise would if they were able to satisfy demand through buying cheaper imports. If their costs are lower, consumers will face lower prices – one of the benefits of trade.

Questions

1. What might have caused cotton prices to be 'relatively high' in 2010/11?
2. Explain some of the problems facing cotton farmers through having to make production decisions many months in advance of receiving revenues from the harvest.
3. Explain the likely effect on cotton prices in Egypt if the government banned foreign imports.
4. How will the import ban affect clothing manufacturers in Egypt?
5. How might clothing manufacturers in Egypt respond to the market conditions they face?

FYI

How to Read This Book

Business Economics is fun – it is dynamic, always raising new issues and problems, interesting approaches and perspectives, but it can also be hard to learn. Our aim in writing this text has been to make it as easy and as much fun as possible to apply basic economic principles to a business context. But you, the student, also have a role to play. Experience shows that if you are actively involved as you study this book, you will enjoy a better outcome, both in your exams and in the years that follow. Here are a few tips about how best to read this book.

1. *Highlighting is not enough.* Running a yellow marker over the text or using the highlight function in an e-book is too passive an activity to keep your mind engaged. Instead, when you come to the end of a section, take a minute and summarize what you have just learnt in your own words, writing your summary in the wide margins we've provided or in the notes section provided in the e-book or, if you don't want to (or are not allowed to) write on the book itself, use a notepad of some description (electronic or paper). When you've finished the chapter, compare your summary with the one at the end of the chapter. Did you pick up the main points?
2. *Test yourself.* Throughout the book, Quick Quizzes offer instant feedback to find out if you've learned what you are supposed to. Take the opportunity. Write your answer using whatever notes writing option you have. The quizzes are meant to test your basic comprehension. If you aren't sure your answer is right, you probably need to review the section. These quizzes will also help you to

think about the issues that have been covered in the text. Thinking in economics is vital if you want to improve and learn what the subject is all about. Never be frightened to think and question – some of the best ideas in economics and business have arisen because people think and question. You may make mistakes when you think but that is one way that we learn.
3. *Practise, practise, practise.* At the end of each chapter, Questions for Review test your understanding, and Problems and Applications ask you to apply and extend the material all set in different business contexts. Perhaps your lecturer will assign some of these exercises as coursework. If so, do them. If not, do them anyway. The more you use your new knowledge, the more solid it becomes.
4. *Study in groups.* After you've read the book and worked through the problems on your own, get together with other students to discuss the material. You will learn from each other – an example of the gains from trade.
5. *Don't forget the real world.* In the midst of all the numbers, graphs and strange new words, it is easy to lose sight of what business economics is all about. The Case Study and In the News boxes sprinkled throughout this book should help remind you. Don't skip them. They show how the theory is tied to business events happening which affect all of our lives. If your study is successful, you won't be able to read a newspaper again or look at a business without thinking about supply, demand and the wonderful world of business economics.

6. *Relate concepts to concrete examples.* Throughout this book we will introduce a number of new concepts – ways of representing things which allow us to bring meaning to our lives. Many of the concepts we introduce will have specific meanings in business economics but also have other meanings in everyday use. For example, the term 'capital' is widely understood by non-economists as meaning 'money'. In business economics capital has a far more precise meaning. We will encounter a number of examples of these concepts which are also in everyday use but which may be interpreted differently in the world of business economics. Ensure, therefore, that you are comfortable in the meaning and use of these concepts.
7. *Think like an economist.* After using this book we hope that you will start to think like an economist. This can be taken to mean that there is a body of knowledge, a set of skills and methods that are used by business economists to identify, analyse and evaluate problems which constitute 'thinking like an economist'. In so doing, those problems become 'economic problems' because they are to do with scarcity, choice, decision making and the outcome of that decision making. To enable economists to be able to represent those problems and provide commentary and solutions, an understanding of a series of concepts is necessary. Some of these concepts are concrete whilst others are very abstract.
8. *Think threshold concepts.* One of the possible approaches to understanding some of these very important

concepts we will introduce is to be found in the notion of threshold concepts (Meyer and Land, 2005[1]). The acquisition of threshold concepts represents a transformation of the student's view of the subject. In essence, a threshold concept represents a portal that opens up a new way of thinking for the learner. Threshold concepts may be intuitively very difficult to comprehend, may be counter-intuitive and in some cases intellectually absurd (Meyer and Land, 2003[2]). Without breaking through this barrier the student will always encounter 'troublesome knowledge' (Perkins, 1999[3]). It could be argued that this troublesome knowledge may well be the source of problems facing students at all levels in business economics with questions that seek to assess the understanding of a number of core concepts. These concepts will remain fuzzy and hazy in the student's mind throughout the period of their study unless they overcome the threshold concept. We will use some of the pedagogic features in the book such as the 'What if...' questions, the 'Pitfall Prevention' and the 'Jeopardy Problem' features to help you come to grips with this troublesome knowledge and enter the portal – make sure that you use these features fully.

CONCLUSION

You now have a taste of what business economics is all about. In the coming chapters we will develop many specific insights about people, businesses, markets and economies. Mastering these insights will take some effort, but it is not an overwhelming task. The field of business economics is based on a few basic ideas that can be applied in many different situations.

Throughout this book we will refer back to the *Ten Principles of Economics* highlighted in this chapter and summarized in Table 1.2. Even the most sophisticated economic analysis is built using the ten principles introduced here.

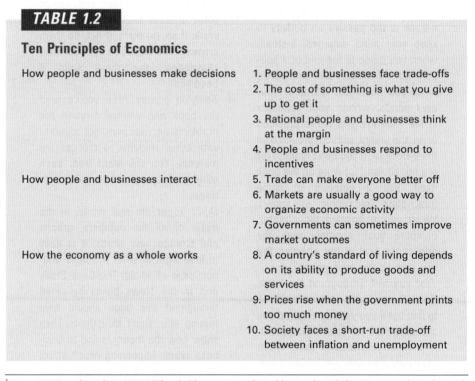

TABLE 1.2

Ten Principles of Economics

How people and businesses make decisions	1. People and businesses face trade-offs
	2. The cost of something is what you give up to get it
	3. Rational people and businesses think at the margin
	4. People and businesses respond to incentives
How people and businesses interact	5. Trade can make everyone better off
	6. Markets are usually a good way to organize economic activity
	7. Governments can sometimes improve market outcomes
How the economy as a whole works	8. A country's standard of living depends on its ability to produce goods and services
	9. Prices rise when the government prints too much money
	10. Society faces a short-run trade-off between inflation and unemployment

[1]Meyer, J.H.F. and Land, R. (2005) 'Threshold concepts and troublesome knowledge 2: epistemological considerations and a conceptual framework for teaching and learning', *Higher Education*, 49: 373–388.

[2]Meyer, J.H.F. and Land, R. (2003) 'Threshold concepts and troublesome knowledge: linkages to ways of thinking and practising within the disciplines'. In: Rust, C. (ed.) *Improving Student Learning – Ten Years On.* Oxford: OCSLD.

[3]Perkins, D. (1999) 'The constructivist classroom: the many faces of constructivism', *Educational Leadership*, 57(3): 6–11.

SUMMARY

- The fundamental lessons about individual decision making are that people and businesses face trade-offs among alternative goals, that the cost of any action is measured in terms of foregone opportunities, that rational people and businesses make decisions by comparing marginal costs and marginal benefits, and that people and businesses change their behaviour in response to the incentives they face.

- The fundamental lessons about interactions among people and businesses are that trade can be mutually beneficial,

that markets are usually a good way of coordinating trade among people and businesses, and that the government can potentially improve market outcomes if there is some market failure or if the market outcome is inequitable.

- The fundamental lessons about the economy as a whole are that productivity is the ultimate source of living standards, that money growth is the ultimate source of inflation, and that society faces a short-run trade-off between inflation and unemployment.

KEY CONCEPTS

stakeholder, p. 4
scarcity, p. 4
economics, p. 4
efficiency, p. 6
equity, p. 7
opportunity cost, p. 8
marginal changes, p. 9

market economy, p. 12
market failure, p. 14
externality, p. 14
market power, p. 14
economic growth, p. 15
gross domestic product (gdp) per head, p. 15

standard of living, p. 16
productivity, p. 16
inflation, p. 16
phillips curve, p. 17
business cycle, p. 17

QUESTIONS FOR REVIEW

1. Give three examples of important trade-offs that a business manufacturing cars might have to face.

2. What is the opportunity cost to a business of hiring four extra workers at an annual salary of €25 000 each?

3. Water is necessary for life. Is the marginal benefit of a glass of water large or small?

4. Why should policy makers think about incentives?

5. Why isn't trade among countries like a game, with some winners and some losers?

6. What does the 'invisible hand' of the marketplace do?

7. Explain the two main causes of market failure and give an example of each.

8. Why is productivity important to businesses and to society as a whole?

9. What is inflation, and what causes it?

10. How are inflation and unemployment related in the short run?

PROBLEMS AND APPLICATIONS

1. Describe some of the trade-offs faced by each of the following:
   a. A decision by an entrepreneur starting a small business to borrow some start-up capital from a bank or raise the funds through borrowing from friends and relations.
   b. A member of the government deciding how much to spend on some new military hardware for the defence industry.
   c. A chief executive officer deciding whether to invest in a new more efficient heating system for the company's headquarters.
   d. A worker in a hotel deciding whether to accept the offer by her manager of extra shifts in the restaurant.

2. You work in a bank and were planning to spend Saturday going to watch your local football team with your son and daughter. However, your boss has asked you if you would help prepare some important financial data for some new regulations that are being introduced by the government. It is not compulsory to come in over the weekend but it is made clear it would be looked upon favourably.
   a. If you decide to go to the football match, what is the true cost to you of that decision?
   b. If you decide to go into work for the weekend to help out your boss, what is the true cost of that decision?

3. A business operated by a sole trader generates €20 000 in profits and has the option of retaining the amount to

reinvest into the business or putting the sum into a bank which would generate 2 per cent interest a year. What would your decision be and why, and what is the opportunity cost of your decision?

4. A smartphone manufacturer invests €20 million in developing a new phone design and 3D interface, but the development is not quite finished. At a recent meeting, your sales people report that a rival has just released a new phone which is estimated to reduce the expected sales of your new product to €12 million. If it would cost €4 million to finish development and make the product, should you go ahead and do so? What is the most that you should pay to complete development? Explain your answer.

5. Three members of the operations management team at a plant manufacturing steel tubing for construction projects are discussing a possible increase in production. Each suggests a way to make this decision.
   a. Team member 1: We should base the decision on whether labour productivity would rise if we increased output.
   b. Team member 2: We need to focus more on cutting our average cost per tube – this will help us to be more competitive against our rivals.
   c. Team member 3: We should only increase output if the extra revenue from selling the additional tubes would be greater than the extra costs.
   Who do you think is right? Why?

6. Two owners of a small business, Hans and Jacques, are investigating how they can make the business more technically and productively efficient. Hans has a qualification in financial accounting whilst Jacques has always had a flair for selling. If Hans does all the accounting whilst Jacques concentrates solely on sales is it likely that the business will achieve its improvement in efficiency?

7. Suppose the European Union adopted central planning for its economy, and you became the Chief Planner. Among the millions of decisions that you need to make for next year are how much food to produce, what land to use and who should receive the food produced and in what quantities.
   a. To make these decisions intelligently, what information would you need about the food industry?
   b. What information would you need about each of the people in the countries making up the European Union?
   c. How would your decisions about food affect some of your other decisions, such as how much farm equipment to produce, how much labour to employ on farms and how much fertilizer to use? How might some of your other decisions about the economy change your views about food?

8. Explain whether each of the following government activities is motivated by a concern about equity or a concern about efficiency. In the case of efficiency, discuss the type of market failure involved.
   a. Regulating gas prices.
   b. Regulating advertising.
   c. Providing students with vouchers that can be used to buy university education.

9. Discuss each of the following statements from the standpoints of equity and efficiency.
   a. 'All students should have free access to higher education'.
   b. 'Businesses making workers redundant should be made to provide at least six months' pay as a redundancy payment to enable those affected time to find a new job'.
   c. 'Businesses should be made to pay more into workers' pension schemes to ensure that people have a decent standard of living when they retire'.

10. Imagine that you are a policy maker trying to decide whether to reduce the rate of inflation in your country. To make an intelligent decision, what would you need to know about inflation, unemployment and the trade-off between them?

2 ECONOMICS AND BUSINESS DECISION MAKING

LEARNING OBJECTIVES

In this chapter you will:

- Cover the basic economic problem of unlimited wants and scarce resources

- See how decision making is governed by estimations of costs and benefits

- Explore the meaning of value in relation to decision-making

- Look at the key areas of business decision making

- Look at the problems facing businesses of acquiring and retaining customers

After reading this chapter you should be able to:

- Give examples of unconscious and conscious decisions by consumers and businesses

- Explain the basic economic problem of scarce resources and unlimited wants

- Give examples about how informed decision making can be based on assumptions about weighing up the value of costs and benefits

- State at least two examples of the difficulties in valuing accurately costs and benefits

- Explain the importance to businesses of decisions on investment, growth and expansion using appropriate examples

- Show how acquiring and keeping customers are important decisions for a business

- Give an example to show how making decisions on keeping customers needs to be assessed carefully

ECONOMICS AS THE SCIENCE OF DECISION MAKING

In every walk of life humans have to make decisions. Many of these decisions are unconscious ones such as choosing when to cross the road, putting butter on toast, filling up the car with fuel and putting on a pair of socks or a skirt, but every decision involves some sort of choice. Many introductory economics texts will tell you that resources are scarce relative to demand and this means that few of us ever have the resources to satisfy all our needs.

The Economic Problem — Scarce Resources and Unlimited Wants and Needs

needs the essentials of life such as food, water, clothing and shelter, without which it would be difficult to survive

wants all the things we would like to have which we believe make our lives more comfortable and happy

scarce resources resources that are insufficient in quantity relative to the demand for them

The central economic problem is one of scarce resources and unlimited wants and needs. The Earth is blessed with resources of all kinds: some we know about and some we still do not know exist. Oil, metals, land, minerals, plants, animals and so on all provide humans with the means to satisfy our **needs**; the essentials of life such as food, water, clothing and shelter, without which it would be difficult to survive, and our **wants** — all the things we would like to have which we believe make our lives more comfortable and happy.

However, these resources are scarce. By **scarce resources** we mean that they are insufficient in quantity relative to the demand for them. Few people have so much money that they can afford to satisfy all their wants and needs (even the phenomenally rich have wants, albeit sometimes highly extravagant!). As a result we have to use our income wisely and make decisions about how we allocate our income and scarce resources to different uses. We have to make decisions.

AT ZEBCO AND ASSOCIATES, THE FILING SYSTEM LEFT A LOT TO BE DESIRED.

P.J CURRIER/MEDIA SELECT INTERNATIONAL

? **what if...**you are living inside the Arctic Circle and are having some guests round to your house for a party. You go to a store which is selling packaged ice cubes in its freezer. Would you buy them? If so why and if not why not?

In choosing between buying one product or another we undertake both conscious and subconscious processing. In seeking to understand decision-making behaviour, economists have made assumptions that help us to model decision-making behaviour. This is based on an assumption that humans weigh up the value of the costs and benefits of a decision. If the value of the benefits of a decision, for example, buying a seat on a flight with one airline rather than another, is greater than the value of the costs then it is reasonable to assume that we will make that decision to buy.

This assumption of rational behaviour may work in many cases; it could be argued that businesses in particular have developed sophisticated ways of making rational decisions. Over the last 30 years, however, advances in technology and research in the field of neuroscience and psychology has opened up new information to how and why humans make decisions which may contradict the assumption of rational behaviour. If we assume rational behaviour as the basis for our model of human behaviour, then deviations from that behaviour can be observed and investigated to find other explanations. As we improve our understanding we can develop new theories which can then be used to make predictions and on which we can make more informed decisions.

Individuals, then, rarely have a sufficient income to satisfy all their wants and needs, businesses rarely have enough cash or assets to be able to satisfy every stakeholder want

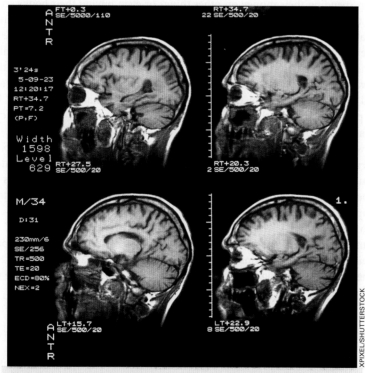

XPIXEL/SHUTTERSTOCK

The use of technology allows researchers to develop an increasingly sophisticated understanding of how the human brain works in decision making under different situations and with different amounts of risk involved.

and need, and governments do not have infinite funds which allow them to meet every want and need of citizens in their own country, and increasingly, in other countries as well, for example in being able to provide aid to less developed countries.

The Effect of Human Decision Making on Businesses

Let us explore the process of decision making in a bit more detail. We might go to the supermarket and, on autopilot, fill up our shopping trolley with similar products to those we purchased last time — almost without thinking. We might be tempted by the end-of-aisle or point-of-sale offers that persuade us to give up our hard earned cash in order to acquire the good in question but this has involved us in a little bit more mental computation than the buying on autopilot.

What has this got to do with business? The answer is a great deal. Every time an individual makes a decision about the purchase of a product it has an effect on a business. Consider the following example.

A new student walks into a university bookshop and looks at the copy of Mankiw, Taylor and Ashwin on the shelf which has been recommended by her lecturer. The student looks at the book, thinks it looks impressive but when she looks at the price she thinks it is a little high. Giving up €50 at that moment in time makes her think twice. She thinks about the freshers' welcome party for new members of the netball team which she is planning on going to, not to mention the freshers' ball at the end of the week. She puts the book back on the shelf and decides she will try her luck in the library instead.

The effect of this decision is that the bookshop will not receive €50 from the sale of the book. This is just another in a long line of decisions being made by students which has seen sales at the bookshop declining. At the end of the month the bookshop returns the unsold stock back to the publisher, Cengage Learning. The publisher has to adjust its inventories (stocks) and now has more stock of the book than it had anticipated.

The bookshop may find that if it cannot encourage more students to use its facilities rather than spending their money on other things or even buying their books second hand or online, then it may not be able to cover the costs of stock, staffing, lighting and heating, administrative costs and rent for the premises. It may have to close down as a result.

For the publisher, the increase in stock means that it will not have to reprint the book at the time it planned to do so. The printing company in China finds that the reprint order it was expecting does not arrive and as a result they cut back on the amount of paper and ink they order from their suppliers. For paper manufacturers the fall in the order for paper means that they now do not need to hire as many workers and so workers are made redundant.

These workers find their incomes are now much lower and so have to cut back on the family spending. They used to eat out at least once every two weeks but now decide they have to cut that out altogether. The restaurant where they used to eat notices a drop in the number of people walking through the door to eat and so do not need to order as many supplies of ingredients as previously …

And so on.

The simple decision by the student on its own may not seem to be that important but the combined effect of millions of decisions made every day by millions of people around the world do have significant effects on businesses. These decisions are important in other ways too.

Value for Money

A decision to buy this book is a message to the publisher and the authors that the book has some value — it helps with study, it makes the subject easier to understand, the support resources are helpful in getting through assessment and ultimately the student can get the grade they are looking for. In other words, a decision to buy this book implies the buyer feels it will give value for money. We can define **value for money** as a situation where the satisfaction gained from using the book (however we choose to measure that satisfaction) is greater than the amount of money the individual had to hand over to acquire it (the price).

If enough students make such a decision this book will be very successful. The authors will be pleased because they will get royalties from the sale of each book and the publisher will be pleased because each sale represents revenue and if enough books are sold to more than cover the total costs of producing and selling the book, it will make a profit.

However, the decision to buy this book has an effect on other books which could have been bought for a Business Economics course. When you are in a book shop or looking at the choices on a website, choosing one book is an endorsement for the producer of that book, but what about the one you decide not to buy? If enough people make the choice to buy this book and not another, then the rival publisher may decide that its book does not have a market and declares the book out of print. The author is likely to get very few, if any, royalties and those people that worked hard to help produce the book may find their jobs in jeopardy if something similar happens to other books they are involved with.

This is why economists spend a great deal of time looking at the working of markets. A **market** is made up of two parties, buyers (consumers) and sellers (producers) coming together to agree on exchange. Businesses make products available and consumers make decisions about whether to buy these products. Every individual consumer decision is important in its own right but in order to get an understanding of the market as a whole we look at the effects of the aggregation of those decisions.

Why consumers make the decisions they do is the subject of continued debate and academic research. The developments in imaging technologies have revealed, in part (there is still much we do not know), how the brain functions when we make decisions. It is opening up fascinating new lines of enquiry and understanding. Neuroscience and developments in psychology are playing their part in helping economists to better understand human behaviour in a variety of contexts, including how they make purchasing decisions. Behavioural economics is becoming an increasingly important branch of the discipline and is being utilized not only by academic economists but also by businesses in a bid to better understand decision making and human behaviour.

> **value for money** a situation (mostly subjective) where the satisfaction gained from purchasing and consuming a product is greater than the amount of money the individual had to hand over to acquire it (the price)

> **market** a group of buyers and sellers of a particular good or service

BUSINESS DECISION MAKING

It is not only consumer behaviour in relation to decision making that businesses are interested in. They are also interested in how businesses make decisions themselves about a whole host of things such as who to hire, when to hire, what to invest in, what not to invest in, how to make decisions that maximize efficiency, whether to pursue an acquisition or not, whether to conduct an advertising campaign and if so how much to spend on it and when, amongst others.

Businesses are also interested in how other stakeholders make decisions — why are some employees apparently 'lazy' and not committed to their work or to the principles and values of the business? How do governments make decisions and what impact will it have on businesses? What decision-making processes take place at suppliers? Are the decisions managers and owners make compatible, and if so how will these decisions affect local communities and the environment?

Quick Quiz Think about a recent purchase decision you made. What were the other options you could have chosen instead? Articulate the reasons why you eventually made the decision to purchase the product you did.

Businesses also have to make decisions every day. There are three important areas we can look at where decision making has to be considered carefully.

Investment

investment making money available to develop a project which will generate future returns including increasing future productive capacity

One of the key decisions that has to be made relates to investment. **Investment**, in this context, is about making money available to develop a project which will generate future returns including increasing future productive capacity:

- It could be a chemical engineering firm deciding to hire a specialist chemist to work on the development of a particular process for a client; it could be a tool making firm investing in a new piece of machinery which helps make the firm more productive; a food manufacturing plant buying a new oven which helps improve temperature regulation of the cooking process or helps to increase the volume of ingredients being processed at any one time.
- A farmer might have to make a decision on whether to install a new milking parlour to replace an existing facility. The new parlour might provide the farmer with more information about the volume and quality of the milk being given by the herd as well as automating some procedures which mean that more cows can be milked in a shorter amount of time. This might then free up the farmer to do other important jobs around the farm.
- A Chinese restaurant owner might have to make a decision about which insurance company to use to renew its insurance policies to cover it for fire, theft, loss of profits, public liability (in case any customer or member of the public is injured or suffers in some way as a result of the business' actions), injury to employees (employers' liability), damage or loss to machinery and equipment and many other possible risks. Does it stick with its existing insurer who has provided good service but is quite expensive, or go with a new insurer with an unknown reputation but which is much cheaper?
- A road haulage company might have to make a decision about investing in a computerized monitoring system for all its fleet of vehicles which travel around Europe to help it improve its logistical planning, adhere to health and safety regulations and help improve tracking in the event of theft.
- A government decision to shift the emphasis towards 'clean' energy and to expand nuclear energy production in the country might mean a 15-year programme to build new nuclear power stations costing around €3 billion per station.

There are some key characteristics which are common to decision making from small decisions such as that of the Chinese restaurant, right up to very large ones such as the nuclear power stations. Any decision will bring with it some costs, both financial and otherwise and it will also bring with it benefits — these benefits could be to the business itself and to stakeholders and the wider society.

In making any decision, therefore, these costs and benefits have to be weighed up. As we have seen, we can make an assumption that a decision is worth taking if the value of the accrued benefits outweighs the value of the total costs of the decision. When you, as an individual, make a decision about which chocolate bar to buy amongst all the ones on display in the shop, you are subconsciously saying that the cost of buying the bar (including the possible effects on your health from its consumption) is less than the satisfaction you will get from eating it *and* that this particular bar gives you more satisfaction at that point in time in relation to the money you are being asked to give up to acquire it than any of the other bars which you could have chosen.

Cook pans in a food manufacturing plant — the decision to purchase these pieces of equipment will have been taken after carefully weighing up the costs and benefits and what contribution they will make to overall production and productivity.

© ANDREW ASHWIN

 what if... you value two chocolate bars equally, how do you make a decision which to buy if you can only afford one of them?

Governments will have to consider these costs and benefits also. Are the costs of building a series of new nuclear power stations, with the potential cost that they could impose on society if there was a catastrophic incident at the station or from the long-term disposal of nuclear waste, deemed less than the benefits which could accrue from relatively cheap, reliable and clean energy supplies?

Economists would argue that in order to make any informed decision we have to have some idea of the value of the relative costs and benefits. It is relatively simple to calculate the financial cost of building and operating a new nuclear power station and to estimate the financial benefits to households. What is not so easy is calculating the cost of a catastrophic failure in the plant which leads to a leakage of radiation, the effect on the ecosystem or the damage to the visual amenity of the area around which the plant will be built.

The more accurately these sort of costs can be calculated the more informed the decision. Economists work at trying to find more effective ways of calculating costs and benefits more accurately but ultimately there is always going to be some error term and a lack of information which will make the calculations and estimates less than perfect.

JEOPARDY PROBLEM

Following a lengthy period of consultation with local communities, businesses and pressure groups, a government agrees to plans to make a busy ten-mile stretch of single carriage roadway connecting a major city to the nearest motorway into a dual carriageway. What sort of factors could have led the government to arrive at this decision?

Growth and Expansion

At some point in time, a business will have to make a decision about growth and expansion. It could be argued that a new business start-up is as much a part of growth and expansion as a decision by a large multinational business to acquire a new business by merger or takeover.

These decisions involve considerable risk to a business. **Risk** is the extent to which a decision leading to a course of action will result in some loss, damage, adverse effect or otherwise undesirable outcome to the decision maker. One of the first questions many businesses may ask themselves when making a decision is 'what could go wrong' and decisions relating to growth and expansion are no different.

risk the extent to which a decision leading to a course of action will result in some loss, damage, adverse effect or otherwise undesirable outcome to the decision maker

A business might grow through internal or external means. Internal growth comes from the business generating sufficient profits to be able to reinvest those profits back into the business to enable it to grow. This reinvestment might be in buying new premises, new plant and equipment, more efficient computer systems or hiring a consultant to help identify new systems and processes of working which allow the business to sell more or taking on more staff.

External growth by contrast is generally much quicker in that a firm can grow by either taking over or merging with another business. Merger and acquisition activity (M&A) tends to fluctuate with the swings in economic activity; when the economy is growing, M&A activity tends to be higher and vice versa. There are often grand claims made by business leaders about the benefits to the business of any such external growth. The word 'synergies' is used regularly to describe how anticipated benefits will accrue to the business. **Synergy** refers to a situation where the combination of two or more businesses or business operations brings total benefits which are greater than those which would arise from the separate business entities. The idea of 2 + 2 = 5 is often used to exemplify the principle.

synergy situation where the combination of two or more businesses or business operations brings total benefits which are greater than those which would arise from the separate business entities

The reality tends to be less spectacular. There have been a number of very high-profile mergers and takeovers which have promised huge benefits to shareholders and customers alike which have proved to be illusory. Some estimates put the success rate of mergers and acquisitions at between 20 and 45 per cent. If we take the lower end of these estimates then only one in five mergers and acquisitions are successful. This, of course, depends on what we mean by 'success'. If the M&A did not bring the benefits promised at the outset then the process could be classed as not being successful although the business might still be in a better position than it was prior to the M&A.

Pitfall Prevention Terms such as 'success' or 'failure' are relative. This means that we have to be careful in how we make judgements in relation to these terms. If a business tells its shareholders that a merger will yield a 40 per cent increase in technical efficiency within 5 years but in the event efficiency only increases by 20 per cent, should this be classed as a failure? Always make sure that you are clear in your definition of what is meant by 'success' or 'failure' when discussing business activity.

Acquiring and Keeping Customers

For any business to survive it must have customers, whether these customers are other businesses buying supplies or final consumers. Acquiring customers involves some cost — marketing, advertising, promotion, putting in place appropriate services, having the right product in the right place at the right time and ensuring that the product meets the expectations of customers in terms of quality. It will also involve making decisions about how much money should be devoted to acquiring new customers? How much budget should a new advertising or promotion campaign be given? What is the best and most efficient way in which customers can be reached and persuaded to try the business' products?

Once a business has acquired customers, there are also decisions to be made about how these customers can be retained and at what cost. What emphasis should the business put on keeping customers in relation to acquiring new ones — should it be 80:20, 70:30, 60:40, 50:50 or some other proportion combination?

At what point is it appropriate to lose a customer? In principle, the answer will be when the cost of retaining that customer becomes higher than the benefits that the customer brings — in other words, the revenue being generated by the customer is less than the cost of retaining that customer.

CASE STUDY

Acquiring Customers

Monica Schnitger is president of the Schnitger Corporation. Her business provides market research and market intelligence services to clients across a range of businesses in the engineering software industry.

In one of a series of blog posts, Monica relates a case where the cost of keeping a customer begins to become questionable but where often a business might be blinded to the fact. The story relates to a computer aided design (CAD) company which built and tested software for one particular customer who provided the business with much needed cash. The cost of running the machinery and platforms both in plant and human terms was relatively high but was it worthwhile to the business to continue to support this high maintenance client?

What was the cost of acquiring this client? Assume that the customer came to the business through responding to a promotional campaign which involved a 'free' consultation by one of the software design team to the business to demonstrate what the company can offer. The cost of that individual's time, the planning and preparation time of the marketing department, producing any necessary documentation, flyers, software demonstration products, getting to the businesses to demonstrate, staff expenses and so on would all have to be considered. Let us assume that the cost of all this was €22 500. As a result of the campaign three new customers were acquired. The cost of acquiring each new customer is thus €7500.

TABLE 2.1

Year	Revenue (€)	Running cost (€)	Net profit (€)
2	15000	6000	9000
3	16000	8000	8000
4	14000	11000	3000
5	13000	12000	1000

In order to make this worthwhile the revenue the customers must bring in must be greater than €7500 each but over what time period? Each year the business will have to spend some money on keeping these customers which also has to be taken into account in looking at whether it is worthwhile doing so.

Let us look at the situation over a period of five years in relation to one of the customers. The cost of maintaining the account is likely to rise over a period of time and revenues may also vary over that time period.

The situation in Year 1 is:

- Initial cost of acquiring customer = €7500
- Revenue in first year = €20000
- Gross profit (the difference between the initial cost and the total revenue) = €12500
- Cost of maintaining the account = €5000 for the year.
- Net profit = gross profit — running costs = €12500 — €5000 = €7500

In subsequent years the costs and revenues are as shown in Table 2.1.

The total cost to the business of this account is €49500. The total revenue is €78000. Overall profit is €28500. It seems from this calculation that this client is clearly beneficial. Schnitger points to the concept of a 'lifetime value' of this account. This value may not be all that it seems because our calculations have not taken into account the fact that the value of the revenues coming in each year is not the same.

The business also faces increases in costs in maintaining the level of service needed to satisfy customer needs. What happens if, in Year 6, the purchaser company insists on an improvement in the service it receives but is not prepared to pay anything more for it? Should the business give in to such a demand in order to keep its customer?

Possibly, but Schnitger points to the fact that consideration has to be given to the real value of the account. By this she is referring to taking into account a concept called the 'present value of money'. We will deal with this concept in more detail in Chapter 15 but at this stage it is sufficient to understand the principle that €1 is not worth as much in 5 years' time as it is today. Inflation will have to be taken into account. For the business, the €15000 it receives in revenue in Year 5 is not worth anything like the same amount as it would have been in Year 1 and the higher the inflation rate the lower will be this value.

The overall profit, therefore, needs to be discounted to take this into consideration. It could be that, after discounting, the business finds that far from operating at a profit it is actually operating at a loss (especially if taking an economic perspective on profit rather than an accounting one). In this case the decision to keep the customer because of loyalty or a belief that it needs the cash and is thus of some strategic importance to the business could be misguided.

The balance between the cost of acquiring and keeping customers changes, depending in part, on the wider economic environment. It is often said that it is much cheaper to keep existing customers than find new ones — a report by the United Nations Conference on Trade and Development (UNCTAD) reported the industry wide ratio of 6:1

meaning that the cost of attracting new customers is six times that of keeping existing ones.

There are a number of factors that can affect the cost of both these things including the rate at which new competitors enter the industry; the extent to which existing competitor bring out new products and how close a substitute they are; pricing tactics being adopted; and levels of customer service. The latter can be important in retaining customers and includes such things as the expectations of customers not being met; the quality of the product in terms of how easy it is to use and how resilient it is; errors in billing customers and general customer service issues like the length of time customers have to wait to speak to someone; how knowledgeable customer service operatives are; the ease of accessing technical help; and how easy a website is to navigate.

All these factors are affected to a greater and lesser extent by the decisions a firm makes. Someone in the organization, for example, makes a decision about what telephone system to use, how many people there are to staff the system, where it is located and what its perceived role is. On the basis of this decision, the company could win and lose customers. Giving customers a frustrating time at the end of a phone but at low unit cost could be false economy.

> **Quick Quiz**   What factors might a business have to consider in making a decision to outsource customer service operations to a low labour-cost economy?

CONCLUSION

Economics can be seen as being a science of decision making. Because we are all affected in some way by scarce resources and unlimited wants and needs, we have to allocate resources to different uses and thus make choices. In making these choices we have to make decisions. There are increasingly more sophisticated ways of looking at how individuals and businesses make decisions but in order to analyse how economies work we make basic assumptions about behaviour. In making these assumptions we can then observe deviations and seek to develop more sophisticated models to understand why and which lead to theories which help us to make predictions.

Every individual consumer decision is important in its own right because that decision sends messages to a business about how the consumer values the products on offer — a decision to purchase can be taken as a positive message whilst a decision to purchase another product is a message that somehow the rival product is more valuable to the consumer for some reason. This collective individual decision making has major effects on the extent to which businesses are successful or not.

Businesses have to understand these reasons in order to improve their offering. In responding to changes or to the messages they receive from consumers, businesses also make decisions every day. These decisions can range from seemingly mundane ones such as whether to order reams of paper from one supplier compared to another, right through to major decisions on new plant and equipment or whether to acquire another business to help meet consumer needs more effectively. Each is important in its own right.

We can look at business decision making in three main areas: decisions on investment in new productive capacity, on growth and expansion, and on acquiring and keeping customers. Collectively these decisions are related and will have knock-on effects on other decisions businesses have to make. For example, if a decision is taken to introduce an enterprise resource planning (ERP) system (a system which brings together management information from inside and outside the business to the whole organization which helps improve flows of information within the business) this might then lead to decisions having to be taken on hiring new staff, maybe reducing staffing in some areas, decisions on training needs for staff and how to manage some of the disruption that will occur during transition.

We work on the basic assumption that businesses will weigh up the costs and benefits of a decision, attempting to quantify as far as possible these costs and benefits, and then making a decision if the value of the benefits outweigh the value of the costs. One of the problems businesses face in making decisions based on this principle is accurately valuing all the costs and benefits.

IN THE NEWS

Investment is crucial to economic growth. Investment referred to in this article as gross fixed capital formation is the amount of money spent by government and business on future productive capacity. We have seen how business has to make careful decisions about investment spending but the overall level of such spending has an effect on the business environment. This is why businesses often look to government to take the lead on investment spending, particularly on infrastructure. This article summarizes investment spending trends in India in late 2011.

Investment in India

The sharp slowdown in investments revealed in the latest GDP numbers is likely to continue going forward, economy watchers say.

Private sector investments are likely to remain weak going forward as policy impediments such as land acquisition issues and problems with environmental clearances weigh down heavily on overall capital formation in the country, they point out.

The investment climate and ease of doing business in infrastructure are critical issues that need to be addressed if India is to achieve the investment rates seen in 2007–2008 and the first half of 2008–2009. The infrastructure space is still not very conducive for private investments.

Although the decline in the investment rate is disconcerting, the government has sought to play down this issue. The second quarter GDP data, released late November 2011, showed gross fixed capital formation (GFCF) declining by 0.6 per cent in real terms to Rs 402994 from Rs 405567.

The investment rate (GFCF as a percentage of GDP at current prices) has come down to 28 per cent in Q2 of current fiscal, lower than the 30.3 per cent seen in Q2 of 2010–2011 and 33–34 per

cent levels achieved in 2007–2008 (at the peak of the India growth story), official data showed.

The investment rate was 28.45 per cent in Q1 of 2011–2012. The steady decline in investment rate is being seen as an important reason for slowdown in GDP growth.

Part of the reason for the steady decline in investment rate could be international factors like the eurozone debt crisis and slowdown in the US economy. Raising finances externally for domestic projects is not all that easy today when compared to the pre-crisis period, economy watchers pointed out. There are issues of availability of funds. The sharp depreciation of the rupee has added to the woes of corporates borrowing abroad.

There is also going to be little support by way of government spending, which has already cooled from a growth of 6.5 per cent in first half of fiscal 2010–2011 to 3.1 per cent in first half of 2011–2012, a research note of Housing Development Finance Corporation (HDFC) Bank pointed out.

Even after factoring in some moderation in net government spending going ahead, the net fiscal deficit for financial year 2011–2012 is likely to be close to 5.4 per cent of GDP against the bud-

geted levels of 4.6 per cent, the research noted added.

'The government has to facilitate a better investment climate. Risk appetite of industry is reducing. There are a number of factors including corruption cases and the uncertainty around government decision making. Many are wary of taking investment decisions in this climate,' Mr Pavan Kumar Vijay, Managing Director, Corporate Professionals, a professional services firm, told Business Line here.

Questions

1. Explain the link between investment and GDP growth in a country like India.
2. Why is infrastructure important for economic growth?
3. What factors might businesses take into account in making investment decisions?
4. What do you think is meant by the term 'risk appetite' in relation to business investment?
5. Explain how the Indian government might 'facilitate a better investment climate'.

Source: http://www.thehindubusinessline .com/industry-and-economy/article2681054.ece accessed 4 December 2011.

SUMMARY

- Decision making is at the heart of economics.
- Millions of decisions are made every day by consumers and these decisions affect businesses in different ways.
- Businesses have to make decisions every day as well and these focus on three main areas. Decisions on:
- investment
- growth and expansion
- acquiring and keeping customers.

- Assessing the value of the costs and benefits is a basis for making decisions.
- If the value of the benefits is greater than the value of the costs then the decision can be justified
- It is not always easy to quantify the value of all the costs and benefits in making a decision.
- Neuroscience is revealing new ways in which people and businesses make decisions which may not always reflect a rational decision based on the value of costs and benefits.

KEY CONCEPTS

needs, p. 24
wants, p. 24
scarce resources, p. 24

value for money, p. 27
market, p. 27
investment, p. 28

risk, p. 29
synergy, p. 29

QUESTIONS FOR REVIEW

1. Explain the difference between a conscious and a subconscious purchasing decision. Which do you think is more reliable and why?
2. Oil is a commodity and there are billions of barrels still waiting to be exploited. Why, then, do we refer to oil as a scarce resource?
3. Using some specific examples, explain the difference between wants and needs.
4. Explain what economists mean by making an informed, rational decision.
5. Explain how a decision by a student to take a bus to a guest lecture by a famous economist at a nearby town hall, rather than a taxi, affects both businesses.

6. You buy a new t-shirt from Holister and have to pay €25 for it. How would you measure the value for money for this t-shirt?
7. Why is it difficult to accurately assess the costs and benefits of a decision such as whether to grant permission to a leisure business to open a new theme park on the outskirts of a town?
8. What is risk in the context of decision making by a business?
9. Why do you think the cost to businesses of acquiring customers is generally much higher than retaining them?
10. Using an appropriate example, outline three factors which could lead to an increase in the cost of keeping customers.

PROBLEMS AND APPLICATIONS

1. When you go into a shop to buy a product, how often do you make decisions based on conscious and subconscious factors?
2. You have to arrange a flight from Amsterdam to Rome and look at a travel website for the choices available to you. List the range of factors you will want to consider in making your choice about which airline to choose to make the flight. To what extent is the decision you arrive at 'rational'?
3. Food is essential for human life. Does this mean that all food items should be classed as 'needs' and not 'wants'?
4. A customer of a mobile phone network contacts the provider to explain that they are changing to another provider. To what extent should the provider be concerned about this decision by the customer? Explain your answer.
5. Two student friends attend a gig showcasing a new band which has had rave reviews from music journalists. At the end of the evening they talk about their experience; one says they thought the band lived up to expectations and the €30 was 'more than worth it'. The other thinks the evening

was a 'waste of money'. Give some possible explanations about why each student had a different perception of value for money in this instance.
6. Some business leaders put faith in 'gut instinct' in making decisions. To what extent would you advise basing decisions on gut instincts rather than 'rational' analysis?
7. Explain how investment in new productive capacity can help a business grow internally.
8. Evaluate the case for a builder's merchant spending more money on retaining its existing customers rather than acquiring new ones.
9. A business calculates that the cost of acquiring a new customer is €250 and the average yearly revenue received from each customer is €260. Should the business go ahead with its customer acquisition spending on this basis?
10. 'There is a science to decision making and a business should take notice of this science in helping to make its own decisions.' To what extent do you agree with this statement?

3 THE BUSINESS ENVIRONMENT

LEARNING OBJECTIVES

In this chapter you will:

- Learn about business and business activity

- Look at the factors of production and how they facilitate the transformation process

- Cover how businesses add value

- See how internal and external factors affect business using the PESTLE framework

- Look at the stakeholder model

After reading this chapter you should be able to:

- Give a definition of the meaning of business and business activity

- List and give examples of the four factors of production

- List the key characteristics and skills of entrepreneurs

- Describe the transformation process and apply this to a series of everyday examples

- Give a definition of the term value added

- Explain the main internal and external factors which affect business activity through using the PESTLE framework

- Give a definition of the terms shareholder value and stakeholders

- Describe how shareholder value can be affected by both increasing revenues and reputation

WHAT IS BUSINESS – THE TRANSFORMATION PROCESS

One of the recurring themes of this book is that of decision making. Successful business is all about making decisions which help the business meet its aims and objectives and, as we have seen, economics can be seen as being a science of decision making. If business is about decision making, what is business? In its simplest terms business activity involves taking a series of inputs and producing an output. The output could be a physical good or a service. The business might provide these goods and services to someone who actually consumes the good or service (the final consumer) or to another business who may either act as an intermediary in getting goods and services to the final consumer or who will do something to those goods and services before selling them on to a final consumer.

Business activity where the business sells goods and services to a final consumer is referred to as **B2C business**. Where a business sells a good or service to another business, this is referred to as **B2B business**. In recent years there are also other forms of activity that could be classed as business activity where consumers interact with other consumers via social networking sites or specialist websites such as eBay, Amazon Marketplace, eBid, OZtion, uBid and Overstock, which facilitate this type of trade. This is referred to as **C2C business**.

B2C business business activity where the business sells goods and services to a final consumer

B2B business business activity where the business sells goods and services to another business

C2C business business activity where consumers exchange goods and services often facilitated by a third party such as an online auction site

transformation process the process in which businesses take factor inputs and process them to produce outputs which are then sold

factors of production a classification of inputs used in business activity which includes land, labour, capital and enterprise

> **Pitfall Prevention** The term 'business' in a question is generic – when considering answers to questions be sure to specify what type of business you are referring to so that you contextualize your answers and show some awareness that different businesses may be affected in different ways.

Factors of Production

There is a common feature which characterizes business activity. This feature is a **transformation process** summarized in Figure 3.1. Any business has to utilize inputs, referred to as **factors of production**, and does something with them to produce an output – a

FIGURE 3.1

The Transformation Process and the External Environment

This diagram is a representation of the business transformation process. Businesses take in inputs which incur costs and combine those inputs in different ways to produce an output which is then sold and generates revenue. Over time the revenue has to exceed the costs in order for the business to survive. The size of the difference between costs and revenues will vary according to different businesses and the aims and objectives of these businesses. Businesses do not carry out this process in isolation, they are affected by various influences classed as political, economic, social, technological, legal and environmental.

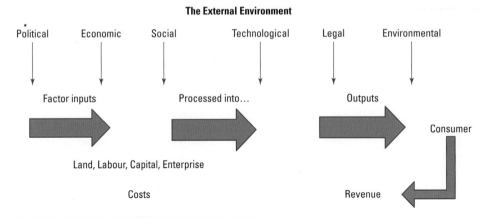

semi-finished product or commodity (raw materials such as rubber, cocoa, coffee, wheat, tin, ores, etc.), which is then sold on to another business or a finished product which is sold to a consumer.

Economists classify these factors of production in four main ways, although there are some that argue for only three factors of production. The four are land, labour, capital and enterprise. Some class enterprise as a specialist form of labour but we will assume it is a separate factor of production.

Land is a term that includes all the natural resources of the Earth and so might not only include pieces of land on which factories or offices are built, or which is farmed, but also things such as fish in the sea, minerals and ores from the ground and so on. **Labour** is all the physical and mental effort that is provided by humans in production. This then includes human activity ranging from the work of a chief executive officer (CEO) at the head of a large public company right through to the person who has to clean the toilets. Look around you at any time and you can see many examples of this human activity.

In everyday language we use the term capital to refer to money. Economists use the term capital in a different way although the two are linked. **Capital** refers to anything that is not used for its own sake but which makes a contribution to production. This might include equipment and machinery, buildings, offices, shops, computers, mainframes, desks, chairs, etc. Of course, in order to get capital, businesses need money but economists view money as a medium of exchange and so it is often more informative to look at what money has been used to purchase rather than how much money has been spent. This is because in making a decision to buy anything we have to make a sacrifice, the opportunity cost involved, and this can tell us a great deal about the relative value that businesses put on decision making.

land all the natural resources of the Earth which can be used in production

labour all the human effort, mental and physical, which is used in production

capital any item used in production which is not used for its own sake but for what it contributes to production

Quick Quiz Choose one product and write down some specific examples of the three factors of production covered so far which are used in the production of this product.

Factors of production like land, labour and capital need organizing before they combine to produce outputs. Iron ore in the ground is useless until someone organizes to bring the labour and capital to bear to extract it and process it ready for another business to use in many different ways. A chemical company will not discover new processes unless humans combine with land and capital to work out what these processes might be and design them so that they are cost effective and viable. As individuals we would have problems cutting and styling our own hair unless someone with the necessary skill brings together the factors of production to enable us to sit and watch as our hair is transformed. That requires land for the salon building, equipment such as sinks, taps, chairs, scissors, dryers, colourings, chemicals, etc., not to mention someone or a group of people taking the risk of setting up the business in the first place.

This is the factor of **enterprise**. Entrepreneurs take the risk of organizing factors of production to generate business activity and in return hope to get a number of rewards which might include profit but might also be less obvious things such as self-satisfaction, personal challenge and the desire to take more control over one's life.

We might often think of entrepreneurs as being exceptional individuals who have seemingly become incredibly successful and very wealthy. The names usually quoted in the same breath as entrepreneurs include Sergey Brin and Larry Page, Richard Branson, Mark Zuckerberg, Debbie Fields, Azim Premji and Lakshmi Mittal, amongst others, but these tend to be extreme examples. The reality is that the world is full of millions of people being entrepreneurial. They might include an individual who has set himself up in business as a painter and decorator, an electrician, builder, plumber, florist, carpet fitter, a child in a

© ANDREW ASHWIN

Look around you any time and business activity is everywhere. A busy city centre is full of people engaging in some sort of business activity. Every non-human thing in this image has been part of the transformation process.

enterprise the act of taking risks in the organization of factors of production to generate business activity

poverty stricken area of India making some money out of recycling rubbish in some way, a farmer running a dairy herd, a financial advisor, tyre fitter and many other examples.

© ANDREW ASHWIN

Can this be classed as an entrepreneurial activity?

The skills necessary to be an entrepreneur are well documented but the extent individuals possess and utilize these skills varies in each case. The reasons why some entrepreneurs go on to make millions whilst others struggle to barely make a living is not simply to do with the degree of determination, initiative, planning, access to finance, asking the right questions, acting on hunches, taking risks, being willing to work hard and make things happen, thinking ahead and thinking creatively, it is also to do with being in the right place at the right time and having a large degree of luck.

Entrepreneurs take risks and many of them fail: the rate of business failure in the three to five years after start up is estimated to be around 30 per cent, although getting precise data is difficult because we have to be careful how we define 'business failure'. It is fairly clear that a business fails if it has to file for insolvency or, in the case of a sole trader, bankruptcy, but if the owner sells on the business after a few years because they do not feel they are getting enough of a return is that also an example of failure?

? **what if…** the number of business failures rises above the 50 per cent level, would this mean that it is not worth taking the risks to start up a new business?

It is clear that setting up a new business is challenging. Potentially high failure rates do not put off millions of people around the world from starting businesses and many will try again after (sometimes many) failures in the hope that lessons have been learned and the next time will see things work.

The skills and qualities of entrepreneurs are many but perhaps the most important is the willingness to take risks. This is one reason why some economists prefer to class enterprise as a factor of production in its own right rather than seeing it as just another form of labour.

Business activity is about bringing these factors of production together to generate a product which is then sold. It is essentially a transformation process, therefore, with some types of business activity being very much more complex and risky than others. This is one reason why prices might be higher for some products compared to others and why some types of labour generate more income than do others.

The Transformation Process

How these factors are brought together, in what proportions and how they work together in the transformation process, could be very different, even in the same type of business operating in the same industry. Rarely are two firms producing cars or chemicals the same although they may have many similarities. One of the key elements of the transformation process is adding value and this could be at any stage in this process.

Added value is what a business does to inputs to convert them to outputs which customers (businesses or final consumers) are prepared to pay for. Adding value could be in the form of a piece or technology that makes a consumer's life much easier in some way or does the job the product is designed for more effectively or more stylishly than other rival products on the market. It might even be that a business creates a product or service that no one has thought of before and which people are prepared to pay enough money for, and over a long enough period (often repeatedly), to enable the business to cover the costs of producing that product and to provide a sufficient return to those who own the business to persuade them to keep producing. There is a great deal of complexity which arises out of this relatively simple statement but it is at the heart of what business activity is about and how a business can survive. If it cannot add value then the business will ultimately fail.

Some products will fail because they do not meet market needs, by which we mean that there are not enough people willing to pay the price being asked which is sufficient to cover the costs of production and provide the return.

> **added value** the difference between the cost of factor inputs into production and the amount consumers are prepared to pay (the value placed on the product by consumers)

> **Pitfall Prevention** Added value is the difference between the cost of inputs and the price consumers are 'prepared to pay' which can be affected by non-tangible things like perceived brand value.

The entrepreneur may have thought there was a market and whilst there invariably are some people who will buy the product, the key is whether there are *enough* people or businesses willing to pay for the product.

In other cases, a perfectly good product which has a market will fail because some other business comes along and offers a product which does something more and better. In other cases the product may fail because times have changed and there is simply no need for that product any more.

Business activity, therefore, is dynamic.

> **Quick Quiz** Think of two products which are now not produced in the volumes they were (if at all). Write down a brief list of why these products have ceased to have any commercial value.

The transitions in mobile phone technology is an excellent example of this dynamic process. The very idea of having a phone which could be used anywhere is relatively new, perhaps only 30 years old, but the changes over that period of time in what these products look like, their size and what they can do have been significant. Initially, merely being able to contact and speak to another person away from the house was a major step forward.

Then being able to send short messages was seen as a revolutionary step forward. After that combining a mobile phone with a device that could access the Internet was a goal of businesses in this Industry, but very quickly it became not only accessing the Internet but being able to send emails, record and transmit video, watch TV, play music, record voices, download and read books, act as a calculator, a personal messaging system, diary, satellite navigation system and so on, which have all become part of our mobile phone to the extent that in many cases people rarely use them for actually making a phone call any more!

It is difficult to imagine the many hours of development and technological change that have led us to the situation we are currently in with mobile phones, and it is probably even harder for us to imagine what these devices might be like in ten years' time. However, the point is that somebody has sat and thought about these things; they have asked what else could the technology allow us to do, what new technologies do we need to enable us to provide some even more wonderful things in the future? What sort of things do people want from these devices and perhaps equally important, what do they not want?

There were probably many different cases of products, phones, technologies that never actually made it past design or market research stage. Many ideas that never worked, but businesses in the industry took those risks, marshalled the factors of production and made the transformations necessary to create that dynamic process whereby competition led us to seeing new products and new technologies which we have been prepared to pay for and which we presumably think improve our lives (although there are always going to be disadvantages). If the advantages or costs outweigh the disadvantages then we tend to buy them and businesses will produce products as a result.

THE PESTLE FRAMEWORK

We have already mentioned that business activity is dynamic. Change will be happening all the time in any business and how they adapt to this change will be an important part of the extent to which the business is a success. In responding to change, there are some factors which the business will have some control over and others which the business does not have control over.

The business can have some control over the inputs it buys and how it combines those inputs to produce its outputs. However, there are a number of external factors over which it has very little control but which it has to respond and react to.

CASE STUDY

A Complex Transformation Process

It is entirely possible that you might be reading this case study on a computer device of some kind, perhaps a laptop, a smart phone, tablet etc. One of the key elements of these technologies is the silicon chip. Intel is one of the largest chip makers in the world and the following case gives some indication as to the complexity of the transformation process.

One of the key inputs is sand which includes large amounts of silicon. The silicon is purified by being melted and then cooled into an ingot – a cylindrical shape around 300 mm in diameter weighing 100 kg. This process is undertaken in Japan by companies like Toshiba Ceramics. Other companies then take these ingots and slice them into thin wafers around 1 mm thick. Each wafer is then polished and

Intel buys them in this state ready for manufacturing at its plants in Arizona and Oregon in the United States.

At these plants (called 'fabs') – which, incidentally are identical in design and building orientation – the wafers are etched with integrated circuits which build layers and which are the result of hundreds of individual processes. Once these processes are complete the wafers are then shipped to Intel's assembly and test plants in Malaysia. Here the wafers are tested and then sliced into pieces called dies and tested again to ensure they work. Those that do not pass this test are discarded and the ones that do are packaged and sent back to warehouses in Arizona. At this stage the packaging is anonymous so that it is not clear that they are from Intel to help reduce the risk of theft in transportation. From the warehouses in Arizona the chips are then shipped to computer manufacturing plants across the world and to different manufacturers. The plants can be in Brazil, Taiwan, China, Malaysia, Ireland and to other parts of the US such as Texas and Tennessee, depending on the manufacturer. Once the chips are put into the device this may then be shipped either to a retail outlet or direct to the customer. The humble chip in your device is likely to have travelled thousands of miles during its production process as it is transformed from sand into an extremely sophisticated electronic component capable of helping process millions of operations in a short amount of time.

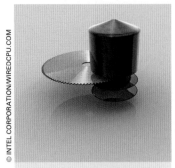

A silicon ingot being sliced into a wafer.

In order to help understand and analyse these external factors, a framework is used which summarizes a number of broad, sometimes highly related and interacting areas, which business has to work within. This framework is referred to as the PESTLE framework with the acronym standing for:

- Political
- Economic
- Social
- Technological
- Legal
- Environment

We will take a brief look at each one in turn.

Political

Politics refers to power – who has power, who makes decisions and how it affects individuals and business. Power can be wielded by local governments, national governments and supranational governments (where decision making or laws are made by groups or states outside national boundaries) such as the European Union (EU). In some countries power lies in the hands of a relatively small number of people, possibly linked to a royal family, tribal or religious group. In others the military may be an important element in the way in which political authority is framed.

In most countries in the EU, government is democratic with political parties submitting themselves for election periodically. Different systems determine who forms governments but one particular party or group of parties in coalition may have been given the power by the people to make decision, policies and laws which affect individuals and businesses in various ways. In other countries it is a ruling elite or the military who make decisions and establish laws and the people in the country may have a very limited, or no say, in the political process. In still other countries, the rule of law may barely exist and in this case business activity may be very difficult to carry out.

Changes to laws, directions in policy or regulations can all affect businesses in different ways. Laws on employment, employee rights and responsibilities, health and safety, taxation, planning, trade, advertising and business governance amongst many other things, all affect business and invariably raise the cost of doing business by either involving the business in additional time, form filling or procedures. In some cases laws or regulations may be passed with the aim of helping a business by giving grants or special dispensation to operate. In this case there may also be a cost in terms of certain conditions to which the business has to adhere to get the benefit. For example, there may be a relaxation of planning regulations which mean a business can establish new premises more quickly but the *quid pro quo* (something given in return for something) is that the business has to remain at the premises for a certain period of time or employ a certain number of people.

Economic

Businesses have to operate within an economic environment. This relates to the extent of economic activity in different 'economies' which could include a very local economy, a regional economy, a national or supranational or global economy. There are also bodies which have supernational powers – the authority to act across different nations – such as the International Monetary Fund (IMF).

Economic activity, as we have seen, refers to the amount of buying and selling that takes place. This activity can be looked at within a local area, a region, nation and on a global scale. The rate at which buying and selling (or the number of transactions) takes place varies at different time periods for different reasons as we will see in more detail in later chapters.

Businesses are affected by these fluctuations in economic activity. For example, a restaurant will be affected by decisions of people to decide to go out for a meal which may, in turn, be affected by how confident these people feel that they will continue to have a job in the future or whether they have recently lost their job. If a restaurant finds that the number of people they serve in a week is falling then they will have to adjust the supplies that they purchase and this will then have an effect on other businesses. Those supplying wine, soft drinks, fresh fruit and vegetables and other ingredients will then be affected by falling sales.

Such an example might be characteristic of a decline in the local economy and can often happen when an area is highly dependent on a single employer who may either scale back operations or even close down. A similar case will occur over regions and whole countries. The south of Italy, for example, suffers from a lower level of economic activity than the north and as such standards of living in the south are lower and opportunities for employment and growth are lower in return. There are similar situations which occur in parts of the former eastern Germany and across different parts of the Middle East. In the Palestinian territories, for example, economic activity is significantly affected by the ongoing political situation and this means that this region has a lower level of economic activity.

Countries can be compared in terms of economic activity and we can see from such comparisons that there are very widely differing levels of economic activity. In some African countries recorded economic activity is tiny in comparison to others in the region such as South Africa and Nigeria.

In recent years much has been made of the global economy and at the time of writing, forecasts for global economic activity are gloomy to say the least and come after a period of slower global economic growth which followed the financial crisis of 2007–2009.

What we can see from the above is that businesses are affected by the swings in economic activity both locally, nationally and globally. In many cases these swings might be triggered by some crisis such as the eurozone debt crisis, or a financial crisis in the banking system or by changes in interest rates, but the effects are magnified by the changes in confidence levels in individuals, businesses and governments.

It is also possible to classify these effects as microeconomic or macroeconomic. The **microeconomic environment** refers to factors and issues that affect an individual firm operating in a particular market or industry. Changes in economic activity can affect some firms in a positive way and others in a negative way. For example, regardless of the level of economic activity, funeral directors may experience relatively stable levels of trade although in times of economic slowdown families may choose to spend smaller amounts on funerals or choose cheaper options than they may do when the economy is performing more strongly.

In times of weak economic growth retail businesses such as supermarkets may also find that whilst there may be changes to the type of products people buy, the volume of trade does not decline that much, meaning they are relatively insulated from declines in economic activity. Retail businesses which sell high end products such as electronic goods or fashion items may find that they are very badly hit by economic slowdown and sales may fall dramatically. Other businesses such as second-hand shops, pawn shops or low price discount stores may actually find their business increases in times of economic slowdown. These are all examples of specific businesses in particular markets.

The **macroeconomic environment** refers to the national or global economy within which the business operates. The things which can affect businesses from macroeconomic changes include variations in exchange rates, interest rates (which may be linked), policies on taxation, planning, competition and so on. Changes in these macroeconomic factors can affect the level of economic activity in the economy as a whole and as a result impact on businesses.

If exchange rates change then businesses will be affected in different ways depending on the extent to which they buy and sell products from abroad and in what proportions. Costs could rise or fall (or a combination of the two) and demand could also rise or fall and the effects can be highly complex in businesses which trade extensively across different regions of the world.

Social

Businesses are affected by various trends, fashions, moods and changes in society. The move to improving the equality between men and women in the workplace, for example, has led to businesses having to adapt their processes and their attitudes to employment, the way their businesses operate and how they monitor the attitudes and behaviour of workers.

Social changes affect our attitudes to things like recycling and the publicity which has been given to the problem of climate change and/or global warming has meant that many businesses now report the extent to which they have taken steps to monitor energy use, recycling, the use of natural resources and where they source raw materials. Building and office construction is changing to try and find ways to improve efficiency and make them 'greener'.

There are broad social changes that are also having an impact on businesses, such as the changing structure of the population. Many European and Middle East economies, for example, are experiencing an ageing population with an increasing proportion of the population over the age of 65. This creates both opportunities and threats to businesses. Retirement ages may well rise in countries as governments struggle to afford state pensions and this changes employment dynamics. Businesses that offer pension support have already found that they have to adjust the type of pension they offer. Final salary schemes, where the pension the employee receives is based on a proportion of their salary at retirement, have been phased out and replaced by contributory pension schemes simply because some businesses were finding that they could not afford to sustain final salary schemes as people were living longer.

microeconomic environment
factors and issues that affect an individual firm operating in a particular market or industry

macroeconomic environment
the national or global economy within which the business operates

Every individual is part of the wider economy and their decisions affect not only the immediate businesses they interact with but the economy as a whole.

DMITRIJS DMITRIJEVS/SHUTTERSTOCK

An ageing population requires resources to be diverted to different uses in order to meet the needs of a different population structure – this provides opportunities for businesses as well as challenges.

For some businesses the ageing population provides opportunities to develop products and services which are targeted at the needs of the growing number of people who are over 65, who tend to be more affluent and who are still relatively healthy and active despite their age. The pattern of housing demand changes, with smaller homes required to take account not only of single pensioners, but also the rising number of single families, which has followed rising divorce rates in many countries.

Manufacturers are looking to develop vehicles which cater for the needs of older drivers through the provision of more intuitive technologies such as automatic parallel parking, sensors which mean the car can effectively 'see round corners', have active safety systems which warn the driver of potential hazards or danger ahead, voice operated functions and wi-fi capability in the car.

Other social changes such as the growth in the use of social networking sites, viral messaging and the Internet have opened up opportunities but also present threats. Facebook and Twitter provide the chance for businesses to showcase themselves and have their brand and message spread to large numbers of people very quickly and at low cost. The flip side of this is that the degree of control a business has over messaging and the reporting of the business is very weak.

Employees can, sometimes innocently, compromise the business and damage the brand or reputation simply through an injudicious use of 140 characters or an ill-judged piece of behaviour which is subsequently broadcast to millions on YouTube or Facebook. It is fair to say that most businesses are still trying to understand the social networking phenomenon and how best to utilize it. The problem is that social networking tends to change more quickly than the ability of a business to understand it and work out how to use it most effectively.

Technological

technology the application or use of knowledge in some way which enables individuals or businesses to have greater control over their environment

It is tempting to think of technology as some electronic gadget but the definition of technology is much wider. **Technology** is the use of knowledge in some way which enables individuals or businesses to have greater control over their environment. Businesses constantly think of ways in which they can employ knowledge in this way because it can help to reduce costs, improve technical and productive efficiency and in many cases social and allocative efficiency. Technology can also help give a firm competitive advantage where the advantage has the key characteristics of being distinctive and defensible.

The last 50 years have seen an explosion in technological developments that have provided both opportunities for businesses and also threats. How businesses respond to these opportunities and threats is a crucial element of business. Technological developments can also help to provide some answers to the most pressing problems that humans face, including the effect on the environment of business activity, how to feed a rapidly growing human population, how to provide access to the essentials of life such as water, how to treat killer diseases, save animals and plants from extinction and tackle global poverty.

Quick Quiz   Outline two examples where you think technology has improved our lives and two examples where you think technology has not led to an improvement in human welfare.

Legal

Laws and regulation can be national or supranational. The legal framework covers all aspects of society and businesses have to abide by these laws. A strong legal system which is respected is fundamental to the principle of good governance, which in turn helps provide confidence in the way in which a business operates and so promotes trade. As we have seen in Chapter 1, trade is beneficial most of the time but businesses will be reluctant to trade and customers put off buying if they do not have confidence in business activity.

For example, customers want to know that if they buy a litre of fuel from a petrol station they do actually get a litre of fuel dispensed from the pump; investors need to know that the information on which they base decisions is as accurate and truthful as possible, if a business comes up with a new idea, process or invention that they can protect the investment in time, money and intellectual capital that they have made.

Much of business success relies on confidence. Confidence between businesses, confidence between businesses and customers and the legal and regulatory framework, which is adhered to by most and which builds in adequate incentives to be adhered to, is an important part of this.

Laws and regulation govern the way in which financial accounts are reported, how labour markets work, what health and safety measures businesses need to put in place, how they can describe and advertise products, what information consumers must be given, what minimum standards must be met, how much pollution a business can create and many more.

Whilst a strong and respected legal and regulatory framework provides confidence, it also comes at a cost; businesses have to pay to implement legal and regulatory requirements and this not only means higher costs for them and possibly an effect on margins, but might also mean higher prices or more inconvenience for consumers. For example, data protection laws mean that husbands and wives often get frustrated at the fact that a business will not discuss issues relating to a spouse or partner.

> **?** **what if…**a business sees an opportunity to sell its goods into a new market in an emerging economy but a report tells them that governance and the rule of law is weak. Should the business enter that market?

Environment

It is now rare for any business to operate without some recognition of the impact of its operations on the environment. This awareness may be as a result of a conscious policy decision to manage its operations to take account of that impact, or through being forced by law or regulation to do so.

Economic growth across many countries around the world has meant that resource use is expanding and as we saw in Chapter 1, resources are scarce in relation to demand. There is also concern about how we use resources, not only in terms of productive and technical efficiency but also from social and allocative efficiency and how we manage the results of resource use in terms of the waste products generated and the impact on ecosystems and land use.

One of the major themes of the last 30 years has been a growing concern that the consequences of human activity could be having a negative effect on the wider ecosystem. There are plenty of studies to suggest that carbon emissions, largely produced by human activity, have been a direct cause of a gradual rise in average global temperatures which in turn could lead to greater volatility in global weather patterns and also bring about a thawing of polar ice caps, rising sea levels and subsequent effects on those living in low-lying areas of the world.

Major efforts have been made to get global agreement on reducing carbon emissions and finding more environmentally friendly ways of producing goods, services and

© ANDREW ASHWIN

The potential for business activity to impact on the environment always exists. The argument centres on the extent to which governments, laws and regulations can help reduce the risk.

energy. This has not been easy to achieve. One of the reasons is that the richer countries who have been accused of being responsible for these carbon emissions are now asking for everyone to take the pain and cost of adjustment and poorer countries are suggesting that such a move would jeopardize their efforts to grow and better provide for their people. They argue that the rich nations are the ones who caused the problems so the rich nations should be the ones who take most of the pain.

To counter this the rich nations say that there is little point in them taking action to reduce emissions if the emerging nations are going to more than replace any reductions they might make several times over in the coming years as they grow rapidly. It seems that whilst there is some consensus that the planet does face a problem, who is responsible and how it should be tackled is less in agreement.

One aspect of thinking like an economist is the necessity of thinking critically, of not accepting everything you hear or read without questioning its validity and reliability. In many countries in Europe, recycling is an obvious and significant feature of everyday life. Almost every business has recycling policies and facilities, universities vie with one another to be the 'greenest' institution, households, local government and businesses are required to recycle and to meet targets set by national and supranational government.

As business economists, we need to be thinking about the costs and benefits of recycling and as a result whether it makes economic sense. Not all recycling is 'good'; if, for example, the amount of resources necessary to recycle metal cans into other products was greater than the cost of producing the cans from scratch, would it be a sensible business decision to do it?

Equally, we need to remember to critically examine claims from 'scientists' about carbon emissions and climate change. If businesses are going to be required to make what are quite possibly very expensive and significant decisions on resource use and allocation, are the reasons for making those decisions based on sound information? How reliable are the studies carried out into the effects of rising carbon emissions? Does the idea of 'global average temperature' actually mean anything? Simply, businesses have to ask the right questions to get the right information in order to make more informed decisions.

Pitfall Prevention Whilst we classify external factors using the PESTLE framework, in analysing real business situations it is often not easy to simply classify factors affecting a business in a simple way – the factors tend to be interrelated and cause and effect are not readily identifiable.

JEOPARDY PROBLEM

A business producing top-of-the-range smartphones with the very latest technology goes into insolvency. What is most likely to have caused this?

SHAREHOLDER VALUE AND STAKEHOLDERS

We have seen how business activity is a transformation process but we have to ask ourselves why businesses carry out this activity and for whom? We can use two concepts to provide at least part of the answer: shareholder value and stakeholders.

Let us assume that shareholders is a term used to represent business owners as a whole rather than simply those people who have purchased shares in a business and become part owners in that business, because the principle is the same. Whoever runs the business on a day-to-day basis, be it managers or in smaller enterprises the owners themselves, the imperative is to seek growth in a variety of things which may include earnings and in larger businesses, dividends and share price. Businesses have to take decisions which help to increase earnings whilst keeping costs under control. These decisions may include what to invest in (and what not) and when to invest as well as how much and what the perceived returns might be. If investment decisions help to generate returns over a period then **shareholder value** will increase. Shareholder value is not simply profit, however, it is also the potential for the business to continue making profits over a period of time and to grow the profits.

Investment decisions can be made which will secure short-term profit growth quickly but which might damage the future capacity of the business to compete and survive in the longer term. Poor decision making can lead to damage in lots of ways, for example, signing up a celebrity to endorse products might help boost sales and earnings in the short term but could lead to longer-term damage if the celebrity happens to get involved in something that affects the reputation of the business. A business could dispose of waste at very low cost and secure short-term profit gains but if that method of waste disposal damages the environment then the longer-term earnings generation potential of the business could be affected in a negative way. In the two examples given, shareholder value could potentially decline in the future.

In addition to considering shareholder value, businesses increasingly have to take into account the fact that their operations affect a much wider group of people or individuals than simply owners. Employees, customers, managers, suppliers, the local community, government and the environment all have an interest in a business from different perspectives. Any individual or group with an interest in a business is called a **stakeholder**.

Most businesses will have to recognize the effect of its operations on these different stakeholders and have to take, often conflicting, perspectives into account when making decisions and running the business. For example, it might be tempting for a business to source new supplies from cheaper operators in emerging economies but in so doing it must consider how this might affect its wider stakeholders. Consumers might be supportive of such moves if it meant that prices are lower but quality is maintained. Suppliers in the domestic economy who lose contracts will be unlikely to support such a decision; some employees might be concerned about losing their jobs as a result and the local community might have a view about the ethical and moral basis for such a decision. Managers may feel the decision is justified if it enhances their reputation for managing complex change projects but owners/shareholders may want to be convinced that the decision really will lead to long-term as well as short-term benefits.

Reconciling the often conflicting interests of stakeholders is one of the most challenging aspects of any business and economics can help in not only identifying the potential costs and benefits but also quantifying these costs and benefits to enable more informed decision making.

shareholder value the overall value delivered to the owners of business in the form of cash generated and the reputation and potential of the business to continue growing over time

stakeholder any group or individual with an interest in a business, such as workers, managers, suppliers, the local community, customers and owners

CONCLUSION

In this chapter we have provided an outline of what business is and how it has to operate in an environment. We have looked at how it takes in resources and transforms them into outputs which are then sold, either to other businesses or final consumers. As part of this transformation process, businesses operate in both an internal and an external environment. The internal environment includes factors over which the business has some control. The business can, for example, take action to control its prices, to get a better understanding about its customers and markets, to change prices, seek cheaper raw materials, outsource parts of its operations to countries with cheaper costs, negotiate with its bankers for cheaper finance and so on.

However, the business has little control over its external environment. We classify this external environment into a number of different areas represented by the acronym PESTLE. Understanding the political, economic, social, technological, legal and environmental influences on a business enables decision makers to be able to analyse the position of the business and devise tactics and strategies to combat them or to put them in a better position to compete and win customers.

Whilst we break down these factors to facilitate ease of analysis, in reality businesses have to deal with all of these factors at the same time and it is often difficult to distinguish which factor is the most significant or which to give greater emphasis to.

For example, a train operating company knows that it has to invest in high quality engines and rolling stock to provide a service to its customers which is perceived as being value for money. It may know that there is a trend for more people to use trains but is this a social trend, an economic one or a political one? Are customers deliberately making decisions to use rail transport because they believe it is more environmentally friendly or are they doing it because the roads are too congested, or is it because work patterns are changing or because people have more disposable income and can afford to travel for business and for leisure? Have governments made decisions to increase the price of petrol to try and encourage reductions in the use of fossil fuels to help reduce the impact on the environment or have they done so to raise money in the form of higher taxes? Has this political decision driven consumers to switch to rail use?

Rail companies will also have to consider the legal and regulatory framework. Safety on the rail networks is a key element of how train operators make decisions. They know that when accidents occur the loss of life and injury can be significant. Should they aim to meet minimum legal and regulatory standards or should they aim to go well beyond them? How much are customers prepared to pay to feel safe when they travel?

They also know that when accidents happen governments tend to tighten regulations and laws to meet increased public concerns. Any increase in legislation on safety will have microeconomic effects on the business – costs will be higher and so fares might have to increase. Technology may be employed to improve train and network safety but businesses will be looking at the balance between the costs of improving safety and the benefits and the relative value of both.

Should a train operating company invest in new, more efficient rolling stock and engines? If so, should it buy the equipment from a local or national provider or should it buy from the supplier who offers the cheapest price for the quality it requires? How far will these sorts of decisions be influenced by political groups? Does the business have a responsibility to its domestic workers or to its supranational workers or to its shareholders? If the cheaper option also happens to be the most environmentally friendly one, should this override national employment considerations?

We can see that any decision is not going to be purely driven or influenced by one factor alone but by a mixture of them all. If decision making was easy then we would all be able to make the right decisions all the time. The fact that businesses ultimately have to make decisions and judgements based on what might possibly be imperfect information will inevitably lead to mistakes being made and less than efficient outcomes as a result.

IN THE NEWS

Social Networking, Businesses and Employees

Businesses have to deal with a myriad of factors which affect their activities. The growth of social networking sites has presented new challenges to business leaders as this article highlights.

Workers Want Employers Out of Their SocNet Biz

Six in ten (60 per cent) business executives believe they have a right to know how their employees portray themselves and their organizations in online social networks because of the risks such activities could present, according to the third annual Deloitte LLP Ethics & Workplace survey.

Many employees, on the other hand, disagree. More than half (53 per cent) of workers say their social networking pages should not be their employer's concern. This is especially true among younger workers, with 63 per cent of 18–34-year-old respondents stating employers have no business monitoring their online activity, Deloitte found.

Though employees express a desire for their employers to stay out of their online social networking business, they nonetheless appear to have a clear understanding of the risks involved in using online social networks. Nearly three-quarters (74 per cent) of employee respondents believe social networks make it easier to damage a company's reputation.

The study, which delves deeply into various ethical and risk-related issues associated with social networking, found that greater executive attention to social networking use is likely warranted.

Few Risk-Management Programmes in Place

Despite the fact that one-third of employees report that they never consider what their boss or customers might think before they post material online, only 17 per cent of execs have programmes in place to monitor and mitigate the possible reputational risks related to social network use, Deloitte reported.

Additionally, less than a quarter of companies have formal policies on social network use among employees, though more guidelines will not likely affect the current levels of risk. Nearly half (49 per cent) of employees indicate defined guidelines will not change their behaviour online.

'This fact alone reinforces how vulnerable brands are as a result of the increased use of social networks,' said Sharon Allen, chairman of the board, Deloitte LLP, who called for greater high-level oversight of social networking activities. 'As business leaders, it is critical that we continue to foster solid values-based cultures that encourage employees to behave ethically regardless of the venue.'

The study found that various 'disconnects' exist with regard to social networking:

- Fifty-six per cent of executives say that using social networks helps their employees achieve a better work–life balance, but only 31 per cent of employees agree.
- Fifty-eight per cent of executives agree that reputational risk and social networking should be a boardroom issue, but only 15 per cent say it actually is.
- Twenty-nine per cent of employees believe the economy is forcing them to be more conservative online for fear that their employers will use anything and everything as an excuse to fire them.
- When asked how often they access social networking sites, 22 per cent of employees said five or more times per week; 23 per cent said one to four times per week.
- Fifty-two per cent of employees choose not to access social networking sites during work hours.
- Twenty-six per cent of employees say their company prevents them from accessing social networking sites from work.
- Thirty-one per cent of employees report that their CEO is on Facebook, while 14 per cent say their CEO has a Twitter profile.

The research also revealed that more than half (55 per cent) of US business executives say their organization does not have an official use of social networking, while 22 per cent say they would like to use social networking in an organizational capacity but haven't figured out how to do so. Less than one-third of companies (30 per cent) say social networking is part of their business operations strategy.

'With the explosive growth of online social networks rapidly blurring the lines between professional and private lives, these virtual communities have increased the potential of reputational risk for many organizations and their brands,' said Allen. 'While the decision to post videos, pictures, thoughts, experiences and observations is personal, a single act can create far reaching ethical consequences for individuals as well as employers.'

Questions

1. Why might business executives want to know 'how employees portray themselves and their organizations'?
2. Do you think a business has the right to monitor its employees' use of social networking sites?
3. Why might brands be 'vulnerable' to increasing use of social networks?
4. Should businesses embrace the use of social networks for their own benefit? Justify your reasoning.
5. How might a business distinguish between professional and personal use of social networking sites for its employees and executives?

Source: http://www.marketingcharts.com/interactive/workers-want-employers-to-butt-out-of-socnet-biz-9228/deloitte-ethics-employees-easy-damage-company-reputation-social-media-may-2009jpg/

SUMMARY

- Business activity involves using factors of production and transforming them into products which are bought either by other businesses or final consumers.

- Business activity has to take place within an environment which is both internal and external.

- Businesses have some control over the internal environment but sometimes limited control over the external environment.

- The external environment can be looked at through the PESTLE framework – political, economic, social, technological, legal and environmental

- Changes in the external environment can provide both opportunities and threats.

- Businesses have a responsibility to a wide range of stakeholders who have some direct or indirect interest in the business.

KEY CONCEPTS

B2C business, p. 36
B2B business, p. 36
C2C business, p. 36
transformation process, p. 36
factors of production, p. 36

land, p. 37
labour, p. 37
capital, p. 37
enterprise, p. 37
added value, p. 39

microeconomic environment, p. 43
macroeconomic environment, p. 43
technology, p. 44
shareholder value, p. 47
stakeholder, p. 47

QUESTIONS FOR REVIEW

1. Using an example of a product of your choice, explain the principle of business activity.

2. Think about a business producing bottled spa water. Identify some examples of the four factors of production which are necessary to produce the output of that businesses.

3. Why do some economists argue for enterprise to be a separate factor of production rather than a specialist form of labour?

4. Think of a good and a service with which you are familiar and sketch a diagram, accompanied by a brief description, of the transformation process which takes place to produce each.

5. Describe the value added at each stage of production of a loaf of bread up to the point it is purchased by the consumer.

6. In a country with a democratic political system, why might a business be concerned about a change in government?

7. Explain the possible differences between the microeconomic and macroeconomic environment effects on a business producing costume jewellery.

8. Explain how a concern over the effect on the environment of business activity can lead to not only environmental change but also technological, social and legal changes which could affect a business.

9. Explain how an investment decision might affect shareholder value in a positive way both in the short run and in the long run.

10. Describe how a plan by a business to increase the price of its goods might cause a conflict between the interests of managers, shareholders, employees and customers.

PROBLEMS AND APPLICATIONS

1. Is there such a thing as a 'science of decision making'? Explain your answer in relation to business decision making.

2. To what extent is it the case that value added is always higher in a B2C business than a B2B business because businesses are more aware of value for money than are consumers?

3. Industries that use large amounts of capital in relation to other factors of production are said to be capital intensive. Is it necessarily the case that capital intensive businesses are more efficient than labour intensive ones? Explain your answer using relevant examples.

4. What do you think separates those entrepreneurs that are deemed massively successful because they are worth millions and those who just about manage to survive running their own business?

5. What do you think is the main reason for the relatively high rate of business failures five years after start-up? Justify your answer.

6. The price of a high-quality diamond ring used for weddings is €250. The price of a tonne of steel is €25. Does this mean that the transformation process in making a diamond ring is ten times more complex and costly than in making a tonne of steel? Explain your answer using the concept of added value.

7. A business making high-quality ball-point pens faces a number of challenges in the next year. It is concerned that a slowdown in the European economy along with a shift to the use of laptops and tablet devices by young people will begin to damage its long-term viability. What advice would you give the owners of this business to respond to these two external challenges? Explain your reasoning.

8. Should businesses be allowed to regulate their own activities or should governments legislate to force them to meet their social and environmental responsibilities? Explain your reasoning and use appropriate examples to illustrate your answer.

9. A pharmaceutical business reads a research report published by a leading university that suggests consumers are 20 per cent less likely to use over-the-counter medicines if these have not been advertised on TV over the last 12 months. What questions might the business want to ask of the research conducted before making any decision on whether to advertise?

10. Do you think that it is ever possible for a business to satisfy the conflicting demands of all stakeholders? Justify your reasoning.

PART 2

MICROECONOMICS –
THE MARKET SYSTEM

4 SUPPLY AND DEMAND: HOW MARKETS WORK

LEARNING OBJECTIVES

In this chapter you will:

- Learn what a competitive market is

- Examine what determines the supply of a good in a competitive market

- Examine what determines the demand for a good in a competitive market

- Distinguish between a movement along and a shift of a curve

- See how supply and demand together set the price of a good and the quantity sold

- Consider the key role of prices in allocating scarce resources in market economies

After reading this chapter you should be able to:

- List the two characteristics of a competitive market

- List the factors that affect the amount that consumers wish to buy in a market

- List the factors that affect the amount that producers wish to sell in a market

- Draw a graph of supply and demand in a market and find the equilibrium price and quantity

- Shift supply and demand curves in response to an economic event and find the new equilibrium price and quantity

- Describe the process by which a new equilibrium is reached

- Explain how price acts as a signal to both producers and consumers

THE MARKET FORCES OF SUPPLY AND DEMAND

We saw in Chapter 2 how a market is made up of two parties – the buyer and the seller. The buyer represents demand and the seller supply. In this chapter we are going to look at a fundamental aspect of business economics, the operation of markets and the interaction between these two 'forces'.

Poor weather conditions in parts of Europe can have an effect on the yield of wheat crops and as a result businesses using wheat in the production of food products face higher costs. High levels of economic growth in China cause the demand for steel to rise and this pushes up prices for businesses across the rest of the world, meaning the price of both semi-finished and finished products rises where steel is a component part in production.

If a report is published linking food products with health risks, firms producing these foods face falling prices and a possible collapse in their markets. A change in exchange rates for currencies can have different effects on different businesses depending on the extent to which they trade with other businesses and customers abroad. Airlines know that they can charge higher prices at certain times of the year to certain destinations than at other times where they may have to cut fares to fill aircraft. What do these events have in common? They all show the workings of supply and demand.

Supply and *demand* are the two words that economists use most often – and for good reason. Supply and demand are the forces that make market economies work. We refer to them as forces because they act in different ways and cause prices to change – the factor that links the two forces. Supply and demand determine the quantity of each good produced and the price at which it is sold. If you want to know how any event or policy will affect the economy and businesses, you must think first about how it will affect supply and demand.

This chapter introduces the theory of supply and demand. It considers how sellers and buyers behave and how they interact with one another. It shows how supply and demand determine prices in a market economy and how prices, in turn, allocate the economy's scarce resources.

At this point it is important to note an important distinction. We use the terms 'price' and 'cost' regularly in everyday life – often interchangeably. In this book we will refer to the two terms in a distinct way. **Price** is the amount of money a buyer (a business or a consumer) has to give up in order to acquire something. **Cost** refers to the payment to factor inputs in production. When we discuss suppliers we will be referring to cost in this sense.

price the amount of money a buyer (a business or a consumer) has to give up in order to acquire something

cost refers to the payment to factor inputs in production

MARKETS AND COMPETITION

The terms *supply* and *demand* refer to the behaviour of businesses and people as they interact with one another in markets. A **market** is a group of sellers and buyers of a particular good or service. The sellers as a group determine the supply of the product and the buyers as a group determine the demand for the product. Before discussing how sellers and buyers behave, let's first consider more fully what we mean by a 'market' and the various types of markets we observe in the economy.

market a group of buyers and sellers of a particular good or service

Competitive Markets

Markets take many forms. Sometimes markets are highly organized, such as the markets for many agricultural commodities and for metals. In these markets, buyers and sellers meet at a specific time and place, where an auctioneer helps set prices and arrange sales.

Many businesses rely on these highly organized markets and are affected by them because they have little control over the prices they have to pay for these products which can affect their costs and margins considerably both in a positive and a negative way.

More often, markets are less organized. For example, consider the market for perfume. Businesses manufacturing and selling perfume are varied and seek to offer different products for sale which they hope will be distinctive and popular. The buyers of perfume do not all meet together at any one time. These buyers are individuals, all of whom have different tastes, One person's ideal fragrance is another person's obnoxious smell and they do not all gather together in a room to shout out the prices they are willing to pay. There is no auctioneer calling out the price of perfume. Each seller of perfume posts a price for a bottle of perfume in their shop, and each buyer either walks past the shop because they do not want perfume or if they do will go to different shops and try different perfumes before making their decision.

Even though it is not organized, the group of perfume sellers and buyers forms a market. Each seller is aware that her product is similar but different to that offered by other sellers. Each buyer knows that there are several sellers from which to choose. The price of perfume and the quantity of perfume sold are not determined by any single buyer or seller. Rather, price and quantity are determined by all sellers and buyers as they interact in the marketplace.

The market for perfume, like most markets in the economy, is competitive. **Competition** exists when two or more firms are rivals for customers. Each firm strives to gain the attention and custom of buyers in the market. Economists use the term *competitive market* in a different way to mean something very specific. A **competitive market** is a market in which there are many buyers and many sellers so that each has a negligible impact on the market price. In the perfume market, sellers may have some limited control over price because of the way they can differentiate their product from competitors. In describing a competitive market in this chapter, we are going to look at a more specific definition of a competitive market and in subsequent chapters look at firm behaviour when the assumptions of perfect competition are relaxed. We are going to look at how sellers and buyers interact in competitive markets and see how the forces of supply and demand determine both the quantity of the good sold and its price.

competition a situation when two or more firms are rivals for customers. Each firm strives to gain the attention and custom of buyers in the market

competitive market a market in which there are many buyers and many sellers so that each has a negligible impact on the market price

Competition: Perfect and Otherwise

The assumptions outlined above refer to markets that are referred to as *perfectly competitive*. Perfectly competitive markets are defined by two main characteristics: (1) the goods being offered for sale are all the same (homogenous) and as a result buyers have no preference between one seller or another; and (2) the buyers and sellers are so numerous that no single buyer or seller can influence the market price. Because buyers and sellers in perfectly competitive markets must accept the price the market determines, they are said to be *price takers*.

There are some markets in which the assumption of perfect competition applies to a very large degree. In the wheat market, for example, there are tens of thousands of farmers who sell wheat and millions of consumers who use wheat and wheat products. Because no single buyer or seller can influence the price of wheat, each takes the price as given.

The reason for making this assumption is so that we can look at how markets operate under these 'ideal' conditions and what the expected outcomes are. If we then observe in reality that these outcomes do not occur as we expect, then we can analyse what imperfections exist which help to explain this behaviour.

Not all goods and services, therefore, are sold in perfectly competitive markets. Some markets have only one seller, and this seller sets the price. Such a seller is called a *monopoly*. Your local water company, for instance, may be a monopoly. Residents in your area probably have only one water company from which to buy this service.

Some markets fall between the extremes of perfect competition and monopoly. One such market, called an *oligopoly*, has a few sellers that do not always compete aggressively. Airline routes are an example. If a route between two cities is serviced by only two or three carriers, the carriers may avoid rigorous competition so they can keep prices high. Another type of market is *monopolistically or imperfectly competitive*; it contains many sellers but each offers a slightly different product. Because the products are not exactly the same, each seller has some ability to set the price for its own product. An example is the market for magazines. Magazines compete with one another for readers and anyone can enter the market by starting a new one, but each magazine offers different articles and can set its own price.

Despite the diversity of market types we find in the world, we begin by studying perfect competition. Perfectly competitive markets are the easiest to analyse. Moreover, because some degree of competition is present in most markets, many of the lessons that we learn by studying supply and demand under perfect competition apply in more complicated markets as well.

> **Quick Quiz** What is the market for processing chips in a computer or mobile phone made up of? • What are the characteristics of a competitive market for milk?

quantity supplied the amount of a good that sellers are willing and able to sell

law of supply the claim that, other things being equal, the quantity supplied of a good rises when the price of the good rises

The distinctive yellow flowers of rape plants make an attractive sight in many countries at certain times of the year. The seed from the plants provides a valuable source of cooking oil.

SUPPLY

We are going to begin our look at markets by considering producers – businesses – and examine the behaviour of sellers. To focus our thinking and provide a context for our analysis, let's consider producers of rape seed which is used to make cooking oil.

The Supply Curve: The Relationship Between Price and Quantity Supplied

The **quantity supplied** of any good or service is the amount that sellers are willing and able to sell. There are many determinants of quantity supplied, but price plays a special role in our analysis. When the price of rape seed is high, selling rape seed is profitable, and so sellers are willing to supply more. Sellers of rape seed work longer hours, devote more planting to rape, invest in research and development on improvements to rape seed growing and hire extra workers in order to ensure supplies to the market rise. By contrast, when the price of rape seed is low, the business is less profitable, and so growers are willing to plant less rape. At a low price, some growers may even choose to shut down, and their quantity supplied falls to zero. Because the quantity supplied rises as the price rises and falls as the price falls, we say that the quantity supplied is *positively related* to the price of the good. This relationship between price and quantity supplied is called the **law of supply**: other things being equal, when the price of a good rises, the quantity producers are willing to supply also rises, and when the price falls, the quantity supplied falls as well.

The table in Figure 4.1 shows the quantity Tramontana, a rape seed grower, is willing to supply, at various prices of rape seed. By convention, the price is on the vertical axis and the quantity supplied on the horizontal axis. At a price below €0.50 per tonne, Tramontana does not supply any rape seed at all. As the price rises, it is willing to supply a greater and greater quantity. This is the **supply schedule**, a table that shows the relationship between the price of a good and the quantity supplied, holding constant everything else that influences how much producers of the good want to sell.

supply schedule a table that shows the relationship between the price of a good and the quantity supplied

FIGURE 4.1

Tramontana's Supply Schedule and Supply Curve

The supply schedule shows the quantity supplied at each price. This supply curve, which graphs the supply schedule, shows how the quantity supplied of the good changes as its price varies. Because a higher price increases the quantity supplied, the supply curve slopes upward.

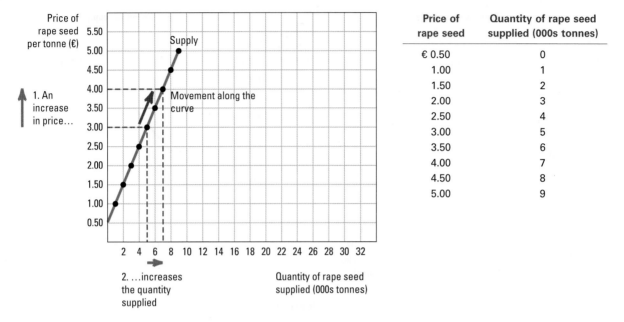

Price of rape seed	Quantity of rape seed supplied (000s tonnes)
€ 0.50	0
1.00	1
1.50	2
2.00	3
2.50	4
3.00	5
3.50	6
4.00	7
4.50	8
5.00	9

The graph in Figure 4.1 uses the numbers from the table to illustrate the law of supply. The curve relating price and quantity supplied is called the supply curve. The **supply curve** slopes upward because, other things being equal, a higher price means a greater quantity supplied.

> **supply curve** a graph of the relationship between the price of a good and the quantity supplied

Market Supply versus Individual Supply

Market supply is the sum of the supplies of all sellers. The table in Figure 4.2 shows the supply schedules for two rape seed producers – Tramontana and Sedona. At any price, Tramontana's supply schedule tells us the quantity of rape seed Tramontana is willing to supply, and Sedona's supply schedule tells us the quantity of rape seed Sedona is willing to supply. The market supply is the sum of the two individual supplies.

The graph in Figure 4.2 shows the supply curves that correspond to the supply schedules. We sum the individual supply curves *horizontally* to obtain the market supply curve. That is, to find the total quantity supplied at any price, we add the individual quantities found on the horizontal axis of the individual supply curves. The market supply curve shows how the total quantity supplied varies as the price of the good varies. In reality, the market supply will be the amount all producers in the market (rape seed manufacturers and sellers in this example) are willing to offer for sale at each price.

> **Pitfall Prevention** Be careful to ensure that you distinguish between individual and market supply in your analysis – the behaviour of one individual business may be different from the whole industry.

FIGURE 4.2

Market Supply as the Sum of Individual Supplies

The quantity supplied in a market is the sum of the quantities supplied by all the sellers at each price. Thus, the market supply curve is found by adding horizontally the individual supply curves. At a price of €2.50, Tramontana is willing to supply 4000 tonnes of rape seed and Sedona is willing to supply 10 000 tonnes. The quantity supplied in the market at this price is 14 000 tonnes of rape seed.

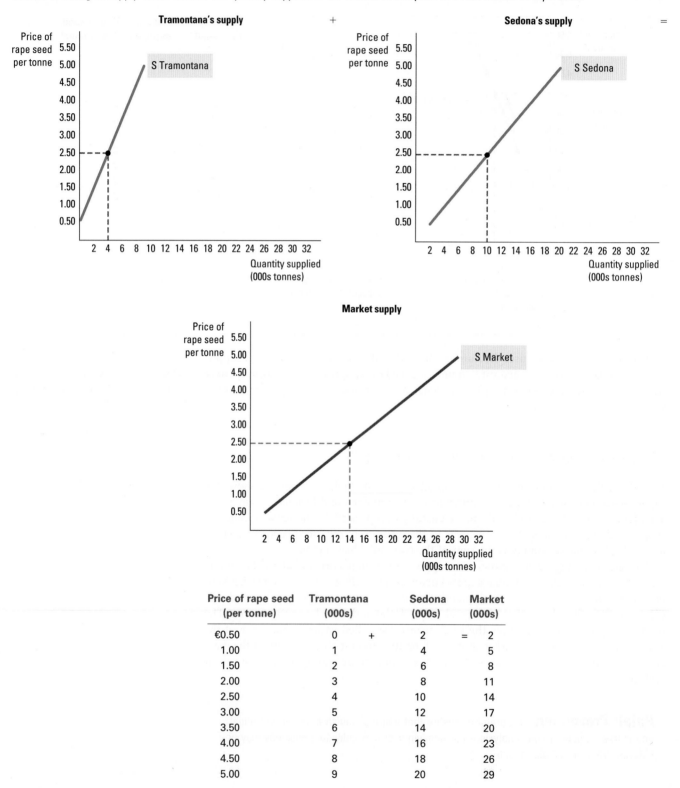

Price of rape seed (per tonne)	Tramontana (000s)		Sedona (000s)		Market (000s)
€0.50	0	+	2	=	2
1.00	1		4		5
1.50	2		6		8
2.00	3		8		11
2.50	4		10		14
3.00	5		12		17
3.50	6		14		20
4.00	7		16		23
4.50	8		18		26
5.00	9		20		29

Shifts versus Movements along the Supply Curve

A distinction must be made between a shift in the supply curve and a movement along the supply curve. A shift in the supply curve is caused by a factor affecting supply other than a change in price. The factors affecting supply are outlined below. If any of these factors change, then the amount sellers are willing to offer for sale changes, whatever the price. The shift in the supply curve is referred to as an *increase or decrease in supply*. A movement along the supply curve occurs when there is a change in price. This may occur because of a change in demand conditions. The factors affecting supply are assumed to be held constant. A change in price leads to a movement along the supply curve and is referred to as a *change in quantity supplied*.

Shifts in the Supply Curve

The supply curve for rape seed shows how much rape seed producers are willing to offer for sale at any given price, holding constant all the other factors beyond price that influence producers' decisions about how much to sell. This relationship can change over time, which is represented by a shift in the supply curve. For example, suppose the price of fertilizer falls. Because fertilizer is an input into producing rape seed, the fall in the price means producing rape seed is now cheaper – the same quantity of rape seed can be made at lower cost which makes selling rape seed more profitable. This raises the supply of rape seed: at any given price, sellers are now willing to offer for sale a larger quantity. Thus, the supply curve for rape seed shifts to the right.

Figure 4.3 illustrates shifts in supply. Any change that raises quantity supplied at every price, such as a fall in the price of fertilizer, shifts the supply curve to the right and is called *an increase in supply*. Similarly, any change that reduces the quantity supplied at every price shifts the supply curve to the left and is called *a decrease in supply*.

There are many variables that can shift the supply curve. Here are some of the most important.

FIGURE 4.3

Shifts in the Supply Curve

Any change that raises the quantity that sellers are willing to produce and offer for sale at a given price shifts the supply curve to the right. Any change that lowers the quantity that sellers are willing to produce and offer for sale at a given price shifts the supply curve to the left.

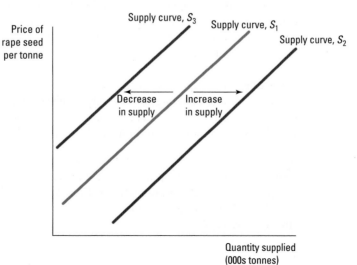

Input Prices To produce their output of rape seed, sellers use various inputs: fertilizer, fuel for tractors, weed killer, harvesting machines and different types of packaging for distribution at various stages in the production process. Growers will also have to pay for computers, machinery, farm buildings and the labour of workers which is used throughout the planting, growing, harvesting and distribution process. When the price of one or more of these inputs rises, producing rape seed is less profitable and firms supply fewer tonnes of rape seed. If input prices rise substantially, some firms might shut down and supply no rape seed at all. If input prices fall for some reason, then production may be more profitable and there is an incentive to supply more at each price. Thus, the supply of a good is negatively related to the price of the inputs used to make the good.

Technology The technology for turning the inputs into rape seed is yet another determinant of supply. This technology might be related to the quality and viability of seed, improvements in plant breeding to create more uniform and productive plants, or in the use of fertilizers to improve soil quality and growth. Advances in technology increase productivity allowing more to be produced using fewer factor inputs. As a result costs, both total and unit, may fall and supply increases. The invention of harvesting machines, for example, reduces the amount of labour necessary to gather and process rape seed. By reducing firms' costs, the advance in technology raises the supply of rape seed.

Expectations The amount of rape seed firms supply today may depend on their expectations of the future. For example, if growers expect the price of rape seed to rise in the future, they may put some of their current stock into storage and supply less to the market today. If government reports from health departments suggest that using cooking oil made from rape seed reduces the chance of heart disease then producers might reasonably expect an increase in sales and so plant more fields to rape in anticipation.

The Number of Sellers Market supply will be affected by the number of firms in the industry. In the EU there are around 20 million tonnes of rape seed produced a year and at a price of approximately €370 per tonne this means a market value around €7.4 billion. If there were more farmers switching to rape production, then the amount of rape seed produced would be likely to rise. Equally, if some of the growers that currently plant rape closed down their operations the amount of rape seed produced would be likely to fall each year.

Natural/Social Factors There are often many natural or social factors that affect supply. These include such things as the weather affecting crops, natural disasters, pestilence and disease, changing attitudes and social expectations (for example, over the production of organic food, the disposal of waste, reducing carbon emissions, ethical supply sourcing and so on) can all have an influence on production decisions. Some or all of these may have an influence on the cost of inputs into production.

Summary The supply curve shows what happens to the quantity supplied of a good when its price varies, holding constant all the other variables that influence sellers. When one of these other variables changes, the supply curve shifts. Table 4.1 lists all the variables that influence how much producers choose to sell of a good.

Quick Quiz Make up an example of a supply schedule for apples, and graph the implied supply curve • Give an example of something that would shift this supply curve • Would a change in the price of apples shift this supply curve?

TABLE 4.1

Variables That Influence Sellers

This table lists the variables that affect how much producers choose to sell of any good. Notice the special role that the price of the good plays: a change in the good's price represents a movement along the supply curve, whereas a change in one of the other variables shifts the supply curve.

Variable	A change in this variable ...
Price	Is represented as a movement along the supply curve
Input prices	Shifts the supply curve
Technology	Shifts the supply curve
Expectations	Shifts the supply curve
Number of sellers	Shifts the supply curve

DEMAND

We now turn to the other side of the market and examine the behaviour of buyers. Once again, to focus our thinking, let's consider the market for rape seed.

The Demand Curve: The Relationship Between Price and Quantity Demanded

The **quantity demanded** of any good is the amount of the good that buyers are willing and able to purchase. As we shall see, many things determine the quantity demanded of any good, but when analysing how markets work, one determinant plays a central role – the price of the good. If the price of rape seed rose, people would buy fewer tonnes of rape seed. Food manufacturers and retailers might switch to another form of cooking oil such as sunflower oil. If the price of rape seed fell to €1 per tonne, people would buy more. Because the quantity demanded falls as the price rises and rises as the price falls, we say that the quantity demanded is *negatively related* to the price. This relationship between price and quantity demanded is true for most goods in the economy and, in fact, is so pervasive that economists call it the **law of demand**: other things being equal, when the price of a good rises, the quantity demanded of the good falls, and when the price falls, the quantity demanded rises.

The table in Figure 4.4 shows how many tonnes of rape seed Hanse, a food manufacturer, is willing and able to buy each year at different prices of rape seed. If rape seed were free, Hanse would be willing to take 10 000 tonnes of rape seed. At €2 per tonne, Hanse would be willing to buy 6000 tonnes of rape seed. As the price rises further, he is willing to buy fewer and fewer tonnes of rape seed. When the price reaches €5.00 per tonne, Hanse would not be prepared to buy any rape seed at all. This table is a **demand schedule**, a table that shows the relationship between the price of a good and the quantity demanded, holding constant everything else that influences how much consumers of the good want to buy.

The graph in Figure 4.4 uses the numbers from the table to illustrate the law of demand. The price of rape seed is on the vertical axis, and the quantity of rape seed demanded is on the horizontal axis. The downward sloping line relating price and quantity demanded is called the **demand curve**.

quantity demanded the amount of a good that buyers are willing and able to purchase at different prices

law of demand the claim that, other things being equal, the quantity demanded of a good falls when the price of the good rises

demand schedule a table that shows the relationship between the price of a good and the quantity demanded

demand curve a graph of the relationship between the price of a good and the quantity demanded

FIGURE 4.4

Hanse's Demand Schedule and Demand Curve

The demand schedule shows the quantity demanded at each price. The demand curve, which graphs the demand schedule, shows how the quantity demanded of the good changes as its price varies. Because a lower price increases the quantity demanded, the demand curve slopes downward.

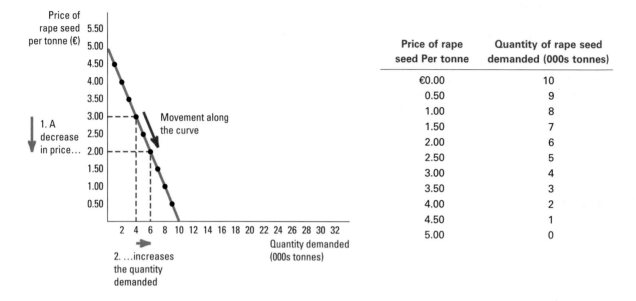

Price of rape seed Per tonne	Quantity of rape seed demanded (000s tonnes)
€0.00	10
0.50	9
1.00	8
1.50	7
2.00	6
2.50	5
3.00	4
3.50	3
4.00	2
4.50	1
5.00	0

Market Demand versus Individual Demand

The demand curve in Figure 4.4 shows an individual's demand for a product. To analyse how markets work, we need to determine the *market demand,* which is the sum of all the individual demands for a particular good or service.

The table in Figure 4.5 shows the demand schedules for rape seed of two food manufacturers – Hanse and Michelle. At any price, Hanse's demand schedule tells us how many tonnes of rape seed he would be willing and able to buy at different prices, and Michelle's demand schedule tells us how many tonnes of rape seed she is willing and able to buy. The market demand at each price is the sum of the two individual demands.

The graph in Figure 4.5 shows the demand curves that correspond to these demand schedules. As we did with the market supply we sum the individual demand curves *horizontally* to obtain the market demand curve.

Because we are interested in analysing how markets work, we shall work most often with the market demand curve. The market demand curve shows how the total quantity demanded of a good varies as the price of the good varies, while all the other factors that affect how much consumers want to buy, such as incomes and taste, amongst other things, are held constant.

Shifts versus Movements along the Demand Curve

As with supply, we must ensure that we distinguish between a shift in the demand curve and a movement along the demand curve. A shift in the demand curve is caused by a factor affecting demand other than a change in price. The factors affecting demand are

FIGURE 4.5

Market Demand as the Sum of Individual Demands

The quantity demanded in a market is the sum of the quantities demanded by all the buyers at each price. Thus, the market demand curve is found by adding horizontally the individual demand curves. At a price of €2, Hanse would like to buy 6000 tonnes of rape seed but Michelle would be prepared to buy 12 000 tonnes of rape seed. The quantity demanded in the market at this price, therefore, is 18 000 tonnes of rape seed.

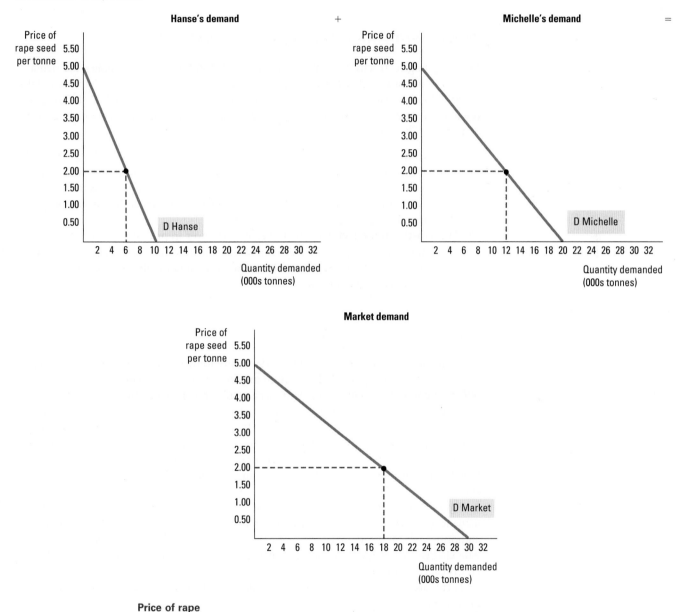

Price of rape seed per tonne	Hanse		Michelle		Market (000s tonnes)
€0.00	10	+	20	=	30
0.50	9		18		27
1.00	8		16		24
1.50	7		14		21
2.00	6		12		18
2.50	5		10		15
3.00	4		8		12
3.50	3		6		9
4.00	2		4		6
4.50	1		2		3
5.00	0		0		0

outlined below. If any of these factors change, then the amount consumers wish to purchase changes, whatever the price. The shift in the demand curve is referred to as an *increase or decrease in demand*. A movement along the demand curve occurs when there is a change in price. This may occur because of a change in supply conditions. The factors affecting demand are assumed to be held constant. A change in price leads to a movement along the demand curve and is referred to as a *change in quantity demanded*.

Movement Along the Demand Curve

We are going to briefly look at the economics behind a movement along the demand curve. Let us assume that the price of a particular variety of rape seed (Excalibur) falls, whilst all other rape seed varieties (Vision, Dimension, Vistive and Fashion) prices remain constant. We know that the fall in price will lead to an increase in quantity demanded. There are two reasons for this increase:

1. **The income effect**. If we assume that incomes remain constant then a fall in the price of Excalibur means that growers who buy this variety can now afford to buy more with their income. In other words, their *real income*, what a given amount of money can buy at any point in time, has increased and part of the increase in quantity demanded can be put down to this effect.
2. **The substitution effect**. Now that Excalibur is lower in price compared to other rape seed varieties, some growers will choose to substitute the more expensive varieties with the now cheaper Excalibur. This switch accounts for the remaining part of the increase in quantity demanded.

Shifts in the Demand Curve

The demand curve for rape seed shows how many tonnes of rape seed people are willing to buy at any given price, holding constant the many other factors beyond price that influence consumers' buying decisions. As a result, this demand curve need not be stable over time. If something happens to alter the demand at any given price, the demand curve shifts. For example, suppose European health authorities discovered that people who regularly use rape seed oil live longer, healthier lives. The discovery would raise the demand for rape seed. At any given price, buyers would now want to purchase a larger quantity of rape seed at all prices and the demand curve for rape seed would shift.

Figure 4.6 illustrates shifts in demand. Any change that increases the quantity demanded at every price, such as our imaginary discovery by the European health authorities, shifts the demand curve to the right and is called *an increase in demand*. Any change that reduces the demand at every price shifts the demand curve to the left and is called *a decrease in demand*.

There are many variables that can shift the demand curve. Here are the most important.

Income What would happen to the demand for rape seed if unemployment increases? Most likely, it would fall (how much it would fall is another question and will be dealt with in the next chapter) because of lower incomes. Lower incomes mean that people have less to spend in total, so they are likely to spend less on some – and probably most – goods. If the demand for a good falls when income falls, the good is called a **normal good**.

normal good a good for which, other things being equal, an increase in income leads to an increase in demand (and vice versa)

FIGURE 4.6

Shifts in the Demand Curve

Any change that raises the quantity that buyers wish to purchase at a given price shifts the demand curve to the right. Any change that lowers the quantity that buyers wish to purchase at a given price shifts the demand curve to the left.

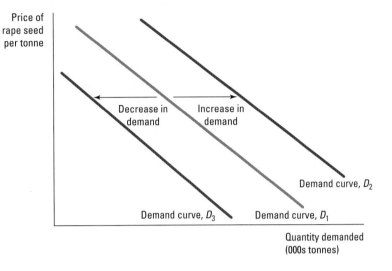

Not all goods are normal goods. If the demand for a good rises when income falls, the good is called an **inferior good**. An example of an inferior good might be bus rides. As income falls, people are less likely to buy a car or take a taxi and more likely to take the bus. As income falls, therefore, demand for bus rides tends to increase. There is a wide range of rape seed oil on the market and we might see consumer behaviour changing when incomes change. More expensive, high-quality luxury oil might be a normal good, whereas oil that could be regarded as being 'standard' might see demand rise when incomes fall as consumers switch from the more expensive, luxury cooking oil to the cheaper, 'standard' oil.

inferior good a good for which, other things being equal, an increase in income leads to a decrease in demand (and vice versa)

Prices of Related Goods   Suppose that the price of sunflower seed oil falls. The law of demand says that people will buy more sunflower seed oil. At the same time, people will probably buy less rape seed oil. Because sunflower seed oil and rape seed oil can both be used for cooking, they satisfy similar desires. When a fall in the price of one good reduces the demand for another good, the two goods are called **substitutes**. Substitutes are often pairs of goods that are used in place of each other, such as beef steak and Wiener schnitzel, pullovers and sweatshirts, and cinema tickets and DVD rentals. The more closely related substitute products are, the more effect we might see on demand if the price of one of the substitutes changes.

substitutes two goods for which an increase in the price of one leads to an increase in the demand for the other

Suppose that the price of woks fall. According to the law of demand, people will buy more woks. Yet, in this case, people will probably buy more rape seed oil as well, because rape seed oil and woks tend to be used together. When a fall in the price of one good raises the demand for another good, the two goods are called **complements**. Complements are often pairs of goods that are used together, such as petrol and cars, computers and software, bread and cheese, strawberries and cream, and bacon and eggs. As with substitutes not only do we need to identify what goods can be classed as complementary, we also need to be aware of the strength of the relationship between the two goods.

complements two goods for which an increase in the price of one leads to a decrease in the demand for the other (and vice versa)

Tastes The most obvious determinant of demand are tastes and fashions. If people like rape seed oil, they buy more of it. Economists are increasingly interested in understanding and explaining people's tastes. The developments in neuroscience mean that we now have an increasing understanding of why people make decisions and this has come into the realm of economics. This helps economists examine what happens, and why, when tastes change. This knowledge is also very important to businesses seeking to get a better understanding of their market, how consumer's behave and why they behave in the ways they do.

Expectations Buyer's expectations about the future may affect their demand for a good or service today. For example, if food manufacturers expect to earn higher revenues next month, they may be more willing to spend some of their current cash reserves buying rape seed oil. As another example, if buyers expect the price of rape seed to fall tomorrow, they may be less willing to buy rape seed at today's price.

The Size and Structure of the Population A larger population, other things being equal, will mean a higher demand for all goods and services. Changes in the way the population is structured also influences demand. Many European countries have an ageing population and this leads to a change in the demand. Goods and services required by the elderly increase in demand as a result. The demand for retirement homes, insurance policies suitable for elderly drivers and smaller cars may increase as a result.

Pitfall Prevention Many students confuse movements along and shifts in demand and supply curves. Using the correct phrasing (change in supply/demand refers to a shift in the curve, change in quantity supplied/demanded refers to a movement along the curve) is one way to help prevent this confusion.

Summary The demand curve shows what happens to the *quantity demanded* of a good when its price varies, holding constant all the other variables that influence buyers. When one or more of these other variables changes, the demand curve shifts leading to an *increase or decrease in demand*. Table 4.2 lists all the variables that influence how much consumers choose to buy of a good.

TABLE 4.2

Variables That Influence Buyers

This table lists the variables that affect how much consumers choose to buy of any good. Notice the special role that the price of the good plays: a change in the good's price represents a movement along the demand curve, whereas a change in one of the other variables shifts the demand curve.

Variable	A change in this variable ...
Price	Is represented as a movement along the demand curve
Income	Shifts the demand curve
Prices of related goods	Shifts the demand curve
Tastes	Shifts the demand curve
Expectations	Shifts the demand curve
Number of buyers	Shifts the demand curve

CASE STUDY

Harvests and Forward Markets

Farmers operate in a highly competitive market – there are many thousands of relatively small firms producing a product that is largely homogenous and farmers are price takers – they have little control over the price they get for their output.

Futures markets exist to enable farmers to buy and sell a specified quantity at an agreed price at some point in the future. Using the futures market can be a useful device for businesses looking to hedge themselves against volatile prices. Farming is a particularly notorious industry for such volatile prices, dependent as it is on climate to determine the size and quality of the harvest. In recent years high temperatures in Russia, disease in Asia, dry weather in Europe and wet weather in Canada have combined to put pressure on the supply of grain, with prices for UK wheat changing dramatically over different periods.

In January 2010, for example, the price of British wheat was around £105 per tonne but by August 2010 it had risen to nearly £160 per tonne, a rise of just over 52 per cent. The price of barley also rose sharply from around £75 per tonne in mid-June 2010 to about £175 per tonne in August of the same year. In early 2012, wheat prices stood at around £146 per tonne. By comparison, in 2009 wheat was trading at around £90 per tonne. It can be seen from this limited example just how volatile prices can be over periods of time and how, as a result, many farmers find it difficult to be able to forecast their revenues with any certainty. High prices in 2012, for example, might benefit some arable farmers who are able to harvest high quality products; for livestock farmers the situation is reversed. High prices of grain mean that their input costs rise because of the role grain plays in livestock feed.

It is precisely this volatility which leads some farmers to 'sell' their output on the forward markets. There is a risk involved in doing this, however. If wheat prices remain relatively high in the period after contracts are agreed, then UK farmers harvesting at that time may well benefit from selling their output at much higher prices, but some will not do so because they entered into contracts to sell their output at agreed prices some time ago. If farmers make a decision to 'sell' their crops at prices around £90–£100 per tonne it may, at the time, seem like a good price, but if actual prices at the time of sale are nearer the £146 per tonne mark then these farmers might be wishing they had hung on and sold their harvest later.

On the flip side, farmers who do lose out this way may decide to enter into forward agreements for next year's crop and if the prices they can get are based around current prices they may benefit in a year's time. Who knows – next year may be a bumper harvest and world grain prices fall sharply as a result. This just highlights the difficult decisions that farmers have to make when they are price takers and operate in volatile markets in which they have limited control over supply, even if they have specific and highly organized markets to help reduce risk.

Stocks can be important in determining how prices on markets for agricultural products change over a period of time.

FOTOKOSTIC/SHUTTERSTOCK

Quick Quiz Make up an example of a demand schedule for pizza, and graph the implied demand curve • Give an example of something that would shift this demand curve • Would a change in the price of pizza shift this demand curve?

DEMAND AND SUPPLY TOGETHER

Having analysed supply and demand separately, we now combine them to see how they determine the quantity of a good sold in a market and its price.

Equilibrium

equilibrium a situation in which the price has reached the level where quantity supplied equals quantity demanded

equilibrium price the price that balances quantity supplied and quantity demanded

equilibrium quantity the quantity supplied and the quantity demanded at the equilibrium price

surplus a situation in which quantity supplied is greater than quantity demanded

Figure 4.7 shows the market supply curve and market demand curve together. Equilibrium is defined as a state of rest, a point where there is no force acting for change. Economists refer to supply and demand as being *market forces*. In any market the relationship between supply and demand exerts force on price. If supply is greater than demand or vice versa, then there is pressure on price to change. Notice, however, that there is one point at which the supply and demand curves intersect. This point is called the market's **equilibrium**. The price at this intersection is called the **equilibrium price**, and the quantity is called the **equilibrium quantity**. Here the equilibrium price is €2.00 per tonne, and the equilibrium quantity is 7000 tonnes bought and sold.

At the equilibrium price, the quantity of the good that buyers are willing and able to buy exactly balances the quantity that sellers are willing and able to sell. The equilibrium price is sometimes called the *market-clearing price* because, at this price, everyone in the market has been satisfied: buyers have bought all they want to buy, and sellers have sold all they want to sell – there is neither a shortage nor a surplus.

The actions of buyers and sellers naturally move markets towards the equilibrium of supply and demand. To see why, consider what happens when the market price is not equal to the equilibrium price.

Suppose first that the market price is above the equilibrium price, as in panel (a) of Figure 4.8. At a price of €2.50 per tonne, the quantity suppliers would like to sell at this price (10000 tonnes) exceeds the quantity which buyers are willing to purchase (4000 tonnes). There is a **surplus** of the good: suppliers are unable to sell all they want at the going price. A surplus is sometimes called a situation of *excess supply*. When there is a surplus in the rape seed market, sellers of rape seed find they cannot sell all the supplies

FIGURE 4.7

The Equilibrium of Supply and Demand

The equilibrium is found where the supply and demand curves intersect. At the equilibrium price, the quantity supplied equals the quantity demanded. Here the equilibrium price is €2: at this price, 7000 tonnes of rape seed are supplied and 7000 tonnes are demanded.

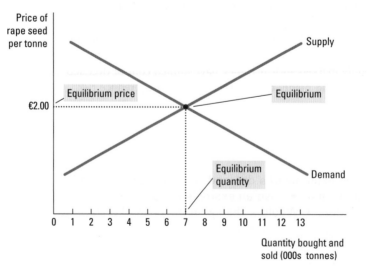

FIGURE 4.8

Markets Not in Equilibrium

In panel (a), there is a surplus. Because the market price of €2.50 is above the equilibrium price, the quantity supplied (10000 tonnes) exceeds the quantity demanded (4000 tonnes). Suppliers try to increase sales by cutting the price of rape seed, and this moves the price toward its equilibrium level. In panel (b), there is a shortage. Because the market price of €1.50 is below the equilibrium price, the quantity demanded (10000 tonnes) exceeds the quantity supplied (4000 tonnes). With too many buyers chasing too few goods, suppliers can take advantage of the shortage by raising the price. Hence, in both cases, the price adjustment moves the market towards the equilibrium of supply and demand.

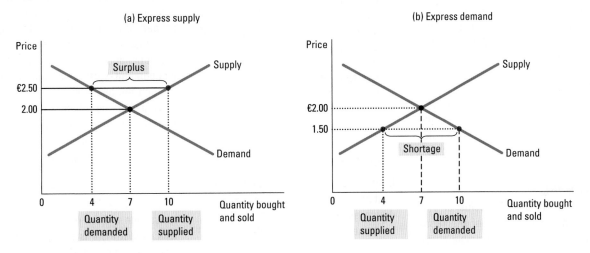

they have and so the market responds to the surplus by cutting prices. Falling prices, in turn, increase the quantity demanded and decrease the quantity supplied. Prices continue to fall until the market reaches the equilibrium.

Suppose now that the market price is below the equilibrium price, as in panel (b) of Figure 4.8. In this case, the price is €1.50 per tonne, and the quantity of the good demanded exceeds the quantity supplied. There is a **shortage** of the good: demanders are unable to buy all they want at the going price. A shortage is sometimes called a situation of *excess demand*. When a shortage occurs in the rape seed market, buyers may find they cannot acquire all the supplies they need. With too many buyers chasing too few goods, the suppliers respond to the shortage by raising prices without losing sales. As the price rises, quantity demanded falls, quantity supplied rises and the market once again moves toward the equilibrium.

Thus, the activities of the many buyers and sellers automatically push the market price towards the equilibrium price. Once the market reaches its equilibrium, all buyers and sellers are satisfied, and there is no upward or downward pressure on the price. How quickly equilibrium is reached varies from market to market, depending on how quickly prices adjust. In most free markets under an assumption of high levels of information available to buyers and sellers, surpluses and shortages are only temporary because prices eventually move towards their equilibrium levels (we will see the significance of the word 'free' later in the book). Indeed, this phenomenon is so pervasive that it is called the **law of supply and demand**: the price of any good adjusts to bring the quantity supplied and quantity demanded for that good into balance.

shortage a situation in which quantity demanded is greater than quantity supplied

law of supply and demand the claim that the price of any good adjusts to bring the quantity supplied and the quantity demanded for that good into balance

JEOPARDY PROBLEM

The market for bicycles has seen falling prices but not a change in the amount of bicycles bought and sold. Explain how this situation might have come about. Use diagrams to illustrate.

FYI

This FYI will be helpful if you have to use maths in your course. If you do not have to use maths then you can safely move on to the next section without affecting your overall understanding of this chapter.

Functions

In economics a lot of use is made of functions. Demand and supply equations are two examples of functions. Typically, functions are expressed as:

$$Y = f(x)$$

or simply $f(x)$

This means that the value of Y is dependent on the value of the terms in the bracket – in our example above there is only one value, x, so the value of Y is dependent on the value of x.

We know from this chapter that there are a number of factors affecting demand and supply. The general form of the function in such a case would look like:

$$Y = f(x_1 \ldots \ldots x_n)$$

where $x_1 \ldots \ldots x_n$ represents a range of variables.

Given the determinants of demand and supply we could write the demand and supply functions as:

$$D = f(P_n, P_n \ldots P_{n-1}, Y, T, P, A, E)$$

Where:

- P_n = Price
- $P_n \ldots P_{n-1}$ = Prices of other goods – substitutes and complements
- Y = Incomes – the level and distribution of income
- T = Tastes and fashions
- P = The level and structure of the population
- A = Advertising
- E = Expectations of consumers

and:

$$S = f(P_n, P_n \ldots P_{n-1}, H, N, F_1 \ldots F_m, E, S_f)$$

Where:

- P_n = Price
- $P_n \ldots P_{n-1}$ = Profitability of other goods in production and prices of goods in joint supply
- H = Technology
- N = Natural shocks
- $F_1 \ldots F_m$ = Costs of production
- E = Expectations of producers
- S_f = Social factors

Linear Equations

Both demand and supply can be represented as linear equations and be drawn as straight line graphs.

A linear equation normally looks like:

$$y = a + bx$$

In this equation, y = the value plotted on the vertical axis (the dependent variable)

x is the value on the horizontal axis (the independent variable)

a is a constant and b is the slope of the line or its gradient.

Remember that demand looks at the relationship between price and the quantity demanded and supply is the relationship between price and the quantity supplied.

In both cases, the quantity demanded and supplied are dependent on the price. So, price is the independent variable and the quantity the dependent variable.

At this point we hit a bit of a snag.

Students of pure maths will notice that in economics, supply and demand graphs are the wrong way round – normally, the vertical Y axis represents the dependent variable and the X axis the independent variable. In supply and demand graphs, price, the independent variable, is drawn on the Y axis and quantity demanded and supplied, the dependent variable, on the X axis.

The switch is attributed to Alfred Marshall (1842–1924) who developed supply and demand analysis in the latter part of the 19th century. It is important, therefore, to remember which is the dependent variable and which the independent variable as we progress through the analysis.

Applying the relationship between price and quantity demanded and supplied we get typical equations such as:

$$Q_d = 2100 - 2.5p$$

$$Q_s = -10 + 6p$$

In the case of the demand curve the minus sign in front of the price variable tells us that there is a negative relationship between price and quantity demanded whereas the plus sign in front of the price in the supply equation tells us that there is a positive relationship between price and quantity supplied.

You may also see demand and supply equations which look like:

$$P = 840 - 0.4Q_d \text{ or}$$

$$P = -120 + 0.8Q_s$$

The equation $P = 840 - 0.4Q_d$ is just the inverse of the demand equation $Q_d = 2100 - 2.5p$. We found this by adopting the following method:

$$Q_d = 2100 - 2.5p$$

$$Q_d + 2.5p = 2100$$

$$2.5p = 2100 - Q_d$$

$$\frac{2.5p}{2.5} = \frac{2100 - Q_d}{2.5}$$

$$P = 840 - 0.4 \, Q_d$$

Remember, however, that because of the switching of supply and demand curves as noted above, you can get some odd looking equations which do not fit with the graphical analysis.

The important thing to remember when manipulating linear equations of this sort is that whatever you do to one side of the equation (multiply, add, divide or subtract a number or element) you must do the same thing to the other side.

Finding Price and Quantity

If we take the original two equations:

$$Q_d = 2100 - 2.5p$$

$$Q_s = -10 + 6p$$

We can dissect them in a bit more detail in relation to the standard $y = a + bx$ linear equation we first introduced.

In our equations, the quantity demanded and supplied are one of the variables in the equation. In this case they are the dependent variable. Their value depends upon the price – the independent variable.

In the case of the demand curve, the quantity demanded will be 2100 minus 2.5 times whatever the price is. If price is €6 then quantity demanded will be $2100 - 2.5(6) = 2085$. If price is €16 then quantity demanded will be $2100 - 2.5 (16) = 2060$

Looking at supply, if the price were €8 then the quantity supplied would be $-10 + 6(8) = 38$ and if price were €16 then quantity supplied would be $-10 + 6(16) = 86$.

If we used the other two equations we looked at:

$$P = 840 - 0.4Q_d$$

Or:

$$P = -120 + 0.8Q_s$$

Then we can arrive at values for P or Q assuming we have at least one of these two variables.

For demand, if p = €6 then the quantity demanded would be:

$$P = 840 - 0.4Q_d$$

$$0.4Q_d = 840 - 6$$

$$\frac{0.4Q_d}{0.4} = \frac{834}{0.4}$$

$$Q_d = 2085$$

In the case of supply, if price = €8:

$$P = -120 + 0.8Q_s$$

$$8 = -120 + 0.8Q_s$$

$$\frac{8}{0.8} = \frac{-120 + 0.8Q_s}{0.8}$$

$$10 = -150 + Q_s$$

$$10 + 150 = Q_s$$

$$Q_s = 160$$

Finding Market Equilibrium
The substitution method

We know that in equilibrium, demand equals supply (D = S).

To find the market equilibrium, therefore, we set the demand and supply equations equal to each other and solve for P and Q.

Take the following demand and supply equations:

$$Q_d = 32 - 3p$$

$$Q_s = 20 + 4p$$

We know that in equilibrium:

$$Q_d = Q_s$$

So, equilibrium in this market will be where:

$$32 - 3p = 20 + 4p$$

This now allows us to solve for P and so find the equilibrium price:

$$32 - 3p = 20 + 4p$$

Subtract 20 from both sides and add 3p to both sides to get:

$$32 - 20 = 4p + 3p$$

$$12 = 7p$$

P = €1.71 (rounded to the nearest whole cent)

We can now substitute the equilibrium price into our two equations to find the equilibrium quantity rounded to the nearest whole number:

$$Q_d = 32 - 3p$$

$$Q_d = 32 - 3(1.71)$$

$$Q_d = 32 - 5.13$$

$$Q_d = 26.87$$

$$Q_d = 27$$

$$Q_s = 20 + 4p$$

$$Q_s = 20 + 4(1.71)$$

$$Q_s = 20 + 6.84$$

$$Q_s = 26.84$$

$$Q_s = 27$$

Note the figures for Q_d and Q_s before rounding differ slightly because we had to round the price. Now look at this example:

$$P = 3 + 0.25Q_s$$

$$P = 15 - 0.75Q_d$$

In this case the equations are defined in terms of price but the principle of working out equilibrium is the same as we have used above.

First, set the two equations equal to each other:

$$3 + 0.25Q_s = 15 - 0.75Q_d$$

Then solve for Q:

Add $0.75Q_d$ to both sides and then subtract 3 from both sides to get:

$$0.75Q_d + 0.25Q_s = 15 - 3$$

$$Q = 12$$

Substitute Q = 12 into one of the equations to find P.

$$P = 3 + 0.25Q_s$$

$$P = 3 + 0.25(12)$$

$$P = 6$$

To check, also substitute into the demand equation:

$$P = 15 - 0.75Q_d$$

$$P = 15 - 0.75(12)$$

$$P = 15 - 9$$

$$P = 6.$$

There is another way to find both the quantity and the price and that is through adopting the approach of solving simultaneous equations. Simultaneous equations require us to find two or more unknowns. In our case it is two unknowns, price and quantity.

The elimination method

Look at the following two equations:

$$Q_d = 20 - 2p$$

$$Q_s = 2 + 2p$$

In this case, the terms are all neatly aligned above each other so it is a relatively simple task to add the two together. Note that we are trying to find equilibrium so $Q_d = Q_s$ so the value of Q is the same. Adding the two together we get:

$$Q_d = 20 - 2p$$
$$Q_s = 2 + 2p$$
$$2Q = 22$$
$$Q = 11$$

Notice that in the above equations we have a very convenient fact that the coefficient of p in each case is the same but with opposite signs. This makes this example very easy to eliminate p to isolate the Q value. This is not always the case, however, but it is important to remember that having two equal values with opposite signs allows us to get rid of them! We will come back to this later.

We can now use the fact that we know Q to find the equilibrium price by substituting Q into one of the equations thus:

$$Q_d = 20 - 2p$$
$$11 = 20 - 2p$$
$$2p = 20 - 11$$
$$2p = 9$$
$$P = 4.5$$

It is always worth checking your answer to make sure you have made no mistakes along the way so in this case we will substitute our known value of Q into the second equation to check we get the same answer (p = 4.5). So:

$$Q_s = 2 + 2p$$
$$11 = 2 + 2p$$
$$11 - 2 = 2p$$
$$9 = 2p$$
$$P = 4.5$$

Sometimes we may have equations where the p and Q values are both on the same side of the equation. In this case we have to use a different technique – the elimination method.

Take the following two equations:

$$-3p + 4Q = 5 \quad (1)$$
$$2p - 5Q = -15 \quad (2)$$

We have labelled these two equations (1) and (2) to allow us to keep track of what we are doing and reduce the risk of making an error.

Remember above when we noted the fact that having a nice convenient equation where the coefficient was equal but the signs opposite enabling us to be able to eliminate one of the values to help solve the equation for the other unknown? That is what we need to do with these two equations. We have to choose to manipulate the two equations to make either the 'p' terms or the 'Q' terms have the same coefficient but opposite signs. A knowledge of factors and lowest common denominators is useful here!

In this example we are going to manipulate the equations to get rid of the 'p' terms. This allows us to isolate the 'Q' terms and thus solve for Q and then find p.

This is how we do this:

$$-3p + 4Q = 5 \quad (1)$$
$$2p - 5Q = -15 \quad (2)$$

To eliminate p, multiply (1) by 2 and (2) by 3

$$-6p + 8Q = 10 \quad (3)$$
$$6p - 15Q = -45 \quad (4)$$

Add together (3) and (4)

$$-6p + 8Q = 10 \quad (3)$$
$$6p - 15Q = -45 \quad (4)$$
$$-7Q = -35$$

Divide both sides by –7

$$Q = 5$$

We can now substitute Q into equations (1) and (2) to find (and check) p If Q = 5 then:

$$-3p + 4(5) = 5$$
$$-3p + 20 = 5$$
$$20 - 5 = 3p$$
$$15 = 3p$$
$$P = 5$$
$$2p - 5(5) = -15$$
$$2p - 25 = -15$$
$$2p = -15 + 25$$
$$2p = 10$$
$$p = 5$$

In this case the equilibrium price is €5 and the equilibrium quantity is 5.

Three Steps to Analysing Changes in Equilibrium

So far we have seen how supply and demand together determine a market's equilibrium, which in turn determines the price of the good and the amount of the good that buyers purchase and sellers produce. Markets are dynamic – demand and supply change all the time and in some markets these changes may be almost every second of every day – in foreign exchange markets, for example. The equilibrium price and quantity depend on the position of the supply and demand curves. When some event shifts one (or both) of these curves, the equilibrium in the market changes. The analysis of such a change is called *comparative statics* because it involves comparing two unchanging situations – an initial and a new equilibrium.

FYI

Prices as Signals

Our analysis so far has only brushed the surface of the way markets operate. Economists have conducted extensive research into the nature and determinants of both demand and supply. It is beyond the scope of this book to go into too much detail on these issues but it is useful to have a little bit of background knowledge on this to help understand markets more effectively.

At the heart of research into demand and supply is why buyers and sellers behave as they do. The development of magnetic resonance imaging (MRI) techniques has allowed researchers to investigate how the brain responds to different stimuli when making purchasing decisions (referred to as *neuroeconomics*). As time goes by our understanding of buyer and seller behaviour will improve and theories will have to be adapted to accommodate this new understanding.

However, much of the theory behind how markets work relies on the assumption of rational behaviour, defined in terms of humans preferring more to less and taking into account information prior to making a decision. The main function of price in a free market is to act as a signal to both buyers and sellers to help in decision making.

For buyers, price tells them something about what they have to give up to acquire the benefits that having the good will confer on them. These benefits are referred to as the *utility* (satisfaction) derived from consumption. If I am willing to pay €10 to go and watch a movie then economists will assume that the value of the benefits I gain from watching the movie is greater than the next best alternative – what else I could have spent my €10 on. Principles 1 and 2 of the *Ten Principles of Economics* state that people face trade-offs and that the cost of something is what you have to give up to acquire it. This is fundamental to the law of demand. At higher prices, the sacrifice being made in terms of the value of the benefits gained from alternatives is greater and so we may be less willing to do so as a result. If the price of a ticket for the movie was €20 (other things being equal) then it might have to be a very good movie to persuade us that giving up what else €20 could buy is worth it.

For sellers price acts as a signal in relation to the profitability of production. For most sellers, increasing the amount of a good produced will incur some additional input costs. A higher price is required in order to compensate for the additional cost and to also enable the producer to gain some reward from the risk they are taking in production. That reward is termed profit.

If prices are rising in a free market then this acts as a different but related signal to buyers and sellers. Rising prices to a seller means that there is a shortage and thus there is an incentive to expand production because the seller knows that she will be able to sell what she produces. For buyers, a rising price changes the nature of the trade-off they have to face. They will now have to give up more in order to acquire the good and they will have to decide whether the value of the benefits they will gain from acquiring the good is worth the extra price they have to pay.

What we do know is that for both buyers and sellers, there are many complex processes that occur in decision making. Whilst we do not fully understand all these processes yet, economists are constantly searching for new insights that might help them understand the workings of markets more fully. All of us go through these complex processes every time we make a purchasing decision – although we may not realize it! Having some appreciation of these processes is fundamental to thinking like an economist.

When analysing how some event affects a market, we proceed in three steps. First, we decide whether the event shifts the supply curve, the demand curve or, in some cases, both curves. Secondly, we decide whether the curve shifts to the right or to the left. Thirdly, we use the supply and demand diagram to compare the initial and the new equilibrium, which shows how the shift affects the equilibrium price and quantity. It is important in the analysis that the process by which equilibrium changes is understood and that the changes involved are not instantaneous (although some schools of thought do refer to instantaneous changes in markets) – some markets will take longer to adjust to changes than others. Table 4.3 summarizes the three steps. To see how this recipe is used, let's consider various events that might affect the market for rape seed.

Example: A Change in Demand Suppose that a government-sponsored research project finds that using rape seed oil helps reduce the risk of heart disease and

TABLE 4.3

A Three-Step Programme for Analysing Changes in Equilibrium
1. Decide whether the event shifts the supply or demand curve (or perhaps both).
2. Decide in which direction the curve shifts.
3. Use the supply and demand diagram to see how the shift changes the equilibrium price and quantity.

strokes. How does this event affect the market for rape seed? To answer this question, let's follow our three steps.

1. The news has a direct effect on the demand curve by changing people's taste for rape seed oil. That is, the report changes the amount of rape seed oil that people want to buy at any given price.
2. Because the report incentivizes people to want to use more rape seed oil, the demand curve shifts to the right. Figure 4.9 shows this increase in demand as the shift in the demand curve from D_1 to D_2. This shift indicates that the quantity of rape seed oil demanded is higher at every price. The shift in demand has led to a shortage of rape seed oil in the market. At a price of €2.00 buyers now want to buy 26 000 tonnes of rape seed but sellers are only offering 12 000 tonnes for sale at this price. There is a shortage of 14 000 tonnes.

FIGURE 4.9

How an Increase in Demand Affects the Equilibrium

An event that raises quantity demanded at any given price shifts the demand curve to the right. The equilibrium price and the equilibrium quantity both rise. Here, the report linking using rape seed oil to reductions in risk of ill health causes buyers to demand more rape seed. The demand curve shifts from D_1 to D_2, which causes the equilibrium price to rise from €2.00 to €3.00 and the equilibrium quantity to rise from 12 000 to 200 000 tonnes.

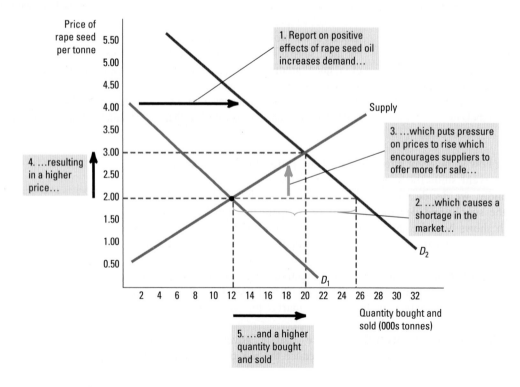

3. As Figure 4.9 shows, the shortage starts to force up prices and encourages growers to plant more rape. The additional production incurs extra costs and so a higher price is required to compensate sellers. This raises the equilibrium price from €2.00 to €3.00 and the equilibrium quantity from 12 000 to 20 000 tonnes. In other words, the report increases the price of rape seed and the quantity of rape seed bought and sold.

Shifts in Curves versus Movements along Curves – a Reminder

When the report drives up the price of rape seed, the quantity of rape seed that growers supply rises, but the supply curve remains in the same position. Economists say there has been an increase in 'quantity supplied' but no change in 'supply'.

'Supply' refers to the position of the supply curve, whereas the 'quantity supplied' refers to the amount suppliers wish to sell at different prices. In this example, we assumed supply does not change. Instead, the report alters consumers' desire to buy at any given price and thereby shifts the demand curve. The increase in demand creates a shortage. The shortage means there are more buyers looking to purchase rape seed than there are sellers willing to sell. As a result, price starts to creep up as buyers are prepared to pay higher prices to get products. When the price rises growers are willing to offer more rape seed for sale and so the quantity supplied rises. This increase in quantity supplied is represented by the movement along the supply curve. The shortage will continue to be competed away by price rising until supply and demand are once again brought into equilibrium. The final result will be a rise in equilibrium price and in the equilibrium amount bought and sold.

To summarize, a shift *in* the supply curve is called a 'change in supply', and a shift *in* the demand curve is called a 'change in demand'. A movement *along* a fixed supply curve is called a 'change in the quantity supplied', and a movement *along* a fixed demand curve is called a 'change in the quantity demanded'.

Example: A Change in Supply Suppose that, during another summer, bad weather destroys part of the seed crop for rape and drives up the world price of rape seed for planting. How does this event affect the market for rape seed? Once again, to answer this question, we follow our three steps.

1. The change in the price of seed, an input needed to grow rape, affects the supply curve. By raising the costs of production, it reduces the amount of rape seed that firms produce and sell at any given price. The demand curve does not change because the higher cost of inputs does not directly affect the amount of rape seed buyers wish to buy.

2. The supply curve shifts to the left because, at every price, the total amount that firms are willing and able to sell is reduced. Figure 4.10 illustrates this decrease in supply as a shift in the supply curve from S_1 to S_2. At a price of €2.00 sellers are now only able to offer 4000 tonnes of rape seed for sale but demand is still 12 000 tonnes of rape seed. The shift in supply to the left has created a shortage in the market. Once again, the shortage will create pressure on price to rise as buyers look to purchase rape seed.

3. As Figure 4.10 shows, the shortage raises the equilibrium price from €2.00 to €2.50 and lowers the equilibrium quantity from 12 000 to 9000 tonnes. As a result of the increase in seed for growing, the price of rape seed rises, and the quantity of rape seed bought and sold falls.

FIGURE 4.10

How a Decrease in Supply Affects the Equilibrium

An event that reduces supply at any given price shifts the supply curve to the left. The equilibrium price rises, and the equilibrium quantity falls. Here, an increase in the price of seed for growing rape plants (an input) causes sellers to supply less rape seed. The supply curve shifts from S_1 to S_2, which causes the equilibrium price of rape seed to rise from €2.00 to €2.50 and the equilibrium quantity to fall from 12000 to 9000 tonnes.

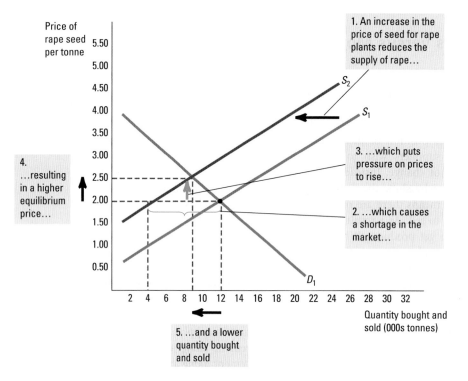

Example: A Change in Both Supply and Demand (i)
Now suppose that the report and the bad weather occur during the same summer. To analyse this combination of events, we again follow our three steps.

1. We determine that both curves must shift. The report affects the demand curve because it alters the amount of rape seed that buyers want to buy at any given price. At the same time, when the bad weather drives up the price of seed for growing rape, it alters the supply curve for rape seed because it changes the amount of rape seed that firms want to sell at any given price.
2. The curves shift in the same directions as they did in our previous analysis: the demand curve shifts to the right, and the supply curve shifts to the left. Figure 4.11 illustrates these shifts.
3. As Figure 4.11 shows, there are two possible outcomes that might result, depending on the relative size of the demand and supply shifts. In both cases, the equilibrium price rises. In panel (a), where demand increases substantially while supply falls just a little, the equilibrium quantity also rises. By contrast, in panel (b), where supply falls substantially while demand rises just a little, the equilibrium quantity falls. Thus, these events certainly raise the price of rape seed, but their impact on the amount of rape seed bought and sold is ambiguous (that is, it could go either way).

FIGURE 4.11

A Shift in Both Supply and Demand (i)

Here we observe a simultaneous increase in demand and decrease in supply. Two outcomes are possible. In panel (a), the equilibrium price rises from P_1 to P_2, and the equilibrium quantity rises from Q_1 to Q_2. In panel (b), the equilibrium price again rises from P_1 to P_2, but the equilibrium quantity falls from Q_1 to Q_2.

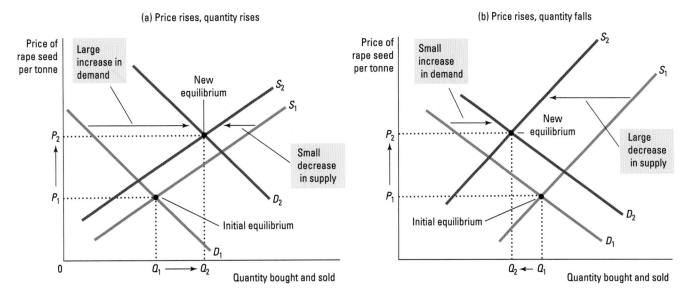

Example: A Change in Both Supply and Demand (ii)

We are now going to look at a slightly different scenario but with both supply and demand increasing together. Assume that the details of the report have been leaked prior to official publication and the findings publicized on TV news stations. We know that the report is likely to increase demand for rape seed and so the demand curve will shift to the right. However, sellers' expectations that sales of rape seed will increase as a result of the forecasts mean that they take steps to expand production of rape seed. This would lead to a shift of the supply curve to the right – more rape seed is now offered for sale at every price. To analyse this particular combination of events, we again follow our three steps.

1. We determine that both curves must shift. The report affects the demand curve because it alters the amount of rape seed that buyers want to buy at any given price. At the same time, the expectations of producers alter the supply curve for rape seed because they change the amount of rape seed that firms want to sell at any given price.
2. Both demand and supply curves shift to the right: Figure 4.12 illustrates these shifts.
3. As Figure 4.12 shows, there are three possible outcomes that might result, depending on the relative size of the demand and supply shifts. In panel (a), where demand increases substantially while supply rises just a little, the equilibrium price and quantity rises. By contrast, in panel (b), where supply rises substantially while demand rises just a little, the equilibrium price falls but the equilibrium quantity rises. In panel (c) the increase in demand and supply are identical and so equilibrium price does not change. Equilibrium quantity will increase, however. Thus, these events have different effects on the price of rape seed although the amount of rape seed bought and sold in each case is higher. In this instance the effect on price is ambiguous.

FIGURE 4.12

A Shift in Both Supply and Demand (ii)

Here, again, we observe a simultaneous increase in demand and supply. Three outcomes are possible. In panel (a) the equilibrium price rises from P_1 to P_2 and the equilibrium quantity rises from Q_1 to Q_2. In panel (b), the equilibrium price falls from P_1 to P_2 but the equilibrium quantity rises from Q_1 to Q_2. In panel (c), there is no change to the equilibrium price but the equilibrium quantity rises from Q_1 to Q_2.

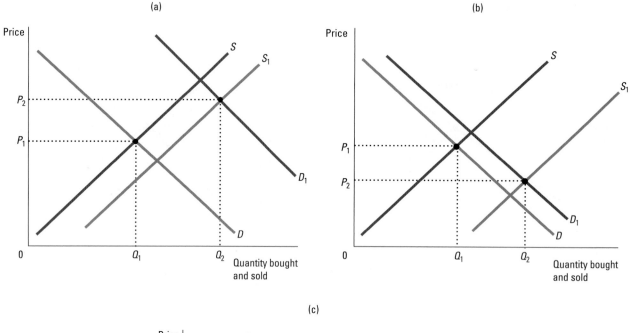

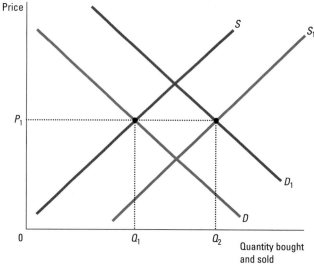

what if…Malmo FF, a Swedish football team, is taken over by a rich Middle East backer. The team is strengthened and produces a series of excellent results which propel them to the top of the Swedish Allsvenskan. Demand for tickets to the 24 000 capacity stadium increases dramatically. Draw a supply and demand diagram to illustrate this market situation. Would the club increase ticket prices? If so, what might fans' reaction be? If the club does not increase prices why might it make this decision? What do you think would be the practical effect on fans and the prices they have to pay for tickets if prices were held at the original level? Assuming the improvement in the club's fortunes continues for several seasons, what might the long-term market situation look like?

The Swedbank Stadion, home of Malmo football club.

Summary

We have just seen four examples of how to use supply and demand curves to analyse a change in equilibrium. Whenever an event shifts the supply curve, the demand curve, or perhaps both curves, you can use these tools to predict how the event will alter the amount bought and sold in equilibrium and the price at which the good is bought and sold. Table 4.4 shows the predicted outcome for any combination of shifts in the two curves. To make sure you understand how to use the tools of supply and demand, pick a few entries in this table and make sure you can explain to yourself why the table contains the prediction it does.

TABLE 4.4

What Happens to Price and Quantity When Supply or Demand Shifts?

As a quick quiz, make sure you can explain each of the entries in this table using a supply and demand diagram.

	No change in supply	An increase in supply	A decrease in supply
No change in demand	P same Q same	P down Q up	P up Q down
An increase in demand	P up Q up	P ambiguous Q up	P up Q ambiguous
A decrease in demand	P down Q down	P down Q ambiguous	P ambiguous Q down

Quick Quiz Analyse what happens to the market for pizza if the price of tomatoes rises. • Analyse what happens to the market for pasta if the price of potatoes falls.

HOW PRICES ALLOCATE RESOURCES

This chapter has analysed supply and demand in a single market. Although our discussion has centred on the market for rape seed, the lessons learned here apply in most other markets as well. Whenever you go to a shop to buy something, you are contributing to the demand for that item. Whenever you look for a job, you are contributing to the supply of labour services. Because supply and demand are such pervasive economic phenomena, the model of supply and demand is a powerful tool for analysis. We shall be using this model repeatedly in the following chapters.

One of the *Ten Principles of Economics* discussed in Chapter 1 is that markets are usually a good way to organize economic activity. Although it is still too early to judge whether market outcomes are good or bad, in this chapter we have begun to see how markets work. In any economic system, scarce resources have to be allocated among competing uses. Market economies harness the forces of supply and demand to serve that end. Supply and demand together determine the prices of the economy's many different goods and services; prices in turn are the signals that guide the allocation of resources.

For example, consider the allocation of property on the seafront in a seaside resort. Because the amount of this property is limited, not everyone can enjoy the luxury of living by the beach. Who gets this resource? The answer is: whoever is willing and able to pay the price. The price of seafront property adjusts until the quantity of property demanded exactly balances the quantity supplied. Thus, in market economies, prices are the mechanism for rationing scarce resources.

Similarly, prices determine who produces each good and how much is produced. For instance, consider farming. Because we need food to survive, it is crucial that some people work on farms. What determines who is a farmer and who is not? In a free society, there is no government planning agency making this decision and ensuring an adequate supply of food. Instead, the allocation of workers to farms is based on the job decisions of millions of workers. This decentralized system works well because these decisions depend on prices. The prices of food and the wages of farm workers (the price of their labour) adjust to ensure that enough people choose to be farmers.

If a person had never seen a market economy in action, the whole idea might seem preposterous. Economies are large groups of people engaged in many interdependent activities. What prevents decentralized decision making from degenerating into chaos? What coordinates the actions of the millions of people with their varying abilities and desires? What ensures that what needs to get done does in fact get done? The answer, in a word, is *prices*. If market economies are guided by an invisible hand, as Adam Smith famously suggested, then prices are the baton that the invisible hand uses to conduct the economic orchestra.

IN THE NEWS

We have used the rape seed market as an example in this chapter to help understand the working of markets. In real life, markets are not isolated but highly interdependent – what happens in one market can have effects on others. This article illustrates just such an example.

Interdependent Markets

Sometimes a great idea comes along that seems to hold the potential for solving a host of problems. The idea receives publicity, is promoted as being the golden key and everyone jumps on the bandwagon. Economists may be part of the problem in that some do take a narrow view of a problem and support solutions that they happen to agree with or which their research tells them has some benefit. However, economists will also tell you that any benefit has some costs attached to it and it is important to look at those costs carefully to assess the true worth of the 'solution'. In economics, markets are highly dependent on one another; if circumstances change in one market they will affect other markets – and the people who both use and rely on them.

Take the case of biofuels. The development of biofuels has been heralded as an opportunity to reduce the reliance on oil, to accelerate the change to renewable energy and to provide a cheaper alternative to oil. Biofuels use crops – often cereal crops – to produce the biofuel. The very word 'biofuel' gives the impression that it is somehow 'good' through the use of the term 'bio'. However, it seems that not everyone is quite so happy that biofuels are a 'good' thing.

Maize can be grown for food manufacture or for fuel.

The charity, Oxfam, has been running a campaign which presents a damning picture of the impact that the move to biofuels is having on the most vulnerable people in the world. The production of biofuel has been partly responsible for increases in basic commodity prices like wheat in recent years. The demand for the raw materials for biofuels has encouraged farmers to switch from production of some crops to others. The resulting output has been diverted between crops going for food and for production of ethanol. The result, say Oxfam, has resulted in an increase in the number of people in poverty, worldwide, of some 30 million and costing poor countries an extra $100 billion in food bills. One of the reasons, says Oxfam, is a shortage of crops (exacerbated by the disruption to supply as a result of bad weather and natural disasters), which has forced food prices much higher. The people who are most affected by these higher prices are the people who are poorest and on the margins of poverty. As food prices rise, these marginal people are dragged into poverty.

Oxfam says that the value to farmers of growing crops for biofuel is higher than that for growing it for food. As a result farmers are diverting production to fuel and this reduces the supply of crops available for food production. The situation is made worse by the subsidies and tax breaks that rich countries have given to encourage the growth in the production and use of biofuel. In addition, the change in land use that is being driven by the move to biofuel is actually adding to carbon emissions, offsetting the environmental benefits of using renewable fuel rather than oil-based fuels. Oxfam suggests that the target that the EU has set for the production of biofuel will lead to carbon emissions rising 70 times by 2020.

The largest producer of bioethanol in Europe, Abengoa Bioenergy, has reacted angrily to the claims and has branded the suggestion that the production of bioethanol can lead to world poverty and extreme hunger as a 'manipulation' and as being 'false statements'. It suggests that production of bioethanol benefits local economies, redistributes global income, creates jobs and increases incomes. There is enough land in the world to make production of cereal-based bioethanol sustainable, it says. In addition it points out that in future, cereal-based bioethanol production will be outstripped by ethanol produced from biomass.

So, where does the truth lie and where should our priorities lie in the production of this type fuel?

Questions

1. In what way is the market for cereals, for food and for biofuel 'interdependent?
2. What factors might influence the decisions of farmers about whether to supply cereal crops for the food or the biofuel industries?
3. Use supply and demand diagrams to show how the growth in biofuels has led to a rise in commodity prices.
4. Why might Oxfam believe the switch from biofuels has caused a rise in poverty?
5. Do you agree with the views of Abengoa Bioenergy that the long-term benefits of biofuel will outweigh any short-term costs?

SUMMARY

- Economists use the model of supply and demand to analyse competitive markets. In a competitive market, there are many buyers and sellers, each of whom has little or no influence on the market price.

- The supply curve shows how the quantity of a good supplied depends on the price. According to the law of supply, as the price of a good rises, the quantity supplied rises. Therefore, the supply curve slopes upward.

- In addition to price, other determinants of how much producers want to sell include input prices, technology, expectations, the number of sellers, and natural and social factors. If one of these factors changes, the supply curve shifts.

- The demand curve shows how the quantity of a good demanded depends on the price. According to the law of demand, as the price of a good falls, the quantity demanded rises. Therefore, the demand curve slopes downward.

- In addition to price, other determinants of how much consumers want to buy include income, the prices of substitutes and complements, tastes, expectations and the number of buyers. If one of these factors changes, the demand curve shifts.

- The intersection of the supply and demand curves determines the market equilibrium. At the equilibrium price, the quantity supplied equals the quantity demanded.

- The behaviour of sellers and buyers naturally drives markets toward their equilibrium. When the market price is above the equilibrium price, there is a surplus of the good, which causes the market price to fall. When the market price is below the equilibrium price, there is a shortage, which causes the market price to rise.

- To analyse how any event influences a market, we use the supply and demand diagram to examine how the event affects the equilibrium price and quantity. To do this we follow three steps. First, we decide whether the event shifts the supply curve or the demand curve (or both). Secondly, we decide which direction the curve shifts. Thirdly, we compare the new equilibrium with the initial equilibrium.

- In market economies, prices are the signals that guide economic decisions and thereby allocate scarce resources. For every good in the economy, the price ensures that supply and demand are in balance. The equilibrium price then determines how much of the good buyers choose to purchase and how much sellers choose to produce.

KEY CONCEPTS

price, p. 56
cost, p. 56
market, p. 56
competition, p. 57
competitive
    market, p. 57
quantity supplied, p. 58
law of supply, p. 58

supply schedule, p. 58
supply curve, p. 59
quantity demanded, p. 63
law of demand, p. 63
demand schedule, p. 63
demand curve, p. 63
normal good, p. 66
inferior good, p. 67

substitutes, p. 67
complements, p. 67
equilibrium, p. 70
equilibrium price, p. 70
equilibrium quantity, p. 70
surplus, p. 70
shortage, p. 71
law of supply and demand, p. 71

QUESTIONS FOR REVIEW

1. What determines the quantity of a good that sellers supply?
2. What are the supply schedule and the supply curve, and how are they related? Why does the supply curve slope upward?

3. Does a change in producers' technology lead to a movement along the supply curve or a shift in the supply curve? Does a change in price lead to a movement along the supply curve or a shift in the supply curve?

4. What determines the quantity of a good that buyers demand?

5. What are the demand schedule and the demand curve, and how are they related? Why does the demand curve slope downward?

6. Does a change in consumers' tastes lead to a movement along the demand curve or a shift in the demand curve? Does a change in price lead to a movement along the demand curve or a shift in the demand curve?

7. Carlos prefers asparagus to spinach. His income declines and as a result he buys more spinach. Is spinach an inferior or a normal good to Carlos? Explain your answer.

8. Define the equilibrium of a market. Describe the forces that move a market toward its equilibrium.

9. Cheese and wine are complements because they are often enjoyed together. When the price of wine rises, what happens to the supply, demand, quantity supplied, quantity demanded and the price in the market for cheese?

10. Describe the role of prices in market economies.

PROBLEMS AND APPLICATIONS

1. Explain each of the following statements using supply and demand diagrams.
   a. When there is a drought in southern Europe, the price of olive oil rises in supermarkets throughout Europe.
   b. When the Olympic Games were held in London in 2012, the price of hotel rooms in central London rose sharply.
   c. When conflict breaks out in the Middle East, the price of petrol in Europe rises and the price of a used Mercedes falls.

2. 'An increase in the demand for mozzarella cheese raises the quantity of mozzarella demanded, but not the quantity supplied.' Is this statement true or false? Explain.

3. Consider the market for large family saloon cars. For each of the events listed here, identify which of the determinants of supply or demand are affected. Also indicate whether supply or demand is increased or decreased. Then show the effect on the price and quantity of large family saloon cars.
   a. People decide to have more children.
   b. A strike by steel workers raises steel prices.
   c. Engineers develop new automated machinery for the production of cars.
   d. The price of estate cars rises.
   e. A stock market crash lowers people's wealth.

4. During the 1990s, technological advances reduced the cost of computer chips. How do you think this affected the market for computers? For computer software? For typewriters?

5. Using supply and demand diagrams, show the effect of the following events on the market for sweatshirts.
   a. A drought in Egypt damages the cotton crop.
   b. The price of leather jackets falls.
   c. All universities require students to attend morning exercise classes in appropriate attire.
   d. New knitting machines are invented.

6. Suppose that in the year 2008 the number of births is temporarily high. How might this baby boom affect the price of baby-sitting services in 2013 and 2023? (Hint: 5-year-olds need babysitters, whereas 15-year-olds can be babysitters.)

7. The market for pizza has the following demand and supply schedules:

Price	Quantity demanded	Quantity supplied
€4	135	26
5	104	53
6	81	81
7	68	98
8	53	110
9	39	121

Graph the demand and supply curves. What is the equilibrium price and quantity in this market? If the actual price in this market were above the equilibrium price, what would drive the market towards the equilibrium? If the actual price in this market were below the equilibrium price, what would drive the market towards the equilibrium?

8. Suppose that the price of tickets to see your local football team play at home is determined by market forces. Currently, the demand and supply schedules are as follows:

Price	Quantity demanded	Quantity supplied
€10	50000	30000
20	40000	30000
30	30000	30000
40	20000	30000
50	10000	30000

   a. Draw the demand and supply curves. What is unusual about this supply curve? Why might this be true?
   b. What are the equilibrium price and quantity of tickets?
   c. Your team plans to increase total capacity in its stadium by 5000 seats next season. What admission price should it charge?

9. Market research has revealed the following information about the market for chocolate bars: the demand schedule can be represented by the equation QD = 1600 − 300P, where QD is the quantity demanded and P is the price. The supply schedule can be represented by the equation QS =1400 + 700P, where QS is the quantity supplied. Calculate the equilibrium price and quantity in the market for chocolate bars.

10. What do we mean by a perfectly competitive market? Do you think that the example of rape seed used in this chapter fits this description? Is there another type of market that better characterizes the market for rape seed?

5 ELASTICITY AND ITS APPLICATIONS

LEARNING OBJECTIVES

In this chapter you will:

- Learn the meaning of the concept of elasticity

- Learn the meaning of the elasticity of supply

- Examine what determines the elasticity of supply

- Apply the concept of elasticity to price, to both supply and demand, to income and demand and the relationship between the changing prices of different products on demand

- Examine what determines the elasticity of demand

- Understand the relevance of elasticity to total expenditure and total revenue

- Apply the concept of elasticity in two different markets

After reading this chapter you should be able to:

- Calculate elasticity using the midpoint method

- Calculate the price elasticity of supply

- Distinguish between an inelastic and elastic supply curve

- Distinguish between the price elasticity of demand for necessities and luxuries

- Calculate different elasticities – price, income and cross

- Demonstrate the impact of the price elasticity of demand on total expenditure and total revenue under conditions of different demand elasticities

ELASTICITY AND ITS APPLICATION

For businesses, the price they charge for the products they produce is a vital part of their product positioning – what the product offering is in relation to competitors. We have seen in Chapter 4 how markets are dynamic and that price acts as a signal to both sellers and buyers; when prices change, the signal is altered and producer and consumer behaviour changes.

Imagine yourself as a producer of silicon chips for use in personal computers, laptops and a variety of other electronic devices. Because you earn all your income from selling silicon chips, you devote much effort to making your factory as productive as it can be. You monitor how production is organized, staff recruitment and motivation levels, check suppliers for cost effectiveness and quality, and study the latest advances in technology. You know that the more chips you manufacture, the more you will have available to sell, and the higher will be your income (assuming you sell them) and your standard of living.

One day a local university announces a major discovery. Scientists have devised a new material to produce chips which would help to increase computing power by 50 per cent. How should you react to this news? Should you use the new material? Does this discovery make you better off or worse off than you were before? In this chapter we will see that these questions can have surprising answers. The surprise will come from applying the most basic tools of economics – supply and demand – to the market for computer chips.

In any competitive market, such as the market for computer chips, the upward sloping supply curve represents the behaviour of sellers, and the downward sloping demand curve represents the behaviour of buyers. The price of the good adjusts to bring the quantity supplied and quantity demanded of the good into balance. To apply this basic analysis to understand the impact of the scientists' discovery, we must first develop one more tool: the concept of *elasticity* also referred to as *price sensitivity*. We know from Chapter 4 that when price rises, demand falls and supply rises. What we did not discuss in the chapter was *how far* demand and supply change in response to changes in price – in other words, how sensitive supply and demand is to a change in prices. When studying how some event or policy affects a market, we can discuss not only the direction of the effects but their magnitude as well. Elasticity, a measure of how much buyers and sellers respond to changes in market conditions, allows us to analyse supply and demand with greater precision.

PRICE ELASTICITY OF SUPPLY

elasticity a measure of the responsiveness of quantity demanded or quantity supplied to one of its determinants

When we introduced supply in Chapter 4, we noted that producers of a good offer to sell more of it when the price of the good rises, when their input prices fall or when their technology improves. To turn from qualitative to quantitative statements about quantity supplied, we use the concept of **elasticity**.

The Price Elasticity of Supply and its Determinants

price elasticity of supply a measure of how much the quantity supplied of a good responds to a change in the price of that good, computed as the percentage change in quantity supplied divided by the percentage change in price

The law of supply states that higher prices raise the quantity supplied. The **price elasticity of supply** measures how much the quantity supplied responds to changes in the price. Supply of a good is said to be *elastic* (or price sensitive) if the quantity supplied responds substantially to changes in the price. Supply is said to be *inelastic* (or price insensitive) if the quantity supplied responds only slightly to changes in the price.

The price elasticity of supply depends on the flexibility of sellers to change the amount of the good they produce. For example, seafront property has an inelastic supply because it is almost impossible to produce more of it quickly – supply is not very sensitive to changes in price. By contrast, manufactured goods, such as books, cars and television sets, have relatively elastic supplies because the firms that produce them can run their factories longer in response to a higher price – supply is sensitive to changes in price.

Elasticity can take any value greater than or equal to zero. The closer to zero the more inelastic, and the closer to infinity the more elastic. We will look at the determinants of supply first and then look in more detail at how elasticity is computed.

The Determinants of Price Elasticity of Supply

The Time Period   In most markets, a key determinant of the price elasticity of supply is the time period being considered. Supply is usually more elastic in the long run than in the short run. We can further distinguish between the short run and the very short run. Over very short periods of time, firms may find it impossible to respond to a change in price by changing output. In the short run firms cannot easily change the size of their factories or productive capacity to make more or less of a good but may have some flexibility. For example, it might take a month to employ new labour but after that time some increase in output can be accommodated. Overall, in the short run, the quantity supplied is not very responsive to the price. By contrast, over longer periods, firms can build new factories or close old ones, hire new staff and buy in more capital and equipment. In addition, new firms can enter a market and old firms can shut down. Thus, in the long run, the quantity supplied can respond substantially to price changes.

Productive Capacity   Most businesses, in the short run, will have a finite capacity – an upper limit to the amount that they can produce at any one time determined by the amount of factor inputs they possess. How far they are using this capacity depends, in turn, on the state of the economy. In periods of strong economic growth, firms may be operating at or near full capacity. If demand is rising for the product they produce and prices are rising, it may be difficult for the firm to expand output to meet this new demand and so supply may be inelastic.

When the economy is growing slowly or is contracting, some firms may find they have to cut back output and may only be operating at 60 per cent of full capacity. In this situation, if demand later increased and prices started to rise, it may be much easier for the firm to expand output relatively quickly and so supply would be more elastic.

The Size of the Firm/Industry   It is possible that as a general rule, supply may be more elastic in smaller firms or industries than in larger ones. For example, consider a small independent furniture manufacturer. Demand for its products may rise and in response the firm may be able to buy in raw materials (wood, for example), to meet this increase in demand. Whilst the firm will incur a cost in buying in this timber, it is unlikely that the unit cost for the material will increase. Compare this to a situation where a steel manufacturer increases its purchase of raw materials (iron ore, for example). Buying large quantities of iron ore on global commodity markets can drive up unit price and, by association, unit costs.

A study of the coffee industry in Papua New Guinea[1] found that the price elasticity of supply of smallholders was around 0.23 whereas that for large estates was much more inelastic at 0.04. The study suggested that these figures compared well to estimates derived in previous studies.

The response of supply to changes in price in large firms/industries, therefore, may be less elastic than in smaller firms/industries. This is also related to the number of firms in

---

[1] http://www.une.edu.au/bepp/working-papers/ag-res-econ/occasional-papers/agecop3.pdf

the industry – the more firms there are in the industry the easier it is to increase supply, other things being equal.

The Mobility of Factors of Production Consider a farmer whose land is currently devoted to producing wheat. A sharp rise in the price of rape seed might encourage the farmer to switch use of land from wheat to rape seed relatively easily. The mobility of the factor of production land, in this case, is relatively high and so supply of rape seed may be relatively elastic.

A number of multinational firms that have plants in different parts of the world now build each plant to be identical. What this means is that if there is disruption to one plant the firm can more easily transfer operations to another plant elsewhere and continue production 'seamlessly'. Car manufacturers provide another example of this interchangeability of parts and operations. The chassis, for example, may be identical across a range of branded car models. This is the case with some Audi, Volkswagen, Seat and Skoda models. This means that the supply may be more elastic as a result.

Different cars? Different brands maybe but there are more similarities to these two cars than there are differences.

Compare this to the supply of highly skilled oncology consultants. An increase in the wages of oncology consultants (suggesting a shortage exists) will not mean that a renal consultant or other doctors can suddenly switch to take advantage of the higher wages and increase the supply of oncology consultants. In this example, the mobility of labour to switch between different uses is limited and so the supply of these specialist consultants is likely to be relatively inelastic.

Ease of Storing Stock/Inventory In some firms, stocks can be built up to enable the firm to respond more flexibly to changes in prices. In industries where inventory build-up is relatively easy and cheap, the price elasticity of supply is more elastic than in industries where it is much harder to do this. Consider the fresh fruit industry, for example. Storing fresh fruit is not easy because it is perishable and so the price elasticity of supply in this industry may be more inelastic.

Computing the Price Elasticity of Supply

Now that we have discussed the price elasticity of supply in general terms, let's be more precise about how it is measured. Economists compute the price elasticity of supply as the percentage change in the quantity supplied divided by the percentage change in the price. That is:

$$\text{Price elasticity of supply} = \frac{\text{Percentage change in quantity supplied}}{\text{Percentage change in price}}$$

For example, suppose that an increase in the price of milk from €2.85 to €3.15 a litre raises the amount that dairy farmers produce from 90 000 to 110 000 litres per month. Using the midpoint method, we calculate the percentage change in price as:

$$\text{Percentage change in price} = (3.15 - 2.85)/3.00 \times 100 = 10\%$$

Similarly, we calculate the percentage change in quantity supplied as:

$$\text{Percentage change in quantity supplied} = (110\,000 - 90\,000)/100\,000 \times 100 = 20\%$$

In this case, the price elasticity of supply is:

$$\text{Price elasticity of supply} = \frac{20\%}{10\%} = 2$$

In this example, the elasticity of 2 reflects the fact that the quantity supplied moves proportionately twice as much as the price.

The Midpoint Method of Calculating Percentage Changes and Elasticities

If you try calculating the price elasticity of supply between two points on a supply curve, you will quickly notice an annoying problem: the elasticity for a movement from point A to point B seems different from the elasticity for a movement from point B to point A. For example, consider these numbers:

$$\text{Point A : Price } = \text{ €4 Quantity Supplied } = \text{ 80}$$
$$\text{Point B : Price } = \text{ €6 Quantity Supplied } = \text{ 125}$$

Going from point A to point B, the price rises by 50 per cent – the change in price divided by the original price × 100 (2/4 × 100) − and the quantity rises by 56.25 per cent – the change in quantity supplied divided by the original supply × 100 (45/80 × 100) − indicating that the price elasticity of supply is 56.25/50, or 1.125. By contrast, going from point B to point A, the price falls by 33 per cent (2/6 × 100), and the quantity falls by 36 per cent (45/125 × 100), indicating that the price elasticity of supply is 36/33, or 1.09.

Note, in the working above we have rounded the fall in price to the nearest whole number (33 per cent). If we had not used this rounding, the price elasticity of supply would be:

$$\frac{\left(\frac{85 - 125}{125}\right)}{\left(\frac{4 - 6}{6}\right)} = 1.08$$

One way to avoid this problem is to use the *midpoint method* for calculating elasticities. In the example above we used a standard way to compute a percentage change – divide the change by the initial level and multiply by 100. By contrast, the midpoint method computes a percentage change by dividing the change by the midpoint (or average) of the initial and final levels. For instance, €5 is the midpoint of €4 and €6. Therefore, according to the midpoint method, a change from €4 to €6 is considered a 40 per cent rise, because $((6 − 4)/5) × 100 = 40$. Similarly, a change from €6 to €4 is considered a 40 per cent fall $((4 − 6)/5) × 100 = −40$. Looking at the quantity, moving from Point A to Point B gives $(125 − 80)/102.5 × 100 = 43.9$ per cent and for a price fall $(80 − 125)/102.5 × 100 = −43.9$ per cent.

Because the midpoint method gives the same answer regardless of the direction of change (as indicated by the negative sign), it is often used when calculating price elasticities between two points. In our example, the midpoint between point A and point B is:

$$\text{Midpoint: Price} = €5 \text{ Quantity} = 102.5$$

According to the midpoint method, when going from point A to point B, the price rises by 40 per cent, and the quantity rises by 43.9 per cent. Similarly, when going from point B to point A, the price falls by 40 per cent, and the quantity falls by 43.9 per cent. In both directions, the price elasticity of supply equals 1.1.

We can express the midpoint method with the following formula for the price elasticity of supply between two points, denoted (Q_1, P_1) and (Q_2, P_2):

$$\text{Price elasticity of supply} = \frac{(Q_2 − Q_1)/([Q_2 + Q_1]/2)}{(P_2 − P_1)/([P_2 + P_1]/2)}$$

The numerator is the percentage change in quantity computed using the midpoint method, and the denominator is the percentage change in price computed using the midpoint method. If you ever need to calculate elasticities, you should use this formula.

The Variety of Supply Curves

Because the price elasticity of supply measures the responsiveness of quantity supplied to the price, it is reflected in the appearance of the supply curve (again, assuming we are using similar scales on the axes of diagrams being used). Figure 5.1 shows five cases. In the extreme case of a zero elasticity, as shown in panel (a), supply is *perfectly inelastic* and the supply curve is vertical. In this case, the quantity supplied is the same regardless of the price. As the elasticity rises, the supply curve gets flatter, which shows that the quantity supplied responds more to changes in the price. At the opposite extreme, shown in panel (e), supply is *perfectly elastic*. This occurs as the price elasticity of supply approaches infinity and the supply curve becomes horizontal, meaning that very small changes in the price lead to very large changes in the quantity supplied.

In some markets, the elasticity of supply is not constant but varies over the supply curve. Figure 5.2 shows a typical case for an industry in which firms have factories with a limited capacity for production. For low levels of quantity supplied, the elasticity of supply is high, indicating that firms respond substantially to changes in the price. In this region, firms have capacity for production that is not being used, such as buildings and machinery sitting idle for all or part of the day. Small increases in price make it profitable for firms to begin using this idle capacity. As the quantity supplied rises, firms begin to reach capacity. Once capacity is fully used, increasing production further

FIGURE 5.1

The Price Elasticity of Supply

The price elasticity of supply determines whether the supply curve is steep or flat (assuming that the scale used for the axes is the same). Note that all percentage changes are calculated using the midpoint method.

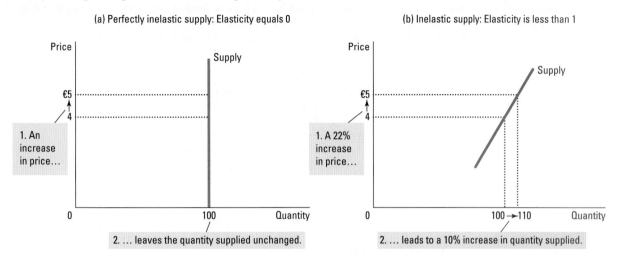

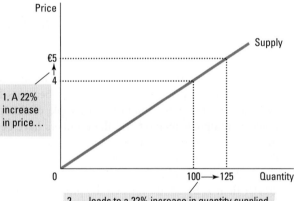

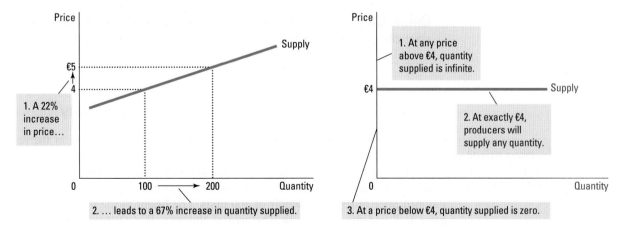

FIGURE 5.2

How the Price Elasticity of Supply Can Vary

Because firms often have a maximum capacity for production, the elasticity of supply may be very high at low levels of quantity supplied and very low at high levels of quantity supplied. Here, an increase in price from €3 to €4 increases the quantity supplied from 100 to 200. Because the increase in quantity supplied of 67 per cent (computed using the midpoint method) is larger than the increase in price of 29 per cent, the supply curve is elastic in this range. By contrast, when the price rises from €12 to €15, the quantity supplied rises only from 500 to 525. Because the increase in quantity supplied of 5 per cent is smaller than the increase in price of 22 per cent, the supply curve is inelastic in this range.

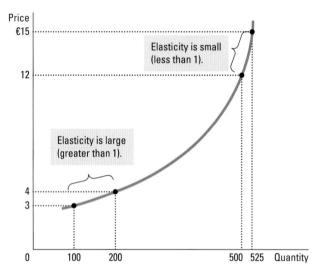

requires the construction of new factories. To induce firms to incur this extra expense, the price must rise substantially, so supply becomes less elastic.

Figure 5.2 presents a numerical example of this phenomenon. In each case we have used the midpoint method and the numbers have been rounded for convenience. When the price rises from €3 to €4 (a 29 per cent increase, according to the midpoint method), the quantity supplied rises from 100 to 200 (a 67 per cent increase). Because quantity supplied moves proportionately more than the price, the supply curve has elasticity greater than 1. By contrast, when the price rises from €12 to €15 (a 22 per cent increase), the quantity supplied rises from 500 to 525 (a 5 per cent increase). In this case, quantity supplied moves proportionately less than the price, so the elasticity is less than 1.

Quick Quiz Define the price elasticity of supply • Explain why the price elasticity of supply might be different in the long run from in the short run.

Total Revenue and the Price Elasticity of Supply

total revenue the amount received by sellers of a good, computed as the price of the good times the quantity sold

When studying changes in supply in a market we are often interested in the resulting changes in the **total revenue** received by producers. In any market, total revenue received by sellers is $P \times Q$, the price of the good times the quantity of the good sold. This is highlighted in Figure 5.3 which shows an upward sloping supply curve with an assumed price of €5 and a supply of 100 units. The height of the box under the supply curve is P and the width is Q. The area of this box, $P \times Q$, equals the total revenue received in this market. In Figure 5.3, where $P = €5$ and $Q = 100$, total revenue is €5 × 100, or €500.

FIGURE 5.3

The Supply Curve and Total Revenue

The total amount received by sellers equals the area of the box under the demand curve, P × Q. Here, at a price of €5, the quantity supplied is 100 and the total revenue is €500.

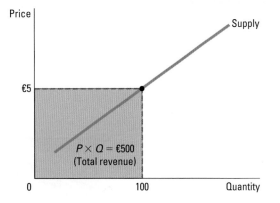

FIGURE 5.4

How Total Revenue Changes When Price Changes: Inelastic Supply

With an inelastic supply curve, an increase in the price leads to an increase in quantity supplied that is proportionately smaller. Therefore, total revenue (the product of price and quantity) increases. Here, an increase in the price from €4 to €5 causes the quantity supplied to rise from 80 to 100, and total revenue rises from €320 to €500.

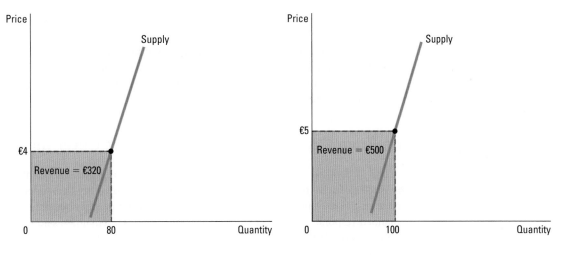

How does total revenue change as one moves along the supply curve? The answer depends on the price elasticity of supply. If supply is inelastic, as in Figure 5.4, then an increase in the price which is proportionately larger causes an increase in total revenue. Here an increase in price from €4 to €5 causes the quantity supplied to rise only from 80 to 100, and so total revenue rises from €320 to €500.

If supply is elastic then a similar increase in price brings about a much larger than proportionate increase in supply. In Figure 5.5, we assume a price of €4 and a supply of 80 with total revenue of €320. Now a price increase from €4 to €5 leads to a much greater than proportionate increase in supply from 80 to 150 with total revenue rising to €750.

FIGURE 5.5

How Total Revenue Changes When Price Changes: Elastic Supply

With an elastic supply curve, an increase in the price leads to an increase in quantity supplied that is proportionately larger. Therefore, total revenue (the product of price and quantity) increases. Here, an increase in the price from €4 to €5 causes the quantity supplied to rise from 80 to 150, and total revenue rises from €320 to €750.

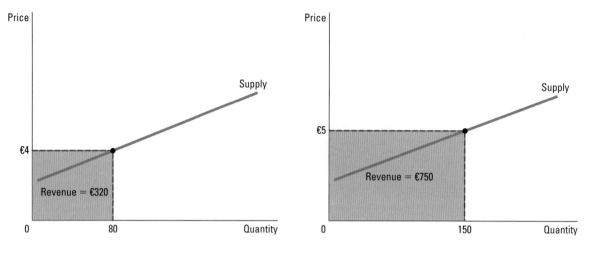

price elasticity of demand a measure of how much the quantity demanded of a good responds to a change in the price of that good, computed as the percentage change in quantity demanded divided by the percentage change in price

THE PRICE ELASTICITY OF DEMAND

Businesses cannot directly control demand. They can seek to influence demand (and do) by utilizing a variety of strategies and tactics but ultimately the consumer decides whether to buy a product or not. One important way in which consumer behaviour can be influenced is through a firm changing the prices of its goods (many firms do have some control over the price it can charge although as we have seen, in perfectly competitive markets this is not the case as the firm is a price taker). An understanding of the price elasticity of demand is important in anticipating the likely effects of changes in price on demand.

The Price Elasticity of Demand and its Determinants

The law of demand states that a fall in the price of a good raises the quantity demanded. The **price elasticity of demand** measures how much the quantity demanded responds to a change in price. Demand for a good is said to be *elastic* or price sensitive if the quantity demanded responds substantially to changes in the price. Demand is said to be *inelastic or price insensitive* if the quantity demanded responds only slightly to changes in the price.

The price elasticity of demand for any good measures how willing consumers are to move away from the good as its price rises. Thus, the elasticity reflects the many economic, social and psychological forces that influence consumer tastes. Based on experience, however, we can state some general rules about what determines the price elasticity of demand.

Availability of Close Substitutes Goods with close substitutes tend to have more elastic demand because it is easier for consumers to switch from that good to others. For example, butter and margarine are easily substitutable. A small increase in the price of butter, assuming the price of margarine is held fixed, causes the quantity of butter sold to fall by a relatively large amount. As a general rule, the closer the substitute the more elastic the good is because it is easier for consumers to switch from one to the other. By contrast, because eggs are a food without a close substitute, the demand for eggs is less elastic than the demand for butter.

Necessities versus Luxuries Necessities tend to have relatively inelastic demands, whereas luxuries have relatively elastic demands. People use gas and electricity to heat their homes and cook their food. If the price of gas and electricity rose together, people would not demand dramatically less of them. They might try and be more energy-efficient and reduce their demand a little, but they would still need hot food and warm homes. By contrast, when the price of sailing dinghies rises, the quantity of sailing dinghies demanded falls substantially. The reason is that most people view hot food and warm homes as necessities and a sailing dinghy as a luxury. Of course, whether a good is a necessity or a luxury depends not on the intrinsic properties of the good but on the preferences of the buyer. For an avid sailor with little concern over her health, sailing dinghies might be a necessity with inelastic demand and hot food and a warm place to sleep a luxury with elastic demand.

Definition of the Market The elasticity of demand in any market depends on how we draw the boundaries of the market. Narrowly defined markets tend to have more elastic demand than broadly defined markets, because it is easier to find close substitutes for narrowly defined goods. For example, food, a broad category, has a fairly inelastic demand because there are no good substitutes for food. Ice cream, a narrower category, has a more elastic demand because it is easy to substitute other desserts for ice cream. Vanilla ice cream, a very narrow category, has a very elastic demand because other flavours of ice cream are almost perfect substitutes for vanilla.

Proportion of Income Devoted to the Product Some products have a relatively high price and take a larger proportion of income than others. Buying a new suite of furniture for a lounge, for example, tends to take up a large amount of income whereas buying an ice cream might account for only a tiny proportion of income. If the price of a three-piece suite rises by 10 per cent, therefore, this is likely to have a greater effect on demand for this furniture than a similar 10 per cent increase in the price of an ice cream. The higher the proportion of income devoted to the product the greater the elasticity is likely to be.

Time Horizon Goods tend to have more elastic demand over longer time horizons. When the price of petrol rises, the quantity of petrol demanded falls only slightly in the first few months. Over time, however, people buy more fuel-efficient cars, switch to public transport and move closer to where they work. Within several years, the quantity of petrol demanded falls more substantially. Similarly, if the price of a unit of electricity rises much above an equivalent energy unit of gas, demand may fall only slightly in the short run because many people already have electric cookers or electric heating appliances installed in their homes and cannot easily switch. If the price difference persists over several years, however, people may find it worth their while to replace their old electric heating and cooking appliances with new gas appliances and the demand for electricity will fall.

Computing the Price Elasticity of Demand

The principles for computing price elasticity of demand are similar to that discussed when we looked at price elasticity of supply. The price elasticity of demand is computed as the percentage change in the quantity demanded divided by the percentage change in the price. That is:

$$\text{Price elasticity of demand} = \frac{\text{Percentage change in quantity demanded}}{\text{Percentage change in price}}$$

For example, suppose that a 10 per cent increase in the price of a packet of breakfast cereal causes the amount you buy to fall by 20 per cent. Because the quantity demanded of a good is negatively related to its price, the percentage change in quantity will always have the opposite sign to the percentage change in price. In this example, the percentage change in price is a *positive* 10 per cent (reflecting an increase), and the percentage change in quantity demanded is a *negative* 20 per cent (reflecting a decrease). For this reason, price elasticities of demand are sometimes reported as negative numbers. In this book we follow the common practice of dropping the minus sign and reporting all price elasticities as positive numbers. (Mathematicians call this the *absolute value.*) With this convention, a larger price elasticity implies a greater responsiveness of quantity demanded to price.

Using this convention we calculate the elasticity of demand as:

$$\text{Price elasticity of demand} = \frac{20\%}{10\%} = 2$$

In this example, the elasticity is 2, reflecting that the change in the quantity demanded is proportionately twice as large as the change in the price.

Pitfall Prevention We have used the term 'relatively' elastic or inelastic at times throughout the analysis so far. It is important to remember that elasticity can be any value greater than or equal to 0. We can look at two goods, therefore, both of which are classed as 'inelastic' but where one is more inelastic than the other. If we are comparing good X, which has an elasticity of 0.2 and good Y, which has an elasticity of 0.5, then both are inelastic but good Y is relatively elastic by comparison. As with so much of economics, careful use of terminology is important in conveying a clear understanding.

Using the Midpoint Method

As with the price elasticity of supply, we use the midpoint method to calculate price elasticity of demand for the same reasons. We can express the midpoint method with the following formula for the price elasticity of demand between two points, denoted (Q_1, P_1) and (Q_2, P_2):

$$\text{Price elasticity of demand} = \frac{(Q_2 - Q_1)/[(Q_2 + Q_1)/2]}{(P_2 - P_1)/[(P_2 + P_1)/2]}$$

The numerator is the proportionate change in quantity computed using the midpoint method, and the denominator is the proportionate change in price computed using the midpoint method.

The Variety of Demand Curves

Economists classify demand curves according to their elasticity. Demand is *elastic* when the elasticity is greater than 1, so that quantity changes proportionately more than the price. Demand is *inelastic* when the elasticity is less than 1, so that quantity moves proportionately less than the price. If the elasticity is exactly 1, so that quantity moves the same amount proportionately as price, demand is said to have *unit elasticity*.

Because the price elasticity of demand measures how much quantity demanded responds to changes in the price, it is closely related to the slope of the demand curve. The following heuristic (rule of thumb) again, assuming we are using comparable scales on the axes, is a useful guide: the flatter the demand curve that passes through a given point, the greater the price elasticity of demand. The steeper the demand curve that passes through a given point, the smaller the price elasticity of demand.

Figure 5.6 shows five cases, each of which uses the same scale on each axis. This is an important thing to remember because simply looking at a graph and the shape of the

FIGURE 5.6

The Price Elasticity of Demand

The steepness of the demand curve indicates the price elasticity of demand (assuming the scale used on the axes are the same). Note that all percentage changes are calculated using the midpoint method.

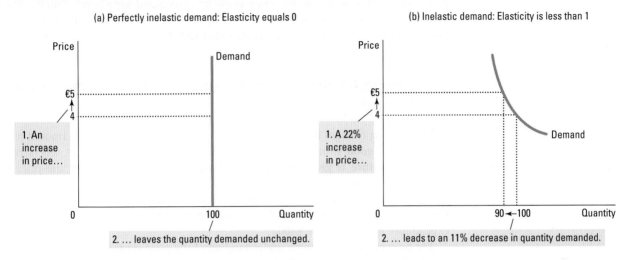

(a) Perfectly inelastic demand: Elasticity equals 0

1. An increase in price...

2. ... leaves the quantity demanded unchanged.

(b) Inelastic demand: Elasticity is less than 1

1. A 22% increase in price...

2. ... leads to an 11% decrease in quantity demanded.

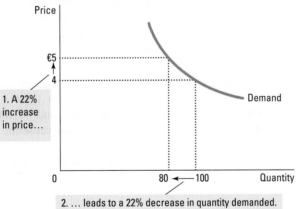

(c) Unit elastic demand: Elasticity equals 1

1. A 22% increase in price...

2. ... leads to a 22% decrease in quantity demanded.

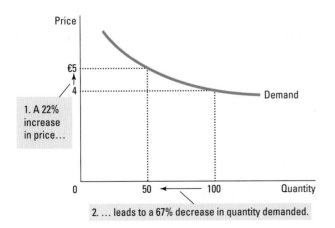

(d) Elastic demand: Elasticity is greater than 1

1. A 22% increase in price...

2. ... leads to a 67% decrease in quantity demanded.

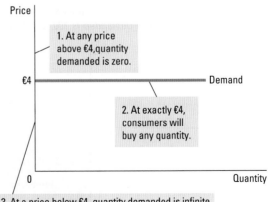

(e) Perfectly elastic demand: Elasticity equals infinity

1. At any price above €4, quantity demanded is zero.

2. At exactly €4, consumers will buy any quantity.

3. At a price below €4, quantity demanded is infinite.

curve without recognizing the scale can result in incorrect conclusions about elasticity. In the extreme case of a zero elasticity shown in panel (a), demand is *perfectly inelastic,* and the demand curve is vertical. In this case, regardless of the price, the quantity demanded stays the same. As the elasticity rises, the demand curve gets flatter and flatter, as shown in panels (b), (c) and (d). At the opposite extreme shown in panel (e), demand is *perfectly elastic.* This occurs as the price elasticity of demand approaches infinity and the demand curve becomes horizontal, reflecting the fact that very small changes in the price lead to huge changes in the quantity demanded.

Total Expenditure, Total Revenue and the Price Elasticity of Demand

total expenditure the amount paid by buyers, computed as the price of the good times the quantity purchased

When studying changes in demand in a market, we are interested in the amount paid by buyers of the good which will in turn represent the total revenue that sellers receive. **Total expenditure** is given by the total amount bought multiplied by the price paid. We can show total expenditure graphically, as in Figure 5.7. The height of the box under the demand curve is P, and the width is Q. The area of this box, $P \times Q$, equals the total expenditure in this market. In Figure 5.7, where $P = €4$ and $Q = 100$, total expenditure is $€4 \times 100$, or $€400$.

For businesses, having some understanding of the price elasticity of demand is important in decision making. If a firm is thinking of changing price how will the demand for its product react? The firm knows that there is an inverse relationship between price and demand but the effect on its revenue will be dependent on the price elasticity of demand. It is entirely possible that a firm could reduce its price and increase total revenue. Equally, a firm could raise price and find its total revenue falling. At first glance this might sound counter-intuitive but it all depends on the price elasticity of demand for the product.

If demand is inelastic, as in Figure 5.8, then an increase in the price causes an increase in total expenditure. Here an increase in price from €1 to €3 causes the quantity demanded to fall only from 100 to 80, and so total expenditure rises from €100 to €240. An increase in price raises $P \times Q$ because the fall in Q is proportionately smaller than the rise in P.

We obtain the opposite result if demand is elastic: an increase in the price causes a decrease in total expenditure. In Figure 5.9, for instance, when the price rises from €4

FIGURE 5.7

Total Expenditure

The total amount paid by buyers, and received as expenditure by sellers, equals the area of the box under the demand curve, $P \times Q$. Here, at a price of €4, the quantity demanded is 100, and total expenditure is €400.

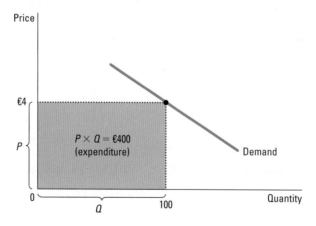

FIGURE 5.8

How Total Expenditure Changes When Price Changes: Inelastic Demand

With an inelastic demand curve, an increase in the price leads to a decrease in quantity demanded that is proportionately smaller. Therefore, total expenditure (the product of price and quantity) increases. Here, an increase in the price from €1 to €3 causes the quantity demanded to fall from 100 to 80, and total expenditure rises from €100 to €240.

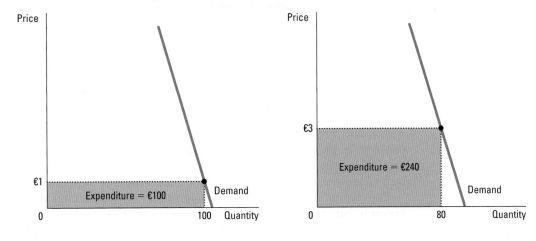

FIGURE 5.9

How Total Expenditure Changes When Price Changes: Elastic Demand

With an elastic demand curve, an increase in the price leads to a decrease in quantity demanded that is proportionately larger. Therefore, total expenditure (the product of price and quantity) decreases. Here, an increase in the price from €4 to €5 causes the quantity demanded to fall from 50 to 20, so total expenditure falls from €200 to €100.

to €5, the quantity demanded falls from 50 to 20, and so total expenditure falls from €200 to €100. Because demand is elastic, the reduction in the quantity demanded is so great that it more than offsets the increase in the price. That is, an increase in price reduces $P \times Q$ because the fall in Q is proportionately greater than the rise in P.

Although the examples in these two figures are extreme, they illustrate a general rule:

- When demand is inelastic (a price elasticity less than 1), price and total expenditure move in the same direction.
- When demand is elastic (a price elasticity greater than 1), price and total expenditure move in opposite directions.
- If demand is unit elastic (a price elasticity exactly equal to 1), total expenditure remains constant when the price changes.

> **?** **what if...** a high street clothes retailer is planning its summer sales campaign and wants to cut prices to help it get rid of stock and also increase footfall (the number of customers entering its premises) and revenue. It knows of the concept of price elasticity of demand but how does it set about estimating the price elasticity of demand for its products so that it can more accurately set price cuts which will achieve its aims?

Elasticity and Total Expenditure Along a Linear Demand Curve

Although some demand curves have an elasticity that is the same along the entire curve, this is not always the case. An example of a demand curve along which elasticity changes is a straight line, as shown in Figure 5.10. A linear demand curve has a constant slope. Recall that slope is defined as 'rise over run', which here is the ratio of the change in price ('rise') to the change in quantity ('run'). This particular demand curve's slope is constant because each €1 increase in price causes the same 2-unit decrease in the quantity demanded.

Even though the slope of a linear demand curve is constant, the elasticity is not. The reason is that the slope is the ratio of *changes* in the two variables, whereas the elasticity is the ratio of *percentage changes* in the two variables. You can see this by looking at the table in Figure 5.10, which shows the demand schedule for the linear demand curve in the graph. The table uses the midpoint method to calculate the price elasticity of

FIGURE 5.10

Elasticity of a Linear Demand Curve

The slope of a linear demand curve is constant, but its elasticity is not. The demand schedule in the table was used to calculate the price elasticity of demand by the midpoint method. At points with a low price and high quantity, the demand curve is inelastic. At points with a high price and low quantity, the demand curve is elastic.

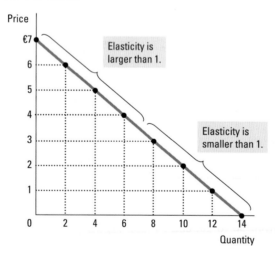

Price	Quantity	Total revenue (Price × Quantity)	Percent change in price	Percent change in quantity	Price elasticity	Quantity description
€7	0	€0	15	200	13.0	Elastic
6	2	12	18	67	3.7	Elastic
5	4	20	22	40	1.8	Elastic
4	6	24	29	29	1.0	Unit elastic
3	8	24	40	22	0.6	Inelastic
2	10	20	67	18	0.3	Inelastic
1	12	12	200	15	0.1	Inelastic
0	14	0				

demand. At points with a low price and high quantity, the demand curve is inelastic. At points with a high price and low quantity, the demand curve is elastic.

The table also presents total expenditure at each point on the demand curve. These numbers illustrate the relationship between total expenditure and elasticity. When the price is €1, for instance, demand is inelastic and a price increase to €2 raises total expenditure. When the price is €5, demand is elastic, and a price increase to €6 reduces total expenditure. Between €3 and €4, demand is exactly unit elastic and total expenditure is the same at these two prices.

In analysing markets, we will use both demand and supply curves on the same diagram. We will refer to changes in total revenue when looking at the effects of changes in equilibrium conditions but remember that revenue for sellers represents the same identity as expenditure for buyers.

CASE STUDY
Putting Bums on Seats!

Imagine you are the owner of a coach company running a scheduled bus service between a rural town and surrounding villages. The service runs every two hours between 6 am and 8 pm. The price passengers pay for a return bus journey is a standard fare priced at €3.00. The maximum capacity of each bus is 80 seats.

You have noticed that the number of passengers on the services is falling and you are considering options to try and increase the demand and fill more seats on each service. You know that price and demand are inversely related and so you are planning on reducing the price to try and encourage more passengers to use your buses. However, a colleague cautions you against doing this until you have thought it through in more detail. She suggests that reducing price might not be the best option and that you might actually be facing two different demand curves with different elasticities.

You decide to investigate this idea in more detail. You look at the pattern of bus usage throughout the day. Your investigations tell you that the occupancy rate for buses (the proportion of seats taken up by passengers) on buses between the hours of 6 am and 8 am is around 95 per cent on average. Between 8 am and 4 pm the occupancy rate falls considerably to only 30 per cent and climbs again to 90 per cent between 4 pm and 6 pm. After 6 pm, the rate falls again to 20 per cent.

The investigation suggests that the demand curve for bus travel in the morning and afternoon rush hour periods is relatively inelastic whereas at other times during the day the demand curve is more elastic. You reason that rather than just reducing the price as you originally planned, you will charge different prices at different times of the day to exploit the different demand curves.

- During the hours of 6 am and 8 am and 4 pm and 6 pm, the price of a return ticket will rise by €1.00 to €4.00.
- Between 8 am and 4 pm the price of a return ticket will fall by 50 per cent to €1.50.
- The bus service will stop running after 6.30 pm.

Your colleague advises you to monitor the effect on occupancy rates once the new prices are introduced. After six months you go back to her with your findings. The increase in the ticket price has resulted in a fall in occupancy rates to 90 per cent in the morning and 87 per cent in the afternoon. During the day, the 50 per cent cut in the price has raised the occupancy rate from an average of 30 per cent to 65 per cent. You are very pleased with the results because although the occupancy rates fell in the morning they only fell by a small amount and the increase in price meant that total revenue increased. At other times during the day the reduction in price encouraged more people to use the service and again, the increase in numbers has led to a rise in revenue.

TADEUS ZIBROM/SHUTTERSTOCK

If the price of a bus ticket was higher would the number of passengers decline?

OTHER DEMAND ELASTICITIES

In addition to the price elasticity of demand, economists also use other elasticities to describe the behaviour of buyers in a market.

The Income Elasticity of Demand

income elasticity of demand a measure of how much the quantity demanded of a good responds to a change in consumers' income, computed as the percentage change in quantity demanded divided by the percentage change in income

The **income elasticity of demand** measures how the quantity demanded changes as consumer income changes. It is calculated as the percentage change in quantity demanded divided by the percentage change in income. That is,

$$\text{Income elasticity of demand} = \frac{\text{Percentage change in quantity demanded}}{\text{Percentage change in income}}$$

As we discussed in Chapter 4, most goods are *normal goods*: higher income raises quantity demanded. Because quantity demanded and income change in the same direction, normal goods have positive income elasticities. A few goods, such as bus rides, are *inferior goods*: higher income lowers the quantity demanded. Because quantity demanded and income move in opposite directions, inferior goods have negative income elasticities.

Even among normal goods, income elasticities vary substantially in size. Necessities, such as food and clothing, tend to have small income elasticities because consumers, regardless of how low their incomes, choose to buy some of these goods. Luxuries, such as caviar and diamonds, tend to have high income elasticities because consumers feel that they can do without these goods altogether if their income is too low.

The Cross-Price Elasticity of Demand

cross-price elasticity of demand a measure of how much the quantity demanded of one good responds to a change in the price of another good, computed as the percentage change in quantity demanded of the first good divided by the percentage change in the price of the second good

The **cross-price elasticity of demand** measures how the quantity demanded of one good changes as the price of another good changes. It is calculated as the percentage change in quantity demanded of good 1 divided by the percentage change in the price of good 2. That is:

$$\text{Cross-price elasticity of demand} = \frac{\text{Percentage change in quantity demanded of good 1}}{\text{Percentage change in the price of good 2}}$$

Whether the cross-price elasticity is a positive or negative number depends on whether the two goods are substitutes or complements. As we discussed in Chapter 4, substitutes are goods that are typically used in place of one another, such as beef steak and Wiener schnitzel. An increase in the price of beef steak induces people to eat Wiener schnitzel instead. Because the price of beef steak and the quantity of Wiener schnitzel demanded move in the same direction, the cross-price elasticity is positive. Conversely, complements are goods that are typically used together, such as computers and software. In this case, the cross-price elasticity is negative, indicating that an increase in the price of computers reduces the quantity of software demanded. As with price elasticity of demand, cross-price elasticity may increase over time: a change in the price of electricity will have little effect on demand for gas in the short run but much stronger effects over several years.

Pitfall Prevention When referring to elasticity it is easy to forget which *type* of elasticity you are referring to. It is sensible to ensure that you use the correct terminology to make sure you are thinking clearly about the analysis and being accurate in your referencing to elasticity. If you are analysing the effect of changes in income on demand then you must specify *income elasticity,* whereas if you are analyzing changes in prices on supply then you must specify *price elasticity of supply* and so on.

Quick Quiz   Define the price elasticity of demand. • Explain the relationship between total expenditure and the price elasticity of demand.

FYI

The Mathematics of Elasticity

We present this section for those who require some introduction to the maths behind elasticity. For those who do not need such a technical explanation, this section can be safely skipped without affecting your overall understanding of the concept of elasticity.

Point Elasticity of Demand

Figure 5.10 showed that the value for elasticity can vary at every point along a straight line demand curve. Point elasticity of demand allows us to be able to be more specific about the elasticity at different points. In the formula repeated below, the numerator (the top half of the fraction) describes

the change in quantity in relation to the base quantity and the denominator the change in price in relation to the base price.

$$ped = \frac{\left(\dfrac{Q_2 - Q_1}{((Q_2 + Q_1)/2)}\right) \times 100}{\left(\dfrac{P_2 - P_1}{((P_2 + P_1)/2)}\right) \times 100}$$

If we cancel out the 100s in the above equation and rewrite it a little more elegantly we get:

$$ped = \frac{\dfrac{\Delta Q}{Q}}{\dfrac{\Delta P}{P}}$$

Where the $\Delta Q = Q_2 - Q_1$

Rearranging the above we get:

$$ped = \frac{\Delta Q}{Q} \times \frac{P}{\Delta P}$$

There is no set order required to this equation so it can be re-written as:

$$ped = \frac{\Delta Q}{\Delta P} \times \frac{P}{Q}$$

The eagle eyed amongst you will notice that the expression $\Delta Q/\Delta P$ is the slope of a linear demand curve. Look at the example in Figure 5.11:

FIGURE 5.11

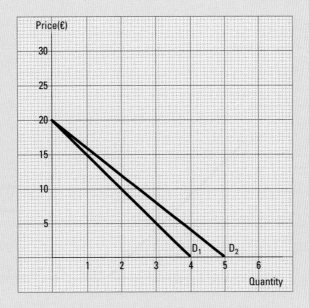

Here we have two demand curves, D_1 and D_2, given by the equations:

$$p = 20 - 5q$$
and
$$Q = 5 - 0.25p$$

For demand curve D_1, the vertical intercept is 20 and the horizontal intercept is 4 and so the slope of the line D_1 is –5.

For demand curve D_2, the vertical intercept is 20 and the horizontal intercept is 5, the slope of the line D_2 is –4.

To verify this let us take demand curve D_1, if price were 10 then the quantity would be $20 - 5q$. Rearranging gives $5q = 20-10$, $5q = 10$ so $q = 20$. (Looking at the inverse of this we would get: $4 - (0.2 \times 10) = 2$).

Looking at demand curve D_2, If price were 10, then the quantity would be $5 - (0.25 \times 10) = 2.5$.

Now let us assume that price falls from 10 to 5 in each case. The quantity demanded for D_1 would now be $4 - (0.2 \times 5) = 3$ and for D_2, $5 - (0.25 \times 5) = 3.75$.

Representing this graphically for demand curve D_1, we get the result shown in Figure 5.12.

The slope of the line as drawn is:

$$\frac{\Delta p}{\Delta q} = \frac{-5}{1} = -5$$

The slope is the same at all points along a linear demand curve. The price which we start with prior to a change will give different ratios at different points on the demand curve. Again, using demand curve D_2, the ratio of P/Q at the initial price of 10 is $10/2 = 5$. At a price of 5, the ratio of P/Q given by the demand curve D_2 would be $5/3 = 1.67$.

Going back to our formula:

$$ped = \frac{\Delta Q}{\Delta P} \times \frac{P}{Q}$$

The first part of the equation ($\Delta Q/\Delta P$) is the slope of the demand curve and the second part of the equation P/Q gives us a specific point on the demand curve relating to a particular price and quantity combination. Multiplying these two terms gives us the price elasticity of demand at a particular point and so is referred to as *point elasticity of demand*.

The price elasticity of demand when price changes from 10 to 5 in demand curve D_2 above, would be:

$$ped = \frac{\Delta Q}{\Delta P} \times \frac{P}{Q}$$

$$ped = \frac{1}{5} \times \frac{10}{2}$$

$$ped = 1$$

If we were looking at a fall in price from 15 to 10 we would get:

$$ped = \frac{\Delta Q}{\Delta P} \times \frac{P}{Q}$$

$$ped = \frac{1}{5} \times \frac{15}{1}$$

$$ped = 3$$

And if looking at a price fall from 5 to 2.5 then we would get:

$$ped = \frac{\Delta Q}{\Delta P} \times \frac{P}{Q}$$

$$ped = \frac{0.5}{5} \times \frac{10}{3}$$

$$ped = 0.33$$

Calculus

The demand curve is often depicted as a linear curve but there is no reason why it should be linear and can be curvilinear. To measure elasticity accurately in this case economists use calculus.

The rules of calculus applied to a demand curve give a far more accurate measurement of *ped* at a particular point.

For a linear demand function, the approximation to the point elasticity

FIGURE 5.12

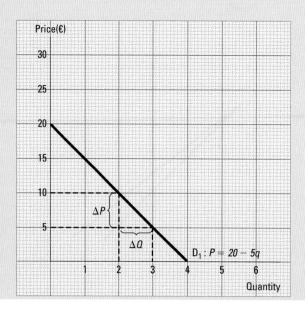

at the initial price and quantity is given by:

$$\frac{(q_2 - q_1)}{(p_2 - p_1)} \cdot \frac{p_1}{q_1}$$

which gives exactly the same result as the point elasticity which is defined in terms of calculus and is given by :

$$\frac{dq}{dp} \cdot \frac{p}{q}$$

Point elasticity defined in terms of calculus give a precise answer; all the other formulae are approximations of some sort.

The formula looks similar but it must be remembered that what we are talking about in this instance is an infinitesimally small change in quantity following an infinitesimally small change in price expressed by the formula:

$$ped = \frac{dq}{dp} \times \frac{P}{Q}$$

where dq/dp is the derivative of a linear function. Given our basic linear equation of the form $q = a - bp$, the power function rule gives dq/dp as the coefficient of $p - (-b)$.

Take the following demand equation:

$$q = 60 - 3p$$

To find the price elasticity of demand when price = 15. First of all we need to find q.

$$q = 60 - 3p$$
$$q = 60 - 3(15)$$
$$q = 15$$

We calculate dq/dp as -3.

Substitute this into the formula to get:

$$ped = -3\left(\frac{15}{15}\right)$$
$$ped = -3$$

Let us frame the demand equation so that p is now being written as a function of q — this is the equation of the inverse demand function.

$$p = 20 - \frac{1}{3}q$$

and we want to find *ped* when price = 24 then:

$$p = 20 - \frac{1}{3}q$$
$$24 = 20 - \frac{1}{3}q$$
$$24 - 20 = -\frac{1}{3}q$$
$$4 = \frac{1}{3}q$$
$$\frac{4}{\frac{1}{3}} = q$$
$$12 = q$$

In this particular case, we must remember that we are now differentiating p with respect to q so we get:

$$dp/dq = -12$$

We cannot simply substitute this number into the formula above, we have to do a bit of rearranging to take account of how we are viewing the relationship between price and quantity in this instance. So using the inverse function rule:

$$\frac{dq}{dp} = \frac{1}{dp/dq}$$
$$\frac{dq}{dp} = -\frac{1}{12}$$

Given that the price is 24 and the quantity is 17.3, the *ped* is:

$$ped = \frac{dq}{dp} \times \frac{P}{Q}$$
$$ped = \frac{1}{12} \times \left[\frac{24}{17.3}\right]$$
$$ped = 0.116$$

It is useful to remember that given an elasticity figure we can calculate the expected change in demand as a result of a change in price. For example, if the *ped* is given as 0.6 then an increase in price of 5 per cent will result in a fall in quantity demanded of 3 per cent.

By using the inverse of the elasticity equation, for any given value of *ped* we can calculate how much of a price change is required to bring about a desired change in quantity demanded.

Suppose that a government wanted to reduce the demand for motor vehicles as part of a policy to reduce congestion and pollution. What sort of price change might be required to bring about a 10 per cent fall in demand?

Assume that the *ped* for motor vehicles is 0.8. The inverse of the basic elasticity formula is:

$$\frac{1}{ped} = \frac{\% \, \Delta p}{\% \, \Delta Q}$$

Substituting our known values into the formula we get:

$$\frac{1}{0.8} = \frac{\% \, Dp}{10}$$
$$1.25 = \frac{\% \, \Delta p}{10}$$
$$\%\Delta p = 12.5$$

To bring about a reduction in demand of 10 per cent, the price of motor vehicles would have to rise by 12.5 per cent.

Other Elasticities

Income and cross-elasticity of demand are all treated in exactly the same way as the analysis of price elasticity of demand above. So:

Point income elasticity would be:

$$yed = \frac{dQ}{dY} \times \frac{Y}{Q}$$

Using calculus:

$$yed = \frac{dq}{dY} \cdot \frac{Y}{q}$$

For cross-elasticity the formulas would be:

$$xed = \frac{\Delta Q_a}{\Delta P_b} \times \frac{P_b}{Q_a}$$

Where Q_a is the quantity demanded of one good, $_a$, and P_b is the price of a related good, $_b$ (either a substitute or a complement).

$$xed = \frac{dq_a}{dP_b} \times \frac{P_b}{Q_a}$$

In Chapter 4 we saw that demand can be expressed as a multivariate function where demand is dependent on a range of variables which include price, incomes, tastes and so on. It is possible to calculate the elasticities of all these other factors using the same principles as those outlined above. In each case it is usual to calculate the elasticity with respect to a change in one of the variables whilst holding the others constant.

For example, take the demand equation $Q = 1400 - 4p + 0.04Y$. This equation tells us that demand is dependent on the price and also the level of income.

From this equation we can calculate the *ped* and *yed*. In this example we will use calculus to find both elasticities assuming $P = 50$ and $Y = 8000$.

Given these values:

$$Q = 1400 - 4(50) + 0.04(8000)$$
$$Q = 1400 - 200 + 320$$
$$Q = 1520$$

Given the formula for *ped*:

$$ped = \frac{dq}{dp} \times \frac{P}{Q}$$
$$dq/dp = -4$$
$$ped = -4(5/1520)$$
$$ped = -0.013$$

Given the formula for *yed*:

$$yed = \frac{dq}{dy} \times \frac{Y}{Q}$$
$$dq/dY = 0.04$$
$$yed = 0.04(8000/1520)$$
$$yed = 0.21$$

Now look at this demand equation:

$$q_a = 100 - 8p_a - 6p_b + 4p_c + 0.015Y$$

This equation gives the relationship between demand and the prices of other goods labelled a, b, and c respectively. We can use this to find the respective cross-elasticities.

Assume that the price of good A is 20, the price of good B 40, the price of good C, 80 and $Y = 20\,000$.

Substituting these into our formula gives:

$$q_a = 100 - 8p_a - 6p_b + 4p_c + 0.015Y$$
$$q_a = 100 - 8(20) - 6(40) + 4(80) + 0.015(20000)$$
$$q_a = 100 - 160 - 240 + 320 + 300$$
$$q_a = 320$$

The *xed* of good A with respect to changes in the price of good B is given by:

$$xed = \frac{dq_a}{dp_b} \times \frac{p_b}{q_a}$$
$$dq_a/dp_b = -6$$

So:

$$xed = -6(40/320)$$
$$xed = -6(0.125)$$
$$xed = -0.75$$

The relationship between good A and B is that they are complements – a rise in the price of good B will lead to a fall in the quantity demanded of good A.

The *xed* of good A with respect to changes in the price of good C is given by:

$$xed = \frac{dq_a}{dp_c} \times \frac{P_c}{Q_a}$$
$$dq_a/dp_c = 4$$
$$xed = 4(80/320)$$
$$xed = 4(0.25)$$
$$xed = 1$$

In this case the relationship between the two goods is that they are substitutes – a rise in the price of good C would lead to a rise in the quantity demanded of good A.

Price Elasticity of Supply

Many of the principles outlined above apply also to the price elasticity of supply. The formula for the price elasticity of supply using the point method is:

$$pes = \frac{\Delta q_s}{\Delta p} \times \frac{p}{q_s}$$

Using calculus:

$$pes = \frac{dq_s}{dp} \times \frac{p}{q_s}$$

However, we need to note a particular issue with *pes* which relates to the graphical representation of supply curves.

This is summarized in the following:

- A straight line supply curve intersecting the y-axis at a positive value has a *pes* > 1

- A straight line supply curve passing through the origin has a *pes* = 1
- A straight line supply curve intersecting the x-axis at a positive value has a *pes* < 1

To see why any straight line supply curve passing through the origin has a *pes* of 1 we can use some basic knowledge of geometry and similar triangles.

Figure 5.13 shows a straight line supply curve S1 passing through the origin. The slope of the supply curve is given by $\frac{\Delta p}{\Delta q_s}$. We have highlighted a triangle shaded blue with the ratio $\frac{\Delta p}{\Delta q_s}$ relating to a change in price of 7.5 and a change in quantity of 1. The larger triangle formed by taking a price of 22.5 and a quantity of 3 shows the ratio of the price and quantity at this point (p/q). The two triangles formed by these are both classed as similar triangles – they have different lengths to their three sides but the internal angles are all the same. The ratio of the sides must therefore be equal as shown by equation 1 below:

$$\frac{\Delta p}{\Delta q_s} = \frac{p}{q_s}$$

Given our definition of point elasticity of supply, if we substitute equation 1 into the formula and rearrange we get:

$$pes = \frac{q_s}{P} \times \frac{P}{q_s}$$

Therefore:

$$pes = 1$$

Elasticity and Total Expenditure/Revenue

We have used the term 'total expenditure' in relation to the demand curve to accurately reflect the fact that demand is related to buyers and when buyers pay for products this represents expenditure. Many books use the term expenditure and revenue interchangeably and in this short section we are going to refer to revenue.

Total revenue is found by multiplying the quantity purchased by the average price paid. This is shown by the formula:

$$TR = P \times Q$$

FIGURE 5.13

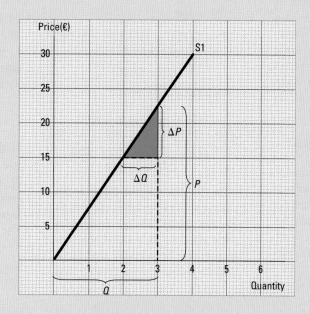

Total revenue can change if either price or quantity, or both, change therefore. This can be seen in Figure 5.14 where a rise in the price of a good from P_0 to P_1 has resulted in a fall in quantity demanded from Q_0 to Q_1.

We can represent the change in price as Δp so that the new price is $(p + \Delta p)$ and the change in quantity as Δq so that the new quantity is $(q + \Delta q)$ so TR can be represented thus:

$$TR = (p + \Delta p)\,(q + \Delta q)$$

If we multiply out this expression as shown then we get:

$$TR = (p + \Delta p)\,(q + \Delta q)$$

$$TR = pq + p\,\Delta q + \Delta pq + \Delta p\Delta q$$

In Figure 5.14, this can be seen graphically.

The original TR is found by multiplying the original price (P_0) by the original quantity (Q_0) and is shown by the brown + blue rectangles.

As a result of the change in price there is an additional amount of

FIGURE 5.14

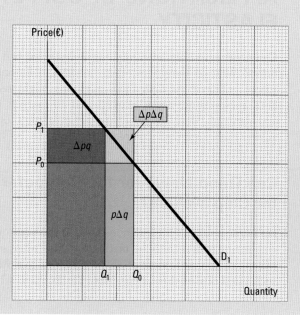

revenue shown by the purple rectangle ($q \, \Delta p$). However, this is offset by the reduction in revenue caused by the fall in quantity demanded as a result of the change in price shown by the blue rectangle ($p \, \Delta q$). There is also an area indicated by the yellow rectangle which is equal to $\Delta p \Delta q$. This leaves us with a formula for the change in TR as:

$$\Delta TR = q \, \Delta p + p \, \Delta q + \Delta p \Delta q$$

Let us substitute some figures into our formula to see how this works in practice. Assume the original price of a product is 15 and the quantity demanded at this price is 750. When price rises to 20 the quantity demanded falls to 500.

Using the equation:

$$TR = pq + p \, \Delta q + \Delta pq + \Delta p \Delta q$$

TR is now:

$$TR = 15(750) + 15(-250) + 5(750)$$
$$+ \, 5(-250)$$
$$TR = 10\,000$$

The change in TR is:

$$\Delta TR = q \Delta p + p \Delta q + \Delta p \Delta q$$
$$\Delta TR = 750(5) + 15(-250) + 5(-250)$$
$$\Delta TR = 3750 - 3750 - 1250$$
$$\Delta TR = -1250$$

In this example the effect of the change in price has been negative on TR. We know from our analysis of price elasticity of demand that this means the percentage change in quantity demand was greater than

the percentage change in price – in other words, *ped* must be elastic at this point (>1). For the change in TR to be positive, therefore, the *ped* must be <1.

We can express the relationship between the change in TR and *ped* as an inequality as follows:

$$ped = \frac{\Delta Q}{\Delta P} \times \frac{P}{Q} > 1$$

When price increases, revenue decreases if *ped* meets this inequality. Equally, for a price increase to result in a rise in revenue *ped* must meet the inequality below:

$$ped = \frac{\Delta Q}{\Delta P} \times \frac{P}{Q} < 1$$

JEOPARDY PROBLEM

A business selling plumbing equipment to the trade (i.e. professional plumbers only) increases the price of copper piping by 4 per cent and reduces the price of radiators by 5 per cent. A year later they analyse their sales figures and find that revenue for copper piping rose in the first three months after the price rise but then fell dramatically thereafter, while the revenue for sales of radiators also fell throughout the period.

Explain what might have happened to bring about this situation. Illustrate your answer with diagrams where appropriate.

APPLICATIONS OF SUPPLY AND DEMAND ELASTICITY

Can good news for the computing industry be bad news for computer chip manufacturers? Why do the prices of ski holidays in Europe rise dramatically over public and school holidays? At first, these questions might seem to have little in common. Yet both questions are about markets and all markets are subject to the forces of supply and demand. Here we apply the versatile tools of supply, demand and elasticity to answer these seemingly complex questions.

Can Good News for the Computer Industry Be Bad News for Chip Makers?

Let's now return to the question posed at the beginning of this chapter: what happens to chip manufacturers and the market for chips when scientists discover a new material for making chips that is more productive than silicon? Recall from Chapter 4 that we answer such questions in three steps. First, we examine whether the supply or demand curve shifts. Secondly, we consider which direction the curve shifts. Thirdly, we use the supply and demand diagram to see how the market equilibrium changes.

This is a situation that is facing chip manufacturers. Scientists are investigating new materials to make computer chips. Such a material may allow the manufacturers to be able to work on building processing power at ever smaller concentrations and increase computing power considerably. In this case, the discovery of the new material affects the supply curve. Because the material increases the amount of computing power that can be produced on each chip, manufacturers are now willing to supply more chips at any given price. In other words, the supply curve for computing power shifts to the right. The demand curve remains the same because consumers' desire to buy chips at any given price is not affected by the introduction of the new material. Figure 5.15 shows an example of such a change. When the supply curve shifts from S_1 to S_2, the quantity of chips sold increases from 100 to 110, and the price of chips falls from €10 per gigabyte to €4 per gigabyte.

FIGURE 5.15

An Increase in Supply in the Market for Computer Chips

When an advance in chip technology increases the supply of chips from S_1 to S_2, the price of chips falls. Because the demand for chips is inelastic, the increase in the quantity sold from 100 to 110 is proportionately smaller than the decrease in the price from €10 to €4. As a result, manufacturers' total revenue falls from €1000 (€10 × 100) to €440 (€4 × 110).

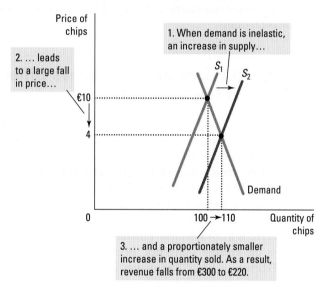

But does this discovery make chip manufacturers better off? As a first stab at answering this question, consider what happens to the total revenue received by chip manufacturers; total revenue is $P \times Q$, the price of each chip times the quantity sold. The discovery affects manufacturers in two conflicting ways. The new material allows manufacturers to produce more chips with greater computing power (Q rises), but now each chip sells for less (P falls).

Whether total revenue rises or falls depends on the elasticity of demand. We can assume that the demand for chips is inelastic; in producing a computer, chips represent a relatively small proportion of the total cost but they also have few good substitutes. When the demand curve is inelastic, as it is in Figure 5.15, a decrease in price causes total revenue to fall. You can see this in the figure: the price of chips falls substantially, whereas the quantity of chips sold rises only slightly. Total revenue falls from €1000 to €440. Thus, the discovery of the new material lowers the total revenue that chip manufacturers receive for the sale of their products.

If manufacturers are made worse off by the discovery of this new material, why do they adopt it? The answer to this question goes to the heart of how competitive markets work. If each chip manufacturer is a small part of the market for chips, he or she takes the price of chips as given. For any given price of chips, it is better to use the new material in order to produce and sell more chips. Yet when all manufacturers do this, the supply of chips rises, the price falls and manufacturers are worse off.

Although this example is only hypothetical, in fact a new material for making computer chips is being investigated. The material is called hafnium and is used in the nuclear industry. In recent years the manufacture of computer chips has changed dramatically. In the early 1990s, prices per megabyte of DRAM (dynamic random access memory) stood at around $55 but fell to under $1 by the early part of the new century. Manufacturers who were first involved in chip manufacture made high profits but as new firms joined the industry, supply increased and as the technology also spread, supply rose and prices fell. The fall in prices led to a number of firms struggling to stay in business. We assumed above that computer chip manufacturers were price takers but in reality the computer chip market is not perfectly competitive. However, the fact that so many smaller manufacturers struggled to survive as chip technology expanded at such a rapid rate from the early 1990s shows that even markets dominated now by a relatively small number of firms exhibit many of the features we have described so far.

When analysing the effects of technology, it is important to keep in mind that what is bad for manufacturers is not necessarily bad for society as a whole. Improvement in computing power technology can be bad for manufacturers who find it difficult to survive unless they are very large, but it represents good news for consumers of this computing power (ultimately the users of PCs, laptops, smartphones and so on) who pay less for computing.

Why Do Prices of Ski Holidays Differ so Much at Different Times of the Season?

Ski holidays in Europe are becoming ever more popular. There were over one million people from the UK who were part of the snowsports travel market in 2011[2]. For an increasing number of people the pleasure of a holiday on the slopes is a part of the winter but people also face considerable changes in the prices that they have to pay for their holiday. For example, a quick check of a ski company website for the 2011–2012 season revealed the prices shown in Table 5.1 for seven-night ski trips per person to Austria leaving from London.

There is a considerable variation in the prices that holidaymakers have to pay – £490 being the greatest difference. Prices are particularly high leaving on 29 December and 12 February – why? The reason is that at this time of the season the demand for ski

TABLE 5.1

Prices for 7-night Ski Holidays in Austria, From London

Departure date	Price per person (£)
29 December 2011	262
8 January 2012	228
15 January 2012	194
22 January 2012	194
29 January 2012	194
5 February 2012	251
12 February 2012	684
19 February 2012	248
26 February 2012	392

[2]http://www.skiclub.co.uk/assets/files/documents/snowsportsanalysis2011.pdf

FIGURE 5.16

The Supply of Ski Holidays in Europe

Panel (a) shows the market for ski holidays in off-peak times. The supply curve S_1 is relatively elastic in the short run. An increase in demand from D_1 to D_2 at this time leads to a relatively small increase in price because the increase can be accommodated by releasing some of the spare capacity that tour operators have. Panel (b) shows the market during peak times. The supply of holidays shown by the curve S_1 is relatively inelastic in the short run. If demand now increases from D_1 to D_2 the result will be a sharp rise in price.

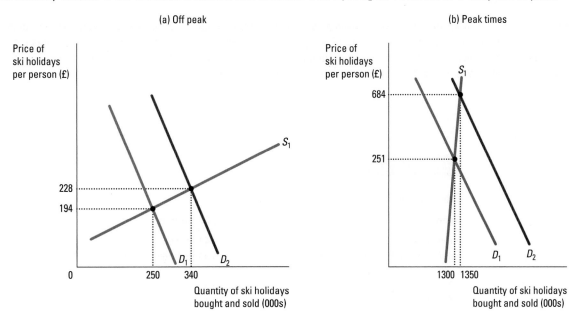

(a) Off peak

(b) Peak times

holidays increases dramatically because they coincide with annual holiday periods; 29 December is part of the Christmas/New Year holidays and when schoolchildren are also on holiday; 12 February is also a major school holiday for many UK children.

The supply of ski holidays does have a limit – there will be a finite number of accommodation places and passes for ski-lifts and so the elasticity of supply is relatively inelastic (see Panel b, Figure 5.16). It is difficult for tour operators to increase supply of accommodation or ski-passes easily in the short run in the face of rising demand at these times. The result is that the increase in demand for ski holidays at these peak times results in prices rising significantly to choke off the excess demand. If holiday-makers are able to be flexible about when they take their holidays then they will be able to benefit from lower prices for the same holiday. Away from these peak periods the demand for ski holidays is lower and so tour operators have spare capacity – the supply curve out of peak times is more elastic in the short run. If there was a sudden increase in demand in mid-January, for example, then tour operators would have the capacity to accommodate that demand so prices would not rise as much as when that capacity is strictly limited.

Cases for which supply is very inelastic in the short run but more elastic in the long run may see different prices exist in the market. Air and rail travel and the use of electricity may all be examples where prices differ markedly at peak times compared with off-peak times because of supply constraints and the ability of firms to be able to discriminate between customers at these times.

Quick Quiz How might a drought that destroys half of all farm crops be good for farmers? If such a drought is good for farmers, why don't farmers destroy their own crops in the absence of a drought?

FYI

Estimates of Elasticities

We have discussed the concept of elasticity in general terms but there is empirical evidence on elasticity of products in the real world. We present some examples of estimates of price elasticity of supply and demand for a range of products in Table 5.2. It must be remembered that the following are estimates and you may find other estimates where the elasticities differ from those given here.

TABLE 5.2

Estimates of Price Elasticity of Supply

Good	PES estimate
Public transport in Sweden	0.44 to 0.64
Labour in South Africa	0.35 to 1.75
Beef	
• Zimbabwe	2.0
• Brazil	0.11 to 0.56
• Argentina	0.67 to 0.96
Corn (short run in US)	0.96
Housing, long run in selected US cities	Dallas: 38.6
	San Francisco: 2.4
	New Orleans: 0.9
	St. Louis: 8.1
Uranium	2.3 to 3.3
Recycled aluminium	0.5
Oysters	1.64 to 2.00
Retail store space	3.2
Natural gas (short run)	0.5

Source: **http://signsofchaos.blogspot.com/2005/11/price-elasticity-of-supply-and-web.html**

Estimates of Price Elasticity of Demand

Good	PED estimate
Tobacco	0.4
Milk	0.3
Wine	0.6
Shoes	0.7
Cars	1.9
Particular brand of car	4.0
Movies	0.9
Entertainment	1.4
Furniture	3.04
Fuel	0.4
Bread	0.25

IN THE NEWS

Price Elasticity of Demand in the Hotel Industry

There are few industries where the concept of elasticity is not relevant but it is just one factor in business decision making. The hotel industry is not a perfectly competitive market but hotels do face considerable competition from rivals. Hotel owners have some influence over the price they charge for the service they provide and a consideration of the concept of elasticity is important in decision making. This article refers to some of these other factors as well as emphasizing the importance of factors affecting price elasticity of demand.

The Making of Mafraq

The National Investor's (TNI) purchase of the 15-year-old Mafraq Hotel in Abu Dhabi in April 2007 was the company's first direct hospitality acquisition. But, with the firm's founding principle being to incubate UAE-based businesses aligned to the Abu Dhabi 2030 vision – in which tourism plays a pivotal role – it was a 'natural choice', recalls TNI vice president, real estate agent, Robert Rowell.

Fast forward four and half years and the company has since invested US $50 million in extending and upgrading the hotel. Far more than a face lift, the full renovation has resulted in a sleek, modern hotel with 250 rooms instead of 120, its dated former self a mere shadow. All achieved while the hotel remained open, not quite on time but most definitely on budget, reveals Rowell. Many owners are forced to invest such sums to bring their properties up to the brand standards of their appointed operators, but this is where Mafraq has a point of difference – TNI decided to manage it in-house and keep the original name.

The general manager, Ghassan Fares, previously a GM at Habtoor Hotels, joined Mafraq in November 2007 to deliver TNI's vision. And for Fares, the freedom bestowed on him by the company has played a major role in the hotel's ongoing success. Rowell and Fares appear to work side by side, finishing each other's sentences and radiating a distinct sense of pride in what they have achieved at Mafraq.

The project marks TNI out as a bold new hospitality investor, avoiding the brand bandwagon and going it alone – controversial perhaps at a time when Abu Dhabi is welcoming numerous global names. It highlights the issue of whether brands are always best and demonstrates that there are indeed other options, so Hotelier paid Mafraq a visit... and was pleasantly impressed with this secluded Abu Dhabi hotel. Here, Rowell and Fares explain the philosophy behind their owner-operator partnership and their 'bullish' approach to 2012.

What was the Mafraq Hotel like when you acquired it?

Rowell: In 2007 we had a four-star hotel that was around 15 years old. It was in need of a refurbishment. The hotel had 120 rooms with one all-day-dining facility. We saw the occupancy levels in the existing hotel and the local demand and realized there was a clear investment case to expand it from 120 rooms to 250 rooms and to fortify the product offering by including a speciality restaurant and a ballroom, within the four-star target.

When will you see return on investment on your acquisition?

Rowell: I think a rule of thumb for modelling investment returns on a hotel would be approximately, or under, 10 years in terms of being able to return the initial amount invested, and I think we'll comfortably be within that return time frame. The hotel has already exceeded our expectations in terms of the room rates which increased rapidly; certainly for

the first couple of years after 2007 the room rates were increasing but the occupancy wasn't decreasing so for us there was a low price elasticity of demand, a low correlation of prices going up and occupancy going down, so that gave us even more encouragement that the asset was a good one and would be good for a long time.

Now the property has its new-look, what will be your approach to driving rates and occupancy?

Fares: We're in line with the market for a four-star property, in the AED 500s. During the Abu Dhabi Grand Prix we did very well.

We are regaining all of our corporate clients because during construction some of them moved out. But we never lost touch with them, we kept visiting them, making sales calls at least weekly, we invited them to different areas, sometimes took them to a different hotel because we didn't have facilities to serve clients here. We stayed proactive on that part of it. They don't believe this is really the property they were staying in before!

I'm not worried at all in keeping this property running and getting profit out of it. We did it in the tough days and when the property was really deteriorated; it wasn't that great in terms of standing, now it's brand new with a lot of facilities. It's a product that can compete with other properties, whereas earlier it was challenging for me to compete with other properties.

We can talk with more confidence now and we can convince clients looking for meetings, incentives, conferences and exhibitions (MICE) business that we are the place for them. The Abu Dhabi Tourism Authority (ADTA) has done well on promoting Abu Dhabi as a MICE sector; earlier we had 3–5 per cent of business in MICE, now we're expecting to have 10 per cent.

What and where is your competition?

Fares: The Yas Island hotels are competing because they are dropping their rates tremendously. There are furnished hotel apartments coming up and that's also a challenge because looking at the business around us it's long-term, when you have a guest that stays with you for a minimum stay of 10 nights, many look for cooking facilities; that's a challenge there for us.

Rowell: It's those other segments that we're not catering for, trying to compete with our segment, possibly a serviced apartment coming in to the area and competing for the long staying guest; or it's the five stars trying to compete on rate, which hurts them in the long run, just to take those clients. Generally it's the closer hotels to us but it's a pretty captive market as there's a limited number around us.

You've now celebrated the official relaunch on November 18, what next?

Rowell: We're very much focused on pushing forward into 2012, we're very bullish on the short, medium and long term of the hotel and the area around it here so we're focusing on operations now. We've just come out of development, so now it's 100 per cent focus on getting the operating efficiency back to where it was and employing staff, retaining the right staff and eventually making profit. We're bullish over the next 12 months despite the upcoming supply.

Questions

1. Why might TNI have wanted to keep the Mafraq Hotel open during renovation and refurbishment?
2. Why might hotel chains establish brands? Use examples to illustrate your answer.
3. What do you think is meant by the phrase 'return on investment'?
4. What factors might influence the price elasticity of supply and demand for hotel accommodation such as that at Mafraq?
5. How might a knowledge of the price elasticity of demand for Mafraq being 'low' be useful to its owners in making pricing decisions?

Source: adapted from **http://www. hoteliermiddleeast.com/13087-the-making-of-mafraq/1/** 11 December 2011, accessed 29 December 2011.

SUMMARY

- The price elasticity of supply measures how much the quantity supplied responds to changes in the price. This elasticity often depends on the time horizon under consideration. In most markets, supply is more elastic in the long run than in the short run.

- The price elasticity of supply is calculated as the percentage change in quantity supplied divided by the percentage change in price. If the elasticity is less than 1, so that quantity supplied moves proportionately less than the price, supply is said to be inelastic. If the elasticity is greater than 1, so that quantity supplied moves proportionately more than the price, supply is said to be elastic.

- The price elasticity of demand measures how much the quantity demanded responds to changes in the price. Demand tends to be more elastic if close substitutes are available, if the good is a luxury rather than a necessity, if the market is narrowly defined or if buyers have substantial time to react to a price change.

- The price elasticity of demand is calculated as the percentage change in quantity demanded divided by the percentage change in price. If the elasticity is less than 1, so that quantity demanded moves proportionately less than the price, demand is said to be inelastic. If the elasticity is greater than 1, so that quantity demanded moves proportionately more than the price, demand is said to be elastic.

- Total revenue, the total amount received by sellers for a good, equals the price of the good times the quantity sold. For inelastic demand curves, total revenue rises as price rises. For elastic demand curves, total revenue falls as price rises.

• The income elasticity of demand measures how much the quantity demanded responds to changes in consumers' income. The cross-price elasticity of demand measures how much the quantity demanded of one good responds to changes in the price of another good.

• The tools of supply and demand can be applied in many different kinds of markets. This chapter uses them to analyse the market for computer chips and the market for ski holidays.

KEY CONCEPTS

elasticity, p. 88
price elasticity of supply, p. 88
total revenue, p. 94

price elasticity of demand, p. 96
total expenditure, p. 100
income elasticity of demand, p. 104

cross-price elasticity of demand, p. 104

QUESTIONS FOR REVIEW

1. How is the price elasticity of supply calculated? Explain what this measures.

2. Is the price elasticity of supply usually larger in the short run or in the long run? Why?

3. What are the main factors that affect the price elasticity of supply? Think of some examples to use to illustrate the factors you cover.

4. Define the price elasticity of demand and the income elasticity of demand.

5. List and explain some of the determinants of the price elasticity of demand. Think of some examples to use to illustrate the factors you cover.

6. If the elasticity is greater than 1, is demand elastic or inelastic? If the elasticity equals 0, is demand perfectly elastic or perfectly inelastic?

7. On a supply and demand diagram, show equilibrium price, equilibrium quantity and the total revenue received by producers.

8. If demand is elastic, how will an increase in price change total revenue? Explain.

9. What do we call a good whose income elasticity is less than 0?

10. In the 2000s, house prices in many parts of the world rose significantly. Outline some of the factors that will affect the elasticity of supply and demand for houses in the short run and the long run.

PROBLEMS AND APPLICATIONS

1. Seafront properties along the promenade at Brighton on the south coast of England have an inelastic supply, and cars have an elastic supply. Suppose that a rise in population doubles the demand for both products (that is, the quantity demanded at each price is twice what it was).
   a. What happens to the equilibrium price and quantity in each market?
   b. Which product experiences a larger change in price?
   c. Which product experiences a larger change in quantity?
   d. What happens to total consumer spending on each product?

2. Because better weather makes farmland more productive, farmland in regions with good weather conditions is more expensive than farmland in regions with bad weather conditions. Over time, however, as advances in technology have made all farmland more productive, the price of farmland (adjusted for overall inflation) has fallen. Use the concept of elasticity to explain why productivity and farmland prices are positively related across space but negatively related over time.

3. For each of the following pairs of goods, which good would you expect to have a more price elastic demand and why?

   a. Required textbooks or mystery novels.
   b. Beethoven recordings or classical music recordings in general.
   c. Heating oil during the next six months or heating oil during the next five years.
   d. Lemonade or water.

4. Suppose that business travellers and holidaymakers have the following demand for airline tickets from Birmingham to Naples:

Price (€)	Quantity demanded (business travellers)	Quantity demanded (holidaymakers)
150	2100	1000
200	2000	800
250	1900	600
300	1800	400

   a. As the price of tickets rises from €200 to €250, what is the price elasticity of demand for (i) business travellers and (ii) holidaymakers? (Use the midpoint method in your calculations.)
   b. Why might holidaymakers have a different elasticity from business travellers?

5. Suppose that your demand schedule for DVDs is as follows:

Price (€)	Quantity demanded (income = €10 000)	Quantity demanded (income = €12 000)
8	40	50
10	32	45
12	24	30
14	16	20
16	8	12

a. Use the midpoint method to calculate your price elasticity of demand as the price of DVDs increases from €8 to €10 if (i) your income is €10 000, and (ii) your income is €12 000.

b. Calculate your income elasticity of demand as your income increases from €10 000 to €12 000 if (i) the price is €12, and (ii) the price is €16.

6. Two drivers – Jan and Lou – each drive up to a petrol station. Before looking at the price, each places an order. Jan says, 'I'd like 30 litres of petrol.' Lou says, 'I'd like €30-worth of petrol.' What is each driver's price elasticity of demand?

7. Consider public policy aimed at smoking.

a. Studies indicate that the price elasticity of demand for cigarettes is about 0.4. If a packet of cigarettes is currently priced at €6 and the government wants to reduce smoking by 20 per cent, by how much should it increase the price?

b. If the government permanently increases the price of cigarettes, will the policy have a larger effect on smoking one year from now or five years from now?

c. Studies also find that teenagers have a higher price elasticity of demand for cigarettes than do adults. Why might this be true?

8. Pharmaceutical drugs have an inelastic demand, and computers have an elastic demand. Suppose that technological advance doubles the supply of both products (that is, the quantity supplied at each price is twice what it was).

a. What happens to the equilibrium price and quantity in each market?

b. Which product experiences a larger change in price?

c. Which product experiences a larger change in quantity?

d. What happens to total consumer spending on each product?

9. Suppose that there is severe flooding in a region in which there is a high concentration of wheat farmers.

a. Farmers whose crops were destroyed by the floods were much worse off, but farmers whose crops were not destroyed benefited from the floods. Why?

b. What information would you need about the market for wheat to assess whether farmers as a group were hurt or helped by the floods?

10. Explain why the following might be true: a drought around the world raises the total revenue that farmers receive from the sale of grain, but a drought only in France reduces the total revenue that French farmers receive.

PART 3

MICROECONOMICS – THE
LIMITATIONS OF MARKETS

6 MARKET FAILURE

LEARNING OBJECTIVES

In this chapter you will:

- Look at the meaning of market failure and the main sources of market failure

- Be introduced to the concepts of consumer and producer surplus as ways of measuring economic welfare

- Look at the difference between positive and negative externalities

- Cover the two main ways in which governments intervene in business to seek to correct market failure

- Cover a formal treatment of taxes and subsidies and how they affect businesses

- Look at public/private solutions to market failure including property rights

- Be introduced to some objections to the economic analysis of pollution

- Explore the meaning of social and ethical responsibility

After reading this chapter you should be able to:

- See how decision making and transactions can often ignore social costs and benefits leading to externalities

- Define market failure and give examples of how it arises

- Explain the difference between private and social costs

- Draw diagrams to show consumer and producer surplus and be able to identify changes in both as a result of changes in price

- Use diagrams to explain how both negative and positive externalities arise and show the welfare costs of inefficient resource allocation

- Discuss different government led solutions to market failure including regulation, taxes and subsidies

- Analyse the use of tradable permits

- Use diagrams to show how taxes and subsidies affect businesses, price and output and how the incidence of tax is shared between consumers and producers

- Evaluate the arguments surrounding the economic analysis of pollution

- Consider some of the issues relating to social and ethical responsibility of firms

- Analyse the use of property rights as a means of correcting externalities

INTRODUCTION

We have looked at markets and how firms operate in those markets. Efficiency has been a recurring feature of the discussion of markets and firms but as noted in Chapter 1, we have to be careful how we define efficiency.

In recent years there has been a far greater awareness of the effects that a firm's operations have on its wider stakeholders which may alter our perception of efficiency. For example, firms that make and sell paper also create, as a by-product of the manufacturing process, a chemical called dioxin. Scientists believe that once dioxin enters the environment it raises the population's risk of cancer, birth defects and other health problems. We know that cigarette and alcohol manufacturers produce products which can result in serious health issues for users and problems for society as a whole. We know that there is a way to reduce the instances of sexually transmitted diseases, including the very serious problem of HIV AIDS, through wider use of condoms, but this is a product which is under-used.

Market theory in its purest sense is based on an assumption that markets work efficiently and when they do, resources are allocated efficiently. The reality is much more complex than this and we know that markets do not work efficiently all the time. Market failure occurs where the market does not allocate resources efficiently.

Mind Map showing the different aspects of market failure.

Sources of Market Failure

There are a number of sources of market failure which can be summarized as follows:

- Imperfect knowledge of and between buyers and sellers. This might arise because consumers do not have adequate technical knowledge or where advertising can mislead or mis-inform. Producers are likely to be unaware of all the opportunities open to them and cannot accurately measure productivity. For both consumers and producers, decisions are often based on past experience rather than future knowledge.
- Goods are not homogenous where differentiation is prevalent in markets. Goods are differentiated through branding, technology and through labelling and product information, amongst other methods.
- Resource immobility – inability of firms to substitute or move factors of production easily. Factors of production are not fully mobile – labour can be both geographically and occupationally immobile, some capital items have limited uses (for example, what else could the Channel Tunnel be used for) and land cannot be moved to where it might be needed nor exploited if it is not suitable.
- Market power – where firms have some element of monopoly power. We have looked at the behaviour of firms with monopoly power and the possibilities which arise for collusion, price fixing, the long term existence of abnormal profits, rigging of markets and the erection of barriers to entry.
- Where services/goods would or could not be provided in sufficient quantity by the market, for example merit goods and public goods (see Chapter 8).
- Where inequality exists in factor or income endowment, for example through unequal wealth distribution, where poverty exists and through discrimination.
- Existence of external costs and benefits.

In this chapter we examine why markets sometimes fail to allocate resources efficiently, how government policies can potentially improve the market's allocation, what kinds of policies are likely to work best and how firms' behaviour is affected.

The market failures examined in this chapter fall under a general category called *externalities*. An externality arises when an individual or business engages in an activity that influences the well-being of a bystander (a third party) who neither pays nor receives any compensation for that effect. If the impact on the bystander is adverse, it is called a *negative externality*; if it is beneficial, it is called a *positive externality*.

Private and Social Costs

We have seen how the operation of markets is based on millions of decisions being made by individuals, businesses and groups. The invisible hand (see Chapter 1) means that individuals, businesses and groups make decisions which are designed to maximize their individual, business or group welfare. In making these decisions there will be private costs and private benefits. In deciding to publish a book, for example, a business incurs various private costs such as the cost of paper, printing, marketing, editorial work, paying author royalties and various overheads such as administration. In publishing a book, there are a number of private benefits which include the share of profits to owners or shareholders, not to mention the employment of individuals within the business. However, in making the decision to publish the book the business may not take into consideration the cost (or benefit) to society that is imposed as a result of that decision. Distribution of the books contributes to congestion, road wear and tear; there are the emissions that the vehicles gives off, the noise pollution and the increased risk of accident which may cause injury or even death to a third party. Firms that make and sell paper, which is used in the production of books, also create, as a by-product of the manufacturing process, a chemical called dioxin. Scientists believe that once dioxin enters the environment it raises the population's risk of cancer, birth defects and other health problems. There may also be some social benefits of the decision; knowledge development is improved as a result of the book being available, employees of the firm will spend the money they earn on goods and services in the local area and workers at paper mills will have jobs, for example.

These social costs and benefits are not necessarily taken into consideration by the business when making the decision to publish the book. The internal costs and benefits may be far more important in the firm's decision making. The social costs and benefits are borne by a third party. The cost of repairing damaged roads, the cost of dealing with accident and injury, delays caused as a result of congestion, the effects and costs of dealing with pollution and so on, all have to be borne by others – often the taxpayer. Equally, any social benefits arising from the decision are gained by those not party to the initial decision without them having to pay for the benefit derived.

In the presence of externalities, society's interest in a market outcome extends beyond the well-being of buyers and sellers who participate in the market; it also includes the well-being of bystanders who are affected indirectly. For a business this might be its wider stakeholders. Because buyers and sellers neglect the external effects of their actions when deciding how much to demand or supply, the market equilibrium is not efficient when there are externalities. That is, the equilibrium fails to maximize the total benefit to society as a whole. The release of dioxin into the environment, for instance, is a negative externality. Self-interested paper firms will not consider the full cost of the pollution they create and, therefore, will emit too much pollution unless the government prevents or discourages them from doing so.

Externalities come in many varieties, as do the policy responses that try to deal with the market failure. Here are some examples.

- The exhaust from cars is a negative externality because it creates smog that other people have to breathe. Drivers do not take into consideration this externality and so tend to drive too much thus increasing pollution. The government attempts to solve this problem by setting emission standards for cars. It also taxes petrol in order to reduce the amount that people drive. These policy remedies have effects on business costs and behaviour which might ultimately have to be passed onto the consumer in the form of higher prices. The benefits might be that more research and development (R&D) into efficient cars is carried out by firms looking to gain some competitive advantage in the market – something that might benefit both firms and consumers.
- Airports create negative externalities because people who live near the airport or on the flight path are disturbed by noise. Airports and airlines do not bear the full cost of the noise and, therefore, may be less inclined to spend money on noise reduction technologies. The government may address this problem by regulating the time that airlines can take-off and land at an airport or providing subsidies to help local homeowners invest in triple glazing and other sound proofing measures for homes on the flight path.
- Research into new technologies provides a positive externality because it creates knowledge that other people can use. Because inventors and business research and development units cannot capture the full benefits of their inventions, they tend to devote too few resources to research. The government addresses this problem partially through the patent and intellectual property system, which gives inventors and businesses an exclusive use over their inventions or right to exploit intellectual property for a period of time, and through the provision of subsidies to encourage firms to invest in R&D.
- The provision of public transport brings benefits to many people not only because it helps them get around more easily but it also helps relieve congestion thus benefiting other road users. Governments are often prepared to subsidize public transport because there are positive benefits to society as a whole.
- Immunization programmes against communicable diseases and infections are often provided free of charge by a country's health service. The benefits not only accrue to the individuals who receive the innoculations but in far wider circles. Those who are inoculated are less likely to pass on infection to others, in particular the more vulnerable

members of society, days lost through work are reduced which in turn helps businesses operate more effectively. Recent studies in the UK suggest that around 180 million working days are lost each year due to illness with an estimated cost to the economy amounting to £2.5 billion (€2.98 billion). The indirect costs due to the fall in consumer service levels as a result of employee absence was estimated at £17 billion (€20.29 billion). If an immunization system contributes to a reduction in the instances of employee absence this can have significant effects on businesses.

In each of these cases, some decision maker fails to take account of the external effects of his or her behaviour. The government responds by trying to influence this behaviour to protect the interests of bystanders.

Immunization programmes are an example of a positive externality – the benefits to third parties are not taken into account by the decision maker but are very real.

EXTERNALITIES

Welfare Economics: An Overview

Firms rely on consumers. Consumers buy products from firms but their behaviour will depend on a variety of factors not least their willingness to pay for a product. Whenever you go into a shop or chose a product online, you are making complex neural calculations – there will be a price which you are prepared to pay to acquire a product and there will be a slightly higher price which for some reason you are not prepared to pay.

Willingness to Pay   The maximum price is the **willingness to pay**, and it measures how much a buyer values the good. Buyers are invariably happy to buy goods at prices less than their willingness to pay but would refuse to buy at a price more than their willingness to pay. We can also assume that the buyer would be indifferent about buying a good at a price exactly equal to his willingness to pay.

When buying a good a consumer can expect to derive some benefit. The willingness to pay is a reflection of the value of the benefit that the buyer expects to receive. This is why firms spend large sums of money trying to understand how consumers value products and what affects their behaviour.

If a consumer buys a product for €10 but would have been prepared to pay €20 we say that the buyer receives *consumer surplus* of €10. **Consumer surplus** is the amount a buyer is willing to pay for a good minus the amount the buyer actually pays for it. We refer to 'getting a bargain' regularly in everyday language. In economics, a bargain means paying much less for something than we expected or anticipated and as a result we get a greater degree of consumer surplus than we expected. Consumer surplus measures the benefit to buyers of participating in a market.

willingness to pay a measure of how much a buyer values a good by the amount they are prepared to pay to acquire the good

consumer surplus the amount a buyer is willing to pay for a good minus the amount the buyer actually pays for it

Using the Demand Curve to Measure Consumer Surplus

Consumer surplus is closely related to the demand curve for a product. The market demand curve represents the willingness and ability to pay of all consumers in the market. Because buyers always want to pay less for the goods they buy, lower prices makes buyers of a good better off. But how much does buyers' well-being rise in response to a lower price? We can use the concept of consumer surplus to answer this question precisely.

Figure 6.1 shows a demand schedule for a market – let's assume that it is the market for tickets for a music festival. If the festival organizers set the price at P_1, Q_1 consumers will want to buy a ticket. The marginal buyer represented by the point Q_1 has a willingness to pay of just P_1; at any price above P_1, this festival goer is not willing to pay. However, all the buyers represented by the amount 0–Q_1 were willing to pay a price higher than P_1 to get tickets. All these buyers gained some degree of consumer surplus shown by the area above the price and below the demand curve. In panel (a) of Figure 6.1, consumer surplus at a price of P_1 is the area of triangle ABC.

FIGURE 6.1

How the Price Affects Consumer Surplus

In panel (a) the price is P_1, the quantity of festival tickets demanded is Q_1 and consumer surplus equals the area of the triangle ABC. If the ticket price is set at P_2 rather than P_1, as in panel (b), the quantity demanded would be Q_2 rather than Q_1, and the consumer surplus rises to the area of the triangle ADF. The increase in consumer surplus (area BCFD) occurs in part because existing consumers now pay less (area BCED) and in part because new consumers enter the market at the lower price (area CEF).

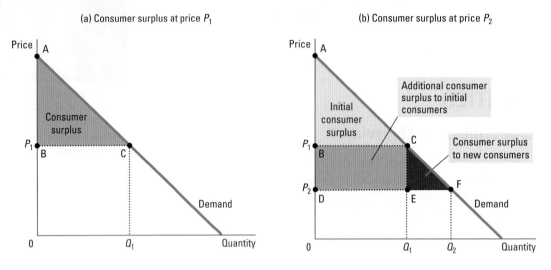

(a) Consumer surplus at price P_1 (b) Consumer surplus at price P_2

Now suppose that the price set by the festival organizers was set at P_2 rather than P_1, as shown in panel (b). The consumer surplus now equals area ADF. The increase in consumer surplus attributable to the lower price is the area BCFD.

This increase in consumer surplus is composed of two parts. First, those buyers who would have bought Q_1 of the good at the higher price P_1 are better off because they now pay less. The increase in consumer surplus of existing buyers is the reduction in the amount they are now being asked to pay; it equals the area of the rectangle BCED. Secondly, some new buyers enter the market because they are now willing and able to buy tickets at the lower price. As a result, the quantity demanded for festival tickets would be Q_2 rather than Q_1. The consumer surplus these newcomers receive is the area of the triangle CEF.

The lesson from this example holds for all demand curves: the area below the demand curve and above the price measures the consumer surplus in a market. The reason is that the height of the demand curve measures the value buyers place on the good, as measured by their willingness to pay for it. The difference between this willingness to pay and the market price is each buyer's consumer surplus. Thus, the total area below the demand curve and above the price is the sum of the consumer surplus of all buyers in the market for a good or service.

What Does Consumer Surplus Measure?

Our goal in developing the concept of consumer surplus is to make normative judgements about the desirability of market outcomes. Firms can also use the concept of consumer surplus in designing branding, advertising and promotion campaigns and deciding on pricing strategies.

Because consumer surplus measures the benefit that buyers receive from a good *as the buyers themselves perceive it*, it is a good measure of economic well-being if policy makers and businesses want to respect and possibly exploit the preferences of buyers.

In most markets consumer surplus can fairly accurately reflect economic well-being. Economists normally presume that buyers are rational when they make decisions and that their preferences should be respected. In this case, consumers are the best judges of how much benefit they receive from the goods they buy.

PRODUCER SURPLUS

We now turn to the other side of the market and consider the benefits sellers receive from participating in a market. As you will see, our analysis of sellers' welfare is similar to our analysis of buyers' welfare.

Cost and the Willingness to Sell

As with our analysis of the buyer side, sellers are willing to offer goods for sale if the price they receive exceeds the cost. Here the term cost should be interpreted as the producer's opportunity cost. Cost is a measure of a firm's willingness to sell their product. Each producer in a market would be eager to sell their products at a price greater than their cost, would refuse to sell their products at a price less than their cost, and would be indifferent about selling their products at a price exactly equal to cost.

If a producer is able to sell a product at a price that is higher than the lowest amount they would be willing to sell that product for then they will receive some benefit. We say that the producer receives *producer surplus*. **Producer surplus** is the amount a seller is paid minus the cost of production. Producer surplus measures the benefit to sellers of participating in a market. The total producer surplus in a market is the value of the sum of all the individual producer surplus.

producer surplus the amount a seller is paid minus the cost of production

Using the Supply Curve to Measure Producer Surplus

Just as consumer surplus is closely related to the demand curve, producer surplus is closely related to the supply curve.

It is not surprising that sellers always want to receive a higher price for the goods they sell. How far sellers' well-being will rise in response to a higher price can be calculated precisely by using the concept of producer surplus.

Figure 6.2 shows a typical upward sloping supply curve. Let us assume that this is the supply curve for firms providing online rental access to movies per time period. At a price of P1, firms can expect to sell Q1 rentals over the time period. The producer surplus is the area below the price and above the supply curve. In panel (a) of Figure 6.2, at the price of P_1 the producer surplus is the area of triangle ABC.

Panel (b) shows what happens if the price of online movie rentals rises from P_1 to P_2. Producer surplus now equals area ADF. This increase in producer surplus has two parts. First, those sellers who were already selling Q_1 of the good at the lower price P_1 are better off because they now get more for what they sell. The increase in producer surplus for existing sellers equals the area of the rectangle BCED. Secondly, some new sellers enter the market because they are now willing to produce the good at the higher price, resulting in an increase in the quantity supplied from Q_1 to Q_2. The producer surplus of these newcomers is the area of the triangle CEF.

As this analysis shows, we use producer surplus to measure the well-being of sellers in much the same way as we use consumer surplus to measure the well-being of buyers.

FIGURE 6.2

How the Price Affects Producer Surplus

In panel (a) the price is P_1, the quantity demanded is Q_1 and producer surplus equals the area of the triangle ABC. When the price rises from P_1 to P_2, as in panel (b), the quantity supplied rises from Q_1 to Q_2 and the producer surplus rises to the area of the triangle ADF. The increase in producer surplus (area BCFD) occurs in part because existing producers now receive more (area BCED) and in part because new producers enter the market at the higher price (area CEF).

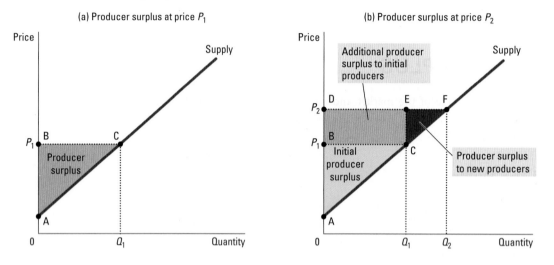

Because these two measures of economic welfare are so similar, it is natural to use them together to analyse market inefficiencies.

These inefficiencies and changes in welfare can be estimated by referring to the deadweight loss. The **deadweight loss** is the fall in total surplus that results when a tax (or some other policy) distorts a market outcome. This can be considered by calculating the changes in both producer and consumer surplus as a result of the tax or policy change minus the benefits (which may be the tax revenue accruing to the government, for example). Figure 6.3 summarizes the effects of a tax by comparing welfare before and after the tax is imposed. The third column in the table in Figure 6.3 shows the changes. The tax causes consumer surplus to fall by the area B + C and producer surplus to fall by the area D + E. Tax revenue rises by the area B + D. Not surprisingly, the tax makes buyers and sellers worse off and the government better off.

The change in total welfare includes the change in consumer surplus (which is negative), the change in producer surplus (which is also negative), and the change in tax revenue (which is positive). When we add these three pieces together, we find that total surplus in the market falls by the area C + E. Thus, the losses to buyers and sellers from a tax exceed the revenue raised by the government. The area C + E measures the size of the deadweight loss.

The area C + E shows the fall in total surplus and is the deadweight loss of the tax.

> **deadweight loss** the fall in total surplus that results from a market distortion, such as a tax

> **Quick Quiz** Draw a supply curve for MP3 downloads. In your diagram show a price of MP3 downloads and the producer surplus that results from that price. Explain in words what this producer surplus measures.

Market Inefficiencies

To make our analysis concrete, we will consider a specific market – the market for aluminium. Figure 6.4 shows the supply and demand curves in the market for aluminium.

FIGURE 6.3

How a Tax Affects Welfare

A tax on a good reduces consumer surplus (by the area B + C) and producer surplus (by the area D + E). Because the fall in producer and consumer surplus exceeds tax revenue (area B + D), the tax is said to impose a deadweight loss (area C + E).

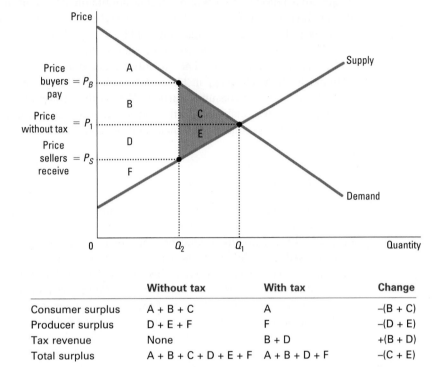

	Without tax	With tax	Change
Consumer surplus	A + B + C	A	–(B + C)
Producer surplus	D + E + F	F	–(D + E)
Tax revenue	None	B + D	+(B + D)
Total surplus	A + B + C + D + E + F	A + B + D + F	–(C + E)

FIGURE 6.4

The Market for Aluminium

The demand curve reflects the value to buyers, and the supply curve reflects the costs of sellers. The equilibrium quantity, Q_{MARKET}, maximizes the total value to buyers minus the total costs of sellers. In the absence of externalities, therefore, the market equilibrium is efficient.

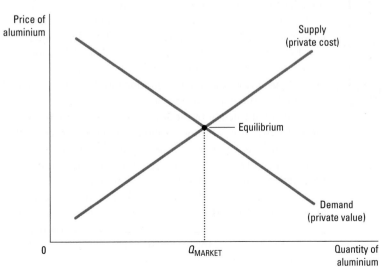

Remember that supply and demand curves contain important information about costs and benefits. The demand curve for aluminium reflects the value of aluminium to consumers, as measured by the prices they are willing to pay. At any given quantity, the height of the demand curve shows the willingness to pay of the marginal buyer. In other words, it shows the value to the consumer of the last unit of aluminium bought. Similarly, the supply curve reflects the costs of producing aluminium. At any given quantity, the height of the supply curve shows the cost of the marginal seller. In other words, it shows the cost to the producer of the last unit of aluminium sold.

In the absence of government intervention, the price adjusts to balance the supply and demand for aluminium. The quantity produced and consumed in the market equilibrium, shown as Q_{MARKET} in Figure 6.4, is efficient in the sense that it maximizes the sum of producer and consumer surplus. That is, the market allocates resources in a way that maximizes the total value to the consumers who buy and use aluminium minus the total costs to the producers who make and sell aluminium.

Negative Externalities

Now let's suppose that aluminium factories emit pollution: for each unit of aluminium produced, a certain amount of a pollutant enters the atmosphere. This pollutant may pose a health risk for those who breathe the air, it is a negative externality. There is a cost involved in dealing with the effects of the pollutant which may be the health care that those affected have to receive. This cost may not be taken into consideration by producers of aluminium who may only consider the private costs of production. How does this externality affect the efficiency of the market outcome?

Because of the externality, the cost to *society* of producing aluminium is larger than the cost to the aluminium producers. For each unit of aluminium produced, the *social (or external) cost* includes the private costs of the aluminium producers plus the costs to those bystanders affected adversely by the pollution. Figure 6.4 shows the social cost of producing aluminium. The social cost curve is above the supply curve because it takes into account the external costs imposed on society by aluminium producers. At every price the social cost is higher than the private cost so we can say that the social cost curve is the sum of the private costs and the social or external cost. The difference between these two curves reflects the social or external cost of the pollution emitted.

What quantity of aluminium should be produced? To answer this question, we can refer to our analysis of consumer and producer surplus. The ideal would be to maximize the total surplus derived from the market – the value to consumers of aluminium minus the cost of producing aluminium with the proviso that the cost of producing aluminium includes the external costs of the pollution.

This ideal would be the level of aluminium production at which the demand curve crosses the social cost curve. This intersection determines the optimal amount of aluminium from the standpoint of society as a whole. As a general principle the socially efficient output occurs where the marginal social cost equals the marginal social benefit at a particular output. Below this level of production, the value of the aluminium to consumers (as measured by the height of the demand curve) exceeds the social cost of producing it (as measured by the height of the social cost curve). Producing any more than this level means the social cost of producing additional aluminium exceeds the value to consumers.

Note that the equilibrium quantity of aluminium, Q_{MARKET}, is larger than the socially optimal quantity, $Q_{OPTIMUM}$. The reason for this inefficiency is that the market equilibrium reflects only the private costs of production. In the market equilibrium, the marginal consumer values aluminium at less than the social cost of producing it. That is, at Q_{MARKET} the demand curve lies below the social cost curve. Thus, reducing aluminium production and consumption below the market equilibrium level raises total economic well-being. We can measure changes in well-being by the welfare loss associated with different market outcomes. We measure the difference in the value placed on each

FIGURE 6.5

Pollution and the Social Optimum

In the presence of a negative externality, such as pollution, the social cost of the good exceeds the private cost. The optimal quantity, $Q_{OPTIMUM}$, is therefore smaller than the equilibrium quantity, Q_{MARKET}.

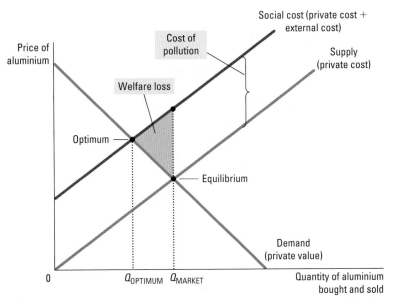

marginal unit of production of aluminium between $Q_{OPTIMUM}$ and Q_{MARKET} by consumers as shown by the shaded triangle in Figure 6.5.

How can society hope to achieve the optimal outcome? The answer is to somehow force the decision maker to take into consideration some or all of the social costs of the decision. In our example, one way to do this would be to tax aluminium producers for each tonne of aluminium sold. The tax would shift the supply curve for aluminium upward by the size of the tax. If the tax accurately reflected the social cost of the pollution released into the atmosphere, the new supply curve would coincide with the social cost curve. In the new market equilibrium, aluminium producers would produce the socially optimal quantity of aluminium.

The use of such a tax is called **internalizing an externality** because it gives buyers and sellers in the market an incentive to take account of the external effects of their actions. Aluminium producers would, in essence, take the costs of pollution into account when deciding how much aluminium to supply because the tax would make them pay for these external costs. The policy is based on one of the *Ten Principles of Economics*: people respond to incentives (see Chapter 1).

Pollution comes in many forms – not just from the actions of firms but from people in general.

internalizing an externality
altering incentives so that people take account of the external effects of their actions

Positive Externalities

Although some activities impose costs on third parties, others yield benefits. For example, consider education. Education yields positive externalities because a more educated population means firms can employ more flexible and productive employees which helps improve productive and technical efficiency and increases the potential for economic growth, which benefits everyone. Notice that the productivity benefit of education is not necessarily an externality: the consumer of education reaps most of the benefit in the form of higher wages. But if some of the productivity benefits of education spill over and benefit other people, as is the case if economic growth is stimulated, then this effect would count as a positive externality as well.

FIGURE 6.6

Education and the Social Optimum

In the presence of a positive externality, the social value of the good exceeds the private value. The optimal quantity, $Q_{OPTIMUM}$, is therefore larger than the equilibrium quantity, Q_{MARKET}.

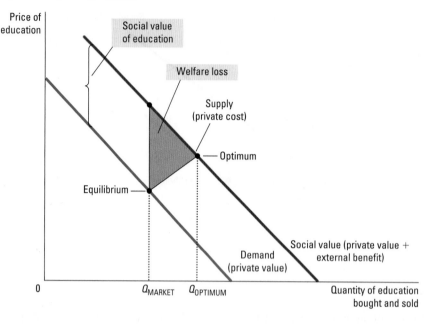

The analysis of positive externalities is similar to the analysis of negative externalities. As Figure 6.6 shows, the demand curve does not reflect the value to society of the good. The value placed on an activity such as education is valued less by consumers than the total value to society. Because the social value (or external benefit) is greater than the private value, the social value curve lies above the demand curve. The social value curve is the private value plus the external benefit to society at each price. At every price the benefit to society is greater than the private benefit, hence the social value curve lies to the right of the private benefit curve. The optimal quantity is found where the social value curve and the supply curve (which represents costs) intersect. Hence, the socially optimal quantity is greater than the quantity determined by the private market.

Once again, the government can correct the market failure by inducing market participants to internalize the externality. The appropriate response in the case of positive externalities is exactly the opposite to the case of negative externalities. To move the market equilibrium closer to the social optimum, a positive externality requires a subsidy. In fact, that is exactly the policy many governments follow by heavily subsidizing education.

To summarize: negative externalities lead markets to produce a larger quantity than is socially desirable. Positive externalities lead markets to produce a smaller quantity than is socially desirable. To remedy the problem, the government can internalize the externality by taxing goods that have negative externalities and subsidizing goods that have positive externalities.

JEOPARDY PROBLEM

From a social efficiency perspective, consider the situation where an orbital motorway around a busy major city is highly congested during the day but is largely deserted between the hours of 11.00 pm and 5.30 am. What steps might be taken to improve the efficiency of such a road system?

CASE STUDY

Technology Spillovers and Industrial Policy

Consider the market for industrial robots. Robots are at the frontier of a rapidly changing technology. Whenever a firm builds a robot, there is some chance that it will discover a new and better design. This new design will benefit not only this firm but society as a whole because the design will enter society's pool of technological knowledge. This type of positive externality is called a *technology spillover*.

In this case, the government can internalize the externality by subsidizing the production of robots. If the government paid firms a subsidy for each robot produced, the supply curve would shift down by the amount of the subsidy, and this shift would increase the equilibrium quantity of robots. To ensure that the market equilibrium equals the social optimum, the subsidy should equal the value of the technology spillover.

Two production lines, two very different approaches. Robots now do the work of humans but are the benefits greater than the costs?

How large are technology spillovers, and what do they imply for public policy? This is an important question because technological progress is the key to why living standards rise over time. Yet it is also a difficult question on which economists often disagree.

Some economists believe that technology spillovers are pervasive and that the government should encourage those industries that yield the largest spillovers. For instance, these economists argue that if making computer chips yields greater spillovers than making fish and chips, then the government should use the tax laws to encourage the production of computer chips relative to the production of fish and chips. Government intervention in the economy that aims to promote technology-enhancing industries is sometimes called *industrial policy*.

In the debate over climate change, some argue that a better way forward for society is to focus efforts on developing new technologies that will reduce our reliance on carbon-based technologies. (Technology, by the way, is defined as the application of knowledge to solve practical problems). Governments throughout Europe, the Middle East and Africa are providing incentives for the development of so-called 'green technologies'. Some claim that development in this area could bring similar change and benefits to those of the information technology revolution which has taken place over the last 30 years. Key areas of green technology relate to energy production and efficiency, construction, green chemistry (using technologies that reduce or eliminate the use or production of substances that are hazardous or present long-term dangers) and green nanotechnology.

This latter technology involves the use of materials at a minute scale and may also incorporate green chemistry. One area where nanotechnology is being developed is the food industry. The technology could lead to more efficient use of pesticides and fertilizers, improving the safety and viability of genetic engineering, dealing with plant and animal pathogens, enhancing food flavours, removing pathogens from food, increasing output and productivity, improving the safety and efficiency of food packaging, and improving the way humans and animals absorb nutrients. The benefits of this technology are being promoted to the developing world, where there are still millions of people who have to suffer starvation and malnutrition, as well as the developed world.

Other economists are sceptical about industrial policy. Even if technology spillovers are common, the success of an industrial policy requires that the government be able to measure the size of the spillovers from different markets. This measurement problem is difficult at best. Moreover, without precise measurements, the political system may end up subsidizing those industries with the most political influence rather than those that yield the largest positive externalities.

Another way to deal with technology spillovers is patent protection. The patent laws protect the rights of inventors by giving them exclusive use of their inventions for a period of time. When a firm makes a technological breakthrough, it can patent the idea and capture much of the economic benefit for itself. The patent is said to internalize the externality by giving the firm a property right over its invention. If other firms want to use the new technology, they have to obtain permission from the inventing firm and pay it some royalty. Thus, the patent system gives firms a greater incentive to engage in research and other activities that advance technology.

Quick Quiz Give an example of a negative externality and a positive externality • Explain why market outcomes are inefficient in the presence of externalities.

GOVERNMENT BUSINESS AND EXTERNALITIES

It is widely acknowledged by firms that their activities result in both positive and negative externalities and that market failure means that resources are not allocated as efficiently as they might be. In virtually every country, governments step in to try and influence business behaviour in an attempt to counter market failure and provide the incentives to change behaviour to generate an outcome which is seen as benefiting society as a whole.

There are two main ways in which governments intervene in business: *command-and-control policies* regulate behaviour directly. *Market-based policies* provide incentives so that private decision makers will choose to solve the problem on their own.

Regulation

The government can remedy an externality by making certain behaviours either required or forbidden. For example, it is a crime in any European country to dump poisonous chemicals into the water supply. In this case, the external costs to society far exceed the benefits to the polluter. The government therefore institutes a command-and-control policy that prohibits this act altogether.

In most cases of pollution, however, the situation is not this simple. Despite the stated goals of some environmentalists, it would be impossible to prohibit all polluting activity. For example, virtually all forms of transport – even the horse – produce some undesirable polluting by-products. But it would not be sensible for the government to ban all transport. Thus, instead of trying to eradicate pollution altogether, society has to weigh the costs and benefits to decide the kinds and quantities of pollution it will allow.

Environmental regulations can take many forms. Sometimes the government may dictate a maximum level of pollution that a factory may emit, or set permitted noise levels for an airline. At other times the government requires that firms adopt a particular technology to reduce emissions or will only grant a licence to operate if certain criteria are met. In all cases, to design good rules, the government regulators need to know the details about specific industries and about the alternative technologies that those industries could adopt. This information is often difficult for government regulators to obtain.

Market-Based Policies – Pigovian Taxes and Subsidies

Instead of regulating behaviour in response to an externality, the government can use market-based policies to align private incentives with social efficiency. For instance, as we saw earlier, the government can internalize the externality by taxing activities that have negative externalities and subsidizing activities that have positive externalities. Taxes enacted to correct the effects of negative externalities are called **Pigovian taxes**, after the English economist Arthur Pigou (1877–1959), an early advocate of their use.

pigovian tax a tax enacted to correct the effects of a negative externality

Economists usually prefer Pigovian taxes over regulations as a way to deal with pollution because such taxes can reduce pollution at a lower cost to society. To see why, let us consider an example.

Suppose that two factories – a paper mill and a steel mill – are each dumping 500 tonnes of effluent into a river each year. The government decides that it wants to reduce the amount of pollution. It considers two solutions:

- *Regulation*. The government could tell each factory to reduce its pollution to 300 tonnes of effluent per year.
- *Pigovian tax*. The government could levy a tax on each factory of €50 000 for each tonne of effluent it emits.

The regulation would dictate a level of pollution, whereas the tax would give factory owners an economic incentive to reduce pollution. Which solution do you think is better?

Most economists would prefer the tax. They would first point out that a tax is just as effective as regulation in reducing the overall level of pollution. The government can achieve whatever level of pollution it wants by setting the tax at the appropriate level. The higher the tax, the larger the reduction in pollution. Indeed, if the tax is high enough, the factories will close down altogether, reducing pollution to zero.

The reason why economists would prefer the tax is that it reduces pollution more efficiently. The regulation requires each factory to reduce pollution by the same amount, but an equal reduction is not necessarily the least expensive way to clean up the water. It is possible that the paper mill can reduce pollution at lower cost than the steel mill. If so, the paper mill would respond to the tax by reducing pollution substantially to avoid the tax, whereas the steel mill would respond by reducing pollution less and paying the tax.

In essence, the Pigovian tax places a price on the right to pollute. Just as markets allocate goods to those buyers who value them most highly, a Pigovian tax allocates pollution to those factories that face the highest cost of reducing it. Whatever the level of pollution the government chooses, it can achieve this goal at the lowest total cost using a tax.

Economists also argue that Pigovian taxes are better for the environment. Under the command-and-control policy of regulation, the factories have no reason to reduce emission further once they have reached the target of 300 tonnes of effluent. By contrast, the tax gives the factories an incentive to develop cleaner technologies, because a cleaner technology would reduce the amount of tax the factory has to pay.

Pigovian taxes are unlike most other taxes. Many taxes distort incentives and move the allocation of resources away from the social optimum. The reduction in economic well-being – that is, in consumer and producer surplus – exceeds the amount of revenue the government raises, resulting in a deadweight loss. By contrast, when externalities are present, society also cares about the well-being of the bystanders who are affected. Pigovian taxes correct incentives for the presence of externalities and thereby move the allocation of resources closer to the social optimum. Thus, while Pigovian taxes raise revenue for the government, they also enhance economic efficiency.

Tradable Pollution Permits

Returning to our example of the paper mill and the steel mill, let us suppose that, despite the advice of its economists, the government adopts the regulation and requires each factory to reduce its pollution to 300 tonnes of effluent per year. Then one day, after the regulation is in place and both mills have complied, the two firms go to the government with a proposal. The steel mill wants to increase its emission of effluent by 100 tonnes. The paper mill has agreed to reduce its emission by the same amount if the steel mill pays it €5 million. Should the government allow the two factories to make this deal?

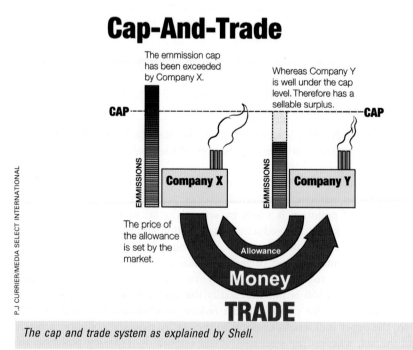

The cap and trade system as explained by Shell.

Source: http://www.shell.com/home/content/shipping_trading/environmental_trading_solutions/markets/basics_environmental_products/

From the standpoint of economic efficiency, allowing the deal is good policy. The deal must make the owners of the two factories better off, because they are voluntarily agreeing to it. Moreover, the deal does not have any external effects because the total amount of pollution remains the same. Thus, social welfare is enhanced by allowing the paper mill to sell its right to pollute to the steel mill.

The same logic applies to any voluntary transfer of the right to pollute from one firm to another. If the government allows firms to make these deals, it will, in essence, have created a new scarce resource: pollution permits. A market to trade these permits will eventually develop, and that market will be governed by the forces of supply and demand. The invisible hand will ensure that this new market efficiently allocates the right to pollute. The firms that can reduce pollution only at high cost will be willing to pay the most for the pollution permits. The firms that can reduce pollution at low cost will prefer to sell whatever permits they have.

One advantage of allowing a market for pollution permits, sometimes referred to as a 'cap and trade' system as outlined in the illustration above, is that the initial allocation of pollution permits among firms does not matter from the standpoint of economic efficiency. Those firms that can reduce pollution most easily would be willing to sell whatever permits they get, and those firms that can reduce pollution only at high cost would be willing to buy whatever permits they need. As long as there is a free market for the pollution rights, the final allocation will be efficient whatever the initial allocation.

Although reducing pollution using pollution permits may seem quite different from using Pigovian taxes, in fact the two policies have much in common. In both cases, firms pay for their pollution. With Pigovian taxes, polluting firms must pay a tax to the government. With pollution permits, polluting firms must pay to buy the permit. (Even firms that already own permits must pay to pollute: the opportunity cost of polluting is what they could have received by selling their permits on the open market.) Both Pigovian taxes and pollution permits internalize the externality of pollution by making it costly for firms to pollute.

The similarity of the two policies can be seen by considering the market for pollution. Both panels in Figure 6.7 show the demand curve for the right to pollute. This curve shows that the lower the price of polluting, the more firms will choose to pollute. In

FIGURE 6.7

The Equivalence of Pigovian Taxes and Pollution Permits

In panel (a) the government sets a price on pollution by levying a Pigovian tax, and the demand curve determines the quantity of pollution. In panel (b) the government limits the quantity of pollution by limiting the number of pollution permits, and the demand curve determines the price of pollution. The price and quantity of pollution are the same in the two cases.

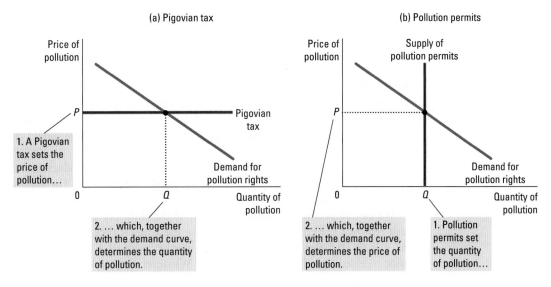

panel (a) the government uses a Pigovian tax to set a price for pollution. In this case, the supply curve for pollution rights is perfectly elastic (because firms can pollute as much as they want by paying the tax), and the position of the demand curve determines the quantity of pollution. In panel (b) the government sets a quantity of pollution by issuing pollution permits. In this case, the supply curve for pollution rights is perfectly inelastic (because the quantity of pollution is fixed by the number of permits), and the position of the demand curve determines the price of pollution. Hence, for any given demand curve for pollution, the government can achieve any point on the demand curve either by setting a price with a Pigovian tax or by setting a quantity with pollution permits.

In some circumstances, however, selling pollution permits may be better than levying a Pigovian tax. Suppose the government wants no more than 600 tonnes of effluent to be dumped into the river. But, because the government does not know the demand curve for pollution, it is not sure what size tax would achieve that goal. In this case, it can simply auction off 600 pollution permits. The auction price would yield the appropriate size of the Pigovian tax.

The idea of the government auctioning off the right to pollute may at first sound like a figment of some economist's imagination. And, in fact, that is how the idea began. But a number of governments around the world have used such a system as a way to control pollution. In 2002, European Union environment ministers unanimously agreed to set up a market to trade pollution permits for carbon dioxide (CO_2), the main so-called greenhouse gas of concern. Pollution permits, like Pigovian taxes, are increasingly being viewed as a cost-effective way to keep the environment clean.

A Formal Analysis of Taxes and Subsidies

Many governments, whether national or local, use taxes to raise revenue for public projects, such as roads, schools and national defence. Businesses in most countries face considerable tax burdens whether it is administering income tax payments to national revenue services, paying value added or sales taxes, paying taxes on profits, excise duties and other taxes such as religious taxes (in countries like Saudi Arabia and Germany, for example) or taxes related to employment referred to as payroll taxes. In some cases, firms can pass on some of the burden of these taxes to consumers.

tax incidence the manner in which the burden of a tax is shared among participants in a market

Economists use the term **tax incidence** to refer to the distribution of a tax burden. We can analyse the incidence of tax by using the tools of supply and demand.

How Taxes on Sellers Affect Market Outcomes

Consider a tax levied on sellers of a good. Suppose the government imposes a tax on sellers of nail varnish remover of €0.50 per bottle. What are the effects of this tax? We can analyse the effect using three steps.

Step One   The immediate impact of the tax is on the sellers of nail varnish remover. The quantity of nail varnish remover demanded at any given price is the same; thus, the demand curve does not change. By contrast, the tax on sellers makes the nail varnish remover business less profitable at any given price, so it shifts the supply curve.

Step Two   Because the tax on sellers raises the cost of producing and selling nail varnish remover, it reduces the quantity supplied at every price. The supply curve shifts to the left (or, equivalently, upward).

We can be precise about the magnitude of the shift. For any market price of nail varnish remover, the effective price to sellers – the amount they get to keep after paying the tax – is €0.50 lower. For example, if the market price of a bottle is €2.00, the effective price received by sellers would be €1.50. Whatever the market price, sellers will supply

FIGURE 6.8

A Tax on Sellers

When a tax of €0.50 is levied on sellers, the supply curve shifts up by €0.50 from S_1 to S_2. The equilibrium quantity falls from 100 to 90 bottles. The price that buyers pay rises from €3.00 to €3.30. The price that sellers receive (after paying the tax) falls from €3.00 to €2.80. Even though the tax is levied on sellers, buyers and sellers share the burden of the tax.

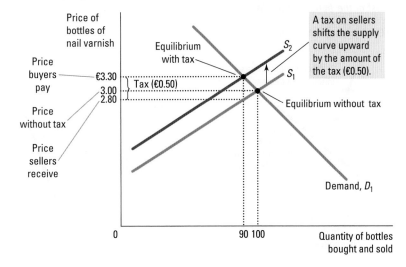

a quantity of nail varnish remover as if the price were €0.50 lower than it is. Put differently, to induce sellers to supply any given quantity, the market price must now be €0.50 higher to compensate for the effect of the tax. Thus, as shown in Figure 6.8, the supply curve shifts *upward* from S_1 to S_2 by exactly the size of the tax (€0.50).

Step Three   Having determined how the supply curve shifts, we can now compare the initial and the new equilibrium. The figure shows that the equilibrium price of nail varnish remover rises from €3.00 to €3.30, and the equilibrium quantity falls from 100 to 90 bottles. The tax reduces the size of the nail varnish remover market and buyers and sellers share the burden of the tax. Because the market price rises, buyers pay €0.30 more for each bottle of nail varnish remover than they did before the tax was enacted. Sellers receive a higher price than they did without the tax, but the effective price (after paying the tax) falls from €3.00 to €2.80.

Implications   A tax on sellers places a wedge between the price that buyers pay and the price that sellers receive. The wedge between the buyers' price and the sellers' price is the same, and would be the same regardless of whether the tax is levied on buyers or sellers. In reality most governments levy taxes on sellers rather than on buyers, however. The wedge shifts the relative position of the supply and demand curves. In the new equilibrium, buyers and sellers share the burden of the tax.

Elasticity and Tax Incidence

When a good is taxed, buyers and sellers of the good share the burden of the tax. But how exactly is the tax burden divided? Only rarely will it be shared equally. To see how the burden is divided, consider the impact of taxation in the two markets in Figure 6.9. In both cases, the figure shows the initial demand curve, the initial supply curve, and a tax that drives a wedge between the amount paid by buyers and the amount received by sellers. The difference in the two panels is the relative elasticity of supply and demand. Panel (a) of Figure 6.9 shows a tax in a market with very elastic supply and relatively

FIGURE 6.9

How the Burden of a Tax is Divided

In panel (a), the supply curve is elastic and the demand curve is inelastic. In this case, the price received by sellers falls only slightly, while the price paid by buyers rises substantially. Thus, buyers bear most of the burden of the tax. In panel (b), the supply curve is inelastic and the demand curve is elastic. In this case, the price received by sellers falls substantially, while the price paid by buyers rises only slightly. Thus, sellers bear most of the burden of the tax.

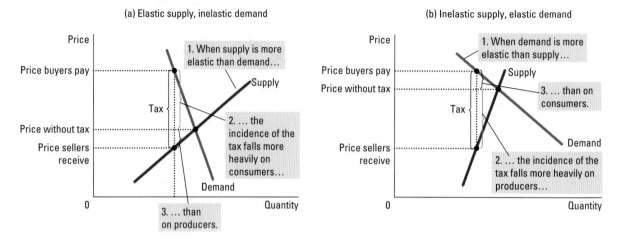

inelastic demand. That is, sellers are very responsive to changes in the price of the good (so the supply curve is relatively flat), whereas buyers are not very responsive (so the demand curve is relatively steep). When a tax is imposed on a market with these elasticities, the price received by sellers does not fall much, so sellers bear only a small burden. By contrast, the price paid by buyers rises substantially, indicating that buyers bear most of the burden of the tax. If the price elasticity of demand is low (represented in Panel (a) by a steep curve) then demand will fall proportionately less in response to a rise in price – buyers are not very price sensitive. The seller can shift the burden of the tax onto the buyer, safe in the knowledge that demand will only fall by a relatively small amount.

Panel (b) of Figure 6.9 shows a tax in a market with relatively inelastic supply and very elastic demand (represented by a flatter curve). In this case, sellers are not very responsive to changes in the price (so the supply curve is steeper), while buyers are very responsive. The figure shows that when a tax is imposed, the price paid by buyers does not rise much, while the price received by sellers falls substantially. Thus, sellers bear most of the burden of the tax. In this case, sellers know that if they try to pass on the tax to buyers that demand will fall by a relatively large amount.

The two panels of Figure 6.9 show a general lesson about how the burden of a tax is divided: a tax burden falls more heavily on the side of the market that is less elastic. Why is this true? In essence, the elasticity measures the willingness of buyers or sellers to leave the market when conditions become unfavourable. A small elasticity of demand means that buyers do not have good alternatives to consuming this particular good. A small elasticity of supply means that sellers do not have good alternatives to producing this particular good. When the good is taxed, the side of the market with fewer good alternatives cannot easily leave the market and must, therefore, bear more of the burden of the tax.

> **Quick Quiz** In a supply and demand diagram, show how a tax on car sellers of €1000 per car affects the quantity of cars sold and the price of cars. In your diagram, show the change in the price paid by car buyers and the change in price received by car sellers.

How Subsidies Affect Market Outcomes

A **subsidy** is the opposite of a tax. Subsidies are levied when governments want to encourage the consumption of a good which they deem is currently underproduced. Subsidies are generally given to sellers and have the effect of reducing the cost of production, as opposed to a tax which increases the cost of production. Subsidies exist in a variety of different areas including education, transport, agriculture, regional development, housing and employment.

Subsidies in education help to make the cost of attending college or higher education lower than it would otherwise be. Most European countries provide subsidies for transport systems and the common agricultural policy oversees subsidies to farmers. In Switzerland some €2.5 billion is spent on subsidies for rail transport, in Germany the figure is nearer to €9 billion, whilst in the UK subsidies account for around €3 billion and in France €6.8 billion.

Figure 6.10 shows how a subsidy works using the rail system as an example. In the absence of a subsidy the equilibrium number of journeys bought and sold is Q_e and the equilibrium train ticket for each journey is price P_e. We again use a three-step approach to analyse the effect.

subsidy a payment to buyers and sellers to supplement income or lower costs and which thus encourages consumption or provides an advantage to the recipient

Step One If the government gives a subsidy of €20 per journey to train operators, it is the supply curve for journeys which is affected; the demand curve is not affected because the number of train journeys demanded at each price stays the same. The subsidy to train operators reduces the cost of providing a train journey and so the supply curve will shift.

Step Two Because the subsidy reduces the cost to the train operators, the supply curve shifts to the right by the amount of the subsidy. If the cost of providing a train journey was an average of €75 and the subsidy was €20 the supply curve would shift so that train operators would now supply train journeys at an effective cost of €20 below

FIGURE 6.10

A Subsidy on Rail Transport

When a subsidy of €20 per journey is given to sellers, the supply curve shifts to the right by €20 from S_1 to S_2. The equilibrium quantity rises from Q_e to Q_1 journeys per year. The price that buyers pay for a journey falls from €75 to €60. The subsidy results in lower prices for passengers and an increased number of journeys available. Even though the subsidy is given to sellers, buyers and sellers share the benefits of the subsidy.

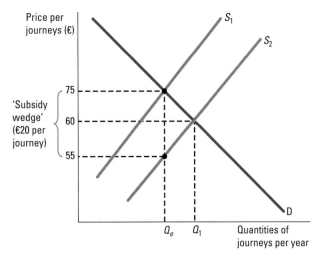

the previous cost. They would now be willing to supply more train journeys at every price.

Step Three   Comparing the initial and the new equilibrium we can see that the equilibrium price of each train journey is now lower at €60 and the equilibrium number of journeys travelled increases to Q_1. Passengers and train operators both benefit from the subsidy as passengers can obtain train tickets at a lower price than before the subsidy and have more journeys available, and sellers receive more revenue than they did before the subsidy allowing them the potential to invest in the service they provide. The precise division of the benefits between buyers and sellers will depend on the relative elasticities of demand and supply.

Implications   There is a considerable debate surrounding the value of subsidies. We have seen from the example how price and quantity can be affected following the imposition of a subsidy. In the case of transport, it may have the effect of altering the incentives for people to travel on the train rather than on the roads, and so have the benefit of reducing congestion on the roads as well as reducing possible pollution that is associated with road use. In the recession of 2008–2009, some countries introduced subsidies to encourage consumers to trade in their old cars for new ones which helped to boost the European motor industry at a time when it was struggling with a downturn in demand. There are also costs associated with subsidies; for one thing someone has to finance the subsidy and it is often the taxpayer. Subsidies may also encourage firms to overproduce which has a wider effect on the market. Subsidies on commodities such as cotton, bananas and sugar distort the workings of the market and change global comparative advantage. Overproduction leads to excess supply on world markets and drives down prices, as well as diverting trade to rich countries who can support producers through subsidies at the expense of poor countries, whose producers cannot compete because prices are lower than the free market price.

> **?**   **what if...** A government imposed a subsidy on a good with a highly inelastic demand curve but a very elastic supply curve. What do you think would be the effects in both the short term and the long term for consumers and businesses in this market?

Property Rights

In some cases, private solutions to externalities can occur but need some form of legal back-up to be able to work. One such example is the establishment of property rights. In order for any economy to work efficiently, a system of property rights has to be established and understood. This is not as easy as it sounds, however. **Property rights** grant the exclusive right of an individual, group or organization to determine how a resource is used. The basic theory is this. If you decided to throw a brick through the window of my house I would be well within my rights to expect legal redress. The reason is that you have caused damage to my property and provided I can prove it was you who caused the damage and that I am the legal owner of the house, I can expect compensation, under the law, to put right the damage. This may include replacing the window pane and for any emotional trauma I have experienced.

With things such as rivers, streams, land and air it is less easy to establish who the legal owners are. If some system could be devised whereby the ownership of property could be established, then those that cause damage to that property can be brought to book! Extending property rights, therefore, might be one area where externalities can be internalized. For example, if property rights over the air that we breathe can be extended, then any firm polluting that air (in whatever way, noise, smell, smoke, etc.) could face

property rights the exclusive right of an individual, group or organization to determine how a resource is used

prosecution for doing so. The threat of prosecution is sufficient to act as an incentive to find ways of not polluting the air.

Extension of property rights also means that the owner of the property (which can be intellectual as well as physical) can also exercise the right to sell or share that property if they so wish at some mutually agreeable price. Extending property rights allows individuals, groups and organizations to be able to arrive at efficient solutions. If, for example, an individual was assigned property rights for the air 1 km above their property, then if a nearby factory wanted to pollute that air they would have to enter into negotiations with the house owner to do so at some mutually agreeable price. The resulting right to pollute could also be sold to another party. A more developed system of property rights can, therefore, improve well-being and it has been identified as playing a crucial role in good governance, particularly relevant for developing countries to be able to attract the sort of inward investment that will help their economies to grow.

Extending property rights – if households were given the rights to the air above and around their homes any violation of that air could be subject to legal claims.

There are problems with extending property rights, however. How do we apportion rights to such things as air, the seas, rivers and land? The cost of establishing property rights and getting international agreement on what they entail is considerable, and may counteract the social benefits they might provide. If property rights were extended to the volume of air 1 km above a person's property, imagine the complexity of the negotiations that would have to be carried out with any business nearby, or airlines and the military for the right to share that air! Property owners may also have insufficient knowledge about their rights and exactly what they mean; it is also not a costless exercise to prove that property rights have been violated.

In the music and movie industry the complexities of property rights have been the subject of debate and countless lawsuits in recent years. It not only relates to the issues of file sharing, pirating, copying CDs and DVDs for personal use and downloading, but also to the artists/actors themselves and the rights to the music that they have written and performed and the performances they have given on stage and screen. Similar issues are also being experienced in the publishing industry as digital technologies mean the traditional printed book is under some pressure and pirating becomes a growing problem.

Intellectual property law is an incredibly complex area and different countries interpret property rights in different ways, making any international agreement even more difficult. Despite the complexities, there have been efforts to extend property rights to help bring social benefits. In many parts of Europe, property rights over public spaces such as national parks, rivers and seas have meant that environmental laws can be established and enforced and this has led to an improvement in well-being for millions who are able to use these spaces, enjoy cleaner rivers and exploit the resources of the sea.

Objections to the Economic Analysis of Pollution

Some environmentalists argue that it is in some sense morally wrong to allow anyone to pollute the environment in return for paying a fee. Clean air and clean water, they argue, are fundamental human rights that should not be debased by considering them in economic terms. How can you put a price on clean air and clean water? The environment is so important, they claim, that we should protect it as much as possible, regardless of the cost.

Economists have little sympathy with this type of argument. To economists, good environmental policy begins by acknowledging the first of the *Ten Principles of Economics* in Chapter 1: people face trade-offs. Certainly, clean air and clean water have value. But their value must be compared to their opportunity cost – that is, to what one must give up to obtain them. Eliminating all pollution is impossible. Trying to eliminate all pollution would reverse many of the technological advances that allow us to enjoy a high standard of living. Few people would be willing to accept poor nutrition, inadequate medical care or shoddy housing to make the environment as clean as possible.

Economists argue that some environmental activists hurt their own cause by not thinking in economic terms. A clean environment is a good like other goods. Like all normal goods, it has a positive income elasticity: rich countries can afford a cleaner environment than poor ones and, therefore, usually have more rigorous environmental protection. In addition, like most other goods, clean air and water obey the law of demand: the lower the price of environmental protection, the more the public will want. The economic approach of using pollution permits and Pigovian taxes reduces the cost of environmental protection and should, therefore, increase the public's demand for a clean environment.

Quick Quiz A glue factory and a steel mill emit smoke containing a chemical that is harmful if inhaled in large amounts. Describe three ways the town government might respond to this externality. What are the pros and cons of each of your solutions?

Social and Ethical Responsibility

Many firms complain about government interference in business and about the taxes they have to pay. Some will also argue that the subsidy system is fundamentally flawed because it is unfair (usually the ones who are most vociferous in this condemnation of subsidies are the ones who do not receive any). There is an argument that government could reduce its involvement in markets if firms behaved more responsibly. Unfortunately, firms do not always behave responsibly (even if we were able to accurately define what the term 'responsible' meant in this context).

Social responsibility refers to the responsibility a firm has for the impact of their product and activities on society. **Ethical responsibilities** refer to the moral basis for business activity and whether what the business does is 'right' and is underpinned by some moral purpose – doing what is 'right'.

The problem arises when asking 'doing what is right for whom?' A private sector firm is primarily responsible to its shareholders – the owners of the business – who in turn

social responsibility the responsibility a firm has for the impact of their product and activities on society

ethical responsibility the moral basis for business activity and whether what the business does 'is right' and is underpinned by some moral purpose – doing what is 'right'

will wish to see the firm grow, expanding sales and profits. In so doing there may be a conflict with the responsibility a firm has to the health and welfare of its customers. Drug companies have a responsibility to develop new products, market them and generate profits for their shareholders. In so doing to what extent should they compromise the health and safety of those who consume their products?

Many businesses will claim to have a socially responsible code of practice that they adhere to as well as an ethical stance to their activities but such claims are sometimes refuted and criticized by opponents. It is all very well claiming to have no artificial colouring and preservative in food products, for example, but this might be disingenuous at the very least if the product is high in salt and sugars which can contribute to obesity, heart disease and high blood pressure if consumed in too high a quantity.

Part of the policy response by governments could be passing legislation that forces businesses to give clearer information on packaging to help consumers make more informed choices about what they buy. Such legislation would impose additional costs on businesses and ultimately would put up the price of the product to the consumer and thus reduce consumer surplus. Are consumers willing to pay such a price for the extra information? If firms do engage in activities that increase levels of responsibility and ethical standards, this comes at a cost. Many European consumers enjoy low prices for clothing whilst some firms in the Middle East who manufacture these products receive very low prices for their efforts. Would consumers in Europe be willing to pay higher prices for their clothes in order that Middle East manufacturers get higher prices and so can improve wages and conditions for employees? It is not at all clear that such a philanthropic approach would be embraced by consumers.

The issues therefore are complex and open, as with so many in business economics, to subjective interpretation. The solution may be to try to arrive at some form of balance between the rights of people to choose their own lifestyle, be informed about the consequences of that lifestyle and to be protected from the unknown by the government. Where that balance lies though is not at all clear.

Child labour – an inexcusable affront to human rights or part of the process of economic development and an opportunity for growth? Social and ethical responsibility is a very challenging area with no easy answers. For people in the developed world, child labour might seem like an abomination but do people in the less developed world see things the same way?

CONCLUSION

The invisible hand is powerful but not omnipotent. A market's equilibrium maximizes the sum of producer and consumer surplus. When the buyers and sellers in the market are the only interested parties, this outcome is efficient from the standpoint of society as a whole. But when there are external effects, such as pollution, evaluating a market outcome requires taking into account the well-being of third parties as well. In this case, the invisible hand of the marketplace may fail to allocate resources efficiently.

Because of the problem of externalities, the government often steps in to try to rectify market failure. When government does intervene in the market, firms are affected either because they have to pay taxes, receive subsidies or through the regulations that are imposed. These interventions invariably impose costs on businesses and in many countries there are complaints from business representatives of the burden of taxes and regulation.

Society as a whole has to make a judgement about the extent to which such government interference confers benefits on society as a whole which are greater than the costs of that intervention. It can be argued that firms should take more responsibility for their actions but getting agreement on what that responsibility should be and whether consumers are prepared to pay for increased social and ethical responsibility in the form of higher prices will always be difficult.

Yet, even now, society should not abandon market forces entirely. Rather, the government can address the problem by requiring decision makers to bear the full costs of their actions. Pigovian taxes on emissions and pollution permits, for instance, are designed to internalize the externality of pollution. Increasingly, they are being seen as effective policies for those interested in protecting the environment. Market forces, properly redirected, are often the best remedy for market failure.

IN THE NEWS

The increasing concern over levels of global carbon emissions has prompted governments around the world to look at so-called 'cap and trade' schemes. Such a scheme imposes limits on the amount of carbon emissions but allows firms to trade surpluses to firms who are not able to meet the limits. Carbon credits are tradable financial instruments measured in tonnes of carbon dioxide equivalent. Markets to trade carbon emission permits have been developed in Europe and countries like China are being encouraged to embrace such ideas in order to arrest the growth of global emissions.

Carbon Trading Permits

European companies have thrown a large number of Chinese emissions reduction projects into doubt by refusing to pay the pre-agreed price following a market plunge, industry insiders said. About half of the Chinese Carbon Development Mechanism (CDM) projects are being renegotiated or terminated, according to estimates. No official figures are available.

China is the world's biggest carbon credit supplier. EU companies agreed to buy most of the credits to help them meet caps under the EU emissions trading scheme. Industrialized countries can buy carbon credits from developing countries under the United Nations Carbon Development Mechanism. The carbon credits help developed nations meet their own emissions targets. By January 2012 the UN had issued 484 million carbon

credits to Chinese CDM projects. Most involved hydro and wind power projects.

However, the international market in carbon credits has plunged and defaults by European firms have surged, said Tang Renhu, general manager of Sino Carbon Innovation and Investment Co.

Many projects are being renegotiated, he said. 'Buyers and sellers were in the same boat when the carbon market was up', but the declining market has changed that, Tang said. Risks facing Chinese sellers grew as the price of carbon credits fell from €25 ($33) a few years ago to record lows of around €4. The average agreed price was around €10, industry insiders said.

'The buyers are looking for loopholes and are trying to terminate or renegotiate agreements,' said an executive of a state-owned CDM developer under condition of anonymity. A CDM consulting company has about 30 projects in its portfolio and about half are being renegotiated, a company source said. 'Obviously buyers want to renegotiate the prices to help them offset the downside risks in the carbon market,' said another developer, who declined to be named. The developer is facing renegotiation and default on two of his wind power projects.

Wind and small hydropower projects are dependent on emissions reduction revenues that make up 20 per cent of their income, Tang said. Investor confidence has been shaken. But not all CDM developers are experiencing turbulence. Judy Fan, manager of the Beijing Tianqing Power International CDM Consulting Co, said most of the projects conducted by the company were performing smoothly. 'Fortunately most of our

customers are big power companies or financial institutions, are financially strong and respect the spirit of the contract, she said.

Tianqing is one of the biggest CDM consulting companies in China with more than 200 projects in its portfolio. But some companies did ask to renegotiate prices in 2012, she added. Zhou Yacheng, a lawyer with Zhong Lun Law Firm, said some Chinese companies failed to pay due diligence when signing the contracts and did not involve a lawyer. The market is expected to rebound in two years. Carbon credits were one of the worst performing commodities in 2011 with prices plunging by about 70 per cent.

Yang Fuqiang, a senior adviser on climate and energy policy with the Natural Resources Defense Council, a New York-based environmental group, said it's time for Chinese companies to transfer their focus from the slumping international carbon market to the domestic market. China is set to unveil plans to impose controls on total energy consumption and that is closely linked to the country's greenhouse gas caps.

China has approved five cities and two provinces to launch carbon emissions trading markets on a pilot basis, probably in 2013. The National Development and Reform Commission

requested that the cities and provinces, including Beijing, Tianjin and Shanghai, set overall emissions control targets and establish a system for carbon trading. 'The European market faces increasing challenges due to sluggish economic growth and uncertainties in the international climate change negotiations,' Yang said.

Questions

1. Explain how a market for carbon credits aims to reduce the overall level of carbon emissions in nations who operate such a system.
2. Outline the key factors in a cap and trade scheme which are necessary to bring about desired reductions in carbon emissions.
3. Why might the price of carbon credits have fallen so far in recent months (use basic supply and demand analysis to help you answer this question).
4. Why might wind and small hydropower products be 'dependent' on emissions reductions revenues?
5. Evaluate the importance of overall emissions control targets to the successful creation of a carbon trading market in China.

Source: http://www.chinadaily.com.cn/china/ 2012-02/09/content_14564340.htm

SUMMARY

- Market failure occurs when resources are not allocated efficiently.
- Typically, market failure occurs because of a lack of perfect information between firms and buyers, because of some element of monopoly power.
- When a transaction between a buyer and seller directly affects a third party, the effect is called an externality. Negative externalities, such as pollution, cause the socially optimal quantity in a market to be less than the equilibrium quantity. Positive externalities, such as technology spillovers,

cause the socially optimal quantity to be greater than the equilibrium quantity.

- Those affected by externalities can sometimes solve the problem privately. For instance, when one business confers an externality on another business, the two businesses can internalize the externality by merging.
- When private parties cannot adequately deal with external effects, such as pollution, the government often steps in. Sometimes the government prevents socially inefficient activity by regulating behaviour. At other times it internalizes

an externality using Pigovian taxes. Another public policy is to issue permits. For instance, the government could protect the environment by issuing a limited number of pollution permits. The end result of this policy is largely the same as imposing Pigovian taxes on polluters.

KEY CONCEPTS

willingness to pay, p. 125
consumer surplus, p. 125
producer surplus, p. 127
deadweight loss, p. 128

internalizing an externality, p. 131
pigovian taxes, p. 135
tax incidence, p. 138
subsidy, p. 141

property rights, p. 142
social responsibility, p. 144
ethical responsibilities, p. 144

QUESTIONS FOR REVIEW

1. Identify, using examples, three sources of market failure.

2. Using an appropriate example, explain the difference between a private cost and a social cost and a private benefit and a social benefit.

3. Give an example of a negative externality and an example of a positive externality.

4. Use a supply-and-demand diagram to explain the effect of a negative externality in production.

5. In a supply-and-demand diagram, show producer and consumer surplus in the market equilibrium.

6. In what way does the patent system help society solve an externality problem?

7. List some of the ways that the problems caused by externalities can be solved without government intervention.

8. How does a tax imposed on a good with a high price elasticity of demand affect the market equilibrium? Who bears most of the burden of the tax in this instance?

9. How does a subsidy on a good affect the price paid by buyers, the price received by sellers and the quantity bought and sold?

10. What are Pigovian taxes? Why do economists prefer them over regulations as a way to protect the environment from pollution?

PROBLEMS AND APPLICATIONS

1. Do you agree with the following statements? Why or why not?

   a. 'The benefits of Pigovian taxes as a way to reduce pollution have to be weighed against the deadweight losses that these taxes cause.'

   b. 'When deciding whether to levy a Pigovian tax on consumers or producers, the government should be careful to levy the tax on the side of the market generating the externality.'

2. Consider the market for fire extinguishers.

   a. Why might fire extinguishers exhibit positive externalities?

   b. Draw a graph of the market for fire extinguishers, labelling the demand curve, the social value curve, the supply curve and the social cost curve.

   c. Indicate the market equilibrium level of output and the efficient level of output. Give an intuitive explanation for why these quantities differ.

   d. If the external benefit is €10 per extinguisher, describe a government policy that would result in the efficient outcome.

3. The cost of producing DVD players has fallen over the past few years. Let's consider some implications of this fact.

   a. Use a supply-and-demand diagram to show the effect of falling production costs on the price and quantity of DVD players sold.

   b. In your diagram, show what happens to consumer surplus and producer surplus.

   c. Suppose the supply of DVD players is very elastic. Who benefits most from falling production costs – consumers or producers of DVD players?

4. The government decides to reduce air pollution by reducing the use of petrol. It imposes €0.50 tax for each litre of petrol sold.

   a. Should it impose this tax on petrol companies or motorists? Explain carefully, using a supply-and-demand diagram.

   b. If the demand for petrol were more elastic, would this tax be more effective or less effective in reducing the quantity of petrol consumed? Explain with both words and a diagram.

   c. Are consumers of petrol helped or hurt by this tax? Why?

   d. Are workers in the oil industry helped or hurt by this tax? Why?

5. Assume that it is rumoured that the Swiss government subsidizes cattle farming, and that the subsidy is larger in

Chapter 6 Market Failure **149**

areas with more tourist attractions. Can you think of a reason why this policy might be efficient?

6. Many observers believe that the levels of pollution in our economy are too high.

   a. If society wishes to reduce overall pollution by a certain amount, why is it efficient to have different amounts of reduction at different firms?

   b. Command-and-control approaches often rely on uniform reductions among firms. Why are these approaches generally unable to target the firms that should undertake bigger reductions?

   c. Economists argue that appropriate Pigovian taxes or tradable pollution rights will result in efficient pollution reduction. How do these approaches target the firms that should undertake bigger reductions?

7. The Pristine River (or the 'Blue Pristine', as it is affectionately known) has two polluting firms on its banks. European Industrial and Creative Chemicals each dump 100 tonnes of effluent into the river each year. The cost of reducing effluent emissions per tonne equals €10 for European Industrial and €100 for Creative. The government wants to reduce overall pollution from 200 tonnes to 50 tonnes per year.

   a. If the government knew the cost of reduction for each firm, what reductions would it impose to reach its overall goal? What would be the cost to each firm and the total cost to the firms together?

   b. In a more typical situation, the government would not know the cost of pollution reduction at each firm. If the government decided to reach its overall goal by imposing uniform reductions on the firms, calculate the reduc-

tion made by each firm, the cost to each firm and the total cost to the firms together.

   c. Compare the total cost of pollution reduction in parts (a) and (b). If the government does not know the cost of reduction for each firm, is there still some way for it to reduce pollution to 50 tonnes at the total cost you calculated in part (a)? Explain.

8. 'A fine is a tax for doing something wrong. A tax is a fine for doing something right.' Discuss.

9. Some people object to market-based policies to reduce pollution, claiming that they place a monetary value on cleaning our air and water. Economists reply that society implicitly places a monetary value on environmental clean-up even under command-and-control policies. Discuss why this is true.

10. (This problem is challenging) There are three industrial firms in Eurovia.

Firm	Initial pollution level	Cost of reducing pollution by 1 unit
A	70 units	€20
B	80	25
C	50	10

The government wants to reduce pollution to 120 units, it gives each firm 40 tradable pollution permits.

   a. Who sells permits and how many do they sell? Who buys permits and how many do they buy? Briefly explain why the sellers and buyers are each willing to do so. What is the total cost of pollution reduction in this situation?

   b. How much higher would the costs of pollution reduction be if the permits could not be traded?

7 THE CONSUMER AND CONSUMER BEHAVIOUR

LEARNING OBJECTIVES

In this chapter you will:

- Cover the assumptions of the standard economic model
- Look at the concepts of value and utility
- See how a budget constraint represents the choices a consumer can afford
- Learn how indifference curves can be used to represent a consumer's preferences
- See how a consumer responds to changes in income and changes in prices
- Decompose the impact of a price change into an income effect and a substitution effect
- Look at the idea of using heuristics as the basis for consumer behaviour
- Learn about market solutions to asymmetric information

After reading this chapter you should be able to:

- Analyse how a consumer's optimal choices are determined
- See how firms use advertising and branding to influence consumer behaviour and the arguments for and against advertising
- Examine the problems caused by asymmetric information
- State the assumptions of the standard economic model
- Calculate total and marginal utility as consumption increases
- Draw a budget constraint on a graph if you are given the value of income and the prices of the goods
- Explain the relationship between the relative prices and the marginal rate of substitution between two goods at the consumer's optimum

- Shift the budget constraint when the price of a good increases

- Demonstrate the income and substitution effect on a graph using indifference curves and budget constraints

- Describe different heuristics and be able to give examples of each

- Present an argument for and against advertising

- Explain how signalling and screening help to reduce asymmetric information

INTRODUCTION

In previous chapters we have looked in detail at the behaviour of firms. Business activity requires a producer and a consumer – businesses cannot survive without some individual, group or other business buying their output. It makes sense, therefore, for businesses to have an understanding of how consumers think and behave. How do consumers make decisions about purchases? What makes a consumer choose one product repeatedly over the many others that are available? How are they influenced by advertising (if at all) and how important are brands in influencing consumer behaviour? We are going to look at all of these issues in this chapter.

First of we all are going to present a classical theory of consumer behaviour based on an assumption of rational behaviour which is referred to as the *standard economic model*. The model presented can explain some consumer behaviour in some situations but as with all models it has its limitations. Over the last 30 years more research has been done into how consumers make purchasing decisions and the existence of technology such as functional magnetic resonance imaging (fMRI) and positive emission tomography (PET) have allowed researchers to analyse how the brain responds to different stimuli and what parts of the brain become active when purchasing decisions are made or when individuals are exposed to stimuli such as advertising.

This research along with that of psychologists and anthropologists amongst other disciplines has led to the development of different, sometimes competing, sometimes complementary theories of consumer behaviour. We are going to look at some of these theories.

We are then going to look at advertising and branding and how businesses can use these to influence consumer behaviour and the extent to which they are successful. In looking at these areas we need to recognize that consumers are not homogenous – it is easy to forget this sometimes. Consumers come in many forms – some are individuals, some are large organizations such as other businesses, government or its agents, and some are small businesses. These are not all going to behave the same and so an understanding of those upon whom you rely is going to be of some importance in a successful business.

The Standard Economic Model

When you walk into a shop, you are invariably confronted with a wide range of goods. Most people have limited financial resources and cannot buy everything they want. How are purchasing choices made, therefore?

One assumption might be that you consider the constraint that is your income, the prices of the various goods being offered for sale and the value they represent (more of this shortly) and choose to buy a bundle of goods that, given your resources, best suits your needs and desires and maximizes value. This is a classic constrained optimization problem that forms the basis of many classical economic theories.

We can summarize some key assumptions of the standard economic model which is important to keep in mind when looking at our first model. These assumptions are:

- Buyers (or economic agents as they are sometimes referred to) are rational.
- More is preferred to less.
- Buyers seek to maximize their utility.
- Consumers act in self-interest and do not consider the utility of others.

Value

value the worth to an individual of owning an item represented by the satisfaction derived from its consumption

utility the satisfaction derived from consumption

A key concept in consumer behaviour is value. Value is a subjective term – what one person or business thinks represents value is often different to that of some other individual or business. **Value** can be seen as the worth to an individual of owning an item represented by the satisfaction derived from its consumption. Classical economists used the term **utility** to refer to the satisfaction derived from consumption. Utility is an ordinal concept; we can use some measure of utility to represent consumer choices in some order but that order tells us nothing about the differences in the values we use. For example, if a group of five people were asked to rank different brands of cola in order of preference using a 10-point scale (with each point referred to as a *util)* we might be able to conclude that brand X was the most popular, followed by brand Y and brand Z. If person 1 ranked brand X at 10 utils whilst person 2 ranked the same brand as a 5 utils we cannot say that person 1 values brand X twice as much as person 2, only that they place it higher in their preferences.

One way in which we can measure value is the amount consumers are prepared to pay. It is highly likely that at some point in your life you will have said something like 'I wouldn't have that if you paid me' or similar. How much of our limited income we are prepared to pay is a reflection of the value we put on acquiring a good. It might not tell us much about the satisfaction from actually consuming the good (the buyer might not be the final consumer) but it does give some idea of value. For example, two friends, Alexa and Monique are in a store looking at DVDs of the latest movie releases. Alexa picks up a copy of *The Artist* priced at €16.99. Monique looks at her friend and asks why on earth she is thinking of buying it? No way would Monique pay that sort of money for such a 'rubbish film'. A discussion ensues about the film; clearly there is a difference of opinion on the quality of the film and thus how much it is 'worth' to own a copy on DVD. If Alexa buys the DVD, then the value to her must be at least €16.99 because that is what she has to give up in money terms in order to acquire it. It may be, as we saw in Chapter 6 that Alexa would have been prepared to pay much more for the DVD in which case she is getting consumer surplus. Monique leaves the store baffled at her friend's purchasing decision. Monique clearly feels that giving up €16.99 to buy that particular DVD was a 'waste of money'.

The amount buyers are prepared to pay for a good, therefore, tells us something about the value they place on it. It is not just the amount of money we hand over that reflects value but what that amount of money could have bought. This highlights one of the *Ten Principles of Economics* – the cost of something is what you have to give up to get it – the opportunity cost. We could make a reasonable assumption that Monique believed there was a way in which she could allocate €16.99 to get more value – in other words, the alternative that €16.99 could buy (whatever that might be) represented greater value than acquiring a copy of *The Artist* on DVD.

Total and Marginal Utility

Given that utility can be used as a word to represent satisfaction derived from consumption we can look at what happens to utility as consumption increases. Given our assumption that consumers prefer more to less, intuition might tell us that total utility increases as consumption increases. This may be true up to a point. To understand this let us use an example.

You have spent two hours in the gym working very hard. You are hot, sweaty and very thirsty. After your shower you go to the nearest café and order a glass of orange juice. If you were asked to rate the satisfaction derived from consuming the orange juice out of 10 (utils) at that time you might rate it at 10. You order a second glass as you are still thirsty; the second glass still brings some satisfaction but if asked to rate it you might give it 8. Total utility is now 18 utils – the second glass has increased total utility. However, you did not rate the second glass quite as high as the first because some of your thirst has been quenched. **Marginal utility** measures the addition to total utility as a result of the consumption of an extra unit. The marginal utility of the first glass was 10 but for the second glass the marginal utility was 8.

marginal utility the addition to total utility as a result of one extra unit of consumption

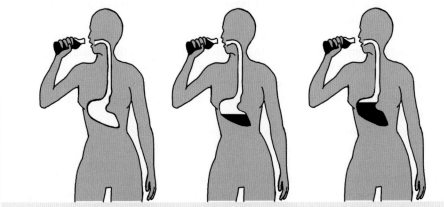

As more drink is consumed, the total utility increases but at a diminishing rate until one extra drink might actually confer negative marginal utility!

If you now ordered a third glass you might rate this at 5. Total utility is now 23 but the marginal utility of the third glass is 5. By the time you get to the fifth or sixth glass the marginal utility is likely to be very low and at some point could even be negative. For example, if you have already had 8 glasses of orange juice your stomach might be telling you that it really does not need another one – having the ninth glass might actually make you physically sick and so the marginal utility of the ninth glass would be negative. It follows that total utility will actually start to decline at this point.

This example illustrates a general principle called the law of **diminishing marginal utility**. This simply states that the more a consumer has of a given commodity the smaller the satisfaction gained from consuming each extra unit. As consumption of a good rises, total utility will rise at first but at a slower rate until some point at which the consumer becomes satiated (has had enough) after which point total utility will fall and marginal utility will be negative.

diminishing marginal utility a 'law' that states that marginal utility will fall as consumption increases

This principle is important in considering the relationship between price and the demand curve. Diminishing marginal utility implies that we value successive units of consumption less than the previous and so it makes sense that consumers are not prepared to pay as much for successive units of consumption. To encourage consumers to buy more, sellers have to reduce prices which partly explains why the demand curve slopes downwards from left to right.

Many firms will be acutely aware that they have rivals competing for consumers and that consumers have a choice. Switching between one good and another is a feature of business. Economists refer to the **marginal rate of substitution** (MRS). The marginal rate of substitution measures how much of one good a consumer requires in order to be compensated for a one-unit reduction in consumption of another good. The marginal rate of substitution between two goods depends on their marginal utilities. For example, if the marginal utility of good X is twice the marginal utility of good Y, then a person would need 2 units of good Y to compensate for losing 1 unit of good X, and the marginal rate of substitution equals 2. More generally, the marginal rate of substitution equals the marginal utility of one good divided by the marginal utility of the other good.

marginal rate of substitution the rate at which a consumer is willing to trade one good for another

What Consumers Can Afford

Most people would like to increase the quantity or quality of the goods they consume – to take longer holidays, drive fancier cars or eat at better restaurants. People consume less than they desire because their spending is *constrained,* or limited, by their income.

To keep things simple, we use a model which examines the decisions facing a consumer who buys only two goods: cola and pizza. Of course, real people buy thousands of different kinds of goods. Yet using this model greatly simplifies the problem without altering the basic insights about consumer choice.

Suppose that the consumer has an income of €1000 per month and that he spends his entire income each month on cola and pizza. The price of a litre of cola is €2 and the price of a pizza is €10.

The table in Figure 7.1 shows some of the many combinations of cola and pizza that the consumer can buy. The first line in the table shows that if the consumer spends all his income on pizza, he can eat 100 pizzas during the month, but he would not be able to buy any cola at all. The second line shows another possible consumption bundle: 90 pizzas and 50 litres of cola. And so on. Each consumption bundle in the table costs exactly €1000.

The graph in Figure 7.1 illustrates the consumption bundles that the consumer can choose. The vertical axis measures the number of litres of cola, and the horizontal axis measures the number of pizzas. Three points are marked on this figure. At point A, the consumer buys no cola and consumes 100 pizzas. At point B, the consumer buys no pizza and consumes 500 litres of cola. At point C, the consumer buys 50 pizzas and 250 litres of cola. Point C, which is exactly at the middle of the line from A to B, is the point at which the consumer spends an equal amount (€500) on cola and pizza. Of course, these are only three of the many combinations of cola and pizza that the consumer can choose. All the points on the line from A to B are possible. This line, called the **budget constraint**, shows the consumption bundles that the consumer can afford. In this case, it shows the trade-off between cola and pizza that the consumer faces.

The slope of the budget constraint measures the rate at which the consumer can trade one good for the other. The slope between two points is calculated as the change in the vertical distance divided by the change in the horizontal distance ('rise over run'). From

budget constraint the limit on the consumption bundles that a consumer can afford

FIGURE 7.1

The Consumer's Budget Constraint

The budget constraint shows the various bundles of goods that the consumer can afford for a given income. Here the consumer buys bundles of cola and pizza. The table and graph show what the consumer can afford if his income is €1000, the price of cola is €2 and the price of pizza is €10.

Litres of cola	Number of pizzas	Spending on cola	Spending on pizza	Total spending
0	100	€0	€1000	€1000
50	90	100	900	1000
100	80	200	800	1000
150	70	300	700	1000
200	60	400	600	1000
250	50	500	500	1000
300	40	600	400	1000
350	30	700	300	1000
400	20	800	200	1000
450	10	900	100	1000
500	0	1000	0	1000

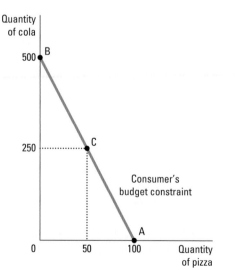

point A to point B, the vertical distance is 500 litres, and the horizontal distance is 100 pizzas. Because the budget constraint slopes downward, the slope is a negative number – this reflects the fact that to get one extra pizza, the consumer has to *reduce* his consumption of cola by five litres. In fact, the slope of the budget constraint (ignoring the minus sign) equals the *relative price* of the two goods – the price of one good compared to the price of the other. A pizza costs 5 times as much as a litre of cola, so the opportunity cost of a pizza is 5 litres of cola. The budget constraint's slope of 5 reflects the trade-off the market is offering the consumer: 1 pizza for 5 litres of cola.

> **Quick Quiz** Draw the budget constraint for a person with income of €1000 if the price of cola is €5 and the price of pizza is €10. What is the slope of this budget constraint?

Preferences – What The Consumer Wants

The consumer's preferences allow him to choose among different bundles of cola and pizza. If you offer the consumer two different bundles, he chooses the bundle that best suits his tastes. If the two bundles suit his tastes equally well, we say that the consumer is *indifferent* between the two bundles.

Just as we have represented the consumer's budget constraint graphically, we can also represent his preferences graphically. We do this with indifference curves. An **indifference curve** shows the bundles of consumption that make the consumer equally happy. In this case, the indifference curves show the combinations of cola and pizza with which the consumer is equally satisfied.

Figure 7.2 shows two of the consumer's many indifference curves. The consumer is indifferent among combinations A, B and C, because they are all on the same curve. Not surprisingly, if the consumer's consumption of pizza is reduced, say from point A to point B, consumption of cola must increase to keep him equally happy. If consumption of pizza is reduced again, from point B to point C, the amount of cola consumed must increase yet again.

indifference curve a curve that shows consumption bundles that give the consumer the same level of satisfaction

FIGURE 7.2

The Consumer's Preferences

The consumer's preferences are represented with indifference curves, which show the combinations of cola and pizza that make the consumer equally satisfied. Because the consumer prefers more of a good, points on a higher indifference curve (I_2 here) are preferred to points on a lower indifference curve (I_1). The marginal rate of substitution (MRS) shows the rate at which the consumer is willing to trade cola for pizza.

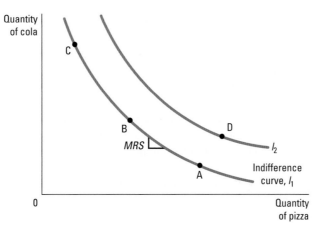

The slope at any point on an indifference curve equals the rate at which the consumer is willing to substitute one good for the other. This is the marginal rate of substitution (MRS). In this case, the marginal rate of substitution measures how much cola the consumer requires in order to be compensated for a one-unit reduction in pizza consumption. Notice that because the indifference curves are not straight lines, the marginal rate of substitution is not the same at all points on a given indifference curve. The rate at which a consumer is willing to trade one good for the other depends on the amounts of the goods he is already consuming. That is, the rate at which a consumer is willing to trade pizza for cola depends on whether he is hungrier or thirstier, which in turn depends on how much pizza and cola he has.

The consumer is equally happy at all points on any given indifference curve, but he prefers some indifference curves to others. We assume that consumers would rather have more of a good than less of it. Because he prefers more consumption to less, higher indifference curves are preferred to lower ones. The idea that buyers can rank preferences from best to worst (or vice versa) is captured by **expected utility theory**. In Figure 7.2, any point on curve I_2 is preferred to any point on curve I_1.

expected utility theory the idea that buyers can rank preferences from best to worst (or vice versa)

A consumer's set of indifference curves gives a complete ranking of the consumer's preferences. That is, we can use the indifference curves to rank any two bundles of goods. For example, the indifference curves tell us that point D is preferred to point A because point D is on a higher indifference curve than point A. (That conclusion may be obvious, however, because point D offers the consumer both more pizza and more cola.) The indifference curves also tell us that point D is preferred to point C because point D is on a higher indifference curve. Even though point D has less cola than point C, it has more than enough extra pizza to make the consumer prefer it. By seeing which point is on the higher indifference curve, we can use the set of indifference curves to rank any combinations of cola and pizza.

> **Pitfall Prevention** Remember that an indifference curve shows bundles of goods which give equal utility so that consumers have no preference between them – they are equally preferred. However, it is assumed that consumers always prefer more to less so would prefer to be on the highest indifference curve possible.

Optimization – What The Consumer Chooses

We have the two pieces necessary to consider the consumer's decision about what to buy. Remembering the assumptions we set out earlier in the chapter, we can state that the consumer would like to end up with the best possible combination of cola and pizza – that is, the combination on the highest possible indifference curve. But the consumer must also end up on or below his budget constraint, which measures the total resources available to him.

Figure 7.3 shows the consumer's budget constraint and three of his many indifference curves. The highest indifference curve that the consumer can reach (I_2 in the figure) is the one that just barely touches the budget constraint. The point at which this indifference curve and the budget constraint touch is called the *optimum*. The consumer would prefer point A, but he cannot afford that point because it lies above his budget constraint. The consumer can afford point B, but that point is on a lower indifference curve and, therefore, provides the consumer less satisfaction. The optimum represents the best combination of consumption of cola and pizza available to the consumer.

Notice that, at the optimum, the slope of the indifference curve equals the slope of the budget constraint. We say that the indifference curve is *tangent* to the budget constraint. The slope of the indifference curve is the marginal rate of substitution between cola and pizza, and the slope of the budget constraint is the relative price of cola and pizza. Thus,

FIGURE 7.3

The Consumer's Optimum

The consumer chooses the point on his budget constraint that lies on the highest indifference curve. At this point, called the optimum, the marginal rate of substitution equals the relative price of the two goods. Here the highest indifference curve the consumer can reach is I_2. The consumer prefers point A, which lies on indifference curve I_3, but the consumer cannot afford this bundle of cola and pizza. In contrast, point B is affordable, but because it lies on a lower indifference curve, the consumer does not prefer it.

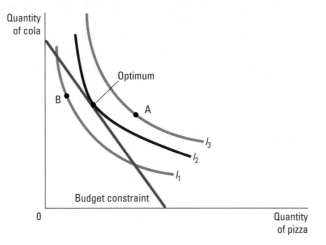

the consumer chooses consumption of the two goods so that the marginal rate of substitution equals the relative price. That is:

$$MRS = P_X/P_Y$$

Because the marginal rate of substitution equals the ratio of marginal utilities, we can write this condition for optimization as:

$$MU_X/MU_Y = P_X/P_Y$$

Now rearrange this expression to become:

$$MU_X/P_X = MU_Y/P_Y$$

This equation has a simple interpretation: at the optimum, the marginal utility per euro spent on good X equals the marginal utility per euro spent on good Y. Why? If this equality did not hold, the consumer could increase utility by changing behaviour, switching spending from the good that provided lower marginal utility per euro and more on the good that provided higher marginal utility per euro. This would be the rational thing to do.

When economists discuss the theory of consumer choice, they might express the theory using different words. One economist might say that the goal of the consumer is to maximize utility. Another economist might say that the goal of the consumer is to end up on the highest possible indifference curve. The first economist would conclude that, at the consumer's optimum, the marginal utility per euro is the same for all goods, whereas the second would conclude that the indifference curve is tangent to the budget constraint. In essence, these are two ways of saying the same thing.

This analysis of consumer choice shows how market prices reflect the marginal value that consumers place on goods. In making his consumption choices, the consumer takes as given the relative price of the two goods and then chooses an optimum at which his marginal rate of substitution equals this relative price. The relative price is the rate at which the *market* is willing to trade one good for the other, whereas the marginal rate of substitution is the rate at which the *consumer* is willing to trade one good for the other. At the consumer's optimum, the consumer's valuation of the two goods (as measured by the marginal rate of substitution) equals the market's valuation (as measured by the relative price). As a result of this consumer optimization, market prices of different goods reflect the value that consumers place on those goods.

How Changes in Income Affect the Consumer's Choices

Now that we have seen how the consumer makes the consumption decision, let's examine how consumption responds to changes in income. To be specific, suppose that income increases. With higher income, the consumer can afford more of both goods. The increase in income, therefore, shifts the budget constraint outward, as in Figure 7.4. Because the relative price of the two goods has not changed, the slope of the new budget constraint is the same as the slope of the initial budget constraint. That is, an increase in income leads to a parallel shift in the budget constraint.

The expanded budget constraint allows the consumer to choose a better combination of cola and pizza. In other words, the consumer can now reach a higher indifference curve. Given the shift in the budget constraint and the consumer's preferences as represented by his indifference curves, the consumer's optimum moves from the point labelled 'initial optimum' to the point labelled 'new optimum'.

Notice that in Figure 7.4 the consumer chooses to consume more cola and more pizza. Although the logic of the model does not require increased consumption of both goods in response to increased income, this situation is the most common one. Remember that if a consumer wants more of a good when his income rises, economists call it a normal good. The indifference curves in Figure 7.4 are drawn under the assumption that both cola and pizza are normal goods.

FIGURE 7.4

An Increase in Income

When the consumer's income rises, the budget constraint shifts out. If both goods are normal goods, the consumer responds to the increase in income by buying more of both of them. Here the consumer buys more pizza and more cola.

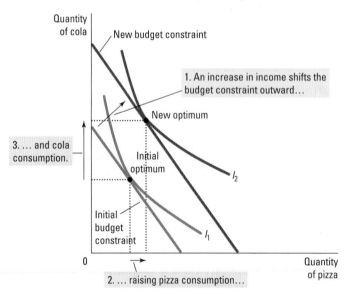

Figure 7.5 shows an example in which an increase in income induces the consumer to buy more pizza but less cola. If a consumer buys less of a good when his income rises, economists call it an inferior good. Figure 7.5 is drawn under the assumption that pizza is a normal good and cola is an inferior good. Although most goods are normal goods, there are some inferior goods in the world. One example is bus rides. High-income consumers are more likely to own cars and less likely to ride the bus than low-income consumers. Bus rides, therefore, are an inferior good.

FIGURE 7.5

An Inferior Good

A good is an inferior good if the consumer buys less of it when his income rises. Here cola is an inferior good: when the consumer's income increases and the budget constraint shifts outward, the consumer buys more pizza but less cola.

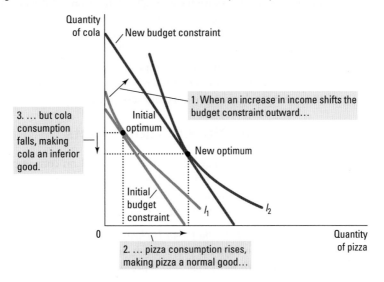

How Changes in Prices Affect the Consumer's Choices

Let's now use this model of consumer choice to consider how a change in the price of one of the goods alters the consumer's choices. Suppose, in particular, that the price of cola falls from €2 to €1 a litre. It is no surprise that the lower price expands the consumer's set of buying opportunities. In other words, a fall in the price of any good causes the budget constraint to pivot. With his available income of €1000 the consumer can now buy twice as many litres of cola than before but the same amount of pizza. Figure 7.6 shows

FIGURE 7.6

A Change in Price

When the price of cola falls, the consumer's budget constraint pivots outward and changes slope. The consumer moves from the initial optimum to the new optimum, which changes his purchases of both cola and pizza. In this case, the quantity of cola consumed rises and the quantity of pizza consumed falls.

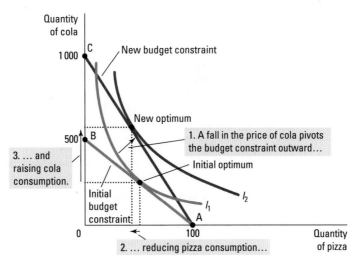

that point A in the figure stays the same (100 pizzas). Yet if the consumer spends his entire income of €1000 on cola, he can now buy 1000 rather than only 500 litres. Thus, the end point of the budget constraint pivots outwards from point B to point C.

Notice that in this case the pivoting of the budget constraint changes its slope. (This differs from what happened previously when prices stayed the same but the consumer's income changed.) As we have discussed, the slope of the budget constraint reflects the relative price of cola and pizza. Because the price of cola has fallen to €1 from €2, while the price of pizza has remained at €10, the consumer can now trade a pizza for 10 rather than 5 litres of cola. As a result, the new budget constraint is more steeply sloped.

How such a change in the budget constraint alters the consumption of both goods depends on the consumer's preferences. For the indifference curves drawn in this figure, the consumer buys more cola and less pizza.

Income and Substitution Effects

income effect the change in consumption that results when a price change moves the consumer to a higher or lower indifference curve

substitution effect the change in consumption that results when a price change moves the consumer along a given indifference curve to a point with a new marginal rate of substitution

The impact of a change in the price of a good on consumption can be decomposed into two effects which we briefly introduced in Chapter 4: an **income effect** and a **substitution effect**. To see what these two effects are, consider how our consumer might respond when he learns that the price of cola has fallen. He might reason in the following ways:

'Great news! Now that cola is cheaper, my income has greater purchasing power – my income now buys me more. I am, in effect, richer than I was. Because I am richer, I can buy both more cola and more pizza.' (This is the income effect.)

'Now that the price of cola has fallen, I get more litres of cola for every pizza that I give up. Because pizza is now relatively more expensive, I should buy less pizza and more cola.' (This is the substitution effect.)

Which statement do you find more compelling?

In fact, both of these statements make sense. The decrease in the price of cola makes the consumer better off. If cola and pizza are both normal goods, the consumer will want to spread this improvement in his purchasing power over both goods. This income effect tends to make the consumer buy more pizza and more cola. Yet, at the same time, consumption of cola has become less expensive relative to consumption of pizza. This substitution effect tends to make the consumer choose more cola and less pizza.

Now consider the end result of these two effects. The consumer certainly buys more cola, because the income and substitution effects both act to raise purchases of cola. But it is ambiguous whether the consumer buys more pizza, because the income and substitution effects work in opposite directions. This conclusion is summarized in Table 7.1.

We can interpret the income and substitution effects using indifference curves. The income effect is the change in consumption that results from the movement to a higher indifference curve. The substitution effect is the change in consumption that results from being at a point on an indifference curve with a different marginal rate of substitution.

TABLE 7.1

Income and Substitution Effects When the Price of Cola Falls

Good	Income effect	Substitution effect	Total effect
Cola	Consumer is richer, so he buys more cola.	Cola is relatively cheaper, so consumer buys more cola.	Income and substitution effects act in same direction, so consumer buys more cola.
Pizza	Consumer is richer, so he buys more pizza.	Pizza is relatively more expensive, so consumer buys less pizza.	Income and substitution effects act in opposite directions, so the total effect on pizza consumption is ambiguous.

FIGURE 7.7

Income and Substitution Effects

The effect of a change in price can be broken down into an income effect and a substitution effect. The substitution effect – the movement along an indifference curve to a point with a different marginal rate of substitution – is shown here as the change from point A to point B along indifference curve I_1. The income effect – the shift to a higher indifference curve – is shown here as the change from point B on indifference curve I_1 to point C on indifference curve I_2.

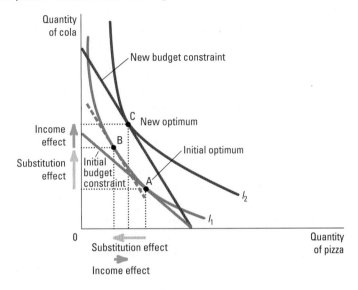

Figure 7.7 shows graphically how to decompose the change in the consumer's decision into the income effect and the substitution effect. When the price of cola falls, the consumer moves from the initial optimum, point A, to the new optimum, point C. We can view this change as occurring in two steps. First, the consumer moves *along* the initial indifference curve I_1 from point A to point B. The consumer is equally happy at these two points, but at point B the marginal rate of substitution reflects the new relative price. (The dashed line through point B reflects the new relative price by being parallel to the new budget constraint.) Next, the consumer *shifts* to the higher indifference curve I_2 by moving from point B to point C. Even though point B and point C are on different indifference curves, they have the same marginal rate of substitution. That is, the slope of the indifference curve I_1 at point B equals the slope of the indifference curve I_2 at point C.

Although the consumer never actually chooses point B, this hypothetical point is useful to clarify the two effects that determine the consumer's decision. Notice that the change from point A to point B represents a pure change in the marginal rate of substitution without any change in the consumer's welfare. Similarly, the change from point B to point C represents a pure change in welfare without any change in the marginal rate of substitution. Thus, the movement from A to B shows the substitution effect, and the movement from B to C shows the income effect.

? **what if…** a rise in prices takes place at the same time as a fall in incomes? How would this affect consumer optimum?

Pitfall Prevention Any change in price will have both income and substitution effects – this is relevant to the analysis of the demand curve we looked at in Chapter 4 where we also mentioned these two effects.

BEHAVIOURAL ECONOMICS

The standard economic model described above has some merits but the key assumption that consumers behave rationally in making purchasing decisions does have some limitations. Why, for example, do consumers complain about a €0.10 increase in a litre of fuel but are happy to spend €10 on a lottery ticket where the chances of winning are less than being struck by lightning? Why do people make pledges to get fitter, eat more healthily or quit habits like smoking but fail in their efforts very quickly? Why do employees get angry if they find out that a colleague is getting a higher pay rise than them? Why do people give up a considerable amount of time to queue (often in very inclement weather) to grab a 'bargain' at the sales when they could have used the time queuing to earn more than they 'save' getting the bargain? Why do people queue for hours to get their hands on the latest technology device from Apple, or the latest version of Halo or the latest version of a Harry Potter novel?

Many of the things we do in life and the decisions we make cannot be explained as those of rational beings. (Rational beings are sometimes referred to by economists as *homoeconomicus*.)

Although in many ways humans resemble the rational, calculating people assumed in economic theory, in reality they are far more complex. They can be forgetful, impulsive, confused, emotional and short-sighted. These imperfections of human reasoning are the bread-and-butter of psychologists, but until recently, economists have neglected them.

Economists have suggested that humans are only 'near rational' or that they exhibit 'bounded rationality'. **Bounded rationality** is the idea that humans make decisions under the constraints of limited, and sometimes unreliable, information, that they face limits to the amount of information they can process and that they face time constraints in making decisions.

Studies of human decision making have tried to detect systematic mistakes that people make. We outline some of the key findings below.

> **bounded rationality** the idea that humans make decisions under the constraints of limited, and sometimes unreliable, information, that they face limits to the amount of information they can process and that they face time constraints in making decisions

People are overconfident
Imagine that you were asked some numerical questions, such as the number of African countries in the United Nations, the height of the tallest mountain in Europe and so on. Instead of being asked for a single estimate, however, you were asked to give a 90 per cent confidence interval – a range such that you were 90 per cent confident the true number falls within it. When psychologists run experiments like this, they find that most people give ranges that are too small: the true number falls within their intervals far less than 90 per cent of the time. That is, most people are too sure of their own abilities.

People give too much weight to a small number of vivid observations
Imagine that you are thinking about buying a new smartphone by company X. To learn about its reliability, you read *Consumer Reports,* which has surveyed 1000 owners of the particular smartphone that you are looking at. Then you run into a friend who owns such a phone and she tells you that she is really unhappy with the phone. How do you treat your friend's observation? If you think rationally, you will realize that she has only increased your sample size from 1000 to 1001, which does not provide much new information. In addition, a process called the *reticular activation system* (RAS) works to bring your attention to instances of this smartphone – you will suddenly start to notice more of them. The RAS is an automatic mechanism in the brain that brings relevant information to our attention. Both these effects – your friend's story is so vivid and you have noticed more of these smartphones around – mean that you may be tempted to attach a disproportionate weight to them in decision making.

People are reluctant to change their mind
People tend to interpret evidence to confirm beliefs they already hold. In one study, subjects were asked to read

and evaluate a research report on whether capital punishment deters crime. After reading the report, those who initially favoured the death penalty said they were more sure in their view, and those who initially opposed the death penalty also said they were more sure in their view. The two groups interpreted the same evidence in exactly opposite ways.

People have a natural tendency to look for examples which confirm their existing view or hypothesis

Nassim Nicholas Taleb calls this 'naïve empiricism'. People identify, select or observe past instances and quote them as evidence for a viewpoint or hypothesis. For example, every extreme weather event that is reported is selected as evidence of climate change or a rise in the price of petrol of 10 per cent is symptomatic of a broader increase in prices of all goods.

People use rules of thumb – heuristics

The standard economic model implies that to act rationally buyers will consider all available information in making purchasing decisions and weigh up this information to arrive at a decision which maximizes utility subject to the budget constraint. In reality it is likely that many consumers will (a) not have access to sufficient information to be able to make a fully rational choice and (b) even if they did they would not be able to process this information fully, partly due to a lack of mental facility (not everyone can do arithmetic quickly in their head nor make statistical calculations on which to base their choices). Instead when making decisions many people will use shortcuts that help simplify the decision-making process. These shortcuts are referred to as **heuristics** or *rules of thumb*. Some of these heuristics can be deep-seated and firms can take advantage of them to influence consumer behaviour.

heuristics rules of thumb or shortcuts used in decision making

There are a number of different types of heuristics. *Anchoring* refers to the tendency for people to start with something they are familiar with or know and make decisions or adjustments based on this anchor. For example, a consumer may base the price they expect to pay for a restaurant meal on the last two prices they paid when eating out. If the price at the next restaurant is higher than this anchor price it may be that the consumer thinks the restaurant is 'expensive' or 'not good value for money' and may choose not to go again, whereas if the price they pay is lower than the anchor price they might see the restaurant as being good value for money and choose to return again. Often these anchors are biased and so the adjustment or decision is flawed in some way.

The *availability* heuristic refers to cases where decisions are made based on an assessment of the risks of the likelihood of something happening. If examples readily come to mind as a result of excessive media coverage, for example, decisions may be taken with a skewed assessment of the risks. If a consumer brings to mind the idea that the last couple of winters have been particularly bad then they might be more likely to buy equipment to help them combat adverse weather for the next winter. Consumers who use commuter trains are more likely to give negative feedback about the service they have received if their recent experience has been of some delays or cancellations even if the overall level of punctuality of the train operator has been very high.

A third heuristic is *representativeness*. In this instance people tend to make judgements by comparing how representative something is to an image or stereotype that they hold. For example, people may be more prepared to pay money to buy a lottery ticket if a close friend has just won a reasonable amount of money on the lottery or make an association that if Bose headphones are good quality then their home theatre systems are also going to be good quality.

Persuasion heuristics are linked to various attributes that a consumer attaches to a product or a brand. For example, it has been shown that size does matter to consumers and so marketers can exploit this by making more exaggerated claims in adverts or using facts and figures to make the product more compelling in the mind of the consumer. The more that the marketers can highlight the positive attributes of their product (and the negative ones of their rivals) the more likely consumers are to make choices in favour of their product. In addition consumers are also persuaded by people they like and

One aspect of behavioural economics involves choice architecture – how choices are presented can help change our behaviour and our purchasing choices to achieve desirable ends.

respect. This may be utilized by firms through the people they use in adverts and celebrity endorsements but may also be important in terms of the people a firm employs to represent them in a sales or marketing capacity. It may also be relevant in cases where friends or colleagues talk about products and is one of the reasons why firms are keen to build a better understanding of how social media like Facebook and Twitter can be exploited. Finally, persuasion heuristics can manifest themselves in the 'bandwagon' effect – if a large number of people go and see a movie and rave about it then there is even more incentive for others to go and see it as well. Firms may look to try and create a bandwagon effect to utilize this persuasion heuristic in their marketing.

Simulation heuristics occur where people use mental processes to establish the likely outcome of something. The easier it is to simulate or visualize that outcome the more likely the individual is to make a decision based on it. For example, if it is easy to imagine a product which makes you look good, then you are more likely to buy it. Pharmaceutical firms know that consumers are more likely to buy and take medicines that deal with known and experienced symptoms (things like headaches, strained muscles, sore throats and runny noses) which are easy to visualize and imagine, than taking regular medicines for something like high cholesterol because it is hard to build a mental process for the effects of high cholesterol.

Expected Utility Theory and Framing Effects
In our discussion of the standard economic model we referred to expected utility theory – the idea that preferences can and will be ranked by buyers. Expected utility theory is important in that every day we have to make decisions based on ranking preferences. Imagine you are faced with buying your first car. You have limited income and so have to go to second-hand dealers. You are wary of the potential problems inherent in buying a second-hand car – you know that if the car develops a mechanical fault it often costs more to repair than to replace so you go to the dealers with this in mind. You find two cars that you like – one is priced at €300 and its age suggests that it has a 50 per cent chance of breaking down in the first year. The second car is €900 but only has a 20 per cent chance of breaking down in the first year. Which do you choose? Expected utility theory says that consumers can rank the preference between these two options. We assumed that if the car breaks down it is more expensive to repair than to replace so our calculations are based on replacing the car rather than repairing it (we are talking rational human beings after all here).

The expected replacement cost of the first car would be the price we paid (€500) × the probability of it breaking down (50 per cent) which works out as €500 × 0.50 = €250. The expected replacement cost of the second car is 0.2 × 900 = €180. The rational choice, therefore, would be to purchase the more expensive car. The problem is that the way in which such choices are presented can affect our judgements and the rational decision is violated.

Behavioural economics has lots of applications. Here a simple mat insert into a public urinal focuses the male attention and helps reduce the costs of cleaning. It's all about understanding behaviour to help change behaviour.

Research into this area is extensive and persuasive. Essentially, choices can be affected by the way in which they are framed. In our example above, if you were faced with the choice of buying a car which has an 80 per cent chance of losing €720 in a year's time, or another car which has a 50 per cent chance of losing €250 after a year, which would you now choose?

In the second case we have just presented the two options differently but based on the same overall figures. The risks now appear different.

Firms are careful to frame the way they present products and information to consumers to try to influence purchasing decisions and exploit these differences in perception. For example, firms selling insurance know that people make judgements about the extent to which they are exposed to risk in deciding whether to take out insurance and how much cover they need. Adverts and marketing, therefore, may be framed to give the impression to consumers that they face increased risk.

ADVERTISING AND BRANDING

Knowledge of these different heuristics is important to firms in advertising. It is nearly impossible to go through a typical day in a modern economy without being bombarded with advertising. Whether you are reading a newspaper, watching television or driving down the motorway, some firm will try to convince you to buy its product. Such behaviour is typical in non-competitive markets where firms sell differentiated products and charge prices above marginal cost. In such markets firms have an incentive to advertise in order to attract more buyers to their particular product.

The amount of advertising varies substantially across products. Firms that sell highly differentiated consumer goods, such as over-the-counter drugs, perfumes, soft drinks, razor blades, breakfast cereals and dog food, typically spend between 10 and 20 per cent of revenue for advertising. Firms that sell industrial products, such as drill presses and communications satellites, typically spend very little on advertising. And firms that sell homogeneous products, such as wheat, peanuts or crude oil, spend nothing at all.

The Debate Over Advertising

There are billions spent on advertising around the world. Is society wasting the resources it devotes to advertising? Or does advertising serve a valuable purpose? Assessing the social value of advertising is difficult and often generates heated argument among economists. Let's consider both sides of the debate.

The Critique of Advertising
Critics of advertising argue that firms advertise in order to manipulate people's tastes. Much advertising is psychological rather than informational. Consider, for example, the typical television advert for some brand of soft drink. The advert most likely does not tell the viewer about the product's price or quality. Instead, it might show a group of happy people at a party on a beach on a beautiful sunny day. In their hands are cans of the soft drink. The goal of the advert is to convey a subconscious (if not subtle) message: 'You too can have many friends and be happy and beautiful, if only you drink our product.' Critics of advertising argue that such an advert creates a desire that otherwise might not exist.

Critics also argue that advertising impedes competition. Advertising often tries to convince consumers that products are more different than they truly are. By increasing the perception of product differentiation and fostering brand loyalty, advertising makes buyers less concerned with price differences among similar goods. With a less elastic demand curve, each firm charges a larger mark-up over marginal cost.

The Defence of Advertising
Defenders of advertising argue that firms use advertising to provide information to customers. Advertising conveys the prices of the

Advertising is becoming ever more sophisticated.

goods being offered for sale, the existence of new products and the locations of retail outlets. This information allows customers to make better choices about what to buy and, thus enhances the ability of markets to allocate resources efficiently.

Defenders also argue that advertising fosters competition. Because advertising allows customers to be more fully informed about all the firms in the market, customers can more easily take advantage of price differences. Thus, each firm has less market power. In addition, advertising allows new firms to enter more easily, because it gives entrants a means to attract customers from existing firms.

CASE STUDY

Advertising – What Does It Really Do?

Ask many people the question 'why do firms advertise?' and they are likely to tell you that it is an attempt by firms to try and increase demand for their products or services. If you consider this view intuitively it might make sense but then ask yourself the question, 'how many times have you seen an advert on the TV and then rushed out to buy the product advertised?' The chances are that this has not (consciously) happened very often at all. So if adverts do not make us rush out to buy products what do they do?

Sutherland and Sylvester (2000)[1] argue that it is largely a myth that adverts are designed to persuade us to buy products or services. They point out that advertising influences the order in which we evoke or notice the alternatives we consider. This does not feel like persuasion and it is not. It is nevertheless effective. Instead of persuasion and other major effects we should look for 'feathers', or minor effects. These can tip the balance when alternative brands are otherwise equal and, through repetition, can grow imperceptibly by small increments over time.

They liken the effect of advertising to that of watching someone grow up. You know that they are growing but the day-to-day changes in the individual are imperceptible. If you have not seen someone for some time, however, you do tend to notice the difference in their height, shape, features and so on. So it is with many advertising campaigns. The primary aim, they argue, is to generate a series of small effects, which ultimately influence our behaviour and may cause us to view differently the products or the brands that we choose, especially in a crowded marketplace with a large amount of competition.

Exactly how adverts work, therefore, is not easy to quantify. Sutherland and Sylvester suggest that many involved in the advertising industry do not really understand why some adverts seem to work and others don't work anything like as well. It has long been recognized that psychology has a lot to do with advertising. Our understanding of the way the brain works has been revolutionized by the developments afforded by magnetic resonance imaging (MRI) scans. The advertising industry has not been slow in looking at this technology and its potential for improving the focus and efficiency of advertising.

In essence, this technique looks at the response of the brain to different images and messages. Using MRI techniques, the areas of the brain that respond to different stimuli can be identified. The field developed as a result of work carried out by a neuroscientist, Read Montague. Montague is Professor in the Department of Neuroscience at Baylor College of Medicine in Houston, Texas. He gave a group of individuals two colas, Pepsi and Coke, to taste and asked them to state which they preferred. The respondents did not know that the two colas were in fact Pepsi and Coke. The results were 50:50 for the two products.

---

[1]Sutherland, M. & Sylvester, A.K. (2000) *Advertising and the Mind of the Consumer: What Works, What Doesn't, and Why.* St Leonards, New South Wales, Allen and Unwin.

However, when the experiment was repeated and the respondents were told what they were drinking, around 75 per cent stated that they preferred Coke. Montague found that brain activity in the medial pre-frontal cortex also showed signs of enhanced activity during the exercise. This area of the brain is associated with higher level thinking. Montague posited that the brain was making an association with the images and messages associated with commercials for Coke that respondents had witnessed over the years. He also suggested that such activity might lead to consumers preferring one product to another, even if there was other evidence to suggest that under normal circumstances, they would not have chosen that product.

Advertising as a Signal of Quality

Many types of advertising contain little apparent information about the product being advertised. Consider a firm introducing a new breakfast cereal. A typical advertisement might have some highly paid actor eating the cereal and exclaiming how wonderful it tastes. How much information does the advertisement really provide?

The answer is: more than you might think. Defenders of advertising argue that even advertising that appears to contain little hard information may in fact tell consumers something about product quality. The willingness of the firm to spend a large amount of money on advertising can itself be a *signal* to consumers about the quality of the product being offered.

Consider the problem facing two firms – Nestlé and Kellogg. Each company has just come up with a recipe for a new breakfast cereal, which it would sell for €3 a box. To keep things simple, let's assume that the marginal cost of making cereal is zero, so the €3 is all profit. Each company knows that if it spends €10 million on advertising, it will get 1 million consumers to try its new cereal. And each company knows that if consumers like the cereal, they will buy it not once but many times.

First consider Nestlé's decision. Based on market research, Nestlé knows that its cereal is only mediocre. Although advertising would sell one box to each of 1 million consumers, the consumers would quickly learn that the cereal is not very good and stop buying it. Nestlé decides it is not worth paying €10 million in advertising to get only €3 million in sales. So it does not bother to advertise. It sends its cooks back to the drawing board to find another recipe.

Kellogg, on the other hand, knows that its cereal is great. Each person who tries it will buy a box a month for the next year. Thus, the €10 million in advertising will bring in €36 million in sales. Advertising is profitable here because Kellogg has a good product that consumers will buy repeatedly. Thus, Kellogg chooses to advertise.

Now that we have considered the behaviour of the two firms, let's consider the behaviour of consumers. We began by asserting that consumers are inclined to try a new cereal that they see advertised. But is this behaviour rational? Should a consumer try a new cereal just because the seller has chosen to advertise it?

In fact, it may be completely rational for consumers to try new products that they see advertised. In our story, consumers decide to try Kellogg's new cereal because Kellogg advertises. Kellogg chooses to advertise because it knows that its cereal is quite good, while Nestlé chooses not to advertise because it knows that its cereal is only mediocre. By its willingness to spend money on advertising, Kellogg signals to consumers the quality of its cereal. Each consumer thinks, quite sensibly, 'Wow, if the Kellogg Company is willing to spend so much money advertising this new cereal, it must be really good.'

What is most surprising about this theory of advertising is that the content of the advertisement is irrelevant. Kellogg signals the quality of its product by its willingness to spend money on advertising. (This example is used for illustrative purposes only and is not meant to infer that Nestlé deliberately produces inferior products!)

What the advertisements say is not as important as the fact that consumers know ads are expensive. By contrast, cheap advertising cannot be effective at signalling quality to consumers. In our example, if an advertising campaign cost less than €3 million, both Nestlé and Kellogg would use it to market their new cereals. Because both good and mediocre cereals would be advertised, consumers could not infer the quality of a new cereal from the fact that it is advertised. Over time, consumers would learn to ignore such cheap advertising.

This theory can explain why firms pay celebrities large amounts of money to make advertisements that, on the surface, appear to convey no information at all. The information is not in the advertisement's content, but simply in its existence and expense.

BRAND NAMES

branding the means by which a business creates an identity for itself and highlights the way in which it differs from its rivals

Advertising is closely related to the existence of **branding**. In many markets, there are two types of firms. Some firms sell products with widely recognized brand names, while other firms sell generic substitutes. For example, in a typical supermarket, you can find Pepsi next to less familiar colas, or Kellogg's cornflakes next to the supermarket's own brand of cornflakes, made for it by an unknown firm. Most often, the firm with the famous brand name spends more on advertising and charges a higher price for its product.

FELIX KNEW THAT IF HE BOUGHT THE NAME BRAND AND THE CHEAP STUFF, HE COULD EASILY SWAP THE LABEL AND HIS FAMILY WOULD NEVER KNOW THAT HE WASN'T BEING THRIFTY. HE'D DONE THIS BEFORE...

Just as there is disagreement about the economics of advertising, there is disagreement about the economics of brand names and branding. Let's consider both sides of the debate.

Critics of brand names argue that branding causes consumers to perceive differences that do not really exist. In many cases, the generic good is almost indistinguishable from the brand-name good. Consumers' willingness to pay more for the brand-name good, these critics assert, is a form of irrationality fostered by advertising. Economist Edward Chamberlin, one of the early developers of the theory of monopolistic competition, concluded from this argument that brand names were bad for the economy. He proposed that the government discourage their use by refusing to enforce the exclusive trademarks that companies use to identify their products.

More recently, economists have defended brand names as a useful way for consumers to ensure that the goods they buy are of high quality. There are two related arguments. First, brand names provide consumers with *information* which cannot be easily judged in advance of purchase. Second, brand names give firms an *incentive* to meet the needs of consumers, because firms have a financial stake in maintaining the reputation of their brand names. Note that branding does not always equate to high quality. Some firms will happily admit their goods are 'cheap and cheerful' but point out that they provide consumers with value for money. A number of discount stores, for example, have expanded over the last five years partly because of the difficult economic times that many countries have experienced. Firms such as Lidl, Netto, Poundstretcher and Poundland are interested in developing their brand names as much as Armani and Ralph Lauren. Consumers were able to associate the brand name with value for money – important when times are difficult.

To see how these arguments work in practice, consider a famous brand name: Ibis hotels. Imagine that you are driving through an unfamiliar town and you need some-where to stay for the night. You see a Hotel Ibis and a local hotel next door to it. Which do you choose? The local hotel may in fact offer better accommodation at lower prices, but you have no way of knowing that. In contrast, Hotel Ibis offers a consistent product across many European cities. Its brand name is useful to you as a way of judging the quality of what you are about to buy.

The Ibis brand name also ensures that the company has an incentive to maintain quality. For example, if some customers were to become very ill from bad food served at breakfast at a Hotel Ibis, the news would be disastrous for the company. Ibis would lose much of the valuable reputation that it has built up over the years and, as a result, it would lose sales and profit, not just in the hotel that served the bad food, but in its many hotels across Europe. By contrast, if some customers were to become ill from bad food served at breakfast in a local hotel, that restaurant might have to close down, but the lost profits would be much smaller. Hence, Ibis has a greater incentive to ensure that its breakfast food is safe.

The debate over brand names thus centres on the question of whether consumers are rational in preferring brand names over generic substitutes. Critics of brand names argue that brand names are the result of an irrational consumer response to advertis-ing. Defenders of brand names argue that consumers have good reason to pay more for brand-name products because they can be more confident in the quality of these products.

Quick Quiz How might advertising make markets less competitive? How might it make markets more competitive? • Give the arguments for and against brand names.

JEOPARDY PROBLEM

A firm manufacturing batteries in a market with a number of competitors spends a large amount of money over a three-year period both advertising its product and building its brand image. It finds, in the following years, that if it increases its price its revenue increases. Its internal research suggests this is contrary to what would have happened prior to the advertising campaign. What has changed in the inter-vening years to lead to this outcome?

ASYMMETRIC INFORMATION

'I know something you don't know.' This statement is a common taunt among children, but it also conveys a deep truth about how people sometimes interact with one another. Many times in life, one person knows more about what is going on than another. A difference in access to relevant knowledge is called an *information asymmetry*.

Examples abound. A worker knows more than his employer about how much effort he puts into his job. A seller of a used car knows more than the buyer about the car's condition. The first is an example of a *hidden action,* whereas the second is an example of a *hidden characteristic.* In each case, the party in the dark (the employer, the car buyer) would like to know the relevant information, but the informed party (the worker, the car seller) may have an incentive to conceal it.

Because asymmetric information is so prevalent, economists have devoted much effort in recent decades to studying its effects. And, indeed, the 2001 Nobel Prize in economics was awarded to three economists (George Akerlof, Michael Spence and Joseph Stiglitz) for their pioneering work on this topic. Let's discuss some of the insights that this study has revealed.

Hidden Actions: Principals, Agents and Moral Hazard

moral hazard the tendency of a person who is imperfectly monitored to engage in dishonest or otherwise undesirable behaviour

agent a person who is performing an act for another person, called the principal

principal a person for whom another person, called the agent, is performing some act

adverse selection the tendency for the mix of unobserved attributes to become undesirable from the standpoint of an uninformed party

Moral hazard is a problem that arises when one person, called the **agent**, is performing some task on behalf of another person, called the **principal**. If the principal cannot perfectly monitor the agent's behaviour, the agent tends to undertake less effort than the principal considers desirable and is not fully responsible for the consequences of their actions. The phrase *moral hazard* refers to the risk, or 'hazard', of inappropriate or otherwise 'immoral' behaviour by the agent.

Moral hazard can lead to **adverse selection**. This means that the market process may end up with 'bad' outcomes because of asymmetric information. Adverse selection is a feature of banking, finance and insurance industries. A bank, for example, sets rules and regulations for its accounts which may lead to some customers, who are not very profitable to the bank, adversely selecting the bank – customers the bank would rather not have. In insurance, the person seeking insurance cover has more information about his or her situation than the insurer. A person who knows they are high risk will look to buy insurance but not necessarily divulge the extent of the risk they pose to the insurance company. How does the insurance company distinguish between its high-risk and low-risk customers? The insurance company would rather take on the low-risk customers than the high-risk ones but high-risk customers adversely select the insurance company. In finance, some investment banks have been accused of putting very risky assets into financial products and clients buying these products do not know the full extent of the risk they are buying – clients are dealing with suppliers who they would have been better off not dealing with. In such a situation, the principal tries various ways to encourage the agent to act more responsibly (such as pricing insurance for high-risk customers higher than for low-risk ones).

> **?** **what if…** governments believed that the market is the best regulator of banks and sought to increase competition in the banking industry. Would this reduce moral hazard?

The employment relationship is the classic example. The employer (business) is the principal, and the worker is the agent. The moral hazard problem is the temptation of imperfectly monitored workers to shirk their responsibilities. How do firms respond to this problem?

- *Better monitoring.* Human resources departments in larger firms develop processes to improve the monitoring of workers and to also put in place performance management systems to help provide incentives for employees to meet their employment responsibilities.
- *High wages.* According to *efficiency wages theories*, some employers may choose to pay their workers a wage above the level that equilibrates supply and demand in the labour market. A worker who earns an above-equilibrium wage is less likely to shirk, because if he is caught and fired, he might not be able to find another high-paying job.
- *Delayed payment.* Firms can delay part of a worker's compensation, so if the worker is caught shirking and is fired, he suffers a larger penalty. One example of delayed compensation is the year-end bonus. Similarly, a firm may choose to pay its workers more later in their lives. Thus, the wage increases that workers get as they age may reflect not just the benefits of experience but also a response to moral hazard.

These various mechanisms to reduce the problem of moral hazard need not be used alone. Employers can use a combination of them.

Beyond the workplace, there are many other examples of moral hazard that affect businesses. Individuals with insurance cover, be it fire, motor vehicle or medical insurance, may behave differently as a result of having that cover. A motorist, for example, might drive more recklessly in the knowledge that in the event of an accident the cost will be met primarily by the insurance company. Similarly, families choosing to live near a river may benefit from the scenic views but the increased risk of flooding imposes a cost to the insurance company and the government in the event of a serious flood. The financial crisis raised the issue of bankers' bonuses. One argument put forward was that banks were acting recklessly in giving large bonuses to workers which encouraged inappropriate and risky investment. Such behaviour was encouraged because bankers 'knew' that governments would step in to prevent banks from failing.

Many regulations are aimed at addressing the problem: an insurance company may require homeowners to buy smoke detectors or pay higher premiums if there is a history of reckless driving (or even refuse to provide insurance cover to the individual), the government may prohibit building homes on land with high risk of flooding and new regulations may be introduced to curb the behaviour of banks. But the insurance company does not have perfect information about how cautious homeowners are, the government does not have perfect information about the risk that families undertake when choosing where to live and regulators do not know fully the risks that bankers take in investment decisions. As a result, the problem of moral hazard persists.

Signalling to Convey Private Information

Markets respond to problems of asymmetric information in many ways. One of them is **signalling**, which refers to actions taken by an informed party for the sole purpose of credibly revealing his private information.

signalling an action taken by an informed party to reveal private information to an uninformed party

We have seen examples of signalling earlier in this chapter; firms may spend money on advertising to signal to potential customers that they have high-quality products. The intention is that the informed party is using a signal to convince the uninformed party that the informed party is offering something of high quality.

What does it take for an action to be an effective signal? Obviously, it must be costly. If a signal were free, everyone would use it, and it would convey no information. For the same reason, there is another requirement: The signal must be less costly, or more beneficial, to the person with the higher-quality product. Otherwise, everyone would have the same incentive to use the signal, and the signal would reveal nothing.

Screening to Induce Information Revelation

When an informed party takes actions to reveal his private information, the phenomenon is called signalling. When an uninformed party takes actions to induce the informed party to reveal private information, the phenomenon is called **screening**.

screening an action taken by an uninformed party to induce an informed party to reveal information

Some screening is common sense. A person buying a used car may ask that it be checked by a car mechanic or a trade association before the sale. A seller who refuses this request reveals his private information that the car is a lemon. The buyer may decide to offer a lower price or to look for another car.

Other examples of screening are more subtle. For example, consider a firm that sells car insurance. The firm would like to charge a low premium to safe drivers and a high premium to risky drivers. But how can it tell them apart? Drivers know whether they are safe or risky, but the risky ones won't admit to it. A driver's history is one piece of information (which insurance companies in fact use), but because of the intrinsic randomness of car accidents, history is an imperfect indicator of future risks.

The insurance company might be able to sort out the two kinds of drivers by offering different insurance policies that would induce them to separate themselves. One policy would have a high premium and cover the full cost of any accidents that occur. Another policy would have low premiums but would have, say, a €1000 excess. (That is, the driver would be responsible for the first €1000 of damage, and the insurance company would cover the remaining risk.) Notice that the excess is more of a burden for risky drivers because they are more likely to have an accident. Thus, with a large enough excess, the low-premium policy with an excess would attract the safe drivers, while the high-premium policy without an excess would attract the risky drivers. Faced with these two policies, the two kinds of drivers would reveal their private information by choosing different insurance policies.

Quick Quiz A person who buys a life insurance policy pays a certain amount per year and receives for his family a much larger payment in the event of his death. Would you expect buyers of life insurance to have higher or lower death rates than the average person? How might this be an example of moral hazard? Of adverse selection? How might a life insurance company deal with these problems?

CONCLUSION

This chapter has examined different but complementary models of consumer behaviour. The standard economic model relies on a set of assumptions with rational human beings at its heart. Economists are always looking to refine their models and the developments in technology and the influence of other disciplines has led to theories of consumer behaviour which go some way to helping understand the imperfections in the standard economic model. Firms are increasingly using these insights to help develop marketing strategies to influence consumer behaviour and increase sales. Advertising and branding are two of these areas which are used by firms to influence consumer behaviour and are features of imperfect competition. Finally we looked at issues which arise from asymmetric information. The very fact that most businesses know more about their product than do consumers gives rise to potential problems, and we looked in particular at moral hazard and adverse selection and how it affects the financial industry.

If there is a unifying theme to these topics, it is that life is messy. Information is imperfect, government is imperfect and people are imperfect. Of course, you knew this long before you started studying economics, but economists need to understand these imperfections as precisely as they can if they are to explain, and perhaps even improve, the world around them.

IN THE NEWS

Asymmetric Information, Valentine's Day and Signalling

On 14 February each year, many people across the world celebrate the love they have for a partner, wife, girlfriend, husband or boyfriend by sending flowers, cards and other gifts. Gift-giving reflects asymmetric information and signalling – what you choose to send or give to your loved one conveys information but the private information of the sender can be quite different to the information of the receiver.

The Valentine's Day Dilemma

For many men, Valentine's Day presents a real dilemma. The problem depends to a large extent on your current romantic situation which can loosely be broken down into four main categories: (a) you are married and have been so for some time in which case Valentine's Day may have a different meaning; (b) you are newly married and the flush of romance and expectation still exists; (c) you are single but have been dating a girl for some time; (d) you are single and have eyes for a lady which is as yet unrequited.

Valentine's Day is a perfect opportunity to send your loved one a message but getting that message right can be problematic. If you are in category (a) then buying a bunch of red roses may almost be expected and routine. In category (b), roses are a sign that you are still smitten with your loved one despite getting married and the roses are an affirmation of your commitment (not to mention the atmosphere in the marital home for the next few weeks); in category (c) roses are a must – after all you may not have committed to marriage yet but this is one of those days of the year when some sign

of effort and commitment is required; and finally category (d) those roses might just be the thing which finally helps you tip the balance in your favour.

Next problem is how many roses to buy – a single red rose is a classic romantic gesture but could be seen as being a bit mean. Three is better but not as good as six and does three or six stems count as a bunch? An associated, and not insignificant question, will have to be the price you have to pay to acquire the roses. Most people will be aware that in the run up to Valentine's Day the price of roses rises significantly. Our understanding of economics means this is not a surprise – demand rises considerably so we would expect price to rise. However, for the buyer the decision then becomes one which involves trying to second guess what your wife, partner, girlfriend, girlfriend-to-be will think as you present the roses. Will a single rose be a sign of a true romantic or be seen as being mean? Will three roses be enough to show your love or is there a minimum of at least six? Will a bunch of 12, or 20, really show that you are totally besotted because you are clearly prepared to lavish significant sums of money on your loved one?

The decision will depend on lots of things, not least your income. A single

married couple, maybe other things are now more important than roses at Valentine's Day (like supporting children), and so spending large sums on lots of roses would just be seen as 'nice' but frivolous. In this case the single rose may be enough to say 'I thought of you and I still love you very much but I am mindful that we have other priorities right now'.

For many men the dilemma is that they just don't know and whatever decision they make – regardless of all good intentions – they will invariably get it wrong. The reason is asymmetric information. The giver does not know for sure how the receiver is going to interpret the decision on the number of roses given.

are sensible enough not to be frivolous. If you have been in a relationship for some time but not yet married, maybe a bunch of roses is a necessity to send that signal that you are really still committed; and for the single person with unrequited love, the bigger the bunch the more impressive the signal because the receiver knows that you will have sacrificed a great deal to send that message.

For the newly-wed, buying a bunch might set a dangerous precedent that such expense will be expected year-after-year. Undoubtedly, your partner will have remembered how many roses you bought last year so any fewer might be saying 'I don't love you quite as much as I did'. If you buy the same amount each year is that a sign that your love is not growing and if you get more each year, when will it ever stop?

Decisions, decisions. It may be the case that most givers never quite get it right but some of the fun might just be in both parties trying to work out what the real signal is!

Questions

1. Whether to buy a dozen red roses, six or three – how would the standard economic model explain how many roses an individual should buy for his/her partner?

2. How might an individual thinking of buying a Valentine's gift for a loved one measure the utility from buying the gift when they are not the ultimate consumers of the gift?

3. What part might the concept of heuristics play in consumer decisions to buy gifts on Valentine's Day?

4. How might asymmetric information in relation to gift-giving between two people who are in a relationship be reduced?

5. 'A signal's credibility is directly related to the cost the signal imposes on the sender.' Explain this statement in relation to gift-giving on Valentine's Day.

P.J. CURRIER/MEDIA SELECT INTERNATIONAL

person on a low income prepared to pay the sort of money needed to buy a dozen red roses might be a real sign of intent and love to that person who has remained elusive to date. But, what happens if the roses are not enough to persuade them that you are really the one for them – what a waste of money that then represents. For the long-term

So the solution is to try and estimate as best as you can how to convey your real intentions and motives – something called signalling. In a long-term relationship you may feel that your partner knows you very well and if you do decide on that single rose that may be enough to convey the message that you really do still care but you

SUMMARY

- The standard economic model assumes humans behave rationally and seek to maximize utility subject to the constraint of limited income.

- Increased consumption raises total utility up to a point but marginal utility falls as consumption increases and is called the law of diminishing marginal utility.

- A consumer's budget constraint shows the possible combinations of different goods he can buy given his income and the prices of the goods. The slope of the budget constraint equals the relative price of the goods.

- The consumer's indifference curves represent his preferences. An indifference curve shows the various bundles of goods that make the consumer equally happy. Points on higher indifference curves are preferred to points on lower indifference curves. The slope of an indifference curve at any point is the consumer's marginal rate of substitution – the rate at which the consumer is willing to trade one good for the other.

- The consumer optimizes by choosing the point on his budget constraint that lies on the highest indifference curve. At this point, the slope of the indifference curve (the marginal rate of substitution between the goods) equals the slope of the budget constraint (the relative price of the goods).

- When the price of a good falls, the impact on the consumer's choices can be broken down into an income effect and a substitution effect. The income effect is the change in consumption that arises because a lower price makes the consumer better off. The substitution effect is the change in consumption that arises because a price change encourages greater consumption of the good that has become relatively cheaper. The income effect is reflected in the movement from a lower to a higher indifference curve, whereas the substitution effect is reflected by a movement along an indifference curve to a point with a different slope.

- The study of psychology and economics reveals that human decision making is more complex than is assumed in conventional economic theory. People are not always rational, they use rules of thumb (heuristics) and are influenced by the way in which information is presented (framing effects) which may alter the outcomes suggested by expected utility theory.

- The product differentiation inherent in imperfectly competitive markets leads to the use of advertising and brand names. Critics of advertising and brand names argue that firms use them to take advantage of consumer irrationality and to reduce competition. Defenders of advertising and brand names argue that firms use them to inform consumers and to compete more vigorously on price and product quality.

- In many economic transactions, information is asymmetric. When there are hidden actions, principals may be concerned that agents suffer from the problem of moral hazard. When there are hidden characteristics, buyers may be concerned about the problem of adverse selection among the sellers. Private markets sometimes deal with asymmetric information with signalling and screening.

KEY CONCEPTS

value, p. 152
utility, p. 152
marginal utility, p. 153
diminishing marginal utility, p. 153
marginal rate of substitution, p. 153
budget constraint, p. 154
indifference curve, p. 155

expected utility theory, p. 156
income effect, p. 160
substitution effect, p. 160
bounded rationality, p. 162
heuristics, p. 163
branding, p. 168
moral hazard, p. 170

agent, p. 170
principal, p. 170
adverse selection, p. 170
signalling, p. 172
screening, p. 172

QUESTIONS FOR REVIEW

1. A consumer goes into a coffee shop and has four cups of coffee. Explain what we might observe about the total utility and marginal utility of the individual. How does your explanation illustrate the law of diminishing returns?

2. A consumer has income of €3000. Bread is priced at €3 a loaf and cheese is priced at €6 a kilo.
   a. Draw the consumer's budget constraint. What is the slope of this budget constraint?

   b. Draw a consumer's indifference curves for wine and cheese. Pick a point on an indifference curve for wine and cheese and show the marginal rate of substitution. What does the marginal rate of substitution tell us?

3. Show a consumer's budget constraint and indifference curves for bread and cheese. Show the optimal consumption choice. If the price of bread is €3 a loaf and the price of

cheese is €6 a kilo, what is the marginal rate of substitution at this optimum?

4. The price of cheese rises from €6 to €10 a kilo, while the price of wine remains at €3 a glass. For a consumer with a constant income of €3000, show what happens to consumption of wine and cheese. Decompose the change into income and substitution effects.

5. Explain and give an example of the following heuristics:
   a. Representative heuristics
   b. Availability heuristics
   c. Simulation heuristics
   d. Adjustment heuristics

PROBLEMS AND APPLICATIONS

1. Jacqueline divides her income between coffee and croissants (both of which are normal goods). An early frost in Brazil causes a large increase in the price of coffee in France.
   a. Show how this early frost might affect Jacqueline's budget constraint.
   b. Show how this early frost might affect Jacqueline's optimal consumption bundle assuming that the substitution effect outweighs the income effect for croissants.
   c. Show how this early frost might affect Jacqueline's optimal consumption bundle assuming that the income effect outweighs the substitution effect for croissants.

2. Surette buys only orange juice and yoghurt.
   a. In 2014, Surette earns €100, orange juice is priced at €2 a carton and yoghurt is priced at €4 a tub. Draw Surette's budget constraint.
   b. Now suppose that all prices increase by 10 per cent in 2015 and that Surette's salary increases by 10 per cent as well. Draw Surette's new budget constraint. How would Surette's optimal combination of orange juice and yoghurt in 2015 compare to her optimal combination in 2014?

3. Economist George Stigler once wrote that, according to consumer theory, 'if consumers do not buy less of a commodity when their incomes rise, they will surely buy less when the price of the commodity rises.' Explain this statement using the concepts of income and substitution effects.

4. Choose three products you purchased recently. Think about the reasons that you made the particular purchase decision in each case in relation to the various heuristics.

5. Look at the following two statements:
   a. Which would you prefer – a 50 per cent chance of winning €150 or a 50 per cent chance of winning €100?
   b. Would you prefer a decision that guarantees a €100 loss or would you rather take a gamble where the chance of winning €50 was rated at 50 per cent but the chance of losing €200 was also rated at 50 per cent?
   c. What would your choice be in a.?
   d. What would your choice be in b.?

6. How might advertising with no apparent informational content in fact convey information to consumers?

7. Explain two benefits that might arise from the existence of brand names.

8. What is moral hazard? List three things an employer might do to reduce the severity of this problem.

9. What is adverse selection? Give an example of a market in which adverse selection might be a problem.

10. Define *signalling* and *screening*, and give an example of each.

   e. What is the difference between these two sets of statements and how do they illustrate the concept of framing?

6. Each of the following situations involves moral hazard. In each case, identify the principal and the agent, and explain why there is asymmetric information. How does the action described reduce the problem of moral hazard?
   a. Landlords require tenants to pay security deposits.
   b. Firms compensate top executives with options to buy company shares at a given price in the future.
   c. Car insurance companies offer discounts to customers who install anti-theft devices in their cars.

7. Some AIDS activists believe that health insurance companies should not be allowed to ask applicants if they are infected with the HIV virus that causes AIDS. Would this rule help or hurt those who are HIV-positive? Would it help or hurt those who are not HIV-positive? Would it exacerbate or mitigate the problem of adverse selection in the market for health insurance? Do you think it would increase or decrease the number of people without health insurance? In your opinion, would this be a good policy?

8. For each of the following pairs of firms, explain which firm would be more likely to engage in advertising:
   a. A family-owned farm or a family-owned restaurant.
   b. A manufacturer of forklift trucks or a manufacturer of cars.
   c. A company that invented a very reliable watch or a company that invented a less reliable watch that costs the same amount to make.

9. The government is considering two ways to help the needy: giving them cash, or giving them free meals at soup kitchens. Give an argument for giving cash. Give an argument, based on asymmetric information, for why the soup kitchen may be better than the cash handout.

10. Describe three adverts that you have seen on TV. In what ways, if any, were each of these adverts socially useful? In what ways were they socially wasteful? Did the adverts affect the likelihood of you buying the product? Why or why not?

PART 4

MICROECONOMICS –
THE ECONOMICS OF FIRMS
IN MARKETS

8 BUSINESS GOALS AND BEHAVIOUR

LEARNING OBJECTIVES

In this chapter you will:

- Look at the distinction between financial and non-financial goals of business

- Identify the point at which a firm maximizes profit

- Consider the break-even point

- Identify the point of revenue maximization

- Look at an alternative approach to the point of cost minimization

- Consider the role of productivity

- Consider tactics and strategies for maximizing market share

- Consider definitions of shareholder value

- Identify issues relating to non-financial objectives such as environmental and social objectives

- Look at an introduction to social enterprise

After reading this chapter you should be able to:

- Explain the point of profit maximization where marginal cost equals marginal revenue and draw a diagram to illustrate

- Show the related point of profit maximization using TR and TC curves and thus the point of revenue maximization

- Explain the relationship between price elasticity of demand, marginal revenue and revenue maximization

- Explain how costs can be minimized at the point where the AC curve is at its lowest

- Outline some basic tactics and strategies for maximizing market share

- Provide alternative definitions of the concept of shareholder value

- Give explanations of non-financial objectives such as environmental and ethical objectives and consider the impact on stakeholders and stakeholder conflicts

- Outline the principles of social enterprise

THE GOALS OF FIRMS

It might seem obvious that businesses exist to make profits and indeed, for many that is a key requirement. However, it is too simplistic to analyse business just based on that assumption. Changes in the last 30 years have led to businesses having to balance a wider range of objectives along with making profit. In some areas of business activity profit may not be the ultimate aim at all – other factors might take precedence. This will depend in part on the nature of the market in which the business operates and the type of good being produced. What we mean by this is not simply whether the good is a chocolate bar or steel but the nature of the good. We can identify such goods by looking at two characteristics:

excludable the property of a good whereby a person can be prevented from using it when they do not pay for it

rival the property of a good whereby one person's use diminishes other people's use

private goods goods that are both excludable and rival

- Is the good **excludable**? Can people who do not pay for the use of a good be prevented from using the good?
- Is the good **rival**? Does one person's use of the good diminish another person's ability to use it?

Using these two characteristics, Figure 8.1 divides goods into four categories:

1. **Private goods** are both excludable and rival. Consider a chocolate bar, for example. A chocolate bar is excludable because it is possible to prevent someone else from eating it – you just don't give it to them. A chocolate bar is rival because if one person eats it, another person cannot eat the same bar. Most goods in the economy are private goods like chocolate bars.

FIGURE 8.1

Four Types of Goods

Goods can be grouped into four categories according to two questions: (1) Is the good excludable? That is, can people be prevented from using it? (2) Is the good rival? That is, does one person's use of the good diminish other people's use of it? This diagram gives examples of goods in each of the four categories.

	Rival?	
Excludable?	**Yes**	**No**
Yes	**Private goods** • Ice cream cornets • Clothing • Congested toll roads	**Natural monopolies** • The fire service • Cable TV • Uncongested toll roads
No	**Common resources** • Fish in the ocean • The environment • Congested non-toll roads	**Public goods** • Flood-control dams • National defence • Uncongested non-toll roads

2. **Public goods** are neither excludable nor rival. That is, people cannot be prevented from using a public good, and one person's use of a public good does not reduce another person's ability to use it. For example, a country's national defence system: it protects all of the country's citizens equally and the fact that one person is being defended does not affect whether or not another citizen is defended.

3. **Common resources** are rival but not excludable. For example, fish in the ocean are a rival good: when one person catches fish, there are fewer fish for the next person to catch. Yet these fish are not an excludable good because, given the vast size of an ocean, it is difficult to stop fishermen from taking fish out of it when, for example, they have not paid for a licence to do so.

4. When a good is excludable but not rival, it is an example of a *natural monopoly*. For instance, consider fire protection in a small town. It is easy to exclude people from using this good: the fire service can just let their house burn down. Yet fire protection is not rival. Firefighters spend much of their time waiting for a fire, so protecting an extra house is unlikely to reduce the protection available to others. In other words, once a town has paid for the fire service, the additional cost of protecting one more house is small.

public goods goods that are neither excludable nor rival

common resources goods that are rival but not excludable

Quick Quiz Define *public goods* and *common resources,* and give an example of each (not the same as the one given in the text).

In this chapter we are going to look at the wide range of factors that might drive business activity. You will have to think about what is the primary objective for the business in each case you look at and for this reason we need to distinguish between aims and objectives and strategies and tactics.

Aims and Objectives

As a general rule, **aims** are the long-term goals of the whole business. These aims are often captured in the business mission and vision statement. **Objectives** are the means by which a business will be able to achieve its aims. They are invariably measurable targets which are set to help the business identify the extent to which it is on target to meet its aims.

aims the long-term goals of a business

objectives the means by which a business will be able to achieve its aims

Many firms will summarize their overall goals through a mission or vision statement. The four examples below are from companies across Europe, the Middle East and Africa (EMEA).

BASF

We combine economic success, social responsibility and environmental protection. Through science and innovation we enable our customers to meet the current and future needs of society.

BASF
The Chemical Company

Source: http://www.basf.com/group/corporate/en/function/conversions:/publish/content/about-basf/facts-reports/reports/2011/BASF_We_create_Chemistry.pdf

KPN

We believe that satisfied customers are the foundation for profitable growth and, as a result, create value for our shareholders. Equally, we believe that our commitment to quality and customer satisfaction can be realized only if our employees are proud to be KPN employees and are motivated to provide the best possible products and services.

We are conscious of our responsibilities to the wider community; it is our policy to use our knowledge and technology to contribute to the well-being of all our stakeholders. We do this by enabling people to stay in touch, with extra attention to those who are hindered by sickness, age or cultural differences. We are also actively taking steps to limit our impact on the environment as a whole.

Source: http://www.kpn.com/corporate/aboutkpn/Company-profile/company-profile/the-company/mission.htm

CAIRO POULTRY COMPANY

Our vision is to be recognized as the brand of choice in market segments in which we choose to compete, while maximizing our stakeholder's values. Our mission is to produce market safe and healthy wide-range of food products and attract, reward and retain the best people in the food industry.

Source: http://www.cpg.com.eg/vision-mission.html

UNION CARRIAGE AND WAGON (UCW)

BUILT IN 1997 BY . . .

NIGEL
UNION
SOUTH AFRICA

UNION CARRIAGE & WAGON CO. (PTY). LTD

WIKIMEDIA/SOLOMON203

Through our unique capabilities and business model, we offer our customers a full spectrum of boundless solutions in the rolling stock sector. Customized rolling stock to meet our customers' unique operational needs, as well as standard product designs in the industry form part of this spectrum. The *'UCW Advantage'* provides customers with quality products on time. Constant emphasis on customer relations, co-operation as well as clear communication with its customers, ensures that the UCW customer enjoys unmatched after sales support to keep the wheels turning!

Source: http://www.ucw.co.za/au_value_proposition.asp

Looking at these four examples it is interesting to note that there is only one reference to profit. There are a number of references, in one form or another to customers, environmental and social responsibility, quality, shareholder value, stakeholder well-being and to employees.

What this highlights is the complex web of stakeholder responsibilities which we outlined in Chapter 3 and which now guides many firms long term goals. Many of these goals are interlinked – references to 'economic success' or 'profitability', for example are linked to shareholder value, quality may not only be associated with customer satisfaction but, depending on the definition, with social and environmental responsibility.

Strategies and Tactics

A **strategy** is generally regarded as being to do with the long term – where the business wants to be at some point in the future. A **tactic**, on the other hand, is seen more as a short-term framework for decision making. Tactics are the 'how' to the question posed by strategy which is the where. To get to where you want to be in the future (the strategy) requires certain steps to be put in place to enable the business to progress towards that place (the tactics).

How long the time period is to define 'the future' is more difficult to identify clearly and there is much debate about the use of the term. For example, one often hears sports managers talking of the 'strategy they devised for the game'. In this case is the 'future' the time period when the game has finished? If the 'strategy' is to win a particularly difficult game against fierce rivals then in the context of decision making this could be seen

strategy a series of actions, decisions and obligations which lead to the firm gaining a competitive advantage and exploiting the firm's core competencies

tactic short-term framework for decision making

as being 'long term'. The team manager will then employ tactics to use in the game to achieve the desired goal of winning the match. These tactics will be the 'how' in terms of what formation is put out, which players will play where, who marks who, whether to focus on defence or attack, which particular opposition players to target to limit their influence on the game and the sort of 'plays', set piece moves etc. that will be used at certain times in the game.

Others would argue that winning the game is not an example of strategy because it is not the long term. The long term would be where the team wants to be at the end of the season, what financial position it wants to be in or where it wants to be in five years' time.

Because there is so much debate on these points we cannot come to any definitive conclusion and this should be borne in mind as you read this book and others (you are likely to see many different interpretations). For the purposes of this book we will use the definitions of strategy and tactics as given above. We will also refer more generally to a firm having 'goals' which is a more generic term which can be understood by all and which does not embroil us in the debate over semantics. This is not meant to detract from the seriousness of the debate, however. Having a clear understanding of what is being done in a business, what decisions are being made, when and why are all vitally important for business success.

Despite the varying goals that exist, a firm must make a profit if it is to survive in the long run – rarely will any business activity be able to continue if costs are consistently greater than revenues. What we have not said anything about at this stage is the size of the profit in question. We will see that there is a theoretical point at which a firm can maximize its profit and this may be something that influences decision making about how much to produce, what price to charge, how to monitor and control costs etc. In balancing out the other objectives a firm has, there will be an inevitable impact on profits. For example, if a firm expresses a goal to reduce its environmental impact then this is likely to have an impact on its costs and this may mean that profit will be less than the maximum that could be made if this focus was not part of its decision making.

The Public Sector and the Private Sector

public sector that part of the economy where business activity is owned, financed and controlled by the government or its agencies on behalf of the public as a whole

The goals of business activity might also be influenced by whether the business operates in the public sector or the private sector. The **public sector** is the part of the economy where goods and services are provided by funds which comes from national or local government on behalf of the population as a whole. The provision of goods and services in the public sector might be through some sort of public corporation which is ultimately responsible to a national parliament but which operates as an independent entity in a similar way to many private sector businesses. The day-to-day decisions will be made by managers but the overall finance for the business comes from a mixture of government funding and charges for goods and services. The goals of such organizations may be to provide high-quality services to customers at reasonable prices such that the operation is able to at least cover its costs. Any profit (or surplus) is used for reinvesting back into the business to improve the quality of the customer provision. These goods and services are sometimes provided free at the point of use and in other cases consumers have to pay a price, although the price might be much lower than would be the case if the good or service was provided by a private sector firm. The aim of public sector activity is to provide services that benefit the public as a whole. This is often because it would be difficult to charge people for the goods and services concerned, or people may not be able to afford to pay for them. Table 8.1 shows some typical examples of business activity which is carried out in the public sector across the EMEA territories. It is clear from this table that some of the goods provided are obviously public goods while there are other examples where the goods are private goods but the public sector may choose to also provide them. This may be because some goods can be classed as merit goods. A **merit good** is one which could be provided by the private sector but which may also be offered

merit good a good which could be provided by the private sector but which may also be offered by the public sector because it is believed that a less than optimal amount would be available to the public if resource allocation was left entirely to the private sector

TABLE 8.1

Business Activity in the Private and Public Sector

Type of good	Public good or both public and private
Health care	Both
Dental care	Both
Pension provision	Both
Street lighting	Public
Roads	Both
Public parks	Public
Beaches	Both
Justice	Public
Police	Public
Refuse collection	Both
Education	Both

by the public sector because it is believed that a less than optimal amount would be available to the public if resource allocation was left entirely to the private sector. This may be because people either would not be able to afford them or because they do not see such purchases as a priority. For example, some people may choose not to take out private health insurance because they think that they will not get ill or would rather spend their money on something that gives more immediate gratification. It is not until they get ill or have an accident and face health cost bills that they realize they may have made an unwise decision.

The examples given in Table 8.1 highlight how some goods can be both public and private goods or very obviously private goods. For example, street lighting is a public good because it is almost impossible for a private business to be able to provide this good and charge individuals for the privilege. Beaches, on the other hand, can be charged for if a business has bought a stretch of beach and is able to allow only certain people to use it following payment. There are plenty of examples of public beaches, but in both cases there is a cost to providing them as they have to be kept clean and have lifeguards provided. In the case of public provision, the taxpayer will ultimately fund the cost of provision, whilst if the beach was owned by a private firm the cost would be covered by the payments members make to access the beach.

In many countries, the public sector accounts for a significant proportion of business activity as highlighted in Table 8.2 which shows government expenditures as a percentage of gross domestic product (GDP) in 2010 for a selection of countries.

TABLE 8.2

Government Expenditures as a Percentage of Gross Domestic Product (Selected Countries), 2010

Country	Government expenditure as a percentage of GDP
Germany	46.7
Netherlands	51.2
Iceland	50.0
United Kingdom	51.0
Greece	49.7
Turkey	37.1
Italy	50.6
Denmark	58.2

Source: OECD – http://stats.oecd.org/Index.aspx

private sector that part of the economy where business activity is owned, controlled and financed by private individuals

Much of the discussion in this chapter will be devoted to firms operating in the private sector. The **private sector** consists of business activity that is owned, financed and run by private individuals. These businesses can be small firms owned by just one person, or large multinational businesses that operate around the world (globally). In the case of large businesses, there might be many thousands of owners involved.

Ultimately, private sector firms have to make a profit to survive, that is they have to at least cover costs in the long run. We can assume, therefore, that no firm in the private sector can afford to take their eye off financial performance but this may be just one goal amongst many.

We are going to split these goals into two sections – financial and non-financial objectives but it is important to remember there may be very close links between the two.

FINANCIAL OBJECTIVES

It might seem obvious to state that businesses have financial objectives. What are these objectives – do all firms seek to follow the classic assumption of profit maximization? If that is the case why do firms engage in price wars or seem to be concerned about their market share? Why do some firms make losses but still keep operating? Are finding ways to improve technical and productive efficiency simply a means of maximizing profits or are there other reasons for a focus on cost minimization? Are any or all of these objectives compatible with maximizing shareholder value (whatever that may mean)? Can financial objectives live side-by-side with non-financial objectives such as a focus on the environmental impact of business operations or social objectives?

We will look at all these questions and hopefully give you the tools to be able to construct some meaningful answers. As with other aspects of business economics we have looked at in other chapters of the book, it is important to remember that some of the models being presented here are simply that – models. They will help to conceptualize what we mean by certain principles and to enable us to understand why businesses make some decisions. We are not suggesting that firms sit down and chart their marginal revenue and marginal costs to find the exact point where they are equal and then announce they are maximizing profits. The point is that these models help explain a principle and so help us understand why, for example, a rail company might charge a different price for the same journey at different times of the day or why an airline or holiday company will slash prices of seats or package holidays at the last minute or why sometimes it is better to think about reducing output rather than constantly looking to increase it. This should be remembered as we go through this chapter and we will try and remind you as we go along.

Profit Maximization

A basic assumption of classical economics is that a firm in a competitive market tries to maximize profit. We have seen how revenue is calculated and that profit is total revenue minus total cost. We will look at the concepts of average revenue and marginal revenue using the example of a competitive firm which we shall call Waterlane Farm Dairy.

Waterlane Farm produces a quantity of milk Q and sells each unit at the market price P. The farm's total revenue is $P \times Q$. For example, if a litre of milk sells for €0.35 and the farm sells 10 000 litres per day, its total revenue is €3500 per day.

Because Waterlane Farm is small compared with the world market for milk, it takes the price as given by market conditions. This means, in particular, that the price of milk does not depend on the quantity of output that Waterlane Farm produces and sells. If Waterlane double the amount of milk they produce, the price of milk remains the

TABLE 8.3

Total, Average and Marginal Revenue for Waterlane Farm Dairy, a Competitive Firm.

Quantity (Q)	Price (P) €	Total revenue (TR = P × Q) €	Average revenue (AR = TR/Q) €	Marginal revenue (MR = ΔTR/ΔQ) €
1 litre	0.35	0.35	0.35	0.35
2	0.35	0.70	0.35	0.35
3	0.35	1.05	0.35	0.35
4	0.35	1.40	0.35	0.35
5	0.35	1.75	0.35	0.35
6	0.35	2.10	0.35	0.35
7	0.35	2.45	0.35	0.35
8	0.35	2.80	0.35	0.35

same, and their total revenue doubles. As a result, total revenue is proportional to the amount of output.

Table 8.3 shows the revenue for Waterlane Farm Dairy. The first two columns show the amount of output the farm produces and the price at which it sells its output. The third column is the farm's total revenue. The table assumes that the price of milk is €0.35 a litre, so total revenue is simply €0.35 times the number of litres.

This allows us to ask two questions:

1. How much revenue does the farm receive for the typical litre of milk?
2. How much additional revenue does the farm receive if it increases production of milk by 1 litre?

The last two columns in Table 8.3 answer these questions.

The fourth column in the table shows **average revenue**, which is total revenue (from the third column) divided by the amount of output (from the first column). Average revenue tells us how much revenue a firm receives for the typical unit sold. In Table 8.3, you can see that average revenue equals €0.35, the price of a litre of milk. This illustrates a general lesson that applies not only to competitive firms but to other firms as well. Total revenue is the price times the quantity ($P \times Q$), and average revenue is total revenue ($P \times Q$) divided by the quantity (Q). Therefore, *in a perfectly competitive market, a firm's, average revenue equals the price of the good.*

The fifth column shows **marginal revenue**, which is the change in total revenue from the sale of each additional unit of output. The sale of one more litre of milk adds €0.35 to total revenue, therefore the marginal revenue is also €0.35. In Table 8.3, marginal revenue equals €0.35, the price of a litre of milk. This result illustrates a lesson that applies only to competitive firms. Total revenue is $P \times Q$, and P is fixed for a competitive firm. Therefore, when Q rises by 1 unit, total revenue rises by P euros. For competitive firms, marginal revenue equals the price of the good.

average revenue total revenue divided by the quantity sold

marginal revenue the change in total revenue from an additional unit sold

> **Quick Quiz** When a competitive firm doubles the amount it sells, what happens to the price of its output and its total revenue?

Let us put together our knowledge of the firm's costs and its revenues to examine how the firm maximizes profit.

Thought Experiment   Before we do this, consider the following thought experiment to help conceptualize what we are about to analyse.

You have €100 in your pocket. You have a collection of souvenir flags for sale. Each flag costs an extra €5 to produce. If you could sell one extra flag to a customer for €10, would you make the transaction? Hopefully your answer is 'yes'. By doing so you will incur an additional cost of €5 to produce the flag but will gain €10 for selling it with the result you have a surplus of €5 which you put into your pocket meaning you now have added to the €100 and now have €105.

If you found it difficult to sell the next flag at €10 but a customer offered you €8, would you be prepared to sell it? Again, your answer ought to be 'yes'. This transaction yields a surplus of €3, not as much as the previous transaction but it still yields a surplus which adds to the amount in your pocket to make the sum €108. Would you prefer to have €108 in your pocket rather than €105? Presumably, the rational person would say 'yes'.

Now consider a situation where you could only persuade a customer to buy the next flag if you charged €4. Would you now make the transaction? In this case you sell the flag for less than the cost of producing the extra flag so you would pay out €5 in costs but only receive €4 in revenue from the sale of the flag. The sale would be made at a loss of €1 and so the money in your pocket would now be €107. Assuming we are behaving rationally, there would be no incentive for you to enter into this particular transaction since it would leave you worse off.

What if you could make a sale of a flag at a price of €5? In this situation you would make neither any surplus nor any loss. Given that you are not any worse off, there is no reason why the transaction should not be carried out.

Identifying the Point of Profit Maximization

Now let's apply this thought experiment to an example using Waterlane Farm. Consider Table 8.4. In the first column of the table is the number of litres of milk Waterlane Farm Dairy produces. The second column shows the farm's total revenue, which is €0.35 times the number of litres. The third column shows the farm's total cost. Total cost includes fixed costs, which are €50 in this example, and variable costs, which depend on the quantity produced.

The fourth column shows the farm's profit, which is computed by subtracting total cost from total revenue. If the farm produces nothing, it has a loss of €200. If it produces 1000 litres, it has a profit of €100. If it produces 2000 litres, it has a profit of €300, and so on. To maximize profit, Waterlane Farm chooses the quantity that makes profit as large as possible. In this example, profit is maximized when the farm produces 4000 or 5000 litres of milk, when the profit is €350.

TABLE 8.4

Profit Maximization: A Numerical Example

Quantity (Q) (000s)	Total revenue (TR) €	Total cost (TC) €	Profit (TR – TC) €	Marginal revenue (MR = ΔTR/ΔQ) €	Marginal cost (MC = ΔTC/ΔQ) €	Change in profit (MR – MC) €
0 litres	0	200	−200			
1	350	250	100	0.35	0.05	0.30
2	700	400	300	0.35	0.15	0.20
3	1050	700	350	0.35	0.30	0.05
4	1400	1050	350	0.35	0.35	0
5	1750	1430	320	0.35	0.38	−0.03
6	2100	1830	270	0.35	0.40	−0.05
7	2450	2250	200	0.35	0.42	−0.07
8	2800	2700	100	0.35	0.45	−0.10

There is another way to look at the Waterlane Farm's decision: it can find the profit-maximizing quantity by comparing the marginal revenue and marginal cost from each unit produced. The fifth and sixth columns in Table 8.4 compute marginal revenue and marginal cost from the changes in total revenue and total cost, and the last column shows the change in profit for each additional litre produced. The first 1000 litres of milk the farm produces has a marginal revenue of €0.35 and a marginal cost of €0.05; hence, producing that extra 1000 litres adds €0.30 per litre to profit (from –€200 to €100). The second 1000 litres produced has a marginal revenue of €0.35 and a marginal cost of €0.15 per litre, so that extra 1000 litres adds €0.20 per litre or €200 in total to profit (from €100 to €300). As long as marginal revenue exceeds marginal cost, increasing the quantity produced adds to profit. Since additional production of milk adds to profit it is worth Waterlane Farm producing this extra milk. Once Waterlane Farm has reached 4000 litres of milk, however, the situation is very different. The next thousand litres would have marginal revenue of €0.35 and marginal cost of €0.38 per litre, so producing it would reduce profit by €30 (from €350 to €320). It does not make sense for Waterlane Farm to produce the extra thousand litres and so as a result, the farm would not produce beyond 4000 litres.

One of the *Ten Principles of Economics* in Chapter 1 is that rational people think at the margin. We now see how Waterlane Farm can apply this principle. If marginal revenue is greater than marginal cost – as it is at 1000, 2000 or 3000 litres – it is worth increasing the production of milk; even making a decision to increase production from 3000 to 4000 litres is worth doing since the MC and MR are the same at this point and as a result the profit level is neither increased nor decreased. If marginal revenue is less than marginal cost – as it is at 5000, 6000 or 7000 litres – the farm should decrease production. This principle of thinking at the margin allows us to identify the point of profit maximization as the output level where MC = MR.

We can use Figure 8.2 to find the quantity of output that maximizes profit. Imagine that the firm is producing at Q_1. At this level of output, marginal revenue is greater than marginal cost. That is, if the firm raised its level of production and sales by 1 unit, the additional revenue (MR_1) would exceed the additional costs (MC_1). Profit, which equals

FIGURE 8.2

Profit Maximization for a Competitive Firm

This figure shows the marginal cost curve (MC), the average total cost curve (ATC) and the average variable cost curve (AVC). It also shows the market price (P), which equals marginal revenue (MR) and average revenue (AR). At the quantity Q_1, marginal revenue MR_1 exceeds marginal cost MC_1, so raising production increases profit. At the quantity Q_2 marginal cost MC_2 is above marginal revenue MR_2, so reducing production increases profit. The profit maximizing quantity Q_{MAX} is found where the horizontal price line intersects the marginal cost curve.

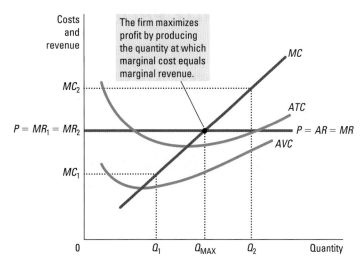

total revenue minus total cost, would increase. Hence, if marginal revenue is greater than marginal cost, as it is at Q_1, the firm can increase profit by increasing production.

A similar argument applies when output is at Q_2. In this case, marginal cost is greater than marginal revenue. If the firm reduced production by 1 unit, the costs saved (MC_2) would exceed the revenue lost (MR_2). Therefore, if marginal revenue is less than marginal cost, as it is at Q_2, the firm can increase profit by reducing production. Where do these marginal adjustments to the level of production end? Regardless of whether the firm begins with production at a low level (such as Q_1) or at a high level (such as Q_2), the firm will eventually adjust production until the quantity produced reaches Q_{MAX}. This analysis confirms the general rule for profit maximization: at the profit-maximizing level of output, marginal revenue and marginal cost are exactly equal.

If we assume that the firm aims to maximize profit then it aims at an output level where MC = MR. In Figure 8.2, that quantity of output is Q_{MAX}.

FYI

The Mathematics of Profit Maximization

Assume that the equations for an inverse demand curve and total cost facing a firm are given as:

$$P = 230 - Q$$

and:

$$TC = 40 + Q^2$$

We know that we have to differentiate both equations to find the marginal revenue and marginal cost and that the power function rule is:

$$\frac{dy}{dx} = nx^{n-1}$$

So, $MC = \dfrac{d(TC)}{dq} = -2q$

$$TR = P \times Q$$

$$TR = (230 - Q)Q$$

$$TR = 230Q - Q^2$$

$$MR = \dfrac{d(TR)}{dq} = 230 - 2q$$

Setting the profit maximizing output at MC = MR gives us:

$$-Q = 230 - 2Q$$

$$Q = 230$$

Profit would be maximized at an output level of 230. It should be noted that that the outcome figures are not always neat round numbers. The point, as has been made earlier, is that this is a model to help firms make decisions and as a result this firm might aim for an output level between two values and know that it is maximizing profit.

JEOPARDY PROBLEM

A firm finds itself in a position of seeing an increase in sales growth of 15 per cent over the previous year and productivity is up by 5 per cent. The firm's directors, however, have reported losses of €25 million compared to a profit of €15 million in the previous year. How could this have happened?

BREAK-EVEN ANALYSIS

break-even the level of output/sales at which total cost equals total revenue found by dividing the fixed costs by the contribution (selling price minus variable costs per unit)

When a new business starts up or if an existing business decides to develop a new product one goal may be to achieve break-even. **Break-even** refers to the output level at which the total costs of production are equal to the total revenue generated from selling that output. Many firms will look at break-even analysis as part of their planning tools.

They can look at the variables involved and how different figures plugged into these variables can affect decision making.

Figure 8.3 shows how we can represent break-even graphically. The vertical axis shows both costs and revenues and the horizontal axis shows output and sales. We know that a firm faces fixed costs which must be paid regardless of whether it produces any output. As a result the Fixed Cost curve FC is represented as a horizontal line at a cost of C_1. Variable costs (VC) are zero when the firm produces no output but rise as output rises. The VC curve shows these costs rising in direct proportion to output. Total cost is the sum of variable costs and fixed cost (TC = VC + FC) and so the TC curve has a vertical intercept equal to the level of fixed costs (C_1) and then rises as output rises. The vertical distance between the TC and VC curve is constant because of the proportional relationship between output and VC assumed above.

The total revenue curve is dependent on the price that the firm chooses to charge for its product. The higher the price charged the steeper the TR curve. The break-even level of output in Figure 8.3 is the amount where TC = TR which is depicted as Q_{BE}. At this output level the TC are C_1 and the TR is the same at R_1 shown by C_1/R_1 in Figure 8.3. At any output level below Q_{BE} the firm will find that its TC is greater than TR and so it will make a loss on that output. The loss made is represented by the area shown by the shaded triangle A.

At output levels above Q_{BE}, for example Q1, the firm's TR, shown by R_2, is greater than its TC, shown by C_2 and as a result it makes profits on this output. The amount of profit made at output Q1 is represented by the shaded triangle B.

If the firm were operating at Q1 then it could experience a fall in sales and still be generating a profit provided sales did not fall below the break-even output Q_{BE}. The distance between the break-even output and current production where TR is greater than TC is called the **margin of safety**.

We can also look at the break-even point in a more mathematical way. A firm needs to aim at selling its output at a price greater than the variable cost of production.

margin of safety the distance between the break-even output and current production where total revenue is greater than total cost

![FIGURE 8.3]

Break-Even Analysis

A break-even chart shows a firm's total cost, made up of fixed and variable costs and its total revenue. The output level where TR = TC is the break-even point shown by output Q_{BE}. Any output level below Q_{BE} would mean that the firm was producing at a loss because TC would be greater than TR but any output above Q_{BE} would mean the firm was operating at a profit. At output level Q_1, the amount of profit is indicated by the shaded triangle B. The distance between Q_{BE} and Q_1 is called the margin of safety and denotes how far sales could fall before the firm starts to make losses.

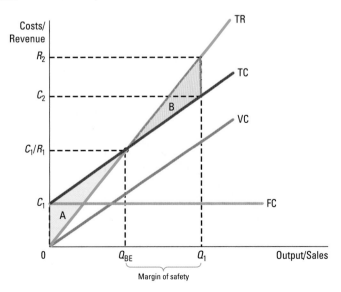

contribution the difference between the selling price and the variable cost per unit

Imagine a firm producing chocolate bars. The ingredient costs are €0.30 per bar and the labour costs are estimated at €0.10 per bar. Total variable costs are €0.40 per bar. If the selling price of the chocolate bar is €0.60 then every bar sold covers the variable costs of production and leaves €0.20 which can be used to help pay off the fixed costs which also have to be paid. This sum is called the **contribution**. The contribution is the difference between the selling price and the variable cost per unit. Knowing the contribution per unit the break-even output can be given by:

$$\text{Break-even} = \frac{\text{Fixed costs}}{\text{Contribution per unit}}$$

The break-even point can be affected by the costs of production, therefore, any change in fixed costs, for example, will shift the FC line up or down and thus the TC curve. Equally, changes in raw materials costs can affect the variable costs and as a result the TC curve.

It may be that the firm has little control over changes to its costs but it can use break-even analysis to assess the impact of the changes and make decisions as a result. What many firms do have control over is the price they charge. We know that TR = P × Q. If a firm changes its price the shape of the TR curve will alter. If a firm chooses to increase its price then the TR curve will pivot and become steeper as shown in Figure 8.4. With the TR curve now indicated as TR_1, the firm will not have to sell as many products to cover its costs and so the break-even output will be lower at Q_{BE2}. A firm might choose to reduce its price in which case the TR curve will become flatter. In this case TR curve will now be represented as TR_2 and the firm will now have to sell more products in order to cover its costs and so the break-even output would rise to Q_{BE3}.

Limitations of break-even analysis   As mentioned above, break-even is best seen as a planning tool and the outline given here is a simplistic one. There are a number of limitations with break-even analysis. Firstly there is an assumption that all output is sold. This is not the case for many firms where production takes place but products are not immediately sold and as such firms have stock (inventory).

FIGURE 8.4

The Effect on Break-Even Output of Changes in Price

Total revenue is found by multiplying price times the quantity sold. If the price is increased the TR curve will become steeper as shown by the curve TR_1. As a result, the firm would now only need to produce output Q_{BE2} in order to break-even. If price was reduced the TR curve becomes flatter indicated by curve TR_2 and the firm would have to sell a higher output level, Q_{BE3} in order to break even.

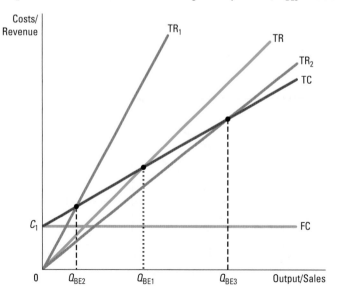

Secondly, the shape of the TR and TC curves is unlikely to be smooth as increases in output can be associated with economies of scale and not every additional product a firm sells can be sold at the same price. Equally, given the dynamic nature of markets, any estimation of costs or revenues are not likely to be relevant for very long.

Thirdly, we know that if a firm changes price, demand will be affected. Break-even analysis says nothing about what the effect of a price change on actual sales will be, nor how long it will take a firm to sell the output level to break even. The effect on sales of a change in price will be dependent on the price elasticity of demand.

CASE STUDY

On 2 February 2011, Rupert Murdoch, the chairman and CEO of News Corporation, launched a new business product *The Daily*. *The Daily* is a newspaper designed exclusively for Apple's iPad. It has a mission to: 'provide the best news experience by combining world-class storytelling with the unique interactive capabilities of the iPad'. Customers can download the app and get two weeks free access before having to subscribe for US$0.99 a week or $39.99 a year.

NEWS INTERNATIONAL

Clearly there will have been a cost to setting the product up in the first place which has been estimated at $30 million. The running costs have been reported to be $500 000 a week or $26 million a year. Given these figures we can get some idea of what the sales of subscriptions need to be for the product to break even. *The Daily* would need some 651 163 subscribers a year just to cover the running costs of the product, let alone the set up costs (which we can loosely refer to as the fixed costs) of $30 million.

What are the chances that it will be able to recruit this number of subscribers? Well, the first thing to note is that the price being charged for subscriptions is relatively low, hence the high numbers needed to break even. To get some idea we might look at data on other subscriptions to online news services. French newspaper *Le Monde* is reported to have around 39 000 web-only subscribers, *The Times*, another of Murdoch's papers, reported subscribers to its digital version as rising to 110 000 in October 2011. A Long Island, New York daily newspaper, *Newsday*, was said to have received just 35 subscriptions after three months of launch. *The Wall Street Journal* is estimated to have around 400 000 online paid subscriptions and *Wired* magazine began its online life with 100 000 subscribers but this fell to 23 000 half a year later. Given these figures, some from established brands, the numbers for *The Daily* do not look promising. Even if subscribers can be encouraged to download the app and pay, Apple will take a cut from the subscription amount so the actual revenues would be lower than that estimated here.

However, a newspaper's revenue does not just come from subscriptions; advertising also brings in revenue. The next question is: is the amount of advertising spend sufficient to make up any gap between costs and subscriber revenue to help *The Daily* break even. Here again, things do not look that promising. Digital intelligence firm, eMarketer, estimates that the total spent on advertising in 2011 was around $1 billion. *The Daily*, therefore, needs to get a share of that spending and given this spending covers all mobile advertising business, it has been estimated that *The Daily* would have to capture around 2.5 per cent of this annual spending.

One other thing to consider is that *The Daily* is only available on iPad and so the number of iPad users represents a constraint on the potential market size. Estimates for total iPad sales up to the end of 2012 since its launch are around 62 million. *The Daily*, therefore, needs to get around 1.05 per cent of iPad users to subscribe to its product and not only to subscribe but to maintain the subscription over a period of time. Is that possible? Of course it is, but the challenges facing *The Daily* to even reach break-even level seem daunting, never mind being able to become profitable.

Revenue Maximization

In recent years there has been some criticism of executives in businesses because their reward packages seem to have grown disproportionately to the performance of the business. One of the problems with this is understanding the definition of 'performance'. Executives might be persuaded to focus on goals which may give an impression of the business doing well such as targeting sales. Other things being equal, a rise in sales is a 'good' thing although of course this might not say anything about the cost involved in achieving any such increase in sales.

We know that total revenue is price multiplied by quantity sold. The goal of revenue maximization may also be referred to as sales revenue maximization. The principle is straight forward. There are three ways to increase sales: do something with price, something to influence how much is sold, or a combination of the two. We have seen how both reducing and increasing price can increase total revenue depending on the price elasticity of demand for the product. There are a number of pricing strategies that can be employed and we will look at these in more detail in Chapter 11. Equally, firms will have a number of strategies and tactics to try and increase sales which will include other elements of the marketing mix apart from price

- the product itself, how consumers are able to access the product (place), how consumers are made aware of the product (promotion), the processes involved which includes things like customer service commitments and the information customers can access, a focus on the people who are involved in the business (the employees and physical evidence), how the firm is viewed in the eyes of its customers, does the view conform with prior assumptions? For example, going into a car showroom and seeing new cars which are dirty and poorly presented in a shabby environment would not be an image most car dealers would want to present.

Graphical Representation of Sales Revenue Maximization

We know from our look at the theory of demand that in order to increase demand, a firm needs to reduce its price. We also know that along a straight line demand curve the elasticity ranges from elastic through to inelastic.

The price elasticity of demand varies at every point along a straight line demand curve. The higher up the demand curve (towards the vertical axis) where price is relatively high but quantity demanded relatively low, *ped* will be elastic, whereas at the lower end of the demand curve (towards the horizontal axis) the price is relatively low but quantity demanded relatively high and as a result *ped* will be inelastic. There will also be a point midway between these two ranges where the *ped* is of unit elasticity.

This knowledge is important for when you look at market structure and imperfect competition such as oligopoly and monopoly where the firm does not face a horizontal demand curve where $P = AR = MR$. In markets where firms are not operating under the assumptions of perfect competition, they will face a downward sloping demand curve. Given that the demand curve slopes down from left to right, in order to sell an additional unit the producer must offer it at a lower price than previous units and so the MR will always be lower than the average revenue. Graphically, the marginal revenue (MR) curve lies below the demand curve (the AR curve) as shown in Figure 8.5. MR is the addition to total revenue as a result of selling one more (or one fewer) units of production. When the addition to total revenue does not change as a result of the sale of one extra unit of production the MR is zero. The definition of unit elasticity is that the percentage change in quantity demanded is equal to the percentage change in price and so there will be no change in total revenue. It follows that the MR curve cuts the horizontal axis where the $ped = 1$. This is summarized in Figure 8.5.

What this tells us is that the total revenue curve will be positive when the price elasticity of the demand curve is elastic, at its maximum when price elasticity is equal to 1 and begins to decline when the price elasticity of the demand curve is inelastic.

FIGURE 8.5

Changing Price Elasticity of Demand Along a Demand Curve and Marginal Revenue

If the firm faces a downward sloping demand curve, then the slope of the curve is constant but the price elasticity of demand is not. In order to sell additional quantities, the firm must reduce price and so the addition to total revenue – the marginal revenue – will be less than the price (average revenue). The MR curve will lie below the demand curve. At the point where ped = unity (1), the addition to TR will be zero and so this represents the horizontal intercept of the MR curve. At points where the ped is less than unity (ped = inelastic), the MR is negative as the addition to TR is falling.

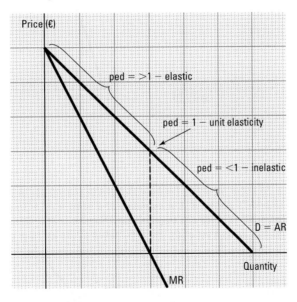

The total revenue curve can be graphed as in Figure 8.6 showing the relationship between sales revenue on the vertical axis in euros and the volume of sales on the horizontal axis. Panel (a) shows the TR for a firm in competitive conditions where $P = AR = AR$ (they are price takers and the demand curve is horizontal). In this situation the TR curve will be a positive curve rising in direct proportion to sales. Panel (b) shows the situation for a firm facing a downward sloping demand curve. The TR curve begins as a positive function of sales rising as more sales are achieved, reaching a maximum at a volume of sales of Q_1 and then declining thereafter. This is because the firm has to reduce prices in order to sell more output and is linked to the explanation given of the shape of the MR and demand curve in Figure 8.5.

We have seen how a firm can achieve profit maximization at the point where MR = MC. At this point the gap between the total revenue curve and the total cost curve is at a maximum. We can transpose the TC curve onto our TR curve given in panel (b) of Figure 8.6 to get the situation depicted in Figure 8.7. From this we can see that the point of profit maximization occurs when sales volumes are at Q_{PM}. At this point the distance between the TR and TC curves is at its maximum. However, the point of sales revenue maximization occurs where sales volume is Q_{SM} to the right of the profit maximizing sales level. This implies that if sales revenue maximization is pursued as a

FIGURE 8.6

The Total Revenue Curve

Panel (a) shows the TR curve for a firm in a competitive market. If the firm is a price taker then P = AR = MR and the demand curve it faces will be horizontal. The TR curve will be a positive curve rising in direct proportion to sales. Panel (b) shows the TR curve for a firm facing a downward sloping demand curve. As sales increase TR starts to rise but the rate of growth in TR will gradually begin to slow, reaching a maximum and then beginning to decline.

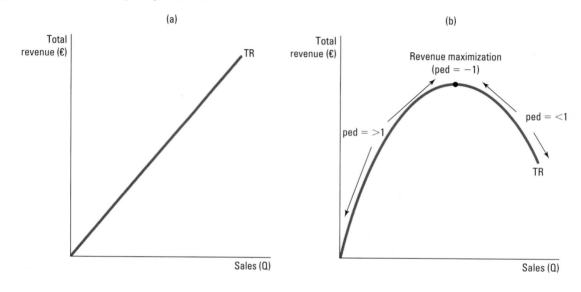

FIGURE 8.7

Profit Maximization and Revenue Maximization

This figure transposes a TC curve onto the TR curve for a firm facing a downward sloping demand curve. The point of profit maximization occurs where the distance between the TR and TC curves is at a maximum at a sales level of Q_{PM}. This is not the sales revenue maximizing position, however; this is achieved where sales are Q_{SM} and the TR curve is at a maximum. If the firm continued to try to push sales growth the TR would start to decline. At a sales level of Q_L, the firm makes a loss as TC is greater than TR at that sales level.

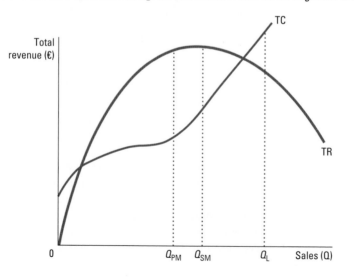

goal by a firm, it may be that it achieves this goal at lower profits, and this is likely to be because the cost of generating additional sales rises faster than the increase in revenue generated. This could be due to very expensive marketing campaigns, for example, or aggressive pricing tactics which drive out rivals but at very reduced margins.

Figure 8.7 also shows a sales volume of Q_L. At this level of sales, TC is greater than TR and the firm is making a loss. Despite generating much higher sales, this is being achieved at greater and greater cost and if continued the firm would continue to make increasing losses.

Pitfall Prevention In the discussion of the difference between profit maximization and sales revenue maximization, it is easy to get confused over the difference between total and marginal values. Ensure that you keep the distinction clear and understand the relationship between the two.

Cost Minimization

Businesses are aware of the concept of the product life cycle. All products go through a process starting with development, launch, growth, maturity and then decline. The **product life cycle** is a simplistic model to describe these typical processes. A typical product life cycle looks like that shown in Figure 8.8 which has sales on the vertical axis and time on the horizontal axis. Sales are clearly zero during the development stage and so at the point of launch the vertical and horizontal intercept will be 0. As the product gains traction in the market, sales will start to rise often picking up speed as a firm's marketing campaigns take effect. At some point sales will start to slow and at this point the market is either saturated as a result of new firms entering to take advantage of profits that exist and which have been highlighted by the product concerned, or where tastes change and the market begins to mature and stagnate. After a certain point, the market will start to decline and sales will gradually taper off. This is the decline stage of the product life cycle.

product life cycle a diagram representing the life cycle of a product from launch through to growth, maturity and decline

FIGURE 8.8

The Product Life Cycle

The product life cycle can be represented by a graph which shows sales on the vertical axis and time on the horizontal axis. At the introduction stage sales begin to rise slowly and then may pick up speed. Sales will continue to grow until the market matures after which time sales will start to decline.

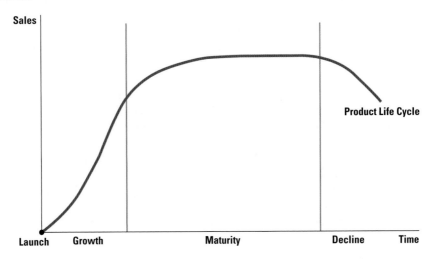

The reason why we have introduced the product life cycle is that there are links between the position of a product and the goal of minimizing cost. It can be assumed that every firm might want to keep costs to a minimum, but as a specific strategy this might be particularly relevant in a mature market, where the product faces little prospect of significant sales growth from year to year although the firm wishes to stay in the market. By sales growth we mean year-on-year increases in sales. For example, assume that unit sales in year X_1 are 1 million. If, in year X_2 sales rise to 1.2 million then sales growth will have been 20 per cent. If in year X_3 sales are 1.25 million then sales growth will have been 4.16 per cent. However, if in year X_4 sales remain at 1.25 million then sales growth will be zero but the firm might still wish to stay in the market because sales are deemed healthy at this level. The firm may see relatively stable revenues from such sales levels being generated for the foreseeable future although the prospect of growing sales in the future is just not feasible.

In such a market how does the firm increase profit? It knows it can do little to increase revenue given the maturity of the market and so the other option is to focus on costs. This could mean looking at making its human resource management more efficient by not only looking at whether it has the optimal number of staff to carry out its operations effectively, but whether those staff are in the right positions, whether talent is being exploited and whether the business can be reorganized to bring about a more optimal structure which allows it to continue meeting customer expectations but at the same time cut costs – both total and unit.

Productivity   One important aspect of this process is a focus on productivity. Productivity is a measure of output per factor of production per unit of time. It can be summarized in the following formula:

$$\text{Productivity} = \frac{\text{Total output}}{\text{Units of the factor}}$$

If, for example, a cutlery manufacturer produced 20000 sets of cutlery per month and employed 200 workers, then output per worker (productivity) would be 100 sets per month. Increasing productivity is an important goal for firms because of the contribution it makes to reducing unit costs.

To see how productivity can help a focus on controlling costs, assume that our cutlery manufacturer sells each set for a price of €75. The current unit cost of production is €50 so the margin on unit sales is just €25. If the firm sells all 20000 units a month it generates revenues of €1.5 million and costs will be €1 million.

The firm makes some organizational changes which include reducing the tiers of management and streamlining the sales function. In addition, new machinery in its factory helps workers to operate more efficiently and as a result of these changes productivity per worker rises to 120 units per month. Clearly there will have been some costs involved in making these changes but if the proportionate increase in costs is less than the proportionate increase in productivity then the firm's unit costs can fall thus improving its margins.

If workers are paid an average of €2500 per month with a productivity level of 100 units per month then we can work out that the unit labour costs to produce the cutlery sets is €25. If wages stay the same but the new changes increase productivity to 120 units per month, the unit labour costs are now only €20.83 per set. Other things being equal, the firm can now increase its margin from €25 to €29.17. Assuming it continues to sell all 20000 units per month its profit increases by €83400 per month.

It is also possible that the firm, in recognition of the changes the workforce are having to adjust to, could even pay the workers a higher wage and still see an increase in profit provided the increase in wages was more than offset by the rise in productivity.

The Supply Chain For many firms the supply chain can be long and complex. The **supply chain** is the various processes, activities, organizations and resources used in moving a product from business to business or business to consumer. Because of the complexities of the supply chain there are lots of opportunities for firms to focus on these activities and processes to find ways of increasing efficiency and reducing both total and unit costs.

One advocate of such a focus is Michael Porter whose theory of competitive advantage has been a foundation of strategic analysis of firms for many years. In his book *Competitive Advantage*[1] Porter states: 'If a firm can achieve and sustain overall cost leadership, then it will be an above-average performer in its industry provided it can command prices at or near the industry average.' A focus on any aspect of the supply chain may help to give the firm a competitive advantage if that advantage is both distinctive and defensible, that is, if it is unique to the business and not easy to copy in the short to medium term by the firm's rivals. Such advantages may be developed through employing specialists to analyse all aspects of the firm's supply chain operations. Investment in new equipment and machinery, designing new processes, putting in place new systems, finding ways to rationalize back-office functions (such activities as administration, payments and accounts offices, IT and human resources management which help keep a business running smoothly but may not have direct contact with customers), streamlining distribution networks and finding cheaper suppliers or outsourcing various aspects of the supply chain.

If these are put in place the firm may well be able to experience benefits which help them to move closer to the minimum point on the short-run average cost curve or, if a change in scale is achieved, a new short-run average cost curve at a lower point on the long-run average cost curve.

> **supply chain** the various processes, activities, organizations and resources used in moving a product from business to business or business to consumer

Shareholder Value

Shareholder value refers to the way in which shareholders receive reward for the risk they have taken in investing in the business. This risk is rewarded through either (or both) an increase in the share price of the business or in the value of the dividends paid to shareholders.

Shareholders are the part owners of a business. Owning a share in a business represents a claim to the future earning of that business. Those earnings will be dependent, in part, on the way in which the business is led and managed. The decisions of the executives and managers in a firm will affect the ability of the firm to generate revenues and to control costs and therefore make profits over time. The profits will be partly distributed to shareholders in the form of dividends. Investors may also buy shares in the hope that the price will rise and as a result the shares can be sold at a personal profit to the investor.

Fundamental to shareholder value is the idea that if a CEO focuses attention on improving the performance of the company through various measures, then the stock price will invariably follow if it is assumed that stock prices accurately reflect fundamental values (something that has been called into question in the years following the financial crisis).

The definition of performance, however, is where there is lots of debate. Should performance include just measures of profit? Do increases in the rate of growth of sales revenue over time signify good performance? Some would suggest firms focus on what is termed **free cash flow**. Free cash flow is the cash generated from the firm's operations minus that spent on capital assets. What this figure represents is the ability of the business to generate cash over and above that necessary to carry out its operations, service its assets and expand those assets. Cash generation is necessary to enable any firm to be able to expand over time and to develop new products and thus maintain its competitiveness.

> **free cash flow** the cash generated from the firm's operations minus that spent on capital assets

---

[1]Porter E.M. (2004) *Competitive Advantage: Creating and sustaining superior performance*, p.13. New York, Free Press.

NON-FINANCIAL OBJECTIVES

The following represents a summary of what we have called non-financial objectives. Of course, in reality, financial and non-financial objectives are often hard to disentangle, partly because as mentioned above, decisions that affect one part of a business are also likely to affect another part. A decision to expand market share, for example, can lead to increases in revenue and profit and as a result improve shareholder value.

Satisficing

The theory of satisficing was developed by Carnegie Tech Nobel-laureate, Herbert Simon in 1956. Simon argued that human beings do not act as rational automatons and are unable to compute optimized outcomes with mathematical precision. For example, CEOs may not have either the time nor brain capacity to sit and calculate the profit maximizing output. Instead they tend to behave using a mix of satisfying and sufficing, termed satisficing. CEOs, for example, have to satisfy shareholder demands and make healthy profits but not necessarily maximizing profit. The profit level must be sufficient to satisfy shareholder demands.

As a result, the assumption of profit maximizing or any other sort of maximizing or minimizing might not hold in the real world where uncertainty, the complexity of organizations and the vagaries of human behaviour mean that decisions are regularly made which are sub-optimal.

Linked to this is so-called **agency theory** whereby managers in a firm are viewed as being agents of shareholders and may pursue their own self-interest rather than the interests of the shareholders. If the interests of shareholders and managers diverge then there can be an agency problem and measures may need to be put into place to more closely align the interests of owners and managers.

agency theory where managers act as the agents of shareholders and as a result there may be a divorce between ownership and control such that managers pursue their own self-interests rather than the interests of shareholders

Market Power

Market power might include a number of different characteristics. It might involve firms seeking growth through acquisition (merger or takeover) both within their core market and outside it. The latter is referred to as conglomerate acquisitions and leads to firms having interests across a range of diverse and often totally unrelated markets. The Indian Tata Group, for example, owns businesses involved with information technology and communications, engineering, automotive, chemicals, energy and consumer products such as beverages and ceramics.

Expanding power can give a firm considerable influence over its market and enable it to have some influence over price or on output. We will look in more detail at the effects on firm behaviour in markets where the assumptions of highly competitive firms is dropped, in later chapters. Part of the drive to expand market power might also involve a desire to increase market share. **Market share** refers to the proportion of total sales in a market accounted for by an individual firm. In the global personal computer (PC) market at the time of writing, for example, Hewlett Packard (HP) accounts for around 16 per cent of total sales, Lenovo for 14 per cent, Dell for around 12.5 per cent, Acer for 8.3 per cent and Apple for 8.5 per cent.

Many CEOs will want to keep an eye on market share, partly because it gives some indication of the market power of the firm, but also because there may be personal gratification in expanding market share ahead of rivals; the CEO network can often be very close and highly competitive.

Market share can be expanded through sub-optimal tactics such as cutting prices. The aim is to encourage consumers to switch and once they have been won over, to then retain them. We saw in Chapter 2 how recruiting and retaining customers have different costs. The tactic of cutting prices to win over customers can be an expensive one in

market share the proportion of total sales accounted for by a product/business in a market

terms of the effect on margins and profits (and hence why it is described as sub-optimal because the firm is not aiming for profit maximization which would be the optimal decision).

Prices might be cut to the point where the firm is selling products at below cost in an attempt to win market share. In the longer term such a tactic is not sustainable as we shall see in the next chapter but in the short term it may well be sufficient to win a significant number of new or returning customers. One example of such a tactic appeared in the tablet market. Apple leads the market with its iPad product and since the introduction of the iPad there have been a number of other technology firms who have launched rival products. Few have been as successful as the iPad, however, and in early 2012, a number of firms announced price cuts for their tablet devices including Research in Motion's BlackBerry PlayBook, the Sony Tablet S and the Motorola Android Xyboard. Some of these price cuts have been up to a quarter off the existing price.

Social, Ethical and Environmental Objectives

Few large firms will neglect the concern amongst their wider stakeholders of the social, ethical and environmental impact of a firm's operations. The vast majority have incorporated some sort of social and environmental responsibility reporting into their operations as well as the annual report of financial accounts. Critics have argued that some firms use social and environmental issues as a cynical marketing tool and this may be true in some cases, but regardless of the reasons for introducing such policies, many firms have changed the way they run their operations to improve levels of social and environmental responsibility.

Examples of the sort of things that have been introduced include a greater awareness of the effects of pollution in all its forms and measures to reduce it through, increasing efficiency in the use of resources, developing operations to utilize cleaner technologies which reduce the environmental impact, sourcing raw materials from renewable sources, looking at options to recycle including making products that are almost fully recyclable, and reducing energy and water use.

Such measures are not only beneficial to the environment as a whole but also to businesses as unit costs can be reduced. Initial investment costs in cleaner energy systems, for example, can be high but the longer-term effects can be significant in terms of reduced unit costs. The social and environmental movement has forced businesses to take a long hard look at themselves and their operations and to make changes to the way they operate and do business and this can be no bad thing for any business looking to find ways of improving – however the definition of 'improving' is framed.

In addition to environmental objectives firms increasingly have developed social and ethical responsibilities in recognition of the wider stakeholders they interact with. Local sponsorship programmes, being involved in charity work, monitoring closely the way workers are treated, especially if the firm outsources part of its operations, basing decision making not simply on profitability but on what is perceived to be 'right and proper', doing work with the local community including getting employees to work with local projects, developing closer relationships with suppliers and promoting diversity.

Ethical decision making involves making decisions and conducting operations which conform to accepted moral codes – doing things the 'right' way. Such decision making includes the way in which a business manages its financial affairs and reports these affairs to help reduce the instances of fraud, bribery and corruption. Other aspects of ethical decision making include giving workers freedom of speech (a particularly relevant point given the increasing use of social media such as Facebook and Twitter as a means of communicating), paying taxes fairly, producing products which are safe (but which may be more costly to produce) and making decisions about who to trade with, who to recruit as suppliers and why those decisions have been made. For example, a firm may choose not to engage in trade with the government of a country which it sees as being repressive, even if such trade could be lucrative.

? **what if…**a firm has been making significant losses for five years which is pushing it to the brink of insolvency. It is offered the prospect of entering into a lucrative trade deal with a very corrupt government which would enable it to not only reverse the losses but also safeguard the jobs of its workers. What should the business do?

Putting into place social, ethical and environmental policies can be expensive and invariably requires considerable changes in a corporate culture and the way the business operates. Many businesses will look at such changes as being long term in their ultimate effects and benefits and part of the process involves convincing shareholders that there are benefits to such changes which outweigh the initial costs. If carefully considered and developed, some of these policies can be seen as being sources of competitive advantage which can be distinctive and defensible and therefore make very good business sense, let alone the impact on the firm's reputation and credibility.

CASE STUDY

Apple's Supplier Responsibility Report

Apple's 2011 *Supplier Responsibility Report* is a fascinating 25-page tour of the world of globalized business. Contained within, and inspired by corporate social responsibility (CSR) standards, are sections on training and development, foreign contract worker protection, preventing firms employing under-age staff, and the use of toxic chemicals in products. What is notable is that many of these areas of enquiry have been insisted on by external parties who make it their business to monitor what Apple gets up to in its business.

While the company's report, published since 2007, tackles what seems to be an exhaustive list of CSR-type concerns, it does not meet the demands of organizations such as As You Sow, which in 2009 urged Apple shareholders to tell the company to produce a formal CSR report, as do its competitors HP, IBM and Dell. Apple refused, saying that formal reporting of its approach to recycling, greenhouse gas emissions and toxins would just involve double reporting and unnecessary time and expense.

Apple has bowed to pressure from this and other groups before: in 2007, it agreed to publish recycling goals just before a shareholder vote on the issue. In the same year, Apple gave in to pressure brought to bear by Greenpeace to be more open about its products' environmental credentials. The green campaign group had ranked Apple near the bottom of its Greener Electronics listing. The Californian firm shrugged off this criticism at first, claiming that the environmental ranking used by Greenpeace was meaningless and that Apple had a strong environmental track record in any case. Eventually, the firm caved in and boss Steve Jobs wound up apologizing for leaving its customers in the dark on environmental issues.

The major headline-grabbing issues associated with Apple's suppliers tend to revolve around its manufacturing and assembly works in mainland China. In particular, a series of well-publicized reports on conditions at Foxconn, a Taiwanese company operating out of super-factories in south China which supplies Apple with iPads (the company also supplies other technology firms such as Nokia, HP, Dell, Samsung and LG with products).The reports cited a spate of worker suicides, accusations of the use of child labour and toxic chemicals at these Original Design Manufacturers (ODMs). While reporting on these practices, many industry-watchers have been fulsome in praise of Apple's efforts to 'hack away at' incidences of corporate wrongdoing at its suppliers' factories.

Other observers point to the litany of 'unsafe working conditions, lack of basic first-aid, bribery, exploitative recruitment fees and unpaid wages' and ask if this is all just a by-product of outsourcing manufacturing to China. It's clearly worth it for Apple to continue to use the globalized model of ODMs in the Far East. But for how long will Apple's auditors need to return to these factories to check on worker abuse? Is there a better way of regulating goods produced in these conditions?

Source: Adapted from Biz/ed http://www.bized.co.uk/blogs/international/2011/02/apple-csr-china

It must be remembered, however, that moves to improve social, ethical and environmental responsibility and the incorporation of policies as part of the goals of a firm do not happen everywhere. The vast majority of businesses are small and medium-sized and it may be impractical for many small businesses to have such goals. In addition, the geographical spread of business means that efforts to promote such policies as business goals may be confined to parts of developed western economies. Problems in securing deals on reducing carbon emissions, for example, highlight the tensions that exist between emerging economies and mature economies. There is still a long way to go.

Brand Recognition

A brand is means of creating awareness and identity in a product or range of products such that consumers come to recognize and associate the product when making purchasing decisions. A brand does not have to be associated with high value, high price or quality. A brand has to reflect clearly to the consumer what the association and personality is – what it means. Brands such as Dolce and Gabbana, for example, have associations with high quality fashion, whereas a brand such as Netto or Poundland have an association with low prices and value for money. If a shopper goes to Netto, they do not expect (nor want) expensively laid out and equipped stores; they expect to be able to buy a range of goods at competitive prices.

Building a brand and subsequent brand recognition may be a goal of business activity. Many firms spend significant sums of money on building brand recognition over time and it should come as no surprise that guarding that hard-earned recognition is something firms are keen to protect. Laws in many countries recognize such efforts and attempts by other firms to imitate a brand can be challenged in the courts.

Ultimately, the goal of brand recognition is designed to influence consumer behaviour. When an individual goes into a fuel station, for example, the array of chocolate bars by the pay station is designed to encourage impulse buying. Brand recognition may be an important factor and is why consumers, almost without thinking, go for a chocolate bar they are aware of and recognize as satisfying their needs. Creating a situation when consumers default to the purchase of one brand ahead of rivals would be the ultimate goal of many businesses in this area and the developments in neuroscience are beginning to reveal more about how brand association and recognition works and influences purchasing decisions.

Reputation and Image

Linked with social, ethical and environmental responsibility and branding is a goal to develop reputation and image. This might be a reputation for high levels of customer service, quality, reliability, value for money, technically sophisticated products, social awareness, design, style – anything that the firm thinks will help it to gain a competitive edge and which it can exploit.

Social enterprises are driven primarily by a social or environmental purpose, not profit.

UNIVERSITY OF LEEDS/ONE/DIVINE CHOCOLATE/THE BIG ISSUE

Social Enterprise

Social enterprises are a combination of charity and business activity. The concept developed in Italy in the 1980s and is a growing feature of business activity throughout Europe. Like any business, social enterprises have to generate a profit (usually referred to as a surplus) in order to survive in the long term, but these surpluses are invested into some social or community-based project rather than being shared between the owners through dividends. These sorts of businesses are also referred to as being part of the not-for-profit or third sector activity.

The goals of the business in such cases might be to generate surpluses to help communities access water supplies in less developed countries, promote recycling or fair trade, provide affordable homes, help young people to take a more active role in society. and so on.

Quick Quiz Are the different business goals outlined above mutually exclusive – i.e. is it possible to be a socially and environmentally responsible business whilst at the same time minimizing cost and maximizing profit?

IN THE NEWS

Tesco is one of the largest retail grocery and supermarket chains in Europe with increasing ambitions to expand even further globally. For many years its success was much vaunted amongst City investors but a change of leadership and a dynamic market environment may mean that the business has to reassess its goals. This article looks at some of the issues facing the business following disappointing sales figures at the end of 2011.

Tesco Share Price Falls 14%

In a trading statement announced in early January 2012, global grocer, Tesco, reported its worst Christmas sales performance in decades, despite a high-profile £500 million price-cutting campaign to attract shoppers back to its stores. The company, which triggered a price war with its promotion at the end of September, said the number of customers drawn in by its latest offer had not been enough to offset its lower prices. The supermarket group, which makes about 70 per cent of its operating profit in Britain, said sales at UK stores open over a year fell 2.3 per cent excluding fuel and value added tax (VAT) in the six weeks ending 7 January 2012. Management warned that it would see minimal profit growth for the year as it is increas-

ing investment into winning back shoppers, particularly in the UK.

The lowering of prices did drive higher sales, but the pressure on margins rendered the promotion unsuccessful. Meanwhile, Tesco's competitors had rather more success over the period, the outlook remains threatening and the company has been forced into something of a profits warning for the year. However, while disappointing, all is not lost. The international businesses continued to make a worthwhile contribution, whilst online sales growth in the UK of over 14 per cent bodes well, particularly given the fact that this could become an area of further focus for the group. Meanwhile, the group's product diversification leaves it well positioned for any upturn, and the dividend yield of around 4 per cent is another attraction.

Prior to [the] decline [in its share price on the announcement of its results], the shares had fallen 5 per cent over the last three months as compared to a gain of 4 per cent for the FTSE 100.

Naturally, it wasn't supposed to be like this. When Sir Terry Leahy passed the Tesco leadership baton to Philip Clarke [in 2011], the succession planning was described as 'perfection' and investors sat back for another decade of financial success.

Instead, Britain's biggest retailer is reeling after its first profit warning in 20 years. About £5 billion was wiped off the company's stock market value after the retailer confessed that its UK chain, which generates more than 60 per cent of group profits, had been wrung dry to fund the creation of Tesco's global empire.

The chain's Christmas sales were the worst in decades and Clarke said Tesco needed to sort out basics like fresh food, product ranges, customer service and staffing levels, to win back shoppers who had defected to Sainsbury's and Waitrose, and even no-frills chains Aldi and Lidl, for their turkeys and sprouts.

Things were so bad Clarke quoted Nietzsche's 'what doesn't kill us makes us stronger' as he briefed reporters. It was not about the Big Price Drop, the £500 million price-cutting campaign that had failed to cut through a 'noisy' market. No: the retailer had to tackle 'long-standing business issues'.

It was all so different last year. When Clarke took over, he said: 'My job is to build on the terrific legacy I have inherited ... that does not mean sweeping changes, a year zero.'

Well, the clock was reset last week, with Clarke earning a seat in the Tesco hall of fame, albeit for the wrong reasons. The 16 per cent fall in Tesco's shares was bigger than that recorded on Black Monday; Evolution Securities analyst Dave McCarthy has dubbed it 'Tesco Thursday'. He says: 'We suspect that when investors look back, they will view this day as the day the market recognized the fundamental changes that are taking and have taken place. A profit warning is the last sign of a company in trouble – and they usually come in threes.'

McCarthy adds: 'Tesco admitted for the first time that it has long-standing problems around range, quality and service. It has slashed wage bills to try to preserve profits and that, like pushing prices up, is a short-term fix at the expense of future profits.'

Over the past five years Tesco has increased the productivity of its UK store staff to record levels. The average number of full-time employees in a 40 000 sq ft superstore has fallen from 275 to 226. Kantar Retail analyst, Bryan Roberts, says the slide in store standards was evident in everything from the queues at the checkouts to customers carrying their groceries home in plastic cones designed for fresh flowers because the carrier bags had run out. 'They probably cut too much from store budgets and service has declined. Grocery shopping doesn't have to be a traumatic ordeal. It can be a fun, engaging thing to do.'

Of course, Tesco is not going bust. The supermarket made profits of £3.7 billion on nearly £68 billion of sales last year. The City was shaken only by the absence of profit growth forecasts when it had already punched 10 per cent into its computers. But there was also another bombshell. Clarke was not sure Tesco needed any more of the sprawling out-of-town Extra stores it has spent so long battling planners to build – and that were vital in its conquest of Britain's retail sector in the 1990s. He didn't want to go as far as to label its more than 200 out-of-town hypermarkets as 'white elephants' but said they were now a 'less potent force' as electricals and clothing sales shifted online.

He has a point, but as all its rivals have followed it out of town, it was a shock for the sector to hear. As Alan Parker, the City grandee trying to rescue Mothercare, put it succinctly last week: 'The whole retail market is restructuring at the moment, away from bricks and into clicks.'

Tesco has also been hurt by stronger competition. After periods in the wilderness, both Sainsbury's and Morrisons are once again forces to be reckoned with, and even its smallest rivals – Waitrose and the discounters Aldi and Lidl – are setting the pace on growth.

Kate Jones, a director at brand consultancy Added Value, says another problem may be that customers do not necessarily 'connect emotionally' with the Tesco brand: 'Its stripped-down communications and focus on the money promise [discounts] does not resonate powerfully enough.'

She adds: 'Fuelled by the credit crunch and the squeeze on incomes, the likes of Aldi have started to make inroads into the British middle class in the way that they have in continental Europe.'

Its indisputable success has given Tesco bragging rights about the calibre of its top executive team, but Leahy's retirement has triggered a changing of the guard, including the departure of Andrew Higginson, its former finance and strategy director, who will step down as head of its retailing services arm in September.

The Big Price Flop, as some analysts now refer to it, also suggests the British arm is missing the influence of Tim Mason, the group's deputy chief executive and Clubcard guru; he currently has his hands full with its heavily loss-making US chain Fresh & Easy.

One former executive argues the top team is depleted and weaker than when 'Terry, Tim and Andy' ran the show, but adds: 'Terry was always going to be a hard act to follow. He was a retail genius.'

When Clarke, who first worked for Tesco in 1974 as a part-time shelf stacker while he was still at school in Liverpool, was appointed to succeed Leahy, their similar backgrounds and immersion in the business suggested they were cast from the same mould. Only time will tell if Clarke can have as much success.

Questions

1. What is meant by the term 'profits warning'?
2. What might the goals be of a retail supermarket chain such as Tesco?
3. Why do you think that the price cutting tactic employed by Tesco was deemed to be a 'flop'?
4. What changes are occurring in the retail grocery sector and how might these changes influence the goals and decision making of a firm like Tesco?
5. If Tesco focused on profit maximization all other goals would naturally come into line'. Comment on this statement.

Sources: http://www.hl.co.uk/news/feature-articles/tesco-share-price-falls-14; http://www.guardian.co.uk/business/2012/jan/15/tesco-growth-megastores?newsfeed=true

SUMMARY

- We have looked at a range of business goals. Some of these can be classified as aims and other objectives.

- The 'traditional' (classical) assumption of profit maximization is one example of a financial objective or goal but increasingly other goals are becoming just as important.

- Brand recognition or a well-developed set of policies to minimize the environmental impact of a business' operations, for example, could be seen as being routes to generate increased sales and thus contribute to higher profits. The aim could still be profit maximization, the objective to help achieve this through promoting brand recognition or environmental responsibility.

- Others might argue that brand recognition or social and environmental awareness is a long-term aim in itself.

- Rather than be overly concerned with such distinctions, it is important to recognize that business goals are varied and dependent in part on the type of business and the type of business organization.

- All these goals are interrelated and can be seen as being parts of a jigsaw. Ultimately, businesses in the private sector need to generate profits – they will have to close down if the business activities are unsustainable.

- Of concern to the business economist, therefore, are the ways in which the stakeholder demands on business can be reconciled.

- It is safe to say that it is unlikely that all stakeholder demands can be met so business owners have to balance these competing demands and find a way of carrying out business which maximizes overall benefits at minimum cost.

- It is important to recognize that there will always be some cost involved in carrying out business and so regardless of the environmental, social and ethical claims of a firm, there will be some areas of operation where criticism can be levelled at the business' activities. How these criticisms are managed is often a crucial part of the role of CEOs and managers.

KEY CONCEPTS

excludable, p. 180	tactic, p. 183	contribution, p. 192
rival, p. 180	public sector, p. 184	product life cycle, p. 197
private goods, p. 180	merit good, p. 184	supply chain, p. 199
public goods, p. 181	private sector, p. 186	free cash flow, p. 199
common resources, p. 181	average revenue, p. 187	agency theory, p. 200
aims, p. 181	marginal revenue, p. 187	market share, p. 200
objectives, p. 181	break-even, p. 190	
strategy, p. 183	margin of safety, p. 191	

QUESTIONS FOR REVIEW

1. Using an example, explain the difference between aims and objectives.

2. Explain why a business can maximize profit where MC = MR.

3. Explain why, at the point of maximum TR, the price elasticity of demand for a good is –1.

4. What is meant by the terms 'break-even point' and 'margin of safety'?

5. What is the meaning of the term 'productivity'?

6. How can increases in factor productivity help a firm to achieve cost minimization?

7. Why might a firm have a goal of increasing market share?

8. Using examples, explain the difference between social and environmental objectives.

9. Explain how an objective to base decisions on strong ethical principles can lead to stakeholder conflict.

10. What is a social enterprise?

PROBLEMS AND APPLICATIONS

1. Why can it be difficult to distinguish between aims and objectives and strategies and tactics?

2. A firm faces the following cost and demand equations:

$$P = 100 - Q$$
$$TC = 10 - 5Q^2$$

Find the profit maximizing output.

3. A firm faces the following cost and revenue schedules:

Output (Q)	TR	TC
0	0	3
1	6	5
2	12	8
3	18	12
4	24	17
5	30	23
6	36	30
7	42	38
8	48	47

Calculate the profit, marginal revenue, marginal cost and state what the profit maximizing output will be for the firm.

4. A firm has the following information available to its managers:
Fixed costs are €1500, price = €8 and the variable costs are €0.50 per unit. What is the break-even output for this firm?

5. The firm in Question 4 above is operating at its break-even output. A discussion is being held about making a decision to change price with the aim of increasing profit. It is operating at 98 per cent capacity. The sales director wants to reduce price but the operations manager wants to increase price. Which of these two options would you recommend the firm take and why?

6. If a firm faces a downward sloping demand curve, why doesn't total revenue continue rising as a firm sells more of its output?

7. Workers in a firm have petitioned the management for a 5 per cent pay increase. How might the firm's management approach negotiations on the pay claim. (Hint – the management may be interested in raising the issue of productivity.)

8. Which of the following do you think is the most important element of shareholder value: the dividend to shareholders, the firm's share price or free cash flow? Explain your answer.

9. How might an energy firm such as BP or Shell claim that they can maximize shareholder value but at the same time emphasize their environmental and social credentials?

10. A firm is operating in a market in which the good it sells is in the maturity stage of its life cycle. How does knowledge of this shape its decisions about what its goals for that product might be? How might these decisions be influenced if the firm had a new product in development which it believed could take significant market share in the future?

9 FIRM BEHAVIOUR AND THE ORGANIZATION OF INDUSTRY

LEARNING OBJECTIVES

In this chapter you will:

- Examine what items are included in a firm's costs of production

- Analyze the link between a firm's production process and its total costs

- Learn the meaning of average total cost and marginal cost and how they are related

- Consider the shape of a typical firm's cost curves

- Examine the relationship between short-run and long-run costs

After reading this chapter you should be able to:

- Explain the difference between economic profit and accounting profit

- Utilize a production function to derive a total cost curve

- Explain why the marginal cost curve must intersect the average total cost curve at the minimum point of the average total cost curve

- Explain why a production function might exhibit increasing marginal product at low levels of output and decreasing marginal product at high levels of output

- Explain why, as a firm expands its scale of operation, it tends to first exhibit economies of scale, then constant returns to scale, then diseconomies of scale

- Show, by using isoquant curves and isocost lines how firms can arrive at the least-cost input combination.

THE COSTS OF PRODUCTION

In Chapters 4 and 5 we looked at how markets operate. In this and subsequent chapters we are going to look in more detail at businesses and how they operate. We will refer to these businesses as 'firms'.

The economy is made up of thousands of firms that produce the goods and services we enjoy every day: Mercedes Benz produces cars, Miele produce kitchen appliances and Nestlé produces food and drink. Some firms, such as these three, are large; they employ thousands of workers and have thousands of shareholders who share in the firms' profits. Other firms, such as the local hairdresser's shop or pizzeria, are small; they employ only a few workers and may be owned by a single person or family.

As we examine firm behaviour in more detail you will gain a better understanding of what decisions lie behind the supply curve in a market which we introduced in Chapter 4. In addition, it will introduce you to a part of economics called *industrial organization* – the study of how firms' decisions regarding prices and quantities depend on the market conditions they face. The town in which you live, for instance, may have several restaurants but only one water supply company. How does this difference in the number of firms affect the prices in these markets and the efficiency of the market outcomes? The field of industrial organization addresses exactly this question.

Before we turn to these issues, however, we need to discuss the costs of production. All firms, from Air France to your local baker's shop, incur costs as they make the goods and services that they sell. A firm's costs are a key determinant of its production and pricing decisions. In this chapter, we define some of the variables that economists use to measure a firm's costs, and we consider the relationships among them. We will also introduce a model to look at how a firm might maximize production given certain constraints such as its budgets and the factors of production it has available.

WHAT ARE COSTS?

We begin our discussion of costs at Primo's Pizza Factory. Primo, the owner of the firm, buys flour, tomatoes, mozzarella cheese, salami and other pizza ingredients. He also buys

Pizza production, like most businesses, relies on some basic factor inputs – land, capital and labour. These are combined to produce products (pizzas in this example) which are then sold to customers and generate revenue. If, over time, the revenue generated by sales of pizzas is greater than the total cost of making them, the firm will make a profit.

the mixers and ovens and hires workers to run this equipment, all of which is housed inside the factory building. He then sells the resulting pizzas to consumers. By examining some of the issues that Primo faces in his business, we can learn some lessons about costs that apply to all firms in the economy.

Total Revenue, Total Cost and Profit

We have seen in Chapter 4 that the amount a firm sells multiplied by the price it sells the products at is the total revenue the firm receives. If Primo sells 500 000 pizzas a year and the average price of each pizza sold is €5 his total revenue will be $5 \times 500\,000 = €2.5$ million.

To produce those 500 000 pizzas, Primo will have had to employ labour, buy machinery and equipment, run and maintain that equipment, buy the raw materials to make the pizzas, pay rent or a mortgage on the factory, pay off loans he may have secured (both the sum borrowed and any interest charged), pay for market research, marketing costs such as advertising and promotion, administration costs (such as managing the firm's payroll, monitoring the finances, processing sales and purchase invoices), and many other everyday payments down to the cost of using the telephone, energy use, postage, maintaining the buildings and so on. These represent Primo's **total cost**.

total cost the market value of the inputs a firm uses in production

If Primo subtracts all the costs over the year from the revenues received in the same year he will either have a surplus (i.e. his revenue will be greater than his costs) or possibly have spent more on costs than received in revenues. **Profit** is a firm's total revenue minus its total cost. That is:

profit total revenue minus total cost

$$\text{Profit} = \text{Total revenue} - \text{Total cost}$$

We can express this in the formula:

$$\pi = \text{TR} - \text{TC}$$

where the Greek letter pi (π) represents profit.

We will look at a firm's objectives in more detail in Chapter 8 but let us assume for the moment that Primo's objective is to make his firm's profit as large as possible – in other words, he wants to maximize profit. Primo needs to be able to measure his total revenue and his total costs. We know how to calculate total revenue, in many cases that is a relatively easy thing to do, but the measurement of a firm's total cost is more subtle and open to different interpretations.

> **Pitfall Prevention** It is important to understand the distinction between profit and cash flow – the latter is the money flowing into and out of a business over a period of time, whereas profit takes into consideration the total revenue and total cost. A firm could be profitable but have cash flow problems which could force it out of business.

Costs as Opportunity Costs

When measuring costs at Primo's Pizza Factory, or any other firm, it is important to keep in mind one of the *Ten Principles of Economics* from Chapter 1: the cost of something is what you give up to get it. Recall that the *opportunity cost* of an item refers to all those things that must be forgone to acquire that item. When economists speak of a firm's cost of production, they include the opportunity costs of making its output of goods and services.

A firm's opportunity costs of production are sometimes obvious but sometimes less so. When Primo pays €1000 for a stock of flour, he can no longer use that €1000 to buy something else; he has to sacrifice what else that €1000 could have purchased. Similarly, when Primo hires workers to make the pizzas, the wages he pays are part of the firm's costs.

Because these costs require the firm to pay out some money, they are called **explicit costs**. By contrast, some of a firm's opportunity costs, called **implicit costs**, do not require a cash outlay. Imagine that Primo is skilled with computers and could earn €100 per hour working as a programmer. For every hour that Primo works at his pizza factory, he gives up €100 in income, and this forgone income is also classed as part of his costs by an economist.

This distinction between explicit and implicit costs highlights an important difference between how economists and accountants analyze a business. Economists are interested in studying how firms make production and pricing decisions. Because these decisions are based on both explicit and implicit costs, economists include both when measuring a firm's costs. By contrast, accountants have the job of keeping track of the money that flows into and out of firms. As a result, they measure the explicit costs but often ignore the implicit costs.

The difference between economists and accountants is easy to see in the case of Primo's Pizza Factory. When Primo gives up the opportunity to earn money as a computer programmer, his accountant will not count this as a cost of his pizza business. Because no money flows out of the business to pay for this cost, it never shows up on the accountant's financial statements. An economist, however, will count the foregone income as a cost because it will affect the decisions that Primo makes in his pizza business. This is an important part of thinking like an economist. If the wage as a computer programmer rose from €100 to €500 per hour, the opportunity cost of running his pizza business might now change his decision making. The opportunity cost of running the business in terms of what Primo is sacrificing in foregone income has risen. Primo might decide he could earn more by closing the business and switching to computer programming.

The Cost of Capital as an Opportunity Cost An important implicit cost of almost every firm is the opportunity cost of the financial capital that has been invested in the business. Suppose, for instance, that Primo used €300 000 of his savings to buy his pizza factory from the previous owner. If Primo had instead left this money deposited in a savings account that pays an interest rate of 5 per cent, he would have earned €15 000 per year (assuming simple interest). To own his pizza factory, therefore, Primo has given up €15 000 a year in interest income. This forgone €15 000 is an implicit opportunity cost of Primo's business. An economist views the €15 000 in interest income that Primo gives up every year as a cost of his business, even though it is an implicit cost. Primo's accountant, however, will not show this €15 000 as a cost because no money flows out of the business to pay for it.

To explore further the difference between economists and accountants, let's change the example slightly. Suppose now that Primo did not have the entire €300 000 to buy the factory but, instead, used €100 000 of his own savings and borrowed €200 000 from a bank at an interest rate of 5 per cent. Primo's accountant, who only measures explicit costs, will now count the €100 000 interest paid on the bank loan every year as a cost because this amount of money now flows out of the firm. By contrast, according to an economist, the opportunity cost of owning the business is still €15 000. The opportunity cost equals the interest on the bank loan (an explicit cost of €10 000) plus the forgone interest on savings (an implicit cost of €5000).

Economic Profit versus Accounting Profit

Now let's return to the firm's objective – profit. Because economists and accountants measure costs differently, they also measure profit differently. An economist measures a firm's **economic profit** as the firm's total revenue minus all the opportunity costs (explicit and implicit) of producing the goods and services sold. An accountant measures the firm's **accounting profit** as the firm's total revenue minus only the firm's explicit costs.

explicit costs input costs that require an outlay of money by the firm

implicit costs input costs that do not require an outlay of money by the firm

economic profit total revenue minus total cost, including both explicit and implicit costs

accounting profit total revenue minus total explicit cost

Economists versus Accountants

Economists include all opportunity costs when analyzing a firm, whereas accountants measure only explicit costs. Therefore, economic profit is smaller than accounting profit.

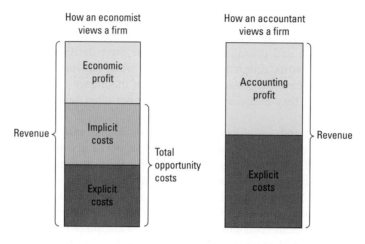

Figure 9.1 summarizes this difference. Notice that because the accountant ignores the implicit costs, accounting profit is usually larger than economic profit. For a business to be profitable from an economist's standpoint, total revenue must cover all the opportunity costs, both explicit and implicit.

> **Quick Quiz** Richard Collishaw is a dairy farmer who is also a skilled metal worker. He makes unique garden sculptures that could earn him €40 an hour. One day, he spends 10 hours milking his dairy herd. The cost of operating the machinery used in the milking process is €200. What opportunity cost has he incurred? What cost would his accountant measure? If the milk produced will yield €400 in revenue, does Richard earn an accounting profit? Does he earn an economic profit? Would you advise Richard to continue as a farmer or switch to metal working?

PRODUCTION AND COSTS

We saw in Chapter 2 how the transformation process was characterized by firms buying inputs to carry out production. There is clearly a relationship between the amount of inputs used, the cost of production and the amount produced. In this section we examine the link between a firm's production process and its total cost using Primo's Pizza Factory as an example.

The Production Function

production function the relationship between quantity of inputs used to make a good and the quantity of output of that good

The relationship between factor inputs can be expressed as a mathematical relationship called a production function. The **production function** shows the amount of output which can be produced given different combinations of factor inputs, land, labour and capital. This should be fairly intuitive – if Primo increases the number of people working in his factory then the amount of pizzas produced would be likely to rise. However, it could also be possible that Primo might decide to cut the number of workers he employs and buy a machine which can do their job and still increase the amount of pizzas produced.

In reality, firms face complex decisions over how to organize production and a whole discipline has grown up around this called operations management which in turn is closely linked to organizational behaviour and organizational design. Some firms rely on large amounts of labour compared to other factors for production and are referred to as *labour intensive*, whereas other firms have relatively small amounts of labour but very large amounts of capital and are referred to as *capital intensive*.

Let us assume there are two factor inputs, labour (L) and capital (K). The production function can be expressed as follows:

$$Q = f (L_1, K_1)$$

This states that the level of output (Q) is dependent upon the amount of labour and capital employed. More complex production functions are developed which include more specific dependent variables which can have different values. For example, we can specify a particular amount of labour, a particular amount of capital, as well as a certain quantity of land. Using this as a model, we can then vary some factor inputs whilst holding the others constant and analyze the effect on the level of output.

Obviously, this is a very simple introduction to the production function and as we will see later, changing the amount of factor inputs can have different consequences.

> **?** **what if…** Primo's factory had a total floor area of 2000 square metres, three-quarters of which was taken up with machinery. Primo employs 50 workers. If he employs a further ten workers, will output of pizzas increase? If he employs another ten will output continue to increase? What do you think would happen to output if Primo continued to increase the number of workers he employs?

The Short Run and the Long Run

In business, the distinction between the short run and the long run is of considerable importance. The **short run** is defined as the period of time in which some factors of production cannot be altered. The **long run** is that period of time when all factors of production can be altered. The distinction is really a conceptual one rather than a specific one. Many businesses will not be able to calculate the short run or the long run but they will know that the distinction will be an important consideration in their decision making. The long run for a market trader in a local street market may be weeks or months but for an energy supply company could be 20 years.

short run the period of time in which some factors of production cannot be changed

long run the period of time in which all factors of production can be altered

For a market trader increasing the amount of labour employed, securing a new pitch and buying a new stall might only take three months; for an energy supply company, building a new power station could take many years as it goes through the process of designing the station, securing planning permission, signing contracts with construction companies and then the actual construction process.

TABLE 9.1

A Production Function and Total Cost: Primo's Pizza Factory

Number of workers	Output (quantity of pizzas produced per hour)	Marginal product of labour	Cost of factory	Cost of workers	Total cost of inputs (cost of factory + cost of workers)
0	0		€30	€0	€30
		50			
1	50		30	10	40
		40			
2	90		30	20	50
		30			
3	120		30	30	60
		20			
4	140		30	40	70
		10			
5	150		30	50	80

Using the short run and the long run we can analyze the effect of decision making. In the short run, let us assume that the size of Primo's factory is fixed (a not unreasonable assumption) but that Primo can vary the quantity of pizzas produced by changing the number of workers.

Table 9.1 shows how the quantity of pizzas Primo's factory produces per hour depends on the number of workers. As you see in the first two columns, if there are no workers in the factory Primo produces no pizzas. When there is 1 worker he produces 50 pizzas. When there are 2 workers he produces 90 pizzas, and so on.

Figure 9.2 (panel (a)) presents a graph of these two columns of numbers. The number of workers is on the horizontal axis, and the number of pizzas produced is on the vertical axis. This is a graph of the production function.

FIGURE 9.2

Primo's Production Function

The production function in panel (a) shows the relationship between the number of workers hired and the quantity of output produced. Here the number of workers hired (on the horizontal axis) is from the first column in Table 9.1, and the quantity of output produced (on the vertical axis) is from the second column. The production function gets flatter as the number of workers increases, which reflects diminishing marginal product. The total cost curve in panel (b) shows the relationship between the quantity of output produced and total cost of production. Here the quantity of output produced (on the horizontal axis) is from the second column in Table 9.1, and the total cost (on the vertical axis) is from the sixth column. The total cost curve gets steeper as the quantity of output increases because of diminishing marginal product.

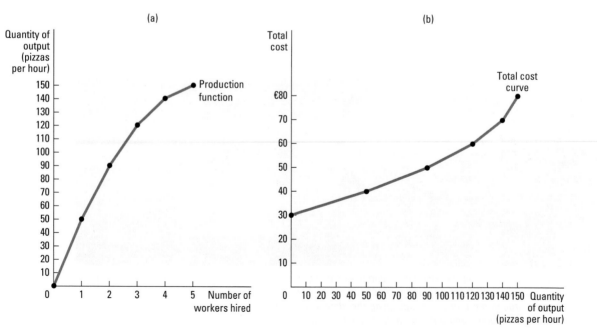

We are interested in the decision making of a firm in such a situation. If Primo is able to estimate his production function, how would such information help him in his decision making? This is what we are trying to model. Remember that a model is a representation of reality. No-one is suggesting that every firm or business person sits down, works out production functions and graphs them (although there are plenty of examples of very sophisticated analysis of this sort which does take place) but the important thing from our perspective is the conceptualization of the decision-making process.

One of the *Ten Principles of Economics* introduced in Chapter 1 is that rational people think at the margin. What does this mean in practice? Think about this proposition. If you were Primo would you want to have some understanding of whether employing an extra worker would affect the amount of pizzas produced? Would you also want to compare that outcome with how much you had to pay the extra worker? If you paid the extra worker €10 per hour and the worker produced 5 pizzas in that hour which you could sell for €5 each, would you employ him or her? What if employing the extra worker required you to pay €30 per hour but the worker still produced 5 pizzas an hour sold at the same price. Would you now employ that extra worker?

To take a step toward understanding these decisions, the third column in the table gives the marginal product of a worker. The **marginal product** of any input in the production process is the increase in the quantity of output obtained from one additional unit of that input. When the number of workers goes from 1 to 2, pizza production increases from 50 to 90, so the marginal product of the second worker is 40 pizzas. And when the number of workers goes from 2 to 3, pizza production increases from 90 to 120, so the marginal product of the third worker is 30 pizzas.

marginal product the increase in output that arises from an additional unit of input

Notice that as the number of workers increases, the marginal product declines. The second worker has a marginal product of 40 pizzas, the third worker has a marginal product of 30 pizzas and the fourth worker has a marginal product of 20 pizzas. This property of the production function is called **diminishing marginal product**. At first, when only a few workers are hired, they have easy access to Primo's kitchen equipment. As the number of workers increases, additional workers have to share equipment and work in more crowded conditions. Hence, as more and more workers are hired, each additional worker contributes less to the production of pizzas.

diminishing marginal product the property whereby the marginal product of an input declines as the quantity of the input increases

Diminishing marginal product is also apparent in Figure 9.2 (panel (a)). The production function's slope ('rise over run') tells us the change in Primo's output of pizzas ('rise') for each additional input of labour ('run'). That is, the slope of the production function measures the marginal product of a worker. As the number of workers increases, the marginal product declines, and the production function becomes flatter.

From the Production Function to the Total Cost Curve

The last three columns of Table 9.1 are reproduced as a graph in Figure 9.2 (panel (b)) to show Primo's cost of producing pizzas. In this example, the cost of operating the factory is €30 per hour and the cost of a worker is €10 per hour. If Primo hires 1 worker, his total cost is €40. If he hires 2 workers, his total cost is €50, and so on. With this information, the table now shows how the number of workers Primo hires is related to the quantity of pizzas he produces and to his total cost of production.

We are interested in studying firms' production and pricing decisions. For this purpose, the most important relationship in Table 9.1 is between quantity produced (in the second column) and total costs (in the sixth column). Panel (b) of Figure 9.2 graphs these two columns of data with the quantity produced on the horizontal axis and total cost on the vertical axis. This graph is called the *total cost curve*.

Now compare the total cost curve in panel (b) of Figure 9.2 with the production function in panel (a). These two curves are opposite sides of the same coin. The total cost curve gets steeper as the amount produced rises, whereas the production function gets flatter as production rises. These changes in slope occur for the same reason. High production of pizzas means that Primo's kitchen is crowded with many workers. Because the kitchen is crowded, each additional worker adds less to production, reflecting diminishing marginal product. Therefore, the production function is relatively flat. But now turn this logic around: when the kitchen is crowded, producing an additional pizza requires a lot of additional labour and is thus very costly. Therefore, when the quantity produced is large, the total cost curve is relatively steep.

> **Quick Quiz** If Farmer Schmidt plants no seeds on his farm, he gets no harvest. If he plants 1 bag of seeds he gets 3 tonnes of wheat. If he plants 2 bags he gets 5 tonnes. If he plants 3 bags he gets 6 tonnes. A bag of seeds is priced at €100, and seeds are his only cost. Use these data to graph the farmer's production function and total cost curve. Explain their shapes.

THE VARIOUS MEASURES OF COST

Our analysis of Primo's Pizza Factory demonstrated how a firm's total cost reflects its production function. From data on a firm's total cost we can derive several related measures of cost. To see how these related measures are derived, we consider the example in Table 9.2. Workers at Primo's factory regularly use Lia's Lemonade Stand.

The first column of the table shows the number of glasses of lemonade that Lia might produce, ranging from 0 to 10 glasses per hour. The second column shows Lia's total cost of producing glasses of lemonade. Figure 9.3 plots Lia's total cost curve. The quantity of lemonade (from the first column) is on the horizontal axis, and total cost (from the second column) is on the vertical axis. Lia's total cost curve has a shape similar to Primo's. In particular, it becomes steeper as the quantity produced rises, which (as we have discussed) reflects diminishing marginal product.

Fixed and Variable Costs

fixed costs costs that are not determined by the quantity of output produced

Lia's total cost can be divided into two types. Some costs, called **fixed costs**, are not determined by the amount of output produced; they can change but not as a result of changes in the amount produced. They are incurred even if the firm produces nothing

TABLE 9.2

The Various Measures of Cost: Lia's Lemonade Stand

Quantity of lemonade glasses (per hour)	Total cost	Fixed cost	Variable cost	Average fixed cost	Average variable cost	Average total cost	Marginal cost
0	€3.00	€3.00	€0.00	–	–	–	
1	3.30	3.00	0.30	€3.00	€0.30	€3.30	€0.30
2	3.80	3.00	0.80	1.50	0.40	1.90	0.50
3	4.50	3.00	1.50	1.00	0.50	1.50	0.70
4	5.40	3.00	2.40	0.75	0.60	1.35	0.90
5	6.50	3.00	3.50	0.60	0.70	1.30	1.10
6	7.80	3.00	4.80	0.50	0.80	1.30	1.30
7	9.30	3.00	6.30	0.43	0.90	1.33	1.50
8	11.00	3.00	8.00	0.38	1.00	1.38	1.70
9	12.90	3.00	9.90	0.33	1.10	1.43	1.90
10	15.00	3.00	12.00	0.30	1.20	1.50	2.10

FIGURE 9.3

Lia's Total Cost Curve

Here the quantity of output produced (on the horizontal axis) is from the first column in Table 9.2, and the total cost (on the vertical axis) is from the second column. As in Figure 9.2, the total cost curve gets steeper as the quantity of output increases because of diminishing marginal product.

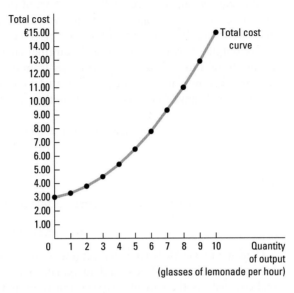

at all. Lia's fixed costs include any rent she pays because this cost is the same regardless of how much lemonade Lia produces. Similarly, if Lia needs to hire bar staff to serve the drinks, regardless of the quantity of lemonade sold, the worker's salary is a fixed cost. The third column in Table 9.2 shows Lia's fixed cost, which in this example is €3.00.

Some of the firm's costs, called **variable costs**, change as the firm alters the quantity of output produced. Lia's variable costs include the cost of lemons, sugar, paper cups and straws: the more lemonade Lia makes, the more of these items she needs to buy. Similarly, if Lia pays her workers overtime to make more lemonade, the wages of these workers are variable costs. The fourth column of the table shows Lia's variable cost. The variable cost is 0 if she produces nothing, €0.30 if she produces 1 glass of lemonade, €0.80 if she produces 2 glasses and so on.

variable costs costs that are dependent on the quantity of output produced

A firm's total cost is the sum of fixed and variable costs. In Table 9.2 total cost in the second column equals fixed cost in the third column plus variable cost in the fourth column.

Average and Marginal Cost

As the owner of her firm, Lia has to decide how much to produce. A key part of this decision is how her costs will vary as she changes the level of production. In making this decision, Lia might ask her production supervisor the following two questions about the cost of producing lemonade:

- How much does it cost to make the typical glass of lemonade?
- How much does it cost to increase production of lemonade by 1 glass?

Although at first these two questions might seem to have the same answer, they do not. Both answers will turn out to be important for understanding how firms make production decisions.

To find the cost of the typical unit produced, we would divide the firm's total costs by the quantity of output it produces. For example, if the firm produces 2 glasses per hour,

average total cost total cost divided by the quantity of output

average fixed cost fixed costs divided by the quantity of output

average variable cost variable costs divided by the quantity of output

marginal cost the increase in total cost that arises from an extra unit of production

its total cost is €3.80, and the cost of the typical glass is €3.80/2, or €1.90. Total cost divided by the quantity of output is called **average total cost**. Because total cost is just the sum of fixed and variable costs, average total cost can be expressed as the sum of average fixed cost and average variable cost. **Average fixed cost** is the fixed cost divided by the quantity of output, and **average variable cost** is the variable cost divided by the quantity of output.

Although average total cost tells us the cost of the typical unit, it does not tell us how much total cost will change as the firm alters its level of production. The last column in Table 9.2 shows the amount that total cost rises when the firm increases production by 1 unit of output. This number is called **marginal cost**. For example, if Lia increases production from 2 to 3 glasses, total cost rises from €3.80 to €4.50, so the marginal cost of the third glass of lemonade is €4.50 minus €3.80, or €0.70.

It may be helpful to express these definitions mathematically:

$$\text{Average total cost} = \text{Total cost/Quantity}$$

$$\text{ATC} = \text{TC/Q}$$

and

$$\text{Marginal cost} = \text{Change in total cost/Change in quantity}$$

$$\text{MC} = \Delta\text{TC}/\Delta\text{Q}$$

Here Δ, the Greek letter delta, represents the change in a variable. These equations show how average total cost and marginal cost are derived from total cost. Average total cost tells us the cost of a typical unit of output if total cost is divided evenly over all the units produced. Marginal cost tells us the increase in total cost that arises from producing an additional unit of output.

Pitfall Prevention Confusion over the relationship between average and marginal concepts is a source of problems in understanding. It is often useful to think of the relationship using something concrete from your own life such as the relationship between the average number of goals/points you score in a hockey, rugby, netball or football match (or whatever sport you take part in) and what happens to your average and marginal points/goal tally as you play additional games.

FYI

The Mathematics of Margins

The concept of the margin refers to small changes in variables such as revenue and costs. We know that total revenue is a function of (is dependent upon) the price and the number of units sold. Total cost is a function of the factor inputs used in production given by the sum of the fixed and variable costs. Given that both total revenue and total cost are functions we can use calculus to derive the respective marginal revenue and marginal costs.

Consider the following demand function:

$$P = 200 - 4Q$$

We know that $TR = P \times Q$

Substituting the demand function into the TR formula we get:

$$TR = (200 - 4Q)\,Q$$

$$TR = 200Q - 4Q^2$$

Using the principle of differentiation outlined in Chapter 4, we can derive marginal revenue (MR) by:

$$MR = \frac{d(TR)}{dq}$$

Using the power function rule for differentiation the MR in the example above is:

$$\frac{d(TR)}{dq} = 200 - 8Q$$

Calculating this allows us to be able to substitute into the demand function and get some indication of marginal revenue at that point. So if demand was 10 pizzas, marginal revenue would be 200 − 8(10) = 120. If demand rose by 1 unit to 11 then total revenue would rise by 200 − 8(11) = 112.

We can apply a similar approach to deriving the marginal cost. Take the TC function TC = Q^2 + 14Q + 20. We can look at the expression Q^2 + 14Q and conclude that this part of the function

is where the value of Q is dependent on some factor and will vary. As a result this is the variable costs component. The last term in the function denoted by the value 20 is not dependent on Q and so is the fixed costs element. We know that when differentiating this term the result is zero. We would expect this to be the case because, by definition, fixed costs are not affected by changes in output. Marginal cost, therefore, relates to changes in the variable costs of production.

To derive the marginal cost, we use:

$$MC = \frac{d(TC)}{dq}$$

Differentiating our TC function gives:

$$MC = \frac{d(TC)}{dq} = 2q + 14$$

If output is 15, then MC = 2(15) + 14 = 44

If output rises to 16 then MC = 2(16) + 44 = 46

As we will see more fully in the next chapter, Lia, our lemonade entrepreneur, will find the concepts of average total cost and marginal cost useful when deciding how much lemonade to produce.

Cost Curves and Their Shapes

Just as in previous chapters we found graphs of supply and demand useful when analyzing the behaviour of markets, we will find graphs of average and marginal cost useful when analyzing the behaviour of firms. Figure 9.4 graphs Lia's costs using the data from Table 9.2. The horizontal axis measures the quantity the firm produces, and the vertical axis measures marginal and average costs. The graph shows four curves: average total cost (*ATC*), average fixed cost (*AFC*), average variable cost (*AVC*), and marginal cost (*MC*).

FIGURE 9.4

Lia's Average Cost and Marginal Cost Curves

This figure shows the average total cost (ATC), average fixed cost (AFC), average variable cost (AVC) and marginal cost (MC) for Lia's Lemonade Bar. All of these curves are obtained by graphing the data in Table 9.2. These cost curves show three features that are typical of many firms: (1) Marginal cost rises with the quantity of output. (2) The average total cost curve is U-shaped. (3) The marginal cost curve crosses the average total cost curve at the minimum of average total cost.

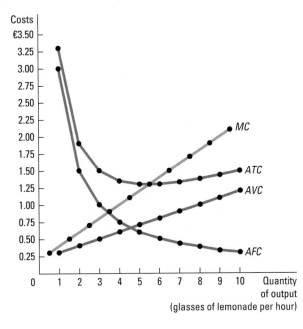

The cost curves shown here for Lia's Lemonade Bar have some features that are common to the cost curves of many firms in the economy. Let's examine three features in particular: the shape of marginal cost, the shape of average total cost, and the relationship between marginal and average total cost.

Rising Marginal Cost

Lia's marginal cost rises with the quantity of output produced. This reflects the property of diminishing marginal product. When Lia is producing a small quantity of lemonade she has few workers and much of her equipment is not being used. Because she can easily put these idle resources to use, the marginal product of an extra worker is large, and the marginal cost of an extra glass of lemonade is small. By contrast, when Lia is producing a large quantity of lemonade her stand is crowded with workers and most of her equipment is fully utilized. Lia can produce more lemonade by adding workers, but these new workers have to work in crowded conditions and may have to wait to use the equipment. Therefore, when the quantity of lemonade being produced is already high, the marginal product of an extra worker is low, and the marginal cost of an extra glass of lemonade is large.

U-Shaped Average Total Cost

Lia's average total cost curve takes on a U-shape. To understand why this is so, remember that average total cost is the sum of average fixed cost and average variable cost. Average fixed cost always declines as output rises because the fixed cost does not change as output rises and so gets spread over a larger number of units. Average variable cost typically rises as output increases because of diminishing marginal product. Average total cost reflects the shapes of both average fixed cost and average variable cost. As shown in Figure 9.4 at very low levels of output, such as 1 or 2 glasses per hour, average total cost is high because the fixed cost is spread over only a few units. Average total cost then declines as output increases until the firm's output reaches 5 glasses of lemonade per hour, when average total cost falls to €1.30 per glass. When the firm produces more than 6 glasses, average total cost starts rising again because average variable cost rises substantially. If further units of output were produced the average total cost curve would continue to slope upwards giving the typical U-shape referred to.

The bottom of the U-shape occurs at the quantity that minimizes average total cost. This quantity is sometimes called the **efficient scale** of the firm. For Lia, the efficient scale is 5 or 6 glasses of lemonade. If she produces more or less than this amount, her average total cost rises above the minimum of €1.30.

efficient scale the quantity of output that minimizes average total cost

The Relationship between Marginal Cost and Average Total Cost

If you look at Figure 9.4 (or back at Table 9.2) you will see something that may be surprising at first. Whenever marginal cost is less than average total cost, average total cost is falling. Whenever marginal cost is greater than average total cost, average total cost is rising. This feature of Lia's cost curves is not a coincidence from the particular numbers used in the example: it is true for all firms and is a basic mathematical relationship.

To see why, refer to your understanding of averages and consider what happens to average cost as output goes up by one unit. If the cost of the extra unit is above the average cost of units produced up to that point, then it will tend to pull up the new average cost of a unit. If the new unit actually costs less than the average cost of a unit up to that point, it will tend to drag the new average down. But the price of an extra unit is what economists call marginal cost, so what we have just asserted is tantamount to saying that if marginal cost is less than average cost, average cost will be falling; and if marginal cost is above average cost, average cost will be rising.

This relationship between average total cost and marginal cost has an important corollary: the marginal cost curve crosses the average total cost curve at its minimum. Why? At low levels of output, marginal cost is below average total cost, so average total cost is falling. But after the two curves cross, marginal cost rises above average total cost. For the reason we have just discussed, average total cost must start to rise at this level of output. Hence, at this point of intersection the cost of an additional unit is the same as the average and so the average does not change and the point is the minimum of average total cost.

Typical Cost Curves

In the examples we have studied so far, the firms' exhibit diminishing marginal product and, therefore, rising marginal cost at all levels of output. Yet actual firms are often a bit more complicated than this. In many firms, diminishing marginal product does not start to occur immediately after the first worker is hired. Depending on the production process, the second or third worker might have higher marginal product than the first because a team of workers can divide tasks and work more productively than a single worker. Such firms would first experience increasing marginal product for a while before diminishing marginal product sets in.

The table in Figure 9.5 shows the cost data for such a firm, called Berit's Bagel Bin. These data are used in the graphs. Panel (a) shows how total cost (*TC*) depends on the quantity produced, and panel (b) shows average total cost (*ATC*), average fixed cost

FIGURE 9.5

Berit's Cost Curves

Many firms, like Berit's Bagel Bin, experience increasing marginal product before diminishing marginal product and, therefore, have cost curves shaped like those in this figure. Panel (a) shows how total cost (TC) depends on the quantity produced. Panel (b) shows how average total cost (ATC), average fixed cost (AFC), average variable cost (AVC) and marginal cost (MC) depend on the quantity produced. These curves are derived by graphing the data from the table. Notice that marginal cost and average variable cost fall for a while before starting to rise.

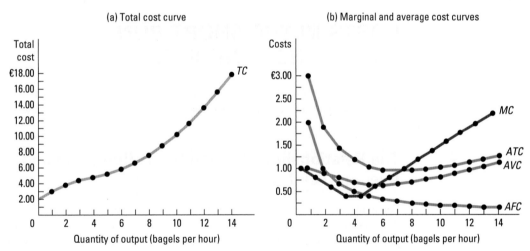

Quantity of bagels (per hour)	Total cost	Fixed cost	Variable cost	Average fixed cost	Average variable cost	Average total cost	Marginal cost
Q	TC = FC + VC	FC	VC	AFC = FC/Q	AVC = VC/Q	ATC = TC/Q	MC = ΔTC/ΔQ
0	€2.00	€2.00	€0.00	–	–	–	
1	3.00	2.00	1.00	€2.00	€1.00	€3.00	€1.00
2	3.80	2.00	1.80	1.00	0.90	1.90	0.80
3	4.40	2.00	2.40	0.67	0.80	1.47	0.60
4	4.80	2.00	2.80	0.50	0.70	1.20	0.40
5	5.20	2.00	3.20	0.40	0.64	1.04	0.40
6	5.80	2.00	3.80	0.33	0.63	0.96	0.60
7	6.60	2.00	4.60	0.29	0.66	0.95	0.80
8	7.60	2.00	5.60	0.25	0.70	0.95	1.00
9	8.80	2.00	6.80	0.22	0.76	0.98	1.20
10	10.20	2.00	8.20	0.20	0.82	1.02	1.40
11	11.80	2.00	9.80	0.18	0.89	1.07	1.60
12	13.60	2.00	11.60	0.17	0.97	1.14	1.80
13	15.60	2.00	13.60	0.15	1.05	1.20	2.00
14	17.80	2.00	15.80	0.14	1.13	1.27	2.20

(AFC), average variable cost *(AVC)* and marginal cost *(MC)*. In the range of output from 0 to 4 bagels per hour, the firm experiences increasing marginal product, and the marginal cost curve falls. After 5 bagels per hour, the firm starts to experience diminishing marginal product, and the marginal cost curve starts to rise. This combination of increasing then diminishing marginal product also makes the average variable cost curve U-shaped.

Despite these differences from our previous example, Berit's cost curves share the three properties that are most important to remember:

* Marginal cost eventually rises with the quantity of output.
* The average total cost curve is U-shaped.
* The marginal cost curve crosses the average total cost curve at the minimum of average total cost.

> **Quick Quiz** Suppose BMW's total cost of producing 4 cars is €225 000 and its total cost of producing 5 cars is €250 000. What is the average total cost of producing 5 cars? What is the marginal cost of the fifth car? • Draw the marginal cost curve and the average total cost curve for a typical firm, and explain why these curves cross where they do.

COSTS IN THE SHORT RUN AND IN THE LONG RUN

We noted earlier in this chapter that a firm's costs might depend on the time horizon being examined. Let's discuss more precisely why this might be the case.

The Relationship Between Short-Run and Long-Run Average Total Cost

For many firms, the division of total costs between fixed and variable costs depends on the time horizon. Consider, for instance, a car manufacturer, such as Renault. Over a period of only a few months, Renault cannot adjust the number or sizes of its car factories. The only way it can produce additional cars is to hire more workers at the factories it already has. The cost of these factories is, therefore, a fixed cost in the short run. By contrast, over a period of several years, Renault can expand the size of its factories, build new factories or close old ones. Thus, the cost of its factories is a variable cost in the long run.

Because many decisions are fixed in the short run but variable in the long run, a firm's long-run cost curves differ from its short-run cost curves. Figure 9.6 shows an example. The figure presents three short-run average total cost curves representing the cost structures for a small, medium and large factory. It also presents the long-run average total cost curve. As the firm adjusts the size of the factory to the quantity of production, it moves along the long-run curve, and it is adjusting the size of the factory to the quantity of production.

This graph shows how short-run and long-run costs are related. The long-run average total cost curve is a much flatter U-shape than the short-run average total cost curve. In addition, all the short-run curves lie on or above the long-run curve. These properties arise because firms have greater flexibility in the long run. In essence, in the long run, the firm chooses which short-run curve it wants to use. But in the short run, it has to use whatever short-run curve it chose in the past.

FIGURE 9.6

Average Total Cost in the Short and Long Runs

Because fixed costs are variable in the long run, the average total cost curve in the short run differs from the average total cost curve in the long run.

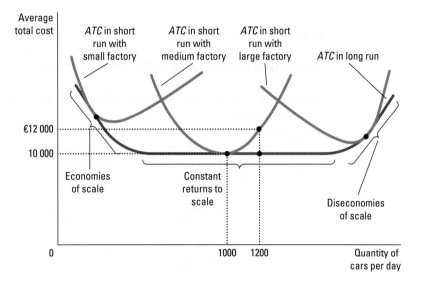

The figure shows an example of how a change in production alters costs over different time horizons. When Renault wants to increase production from 1000 to 1200 cars per day, it has no choice in the short run but to hire more workers at its existing medium-sized factory. Because of diminishing marginal product, average total cost rises from €10 000 to €12 000 per car. In the long run, however, Renault can expand both the size of the factory and its workforce, and average total cost returns to €10 000.

Economies and Diseconomies of Scale

The shape of the long-run average total cost curve conveys important information about the technology for producing a good. When long-run average total cost declines as output increases, there are said to be **economies of scale**. When long-run average total cost rises as output increases, there are said to be **diseconomies of scale**. When long-run average total cost does not vary with the level of output, there are said to be **constant returns to scale**. In this example, Renault has economies of scale at low levels of output, constant returns to scale at intermediate levels of output and diseconomies of scale at high levels of output.

What might cause economies or diseconomies of scale? Economies of scale often arise because higher production levels allow *specialization* among workers and increase the possibility that technology can be used, which permits each worker to become better at his or her assigned tasks. For instance, modern assembly line production may require fewer workers in relation to the technology used but still produce more cars. If Renault were producing only a small quantity of cars, it could not take advantage of this approach and would have higher average total cost. Diseconomies of scale can arise because of *coordination problems* that are inherent in any large organization. The more cars Renault produces, the more stretched the management team becomes, and the less effective the managers become at keeping costs down.

This analysis shows why long-run average total cost curves are often U-shaped. At low levels of production, the firm benefits from increased size because it can take advantage of greater specialization. Coordination problems, meanwhile, are not yet acute. By

economies of scale the property whereby long-run average total cost falls as the quantity of output increases

diseconomies of scale the property whereby long-run average total cost rises as the quantity of output increases

constant returns to scale the property whereby long-run average total cost stays the same as the quantity of output changes

contrast, at high levels of production, the benefits of specialization have already been realized, and coordination problems become more severe as the firm grows larger. Thus, long-run average total cost is falling at low levels of production because of increasing specialization and rising at high levels of production because of increasing coordination problems.

CASE STUDY

The Implications of Economies of Scale

Economies of scale are the advantages of large-scale production that result in lower average or unit costs.

Imagine a firm which makes bricks. The current plant has a maximum capacity of 100 000 bricks per week and the total costs are €200 000 per week. The average cost for each brick, therefore, is €2. The firm sets a price of €2.20 per brick giving it a profit margin of €0.20 per brick.

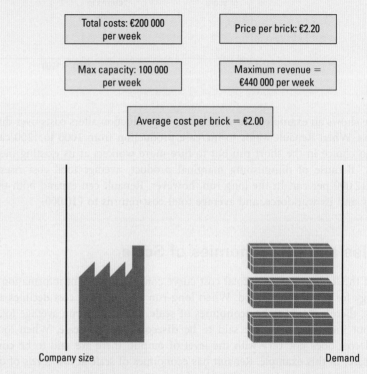

Now imagine that in the long run the firm expands. It doubles the size of its plant. The total costs, obviously, increase – they are now using more land and putting up more buildings, as well as hiring extra labour and buying more equipment and raw materials. All of this expansion will increase the total cost. However, it is not the case that a doubling of capacity will also lead to a doubling of the cost.

Assume TC is now €350 000 per week. The expansion of the plant means that the firm can double its output so its capacity is now 200 000 bricks per week. The proportionate increase in the total costs is less than the proportionate increase in output. Total costs have risen by €150 000 or 75 per cent and total output by 100 per cent, which means that the average cost per brick is now €1.75 per brick.

The firm now faces two scenarios. In Scenario 1, the firm could maintain its price at €2.20 and increase its profit margin on each brick sold from €0.20 to €0.45. Assuming it sells all the bricks it produces its revenue would increase to €440 000 per week.

Scenario 1

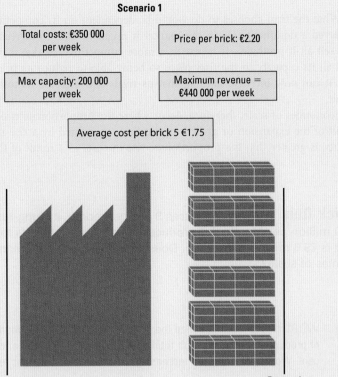

Total costs: €350 000 per week

Price per brick: €2.20

Max capacity: 200 000 per week

Maximum revenue = €440 000 per week

Average cost per brick 5 €1.75

Company size

Demand

In scenario 2, the firm might choose to reduce its price to improve its competitiveness against its rivals. It could maintain its former profit margin of €0.20 and reduce the price to €1.95 improving the chances of increasing its competitive advantage. In this case, if it sells all it produces its revenue would be €390 000 per week.

Scenario 2

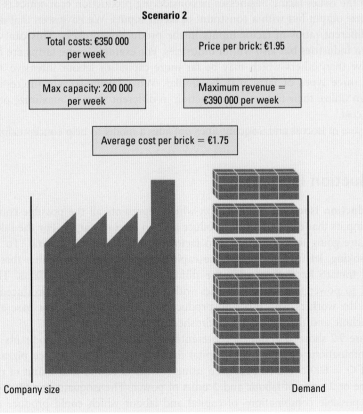

Total costs: €350 000 per week

Price per brick: €1.95

Max capacity: 200 000 per week

Maximum revenue = €390 000 per week

Average cost per brick = €1.75

Company size

Demand

What the firm chooses to do would be dependent on its competitive position. If it played a dominant role in the market it might be able to increase its price and still sell all it produces. If it was in a more competitive market it might not have sold all its capacity in the first place so being able to reduce its price might mean that it can now increase sales against its rivals and increase its total revenue as a result.

Economies of scale, therefore, occur where the proportionate rise in output as a result of the expansion or growth of the firm, as defined by a rise in all the factor inputs, is greater that the proportionate rise in costs as a result of the expansion.

Quick Quiz If Airbus produces 9 jets per month, its long-run total cost is €9.0 million per month. If it produces 10 jets per month, its long-run total cost is €9.5 million per month. Does Airbus exhibit economies or diseconomies of scale?

? **what if…**a firm expanded the scale of its operations by doubling all the factors of production but as a result total cost rose by 150 per cent and output by 120 per cent. Would the firm face increasing, decreasing or constant returns to scale?

ISOQUANTS AND ISOCOSTS

One of the issues facing businesses in considering production economics is to attempt to maximize output but with a constraint of factor inputs. We have seen that different firms have different ratios of factor inputs in the production process. This can vary not only between industries but also within industries. For example, some farms are far more land intensive than others which may be far more capital or labour intensive. Output levels for all three types of farm may be similar. What businesses are interested in is how they can utilize their factors of production in different ways to maximize output at minimum cost.

The use of isocost and isoquant lines provides a model to help conceptualize the process.

Production Isoquants

production isoquant a function which represents all the possible combinations of factor inputs that can be used to produce a given level of output

A **production isoquant** is a function which represents all the possible combinations of factor inputs that can be used to produce a given level of output. For the sake of simplicity we are going to assume just two factor inputs, labour and capital. To further focus our thinking, let us assume that the capital in question is a machine that coats pizzas with a tomato base, then adds the filling and then bakes the pizzas. The electricity needed to power this machine varies with the amount of pizzas produced. The labour will be the workers who mix and produce the dough for the pizza base and who feed the machine and then package the finished pizzas.

Figure 9.7 shows a graphical representation of the production isoquants that relate to the combinations of labour and capital that can be used to produce pizzas. An output level of Q = 600 could be produced using 5 units of labour and 1 unit of power for the machine or 2 units of labour and 2 units of power. The isoquant line Q = 600 connects all the possible combinations of capital and labour which could produce an output of

FIGURE 9.7

Production Isoquants for Primo's Pizza Factory

Given the possibility of employing different amounts of capital and labour, the isoquant map connects together combinations of capital and labour which could be employed to produce different levels of output of pizzas. For an output level Q = 600, 4 units of power for the machine and 1 unit of labour could produce 600 pizzas but so could the combination 2 units of power for the machine and 2 units of labour. 5 units of power and 5 units of labour could produce an output level Q = 900; a combination of 2 units of power and 10 units of labour could also produce 900 pizzas.

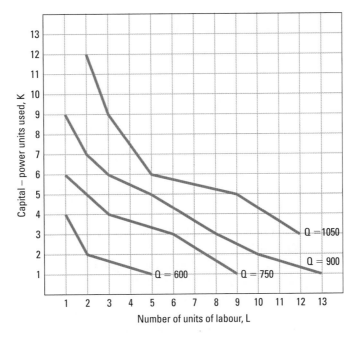

600 pizzas. Given the level of capital and labour inputs for Primo's factory, a series of isoquants can be drawn for different levels of output. Figure 9.7 shows the isoquants for output levels of Q = 600, Q = 750, Q = 900 and Q = 1050. In theory, the whole of the graphical space could be covered with isoquants all relating to the different levels of possible output.

As mentioned previously, few businesses will sit down and draw out isoquants in the way we have done here but the reality is that firms do regularly make decisions about factor combinations in deciding output. Firms will often look at the option of substituting capital for labour by making staff redundant and investing instead in new equipment. Firms may also look at replacing existing machinery for new ones or look for outsourcing opportunities both of which would have an effect on the shape and position of the isoquants.

Substituting one factor for another will have costs. It may not be easy to substitute one factor for another; machinery may be highly specialized and worker may have skills that machines simply cannot replicate (the ability to make clients feel confident and at ease, for example). The slope of the isoquant represents the **marginal rate of technical substitution** (MRTS). This is the rate at which one factor input can be substituted for another at a given level of output. Referring to Figure 9.7, take the output level Q = 1050 and a combination of labour and capital at 5 and 6 units respectively. If Primo considered cutting 2 units of labour he would have to increase the amount of power used on the machine employed by 3 to 9 in order to maintain output at 1050. The MRTS would be given by the ratio of the change in capital to the change in labour, $\Delta K/\Delta L$. The change in capital is from 6 to 9 units and the change in labour is from 5 to 3. The MRTS = 3/−2 or −1.5. (Note, these changes are in opposite directions and so the MRTS would be a negative number.) This tells us that Primo has to increase the

marginal rate of technical substitution the rate at which one factor input can be substituted for another at a given level of output

FIGURE 9.8

Production Isoquants

It is common to represent production isoquants as a series of smooth curves representing the different combinations of capital and labour which would be used to produce different levels of output represented in this Figure as Q = X, Q = X₁, Q = X₂, etc.

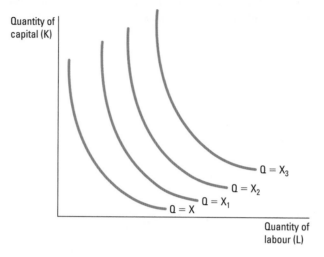

amount of power used by 1.5 for every 1 unit of labour released to maintain production at Q = 1050.

The way we have drawn the isoquants in Figure 9.7 would suggest different MRTS because the slope of each isoquant is different.

It is common to see isoquants drawn as smooth curves as shown in Figure 9.8. Clearly, in such a situation the use of calculus to calculate the MRTS would be advantageous because it would provide a very much more accurate value at every point on each curve. Using calculus the derivative of capital with respect to labour $\frac{dK}{dL}$ would give us this precise value.

Isocost Lines

Our analysis so far has looked at different combinations of factor inputs to produce given outputs. A business has to take into consideration the obvious fact that factor inputs cost money. Labour has to be paid, wages and salaries and energy to power the machines has to be purchased. Firms have budgets which have to be adhered to.

isocost line the different combination of factor inputs which can be purchased with a given budget

Isocost lines take the cost of factor inputs into consideration. An **isocost line** shows the different combination of factor inputs which can be purchased with a given budget.

Assume that the price of power to operate the pizza machine Primo has to buy is given by the general form P_kK, and the price of labour is given the general form P_LL. Given a cost constraint represented by TC_{CL} we can express the relationship as:

$$P_kK + P_LL = TC_{kL}$$

Now assume that the price of capital per unit to make pizzas is €1000 per month and the price of labour, €500 per month. Our formula would look like this:

$$1000K + 500L = TC_{kL}$$

Using 3 capital units and 9 units of labour would cost 1000(3) + 500(9) = €7500. Are there other combinations of capital and labour that would produce pizzas at a cost of €7500? We can find this out by rearranging the equation to give:

$$€7500 = 1000K + 500L$$

TABLE 9.3

Factor combinations to satisfy the equation K = 7.5 – 0.5L

K	L
7.0	1
6.5	2
6.0	3
5.5	4
5.0	5
4.5	6
4.0	7
3.5	8
3.0	9
2.5	10
2.0	11
1.5	12
1.0	13
0.5	14
0.0	15

We can now find values for K and L which satisfy this equation. For example, dividing both sides by 1000 and solving for K we get:

$$K = \frac{7500}{1000} - \frac{500L}{1000}$$

$$K = 7.5 - 0.5L$$

Table 9.3 shows combinations of capital and labour that satisfy this equation. For example, if 6 units of labour were used then K = 7.5 − 0.5(6)

$$K = 7.5 - 3.0, K = 4.5.$$

The information can be graphed as in Figure 9.9 with units of capital on the vertical axis and units of labour on the horizontal axis. The isocost line $TC_{kL = 7500}$ connects all the combinations of labour and capital to make pizzas which cost €7500. At point A, 4.5 units of capital and 6 units of labour will have a total cost of €7500 but so will the combination of 1.5 units of capital and 12 units of labour at point B.

Other isocost lines could be drawn connecting combinations of capital and labour at different levels of total cost. For each of these isocost lines, the vertical intercept shows how many units of capital Primo could buy with his budget constraint if he employed zero units of labour. The horizontal intercept shows how many units of labour Primo could buy if zero units of capital were purchased. The isocost line shows the combinations of capital and labour that Primo could purchase given his budget constraint.

The slope of the isocost line is the ratio of the price of labour to capital P_L/p_k. As the isocost line is a straight line the slope is constant throughout. In this example, the slope is 500/1000 = 0.5. This tells us that for every one additional unit of labour employed he has to reduce the amount of capital by 0.5 and for every one additional unit of capital employed he must reduce labour by 2 units.

The Least-Cost Input Combination

We now know the combination of factor inputs needed to produce given quantities of output (pizzas in our case) given by the isoquant curves and the cost of using different factor combinations given by the isocost lines. We can put these together to find the least cost input combination.

FIGURE 9.9

Isocost Lines

Isocost lines connect combinations of capital and labour that a business can afford to buy given a budget constraint. The isocost line shown relates to a budget constraint of €7500. With this budget constraint Primo could spend all the money on 7 units of capital but would not be able to afford any workers giving the vertical intercept. If the business chose to spend the budget entirely on labour then it would be able to purchase 15 units of labour but no machines. Any point on the isocost line between these two extremes connects together combinations of capital and labour that could be purchased with the available budget. At point A, Primo could afford to buy 4.5 units of capital and 6 units of labour; at point B, he could afford to buy 1.5 units of labour and 12 units of labour.

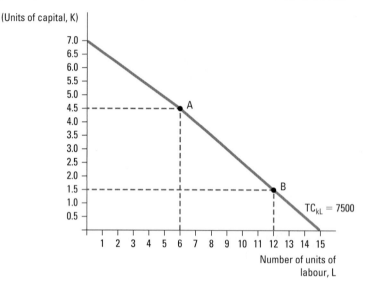

FIGURE 9.10

The Least-Cost Input Combination

The figure shows different isoquants relating to three different output levels Q = X, Q = X₁ and Q = X₂ and three isocost lines relating to three different budget constraints TC_{kL1}, TC_{kL2} and TC_{kL3}. Given isocost line TC_{kL3} any of the outputs represented by A–E are possible but the optimum is at point E where the isoquant Q = X₂ is tangential to the isocost line.

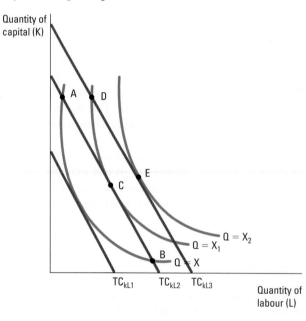

Figure 9.10 shows different isoquants relating to three different output levels Q = X, Q = X₁ and Q = X₂ and three isocost lines relating to three different budget constraints TC_{kL1}, TC_{kL2} and TC_{kL3}.

Any point where the isocost line cuts the isoquant line is a possible combination of factors that could be used. The more resources a business has at its disposal the higher the output it can produce. The question we want to ask is: what is the best or optimum combination? Let us assume that Primo has a budget constraint of TC_{kL2}. He could produce output Q = X and employ the combination of factors of production at point A. Similarly he could employ fewer units of capital and more units of labour and afford to produce the same output at point B. However, we could reasonably assume that if there was a way in which a business could use its existing budget and resources to produce more output then it would do so. It may make such a decision if it thought that it could sell more output.

Starting at point A, therefore, Primo could reduce the amount of capital used and increase the amount of labour to produce a higher output level Q = X_1 at point C. Primo might like to produce an output Q = X_1 using the combination of factors given by point D, however, that combination falls on a different isocost line, TC_{kL3}. Primo does not have the funds to be able to afford this combination; however, he can afford to employ capital and labour in the combination where the combination of factors given at point C is exactly the same as the cost of employing those factors. At point C the isoquant curve is tangential to the isocost line. This is the least-cost input combination. Given Primo's budget constraint there is no incentive for him to change the combination of factors of production employed at this point because to do so would mean that those resources would not be producing at maximum efficiency at minimum cost. Primo might like to produce an output level given by Q = X_2 given his budget constraint he cannot afford to produce that level of output. The optimum point, therefore, given existing productivity levels of factor inputs and the price of factor inputs, is C.

At this point of tangent, the point of least-cost input occurs where the marginal rate of technical substitution is equal to the ratio of the prices of factors. This is represented by the equation:

$$\frac{MP_L}{MP_K} = \frac{P_L}{P_K}$$

This is also sometimes given as:

$$\frac{MP_L}{P_L} = \frac{MP_K}{P_K}$$

JEOPARDY PROBLEM

Primo has been able to increase the amount of pizzas he is producing without increasing the budget he has available. How might this outcome be possible?

Summary

Let us just summarize this section by thinking through this logically. If you were Primo faced with a budget constraint, you would want to ensure that you use your money in the best way possible to produce the maximum amount possible. Taking a factor input combination such as that at A, if there was a way in which you could reorganize those factor inputs so that they did not cost you any more, but you could produce more pizzas, it would make sense to do so.

Cutting back on the use of capital and increasing labour means the additional output produced is greater but does not cost any more. Provided the benefit of doing this is greater than the cost incurred it makes sense to make such a decision. If there is still a way to continue cutting capital use and increasing labour which would bring about increased production of pizzas, then it is clearly sensible to continue doing so until you reach a point where there is no benefit in shifting resources any further.

The least-cost input combination can change if the cost of labour or capital changes (in which case the slope of the isocost line would change) or if both prices changed equally then the isocost line would shift either inwards or outwards depending on the direction of the price change. The shape of the isoquant curve might also change if the marginal productivity of either capital or labour changed.

Remember early in this analysis how we mentioned that this approach was a way of conceptualizing how businesses behave. The assumption is that firms want to maximize output at minimum cost. Firms will have some idea of the productivity of factor inputs and also of the cost of buying in factors. They will continually be looking to find ways to reorganize factors of production they employ to increase output but keep costs under control. The use of this model helps us to understand the logic behind business restructuring, outsourcing, seeking out cheaper suppliers, using different raw materials in different ways, spending money on training workers to be more effective in their jobs and other ways of influencing productivity, and helps explain why businesses are dynamic and constantly changing and evolving organizations.

CONCLUSION

The purpose of this chapter has been to develop some tools that we can use to study how firms make production and pricing decisions. You should now understand what economists mean by the term *costs* and how costs vary with the quantity of output a firm produces. To refresh your memory, Table 9.4 summarizes some of the definitions we have encountered.

By themselves, of course, a firm's cost curves do not tell us what decisions the firm will make. But they are an important component of that decision.

TABLE 9.4

The Many Types of Cost: A Summary

Term	Definition	Mathematical description
Explicit costs	Costs that require an outlay of money by the firm	–
Implicit costs	Costs that do not require an outlay of money by the firm	–
Fixed costs	Costs that do not vary with the quantity of output produced	FC
Variable costs	Costs that do vary with the quantity of output produced	VC
Total cost	The market value of all the inputs that a firm uses in production	TC = FC + VC
Average fixed cost	Fixed costs divided by the quantity of output	AFC = FC/Q
Average variable cost	Variable costs divided by the quantity of output	AVC = VC/Q
Average total cost	Total cost divided by the quantity of output	ATC = TC/Q
Marginal cost	The increase in total cost that arises from an extra unit of production	$\dfrac{d(TC)}{dq}$

IN THE NEWS

In this chapter we have noted how businesses are dynamic and constantly looking to exploit new opportunities which involve changing the way they operate production. What might not have been a success for some firms does not mean to say that there are not other firms that will be able to benefit. This article shows how problems faced by one firm in making sufficient profits are not necessarily shared by other firms as the use of factor inputs is changed.

Best Buy Fails to Break UK Market

US electrical retailer, Best Buy, made an attempt to enter the UK electrical retail market in 2010. The retailer is known across the United States for its high quality sales staff and discount prices and attempted to bring its business model to the crowded UK market which features the likes of Currys, Argos, Dixons and Comet.

The plans to enter the UK market arose when Best Buy Inc bought half of The Carphone Warehouse's retail interests. Plans were made to open up to 200 so-called 'Big Box' stores throughout the UK with the first one opening in Thurrock, Essex in April 2010. However, facing strong competition, a lack of brand recognition by UK consumers and the rapid growth of online retailing from firms like Amazon, Best Buy found things difficult and by January 2012 a decision was made to close down its 11 bricks and mortar retail operations following losses of around £62 million.

The decision to close down was made after consideration was given to commit more capital to its operations in an attempt to secure the advantages of large-scale production – economies of scale. In the end the cost of such an investment in relation to the expected benefits in a market which was challenging (given the economic situation in the UK, the income elasticity of demand for electrical goods in general and the increasing use of online as the medium of choice for shoppers), meant that option was discounted.

The decision to close down operations will have been taken in the light of the expected costs of trying to maintain its presence on the high street and the future of the industry as a whole. It would not have been taken lightly as reports suggested closing down would cost Best Buy and Carphone Warehouse around £100 million.

One option being considered was selling its stores to the UK's fourth largest supermarket group by market share, Morrisons. Morrisons were reported to have expressed interest in acquiring the stores, mostly in large out-of-town retail sites, for its Kiddicare brand of baby, infant and small children's products such as toys, pushchairs, cots and so on.

The reports caused interest in the markets and some surprise given the challenges that exist in that market for some of the same reasons that Best Buy found life difficult. An increasing trend to purchase goods online and the economic climate had already seen retailers like Mothercare and its Early Learning Centre stores facing declining sales and profits. Kiddicare had been an almost exclusively online operation and so the decision by Morrisons to move into the bricks and mortar sector was seen as a high-risk move.

Questions

1. For Morrisons, what is the difference between the short run and the long run in this case?
2. Explain some of the reasons why Best Buy made such losses in the UK given its global size.
3. How might Carphone Warehouse and Best Buy have gained economies of scale if they had 'committed new capital'? Explain your reasoning.
4. Why might Carphone Warehouse and Best Buy 'incur a cost of as much as £100 million' in closing down the stores?
5. If Mothercare is 'troubled' why might Morrisons believe it can succeed with Kiddicare?

SUMMARY

- Profit equals total revenue minus total cost.
- When analyzing a firm's behaviour, it is important to include all the opportunity costs of production. Some of the opportunity costs, such as the wages a firm pays its workers, are explicit. Other opportunity costs, such as the wages the firm owner gives up by working in the firm rather than taking another job, are implicit.
- A firm's costs reflect its production process. A typical firm's production function gets flatter as the quantity of an input increases, displaying the property of diminishing marginal product. As a result, a firm's total cost curve gets steeper as the quantity produced rises.
- A firm's total costs can be divided between fixed costs and variable costs. Fixed costs are costs that are not determined by the quantity of output produced. Variable costs are costs that directly relate to the amount produced and so change when the firm alters the quantity of output produced.
- From a firm's total cost, two related measures of cost are derived. Average total cost is total cost divided by the quantity of output. Marginal cost is the amount by which total cost changes if output increases (or decreases) by 1 unit.
- When analyzing firm behaviour, it is often useful to graph average total cost and marginal cost. For a typical firm, marginal cost rises with the quantity of output. Average total cost first falls as output increases and then rises as output increases further. The marginal cost curve always crosses the average total cost curve at the minimum of average total cost.
- A firm's costs often depend on the time horizon being considered. In particular, many costs are fixed in the short run but variable in the long run. As a result, when the firm changes its level of production, average total cost may rise more in the short run than in the long run.
- The use of isoquants and isocosts helps conceptualize the reasons why firms make decisions to change factor combinations used in production and how the prices of factor combinations can also influence those decisions.

KEY CONCEPTS

total cost, p. 210
profit, p. 210
explicit costs, p. 211
implicit costs, p. 211
economic profit, p. 211
accounting profit, p. 211
production function, p. 212
short run, p. 213
long run, p. 213

marginal product, p. 215
diminishing marginal product, p. 215
fixed costs, p. 216
variable costs, p. 217
average total cost, p. 218
average fixed cost, p. 218
average variable cost, p. 218
marginal cost, p. 218
efficient scale, p. 220

economies of scale, p. 223
diseconomies of scale, p. 223
constant returns to scale, p. 223
production isoquant, p. 226
marginal rate of technical substitution, p. 227
isocost line, p. 228

QUESTIONS FOR REVIEW

1. What is the relationship between a firm's total revenue, profit and total cost?
2. Give an example of an opportunity cost that an accountant might not count as a cost. Why would the accountant ignore this cost?
3. What is marginal product, and what does it mean if it is diminishing?
4. Draw a production function that exhibits diminishing marginal product of labour. Draw the associated total cost curve. (In both cases, be sure to label the axes.) Explain the shapes of the two curves you have drawn.
5. Define total cost, average total cost and marginal cost. How are they related?
6. Draw the marginal cost and average total cost curves for a typical firm. Explain why the curves have the shapes that they do and why they cross where they do.
7. How and why does a firm's average total cost curve differ in the short run and in the long run?

8. Define economies of scale and explain why they might arise. Define diseconomies of scale and explain why they might arise.

9. Define an isoquant, an isocost line and the least-cost input combination.

PROBLEMS AND APPLICATIONS

1. This chapter discusses many types of costs: opportunity cost, total cost, fixed cost, variable cost, average total cost and marginal cost. Fill in the type of cost that best completes each phrase below.
   a. The true cost of taking some action is its _____.
   b. _____ is falling when marginal cost is below it, and rising when marginal cost is above it.
   c. A cost that does not depend on the quantity produced is a _____.
   d. In the breakfast cereal industry in the short run, _____ includes the cost of cereals such as wheat and corn and sugar, but not the cost of the factory.
   e. Profits equal total revenue minus _____.
   f. The cost of producing an extra unit of output is the _____.

2. Patrice is thinking about opening a café. He estimates that it would cost €500 000 per year to rent the premises, buy the equipment to make hot drinks and snacks and to buy in the ingredients. In addition, he would have to leave his €50 000 per year job as an accountant.
   a. Define opportunity cost.
   b. What is Patrice's opportunity cost of running the café for a year? If Patrice thought he could sell €510 000 worth of coffee and snacks in a year, should he open the café? Explain your answer.

3. A commercial fisherman notices the following relationship between hours spent fishing and the quantity of fish caught:

Hours	Quantity of fish (in kilograms)
0	0
1	10
2	18
3	24
4	28
5	30

   a. What is the marginal product of each hour spent fishing?
   b. Use these data to graph the fisherman's production function. Explain its shape.
   c. The fisherman has a fixed cost of €10 (his fishing rod). The opportunity cost of his time is €5 per hour. Graph the fisherman's total cost curve. Explain its shape.

4. Clean Sweep is a company that makes brooms and then sells them door-to-door. Here is the relationship between

the number of workers and Clean Sweep's output in a given day:

Workers	Output	Marginal product	Average total cost	Marginal cost
0	0			
1	20			
2	50			
3	90			
4	120			
5	140			
6	150			
7	155			

a. Fill in the column of marginal product. What pattern do you see? How might you explain it?
b. A worker costs €100 a day, and the firm has fixed costs of €200. Use this information to fill in the column for total cost.
c. Fill in the column for average total cost. (Recall that $ATC = TC/Q$.) What pattern do you see?
d. Now fill in the column for marginal cost. (Recall that $MC = \Delta TC/Q$.) What pattern do you see?
e. Compare the column for marginal product and the column for marginal cost. Explain the relationship.
f. Compare the column for average total cost and the column for marginal cost. Explain the relationship.

5. Suppose that you and your roommate have started a bagel delivery service on campus. List some of your fixed costs and describe why they are fixed. List some of your variable costs and describe why they are variable.

6. Consider the following cost information for a pizzeria:

Q (dozens)	Total cost	Variable cost
0	€300	€0
1	350	50
2	390	90
3	420	120
4	450	150
5	490	190
6	540	240

a. What is the pizzeria's fixed cost?
b. Construct a table in which you calculate the marginal cost per dozen pizzas using the information on total cost. Also calculate the marginal cost per dozen pizzas using the information on variable cost. What is the relationship between these sets of numbers? Comment.

10. Using the isocost, isoquant model, explain why firms might make a decision to cut the labour force and invest in capital equipment instead.

7. You are thinking about setting up a lemonade bar. The bar itself costs €200 a week to rent. The ingredients for each cup of lemonade cost €0.50.
   a. What is your fixed cost of doing business? What is your variable cost per cup?
   b. Construct a table showing your total cost, average total cost and marginal cost for output levels varying from 0 to 100 litres. (Hint: there are 4 cups in a litre.) Draw the three cost curves.

8. Healthy Harry's Juice Bar has the following cost schedules:

Q (vats)	Variable cost	Total cost
0	€0	€30
1	10	40
2	25	55
3	45	75
4	70	100
5	100	130
6	135	165

   a. Calculate average variable cost, average total cost and marginal cost for each quantity.
   b. Graph all three curves. What is the relationship between the marginal cost curve and the average total cost curve? Between the marginal cost curve and the average variable cost curve? Explain your answer.

9. Consider the following table of long-run total cost for three different firms:

Quantity	1	2	3	4	5	6	7
Firm A	€60	€70	€80	€90	€100	€110	€120
Firm B	11	24	39	56	75	96	119
Firm C	21	34	49	66	85	106	129

Does each of these firms experience economies of scale or diseconomies of scale?

10. Given the equation K = 2000 – 250L, calculate the combination of capital and labour between L = 1 and L = 10 which would produce an output with a total cost of €400. Draw the resulting isocost curve with this data.

On your diagram draw a series of isoquants and explain how a business would either find the point where they minimized total cost given a constraint on output or maximize output given a budget constraint.

10 THE FIRM'S PRODUCTION DECISIONS

LEARNING OBJECTIVES

In this chapter you will:

- Revisit the meaning of competition and a competitive market

- Look at the conditions under which a competitive firm will shut down temporarily

- Examine the conditions under which a firm will choose to exit a market

- See why sunk costs can be ignored in production decisions

- Cover the difference between normal and abnormal profit and how making normal or zero profit still means it is worth continuing in production

- See how the supply curve for a competitive firm is derived in the short run and the long run

- Cover the difference in the equilibrium position of a competitive firm in the short run and the long run

After reading this chapter you should be able to:

- State the assumptions of the model of a highly competitive firm

- Calculate and draw cost and revenue curves and show the profit-maximizing output

- Show, using diagrams and basic maths, the conditions under which a firm will shut down temporarily and exit the market in the long run

- Explain the difference between normal and abnormal profit

- Explain why a firm will continue in production even if it makes zero profit

- Use diagrams to explain the short- and long-run equilibrium position for a firm in a highly competitive market

INTRODUCTION

In Chapters 8 and 9 we looked at a firm's costs and revenues and the various goals of a business. In this chapter we are going to look at the implications of these for decisions about how much to supply and about when to cease production. Chapter 8 introduced the concept of the product life cycle. Most products will have a product life cycle which includes the phases from launch, through growth maturity and decline. Firms will have to make decisions about levels of production during these phases and when a product reaches the decline stage a decision will need to be made about whether to continue production.

Firms are affected by the general state of the economy and changing tastes and fashions. In times of economic downturn, some firms will find that demand for their product falls to such an extent that it becomes impossible to continue production and so close down. VHS video recorders and cathode ray tube TVs are no longer produced by most of the major electrical manufacturers for example. Such external effects mean that decisions will have to be taken on changes to production levels and indeed whether production should continue at all. We will look at the principles governing these decisions in this chapter.

Competitive Markets – A Refresher

In Chapter 4 we looked at the nature of competitive markets. As background to the material we are going to cover in this chapter, let us remind ourselves of the main principles. If an individual petrol station raised the price it charges for petrol by 20 per cent it would be likely to see a large drop in the amount of petrol it sold. Its customers would quickly switch to buying their petrol at other petrol stations. By contrast, if your regional water company raised the price of water by 20 per cent, it would see only a small decrease in the amount of water it sold. People might look to use water in more efficient ways but they would be hard pressed to reduce water consumption greatly and would be unlikely to find another supplier. The difference between the petrol market and the water market is obvious: there are many firms selling petrol in many areas but there is only one firm selling water. As you might expect, this difference in market structure shapes the pricing and production decisions of the firms that operate in these markets.

Recall that a market is competitive if each buyer and seller is small compared to the size of the market and, therefore, has little ability to influence market prices. By contrast, if a firm can influence the market price of the good it sells, it is said to have *market power*. We will examine the behaviour of firms with market power in a later chapter.

Our analysis of competitive firms in this chapter will shed light on the decisions that lie behind the supply curve in a competitive market. Not surprisingly, we will find that a market supply curve is tightly linked to firms' costs of production. Among a firm's various costs – fixed, variable, average and marginal – which ones are most relevant for its decision about the quantity to supply at any given price? We will see that all these measures of cost play important and interrelated roles.

The following represents some basic principles underlying competition and competitive markets:

- Where more than one firm offers the same or a similar product there is competition – the more firms there are in the market the more competition there is but the size of each firm relative to the total market is important in our analysis.
- Where firms are small in relation to the total market their influence on price is limited and they take on more characteristics of being price takers.
- Competition will manifest itself where substitutes exist: for example, gas and electricity are separate markets but there is the opportunity for consumers to substitute gas cookers for electric ones and so some element of competition exists.
- The closer the degree of substitutability the greater will be the competition that exists.

- Firms may influence the level of competition through the way they build relationships with consumers, encourage purchasing habits, provide levels of customer service and after sales service, and so on.

Markets will have different degrees of competition. For a market to be at the highly competitive end of the scale, a number of characteristics have to exist:

- There are many buyers and many sellers in the market.
- The goods offered by the various sellers are largely the same (if identical the goods are described as being 'homogenous').
- Firms can freely enter or exit the market.
- There is a high degree of information available to buyers and sellers in the market.

An example is the market for milk. No single buyer of milk can influence the price of milk because each buyer purchases a small amount relative to the size of the market. Similarly, each seller of milk has limited control over the price because many other sellers are offering milk that is essentially identical. It is assumed that because each seller is small they can sell all they want at the going price. There is little reason to charge less, and if a higher price is charged, buyers will go elsewhere. Buyers and sellers in competitive markets must accept the price the market determines and, therefore, are said to be *price takers*.

Entry into the dairy industry is relatively easy – anyone can decide to start a dairy farm and for existing dairy farmers it is relatively easy to leave the industry. It should be noted that much of the analysis of competitive firms does not rely on the assumption of free entry and exit because this condition is not necessary for firms to be price takers. But as we will see later in this chapter, entry and exit are often powerful forces shaping the long-run outcome in competitive markets.

The developments in technology now mean that many more people have access to information about firms. Price comparison websites, blogs, review sites and so on mean that it is much easier for consumers to find out about the prices being charged by different firms in a market, as well as the sort of service and quality they offer. Firms can also make use of this information and are aware that they are subject to increasing transparency over the way they conduct their business. This can affect their behaviour.

Having stated these assumptions we can look at how firms behave in such markets. Remember this is a model which allows us to be able to analyze behaviour under these assumptions. We can then begin to drop some of these assumptions and analyze how firm behaviour may differ as a result.

The dairy industry is not just about having cows and a field – there is plenty of capital investment needed as well to maximize yields.

The Marginal Cost Curve and the Firm's Supply Decision

In Chapter 8 we identified the point of profit maximization as the output level where marginal cost = marginal revenue (MC = MR). Consider the profit-maximizing position for a competitive firm as shown in Figure 10.1. The figure shows a horizontal line at the market price (P). The price line for a highly competitive firm is horizontal because the firm is a price taker: the price of the firm's output is the same, regardless of the quantity that the firm decides to produce. Remember we are assuming the firm is operating in a highly competitive market. For a competitive firm, the firm's price equals both its average revenue (AR) and its marginal revenue (MR). This is because the firm is so small relative to the market that it cannot influence price. We also assumed the firm can sell all it wants at the reigning market price. If the firm is currently selling 100 units and the market price is €2 per unit then the average revenue ($AR = TR/Q$) will be 200/100 = €2. If it now sells an additional unit at €2 its average revenue will be 202/101 = €2 and the marginal revenue (the addition to total revenue as a result of selling one extra unit) will also be €2. Therefore under these highly competitive conditions, P = AR = MR.

FIGURE 10.1

Profit Maximization for a Competitive Firm

This figure shows the marginal cost curve (MC), the average total cost curve (ATC) and the average variable cost curve (AVC). It also shows the market price (P), which equals marginal revenue (MR) and average revenue (AR). At the quantity Q_1, marginal revenue MR_1 exceeds marginal cost MC_1, so raising production increases profit. At the quantity Q_2 marginal cost MC_2 is above marginal revenue MR_2, so reducing production increases profit. The profit-maximizing quantity Q_{MAX} is found where the horizontal price line intersects the marginal cost curve.

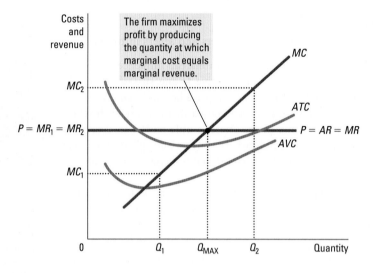

FIGURE 10.2

Marginal Cost as the Competitive Firm's Supply Curve (1)

An increase in the price from P_1 to P_2 leads to an increase in the firm's profit-maximizing quantity from Q_1 to Q_2. Because the marginal cost curve shows the quantity supplied by the firm at any given price, it is the firm's supply curve.

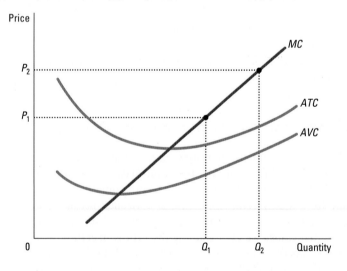

Figure 10.2 shows how a competitive firm responds to an increase in the price which may have been caused by a change in global market conditions. Remember that competitive firms are price takers and have to accept the market price for their product. Prices of commodities such as grain, metals, sugar, cotton, coffee, pork bellies, oil and so on are set by organized international markets and so the individual firm has no power to influence price. When the price is P_1, the firm produces quantity Q_1, the

FIGURE 10.3

Marginal Cost as the Competitive Firm's Supply Curve (2)

A fall in the price from P_1 to P_2 leads to a decrease in the firm's profit-maximizing quantity from Q_1 to Q_2. The marginal cost curve shows the quantity supplied by the firm at any given price.

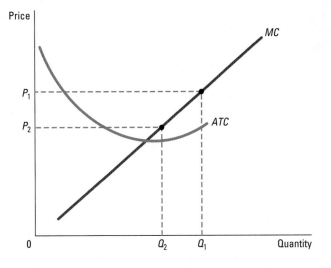

quantity that equates marginal cost to the price (which remember is the same as marginal revenue). Assume that an outbreak of tuberculosis results in the need to slaughter a large proportion of dairy cattle and as a result there is a shortage of milk on the market. When the price rises to P_2, the individual firm finds that marginal revenue is now higher than marginal cost at the previous level of output, so the firm will seek to increase production (assuming it is not one of the firms whose dairy herd has been wiped out). The new profit-maximizing quantity is Q_2, at which marginal cost equals the new higher price. In essence, because the firm's marginal cost curve determines the quantity of the good the firm is willing to supply at any price, it is the competitive firm's supply curve.

A similar, but reversed, situation would occur if the price fell for some reason as shown in Figure 10.3. In this situation, the firm would find that at the initial equilibrium output level, Q_1, marginal cost would be greater than marginal revenue with a new price of P_2 and so the firm would look to cut back production to the new profit-maximizing output level Q_2.

The Firm's Short-Run Decision to Shut Down

Clearly, in reality, the profit-maximizing output might be hard to identify because it relies on the firm being able to identify all its costs and revenues accurately over a period of time and to have the capacity to expand and contract quickly in response to changing market conditions.

We also know that firms make losses – sometimes very big losses. If we assume that a firm exists to make a profit do we conclude that if it makes a loss it will shut down its operations? This is obviously not the case in some situations although at some point a decision to cease operating will be taken. How does the firm make that sort of decision?

We can distinguish between a temporary shutdown of a firm and the permanent exit of a firm from the market. A *shutdown* refers to a short-run decision not to produce anything during a specific period of time because of current market conditions. This was the case with some firms in the automotive industry during the aftermath of the financial crisis in 2008–2010. A number of firms decided to suspend production for varying periods of time while the market recovered and stocks were reduced.

The decision to shut down a firm affects large numbers of people, not just employees who may lose their jobs, and can be a lengthy process and a costly decision to make.

This is different to a complete cessation of operations referred to as exit. *Exit* is a long-run decision to leave the market. The short-run and long-run decisions differ because most firms cannot avoid their fixed costs in the short run but can do so in the long run. A firm that shuts down temporarily still has to pay its fixed costs, whereas a firm that exits the market saves both its fixed and its variable costs.

For example, consider the production decision that an oil producer faces. The cost of the land, and the capital equipment to drill and process oil, form part of the producer's fixed costs. If the firm decides to suspend the supply of oil for two months, the cost of the land and capital cannot be recovered. When making the short-run decision whether to shut down production for a period, the fixed cost of land and capital is said to be a *sunk cost*. By contrast, if the oil producer decides to leave the industry altogether, it can sell the land and some of the capital equipment. When making the long-run decision whether to exit the market, the cost of land and capital is not sunk. (We return to the issue of sunk costs shortly.)

Now let's consider what determines a firm's shutdown decision in the short run. If the firm shuts down, it loses all revenue from the sale of the products it is not now producing and which could be sold. At the same time, it does not have to pay the variable costs of making its product (but must still pay the fixed costs). Common sense would tell us that a firm shuts down if the revenue that it would get from producing is less than its variable costs of production; it is simply not worth producing a product which costs more to produce than the revenue generated by its sale. Doing so would reduce profit or make any existing losses even greater.

A little bit of mathematics can make this shutdown criterion more useful. If *TR* stands for total revenue and *VC* stands for variable costs, then the firm's decision can be written as:

$$\text{Shut down if } TR < VC$$

The firm shuts down if total revenue is less than variable cost. By dividing both sides of this inequality by the quantity *Q*, we can write it as:

$$\text{Shut down if } TR/Q < VC/Q$$

Notice that this can be further simplified. *TR/Q* is total revenue divided by quantity, which is average revenue (*AR*). For a competitive firm average revenue is simply the good's price *P*. Similarly, *VC/Q* is average variable cost *AVC*. Therefore, the firm's shutdown criterion is:

$$\text{Shut down if } P < AVC$$

That is, a firm chooses to shut down if the price of the good is less than the average variable cost of production. This is our common sense interpretation: when choosing to produce, the firm compares the price it receives for the typical unit to the average variable cost that it must incur to produce the typical unit. If the price doesn't cover the average variable cost, the firm is better off stopping production altogether. The firm can reopen in the future if conditions change so that price exceeds average variable cost.

 what if...the price the firm received was equal to AVC in the long run – would the firm still be able to continue in production indefinitely?

We now have a full description of a competitive firm's profit-maximizing strategy. If the firm produces anything, it produces the quantity at which marginal cost equals the price of the good. Yet if the price is less than average variable cost at that quantity, the firm is better off shutting down and not producing anything. These results are illustrated in Figure 10.4. The competitive firm's short-run supply curve is the portion of its marginal cost curve that lies above average variable cost.

FIGURE 10.4

The Competitive Firm's Short-Run Supply Curve

In the short run, the competitive firm's supply curve is its marginal cost curve (MC) above average variable cost (AVC). If the price falls below average variable cost, the firm is better off shutting down.

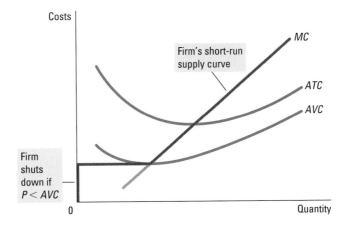

Sunk Costs Economists say that a cost is a **sunk cost** when it has already been committed and cannot be recovered. In a sense, a sunk cost is the opposite of an opportunity cost: an opportunity cost is what you have to give up if you choose to do one thing instead of another, whereas a sunk cost cannot be avoided, regardless of the choices you make. Because nothing can be done about sunk costs, you can ignore them when making decisions about various aspects of life, including business strategy.

sunk cost a cost that has already been committed and cannot be recovered

Our analysis of the firm's shutdown decision is one example of the importance of recognizing sunk costs. We assume that the firm cannot recover its fixed costs by temporarily stopping production. As a result, the firm's fixed costs are sunk in the short run, and the firm can safely ignore these costs when deciding how much to produce. The firm's short-run supply curve is the part of the marginal cost curve that lies above average variable cost, and the size of the fixed cost does not matter for this supply decision.

The Firm's Long-Run Decision to Exit or Enter a Market

The firm's long-run decision to exit the market is similar to its short-run decision in some respects. If the firm exits, it again will lose all revenue from the sale of its product, but now it saves on both fixed and variable costs of production. Thus, the firm exits the market if the revenue it would get from producing is less than its total costs.

We can again make this criterion more useful by writing it mathematically. If *TR* stands for total revenue and *TC* stands for total cost, then the firm's criterion can be written as:

$$\text{Exit if } TR < TC$$

The firm exits if total revenue is less than total cost in the long run. By dividing both sides of this inequality by quantity *Q*, we can write it as:

$$\text{Exit if } TR/Q < TC/Q$$

We can simplify this further by noting that *TR/Q* is average revenue, which, of course for a competitive firm is the same as the price *P*, and that *TC/Q* is average total cost *ATC*. Therefore, the firm's exit criterion is:

$$\text{Exit if } P < ATC$$

That is, a firm chooses to exit if the price of the good is less than the average total cost of production.

The Competitive Firm's Long-Run Supply Curve

In the long run, the competitive firm's supply curve is its marginal cost curve (MC) above average total cost (ATC). If the price falls below average total cost, the firm is better off exiting the market.

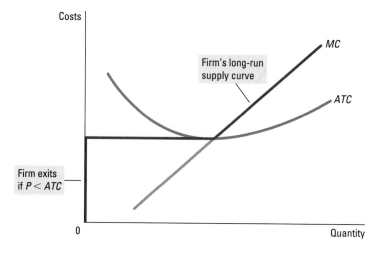

One of the financial objectives for new firms starting up is to make profit. The entry criterion where some profit will be made is:

$$\text{Enter if } P > ATC$$

The criterion for entry is exactly the opposite of the criterion for exit.

We can now describe a competitive firm's long-run profit-maximizing strategy. If the firm is in the market, it aims to produce at the quantity at which marginal cost equals the price of the good. Yet if the price is less than average total cost at that quantity, the firm chooses to exit (or not enter) the market. These results are illustrated in Figure 10.5. The competitive firm's long-run supply curve is the portion of its marginal cost curve that lies above average total cost.

CASE STUDY

Production Shutdowns

Potash Corp, based in Saskatchewan, Canada, produces fertilizers for agriculture. It supplies around 20 per cent of the world's supply of potash, a key element in crop nutrients. Given its size, Potash Corp cannot be described as a highly competitive firm but it still faces many of the issues that firms in our model face.

Demand for the firm's products is dependent on the state of the agriculture industry. The more acres of land that are farmed the higher the demand for fertilizers like potash and so the more incentive there is for Potash Corp to supply the market. However, if demand for its products falls then

By shutting down temporarily, Potash Corp will not have to pay the variable costs of operating machinery and mining potash given that sluggish demand for potash means prices may be lower than the variable costs of production.

the company has to make decisions about production levels. In February 2012, the company announced a decision to temporarily shutdown production at one of its plants in Saskatchewan for four weeks. This decision followed temporary shutdowns in two other plants in Canada, one for 6 weeks which started in late December 2011 and the other from January 2012 for 8 weeks.

The reason for the announcements was that demand for potash had slowed, partly due to the global economic position. Buyers were not replenishing stocks at a rate which made it viable to continue production and so the company moved to reduce supply until demand began to pick up. Potash Corp executives suggested that demand was expected to pick up in the northern hemisphere spring due to relatively high prices of crops and decisions by farmers to plant more acres as a result to take advantage of the higher crop prices.

Annual production at the firm's Allan mine would be reduced by between 150 000 to 160 000 metric tonnes; according to reports, around 1.6 per cent of the firm's total annual production of potash. Potash Corp noted that workers at the plants would not be laid off, however, but instead would be deployed to other work within the company during the shutdown period.

Measuring Profit in Our Graph for the Competitive Firm

As we analyze exit and entry, it is useful to be able to analyze the firm's profit in more detail. Recall that profit (π) equals total revenue (TR) minus total cost (TC):

$$\pi = TR - TC$$

We can rewrite this definition by multiplying and dividing the right-hand side by Q:

$$\pi = ((TR/q) - (TC/q)) \times q$$

But note that TR/Q is average revenue, which is the price P, and TC/Q is average total cost ATC. Therefore:

$$\pi = (P - ATC) \times Q$$

This way of expressing the firm's profit allows us to measure profit in our graphs.

Panel (a) of Figure 10.6 shows a firm earning positive profit. As we have already discussed, the firm maximizes profit by producing the quantity at which price equals

FIGURE 10.6

Profit as the Area Between Price and Average Total Cost

The area of the shaded box between price and average total cost represents the firm's profit. The height of this box is price minus average total cost (P − ATC), and the width of the box is the quantity of output (Q). In panel (a), price is above average total cost, so the firm has positive profit. In panel (b), price is less than average total cost, so the firm has losses.

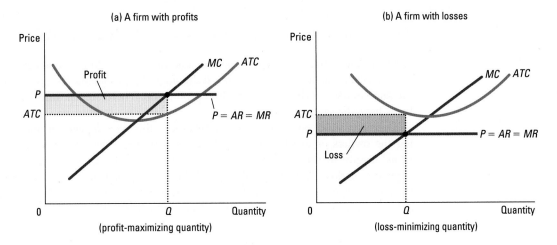

marginal cost. Now look at the shaded rectangle. The height of the rectangle is $P - ATC$, the difference between price and average total cost. The width of the rectangle is Q, the quantity produced. Therefore, the area of the rectangle is $(P - ATC) \times Q$, which is the firm's profit.

Similarly, panel (b) of this figure shows a firm with losses (negative profit). In this case, maximizing profit means minimizing losses, a task accomplished once again by producing the quantity at which price equals marginal cost. Now consider the shaded rectangle. The height of the rectangle is $ATC - P$, and the width is Q. The area is $(ATC - P) \times Q$, which is the firm's loss. Because a firm in this situation is not making enough revenue to cover its average total cost, the firm would choose to exit the market.

> **Quick Quiz** How does the price faced by a profit-maximizing competitive firm compare to its marginal cost? Explain. • When does a profit-maximizing competitive firm decide to shut down? When does a profit-maximizing competitive firm decide to exit a market?

THE SUPPLY CURVE IN A COMPETITIVE MARKET

Now that we have examined the supply decision of a single firm, we can discuss the supply curve for a market. There are two cases to consider. First, we examine a market with a fixed number of firms. Secondly, we examine a market in which the number of firms can change as old firms exit the market and new firms enter. Both cases are important, for each applies over a specific time horizon. Over short periods of time it is often difficult for firms to enter and exit, so the assumption of a fixed number of firms is appropriate. But over long periods of time, the number of firms can adjust to changing market conditions.

The Short Run: Market Supply with a Fixed Number of Firms

Consider first a market with 1000 identical firms. For any given price, each firm supplies a quantity of output so that its marginal cost equals the price, as shown in panel (a) of Figure 10.7. That is, as long as price is above average variable cost, each firm's marginal cost curve is its supply curve. The quantity of output supplied to the market equals the sum of the quantities supplied by each of the 1000 individual firms. Thus, to derive the market supply curve, we add the quantity supplied by each firm in the market. As panel (b) of Figure 10.7 shows, because the firms are identical, the quantity supplied to the market is 1000 times the quantity supplied by each firm.

The Long Run: Market Supply with Entry and Exit

Now consider what happens if firms are able to enter or exit the market. Let's suppose that everyone has access to the same technology for producing the good and access to the same markets to buy the inputs into production. Therefore, all firms and all potential firms have the same cost curves.

Decisions about entry and exit in a market of this type depend on the incentives facing the owners of existing firms and the entrepreneurs who could start new firms. If firms already in the market are profitable, then new firms will have an incentive to enter the market. This entry will expand the number of firms, increase the quantity of the good supplied, and drive down prices and profits. Conversely, if firms in the market are making losses, then some existing firms will exit the market. Their exit will reduce

FIGURE 10.7

Market Supply with a Fixed Number of Firms

When the number of firms in the market is fixed, the market supply curve, shown in panel (b), reflects the individual firms' marginal cost curves, shown in panel (a). Here, in a market of 1000 firms, the quantity of output supplied to the market is 1000 times the quantity supplied by each firm.

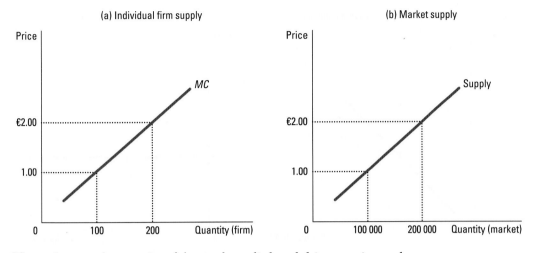

the number of firms, decrease the quantity of the good supplied, and drive up prices and profits. At the end of this process of entry and exit, firms that remain in the market must be making zero economic profit.

> **Pitfall Prevention** When talking about zero economic profit, it is important to remember the distinction between economic profit and accounting profit introduced in Chapter 9. When an economist talks of zero profit they are referring to economic profit.

Recall that we can write a firm's profits as:

$$\text{Profit} = (P - ATC) \times Q$$

This equation shows that an operating firm has zero profit if and only if the price of the good equals the average total cost of producing that good. If price is above average total cost, profit is positive, which encourages new firms to enter. If price is less than average total cost, profit is negative, which encourages some firms to exit. The process of entry and exit ends only when price and average total cost are driven to equality.

This analysis has a surprising implication. We noted earlier in the chapter that competitive firms produce so that price equals marginal cost. We just noted that free entry and exit forces price to equal average total cost. But if price is to equal both marginal cost and average total cost, these two measures of cost must equal each other. Marginal cost and average total cost are equal, however, only when the firm is operating at the minimum of average total cost. Recall from Chapter 9 that the level of production with lowest average total cost is called the firm's efficient scale. Therefore, the long-run equilibrium of a competitive market with free entry and exit must have firms operating at their efficient scale.

Panel (a) of Figure 10.8 shows a firm in such a long-run equilibrium. In this figure, price *P* equals marginal cost *MC*, so the firm is profit-maximizing. Price also equals average total cost *ATC*, so profits are zero. New firms have no incentive to enter the market, and existing firms have no incentive to leave the market.

From this analysis of firm behaviour, we can determine the long-run supply curve for the market. In a market with free entry and exit, there is only one price consistent with zero profit – the minimum of average total cost. As a result, the long-run market supply curve must be horizontal at this price, as in panel (b) of Figure 10.8. Any price above

FIGURE 10.8

Market Supply with Entry and Exit

Firms will enter or exit the market until profit is driven to zero. Thus, in the long run, price equals the minimum of average total cost, as shown in panel (a). The number of firms adjusts to ensure that all demand is satisfied at this price. The long-run market supply curve is horizontal at this price, as shown in panel (b).

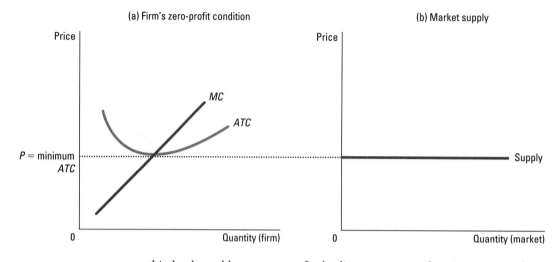

(a) Firm's zero-profit condition

(b) Market supply

this level would generate profit, leading to entry and an increase in the total quantity supplied. Any price below this level would generate losses, leading to exit and a decrease in the total quantity supplied. Eventually, the number of firms in the market adjusts so that price equals the minimum of average total cost, and there are enough firms to satisfy all the demand at this price.

Why Do Competitive Firms Stay in Business If They Make Zero Profit?

At first, it might seem odd that competitive firms earn zero profit in the long run. After all, people start businesses to make a profit. If entry eventually drives profit to zero, there might seem to be little reason to stay in business.

To understand the zero-profit condition more fully, recall that profit equals total revenue minus total cost, and that total cost includes all the opportunity costs of the firm. In particular, total cost includes the opportunity cost of the time and money that the firm owners devote to the business. In the zero-profit equilibrium, the firm's revenue must compensate the owners for the time and money that they expend to keep their business going.

Consider an example. Suppose that a farmer had to invest €1 million to open his farm, which otherwise he could have deposited in a bank to earn €50 000 a year in interest. In addition, he had to give up another job that would have paid him €30 000 a year. Then the farmer's opportunity cost of farming includes both the interest he could have earned and the forgone wages – a total of €80 000. This sum must be calculated as part of the farmer's total costs. In some situations zero profit is referred to as **normal profit** – the minimum amount required to keep factor inputs in their current use. Even if his profit is driven to zero, his revenue from farming compensates him for these opportunity costs.

normal profit the minimum amount required to keep factors of production in their current use

Keep in mind that accountants and economists measure costs differently. As we discussed in Chapter 9, accountants keep track of explicit costs but usually miss implicit costs. That is, they measure costs that require an outflow of money from the firm, but they fail to include opportunity costs of production that do not involve an outflow of money. As a result, in the zero-profit equilibrium, economic profit is zero, but accounting profit is positive. Our farmer's accountant, for instance, would conclude that the farmer earned an accounting profit of €80 000, which is enough to keep the farmer in business. In the short run as we shall see, profit can be above zero or normal profit which is referred to as **abnormal profit**.

abnormal profit the profit over and above normal profit

? **what if…**a firm earned profit which was only 1 per cent less than zero profit. Would it still be worthwhile continuing in production?

A Shift in Demand in the Short Run and Long Run

Because firms can enter and exit a market in the long run but not in the short run, the response of a market to a change in demand depends on the time horizon. To see this, let's trace the effects of a shift in demand. This analysis will show how a market responds over time, and it will show how entry and exit drive a market to its long-run equilibrium.

Suppose the market for milk begins in long-run equilibrium. Firms are earning zero profit, so price equals the minimum of average total cost. Panel (a) of Figure 10.9 shows the situation. The long-run equilibrium is point A, the quantity sold in the market is Q_1, and the price is P_1.

Now suppose scientists discover that milk has miraculous health benefits. As a result, the demand curve for milk shifts outward from D_1 to D_2, as in panel (b). The short-run equilibrium moves from point A to point B; as a result, the quantity rises from Q_1 to Q_2 and the price rises from P_1 to P_2. All of the existing firms respond to the higher price by raising the amount produced. Because each firm's supply curve reflects its marginal cost curve, how much they each increase production is determined by the marginal cost curve. In the new short-run equilibrium, the price of milk exceeds average total cost, so the firms are making positive or abnormal profit.

Over time, the profit in this market encourages new firms to enter. Some farmers may switch to milk production from other farm products, for example. As the number of firms grows, the short-run supply curve shifts to the right from S_1 to S_2, as in panel (c), and this shift causes the price of milk to fall. Eventually, the price is driven back down to the minimum of average total cost, profits are zero and firms stop entering. Thus, the market reaches a new long-run equilibrium, point C. The price of milk has returned to P_1, but the quantity produced has risen to Q_3. Each firm is again producing at its efficient scale, but because more firms are in the dairy business, the quantity of milk produced and sold is higher.

JEOPARDY PROBLEM

When the Channel Tunnel was built between the United Kingdom and France, the cost of production rose dramatically but not surprisingly given the technical challenges of such an engineering project. Once opened it soon became clear that the firm which operated the tunnel, Eurotunnel, would never break even. Why might this situation have arisen and why is the tunnel still operational despite being loss making?

NAUFRAGO PLANETÁRIO

The Channel Tunnel – what other use could it possibly have? Does this affect decisions on whether to shut or restructure the business?

FIGURE 10.9

An Increase in Demand in the Short Run and Long Run

The market starts in a long-run equilibrium, shown as point A in panel (a). In this equilibrium, each firm makes zero profit, and the price equals the minimum average total cost. Panel (b) shows what happens in the short run when demand rises from D_1 to D_2. The equilibrium goes from point A to point B, price rises from P_1 to P_2, and the quantity sold in the market rises from Q_1 to Q_2. Because price now exceeds average total cost, firms make profits, which over time encourage new firms to enter the market. This entry shifts the short-run supply curve to the right from S_1 to S_2 as shown in panel (c). In the new long-run equilibrium, point C, price has returned to P_1 but the quantity sold has increased to Q_3. Profits are again zero, price is back to the minimum of average total cost, but the market has more firms to satisfy the greater demand.

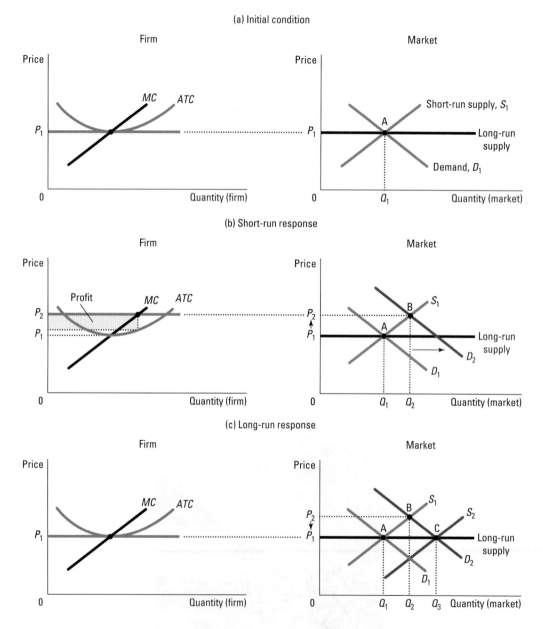

Why the Long-Run Supply Curve Might Slope Upward

So far we have seen that entry and exit can cause the long-run market supply curve to be horizontal. The essence of our analysis is that there are a large number of potential entrants, each of which faces the same costs. As a result, the long-run market supply curve is horizontal at the minimum of average total cost. When the demand for the good increases, the long-run result is an increase in the number of firms and in the total quantity supplied, without any change in the price.

The reality is that the assumptions we have made in our model do not hold in all cases. There are, as a result, two reasons that the long-run market supply curve might slope upward. The first is that some resources used in production may be available only in limited quantities. For example, consider the market for farm products. Anyone can choose to buy land and start a farm, but the quantity and quality of land is limited. As more people become farmers, the price of farmland is bid up, which raises the costs of all farmers in the market. Thus, an increase in demand for farm products cannot induce an increase in quantity supplied without also inducing a rise in farmers' costs, which in turn means a rise in price. The result is a long-run market supply curve that is upward sloping, even with free entry into farming.

A second reason for an upward sloping supply curve is that firms may have different costs. For example, consider the market for painters. Anyone can enter the market for painting services, but not everyone has the same costs. Costs vary in part because some people work faster than others, use different materials and equipment and because some people have better alternative uses of their time than others. For any given price, those with lower costs are more likely to enter than those with higher costs. To increase the quantity of painting services supplied, additional entrants must be encouraged to enter the market. Because these new entrants have higher costs, the price must rise to make entry profitable for them. Thus, the market supply curve for painting services slopes upward even with free entry into the market.

Notice that if firms have different costs, some firms earn profit even in the long run. In this case, the price in the market reflects the average total cost of the *marginal firm* – the firm that would exit the market if the price were any lower. This firm earns zero profit, but firms with lower costs earn positive profit. Entry does not eliminate this profit because would-be entrants have higher costs than firms already in the market. Higher-cost firms will enter only if the price rises, making the market profitable for them.

Thus, for these two reasons, the long-run supply curve in a market may be upward sloping rather than horizontal, indicating that a higher price is necessary to induce a larger quantity supplied. Nevertheless, the basic lesson about entry and exit remains true. Because firms can enter and exit more easily in the long run than in the short run, the long-run supply curve is typically more elastic than the short-run supply curve.

Quick Quiz In the long run with free entry and exit, is the price in a market equal to marginal cost, average total cost, both, or neither? Explain with a diagram.

CONCLUSION: BEHIND THE SUPPLY CURVE

We have been discussing the behaviour of competitive profit-maximizing firms. You may recall from Chapter 1 that one of the *Ten Principles of Economics* is that rational people think at the margin. This chapter has applied this idea to the competitive firm. Marginal analysis has given us a theory of the supply curve in a competitive market and, as a result, a deeper understanding of market outcomes.

We have learned that when you buy a good from a firm in a competitive market, you can be assured that the price you pay is close to the cost of producing that good. In particular, if firms are competitive and profit-maximizing, the price of a good equals the marginal cost of making that good. In addition, if firms can freely enter and exit the market, the price also equals the lowest possible average total cost of production.

Although we have assumed throughout this chapter that firms are price takers, many of the tools developed here are also useful for studying firms in less competitive markets. In subsequent chapters we will examine the behaviour of firms with market power. Marginal analysis will again be useful in analyzing these firms, but it will have quite different implications.

IN THE NEWS

The Tablet Market

Businesses like Apple, Samsung and Microsoft are hardly the epitome of the perfectly competitive firm that we have been describing, but the market dynamics in which they operate can bear some comforting resemblances to the model outlined in this chapter.

Tablet Growth

There are few people in the world today who are not touched in some way by mobile devices. Ever since the mobile phone became a product accessible to very large numbers of people, firms have been looking to find ways of expanding the mobile technology market. The development of text messaging, emails, the web, listening to music, playing games and watching video have all been included on mobile devices with varying degrees of success over the last ten years.

Apple's introduction of the iPad developed a new concept in mobile devices – the tablet. Tablet computers are a mobile device that function very similarly to a personal computer and are characterized by a touch screen which can be operated by hands or some sort of pen device.

The iPad was launched in January 2010. Since that time sales rose quickly reaching 1 million by May 2010 and around 25 million by June 2011. The iPad 2 was released in March 2011 and the iPad 3 a year later. The success of the iPad made it clear that there was a demand for these types of devices and that there were potential profits to be made – Apple reported its fiscal

fourth quarter profits of $6.62 billion in October 2011 (not all of this profit is attributed to the iPad of course). Apple was one of the first companies to launch a tablet PC but other electrical manufacturers were not far behind and saw the market potential.

When the iPad was first introduced, the price was relatively high at between €500 to €950 depending on the model. The abnormal profits that could be earned on these devices meant that there was an incentive for rivals to follow suit and launch their own tablet PC versions. Amazon had launched its Kindle in 2007 but this device did not have the functionality of an iPad and was more of an eBook service than a tablet PC. There had been other tablet PC devices prior to the iPad but Apple did have the advantage of launching at a time when 3G and wi-fi access was more widely available and accessible.

Following the release of the iPad, the Galaxy Tab from Samsung, Research in Motion's BlackBerry Playbook, Vizio's Via, the Toshiba Thrive, LG's Optimus and the Motorola Xoom all appeared on the market. Amazon sought to get in on the act by updating its Kindle to the Kindle Fire which included far more functionality, mimick-

ing a tablet PC. A host of other technology firms also introduced tablets such as Disgo, Creative, Acer, Archos, HTC and Dell.

How the market reacts to this influx of supply is dependent on the degree of substitutability between these different devices. This is not a perfect market with homogenous products and each device is different in terms of looks, functionality and usability. We are not talking about an industry supply curve, therefore, that is the summation of individual firm's supply curves.

However, for the consumer, the effect is that they have a far wider choice and with greater choice and competition between sellers, the pressure on prices to fall exists. Along with greater competition come the improvements in production techniques and knowledge, which individual manufacturers will be looking to exploit to lower production costs and increase productivity and efficiency, thus allowing them to have more flexibility on pricing in what is a growing and increasingly competitive market.

The result has been a gradual reduction in the prices of tablet PCs as competition and production efficiencies rise. The iPad 2, for example, was launched at prices around €50 per model less than the iPad 1. Other devices are being marketed at prices between €50 and €500. According to analysts' reports, the tablet PC market is in the early phases of its life cycle. The predictions for tablets based on an optimistic, a most likely and worst case scenario suggests that the growth of the tablet has a long way to go yet.

Questions

1. Apple was one of the first businesses to enter the tablet PC market. What costs would it have had to take into account in deciding whether the market was worth entering?
2. Our model assumes freedom of entry and exit for a market that may not be present in markets which are not highly competitive. Outline some factors that might prevent entry into the tablet PC market.
3. Using diagrams, explain how short-run profits in the tablet PC industry might be competed away in the long term to lead to normal profits being made in this market.
4. What factors might affect the length of time which could constitute the long run in the tablet PC market?
5. Assess the factors which would allow a firm like Apple to continue making abnormal profits in the long run in this market.

SUMMARY

- Because a competitive firm is a price taker, its revenue is proportional to the amount of output it produces. The price of the good equals both the firm's average revenue and its marginal revenue.

- To maximize profit, a firm chooses a quantity of output such that marginal revenue equals marginal cost. Because marginal revenue for a competitive firm equals the market price, the firm chooses quantity so that price equals marginal cost. Thus, the firm's marginal cost curve is its supply curve.

- In the short run when a firm cannot recover its fixed costs, the firm will choose to shut down temporarily if the price of the good is less than average variable cost. In the long run

when the firm can recover both fixed and variable costs, it will choose to exit if the price is less than average total cost.

- In a market with free entry and exit, profits are driven to zero in the long run. In this long-run equilibrium, all firms produce at the efficient scale, price equals the minimum of average total cost, and the number of firms adjusts to satisfy the quantity demanded at this price.

- Changes in demand have different effects over different time horizons. In the short run, an increase in demand raises prices and leads to profits, and a decrease in demand lowers prices and leads to losses. But if firms can freely enter and exit the market, then in the long run the number of firms adjusts to drive the market back to the zero-profit equilibrium.

KEY CONCEPTS

sunk cost, p. 243   normal profit, p. 248   abnormal profit, p. 249

QUESTIONS FOR REVIEW

1. What is meant by a competitive firm?
2. Draw the cost curves for a typical firm. For a given price, explain how the firm chooses the level of output that maximizes profit.
3. Under what conditions will a firm shut down temporarily? Explain.
4. Under what conditions will a firm exit a market? Explain.
5. Under what conditions will a firm enter a market? Explain.
6. Does a firm's price equal marginal cost in the short run, in the long run, or both? Explain.

7. Does a firm's price equal the minimum of average total cost in the short run, in the long run, or both? Explain.
8. Explain why a firm will continue in production even if it makes zero profit.
9. If a firm is making abnormal profit in the short run, what will happen to these profits in the long run assuming the conditions for a highly competitive market exist?
10. Are market supply curves typically more elastic in the short run or in the long run? Explain.

PROBLEMS AND APPLICATIONS

1. What are the characteristics of a competitive market? Which of the following drinks do you think is best described by these characteristics? Why aren't the others?
   a. tap water
   b. bottled water
   c. cola
   d. beer

2. Your flatmate's long hours in the chemistry lab finally paid off – she discovered a secret formula that lets people do an hour's worth of studying in 5 minutes. So far, she's sold 200 doses, and faces the following average total cost schedule:

Q	Average total cost
199	€199
200	200
201	201

   If a new customer offers to pay your flatmate €300 for one dose, should she make one more? Explain.

3. You go out to the best restaurant in town and order a lobster dinner for €40. After eating half of the lobster, you realize that you are quite full. Your date wants you to finish your dinner, because you can't take it home and because 'you've already paid for it'. What should you do? Relate your answer to the material in this chapter.

4. PC Camera GmBH faces costs of production as follows:

Quantity	Total fixed costs (€)	Total variable costs (€)
0	100	0
1	100	50
2	100	70
3	100	90
4	100	140
5	100	200
6	100	360

   a. Calculate the company's average fixed costs, average variable costs, average total costs and marginal costs at each level of production.
   b. The price of a PC camera is €50. Seeing that he can't make a profit the chief executive officer (CEO) decides to shut down operations. What are the firm's profits/losses? Was this a wise decision? Explain.
   c. Vaguely remembering her introductory business economics course, the chief financial officer (CFO) tells the CEO it is better to produce 1 PC camera because marginal revenue equals marginal cost at that quantity. What are the firm's profits/losses at that level of production? Was this the best decision? Explain.

5. 'High prices traditionally cause expansion in an industry, eventually bringing an end to high prices and manufacturers' prosperity.' Explain, using appropriate diagrams.

6. Suppose the book printing industry is competitive and begins in long-run equilibrium.
   a. Draw a diagram describing the typical firm in the industry.
   b. Hi-Tech Printing Company invents a new process that sharply reduces the cost of printing books. What happens to Hi-Tech's profits and the price of books in the short run when Hi-Tech's patent prevents other firms from using the new technology?
   c. What happens in the long run when the patent expires and other firms are free to use the technology?

7. Many small boats are made of fibreglass, which is derived from crude oil. Suppose that the price of oil rises.
   a. Using diagrams, show what happens to the cost curves of an individual boat-making firm and to the market supply curve.
   b. What happens to the profits of boat-makers in the short run? What happens to the number of boat-makers in the long run?

8. Suppose that the European Union textile industry is competitive, and there is no international trade in textiles. In long-run equilibrium, the price per unit of cloth is €30.
   a. Describe the equilibrium using graphs for the entire market and for an individual producer.
      Now suppose that textile producers in non-EU countries are willing to sell large quantities of cloth in the EU for only €25 per unit.
   b. Assuming that EU textile producers have large fixed costs, what is the short-run effect of these imports on the quantity produced by an individual producer? What is the short-run effect on profits? Illustrate your answer with a graph.
   c. What is the long-run effect on the number of EU firms in the industry?

9. Assume that the gold-mining industry is competitive.
   a. Illustrate a long-run equilibrium using diagrams for the gold market and for a representative gold mine.
   b. Suppose that an increase in jewellery demand induces a surge in the demand for gold. Using your diagrams from part (a), show what happens in the short run to the gold market and to each existing gold mine.
   c. If the demand for gold remains high, what would happen to the price over time? Specifically, would the new long-run equilibrium price be above, below or equal to the short-run equilibrium price in part (b)? Is it possible for the new long-run equilibrium price to be above the original long-run equilibrium price? Explain.

10. The liquorice industry is competitive. Each firm produces 2 million liquorice bootlaces per year. The bootlaces have an average total cost of €0.20 each, and they sell for €0.30.
    a. What is the marginal cost of a liquorice bootlace?
    b. Is this industry in long-run equilibrium? Why or why not?

11 CORPORATE STRATEGY AND PRICING POLICY

LEARNING OBJECTIVES

In this chapter you will:

- Look at the meaning of strategy

- Be shown the key stages in developing and implementing strategy

- Cover a variety of pricing strategies that firms can use

After reading this chapter you should be able to:

- Give a clear definition of strategy

- Outline at least two frameworks for strategic analysis

- Outline some benefits and limitations of strategic planning

- Outline the main features of the resource-based model

- Explain the idea of emergent strategy

- Outline the idea of logical incrementalism

- Explain the main features of market-based strategies including value chain analysis, cost leadership, differentiation and niche marketing

- Analyze the processes and challenges of implementing strategy

- Explain the concept of the margin

- Discuss the issues facing firms in making pricing decisions covering a range of pricing strategies

INTRODUCTION

In this chapter we will be looking at aspects of corporate strategy and pricing policy. Strategy is a controversial subject with many different points of view but we will present an outline of the key issues. We are going to start by looking at the idea of corporate strategy and then at some of the principal pricing strategies that firms in imperfectly competitive markets can adopt. Pricing strategies are not relevant in perfect competition because firms are price takers and have no control over the price they charge.

BUSINESS STRATEGY

As noted above, the concept of strategy is a controversial one. There are many books written on the subject and intense debates between academics, between business leaders and between academics and business leaders about exactly what it means. What follows is an outline of the main schools of thought. Whenever you read about strategy, the important thing to consider is that if anyone really knew what strategy was about they would be making many millions. The very fact that there is no one magic formula would suggest that it is highly complex and differs from organization to organization.

What is Strategy?

To take a broad definition, strategy can be seen as a series of actions, decisions and obligations which lead to the firm gaining a competitive advantage and exploiting the firm's core competencies. This definition implies the future and as such we can shorten this definition to note that strategy is about where the business wants to be at some point in the future and what steps it needs to take to get there. It is, therefore, about setting the overall direction of the business but in times of change much of this direction will be carried out in an environment of uncertainty. In Chapter 8 we noted how firms set mission and value statements to try and capture the essence of what they are about. In many cases, these mission and value statements can be seen as being an attempt to summarize the firm's strategy.

The Strategic Hierarchy

Typically we might expect the strategic direction of the firm to be formulated at the highest levels of the business and this strategy then informs decisions and behaviour lower down the organization. This may be the case in many firms but we must also be aware that organizations now recognize that the senior team do not always have all the answers and increasingly strategy is formulated at lower levels of the organization. Such strategic formulation and management is likely to be carried out in the context of the firm's overall strategy but that overall strategy may be formulated around a series of strategic intents rather than being anything specific. **Strategic intent** was picked up by Max Boisot in 1995 following the development of the idea by Gary Hamel and C.K. Prahalad in an article in the *Harvard Business Review* in 1989.

strategic intent a framework for establishing and sharing a vision of where a business wants to be at some point in the future and encouraging all those involved in the business to understand and work towards achieving this vision

C.K. Prahalad and Gary Hamel, pioneers of the idea of core competencies.

It refers to establishing and sharing a vision of where a business wants to be at some point in the future and encouraging all those involved in the business to understand and work towards achieving this vision. Strategic intent can be thought of as a framework for decision making in an uncertain environment where detailed plans can be very quickly blown off course. Whenever key decisions need to be made, the decision maker/s need to refer back to the strategic intent and ask themselves the question: what decision would help to allow the firm to operate at a higher level in line with the vision?

Strategic Planning

If a firm is able to articulate where it wants to be in the future then it needs to put something in place to help it achieve that goal and this might be a plan of some description. Strategic planning aims to put in place a system for decision making which is designed to help the business achieve its long-term goals. Such a plan may include four elements; establishing the purpose, the objectives, strategies and tactics, commonly referred to by the acronym POST.

In order to develop the plan some understanding needs to be developed about the organization and where it stands in relation to its external environment. Such an awareness-building exercise might start with an analysis of the firm and its market, its place within that market and to understand the market.

This might be carried out by various means such as a **SWOT analysis** (an analysis of the firm's strengths, weaknesses, opportunities and threats) or analyzing its product portfolio using the Boston Consulting Group's matrix. This matrix classifies the firm's products in four ways: as cash cows, rising stars, problem children or dogs. Each of these classifications relates to the extent to which the product is part of a growing market and the proportion of market share the product has.

SWOT analysis an analysis of the firm's strengths, weaknesses, opportunities and threats

A cash cow, for example, will be a product that is in a mature market – the market is not growing but the product has a high market share and as such does not require significant expenditure to maintain sales. A problem child will be a product which has a low market share in a growing market. There might be something that is preventing the product from capturing more of the market and the firm may have to invest more money if the product is to go anywhere in the market. The firm may have to make a decision about whether to continue to support the product or whether it might be better to withdraw it from the market – something which would be sensible if the cost of supporting it was much higher than the revenues it was going to bring in. A rising star is a product which is part of a growing market whose market share is also rising. This type of product may be a future cash cow. A dog is a product in a market which is declining and it may also have a low market share. This is a product which is a candidate for withdrawal from the market.

FIGURE 11.1

The Boston Consulting Group Matrix

The Boston Consulting Group matrix classifies products in relation to market share (horizontal axis) and the extent to which it is a part of a growing market (vertical axis). The matrix then groups products into four classifications: Stars, Dogs, Cash Cows and Problem Children

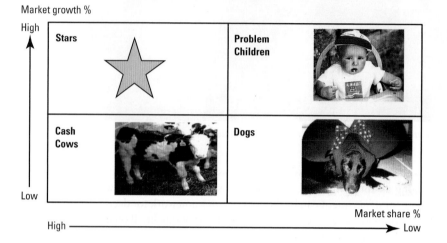

Many larger firms have large product portfolios so using the Boston Matrix may be a way in which it can analyze this portfolio and enable it to make decisions about supporting products, on whether new product development needs to be carried out on cash flows and its overall market presence. It is a framework, therefore, for making decisions about the future and reflects the firm's obligations and where it wants to be in the future.

Similarly, a firm might use a framework referred to as Porter's Five Forces. This was developed by Michael Porter in the 1980s and is cited extensively in the literature. The Five Forces framework allows a firm to analyze its own competitive strength set in the context of external factors. The firm can analyze the existing competitive rivalry between suppliers in the market, the potential threat posed by new entrants into the market, how much bargaining power buyers and suppliers in the market have and what threat is provided by substitute products.

The Five Forces model has been, and remains, extremely influential in business strategy. It is not, however, without its limitations. In particular, the movement of businesses to build collaboration through things such as joint ventures, supplier agreements, buyer agreements, research and development collaboration, and cost sharing all mean that buyer and supplier power might be moderated and not simply be seen as a threat. It is also important that a business recognizes the importance and role of its internal culture and the quality of its human resources in influencing its competitive strategy.

Regardless of the model used, the firm needs to have a clear understanding of its position in the market and that of its competitors to be able to formulate actions that will enable it to be where it wants to be in the future. Some element of planning, therefore, will be essential but the dynamic nature of business means that plans have to be flexible and subject to constant amendment if they are to be of any longer term benefit. Few firms would create a plan and then stick rigidly to it. The strategic plan may be a way in which the firm outlines its strategy but how does it choose this strategy in the first place?

There are a number of different approaches which have been suggested. The following provides a brief outline of each.

Resource-Based Model

Every firm uses resources. It could be argued that each firm has a unique set of resources and it can use this uniqueness as the basis for choosing its strategy. Resources could be unique because the firm owns a particular set of assets which few other firms have, or employs a particularly brilliant team of production designers; it could be the location of the business that is unique or the way in which the firm has designed and organized its production operations. These resources can be analyzed to find, identify and isolate **core competencies**. Core competencies are the things a business does which are the source of competitive advantage over its rivals. Firms can be in the same industry and have access to similar resources but for some reason one firm might better utilize these resources to achieve returns that are above others in the industry. The firm's strategy can be developed once these unique features have been identified and exploited and it is this which helps provide the competitive advantage.

<aside>**core competencies** the things a business does which are the source of competitive advantage over its rivals</aside>

Remember that competitive advantage refers to the advantages a firm has over its rivals which are both distinctive and defensible. What this tells us is if a firm is able to identify its core competencies it can exploit these in order to achieve greater returns and its rivals will not be able to quickly or cheaply find a way to emulate what the firm does in order to erode the advantage/s the firm has.

If a firm develops a strategy that starts to move away from its core competencies then there is a potential for failure unless it can develop core competencies in this new area. For example, a firm like 3M has core competencies in substrates (the base material onto which something will be printed or laminated or protected), coatings and adhesives. It might use its expertise in these areas to formulate a strategy which seeks to exploit these competencies but if it decides that it will branch out to another area, for example, into cleaning products to complement its Scotchguard protection brand, then it might find the expertise needed in that area is not something it possesses and as such may end up making below average returns.

There are plenty of examples of firms that have tried to branch out into new areas outside their expertise and have failed. Harley Davidson, for example, attempted to move into the perfume market, Bic, the ball point pen manufacturer, into ladies underwear and the women's magazine, *Cosmopolitan*, attempted to launch a range of yoghurts. In each case the moves were unsuccessful, partly because consumers failed to understand the association between what were established brands and a new departure, but also because the new ideas did not represent the core competencies of each firm.

Is the brand association of a firm like Harley Davidson so ingrained that moving into an unrelated market becomes difficult?

Emergent Strategy

The dynamic and often chaotic nature of the business environment means that whatever plans a business has are likely to be outdated almost as soon as they are written, or overtaken by events which occur and which are outside the control of the business. The model of emergent strategy recognizes this reality.

A firm might start off with an intended (sometimes referred to as deliberate) strategy which is planned, deliberate and focused on achieving stated long-term goals. However, it is highly likely that some part of this intended strategy will not be realized and as situations and circumstances change the firm will have to make decisions. These decisions are made with the overall intended strategy in mind but adjusted to take account of the changed circumstances.

Over time this decision making forms a pattern which becomes emergent strategy. This implies that firms may adopt broad policies of intent rather than detailed plans so that they can respond to changed circumstances and also that they can learn as they go along.

Logical Incrementalism

The term logical incrementalism was used by James Brian Quinn, a professor of management at Amos Tuck School, Dartmouth, Colorado. Quinn suggests that managers might be seen to be making various incremental decisions in response to events which may not seem to have any coherent structure. However, these responses may have some rational basis whereby the firm has an overall strategy but local managers respond to local situations. The overall strategy can be realized but incrementally. Such incremental decisions may be affected by resource constraints at a local level which mean that trade-offs and compromises have to be made in order to adjust to these local conditions.

Market-Based Strategy

Market-based strategy turns the focus onto the business environment in which the firm operates and strategy is chosen based on an understanding of the competitive environment that the firm operates. Analysis of the competitive environment is focused on two key areas – the firm's cost structure and how it differentiates itself from its rivals.

It is often assumed that a firm can adopt pricing strategies regardless of other factors in an attempt to win market share or expand sales, but as will be noted later in this chapter, flexibility on the choice of pricing strategy is partly dependent on whether a firm can afford to adopt a pricing strategy. For example, it is only possible to adopt prices that are lower in comparison to rivals if the firm's cost base allows it to do so.

Value Chain Analysis   One of the first things a business has to do, therefore, is to look at its value chain and examine every aspect to determine where inefficiencies may exist and where cost benefits can be gained. The term **value chain** refers to all the activities and operations which a firm carries out and how value is added at each of these stages. If the value created is greater than the cost of making the good or service available to the consumer then the firm will generate profit. It makes sense, therefore, to focus on these value stages and extract maximum value at minimum cost as the basis of creating sustainable competitive advantage.

Crucially, value chain analysis can focus on aspects of the business which may have been seen as being unimportant but necessary. For example, publishers have warehouses where stock is processed prior to delivery to customers, whoever those customers may be – book shops, university campuses, online retailers and so on. Time spent looking at

value chain the activities and operations which a firm carries out and how value is added at each of these stages

ways in which orders can be processed and shipped in the minimum time possible and at minimum cost could help create competitive advantage. Not only is the operation efficient but the reputation the publisher gets through having a highly efficient processing and distribution system can be worth additional sales in the market when competition is strong. Two business economics textbooks may be as good as each other but if one publisher can guarantee order-shipment-delivery times weeks ahead of the other, and with 99.99 per cent reliability, then this may be the reason why a customer chooses one book over another.

Porter outlined a number of key value chain activities.

- Inbound logistics includes goods inwards, warehousing and stock control; operations relates to the processes that transform inputs into outputs; outbound logistics focus on fulfilling orders, shipping and distribution, marketing and sales which deals with making consumers aware of the product and ensuring that products get to consumers at the right time and at the right place, the right price and in sufficient quantities; and finally, service which is associated with the functions that help build product value and reputation and which include customer relations, customer service and maintenance and repair (or lack of it).

By exploiting value chain analysis a firm can identify ways of reducing its costs below that of its competitors and thus gain competitive advantage, which, remember, must be distinctive and defensible. This is the essence of **cost leadership**. A firm might be able to identify particular efficiencies as described above or exploit possible economies of scale to gain the advantage over its rivals. As the firm progresses through these processes it can also benefit from the *learning curve* (sometimes also referred to as the *experience curve*). This states that as tasks and processes are repeated, the firm will become more efficient and effective at carrying out those tasks and in a cumulative way, build in further improvements and efficiencies as time progresses.

cost leadership a strategy to gain competitive advantage through reducing costs below competitors

Cost leadership may be beneficial in markets where price competition is fierce, where there is a limit to the degree of differentiation of the product possible, where the needs of consumers are similar and where consumers can relatively easily substitute one rival product for another – in other words, they incur low switching costs.

Quick Quiz Why might a firm want to reduce maintenance and repair to a bare minimum as a means of increasing value?

A detailed analysis of every aspect of the firm's value chain can reveal small but possibly important activities where efficiencies can be improved to generate added value and reduce cost. Ensuring that the various functions and activities are coordinated and can also help generate competitive advantage.

Travelling around many countries these days, you might notice extremely large distribution centres located near to major arterial roadways, airports, ports or railways. The development of these massive distribution centres has come through value chain analysis. A number of retail chain stores have such a system where the distribution centre acts as a hub receiving supplies and distributing them along 'spokes'. Such systems have helped give firms cost advantages as well as improving reputation for efficient delivery and order processing. Hub-and-spoke systems are also used by airlines to help simplify routes and keep costs under control as well as get passengers to their destinations as efficiently as possible.

If a firm is able to generate cost advantages through value chain analysis it can gain a position of being a cost leader and as such has greater flexibility in being able to set prices which help maximize revenues or profit.

MARCIN BALCERZAK/SHUTTERSTOCK

An interior view of part of the baby and children's retailer, Mothercare, which also links in with the Early Learning Centre's, distribution centre in Daventry in Northamptonshire, UK. Daventry is a town located within a few miles of major arterial motorways connecting to all parts of the UK including the M1, M40 and M6 motorways and close to London and Birmingham, the first and second cities in the UK respectively.

differentiation the way in which a firm seeks to portray or present itself as being different or unique in some way

Differentiation   The second focus of market-based strategies is on differentiation. **Differentiation** is the way in which a firm seeks to portray or present itself as being different or unique in some way. This can be physical in the form of the actual product itself or mental and emotional through the way in which the business is able to develop its brands, advertise and promote itself and create emotional attachments to its products. Firms attempting to differentiate themselves do need to be aware of the importance of taking into account changing tastes and fashions. What differentiates a firm one year might become a burden the next and the perception of the business becomes difficult to change as time moves on.

Apple has been very successful at differentiating itself from its rivals both in terms of the functionality of its products but also in its design and the way in which it creates a loyal following of customers who are keen to snap up its products whenever they are released. Similarly, firms like Bose and Bang & Olufsen have created a reputation for high-quality sound systems and enviable design which set them apart from their rivals. Food manufacturers like Heinz increasingly place an emphasis on quality, on the use of natural ingredients and low fat and sodium as a means of differentiating themselves. Hotel chains such as Holiday Inn place an emphasis on consistency so that wherever a guest stays, in whatever country it may be, there are certain features that are familiar and comforting so that guests do not experience any shocks.

market niche a small segment of an existing market with specific wants and needs which are not currently being met by the market

Niche Strategies   A **market niche** is an (often) small segment of an existing market with specific wants and needs which are not currently being met by the market. Focusing on a niche might allow a business to identify some very specific customer requirements which it can meet profitably. Imagine a firm which develops flip-flops which have a built in supportive arch. It is unlikely that 'everyone' will buy this product but for those people who suffer from foot problems, such as fallen arches or flat feet, the product might be extremely useful – so much so that they are prepared to pay a premium price for the comfort they bring. The niche market in this case is a small section of the overall market for summer footwear who have podiatry problems (a podiatrist is a specialist in the treatment of foot problems).

Niche strategies are often beneficial to small firms which have developed specialized products but are certainly not unique to these types of business. Small businesses, in addition, may not have the resources to compete in terms of cost and in producing a mass market product have problems in differentiating themselves from their bigger rivals. In such cases, niche marketing may be an appropriate strategy to follow.

Larger firms may also target niche markets by creating trademarks, brands or securing patents. In such cases, firms may be able to not only target a wider market but also specific niches within it. In our flip-flop example, a large firm such as SSL, the owner of the Dr Scholl footwear brand, might patent the design of foot support flip-flops and secure the niche market as a result.

Quick Quiz   What are the key features of a market niche? Give three examples of niche products with which you are familiar.

Strategic Implementation

Having analyzed the firm and the market and then decided on some strategy, the next phase is to implement this strategy. This is invariably the most challenging part of strategic management. Implementation involves the way in which the plans and direction are actually put into practice and decisions that a firm takes to translate words into action.

Those who have created the strategy – often the senior leaders and managers in a business – have to communicate the vision and strategy to a range of stakeholders (not just the employees) and then make sure that the structures, design, people and operations are in place to deliver the strategy. In addition, the senior team will have to put in place systems to monitor progress of the strategy. This is not to suggest that the whole process is simply a top-down approach; as noted earlier, an increasing number of firms recognize that strategy has to be a focus at all levels of the business and that individuals and groups lower down the hierarchy have to have the flexibility and freedom to make choices and decisions. The caveat is seeking to ensure that these choices and decisions are made with the overall strategy in mind.

One framework which has been suggested for managing strategic implementation is the FAIR framework. This stands for Focus, Alignment, Integration and Review. In the focus phase, senior managers identify shorter-term objectives in conjunction with departmental or functional heads and in line with the overall strategic goals. These shorter-term objectives then have to be aligned throughout the functional and departmental areas of the organization, with resourcing and practical implications considered and worked through. These plans are then integrated into the day-to-day operational processes and workflows but management of these processes has to be reviewed periodically to see the extent to which the strategy is being implemented and what the results are.

Summary

This brief overview of a very complex topic has outlined some of the issues and thinking on strategy. There are many excellent books and articles on strategy and strategic management, many of which go into much greater detail about the debates and differing perspectives that characterize the field of strategy. Ultimately, however, a firm has to have some understanding of itself and its market, identify and articulate a clear vision about where it wants to be in the future and find ways of implementing the strategic choices it has made.

PRICING STRATEGIES

One of the key decisions any firm has to make is on the price to charge for its products. There are a number of pricing strategies (some argue they should properly be called tactics). The purpose of pricing strategies is to influence sales in some way or to reflect something about the product that the firm wishes to communicate to its customers and potential customers. At its simplest, there are only a few things a firm can do – either set price lower than its rivals, set price higher in order to reflect a standard or some suggestion of quality, or seek to set price at a similar level to that of its rivals.

Of course, the ability of the firm to use price as a means of influencing sales depends to a large extent on its costs. The difference between the cost of production and price can be looked at as a **margin** – the amount of profit a firm makes on each sale. Of course, this definition does depend on how 'cost of production' is calculated and what costs are included. However, for our purposes, looking at margins as the profit a firm makes from each sale is sufficient for our analysis. A firm operating at a higher cost base than its rivals will struggle in the long term to match the low prices its rivals may be able to charge because they have a lower average cost.

margin the amount of profit a firm makes on each sale

Cost-plus pricing

This is perhaps the simplest form of pricing. The firm calculates the cost of production per unit and then sets price above this cost. The price can therefore reflect the margin or mark-up that the firm desires. For this reason cost plus pricing is also referred to as mark-up pricing or full-cost pricing. Let us take an example. Assume that a hairdresser calculates the average cost of a styling to include the cost of the stylist's time, the chemicals used during the styling as well as working out how the fixed costs could be attributed to each customer (for example, the cost of heating and lighting, rent on the premises, rates, insurance, drinks and magazines given to customers, performing rights fees for music played in the salon and so on) at €30. If the salon owner desired a profit margin of 10 per cent then they should charge a price of €33 but if a mark-up of 50 per cent was required then the customer will be charged €45. The formula for calculating price given a desired mark-up percentage is:

Selling price = Total cost per unit × (1 + percentage mark-up expressed as a proportion)

If our salon owner calculated the total cost per customer of a simple wash, cut and blow-dry at €12 and the desired mark-up was 25 per cent then the price charged would be 12 × (1 + 0.25) = 12 × 1.25 = €15.

One of the benefits of cost-plus pricing is that the firm can see very easily what overall profit it is likely to make if it sells the desired number of units. It is also possible to set different prices with the same mark-up as shown in the examples above. The total cost per unit of doing a simple wash, cut and blow-dry is not the same as someone having a completely new style with highlights, but by using this formula the salon owner could be sure that the different prices charged generate the same percentage mark-up.

However, one of the problems is that basing price simply on a desired mark-up does not take into account market demand and the competition. In reality many firms will take these factors into consideration and adjust the size of the mark-up accordingly. Assume that our salon owner knows that there is another salon in town which charges €14 for a wash, cut and blow-dry and that the owner wants to undercut the rival. They set the price at €13. What is the mark-up now?

To calculate the mark-up in this case we use the formula:

Mark-up (per cent) = (Selling price – Total cost per unit/Total cost) × 100

The mark-up percentage, therefore, will be ((13 − 12)/12) × 100 = 8.3 per cent.

The mark-up is not the same as the margin. In the example above the margin is the difference between the selling price and total cost per unit which as €1. This margin is then expressed as a percentage of the selling price and so would be (1/13) × 100 = 7.69 per cent.

It is possible that the salon owner might have a desired margin level (let's say it is 20 per cent) in which case this can be used to determine the selling price using the formula:

Selling price = Total cost per unit /(1 − Margin)

In our example the selling price will now be 12/(1 − 0.20) = 12/0.8 = €15.

Quick Quiz Using examples, explain the difference between mark-up and margin.

Contribution or Absorption Cost Pricing

This is related to cost-plus pricing and is based on the same principles but instead of attempting to calculate the total cost per unit, the firm will estimate the variable cost only and then add some mark-up to determine the selling price. The difference between the variable cost per unit and the selling price is called the contribution. This sum represents a contribution to the fixed costs which must also be paid. Recall the analysis of the break-even point in Chapter 8. As the firm sells more and more units the contribution eventually covers the fixed costs and, for all subsequent sales, the contribution will add to profit.

Contribution pricing may be useful if it is difficult for the firm to ascribe fixed costs to output easily, which may be the case in some service industries.

Psychological Pricing

The basis of psychological pricing is that humans respond to different prices in different ways and for some reason may, as a result, behave differently or have a different emotional response. The classic example of psychological pricing is that of a firm charging €5.99 for a product rather than €6.00. This is partly due to the way we view things – many people may look at the first figure in a price and pay little attention to the last two digits (called the *left-digit effect*). If the firm believes that customers would see the number '5' as being 'reasonable' but '6' as being too expensive then setting the price at €5.99 might encourage consumers to purchase believing they are getting some sort of discount.

Psychological pricing is based on a fundamental assumption that consumers do not behave rationally. If they did then why would they be willing to buy something at €15.49 but not at €15.50? It could also be argued that psychological pricing treats consumers as if they are not very bright and cannot see through the tactic. One can only conclude that the prevalence of use of this tactic would suggest that it does work.

Penetration Pricing

As the name suggests, penetration pricing is a tactic that is used to gain some penetration in a market. The firm sets its price at the lowest possible level in order to capture sales and market share. This is a tactic that may be used when a firm launches a new product onto the market and wants to capture market share. Once that market share has been captured and some element of brand loyalty built up, the firm may start to push up the price. If this is the longer-term aim then there could be a problem with consumers getting used to low prices and being put off when prices begin to rise. At this point, the price elasticity of demand is crucial to the longer-term success of the product. If consumers are sensitive about price then increases might lead to a switch to substitutes or the consumer leaving the market altogether.

Penetration pricing assumes that firms will operate at low margins whilst pursuing such a tactic, but if successful and sales volumes are high, then total profit could still be relatively high. Penetration pricing implies that a firm needs to have considerable control over its costs to enable it to operate at low margins.

Some products may be priced at a low level but sell in very large volumes and so make high profits as a result.

Quick Quiz Why does penetration pricing tend to be a tactic that is associated with high-volume products?

Market Skimming

Market or price skimming is a tactic that can be used to exploit some advantage a firm has which allows it to sell its products at a high price. The term 'skimming' refers to the fact that the firm is trying to 'skim' profits while market conditions prevail by setting price as high as demand will allow.

Such a situation can arise when a firm launches a new product onto the market which has been anticipated for some time. Companies like Apple are very good at building such anticipation (some would call it hype) so that when the product does finally launch the market price can be relatively high. It may be that some months later the price of the product starts to fall, partly because of the need to persuade consumers who are marginal

Loss-leaders are designed to create interest in the business in the hope of generating wider sales on products which have higher profit margins.

buyers, i.e. those that are not devoted to the product and would only consider buying at lower prices, or because the competition has reacted and launched substitutes.

The high initial prices imply that the firm is able to generate relatively high margins in the early stages of the product which may be used to help offset the development costs, which in the case of technology products like smartphones, tablets and gaming consoles (where market skimming is not unusual as a pricing tactic) can be relatively high.

Destroyer or Predatory Pricing

This is a tactic designed to drive out competition. A firm uses its dominance in the market and its cost advantages to set price below a level its competitors are able to match. The intention is that some rivals will be forced from the market and so competition is reduced. Ultimately the firm which instigated the strategy is able to operate with greater monopoly power. This tactic is illegal in many countries and comes under anti-competitive laws; however it is often difficult to prove.

Loss-Leader

The use of loss-leaders is a tactic that is often seen in larger businesses and especially in supermarkets. A loss-leader is a product deliberately sold below cost and therefore at a loss in an attempt to encourage sales of other products. At holiday times, for example, many supermarkets will sell drinks at prices below cost and advertise this in the hope and expectation that consumers will come into the store, buy the drinks which are on offer but also buy other things as well. The other items that are bought generate a profit and this profit offsets the losses made on the loss-leader.

The type of product chosen to be the loss-leader can be important. Often a firm will choose something that it thinks consumers will have a good understanding of in terms of value and original price. By doing this it hopes that the 'incredible' offer it is making will be noticed more obviously by the consumer and thus encourage the consumer to take advantage.

Products which are complements may also be the target of such a tactic. For example, selling a blu-ray DVD player at a loss may encourage consumers to buy blu-ray DVDs; or a firm sells wet shavers at low prices but consumers find that replacement blades tend to be sold at relatively high prices (and often packaged in large quantities so that not just one new blade can be purchased). Potential drawbacks could occur if the consumer is highly disciplined and only buys the goods on offer, but evidence suggests this is relatively unusual.

> **Quick Quiz** How might a firm calculate whether a loss-leader has been a successful tactic?

Premium or Value Pricing

The type of market a firm operates in can be a determinant of the pricing strategy it adopts. On the one hand, fast selling consumer goods might generate large volume sales for firms but at a price which is competitive and yields low margins (such as chocolate bars, newspapers and ball point pens) but at the other end of the scale, a firm might deliberately set its price high to reflect the quality or exclusivity of the product. It knows that sales volumes will be low but that the margins are high and as a result profits can still be high on low sales.

Premium pricing may be a feature of certain types of technology-based products, luxury yachts, some motor cars, jewellery, designer fashion items, hotels, perfumes and first class travel. In each of these cases the firm may deliberately set prices high or output is restricted so that price rises relative to demand.

Competition Pricing

Competition pricing occurs where a firm will note the prices charged by its rivals and either set its own price at the same level or below in order to capture sales. One of the problems facing firms who use this strategy is that firms have to have an understanding of their competitors. For example, if a rival firm was charging a particular price for a product because it benefited from economies of scale and had lower average costs, then a new firm coming into the market and looking to compete on price might find that it cannot do so because it does not have the cost advantages. It could also be the case that a rival has set price based on established brand loyalty and as such simply setting a price at or below this in an attempt to capture sales may not work because the price difference is insufficient to break the loyalty that consumers have for the branded product.

In markets where competition is limited, 'going rate' pricing may be applicable and each firm charges similar prices to that of its rivals and in each case price may be well above marginal cost. Such a situation might be applicable to the banking sector, petrol and fuel, supermarkets and some electrical goods where prices tend to be very similar across different sellers.

Price Leadership

In some markets, a firm may be dominant and is able to act as a price leader. In such cases, rivals have difficulty in competing on price; if they charge too high a price they risk losing market share and forcing prices lower could result in the price leader matching price and forcing smaller rivals out of the market. The other option, therefore, is to act as a follower and follow the pricing leads of rivals especially where those rivals have a clear dominance of market share.

> **?** **what if…** a firm which is seen as a price leader increases prices by 10 per cent but its rivals who are classed as followers decide not to raise price in this case?

Marginal-Cost Pricing

This typically occurs when a firm faces a situation where the marginal cost of producing an extra unit is very low and where the bulk of the costs are fixed costs. In such a situation the cost of selling an additional unit is either very low or non-existent and as a result the firm is able to be flexible about the prices it can charge.

An example occurs in the transport industry on airlines and trains. If an airline operates a scheduled flight with 300 seats available from Amsterdam to Riyadh, then the bulk of the costs will be incurred regardless of how many seats are sold. Let us assume that five days prior to departure only half of the seats have been sold and it does not look as if demand is going to rise in the time leading up to the flight departing. If the firm calculates that the cost of taking an extra passenger is €5 (the additional cost of fuel, food and processing) then it makes sense for the firm to accept any price above €5 in the time leading up to departure.

The main costs of an airline flight are fixed. The cost of filling an extra seat is minimal which gives airlines flexibility in pricing.

If the standard ticket was priced at €300 but demand is weak then it is clear that the airline ought to reduce price. It could conceivably keep reducing prices down to €5 in order to fill all the seats because every additional €1 above this amount would contribute to the fixed costs and thus make it worthwhile for the airline.

Pitfall Prevention We have covered a range of pricing strategies in this section. However, it is important to remember that firms do not make pricing decisions in isolation – i.e. if a firm decides to adopt a price skimming strategy it will not do this without taking into account many other factors including what its competitors are charging, what type of product they are selling and so on, all of which may be factors that are characteristic of decision making in other pricing strategies.

CASE STUDY

J.C. Penney's Pricing Strategy

J.C. Penney is a US retailer. It runs around 1100 department stores in the US and Puerto Rico with annual sales of around $17.5 billion. In January 2012, the company announced a new pricing strategy. The company noted that over a period of a year it had numerous sales and customers had clearly got wise to this and tended to wait for sales periods to come round. Like many such stores, J.C. Penney found that it had very busy periods during sales times but very quiet periods in non-sales times.

Its new pricing strategy is designed to reduce this guessing game where customers wait for sales periods and instead the company announced that it would cut the price of all its merchandise by 40 per cent from the previous year's prices and thus offer customers a much simpler pricing structure. It called this strategy 'Every day pricing'.

The new strategy was introduced by Ron Johnson, the chief executive officer of J.C. Penney. Johnson came to the position from Apple where he was Vice President for retail and had been partly responsible for the success of the Apple store concept. Johnson believes that pricing is a simple thing and that customers are savvy and will not pay more than how much they value the product at – which is not an unreasonable statement. If a customer is willing to buy an item then they must place at least a value on that product that they are willing to pay – if they do not buy it then presumably they do not believe the price being asked is sufficient to compensate them for the value they expect to get from the good.

So Johnson is introducing a strategy which means that customers will face a great deal more predictability in pricing. Sale prices become the norm rather than the exception – hence the use of the term 'every day pricing'. The firm will still have sales but they will not be as frequent as in previous year's and will tend to be more targeted. For example, gift items for Easter might go on sale for the month prior to the holidays (called 'Month-Long Value') and clearance items offered at particular times to coincide with when workers get paid – typically the first and third Friday of each month. To distinguish these prices from the rest they will be referred to as 'Best Prices'. The simple pricing principle will be further reinforced with goods being given specific price tags to alert customers to the three different pricing structures and in addition, prices will always be expressed in round numbers – no psychological pricing here.

New pricing tactics at J.C. Penney – but will they work?

The new pricing strategy was launched with an advertising campaign, new logo, a catalogue mailed to customers, a new spokesperson and other promotions. It may sound like a bold strategy and analysts are complementing Johnson on his vision but at the same time urging caution. The strategy is being launched at a time when the USA has been struggling with slow economic growth and for some years the US consumer has been used to retailers offering excellent discounts through regular sales. How consumers respond to the idea of cutting back on sales when they are used to bargain hunting and to a different approach to pricing which requires them to change habits will be the key to whether Johnson can help improve the fortunes of J.C. Penney.

IN THE NEWS

Strategy and Pricing in the Digital Imaging Market

You might think that a firm which invents a product which revolutionizes the market might be in a position to exploit the market and achieve long-term success. Not so – the case of Eastman Kodak is a good example of how strategic choices rely ultimately on human judgement which can often be found to be wanting as time marches on.

Strategy and Pricing in the Digital Imaging Market

Eastman Kodak was founded over 130 years ago. It has become synonymous with photography and imaging and one might assume that it is in these areas where its core competencies lie. Back in 1995, *Bloomberg Businessweek* ran an article on George M.C. Fisher who took over as CEO for Kodak in 1993. The article noted that Fisher had inherited 'a powerhouse brand name ... trapped in the slow-growth photography industry, hobbled by huge debts, a dysfunctional management culture, and a dispirited workforce.'[1] At that time Kodak was operating in a market which had a large number of competitors (the *Businessweek* article reported some 599 global competitors) which meant increased supply and lower prices. To maintain profit levels in a market in

[1] http://www.businessweek.com/archives/1995/b340974.arc.htm accessed 11 February 2012.

which sales growth was slow, Kodak would have to cut manufacturing costs, as well as investing in new products in what was then the infant digital imaging market. Fisher had sold off other businesses such as health care and household products which Kodak had sought to expand into and instead decided to focus more on the firm's core competencies. One of these areas was digital imaging. Digital imaging is not a new idea – it has been around since the 1970s and Kodak had been at the forefront of research and development into the area since that time. One of the problems that Kodak faced was that the development of digital imaging products such as scanners and cameras had the potential to cannibalize its photographic film and handheld camera market. Some of the most profitable parts of the business were centred on the sale of film (for cameras and in the entertainment industry), chemicals and photographic paper. In 1976, for example, Kodak

had a 90 per cent market share in film and 85 per cent market share in cameras in the USA. The arrival of digital imaging threatened these revenue earning parts of the business.

Kodak is credited with being one of the inventors of the digital camera. A Kodak engineer, Steve Sasson, spent around a year working on the development of the product as far back as 1975. In terms of the amount of funds it invested in digital imaging, it could be argued that Kodak had first mover advantage in the market. Over the next 35 years, however, Kodak could not seem to square the inevitable trade-off between digital and film-based photography and as technology changed rapidly key competitors such as Canon, Fujitsu, Hewlett Packard, Nikon and Sony embraced digital imagery far quicker than Kodak.

The result has been that in January 2012, Kodak filed for Chapter 11 bankruptcy in the USA to protect itself whilst it restructured. The company also announced that it would withdraw from the digital camera, pocket video camera and digital picture frames businesses. It decided to exit these businesses because it could not compete with rivals on both price and operational efficiency. Instead the company said that its strategy would focus on its inks and printer business, would licence its brand name to other image capturing based firms and on its online and retail photo printing.

Kodak said that these business areas were where it had seen some success in terms of market growth and the opportunity to increase margins. Its decision to reduce the focus of its business and its product portfolio was based on an 'analysis of the industry trends' according to Kodak's chief

marketing officer, Pradeep Jotwani. The new strategy does not come without a cost, however. The company has a number of manufacturing contracts with other firms and ending these contracts will incur some costs. It also has sponsorship deals with organizations such as the Oscars but it was not able to escape early from some of these contracts and so will have to incur costs in this respect also. Estimates suggest that the cost of exit will be around $30 million but that the overall benefits to the business will be up to $100 million.

Questions

1. Use the Boston Consulting Group Matrix to analyze the position of Kodak's digital cameras, handheld film cameras, and camera and movie film. Explain your reasoning.
2. One of the reasons why Kodak said that it was exiting some markets was because it could not compete on price and efficiency with its rivals. What factors might have contributed to this situation?
3. Explain why exiting the market costs so much money.
4. Evaluate the decision of the current Kodak senior team to refocus its strategy in the way outlined in the article.
5. Discuss the factors which may have convinced the senior managers of Kodak to not exploit its first mover advantage in digital imaging.

SUMMARY

- Strategy looks at where a firm wants to be in the future.
- Strategy involves an analysis of the firm and its market, making strategic choices and then implementing those choices.
- Firms have to consider a wide range of factors prior to adopting any strategy, not least the sort of market structure it operates in; what rivals might do in response; how consumers value the product; what its cost structures are and how these compare to rivals; the extent to which brand loyalty affects demand; and the price elasticity of demand.

- There is considerable debate over strategy – ultimately we might conclude that if it was easy then everyone would do it well and be successful!
- There are a range of pricing strategies (or tactics).
- Price is only one aspect of positioning a product – i.e. where the product sits in relation to the market.
- Any decision on price will be one part of the overall strategy of the firm.

KEY CONCEPTS

strategic intent, p. 256
SWOT analysis, p. 257
core competencies, p. 259

value chain, p. 260
cost leadership, p. 261
differentiation, p. 262

market niche, p. 262
margin, p. 263

QUESTIONS FOR REVIEW

1. Give a definition of the term 'strategy'.
2. Explain how the idea of 'strategic intent' helps a firm provide a framework for strategic decision making.
3. Outline two frameworks which a business might use in strategic analysis.

4. Give a bullet point list to outline the main features of the:
   a. Resource-based model
   b. Emergent strategy
   c. Logical incrementalism

5. How can value chain analysis help a firm establish an appropriate pricing policy?

6. Why might niche market strategies be beneficial to small and medium-sized firms?

7. Outline three challenges facing a business in implementing strategy.

8. Explain the relevance of the concept of the margin in pricing decisions.

9. Outline two advantages and two disadvantages to a firm of using cost-based pricing policies.

10. Explain the difference between market skimming and price penetration strategies.

PROBLEMS AND APPLICATIONS

1. A chemical firm believes it has a core competency in identifying and exploiting particular chemical processes in intermediate products (i.e. chemical products which will be used to help make other chemical products/drugs etc.). How might this core competency lead to competitive advantage?

2. 'The thicker the strategic plan the less relevant it will be'. (Quote adapted from Davies, B. and Ellison, L. 1999. *Strategic Direction and Development of the School.* London: Routledge.) To what extent to you agree with this view? Explain your reasoning.

3. Consider the models of emergent strategy and logical incrementalism. To what extent would you agree with the view that they are effectively describing the same thing – the reality of decision making in an uncertain environment.

4. Using an appropriate example, explain how value chain analysis can be a source of cost leadership and competitive advantage.

5. Choose a product with which you are familiar. Explain how the firm producing that product tries to differentiate it from rivals.

6. A firm producing fancy dress costumes estimates the fixed costs per costume at €20 and the variable costs at €5.
   a. Using this information, calculate the price if:
      i. The desired profit margin is 75 per cent.
      ii. The desired mark-up is 45 per cent.

   b. The firm knows that its rivals charge €50 per costume and it wants to undercut its rivals by 10 per cent.
      i. Calculate the price, the profit margin and the mark-up.

7. Two firms operate in different markets and introduce a new product into their respective markets. One uses a price penetration strategy and the other a market skimming strategy. At the end of the first year they both make the same amount of profit. Explain how this situation could arise.

8. Explain why predatory pricing is illegal in many countries. Do you agree that it should be illegal or is this pricing strategy just an inevitable consequence of competition? Explain your reasoning.

9. The tactic of using loss leaders is sometimes referred to as the 'razor strategy' because firms who sell razors do so below cost but then charge high prices for replacement blades. What sort of razors do you think this sort of tactic would work with. (Hint: think of the difference between a product such as the Gillette Fusion and disposable razors such as those produced by Bic.) How does a firm prevent consumers treating the razors used as loss-leaders from being treated as disposable?

10. What other factors does a firm have to have in place in order to adopt a premium pricing strategy?

12 MARKET STRUCTURES

LEARNING OBJECTIVES

In this chapter you will:

- See how imperfect competition differs from perfect competition

- Learn why some markets have only one seller

- Analyze how a monopoly determines the quantity to produce and the price to charge

- See how the monopoly's decisions affect economic well-being

- Consider the various public policies aimed at solving the problem of monopoly

- See why monopolies try to charge different prices to different customers

After reading this chapter you should be able to:

- List three reasons why a monopoly can remain the sole seller of a product in a market

- Use a monopolist's cost curves and the demand curve it faces to show the profit earned by a monopolist

- Show the deadweight loss from a monopolist's production decision

- Show why forcing a natural monopoly to set its selling price equal to its marginal cost of production creates losses for the monopolist

- Demonstrate the surprising result that price discrimination by a monopolist can raise economic welfare above that generated by standard monopoly pricing

INTRODUCTION

If you own a personal computer, it probably uses some version of Windows, the operating system sold by the US company, Microsoft Corporation. When Microsoft first designed Windows many years ago, it applied for and received a copyright, first from the US government and then from many of the governments of the world. The copyright gives Microsoft the exclusive right to make and sell copies of the Windows operating system. So if a person wants to buy a copy of Windows, he or she has little choice but to give Microsoft the price that the firm has decided to charge for its product. Windows is the operating system used by around 85 per cent of the PCs in the world. Microsoft is said to have a *monopoly* in the market for Windows.

If you use a PC or laptop, there is a very high chance that when you use a search engine it will be Google which dominates the search engine market with a market share of around 64 per cent.

In most countries, the option for consumers to purchase utilities like gas, water and electricity is limited to a very small number of firms and in some cases there might only be one supplier.

Across many parts of Europe, consumers have choice in where they do their weekly grocery shopping but the market is likely to be dominated by a relatively small number of very large firms. Once in those large supermarkets, the choice may seem very wide indeed but it might be a surprise to learn that many of the choices on offer are actually produced by a small number of firms.

In the breakfast cereal aisle, for example, there is a very wide range of choice available but most are produced by four very large firms, Nestlé, Kellogg, General Mills and Quaker. Equally, toothpaste, detergents, soaps, washing up liquid and so on are likely to be made by Procter & Gamble, Colgate-Palmolive, Kimberley-Clarke and Unilever.

A variety of well-known products which all have something in common; they are all brands owned by the multinational firm Procter & Gamble, which has 4.4 billion customers around the world.

There is a choice in the purchase of mobile phones and mobile phone service providers but again the market is dominated by a small number of very large firms. Apple, Nokia, Samsung, LG, Research in Motion (the makers of the BlackBerry brand), Motorola, HTC and Sony Ericsson are the main suppliers of handsets, Orange, O2, Vodafone, Verizon, T-Mobile, AT&T, Etisalat and Orascom being very large firms across Europe and the Middle East which dominate mobile phone service provision.

If you are a business and want to employ a firm of accountants to check your books and provide financial advice, it is very likely that you might turn to one of the so-called 'Big-Four' accounting firms, KPMG, Deloitte, PwC (PriceWaterhouseCoopers) and Ernst & Young.

You might think there is lots of choice if you want to buy some takeaway food or go to a restaurant or bar. How often, in reality, do you go back to the same place on a regular basis? If you analyze your behaviour it is likely that you will tend to have a degree of loyalty to particular brands for a variety of reasons.

What these examples highlight is that our everyday lives are influenced to a very large extent by interaction with a relatively small number of very large firms. Many markets are not characterized by a large number of relatively small firms who are price takers and have no influence of price selling products that are very similar (homogenous). Even if we do have to buy an homogenous product like petrol or diesel, for example, we will tend to buy from a small number of very big suppliers such as BP, Shell, Texaco and Esso.

IMPERFECT COMPETITION

The business decisions of many of these firms we have used as examples are not well described by the model of a competitive market we have been assuming in the previous chapters. The reality is that firms can be *price makers* rather than having to be *price takers* and do not sell homogenous products. In some way or another, either because of some physical difference or because our psychology tells us, products are not homogenous and the degree to which one product is a substitute for another can be influenced by firms. If firms can influence price or control the amount they supply or in some way present their product as being something very different, then they have some element of market power. A firm such as Microsoft has few close competitors and such a dominant market share that it can influence the market price of its product. When a firm has some element of market power its behaviour is different to that under the assumptions which characterized a highly competitive market.

> **Pitfall Prevention** Care is needed when using the word 'competitive' in economic analysis. In everyday usage, we use competitive to describe the degree of rivalry between groups or individuals. In economics, a firm in a competitive market is one which operates under the assumptions of a competitive market structure. Once we relax those assumptions we are interested in how a firm's behaviour changes. Competition between firms in market structures where there is considerable market power is certainly intense but the options available to firms and their behaviours are different to those firms operating under more perfectly competitive conditions.

In this chapter we examine the idea of imperfect competition and in particular the extreme form of imperfect competition, monopoly. In the next chapter we will look at other forms of imperfect competition.

An imperfectly competitive market is one where the assumptions of perfect competition do not hold. Just as the very extreme of the perfectly competitive model assumes homogeneity of product, perfect information, perfect substitutability of goods, a large number of small firms with no influence on market price able to sell all they produce at the going market price, the extreme of imperfect competition is monopoly.

A monopoly, in the extreme case, is a single supplier of a good with no competitors. Just as the extreme model of perfect competition does not exist in its purest form, there are few examples of a perfect monopoly. However, what we can identify are certain characteristics in particular markets where firms behave as if they are a monopoly supplier. A firm with an 85 per cent market share such as Microsoft in the Windows operating system market is not a pure monopoly – there are other operating systems such as Apple's iOS, Java, Linux, Android and Symbian, for example, but the market power that Microsoft can wield is considerable.

Where firms have some element of market power it can alter the relationship between a firm's costs and the price at which it sells its product to the market. A competitive firm takes the price of its output as given by the market and then chooses the quantity it will supply so that price equals marginal cost. By contrast, the price charged by firms with market power exceeds marginal cost. This result is clearly true in the case of Microsoft's Windows. The marginal cost of Windows – the extra cost that Microsoft would incur by printing one more copy of the program onto a CD – is only a few euros. The market price of Windows is many times marginal cost.

It is perhaps not surprising that firms with considerable market power can charge relatively high prices for their products. Customers of monopolies might seem to have little choice but to pay whatever the monopoly charges. But, if so, why is a copy of Windows priced at about €50 and not €500? Or €5000? The reason, of course, is that if Microsoft set the price that high, fewer people would buy the product. People would buy fewer computers, switch to other operating systems or make illegal copies. Monopolies cannot achieve any level of profit they want because high prices reduce the amount that their customers buy. Although monopolies can control the prices of their goods, their profits are not unlimited. In other words, under conditions of imperfect competition firms do not face a horizontal demand curve which suggests they can sell any amount they offer at the going market price. Instead, firms face a downward sloping demand curve which means that if they want to sell more products they have to accept lower prices. If this is the case then price does not equal average revenue and marginal revenue is lower. This is partly what leads to changed behaviour.

We are going to start our analysis of behaviour of firms under imperfect competition by looking at monopolies. A **monopoly** is a firm which is the sole supplier of a product in a market. In reality we describe firms as monopolies even though there are other suppliers, as we have seen in the case of operating systems. Because there are concerns about the effect of market power on consumers and suppliers, most national competition policy defines monopolies in a much stricter way. A firm might be able to exercise some monopoly power if it has 25 per cent or more of the market. However, for the purposes of our analysis let us assume that there is only one supplier in the market. Remember that features of our analysis will apply fairly closely to situations where a firm dominates the market even though there are other suppliers. When we looked at firms under highly competitive conditions we saw that the profit maximizing output would occur where MC = MR. We also saw that if market conditions change any abnormal or subnormal profit would disappear in the long run as new firms enter and leave the industry. In a competitive market firms are price takers and P = AR = MR. A firm operating as a monopoly does not face these same conditions and so production and pricing decisions are different.

As we examine the production and pricing decisions of monopolies, we also consider the implications of monopoly for society as a whole. We base our analysis of monopoly firms, like competitive firms, on the assumption that they aim to maximize profit. But this goal has very different ramifications for competitive and monopoly firms. In a competitive market, price is equal to marginal cost and in the long run the firm operates at the lowest point on the average cost curve. This implies that firms are operating efficiently and consumers not only have choice but pay low prices. Because monopoly firms face different market conditions, the outcome in a market with a monopoly is often different and not always in the best interest of society. It is these market imperfections that are so interesting and form the basis for so much government policy.

One of the *Ten Principles of Economics* in Chapter 1 is that governments can sometimes improve market outcomes. The analysis in this chapter will shed more light on this principle. As we examine the problems that monopolies raise for society, we will also discuss the various ways in which government policy makers might respond to these problems. The Competition Commission in Europe, for example, has been keeping a close eye on Microsoft for some years. Microsoft was accused of preventing fair competition because it bundled its web browser, Internet Explorer (IE), with its Windows operating system (this is known as 'tying'). Companies have complained about the way in which Microsoft allegedly makes it more difficult for other browsers to be interoperable – that is, work within a range of other platforms. The Commission imposed a fine of $1.4 billion in 2008 on Microsoft for breaching EU competition rules. As part of that investigation, the EU insisted that Microsoft made more of its code available to other software manufacturers to ensure greater interoperability. Microsoft had argued that such a move would compromise its security and that the code constituted sensitive commercial information.

monopoly a firm that is the sole seller of a product without close substitutes

GETTY IMAGES

The battle between Microsoft and the European Commission over tying has been going on for many years with accusations that Microsoft's inclusion of IE with its Windows operating system constitutes anti-competitive behaviour.

MONOPOLY

The fundamental cause of monopoly is *barriers to entry*: a monopoly remains the only seller in its market because other firms cannot enter the market and compete with it. Barriers to entry, in turn, have four main sources which we will briefly discuss.

Monopoly Resources

The simplest way for a monopoly to arise is for a single firm to own a key resource. For example, consider the market for water in a small town on a remote Scottish island not served by the water company from the mainland. If dozens of town residents on the island have working wells, the competitive model we have previously described is likely to hold. In such a situation the price of a litre of water is driven to equal the marginal cost of pumping an extra litre. But if there is only one well in town and it is impossible to get water from anywhere else, then the owner of the well has a monopoly on water. Not surprisingly, the monopolist has much greater market power than any single firm in a competitive market. In the case of a necessity like water, the monopolist could command quite a high price, even if the marginal cost is low.

Although exclusive ownership of a key resource is a potential cause of monopoly, in practice monopolies rarely arise for this reason. Actual economies are large, and resources are owned by many people. Indeed, because many goods are traded internationally, the natural scope of their markets is often worldwide. There are, therefore, few examples of firms that own a resource for which there are no close substitutes.

Government-Created Monopolies

In many cases, monopolies arise because the government has given one person or firm the exclusive right to sell some good or service. European kings, for example, once granted exclusive business licences to their friends and allies in order to raise money – a highly prized monopoly being the exclusive right to sell and distribute salt in a particular region of Europe. Even today, governments sometimes grant a monopoly (perhaps even to itself) because doing so is viewed to be in the public interest. In Sweden, the retailing of alcoholic beverages is carried out under a state-owned monopoly known as the Systembolaget, because the Swedish government deems it to be in the interests of public health to be able to control directly the sale of alcohol.

As a member of the EU, questions have been raised about this policy but Sweden seems keen to maintain its control of alcohol sales. In a recent study commissioned by the Swedish National Institute for Public Health, researchers concluded that if retail alcohol sales were privatized, the net effects on the country would be negative with an increase in alcohol-related illness and deaths, fatal accidents, suicides and homicides and a large increase in the number of working days lost to sickness.[1]

The patent and copyright laws are two important examples of how the government creates a monopoly to serve the public interest. When a pharmaceutical company discovers a new drug, it can apply to the government for a patent. If the government deems the drug to be truly original, it approves the patent, which gives the company the exclusive right to manufacture and sell the drug for a fixed number of years – often 20 years. Similarly, when a novelist finishes a book, they can copyright it. The copyright is a government guarantee that no one can print and sell the work without the author's permission. The copyright makes the novelist a monopolist in the sale of their novel.

The effects of patent and copyright laws are easy to see. Because these laws give one producer a monopoly, they lead to higher prices than would occur under competition. But by allowing these monopoly producers to charge higher prices and earn higher profits, the laws also encourage some desirable behaviour. Drug companies are allowed to be monopolists in the drugs they discover in order to encourage research. Authors are allowed to be monopolists in the sale of their books to encourage them to write more and better books.

Thus, the laws governing patents and copyrights have benefits and costs. The benefits of the patent and copyright laws are the increased incentive for creative activity. These benefits are offset, to some extent, by the costs of monopoly pricing, which we examine fully later in this chapter.

---

[1]Holder, H. (ed) (2007) *If retail alcohol sales in Sweden were privatized, what would be the potential consequences?* **http://www.systembolagetkampanj.se/forskarrapport_en/downloads/Hela_rapporten.pdf**

Natural Monopolies

An industry is a **natural monopoly** when a single firm can supply a good or service to an entire market at a lower cost than could two or more firms. A natural monopoly arises when there are economies of scale over the relevant range of output. Figure 12.1 shows the average total costs of a firm with economies of scale. In this case, a single firm can produce any amount of output at least cost. That is, for any given amount of output, a larger number of firms leads to less output per firm and higher average total cost.

natural monopoly a monopoly that arises because a single firm can supply a good or service to an entire market at a smaller cost than could two or more firms

FIGURE 12.1

Economies of Scale as a Cause of Monopoly

When a firm's average total cost curve continually declines, the firm has what is called a natural monopoly. In this case, when production is divided among more firms, each firm produces less, and average total cost rises. As a result, a single firm can produce any given amount at the smallest cost.

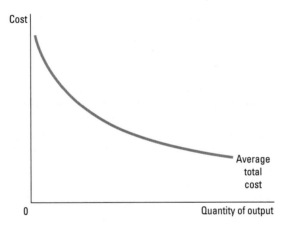

An example of a natural monopoly is the distribution of water. To provide water to residents of a town, a firm must build a network of pipes throughout the town. If two or more firms were to compete in the provision of this service, each firm would have to pay the fixed cost of building a network. Thus, the average total cost of water is lowest if a single firm serves the entire market.

When a firm is a natural monopoly, it is less concerned about new entrants eroding its monopoly power. Normally, a firm has trouble maintaining a monopoly position without ownership of a key resource or protection from the government. The monopolist's profit attracts entrants into the market, and these entrants make the market more competitive. By contrast, entering a market in which another firm has a natural monopoly is unattractive. Would-be entrants know that they cannot achieve the same low costs that the monopolist enjoys because, after entry, each firm would have a smaller piece of the market.

External Growth

Many of the largest firms in the world have grown partly through acquisition, merger or takeover of other firms. As they do so, the industry becomes more concentrated; there are fewer firms in the industry. Earlier we mentioned the Big Four accounting firms. This is an example where smaller accounting firms have merged or been taken over and has resulted in a number of large firms dominating the industry. One effect of this type of growth is that a firm might be able to develop monopoly power over its rivals and erect barriers to entry to make it harder for new firms to enter. It is for this reason that governments monitor such acquisitions to see if there are implications for competition. In the UK, for example, any merger that gives a firm 25 per cent or more of the market may be investigated to see if the acquisition is in the public interest.

HOW MONOPOLIES MAKE PRODUCTION AND PRICING DECISIONS

Now that we know how monopolies arise, we can consider how a monopoly firm decides how much of its product to make and what price to charge for it. The analysis of monopoly behaviour in this section is the starting point for evaluating whether monopolies are desirable and what policies the government might pursue in monopoly markets.

Monopoly versus Competition

The key difference between a competitive firm and a monopoly is the monopoly's ability to influence the price of its output. A competitive firm is small relative to the market in which it operates and, therefore, takes the price of its output as given by market conditions and is assumed to be able to sell all its output. By contrast, because a monopoly is the sole producer in its market, it can alter the price of its good by adjusting the quantity it supplies to the market.

Because a monopoly is the sole producer in its market, its demand curve is the market demand curve. Thus, the monopolist's demand curve slopes downward for all the usual reasons, as in panel (b) of Figure 12.2. If the monopolist raises the price of its good, consumers buy less of it. Looked at another way, if the monopolist reduces the quantity of output it sells, the price of its output increases.

FIGURE 12.2

Demand Curves for Competitive and Monopoly Firms

Because competitive firms are price takers, they in effect face horizontal demand curves, as in panel (a). Because a monopoly firm is the sole producer in its market, it faces the downward sloping market demand curve, as in panel (b). As a result, the monopoly has to accept a lower price if it wants to sell more output.

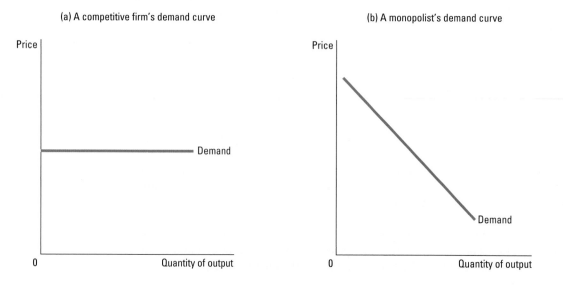

Pitfall Prevention Because a monopolist faces a downward sloping demand curve it can either set price and accept the level of demand to determine its sales or it can fix output at a certain level and allow the market to determine the price it can charge – it cannot do both, i.e., it cannot fix price *and* output together.

The market demand curve provides a constraint on a monopoly's ability to profit from its market power. A monopolist would prefer, if it were possible, to charge a high price and sell a large quantity at that high price. The market demand curve makes that outcome impossible. In particular, the market demand curve describes the combinations of price and quantity that are available to a monopoly firm. By adjusting the quantity produced (or, equivalently, the price charged), the monopolist can choose any point on the demand curve, but it cannot choose a point off the demand curve.

What point on the demand curve will the monopolist choose? As with competitive firms, we assume that the monopolist's goal is to maximize profit. Because the firm's profit is total revenue minus total costs, our next task in explaining monopoly behaviour is to examine a monopolist's revenue.

A Monopoly's Revenue

Consider a town with a single producer of water. Table 12.1 shows how the monopoly's revenue might depend on the amount of water produced.

The first two columns show the monopolist's demand schedule. If the monopolist produces just 1 litre of water, it can sell that litre for €1. If it produces 2 litres, it must lower the price to €0.90 in order to sell both litres. And if it produces 3 litres, it must lower the price to €0.80, and so on. If you graphed these two columns of numbers, you would get a typical downward sloping demand curve.

The third column of the table presents the monopolist's *total revenue*. It equals the quantity sold (from the first column) times the price (from the second column). The fourth column computes the firm's *average revenue,* the amount of revenue the firm receives per unit sold. We compute average revenue by taking the number for total revenue in the third column and dividing it by the quantity of output in the first column. As we discussed in the previous chapter, average revenue always equals the price of the good. This is true for monopolists as well as for competitive firms.

The last column of Table 12.1 computes the firm's *marginal revenue,* the amount of revenue that the firm receives for each additional unit of output. We compute marginal revenue by taking the change in total revenue when output increases by 1 unit. For

TABLE 12.1

A Monopoly's Total, Average and Marginal Revenue

Quantity of water	Price €	Total revenue €	Average revenue €	Marginal revenue €
(Q)	(P)	(TR = P × Q)	(AR = TR/Q)	(MR = $\Delta TR/\Delta Q$)
0 litres	1.1	0.0	–	
				1.0
1	1.0	1.0	1.0	
				0.8
2	0.9	1.8	0.9	
				0.6
3	0.8	2.4	0.8	
				0.4
4	0.7	2.8	0.7	
				0.2
5	0.6	3.0	0.6	
				0.0
6	0.5	3.0	0.5	
				−0.2
7	0.4	2.8	0.4	
				−0.4
8	0.3	2.4	0.3	

example, when the firm is producing 3 litres of water it receives total revenue of €2.40. Raising production to 4 litres increases total revenue to €2.80. Thus, marginal revenue is €2.80 minus €2.40, or €0.40.

Table 12.1 shows a result that is important for understanding monopoly behaviour: a monopolist's marginal revenue is always less than the price of its good. For example, if the firm raises production of water from 3 to 4 litres, it will increase total revenue by only €0.40, even though it will be able to sell each litre for €0.70. For a monopoly, marginal revenue is lower than price because a monopoly faces a downward sloping demand curve. To increase the amount sold, a monopoly firm must lower the price of its good. Hence, to sell the fourth litre of water, the monopolist must get less revenue for each of the first three litres.

Marginal revenue for monopolies is very different from marginal revenue for competitive firms. When a monopoly increases the amount it sells, it has two effects on total revenue ($P \times Q$):

- *The output effect.* More output is sold, so Q is higher, which tends to increase total revenue.
- *The price effect.* The price falls, so P is lower, which tends to decrease total revenue.

Because a competitive firm can sell all it wants at the market price, there is no price effect. When it increases production by 1 unit, it receives the market price for that unit, and it does not receive any less for the units it was already selling. That is, because the competitive firm is a price taker, its marginal revenue equals the price of its good. By contrast, when a monopoly increases production by 1 unit, it must reduce the price it charges for every unit it sells, and this cut in price reduces revenue on the units it was already selling. As a result, a monopoly's marginal revenue is less than its price.

Figure 12.3 graphs the demand curve and the marginal revenue curve for a monopoly firm. (Because the firm's price equals its average revenue, the demand curve is also the average revenue curve.) These two curves always start at the same point on the vertical axis because the marginal revenue of the first unit sold equals the price of the good. But thereafter, for the reason we just discussed, the monopolist's marginal revenue is less than the price of the good. Thus, a monopoly's marginal revenue curve lies below its demand curve. (We analyzed the maths of this in Chapter 8, Figure 8.5)

FIGURE 12.3

Demand and Marginal Revenue Curves for a Monopoly

The demand curve shows how the quantity affects the price of the good. The marginal revenue curve shows how the firm's revenue changes when the quantity increases by 1 unit. Because the price on all units sold must fall if the monopoly increases production, marginal revenue is always less than the price.

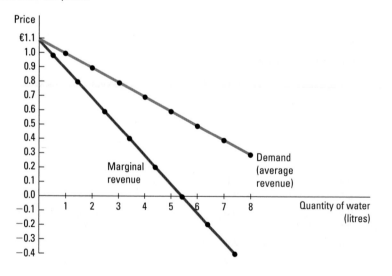

You can see in Figure 12.3 (as well as in Table 12.1) that marginal revenue can even become negative. Marginal revenue is negative when the price effect on revenue is greater than the output effect. In this case, when the firm produces an extra unit of output, the price falls by enough to cause the firm's total revenue to decline, even though the firm is selling more units.

Profit Maximization

Now that we have considered the revenue of a monopoly firm, we are ready to examine how such a firm maximizes profit. We apply the logic of marginal analysis to the monopolist's decision about how much to produce.

Figure 12.4 graphs the demand curve, the marginal revenue curve and the cost curves for a monopoly firm. All these curves should seem familiar: the demand and marginal revenue curves are like those in Figure 12.3, and the cost curves are like those we encountered in earlier chapters. These curves contain all the information we need to determine the level of output that a profit-maximizing monopolist will choose.

Suppose, first, that the firm is producing at a low level of output, such as Q_1. In this case, marginal cost is less than marginal revenue. If the firm increased production by 1 unit, the additional revenue would exceed the additional costs, and profit would rise. Thus, when marginal cost is less than marginal revenue, the firm can increase profit by producing more units.

A similar argument applies at high levels of output, such as Q_2. In this case, marginal cost is greater than marginal revenue. If the firm reduced production by 1 unit, the costs saved would exceed the revenue lost. Thus, if marginal cost is greater than marginal revenue, the firm can raise profit by reducing production.

In the end, the firm adjusts its level of production until the quantity reaches Q_{MAX}, at which marginal revenue equals marginal cost. Thus, the monopolist's profit-maximizing quantity of output is determined by the intersection of the marginal revenue curve and the marginal cost curve. In Figure 12.4, this intersection occurs at point A.

FIGURE 12.4

Profit Maximization for a Monopoly

A monopoly maximizes profit by choosing the quantity at which marginal revenue equals marginal cost (point A). It then uses the demand curve to find the price that will induce consumers to buy that quantity (point B).

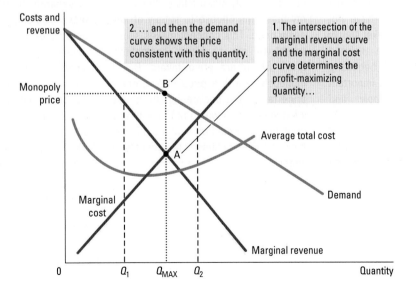

Remember that competitive firms choose to produce at the quantity of output at which marginal revenue equals marginal cost. In following this rule for profit maximization, competitive firms and monopolies are alike. But there is also an important difference between these types of firm: the marginal revenue of a competitive firm equals its price, whereas the marginal revenue of a monopoly is less than its price. That is:

$$\text{For a competitive firm: } P = MR = MC$$

$$\text{For a monopoly firm: } P > MR = MC$$

Assuming profit maximization, the decision to produce at a point where marginal revenue and marginal cost are equal is the same for both types of firm. What differs is the relationship of the price to marginal revenue and marginal cost.

How does the monopoly find the profit-maximizing price for its product? The demand curve answers this question because the demand curve relates the amount that customers are willing to pay to the quantity sold. Thus, after the monopoly firm chooses the quantity of output that equates marginal revenue and marginal cost, it uses the demand curve to find the price consistent with that quantity. In Figure 12.4, the profit-maximizing price is found at point B.

We can now see a key difference between markets with competitive firms and markets with a monopoly firm: in competitive markets, price equals marginal cost. In monopolized markets, price exceeds marginal cost. As we will see in a moment, this finding is crucial to understanding the social cost of monopoly.

FYI

Why a Monopoly Does Not Have a Supply Curve

You may have noticed that we have analyzed the price in a monopoly market using the market demand curve and the firm's cost curves. We have not made any mention of the market supply curve. By contrast, when we analyzed prices in competitive markets beginning in Chapter 4, the two most important words were always *supply* and *demand*.

What happened to the supply curve? Although monopoly firms make decisions about what quantity to supply (in the way described in this chapter), a monopoly does not have a supply curve. A supply curve tells us the quantity that firms choose to supply at any given price. This concept makes sense when we are analyzing competitive firms, which are price takers. But a monopoly firm is a price maker, not a price taker. It is not meaningful to ask what such a firm would produce at any price because the firm sets the price at the same time it chooses the quantity to supply.

Indeed, the monopolist's decision about how much to supply is impossible to separate from the demand curve it faces. The shape of the demand curve determines the shape of the marginal revenue curve, which in turn determines the monopolist's profit-maximizing quantity. In a competitive market, supply decisions can be analyzed without knowing the demand curve, but that is not true in a monopoly market. Therefore, we never talk about a monopoly's supply curve.

A Monopoly's Profit

How much profit does the monopoly make? To see the monopoly's profit, recall that profit equals total revenue (*TR*) minus total costs (*TC*):

$$\text{Profit} = TR - TC$$

We can rewrite this as:

$$\text{Profit} = (TR/Q - TC/Q) \times Q$$

TR/Q is average revenue, which equals the price *P*, and *TC/Q* is average total cost *ATC*. Therefore:

$$\text{Profit} = (P - ATC) \times Q$$

This equation for profit (which is the same as the profit equation for competitive firms) allows us to measure the monopolist's profit in our graph.

Consider the shaded box in Figure 12.5. The height of the box (the segment BC) is price minus average total cost, $P - ATC$, which is the profit on the typical unit sold. The width of the box (the segment DC) is the quantity sold Q_{MAX}. Therefore, the area of this box is the monopoly firm's total profit.

FIGURE 12.5

The Monopolist's Profit

The area of the box BCDE equals the profit of the monopoly firm. The height of the box (BC) is price minus average total cost, which equals profit per unit sold. The width of the box (DC) is the number of units sold.

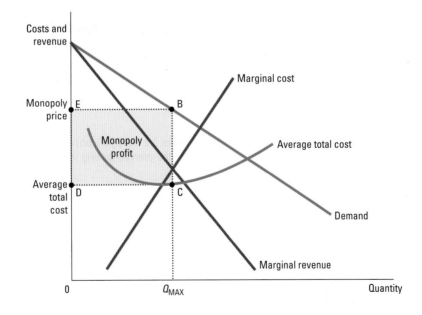

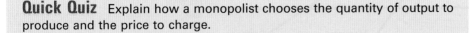

Quick Quiz Explain how a monopolist chooses the quantity of output to produce and the price to charge.

CASE STUDY

Monopoly Drugs versus Generic Drugs

According to our analysis, prices are determined quite differently in monopolized markets from the way they are in competitive markets. A natural place to test this theory is the market for pharmaceutical drugs, because this market takes on both market structures. When a firm discovers a new drug, patent laws give the firm a monopoly on the sale of that drug. But eventually the firm's patent runs out, and any company can make and sell the drug. At that time, the market switches from being monopolistic to being competitive.

What should happen to the price of a drug when the patent runs out? Figure 12.6 shows the market for a typical drug. In this figure, the marginal cost of producing the drug is constant. (This is approximately true for many drugs.) During the life of the patent, the monopoly firm maximizes profit by producing the quantity at which marginal revenue equals marginal cost and charging a price well above marginal cost. But when the patent runs out, the profit from making the drug should encourage new firms to enter the market. As the market becomes more competitive, the price should fall to equal marginal cost.

Experience is, in fact, consistent with our theory. When the patent on a drug expires, other companies quickly enter and begin selling so-called generic products that are chemically identical to the former monopolist's brand-name product. And just as our analysis predicts, the price of the competitively produced generic drug is well below the price that the monopolist was charging.

The expiration of a patent, however, does not cause the monopolist to lose all its market power. Some consumers remain loyal to the brand-name drug, perhaps out of fear that the new generic drugs are not actually the same as the drug they have been using for years. As a result, the former monopolist can continue to charge a price somewhat above the price charged by its new competitors.

FIGURE 12.6

The Market for Drugs

When a patent gives a firm a monopoly over the sale of a drug, the firm charges the monopoly price, which is well above the marginal cost of making the drug. When the patent on a drug runs out, new firms enter the market, making it more competitive. As a result, the price falls from the monopoly price to marginal cost.

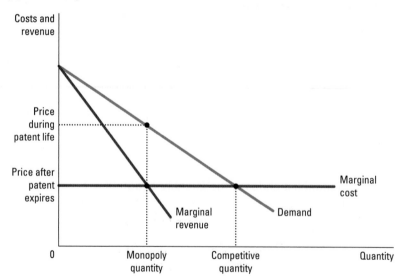

THE WELFARE COST OF MONOPOLY

Is monopoly a good way to organize a market? We have seen that a monopoly, in contrast to a competitive firm, charges a price above marginal cost. From the standpoint of consumers, this high price makes monopoly undesirable. At the same time, however, the monopoly is earning profit from charging this high price. From the standpoint of the owners of the firm, the high price makes monopoly very desirable. Is it possible that the benefits to the firm's owners exceed the costs imposed on consumers, making monopoly desirable from the standpoint of society as a whole?

We can answer this question using the concepts of consumer and producer surplus as our measure of economic well-being. Total surplus is the sum of consumer surplus and producer surplus. Consumer surplus is consumers' willingness to pay for a good minus the amount they actually pay for it. Producer surplus is the amount producers receive for a good minus their costs of producing it. In this case, there is a single producer – the monopolist.

The Deadweight Loss

We begin by considering what the monopoly firm would do if it were run by a benevolent social planner. The social planner cares not only about the profit earned by the firm's owners but also about the benefits received by the firm's consumers. The planner tries to maximize total surplus, which equals producer surplus (profit) plus consumer surplus. Keep in mind that total surplus equals the value of the good to consumers minus the costs of making the good incurred by the monopoly producer.

Figure 12.7 analyzes what level of output a benevolent social planner would choose. The demand curve reflects the value of the good to consumers, as measured by their willingness to pay for it. The marginal cost curve reflects the costs of the monopolist. Thus, the socially efficient quantity is found where the demand curve and the marginal cost curve intersect. Below this quantity, the value to consumers exceeds the marginal cost of providing the good, so

FIGURE 12.7

The Efficient Level of Output

A benevolent social planner who wanted to maximize total surplus in the market would choose the level of output where the demand curve and marginal cost curve intersect. Below this level, the value of the good to the marginal buyer (as reflected in the demand curve) exceeds the marginal cost of making the good. Above this level, the value to the marginal buyer is less than marginal cost.

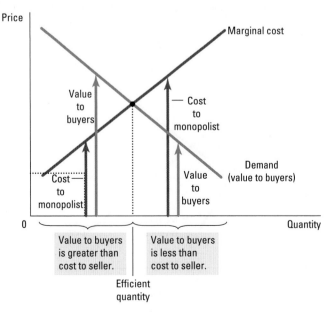

increasing output would raise total surplus. Above this quantity, the marginal cost exceeds the value to consumers, so decreasing output would raise total surplus.

If the social planner were running the monopoly, the firm could achieve this efficient outcome by charging the price found at the intersection of the demand and marginal cost curves. Thus, like a competitive firm and unlike a profit maximizing monopoly, a social planner would charge a price equal to marginal cost. Because this price would give consumers an accurate signal about the cost of producing the good, consumers would buy the efficient quantity.

We can evaluate the welfare effects of monopoly by comparing the level of output that the monopolist chooses to the level of output that a social planner would choose. As we have seen, the monopolist chooses to produce and sell the quantity of output at which the marginal revenue and marginal cost curves intersect; the social planner would choose the quantity at which the demand and marginal cost curves intersect. Figure 12.8 shows the comparison. The monopolist produces less than the socially efficient quantity of output.

We can also view the inefficiency of monopoly in terms of the monopolist's price. Because the market demand curve describes a negative relationship between the price and quantity of the good, a quantity that is inefficiently low is equivalent to a price that is inefficiently high. When a monopolist charges a price above marginal cost, some potential consumers value the good at more than its marginal cost but less than the monopolist's price. These consumers do not end up buying the good. Because the value these consumers place on the good is greater than the cost of providing it to them, this result is inefficient. Thus, monopoly pricing prevents some mutually beneficial trades from taking place.

The inefficiency of monopoly can be measured in Figure 12.8 which shows the dead-weight loss. Recall that the demand curve reflects the value to consumers and the marginal cost curve reflects the costs to the monopoly producer. Thus, the area of the deadweight loss triangle between the demand curve and the marginal cost curve equals the total surplus lost because of monopoly pricing.

The deadweight loss is caused because a monopoly exerts its market power by charging a price above marginal cost, creating a wedge. The wedge causes the quantity sold to fall short of the social optimum. In this situation a private firm gets the monopoly profit.

FIGURE 12.8

The Inefficiency of Monopoly

Because a monopoly charges a price above marginal cost, not all consumers who value the good at more than its cost buy it. Thus, the quantity produced and sold by a monopoly is below the socially efficient level. The deadweight loss is represented by the area of the triangle between the demand curve (which reflects the value of the good to consumers) and the marginal cost curve (which reflects the costs of the monopoly producer).

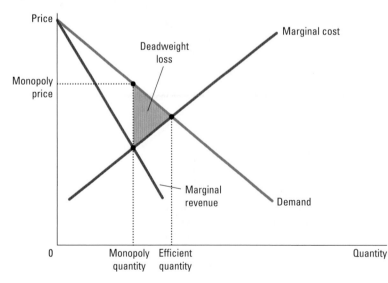

JEOPARDY PROBLEM

How might a situation arise through which a government granting monopoly rights to a TV company to provide national TV broadcasting leads to an overall increase in welfare in society?

The Monopoly's Profit: A Social Cost?

It is tempting to decry monopolies for 'profiteering' at the expense of the public. And, indeed, a monopoly firm does earn a higher profit by virtue of its market power. According to the economic analysis of monopoly, however, the firm's profit is not in itself necessarily a problem for society.

Welfare in a monopolized market, like all markets, includes the welfare of both consumers and producers. Whenever a consumer pays an extra euro to a producer because of a monopoly price, the consumer is worse off by a euro, and the producer is better off by the same amount. This transfer from the consumers of the good to the owners of the monopoly does not affect the market's total surplus – the sum of consumer and producer surplus. In other words, the monopoly profit itself does not represent a shrinkage in the size of the economic pie; it merely represents a bigger slice for producers and a smaller slice for consumers. Unless consumers are for some reason more deserving than producers – a judgement that goes beyond the realm of economic efficiency – the monopoly profit is not a social problem.

The problem in a monopolized market arises because the firm produces and sells a quantity of output below the level that maximizes total surplus. The deadweight loss measures how much the economic pie shrinks as a result. This inefficiency is connected to the monopoly's high price: consumers buy fewer units when the firm raises its price above marginal cost. But keep in mind that the profit earned on the units that continue to be sold is not the problem. The problem stems from the inefficiently low quantity of output. Put differently, if the high monopoly price did not discourage some consumers from buying the good, it would raise producer surplus by exactly the amount it reduced consumer surplus, leaving total surplus the same as could be achieved by a benevolent social planner.

There is, however, a possible exception to this conclusion. Suppose that a monopoly firm has to incur additional costs to maintain its monopoly position. For example, a firm with a government-created monopoly might need to hire lobbyists to convince lawmakers to continue its monopoly. In this case, the monopoly may use up some of its monopoly profits paying for these additional costs. If so, the social loss from monopoly includes both these costs and the deadweight loss resulting from a price above marginal cost.

Quick Quiz How does a monopolist's quantity of output compare to the quantity of output that maximizes total surplus?

 what if… a monopolist did not have a primary goal of maximizing profit. Would the welfare losses still be as high?

PRICE DISCRIMINATION

So far we have been assuming that the monopoly firm charges the same price to all customers. Yet in many cases firms try to sell the same good to different customers for different prices, even though the costs of producing for the two customers are the same. This practice is called **price discrimination**.

Before discussing the behaviour of a price-discriminating monopolist, we should note that price discrimination is not possible when a good is sold in a competitive market. In a competitive market, there are many firms selling the same good at the market price. No firm is willing to charge a lower price to any customer because the firm can sell all it wants at the market price. And if any firm tried to charge a higher price to a customer, that customer would buy from another firm. For a firm to price discriminate, it must have some market power.

A Parable About Pricing

To understand why a monopolist would want to price discriminate, let's consider a simple example. Imagine that you are the chief executive officer of Readalot Publishing Company. Readalot's best-selling author has just written her latest novel. To keep things simple, let's imagine that you pay the author a flat €2 million for the exclusive rights to publish the book. Let's also assume – for simplicity – that the cost of printing the book is zero. Readalot's profit, therefore, is the revenue it gets from selling the book minus the €2 million it has paid to the author. Given these assumptions, how would you, as Readalot's CEO, decide what price to charge for the book?

Your first step in setting the price is to estimate what the demand for the book is likely to be. Readalot's marketing department tells you that the book will attract two types of readers. The book will appeal to the author's 100 000 diehard fans. These fans will be willing to pay as much as €30 for the book. In addition, the book will appeal to about 400 000 less enthusiastic readers who will be willing to pay up to €5 for the book.

What price maximizes Readalot's profit? There are two natural prices to consider: €30 is the highest price Readalot can charge and still get the 100 000 diehard fans, and €5 is the highest price it can charge and still get the entire market of 500 000 potential readers. It is a matter of simple arithmetic to solve Readalot's problem. At a price of €30, Readalot sells 100 000 copies, has revenue of €3 million, and makes profit of €1 million. At a price of €5, it sells 500 000 copies, has revenue of €2.5 million, and makes profit of €500 000. Thus, Readalot maximizes profit by charging €30 and forgoing the opportunity to sell to the 400 000 less enthusiastic readers.

Notice that Readalot's decision causes a deadweight loss. There are 400 000 readers willing to pay €5 for the book, and the marginal cost of providing it to them is zero. Thus, €2 million of total surplus is lost when Readalot charges the higher price. This deadweight loss is the usual inefficiency that arises whenever a monopolist charges a price above marginal cost.

Now suppose that Readalot's marketing department makes an important discovery: these two groups of readers are in separate markets. All the diehard fans live in Switzerland and all the other readers live in Turkey. Moreover, it is difficult for readers in one country to buy books in the other. How does this discovery affect Readalot's marketing strategy?

In this case, the company can make even more profit. To the 100 000 Swiss readers, it can charge €30 for the book. To the 400 000 Turkish readers, it can charge €5 for the book (or the Turkish lira equivalent). In this case, revenue is €3 million in Switzerland and €2 million in Turkey, for a total of €5 million. Profit is then €3 million, which is substantially greater than the €1 million the company could earn charging the same €30 price to all customers. Not surprisingly, Readalot chooses to follow this strategy of price discrimination.

Although the story of Readalot Publishing is hypothetical, it describes accurately the business practice of many publishing companies. Textbooks, for example, are often sold at a different price in Europe from in the United States, the Middle East and Africa. Even more important is the price differential between hardcover books and paperbacks. New novels are often initially released as an expensive hardcover edition and later released in a cheaper paperback edition. The difference in price between these two editions far exceeds the difference in printing costs. The publisher's goal is just as in our example. By selling the hardcover to diehard fans (and libraries) who must have the book as soon as it is published and the paperback to less enthusiastic readers who don't mind waiting, the publisher price discriminates and raises its profit.

?   **what if**…the price elasticity of demand is not that different in different markets – would a monopolist still be able to practise price discrimination?

The Moral of the Story

Like any parable, the story of Readalot Publishing is stylized. Yet, also like any parable, it teaches some important and general lessons. In this case, there are three lessons to be learned about price discrimination.

The first and most obvious lesson is that price discrimination is a rational strategy for a profit-maximizing monopolist. In other words, by charging different prices to different customers, a monopolist can increase its profit. In essence, a price-discriminating monopolist charges each customer a price closer to his or her willingness to pay than is possible with a single price.

The second lesson is that price discrimination requires the ability to separate customers according to their willingness to pay. In our example, customers were separated geographically. But sometimes monopolists choose other differences, such as age or income, to distinguish among customers. Energy companies are able to discriminate through setting different prices at different times of the day with off-peak usage priced lower than peak time. Similarly, rail companies charge different prices to passengers at certain times of the day with peak travel attracting a much higher price than off-peak travel. Where there is a difference in the price elasticity of demand the monopolist can exploit this and practise price discrimination. Between the hours of 6.00am and 9.30am on weekday mornings, for example, the price elasticity of demand for rail travel is relatively low, whereas between 9.30am and 4.00pm it tends to be relatively high. A higher price can be charged at the peak time but during the off-peak period, the firm may benefit from charging a lower price and encouraging more passengers to travel; the cost of running the train is largely fixed and the marginal cost of carrying an additional passenger is almost zero. Lowering the price, therefore, is a way of utilizing the capacity on the train and adding to profit.

A corollary to this second lesson is that certain market forces can prevent firms from price discriminating. In particular, one such force is *arbitrage*, the process of buying a good in one market at a low price and selling it in another market at a higher price in order to profit from the price difference. In our example, suppose that Swiss bookshops could buy the book in Turkey for €5 and resell it to Swiss readers at a price well below €30. This arbitrage would prevent Readalot from price discriminating because no Swiss resident would buy the book at the higher price. In fact, the increased use of the Internet for buying books and other goods through companies like Amazon and eBay is likely to affect the ability of companies to price discriminate internationally. Where firms can enforce the division of the market, as in the case of rail fares, it can practise price discrimination. A passenger buying a ticket at off-peak rates is not allowed to travel on a train running during peak periods, and hence arbitrage is circumvented.

The third lesson from our parable is perhaps the most surprising: price discrimination can raise economic welfare. Recall that a deadweight loss arises when Readalot charges a single €30 price, because the 400 000 less enthusiastic readers do not end up with the book, even though they value it at more than its marginal cost of production. By contrast, when Readalot price discriminates, all readers end up with the book, and the outcome is efficient. Thus, price discrimination can eliminate the inefficiency inherent in monopoly pricing.

Note that the increase in welfare from price discrimination shows up as higher producer surplus rather than higher consumer surplus. In our example, consumers are no better off for having bought the book: the price they pay exactly equals the value they place on the book, so they receive no consumer surplus. The entire increase in total surplus from price discrimination accrues to Readalot Publishing in the form of higher profit.

The Analytics of Price Discrimination

Let us consider a little more formally how price discrimination affects economic welfare. We begin by assuming that the monopolist can price discriminate perfectly. *Perfect price discrimination* describes a situation in which the monopolist knows exactly the willingness to pay of each customer and can charge each customer a different price. In this case, the monopolist charges each customer exactly his willingness to pay, and the monopolist gets the entire surplus in every transaction.

Figure 12.9 shows producer and consumer surplus with and without price discrimination. Without price discrimination, the firm charges a single price above marginal cost,

FIGURE 12.9

Welfare With and Without Price Discrimination

Panel (a) shows a monopolist that charges the same price to all customers. Total surplus in this market equals the sum of profit (producer surplus) and consumer surplus. Panel (b) shows a monopolist that can perfectly price discriminate. Because consumer surplus equals zero, total surplus now equals the firm's profit. Comparing these two panels, you can see that perfect price discrimination raises profit, raises total surplus and lowers consumer surplus.

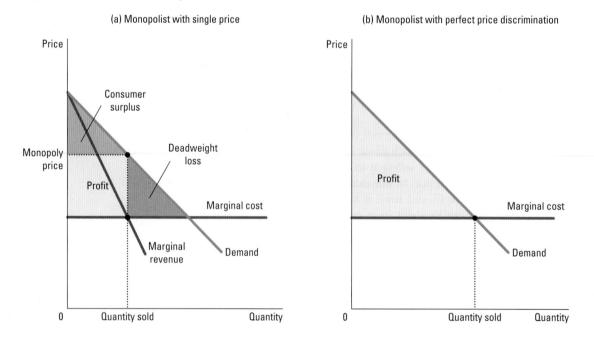

as shown in panel (a). Because some potential customers who value the good at more than marginal cost do not buy it at this high price, the monopoly causes a deadweight loss. Yet when a firm can perfectly price discriminate, as shown in panel (b), each customer who values the good at more than marginal cost buys the good and is charged his willingness to pay. All mutually beneficial trades take place, there is no deadweight loss, and the entire surplus derived from the market goes to the monopoly producer in the form of profit.

In reality, of course, price discrimination is not perfect. Customers do not walk into shops with signs displaying their willingness to pay. Instead, firms price discriminate by dividing customers into groups: young versus old, weekday versus weekend shoppers, Germans versus British, and so on. Unlike those in our parable of Readalot Publishing, customers within each group differ in their willingness to pay for the product, making perfect price discrimination impossible.

How does this imperfect price discrimination affect welfare? The analysis of these pricing schemes is quite complicated, and it turns out that there is no general answer to this question. Compared to the monopoly outcome with a single price, imperfect price discrimination can raise, lower or leave unchanged total surplus in a market. The only certain conclusion is that price discrimination raises the monopoly's profit – otherwise the firm would choose to charge all customers the same price.

Examples of Price Discrimination

Firms use various business strategies aimed at charging different prices to different customers. Now that we understand the economics of price discrimination, let's consider some examples.

Cinema Tickets   Many cinemas charge a lower price for children and senior citizens than for other patrons. This fact is hard to explain in a competitive market. In a competitive market, price equals marginal cost, and the marginal cost of providing a seat for a child or senior citizen is the same as the marginal cost of providing a seat for anyone else. Yet this fact is easily explained if cinemas have some local monopoly power and if children and senior citizens have a lower willingness to pay for a ticket. In this case, cinemas raise their profit by price discriminating.

Airline Prices   Seats on aeroplanes are sold at many different prices. Most airlines charge a lower price for a round-trip ticket between two cities if the traveller stays over a Saturday night. At first this seems odd. Why should it matter to the airline whether a passenger stays over a Saturday night? The reason is that this rule provides a way to separate business travellers and personal travellers. A passenger on a business trip has a high willingness to pay and, most likely, does not want to stay over a Saturday night. By contrast, a passenger travelling for personal reasons has a lower willingness to pay and is more likely to be willing to stay over a Saturday night. Thus, the airlines can successfully price discriminate by charging a lower price for passengers who stay over a Saturday night.

Discount Coupons   Many companies offer discount coupons to the public in newspapers and magazines. A buyer simply has to cut out the coupon in order to get €0.50 off his next purchase. Why do companies offer these coupons? Why don't they just cut the price of the product by €0.50?

The answer is that coupons allow companies to price discriminate. Companies know that not all customers are willing to spend the time to cut out coupons. Moreover, the willingness to clip coupons is related to the customer's willingness to pay for the good. A rich and busy executive is unlikely to spend her time cutting discount coupons out of the newspaper, and she is probably willing to pay a higher price for many goods. A person who is unemployed is more likely to clip coupons and has a lower willingness to pay. Thus, by charging a lower price only to those customers who cut out coupons, firms can successfully price discriminate.

Quantity Discounts So far in our examples of price discrimination the monopolist charges different prices to different customers. Sometimes, however, monopolists price discriminate by charging different prices to the same customer for different units that the customer buys. Traditionally, English bakers would give you an extra cake for nothing if you bought 12. While the quaint custom of the 'baker's dozen' (i.e. 13 for the price of 12) is largely a thing of the past, many firms offer lower prices to customers who buy large quantities. This is a form of price discrimination because the customer effectively pays a higher price for the first unit bought than for last. Quantity discounts are often a successful way of price discriminating because a customer's willingness to pay for an additional unit declines as the customer buys more units.

> **Quick Quiz** Give two examples of price discrimination. • How does perfect price discrimination affect consumer surplus, producer surplus and total surplus?

PUBLIC POLICY TOWARDS MONOPOLIES

We have seen that monopolies, in contrast to competitive markets, fail to allocate resources efficiently. Monopolies produce less than the socially desirable quantity of output and, as a result, charge prices above marginal cost. Policy makers in the government can respond to the problem of monopoly in one of four ways, by:

- trying to make monopolized industries more competitive
- regulating the behaviour of the monopolies
- turning some private monopolies into public enterprises
- doing nothing at all.

All industrialized countries have some sort of process for legally prohibiting mergers that are against the public interest.

The earliest moves towards using legal remedies to monopoly power were taken in the US in the late 19th and early 20th centuries, forming the basis of legislation that has become known in the USA as the anti-trust laws (in the UK and the rest of Europe, anti-trust law and anti-trust policy are more commonly referred to as competition law and competition policy, although usage of both terms is becoming widespread). These laws cover proposed mergers between two companies which already have substantial market share and are closely examined by the authorities, who might well decide that the merger would make the industry in question substantially less competitive and, as a result, would reduce the economic well-being of the country or region as a whole.

In Europe, each country has a competition authority. In the UK it is the Competition Commission; in Germany it is the Federal Cartel Office (*Bundeskartellamt*); in 2009 the French Competition Authority began discharging its regulatory powers following reform of competition regulation; and in Italy the Anti-trust Authority (*Autorità garante della concorrenza e del mercato*) oversees competition issues. National competition authorities such as these cooperate with each other and with the EU Competition Commission through the European Competition Network (ECN). The aim of the network is to coordinate activities and share information to help enforce EU competition law in member states where the opportunities for cross-border business have increased as the EU has developed and expanded.

Whilst each national country can enforce its own competition legislation, these laws have to be in line with overall EU competition legislation. In the UK, for example, the Competition Act 1998 and the Enterprise Act 2002 both deal with competition issues within the UK but cross-border competition cases would be dealt with under EU law. There are well-defined criteria for deciding whether a proposed merger of companies belonging to more than one European Union country is subject to reference exclusively to the European Commission rather than to national authorities, such as the size of the worldwide or European turnover of the companies in question.

Competition legislation covers three main areas:

- Acting against cartels and cases where businesses engage in restrictive business practices which prevent free trade.
- Banning pricing strategies which are anti-competitive such as price fixing, predatory pricing, price gouging and so on, and through behaviour which might lead to a restriction in competition such as the sharing of information or carving up markets between different firms, rigging bids in tender processes or deliberately restricting production to reduce competition.
- Monitoring and supervising acquisitions and joint ventures.

The legislation allows competition authorities the right to fine firms who are found guilty of restricting competition, ordering firms to change behaviour and banning proposed acquisitions. The investigation will consider whether the acquisition, regardless of what size company it produces, is in the public interest. This is in recognition of the fact that companies sometimes merge not to reduce competition but to lower costs through more efficient joint production. These benefits from mergers are often called *synergies*.

Clearly, the government must be able to determine which mergers are desirable and which are not. That is, it must be able to measure and compare the social benefit from synergies to the social costs of reduced competition.

Regulation

Another way in which the government deals with the problem of monopoly is by regulating the behaviour of monopolists. This solution is common in the case of natural monopolies, for instance utility companies like water, gas and electricity companies. These companies are not allowed to charge any price they want. Instead, government agencies regulate their prices.

Marginal Cost Pricing For a Natural Monopoly

Because a natural monopoly has declining average total cost, marginal cost is less than average total cost. Therefore, if regulators require a natural monopoly to charge a price equal to marginal cost, price will be below average total cost, and the monopoly will lose money.

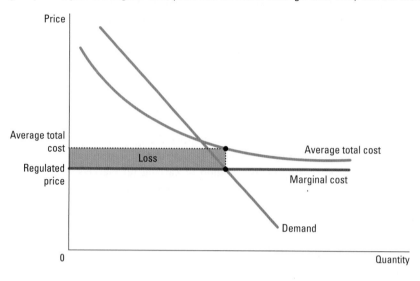

What price should the government set for a natural monopoly? This question is not as easy as it might at first appear. One might conclude that the price should equal the monopolist's marginal cost. If price equals marginal cost, customers will buy the quantity of the monopolist's output that maximizes total surplus, and the allocation of resources will be efficient.

There are, however, two practical problems with marginal-cost pricing as a regulatory system. The first is illustrated in Figure 12.10. Natural monopolies, by definition, have declining average total cost. When average total cost is declining, marginal cost is less than average total cost. If regulators are to set price equal to marginal cost, that price will be less than the firm's average total cost, and the firm will lose money. Instead of charging such a low price, the monopoly firm would just exit the industry.

Regulators can respond to this problem in various ways, none of which is perfect. One way is to subsidize the monopolist. In essence, the government picks up the losses inherent in marginal-cost pricing. Yet to pay for the subsidy, the government needs to raise money through taxation, which involves its own deadweight losses. Alternatively, the regulators can allow the monopolist to charge a price higher than marginal cost. If the regulated price equals average total cost, the monopolist earns exactly zero economic profit. Yet average-cost pricing leads to deadweight losses, because the monopolist's price no longer reflects the marginal cost of producing the good. In essence, average-cost pricing is like a tax on the good the monopolist is selling.

The second problem with marginal-cost pricing as a regulatory system (and with average-cost pricing as well) is that it gives the monopolist no incentive to reduce costs. Each firm in a competitive market tries to reduce its costs because lower costs mean higher profits. But if a regulated monopolist knows that regulators will reduce prices whenever costs fall, the monopolist will not benefit from lower costs. In practice, regulators deal with this problem by allowing monopolists to keep some of the benefits from lower costs in the form of higher profit, a practice that requires some departure from marginal-cost pricing.

For example, in the UK, utility companies have often been subject to price caps whereby the regulator determines that the real price of the company's product – a kilowatt hour of electricity, for example – should fall by a given number of percentage points each year, reflecting productivity rises. Say, for example, this is 2 per cent. The company would then be allowed to raise its prices each year by the inflation rate *minus* 2 per cent. If the company increases its productivity by, say 4 per cent each year, however (in other words it can produce the same amount of output with 4 per cent fewer inputs), then in real terms its profits will go up each year. In this way, the system of price caps aims to give natural monopolies the motivation to improve efficiency and productivity that would be supplied by the invisible hand in a competitive market.

Public Ownership

The third policy used by the government to deal with monopoly is public ownership. That is, rather than regulating a natural monopoly that is run by a private firm, the government can run the monopoly itself. An industry owned by the government is called a nationalized industry. This solution is common in many European countries, where the government owns and operates utilities such as the telephone, water and electric companies.

Economists usually prefer private to public ownership of natural monopolies. The key issue is how the ownership of the firm affects the costs of production. Private owners have an incentive to minimize costs as long as they reap part of the benefit in the form of higher profit. If the firm's managers are doing a bad job of keeping costs down, the firm's owners will fire them. By contrast, if the government bureaucrats who run a monopoly do a bad job, the losers are the customers and taxpayers, whose only recourse is the political system. The bureaucrats may become a special interest group and attempt to block cost reducing reforms. Put simply, as a way of ensuring that firms are well run, the voting booth is less reliable than the profit motive.

Doing Nothing

Each of the foregoing policies aimed at reducing the problem of monopoly has drawbacks. As a result, some economists argue that it is often best for the government not to try to remedy the inefficiencies of monopoly pricing. Here is the assessment of economist George Stigler, who won the Nobel Prize for his work in industrial organization, writing in the *Fortune Encyclopedia of Economics*:

> *A famous theorem in economics states that a competitive enterprise economy will produce the largest possible income from a given stock of resources. No real economy meets the exact conditions of the theorem, and all real economies will fall short of the ideal economy – a difference called 'market failure'. In my view, however, the degree of 'market failure' for the American economy is much smaller than the 'political failure' arising from the imperfections of economic policies found in real political systems.*

As this quotation makes clear, determining the proper role of the government in the economy requires judgements about politics as well as economics.

Quick Quiz Describe the ways policy makers can respond to the inefficiencies caused by monopolies. List a potential problem with each of these policy responses.

CONCLUSION: THE PREVALENCE OF MONOPOLY

This chapter has discussed the behaviour of firms that have control over the prices they charge. We have seen that these firms behave very differently from the competitive firms studied in the previous chapter. Table 12.2 summarizes some of the key similarities and differences between competitive and monopoly markets.

From the standpoint of public policy, a crucial result is that monopolists produce less than the socially efficient quantity and charge prices above marginal cost. As a result, they cause deadweight losses. In some cases, these inefficiencies can be mitigated through price discrimination by the monopolist, but at other times they call for policy makers to take an active role.

How prevalent are the problems of monopoly? There are two answers to this question.

In one sense, monopolies are common. Most firms have some control over the prices they charge. They are not forced to charge the market price for their goods, because their goods are not exactly the same as those offered by other firms. A Honda Accord is not the same as a Volkswagen Passat. Ben and Jerry's ice cream is not the same as Wall's. Each of these goods has a downward sloping demand curve, which gives each producer some degree of monopoly power.

Yet firms with substantial monopoly power are quite rare. Few goods are truly unique. Most have substitutes that, even if not exactly the same are very similar. Ben and Jerry can raise the price of their ice cream a little without losing all their sales; but if they raise it very much, sales will fall substantially.

In the end, monopoly power is a matter of degree. It is true that many firms have some monopoly power. It is also true that their monopoly power is usually limited. In these cases, we will not go far wrong assuming that firms operate in competitive markets, even if that is not precisely the case.

TABLE 12.2

Competition versus Monopoly: A Summary Comparison

	Competition	Monopoly
Similarities		
Goal of firms	Maximize profits	Maximize profits
Rule for maximizing	$MR = MC$	$MR = MC$
Can earn economic profits in the short run?	Yes	Yes
Differences		
Number of firms	Many	One
Marginal revenue	$MR = P$	$MR < P$
Price	$P = MC$	$P > MC$
Produces welfare-maximizing level of output?	Yes	No
Entry in long run?	Yes	No
Can earn economic profits in long run?	No	Yes
Price discrimination possible?	No	Yes

IN THE NEWS

Monopoly in Postal Services

The collection and delivery of mail in many countries is placed is the hands of a single operator. Part of the reason for this is that private firms might charge those who live in rural or remote parts of the country much higher prices to reflect the additional costs of servicing these customers. In recent years, however, these national monopolies have begun to be broken up and competition introduced. As this has happened, some confusion has developed about what competitors are and are not allowed to do as this example from Poland illustrates.

Weighty Court Victory for InPost Against Polish Mail Monopoly

Poland's national postal service Polish Post has lost a key court battle against a private sector competitor it claimed was delivering mail in violation of the country's monopoly protections.

The verdict of the district court in Krakow is open to a possible appeal. Although Poland has to fully open up its postal market to competition from the private sector from 2013, under EU postal legislation, the country still currently has restrictions against anyone other than Polish Post delivering mail pieces lighter than 50g.

The restrictions mean that private sector companies delivering sub-50g letters would have to charge at least 2.5 times the rate charged by Polish Post. For years, private sector mail company InPost, part of Integer.pl Group, has been bypassing the restrictions by offering delivery services in which small metal plates are added to individual letters to bring them into the competitive market [by increasing the weight above the restricted limit]. The company has previously argued that the plates were

seals, protecting mail against unauthorized opening, but even at the higher weight category was delivering the letters for a lower rate than Polish Post's equivalent sub-50g rate.

On Wednesday [25 January 2012], the commercial division of the district court in Krakow threw out Polish Post's demand for compensation for what it saw as an illegal act circumventing Poland's monopoly protections.

Polish Post had been demanding that InPost should return 60.71m Polish Zloty (PLN), [around $18.97m or €14.37m] in 'improperly obtained financial benefits', plus interest since November 2010, claiming that InPost had engineered its mail in such a way that it illegally circumvented the requirement to charge a rate above that of Polish Post.

The Post had also wanted InPost banned from accepting, transporting or delivering any mail items posted in a manner that would prevent them from being assessed against the protections of the universal postal service. However, the court dismissed the case, despite the fact that Polish Post's claims were based on a review by Poland's Office of Electronic Communications.

Commenting on the dismissal, Polish Post said in a statement that it would be considering its options once it had fully reviewed the court's order. The company said in a statement: 'Polish Post respects the order of the court, but is convinced of the merits of its case. After reviewing the written reasons for the order, Polish Post will take all possible actions to protect the economic and legal interests of the company.'

In a statement commenting on the court's dismissal, InPost and Integer.pl Group president Rafal Brzoska noted that Polish Post's claims had been 'dismissed entirely', but he added that the state-run postal service does have the right to appeal. The company president said he fully accepted the judgement of the Krakow court, although it was not necessarily final and binding. Brzoska said: 'The board of InPost and Integer.pl shall ensure once again, based on the results of the inspection carried out within the company by the Office of Electronic Communications, that companies within the Group operate in compliance with the Postal Act and its interpretation.'

Questions

1. What is the source of monopoly power for Polish Post?
2. Examine two possible reasons why national governments might want to introduce competition into the postal service market.
3. Why might the restrictions placed on competitor firms mean they would have to charge 2.5 times the price that Polish Post currently charge?
4. Why might InPost have been able to offer lower prices even though it is adding weight to its letters to 'circumvent the restrictions'?
5. Discuss the welfare implications of monopoly postal providers like Polish Post.

Source: **http://postandparcel.info/45188/news/ companies/weighty-court-victory-for-inpost- against-polish-mail-monopoly/** Accessed 29 January 2012.

SUMMARY

- Imperfect competition is where the assumptions of perfect competition are dropped and firms have some degree of market power.

- Having market power means firms behaviour may be different to that which operates under competitive conditions.

- At the extreme of imperfect competition is monopoly.

- A monopoly is a firm that is the sole seller in its market. A monopoly arises when a single firm owns a key resource, when the government gives a firm the exclusive right to produce a good, or when a single firm can supply the entire market at a smaller cost than many firms could.

- Because a monopoly is the sole producer in its market, it faces a downward sloping demand curve for its product. When a monopoly increases production by 1 unit, it causes the price of its good to fall, which reduces the amount of revenue earned on all units produced. As a result, a monopoly's marginal revenue is always below the price of its good.

- Like a competitive firm, a monopoly firm maximizes profit by producing the quantity at which marginal revenue equals marginal cost. The monopoly then chooses the price at which that quantity is demanded. Unlike a competitive firm, a monopoly firm's price exceeds its marginal revenue, so its price exceeds marginal cost.

- A monopolist's profit-maximizing level of output is below the level that maximizes the sum of consumer and producer surplus. That is, when the monopoly charges a price above marginal cost, some consumers who value the good more than its cost of production do not buy it. As a result, monopoly causes deadweight losses.

- Policy makers can respond to the inefficiency of monopoly behaviour in four ways. They can use competition law to try to make the industry more competitive. They can regulate the prices that the monopoly charges. They can turn the monopolist into a government-run enterprise. Or, if the market failure is deemed small compared to the inevitable imperfections of policies, they can do nothing at all.

- Monopolists often can raise their profits by charging different prices for the same good based on a buyer's willingness to pay. This practice of price discrimination can raise economic welfare by getting the good to some consumers who otherwise would not buy it. In the extreme case of perfect price discrimination, the deadweight losses of monopoly are completely eliminated. More generally, when price discrimination is imperfect, it can either raise or lower welfare compared to the outcome with a single monopoly price.

KEY CONCEPTS

monopoly, p. 275

natural monopoly, p. 277

price discrimination, p. 288

QUESTIONS FOR REVIEW

1. Explain the difference between a perfectly competitive market and an imperfectly competitive market.

2. Do firms which operate in a market where there is a dominant firm not face competition? Explain.

3. Give an example of a government-created monopoly. Is creating this monopoly necessarily bad public policy? Explain.

4. Define natural monopoly. What does the size of a market have to do with whether an industry is a natural monopoly?

5. Why is a monopolist's marginal revenue less than the price of its good? Can marginal revenue ever be negative? Explain.

6. Draw the demand, marginal revenue and marginal cost curves for a monopolist. Show the profit-maximizing level of output. Show the profit-maximizing price.

7. In your diagram from the previous question, show the level of output that maximizes total surplus. Show the deadweight loss from the monopoly. Explain your answer.

8. What gives the government the power to regulate mergers between firms? From the standpoint of the welfare of society, give a good reason and a bad reason that two firms might want to merge.

9. Describe the two problems that arise when regulators tell a natural monopoly that it must set a price equal to marginal cost.

10. Give two examples of price discrimination. In each case, explain why the monopolist chooses to follow this business strategy.

PROBLEMS AND APPLICATIONS

1. A publisher faces the following demand schedule for the next novel of one of its popular authors:

Price (€)	Quantity demanded
100	0
90	100 000
80	200 000
70	300 000
60	400 000
50	500 000
40	600 000
30	700 000
20	800 000
10	900 000
0	1 000 000

The author is paid €2 million to write the book, and the marginal cost of publishing the book is a constant €10 per book.

a. Compute total revenue, total cost and profit at each quantity. What quantity would a profit-maximizing publisher choose? What price would it charge?

b. Compute marginal revenue. (Recall that $MR = \Delta TR/\Delta Q$.) How does marginal revenue compare to the price? Explain.

c. Graph the marginal revenue, marginal cost and demand curves. At what quantity do the marginal revenue and marginal cost curves cross? What does this signify?

d. In your graph, shade in the deadweight loss. Explain in words what this means.

e. If the author was paid €3 million instead of €2 million to write the book, how would this affect the publisher's decision regarding the price to charge? Explain.

f. Suppose the publisher was not profit-maximizing but was concerned with maximizing economic efficiency. What price would it charge for the book? How much profit would it make at this price?

2. Suppose that a natural monopolist was required by law to charge average total cost. On a diagram, label the price charged and the deadweight loss to society relative to marginal-cost pricing.

3. Consider the delivery of mail. In general, what is the shape of the average total cost curve? How might the shape differ between isolated rural areas and densely populated urban areas? How might the shape have changed over time? Explain.

4. Suppose the Eau de Jeunesse Water Company has a monopoly on bottled water sales in France. If the price of tap water increases, what is the change in Eau de Jeunesse's profit-maximizing levels of output, price and profit? Explain in words and with a graph.

5. The Wise Economists, a top rock band, have just finished recording their latest music CD. Their record company's marketing department determines that the demand for the CD is as follows:

Price (€)	Number of CDs
24	10 000
22	20 000
20	30 000
18	40 000
16	50 000
14	60 000

The company can produce the CD with no fixed cost and a variable cost of €5 per CD:

a. Find total revenue for quantity equal to 10 000, 20 000 and so on. What is the marginal revenue for each 10 000 increase in the quantity sold?

b. What quantity of CDs would maximize profit? What would the price be? What would the profit be?

c. If you were The Wise Economists agent, what recording fee would you advise them to demand from the record company? Why?

6. A company is considering building a bridge across a river. The bridge would cost €2 million to build and nothing to maintain. The following table shows the company's anticipated demand over the lifetime of the bridge:

Price per crossing (€)	Number of crossings (in thousands)
8	0
7	100
6	200
5	300
4	400
3	500
2	600
1	700
0	800

a. If the company were to build the bridge, what would be its profit-maximizing price? Would that be the efficient level of output? Why or why not?

b. If the company is interested in maximizing profit, should it build the bridge? What would be its profit or loss?

c. If the government were to build the bridge, what price should it charge for passengers and vehicles to use the bridge? Explain your answer.

d. Should the government build the bridge? Explain.

7. The Placebo Drug Company holds a patent on one of its discoveries.

a. Assuming that the production of the drug involves rising marginal cost, draw a diagram to illustrate Placebo's profit-maximizing price and quantity. Also show Placebo's profits.

b. Now suppose that the government imposes a tax on each bottle of the drug produced. On a new diagram, illustrate Placebo's new price and quantity. How does each compare to your answer in part (a)?

c. Although it is not easy to see in your diagrams, the tax reduces Placebo's profit. Explain why this must be true.

d. Instead of the tax per bottle, suppose that the government imposes a tax on Placebo of €110 000 regardless of how many bottles are produced. How does this tax affect Placebo's price, quantity and profits? Explain.

8. Pablo, Dirk and Franz run the only bar in town. Pablo wants to sell as many drinks as possible without losing money. Dirk wants the bar to bring in as much revenue as possible. Franz wants to make the largest possible profits. Using a single diagram of the bar's demand curve and its cost curves, show the price and quantity combinations favoured by each of the three partners. Explain.

9. The Best Computer Company just developed a new computer chip, on which it immediately acquires a patent.

a. Draw a diagram that shows the consumer surplus, producer surplus and total surplus in the market for this new chip.

b. What happens to these three measures of surplus if the firm can perfectly price discriminate? What is the change in deadweight loss? What transfers occur?

10. Many schemes for price discriminating involve some cost. For example, discount coupons take up time and resources from both the buyer and the seller. This question considers the implications of costly price discrimination. To keep things simple, let's assume that our monopolist's production costs are simply proportional to output, so that average total cost and marginal cost are constant and equal to each other.

a. Draw the cost, demand and marginal revenue curves for the monopolist. Show the price the monopolist would charge without price discrimination.

b. In your diagram, mark the area equal to the monopolist's profit and call it X. Mark the area equal to consumer surplus and call it Y. Mark the area equal to the deadweight loss and call it Z.

c. Now suppose that the monopolist can perfectly price discriminate. What is the monopolist's profit? (Give your answer in terms of X, Y and Z.)

d. What is the change in the monopolist's profit from price discrimination? What is the change in total surplus from price discrimination? Which change is larger? Explain. (Give your answer in terms of X, Y and Z.)

e. Now suppose that there is some cost of price discrimination. To model this cost, let's assume that the monopolist has to pay a fixed cost C in order to price discriminate. How would a monopolist make the decision whether to pay this fixed cost? (Give your answer in terms of X, Y, Z and C.)

f. How would a benevolent social planner, who cares about total surplus, decide whether the monopolist should price discriminate? (Give your answer in terms of X, Y, Z and C.)

g. Compare your answers to parts (e) and (f). How does the monopolist's incentive to price discriminate differ from the social planner's? Is it possible that the monopolist will price discriminate even though it is not socially desirable?

13 OTHER TYPES OF IMPERFECT COMPETITION

LEARNING OBJECTIVES

In this chapter you will:

- Analyze competition among firms that sell differentiated products

- Compare the outcome under monopolistic competition and under perfect competition

- Consider the desirability of outcomes in monopolistically competitive markets

- Examine what outcomes are possible when a market is an oligopoly

- Learn about the prisoners' dilemma and how it applies to oligopoly and other issues

- Consider how competition laws try to foster competition in oligopolistic markets

After reading this chapter you should be able to:

- Show the long-run adjustment that takes place in a monopolistically competitive market when a firm generates economic profits

- Show why monopolistically competitive firms produce at less-than-efficient scale in the long run

- Discuss the inefficiencies of monopolistically competitive markets

- Describe the characteristics of oligopoly and monopolistic competition

- Describe the conditions under which an oligopolistic market generates the same outcome as a monopolistic market

- Show why the outcome of the prisoners' dilemma may change if the game is repeated

- Show why some business practices that appear to reduce competition may have a legitimate business purpose

INTRODUCTION

In Chapter 12 we looked at an extreme form of imperfect competition – monopoly. We saw how a firm's behaviour might be different to that of a competitive market if it was the only supplier in the market.

In most markets we do not see the extremes described in perfect competition or monopoly, instead there are often many firms competing with each other but with some very much larger than others. The competition between firms might be very localized, for example, between a number of restaurants in a typical city centre, be based on differences in price, on differences in the product or the quality of the service provided, or through exploiting human psychology to make it appear there is some difference between the product or encouraging some sort of loyalty to a product.

These things and more are all characteristic of imperfect competition. In conditions of imperfect competition, products are not homogenous. There might be many substitutes for a good in the market but in some way or another, the firm tries to make their product different to rivals so that the degree of substitutability is reduced. In differentiating products the firm is able to have some control over the price that they charge. The sellers in this market are price makers rather than price takers and price will be above marginal cost.

Monopolistic Competition

monopolistic competition a market structure in which many firms sell products that are similar but not identical

Because these markets have some features of competition and some features of monopoly it is called **monopolistic competition**. Monopolistic competition describes a market with the following attributes:

* *Many sellers.* There are many firms competing for the same group of customers with each firm being small compared to the market as a whole.
* *Product differentiation.* Each firm produces a product that is at least slightly different from those of other firms. The firm is able to have some control over the extent to which it can differentiate its product from its rivals, thus reducing the degree of substitutability and garnering an element of customer or brand loyalty. Therefore, rather than being a price taker, each firm faces a downward sloping demand curve.
* *Free entry.* Firms can enter (or exit) the market without restriction. Thus, the number of firms in the market adjusts until economic profits are driven to zero.

Table 13.1 lists examples of the types of market with these attributes.

Four different toothpastes, one firm. How different are these products and how does the consumer know they are different?

TABLE 13.1

Examples of Markets Which Have Characteristics of Monopolistic Competition

Computer games	Vets
Restaurants	Hotel accommodation
Conference organizers	Air conditioning systems
Wedding planners	Pest control
Plumbing	Removal services
Coach hire	Beauty consultants
Funeral directors	Shop fitters
Fabric manufacturers	Waste disposal
Tailors	Dentists
Music teachers	Children's entertainers
Books	Gas engineers
CDs/DVDs	Steel fabricators
Landscape architects	Driving schools
Environmental consultants	Opticians
Furniture manufacturers	Chimney sweeps

COMPETITION WITH DIFFERENTIATED PRODUCTS

To understand monopolistically competitive markets, we first consider the decisions facing an individual firm. We then examine what happens in the long run as firms enter and exit the industry. Next, we compare the equilibrium under monopolistic competition to the equilibrium under perfect competition. Finally, we consider whether the outcome in a monopolistically competitive market is desirable from the standpoint of society as a whole.

The Monopolistically Competitive Firm in the Short Run

Each firm in a monopolistically competitive market is, in many ways, like a monopoly. Because its product is different from those offered by other firms, it faces a downward sloping demand curve. If we assume that a monopolistically competitive firm aims for profit maximization it chooses the quantity at which marginal revenue equals marginal cost and then uses its demand curve to find the price consistent with that quantity.

Figure 13.1 shows the cost, demand and marginal revenue curves for two typical firms, each in a different monopolistically competitive industry. In both panels of this figure, the profit-maximizing quantity is found at the intersection of the marginal revenue and marginal cost curves. The two panels in this figure show different outcomes for the firm's profit. In panel (a), price exceeds average total cost, so the firm makes a profit. In panel (b), price is below average total cost. In this case, the firm is unable to make a positive profit, so the best the firm can do is to minimize its losses.

All this should seem familiar. A monopolistically competitive firm chooses its quantity and price just as a monopoly does. In the short run, these two types of market structure are similar.

FIGURE 13.1

Monopolistic Competitors in the Short Run

Monopolistic competitors maximize profit by producing the quantity at which marginal revenue equals marginal cost. The firm in panel (a) makes a profit because, at this quantity, price is above average total cost. The firm in panel (b) makes losses because, at this quantity, price is less than average total cost.

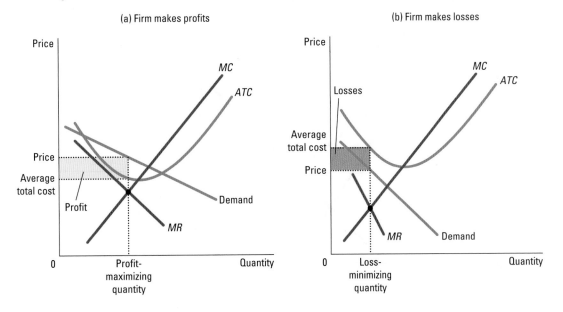

The Long-Run Equilibrium

The situations depicted in Figure 13.1 do not last long. When firms are making profits, as in panel (a), new firms have an incentive to enter the market (remember that there is free entry and exit into the market). This entry means that more firms are now offering products for sale in the industry. The increase in supply causes the price received by all firms in the industry to fall. If an existing firm wishes to sell more, then it must reduce its price. There are now more substitutes available in the market and so the effect for firms is to shift the demand curve to the left. The effect is that there is an increase in the number of products from which customers can now choose and, therefore, reduces the demand faced by each firm already in the market. In other words, profit encourages entry, and entry shifts the demand curves faced by the incumbent firms to the left. As the demand for incumbent firms' products falls, these firms experience declining profit.

Conversely, when firms are making losses, as in panel (b), firms in the market have an incentive to exit. As firms exit, the supply will fall and price will rise. There are now fewer substitutes and so customers have fewer products from which to choose. This decrease in the number of firms effectively expands the demand faced by those firms that stay in the market. In other words, losses encourage exit, and exit has the effect of shifting the demand curves of the remaining firms to the right. As the demand for the remaining firms' products rises, these firms experience rising profit (that is, declining losses).

This process of entry and exit continues until the firms in the market are making exactly zero economic profit. Figure 13.2 depicts the long-run equilibrium. Once the market reaches this equilibrium, new firms have no incentive to enter, and existing firms have no incentive to exit.

 what if…a firm operating in a very localized market making short-run abnormal profit could erect some sort of barrier to entry – would it still be able to make abnormal profits in the long run?

FIGURE 13.2

A Monopolistic Competitor in the Long Run

In a monopolistically competitive market, if firms are making profit, new firms enter and the demand curves for the incumbent firms shift to the left. Similarly, if firms are making losses, old firms exit and the demand curves of the remaining firms shift to the right. Because of these shifts in demand, a monopolistically competitive firm eventually finds itself in the long-run equilibrium shown here. In this long-run equilibrium, price equals average total cost, and the firm earns zero profit.

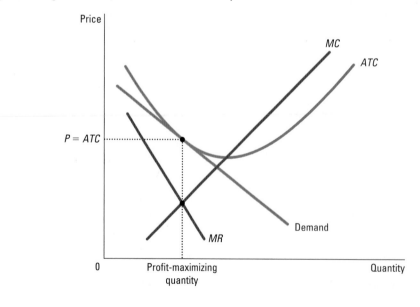

Notice that the demand curve in this figure just barely touches the average total cost curve. Mathematically, we say the two curves are *tangent* to each other. These two curves must be tangent once entry and exit have driven profit to zero. Because profit per unit sold is the difference between price (found on the demand curve) and average total cost, the maximum profit is zero only if these two curves touch each other without crossing.

To sum up, two characteristics describe the long-run equilibrium in a monopolistically competitive market:

- As in a monopoly market, price exceeds marginal cost. This conclusion arises because profit maximization requires marginal revenue to equal marginal cost and because the downward sloping demand curve makes marginal revenue less than the price.
- As in a competitive market, price equals average total cost. This conclusion arises because free entry and exit drive economic profit to zero.

The second characteristic shows how monopolistic competition differs from monopoly. Because a monopoly is the sole seller of a product without close substitutes, it can earn positive economic profit, even in the long run. By contrast, because there is free entry into a monopolistically competitive market, the economic profit of a firm in this type of market is driven to zero.

Monopolistic versus Perfect Competition

Figure 13.3 compares the long-run equilibrium under monopolistic competition to the long-run equilibrium under perfect competition. There are two noteworthy differences between monopolistic and perfect competition – excess capacity and the mark-up.

Excess Capacity As we have just seen, entry and exit drive each firm in a monopolistically competitive market to a point of tangency between its demand and average

FIGURE 13.3

Monopolistic versus Perfect Competition

Panel (a) shows the long-run equilibrium in a monopolistically competitive market, and panel (b) shows the long-run equilibrium in a perfectly competitive market. Two differences are notable. (1) The perfectly competitive firm produces at the efficient scale, where average total cost is minimized. By contrast, the monopolistically competitive firm produces at less than the efficient scale. (2) Price equals marginal cost under perfect competition, but price is above marginal cost under monopolistic competition.

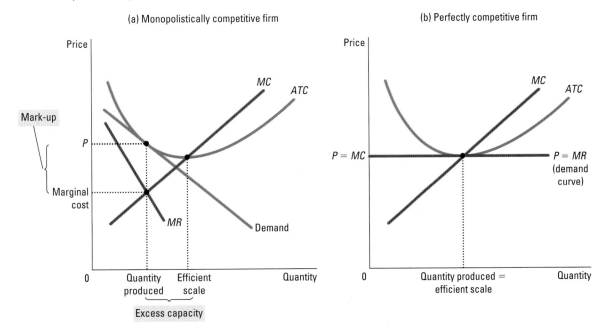

total cost curves. Panel (a) of Figure 13.3 shows that the quantity of output at this point is smaller than the quantity that minimizes average total cost. Thus, under monopolistic competition, firms produce on the downward sloping portion of their average total cost curves. In this way, monopolistic competition contrasts starkly with perfect competition. As panel (b) of Figure 13.3 shows, free entry in competitive markets drives firms to produce at the minimum of average total cost.

The quantity that minimizes average total cost is called the *efficient scale* of the firm. In the long run, perfectly competitive firms produce at the efficient scale, whereas monopolistically competitive firms produce below this level. Firms are said to have *excess capacity* under monopolistic competition. In other words, a monopolistically competitive firm, unlike a perfectly competitive firm, could increase the quantity it produces and lower the average total cost of production.

Mark-Up Over Marginal Cost   A second difference between perfect competition and monopolistic competition is the relationship between price and marginal cost. For a competitive firm, such as that shown in panel (b) of Figure 13.3, price equals marginal cost. For a monopolistically competitive firm, such as that shown in panel (a), price exceeds marginal cost, because the firm always has some market power.

How is this mark-up over marginal cost consistent with free entry and zero profit? The zero-profit condition ensures only that price equals average total cost. It does *not* ensure that price equals marginal cost. Indeed, in the long-run equilibrium, monopolistically competitive firms operate on the declining portion of their average total cost curves, so marginal cost is below average total cost. Thus, for price to equal average total cost, price must be above marginal cost. Because of this a monopolistically competitive firm is always eager to get another customer. Because its price exceeds marginal cost, an extra unit sold at the posted price means more profit.

One characteristic of monopolistic competition is the use of advertising and establishment of brand names. We looked at advertising and branding in Chapter 7 and suffice to say that these are important in understanding the behaviour of firms in imperfect competition.

Summary

- A monopolistically competitive market is characterized by three attributes: many firms, differentiated products and free entry.
- The equilibrium in a monopolistically competitive market differs from that in a perfectly competitive market in two related ways. First, each firm in a monopolistically competitive market has excess capacity. That is, it operates on the downward sloping portion of the average total cost curve. Secondly, each firm charges a price above marginal cost.
- Monopolistic competition does not have all the desirable properties of perfect competition. There is the standard deadweight loss of monopoly caused by the mark-up of price over marginal cost. In addition, the number of firms (and thus the variety of products) can be too large or too small. In practice, the ability of policy makers to correct these inefficiencies is limited.
- The product differentiation inherent in monopolistic competition leads to the use of advertising and brand names.

Table 13.2 summarizes the differences between monopolistic competition, perfect competition and monopoly.

Quick Quiz   List the three key attributes of monopolistic competition.
• Draw and explain a diagram to show the long-run equilibrium in a monopolistically competitive market. How does this equilibrium differ from that in a perfectly competitive market?

TABLE 13.2

Monopolistic Competition: Between Perfect Competition and Monopoly Market Structure

	Market Structure		
	Perfect competition	Monopolistic competition	Monopoly
Features that all three market structures share			
Goal of firms	Maximize profits	Maximize profits	Maximize profits
Rule for maximizing	MR = MC	MR = MC	MR = MC
Can earn economic profits in the short run?	Yes	Yes	Yes
Features that monopoly and monopolistic competition share			
Price taker?	Yes	No	No
Price	P = MC	P > MC	P > MC
Produces welfare-maximizing level of output?	Yes	No	No
Features that perfect competition and monopolistic competition share			
Number of firms	Many	Many	One
Entry in long run?	Yes	Yes	No
Can earn economic profits in long run?	No	No	Yes

FYI

Contestable Markets

Most economics textbooks up to the late 1970s covered market structures ranging from perfect competition at one extreme to monopoly at the other. Changes in the way businesses actually operated in the real world meant that there were some gaps between the theory and the observed behaviour of firms. This led to the development of a new theory which was incorporated into the explanation of market structures. The theory of contestable markets was developed by William J. Baumol, John Panzar and Robert Willig in 1982.

The key characteristic of a perfectly contestable market (the benchmark to explain firms' behaviours) was that firms were influenced by the threat of new entrants into a market. We have seen how, in monopolistically competitive markets, despite the fact that each firm has some monopoly control over its product, the ease of entry and exit means that in the long run profits can be competed away as new firms enter the market. This threat of new entrants may make firms behave in a way that departs from what was assumed to be the traditional goal of firms – to maximize profits. The suggestion by Baumol and colleagues was that firms may deliberately limit profits made to discourage new entrants. The other characteristics of a perfectly contestable market are that there are no barriers to entry or exit and no sunk costs. Profits might be limited by what was termed *entry limit pricing*. This refers to a situation where a firm will keep prices lower than they could be in order to deter new entrants. Similarly, firms may also practise *predatory or destroyer pricing* whereby the price is held below average cost for a period to try and force out competitors or prevent new firms from entering the market. Incumbent firms may be in a position to do this because they may have been able to gain some advantages of economies of scale which new entrants may not be able to exploit.

In a contestable market firms may also erect other artificial barriers to prevent entry into the industry by new firms. Such barriers might include operating at over-capacity, which provides the opportunity to flood the market and drive down price in the event of a threat of entry. Firms will also carry out aggressive marketing and branding strategies to 'tighten' up the market or find ways of reducing costs and increasing efficiency to gain competitive advantage. Searching out sources of competitive advantage was a topic written on extensively by Michael Porter, who defined competitive advantage as being the advantages firms can gain over another which are both distinctive and defensible. These sources are not simply to be found in terms of new product development but through close investigation and analysis of the supply chain, where little changes might make a difference to the cost base of a firm which it can then exploit to its advantage.

Hit-and-run tactics might be evident in a contestable market where firms enter the industry, take the profit and get out quickly (possible because of the freedom of entry and exit). In other cases firms may indulge in what is termed *cream-skimming* – identifying parts of the market that are high in value added and exploiting those markets.

The theory of contestable markets has been widely adopted as a beneficial addition to the theory of the firm and there has been extensive research into its application. There are numerous examples of markets exhibiting contestability characteristics including financial services; airlines, especially flights on domestic routes; the IT industry and in particular internet service providers (ISPs), software and web developers; energy supplies and the postal service.

OLIGOPOLY

oligopoly competition amongst the few – a market structure in which only a few sellers offer similar or identical products and dominate the market

The Europeans love chocolate. The average German eats about 180 62-gram bars of chocolate a year. The Belgians are not far behind at 177 bars, the Swiss around 173 and the British eat around 164 bars per year. There are many firms producing chocolate in Europe including Anthon Berg in Denmark, Camille Bloch, Lindt and Favarger in Switzerland, Guylian and Godiva in Belgium, and Hachez in Germany. However, Europeans are likely to find that what they are eating has probably been made by one of three companies: Cadbury (now owned by US firm Kraft), Mars or Nestlé. These firms dominate the chocolate industry in the European Union. Being so large and dominant they are able to influence the quantity of chocolate bars produced and, given the market demand curve, the price at which chocolate bars are sold.

The European market for chocolate bars fits a model of imperfect competition called **oligopoly** – literally, competition amongst the few. The essence of an oligopolistic market is that there are a few sellers which dominate the market and where the products they sell are identical or near identical. In this situation, competition between these large firms might be focused on strategic interactions among them. As a result, the actions of any one seller in the market can have a large impact on the profits of all the other sellers. That is, oligopolistic firms are interdependent in a way that competitive firms are not.

There is no magic number that defines 'few' from 'many' when counting the number of firms. Do the approximately dozen companies that now sell cars in Europe make this market an oligopoly or more competitive? The answer is open to debate. Similarly, there is no sure way to determine when products are differentiated and when they are identical. Are different brands of milk really the same? Again, the answer is debatable. When analyzing actual markets, economists have to keep in mind the lessons learned from studying all types of market structure and then apply each lesson as it seems appropriate.

Our goal is to see how the interdependence that characterizes oligopolistic markets shapes the firms' behaviour and what problems it raises for public policy.

MARKETS WITH ONLY A FEW DOMINANT SELLERS

If a market is dominated by a relatively small number of sellers it is said to be *concentrated*. The *concentration ratio* refers to the proportion of the total market share accounted for by the top x number of firms in the industry. For example, a five-firm concentration ratio of 80 per cent means that five firms account for 80 per cent of market share; a three-firm concentration ratio of 72 per cent would indicate that three firms account for 72 per cent of total market sales and so on.

There are a number of examples of oligopolistic market structures including brewing, banking, mobile phone networks, the chemical and oil industries, the grocery/supermarket industry, detergents, and entertainment. Note that in each of these industries there might be many sellers in the industry (there are thousands of small independent breweries across Europe, for example) but sales are dominated by a relatively small number of firms. In brewing, the industry is dominated by A-BInBev, Heineken, Carlsberg and SABMiller.

A key feature of oligopoly is the tension that exists between the firms of cooperation and self-interest. The group of oligopolists is best off cooperating and acting like a monopolist – producing a small quantity of output and charging a price above marginal cost. Yet because each oligopolist cares about only its own profit, there are powerful incentives at work that hinder a group of firms from maintaining the monopoly outcome.

A Duopoly Example

To understand the behaviour of oligopolies, let's consider an oligopoly with only two members, called a *duopoly*. Duopoly is the simplest type of oligopoly. Oligopolies with three or more members face the same problems as oligopolies with only two members, so we do not lose much by starting with the case of duopoly.

Imagine a town in which only two residents – Ishaq and Coralie – own wells that produce water safe for drinking. Each Saturday, Ishaq and Coralie decide how many litres of water to pump, bring the water to town, and sell it for whatever price the market will bear. To keep things simple, suppose that Ishaq and Coralie can pump as much water as they want without cost. That is, the marginal cost of water equals zero.

Table 13.3 shows the town's demand schedule for water. The first column shows the total quantity demanded, and the second column shows the price. If the two well owners sell a total of 10 litres of water, water goes for €110 a litre. If they sell a total of 20 litres, the price falls to €100 a litre. And so on. If you graphed these two columns of numbers, you would get a standard downward sloping demand curve.

The last column in Table 13.3 shows the total revenue from the sale of water. It equals the quantity sold times the price. Because there is no cost to pumping water, the total revenue of the two producers equals their total profit.

Let's now consider how the organization of the town's water industry affects the price of water and the quantity of water sold.

A duopoly sees two dominant firms competing against each other – will it always be a fight?

TABLE 13.3

The Demand Schedule for Water

Quantity (in litres)	Price €	Total revenue (and total profit) €
0	120	0
10	110	1100
20	100	2000
30	90	2700
40	80	3200
50	70	3500
60	60	3600
70	50	3500
80	40	3200
90	30	2700
100	20	2000
110	10	1100
120	0	0

Competition, Monopolies and Cartels

Consider what would happen if the market for water were perfectly competitive. In a competitive market, the production decisions of each firm drive price equal to marginal cost. In the market for water, marginal cost is zero. Thus, under competition, the equilibrium price of water would be zero, and the equilibrium quantity would be 120 litres. The price of water would reflect the cost of producing it, and the efficient quantity of water would be produced and consumed.

Now consider how a monopoly would behave. Table 13.3 shows that total profit is maximized at a quantity of 60 litres and a price of €60 a litre. A profit-maximizing monopolist, therefore, would produce this quantity and charge this price. As is standard for monopolies, price would exceed marginal cost. The result would be inefficient, for the quantity of water produced and consumed would fall short of the socially efficient level of 120 litres.

What outcome should we expect from our duopolists? One possibility is that Ishaq and Coralie get together and agree on the quantity of water to produce and the price to charge for it. Such an agreement among firms over production and price is called **collusion**, and the group of firms acting in unison is called a **cartel**. Once a cartel is formed, the market is in effect served by a monopoly, and we can apply our analysis from Chapter 12. That is, if Ishaq and Coralie were to collude, they would agree on the monopoly outcome because that outcome maximizes the total profit that the producers can get from the market. Our two producers would produce a total of 60 litres, which would be sold at a price of €60 a litre. Once again, price exceeds marginal cost, and the outcome is socially inefficient.

collusion an agreement amongst firms in a market about quantities to produce or prices to charge

cartel a group of firms acting in unison

 what if…one of the firms entering into a cartel had much more market power than the other firms in the agreement – would this mean the cartel is more likely to succeed or not?

A cartel must agree not only on the total level of production but also on the amount produced by each member. In our case, Ishaq and Coralie must agree how to split between themselves the monopoly production of 60 litres. Each member of the cartel will want a larger share of the market because a larger market share means larger profit. If Ishaq and Coralie agreed to split the market equally, each would produce 30 litres, the price would be €60 a litre and each would get a profit of €1800.

CASE STUDY

OPEC and the World Oil Market

Our story about the town's market for water is fictional, but if we change water to crude oil, and Ishaq and Coralie to Iran and Iraq, the story is close to being true. Much of the world's oil is produced by a few countries, mostly in the Middle East. These countries together make up an oligopoly. Their decisions about how much oil to pump are much the same as Ishaq and Coralie's decisions about how much water to pump.

The countries that produce most of the world's oil have formed a cartel, called the Organization of Petroleum Exporting Countries (OPEC). As originally formed in 1960, OPEC included Iran, Iraq, Kuwait, Saudi Arabia, and Venezuela. By 1973, eight other nations had joined: Qatar, Indonesia, Libya, the United Arab Emirates, Algeria, Nigeria, Ecuador and Gabon. These countries control about three-fourths of the world's oil reserves. Like any cartel, OPEC tries to raise the price of its product through a coordinated reduction in quantity produced. OPEC tries to set production levels for each of the member countries.

The problem that OPEC faces is much the same as the problem that Ishaq and Coralie face in our story. The OPEC countries would like to maintain a high price for oil. But each member of the cartel is tempted to increase its production to get a larger share of the total profit. OPEC members frequently agree to reduce production but then cheat on their agreements.

OPEC was most successful at maintaining cooperation and high prices in the period from 1973 to 1985. The price of crude oil rose from $3 a barrel in 1972 to $11 in 1974 and then to $35 in 1981. But in the mid-1980s, member countries began arguing about production levels, and OPEC became ineffective at maintaining cooperation. By 1986 the price of crude oil had fallen back to $13 a barrel.

In recent years, the members of OPEC have continued to meet regularly, but the cartel has been less successful at reaching and enforcing agreements. Although the price of oil rose significantly in 2007 and 2008, the primary cause was increased demand in the world oil market, in part from a booming Chinese economy, rather than restricted supply. While this lack of cooperation among OPEC nations has reduced the profits of the oil-producing nations below what they might have been, it has benefited consumers around the world.

The Equilibrium For an Oligopoly

Although oligopolists would like to form cartels and earn monopoly profits, often that is not possible. Competition laws prohibit explicit agreements among oligopolists as a matter of public policy. In addition, squabbling among cartel members over how to divide the profit in the market sometimes makes agreement among them impossible. Let's therefore consider what happens if Ishaq and Coralie decide separately how much water to produce.

At first, one might expect Ishaq and Coralie to reach the monopoly outcome on their own, for this outcome maximizes their joint profit. In the absence of a binding agreement, however, the monopoly outcome is unlikely. To see why, imagine that Ishaq expects Coralie to produce only 30 litres (half of the monopoly quantity). Ishaq might reason as follows:

I could produce 30 litres as well. In this case, a total of 60 litres of water would be sold at a price of €60 a litre. My profit would be €1800 (30 litres × €60 a litre). Alternatively, I could produce 40 litres. In this case, a total of 70 litres of water would be sold at a price of €50 a litre. My profit would be €2000 (40 litres × €50 a litre). Even though total profit in the market would fall, my profit would be higher, because I would have a larger share of the market.

Of course, Coralie might reason the same way. If so, Ishaq and Coralie would each bring 40 litres to town. Total sales would be 80 litres, and the price would fall to €40. Thus, if the duopolists individually pursue their own self-interest when deciding how much to produce, they produce a total quantity greater than the monopoly quantity, charge a price lower than the monopoly price and earn total profit less than the monopoly profit.

Although the logic of self-interest increases the duopoly's output above the monopoly level, it does not push the duopolists to reach the competitive allocation. Consider what happens when each duopolist is producing 40 litres. The price is €40, and each duopolist makes a profit of €1600. In this case, Ishaq's self-interested logic leads to a different conclusion:

Right now my profit is €1600. Suppose I increase my production to 50 litres. In this case, a total of 90 litres of water would be sold, and the price would be €30 a litre. Then my profit would be only €1500. Rather than increasing production and driving down the price, I am better off keeping my production at 40 litres.

Nash equilibrium a situation in which economic actors interacting with one another each choose their best strategy given the strategies that all the other actors have chosen

The outcome in which Ishaq and Coralie each produce 40 litres looks like some sort of equilibrium. In fact, this outcome is called a **Nash equilibrium** (named after economic theorist John Nash, whose life was portrayed in the book, *A Beautiful Mind,* and the film of the same name). A Nash equilibrium is a situation in which economic actors interacting with one another each choose their best strategy given the strategies the others have chosen. In this case, given that Coralie is producing 40 litres, the best strategy for Ishaq is to produce 40 litres. Similarly, given that Ishaq is producing 40 litres, the best strategy for Coralie is to produce 40 litres. Once they reach this Nash equilibrium, neither Ishaq nor Coralie has an incentive to make a different decision.

This example illustrates the tension between cooperation and self-interest. Oligopolists would be better off cooperating and reaching the monopoly outcome. Yet because they pursue their own self-interest, they do not end up reaching the monopoly outcome and maximizing their joint profit. Each oligopolist is tempted to raise production and capture a larger share of the market. As each of them tries to do this, total production rises, and the price falls.

At the same time, self-interest does not drive the market all the way to the competitive outcome. Like monopolists, oligopolists are aware that increases in the amount they produce reduce the price of their product. Therefore, they stop short of following the competitive firm's rule of producing up to the point where price equals marginal cost.

In summary, when firms in an oligopoly individually choose production to maximize profit, they produce a quantity of output greater than the level produced by monopoly and less than the level produced by competition. The oligopoly price is less than the monopoly price but greater than the competitive price (which equals marginal cost).

JEOPARDY PROBLEM

An oligopolistic market consists of a four-firm concentration ratio of 80 per cent. An economist does some research on this market and finds that prices have remained stable in the market for the last five years. What might the explanation be for this behaviour?

How the Size of an Oligopoly Affects the Market Outcome

We can use the insights from this analysis of duopoly to discuss how the size of an oligopoly is likely to affect the outcome in a market. Suppose, for instance, that Jean and Patrice suddenly discover water sources on their property and join Ishaq and Coralie in the water oligopoly. The demand schedule in Table 13.3 remains the same, but now more producers are available to satisfy this demand. How would an increase in the number of sellers from two to four affect the price and quantity of water in the town?

If the sellers of water could form a cartel, they would once again try to maximize total profit by producing the monopoly quantity and charging the monopoly price. Just as when there were only two sellers, the members of the cartel would need to agree on production levels for each member and find some way to enforce the agreement. As the cartel grows larger, however, this outcome is less likely. Reaching and enforcing an agreement becomes more difficult as the size of the group increases.

If the oligopolists do not form a cartel – perhaps because competition laws prohibit it – they must each decide on their own how much water to produce. To see how the increase in the number of sellers affects the outcome, consider the decision facing each seller. At any time, each well owner has the option to raise production by 1 litre. In making this decision, the well owner weighs two effects:

- *The output effect.* Because price is above marginal cost, selling 1 more litre of water at the going price will raise profit.
- *The price effect.* Raising production will increase the total amount sold, which will lower the price of water and lower the profit on all the other litres sold.

If the output effect is larger than the price effect, the well owner will increase production. If the price effect is larger than the output effect, the owner will not raise production. (In fact, in this case, it is profitable to reduce production.) Each oligopolist continues to increase production until these two marginal effects exactly balance, taking the other firms' production as given.

Now consider how the number of firms in the industry affects the marginal analysis of each oligopolist. The larger the number of sellers, the less concerned each seller is about its own impact on the market price. That is, as the oligopoly grows in size, the magnitude of the price effect falls. When the oligopoly grows very large, the price effect disappears altogether, leaving only the output effect. In this extreme case, each firm in the oligopoly increases production as long as price is above marginal cost.

We can now see that a large oligopoly is essentially a group of competitive firms. A competitive firm considers only the output effect when deciding how much to produce: because a competitive firm is a price taker, the price effect is absent. Thus, as the number of sellers in an oligopoly grows larger, an oligopolistic market looks more and more like a competitive market. The price approaches marginal cost, and the quantity produced approaches the socially efficient level.

Pitfall Prevention Remember that in an oligopolistic market structure there can be many hundreds, and in some cases, thousands of firms but the crucial thing to remember is that the market is dominated by a small number of very large firms.

This analysis of oligopoly offers a new perspective on the effects of international trade. Imagine that Toyota and Honda are the only car manufacturers in Japan, Volkswagen and BMW are the only car manufacturers in Germany, and Citroën and Peugeot are the only car manufacturers in France. If these nations prohibited international trade in cars, each would have a motorcar oligopoly with only two members, and the market outcome would likely depart substantially from the competitive ideal. With international trade, however, the car market is a world market, and the oligopoly in this example has six members. Allowing free trade increases the number of producers from whom each consumer can choose, and this increased competition keeps prices closer to marginal cost. Thus, the theory of oligopoly provides another reason why all countries can benefit from free trade.

> **Quick Quiz** If the members of an oligopoly could agree on a total quantity to produce, what quantity would they choose? • If the oligopolists do not act together but instead make production decisions individually, do they produce a total quantity more or less than in your answer to the previous question? Why?

GAME THEORY AND THE ECONOMICS OF COMPETITION

As we have seen, oligopolies would like to reach the monopoly outcome, but doing so requires cooperation, which at times is difficult to maintain. In this section we look more closely at the problems people face when cooperation is desirable but difficult. To analyze the economics of cooperation, we need to learn a little about game theory.

game theory the study of how people behave in strategic situations

Game theory is the study of how people behave in strategic situations. By 'strategic' we mean a situation in which each person, when deciding what actions to take, must consider how others might respond to that action. Because the number of firms in an oligopolistic market is small, each firm must act strategically. Each firm knows that its profit depends not only on how much it produces but also on how much the other firms produce. In making its production decision, each firm in an oligopoly should consider how its decision might affect the production decisions of all the other firms. Game theory is quite useful for understanding the behaviour of oligopolies.

prisoners' dilemma a particular 'game' between two captured prisoners that illustrates why cooperation is difficult to maintain even when it is mutually beneficial

A particularly important 'game' is called the **prisoners' dilemma**. This game provides insight into the difficulty of maintaining cooperation. Many times in life, people fail to cooperate with one another even when cooperation would make them all better off. An oligopoly is just one example. The story of the prisoners' dilemma contains a general lesson that applies to any group trying to maintain cooperation among its members.

The Prisoners' Dilemma

The prisoners' dilemma is a story about two criminals who have been captured by the police. Let's call them Mr Green and Mr Blue. The police have enough evidence to convict Mr Green and Mr Blue of a relatively minor crime, possessing stolen property, so that each would spend a year in jail. The police also suspect that the two criminals have committed an armed jewellery robbery together, but they lack hard evidence to convict them of this major crime. The police question Mr Green and Mr Blue in separate rooms, and they offer each of them the following deal:

Right now we can lock you up for 1 year. If you confess to the jewellery robbery and implicate your partner, however, we'll give you immunity and you can go free. Your partner will get 20 years in jail. But if you both confess to the crime, we won't need your testimony and we can avoid the cost of a trial, so you will each get an intermediate sentence of 8 years.

If Mr Green and Mr Blue, heartless criminals that they are, care only about their own sentences, what would you expect them to do? Would they confess or remain silent? Figure 13.4 shows their choices. Each prisoner has two strategies: confess or remain silent. The sentence each prisoner gets depends on the strategy he chooses and the strategy chosen by his partner in crime.

FIGURE 13.4

The Prisoners' Dilemma

In this game between two criminals suspected of committing a crime, the sentence that each receives depends both on his decision whether to confess or remain silent and on the decision made by the other.

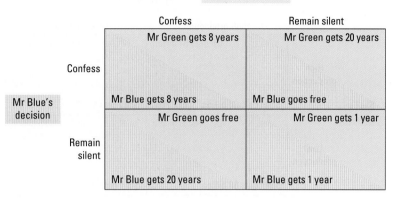

Consider first Mr Green's decision. He reasons as follows:

I don't know what Mr Blue is going to do. If he remains silent, my best strategy is to confess, since then I'll go free rather than spending a year in jail. If he confesses, my best strategy is still to confess, since then I'll spend 8 years in jail rather than 20. So, regardless of what Mr Blue does, I am better off confessing.

In the language of game theory, a strategy is called a **dominant strategy** if it is the best strategy for a player to follow regardless of the strategies pursued by other players. In this case, confessing is a dominant strategy for Mr Green. He spends less time in jail if he confesses, regardless of whether Mr Blue confesses or remains silent.

Now consider Mr Blue's decision. He faces exactly the same choices as Mr Green, and he reasons in much the same way. Regardless of what Mr Green does, Mr Blue can reduce his time in jail by confessing. In other words, confessing is also a dominant strategy for Mr Blue.

In the end, both Mr Green and Mr Blue confess, and both spend 8 years in jail. Yet, from their standpoint, this is a terrible outcome. If they had *both* remained silent, both of them would have been better off, spending only 1 year in jail on the possession charge. By each pursuing his own interests, the two prisoners together reach an outcome that is worse for each of them.

To see how difficult it is to maintain cooperation, imagine that, before the police captured Mr Green and Mr Blue, the two criminals had made a pact not to confess. Clearly, this agreement would make them both better off *if* they both live up to it, because they would each spend only 1 year in jail. But would the two criminals in fact remain silent, simply because they had agreed to? Once they are being questioned separately, the logic of self-interest takes over and leads them to confess. Cooperation between the two prisoners is difficult to maintain, because cooperation is individually irrational.

> **dominant strategy** a strategy that is best for a player in a game regardless of the strategies chosen by the other players

Oligopolies as a Prisoner's Dilemma

What does the prisoners' dilemma have to do with markets and imperfect competition? It turns out that the game oligopolists play in trying to reach the monopoly outcome is similar to the game that the two prisoners play in the prisoners' dilemma.

FIGURE 13.5

An Oligopoly Game

In this game between members of an oligopoly, the profit that each earns depends on both its production decision and the production decision of the other oligopolist.

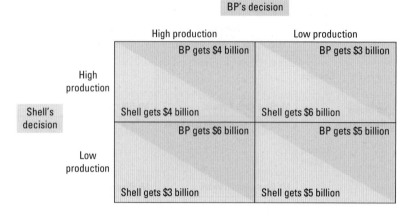

Consider an oligopoly with two firms, BP and Shell. Both firms refine crude oil. After prolonged negotiation, the two firms agree to keep refined oil production low in order to keep the world price of refined oil high. After they agree on production levels, each firm must decide whether to cooperate and live up to this agreement or to ignore it and produce at a higher level. Figure 13.5 shows how the profits of the two firms depend on the strategies they choose.

Suppose you are the CEO of BP. You might reason as follows:

I could keep production low as we agreed, or I could raise my production and sell more refined oil on world markets. If Shell lives up to the agreement and keeps its production low, then my firm earns profit of $6 billion with high production and $5 billion with low production. In this case, BP is better off with high production. If Shell fails to live up to the agreement and produces at a high level, then my firm earns $4 billion with high production and $3 billion with low production. Once again, BP is better off with high production. So, regardless of what Shell chooses to do, my firm is better off reneging on our agreement and producing at a high level.

Producing at a high level is a dominant strategy for BP. Of course, Shell reasons in exactly the same way, and so both countries produce at a high level. The result is the inferior outcome (from BP and Shell's standpoint) with low profits for each firm.

This example illustrates why oligopolies have trouble maintaining monopoly profits. The monopoly outcome is jointly rational for the oligopoly, but each oligopolist has an incentive to cheat. Just as self-interest drives the prisoners in the prisoners' dilemma to confess, self-interest makes it difficult for the oligopoly to maintain the cooperative outcome with low production, high prices and monopoly profits.

Other Examples of the Prisoners' Dilemma

We have seen how the prisoners' dilemma can be used to understand the problem facing oligopolies. The same logic applies to many other situations as well. Here we consider two examples in which self-interest prevents cooperation and leads to an inferior outcome for the parties involved.

Advertising When two firms advertise to attract the same customers, they face a problem similar to the prisoners' dilemma. For example, consider the decisions facing two cigarette companies, Marlboro and Camel. If neither company advertises, the two companies split the market. If both advertise, they again split the market, but profits are lower, since each company must bear the cost of advertising. Yet if one company advertises while the other does not, the one that advertises attracts customers from the other.

Figure 13.6 shows how the profits of the two companies depend on their actions. You can see that advertising is a dominant strategy for each firm. Thus, both firms choose to advertise, even though both firms would be better off if neither firm advertised.

A test of this theory of advertising occurred in many countries during the 1970s and 1980s, when laws were passed in Europe and North America banning cigarette advertisements on television. To the surprise of many observers, cigarette companies did not use their political influence to oppose these bans. When the laws went into effect, cigarette advertising fell and the profits of cigarette companies rose. The television advertising bans did for the cigarette companies what they could not do on their own: they solved the prisoners' dilemma by enforcing the cooperative outcome with low advertising and high profit.

Common Resources Common resources tend to be subject to overuse because they are rival in consumption but not excludable, for example, fish in the sea. One can view this problem as an example of the prisoners' dilemma.

Imagine that two mining companies – Kazakhmys and Vedanta – own adjacent copper mines. The mines have a common pool of copper worth €12 million. Drilling a shaft

FIGURE 13.6

An Advertising Game

In this game between firms selling similar products, the profit that each earns depends on both its own advertising decision and the advertising decision of the other firm.

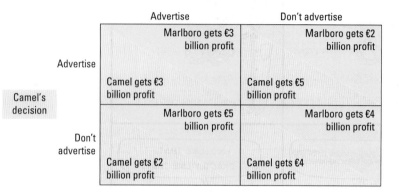

to mine the copper costs €1 million. If each company drills one shaft, each will get half of the copper and earn a €5 million profit (€6 million in revenue minus €1 million in costs).

Because the pool of copper is a common resource, the companies will not use it efficiently. Suppose that either company could drill a second shaft. If one company has two of the three shafts, that company gets two-thirds of the copper, which yields a profit of €6 million. The other company gets one-third of the copper, for a profit of €3 million. Yet if each company drills a second shaft, the two companies again split the copper. In this case, each bears the cost of a second shaft, so profit is only €4 million for each company.

Figure 13.7 shows the game. Drilling two wells is a dominant strategy for each company. Once again, the self-interest of the two players leads them to an inferior outcome.

FIGURE 13.7

A Common Resources Game

In this game between firms mining copper from a common pool, the profit that each earns depends on both the number of shafts it drills and the number of shafts drilled by the other firm.

Vedanta's decision

	Drill two shafts	Drill one shaft
Drill two shafts	Vedanta gets €4 million profit / Kazakhmys gets €4 million profit	Vedanta gets €3 million profit / Kazakhmys gets €6 million profit
Drill one shaft	Vedanta gets €6 million profit / Kazakhmys gets €3 million profit	Vedanta gets €5 million profit / Kazakhmys gets €5 million profit

Kazakhmy's decision

Why Firms Sometimes Cooperate

The prisoners' dilemma shows that cooperation is difficult. But is it impossible? Not all prisoners, when questioned by the police, decide to turn in their partners in crime. Cartels sometimes do manage to maintain collusive arrangements, despite the incentive for individual members to defect. Very often, the reason that players can solve the prisoners' dilemma is that they play the game not once but many times.

To see why cooperation is easier to enforce in repeated games, let's return to our duopolists, Ishaq and Coralie. Recall that Ishaq and Coralie would like to maintain the monopoly outcome in which each produces 30 litres, but self-interest drives them to an equilibrium in which each produces 40 litres. Figure 13.8 shows the game they play. Producing 40 litres is a dominant strategy for each player in this game.

Imagine that Ishaq and Coralie try to form a cartel. To maximize total profit they would agree to the cooperative outcome in which each produces 30 litres. Yet, if Ishaq and Coralie are to play this game only once, neither has any incentive to live up to this agreement. Self-interest drives each of them to renege and produce 40 litres.

Now suppose that Ishaq and Coralie know that they will play the same game every week. When they make their initial agreement to keep production low, they can also specify what happens if one party reneges. They might agree, for instance, that once one of them reneges and produces 40 litres, both of them will produce 40 litres forever after. This penalty is easy to enforce, for if one party is producing at a high level, the other has every reason to do the same.

The threat of this penalty may be all that is needed to maintain cooperation. Each person knows that defecting would raise his or her profit from €1800 to €2000. But this benefit would last for only one week. Thereafter, profit would fall to €1600 and stay there. As long as the players care enough about future profits, they will choose to forgo the one-time gain from defection. Thus, in a game of repeated prisoners' dilemma, the two players may well be able to reach the cooperative outcome.

Quick Quiz Tell the story of the prisoners' dilemma. Write down a table showing the prisoners' choices and explain what outcome is likely. • What does the prisoners' dilemma teach us about oligopolies?

FIGURE 13.8

Ishaq and Coralie's Oligopoly Game

In this game between Ishaq and Coralie, the profit that each earns from selling water depends on both the quantity he or she chooses to sell and the quantity the other chooses to sell.

Coralie's decision	Ishaq's decision: Sell 40 litres	Ishaq's decision: Sell 30 litres
Sell 40 litres	Ishaq gets €1600 profit; Coralie gets €1600 profit	Ishaq gets €1500 profit; Coralie gets €2000 profit
Sell 30 litres	Ishaq gets €2000 profit; Coralie gets €1500 profit	Ishaq gets €1800 profit; Coralie gets €1800 profit

Models of Oligopoly

Earlier we noted that firms are interdependent. Most firms will have a reasonable idea of the size of the market in which they operate and what position they hold in that market. Let us assume a duopoly again to illustrate how firms might behave.

Assume that Firm A has conducted research and that the size of the market it operates in is 1 million units or a value of €1 million a year. We will also assume that the marginal cost is constant. Figure 13.9 illustrates this situation. If Firm A were the only producer in the market it would produce where the MR curve cuts the MC curve and supply the whole 1 million units at Q_1. However, Firm A knows that Firm B also operates in the market and supplies 20 per cent of the market. The demand curve it faces is thus not D_1 but D_2 which is referred to as a residual demand curve. D_2 has an associated marginal revenue curve MR_2. Firm A's profit-maximizing output is now Q_2 where MR_2 cuts the MC curve. **Residual demand** is defined as the difference between the market demand curve and the amount supplied by other firms in the market. The residual demand curve depends on the output decision of the other firms in the market. Firm A might expend some time and effort trying to find out or at the very least estimate what this output level might be. In other words, Firm A needs to have some idea of the residual demand curve it faces or risk producing an output which would drive down the market price it faced. If, for example, it produced 1 million units and Firm B produced 200 000 units then there would be excess supply and the price it faces would fall. Knowing what your rival is planning to do is important in adopting the right strategy to ensure profit-maximizing output.

If Firm B supplied 40 per cent of the market then Firm A would face a different residual demand curve D_3 and would set output at Q_3 where MR_3 cuts the MC curve. It would be possible to conceptualize a situation where Firm A could map all possible outputs by Firm B and thus how it would react to these output levels.

residual demand the difference between the market demand curve and the amount supplied by other firms in the market

---

FIGURE 13.9

Residual Demand

If Firm A supplied the whole market (i.e. it assumes Firm B produces nothing) then the profit-maximizing output would be Q_1. If Firm A assumes Firm B produces 20 per cent of the market (shown by demand curve D_2) then its new profit-maximizing output will be Q_2 where the MR curve associated with the residual demand curve D_2. If Firm B was assumed to produce 40 per cent of the market output then Firm A would produce where MR_3 associated with residual demand D_3 cuts the MC curve at output Q_3.

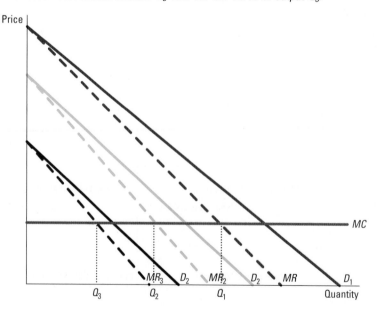

The result of this analysis by Firm A would give it its reaction function. The **reaction function** outlines the profit-maximizing output for a firm given the simultaneous output decisions of its rivals. Firm B will also have a reaction function derived from its analysis of how it would react to the output decisions of Firm A. The respective reaction functions show how Firm A would react if Firm B changed its output decisions and vice versa. This model of oligopoly was developed by Augustin Cournot in 1838. Cournot assumed that given two firms in a duopoly, each firm determines its profit-maximizing output on the assumption of the output of the other firm and that the decision of the other firm will not change in a given time period. In a given time period, therefore, Firm A, for example, could alter its output decision and its rival would not react. However, Firm B makes its decision under the same assumptions. This simultaneous decision making whereby each firm is trying to increase its profits but assuming its rivals will not react over different time periods eventually leads to an equilibrium position.

> **reaction function** the profit-maximizing output for a firm given the simultaneous output decisions of its rivals

We can represent this equilibrium in Figure 13.10. Firm A's output is on the vertical axis and Firm B's output on the horizontal axis. If Firm A assumed Firm B would produce zero then it would supply the whole market and the vertical intercept would be given by point C_1. If Firm B produced all the market output then Firm A would produce nothing indicated by point C_2. All other points in between show combinations of output for Firm A given a corresponding output decision by Firm B. The red line is Firm A's reaction function.

Equally we can graph Firm B's reaction function which will be the symmetrical opposite of Firm A's. If Firm A produces all the market output Firm B will produce nothing (point T_1) and if Firm A produced nothing Firm B would produce all the market output (point T_2). Connecting these points gives Firm B's reaction function indicated by the blue line.

FIGURE 13.10

Reaction Functions

The reaction functions given by the red and blue lines show combinations of output produced by Firm A and Firm B respectively given simultaneous decisions on output. If Firm A assumed Firm B will produce all the output in the market it produces zero shown by the horizontal intercept C_1. If Firm B produced nothing, Firm A will act as a monopolist and produce all the output shown by the vertical intercept C_2. The points in between show the various combinations of output Firm A would produce given Firm B's reaction and give Firm A's reaction function shown by the red line.

Equally, if Firm A produced nothing, Firm B would act as the monopolist and produce all the output shown by the horizontal intercept T_1. If Firm A produced all the output Firm B would produce nothing shown by the vertical intercept T_2. The points in between give Firm B's reaction function shown by the blue line. If either firm produced off its reaction function at different time periods there would be an incentive for the other to change its output in subsequent time periods until equilibrium was reached at Q_1, Q_2. This represents a Nash equilibrium because both firms make optimum decisions based on what its rivals are doing and a change in strategy by either firm would result in a less than optimum outcome.

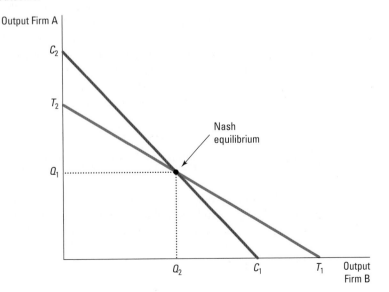

The point where the two reaction functions cross is a Nash equilibrium. At this point neither firm has any incentive to change its output – both firms maximize profit given its own decision and the decision of its rival.

An alternative model is the Bertrand model. In this model firms assume that the price fixed by its rivals is given. If Firm B, for example, sets price, Firm A will select a price and output level which maximizes this profit.

Assume that Firm B sets a price which is above MC. Firm A has the incentive to set its price slightly below that of Firm B and capture market share. In such a situation how would Firm B react? It would react by cutting its price. In turn Firm A would cut its price and the process will continue until P = MC and there is no incentive for either to change. What the Bertrand model predicts, therefore, is that the equilibrium in an oligopoly will give an outcome the same as that in perfect competition with P = MC. In such a situation each firm will be making its own pricing decision based on its own optimal outcome given the optimal behaviour of its rivals. Once again, this is a Nash equilibrium.

In reality, of course, firms do not make simultaneous decisions and game theory tells us that a firm will look to make decisions based on what it thinks its rivals will do in response and that it will learn from repeated instances of this 'game'. The Stackelberg model takes these new assumptions into account. This model looks at what equilibrium output would be for the two firms if one firm was the leader taking decisions first but considering what the other firm would do in response. If Firm A announces that it is going to produce output Q_1, it has to think about what Firm B will do in response. Firm A will have to consider a range of outputs and the response of Firm B to determine what its optimal output and profit level will be.

The Stackelberg model describes the advantages a firm can gain through moving before that of its rivals – so called *first mover advantage*. If Firm A is the leader and Firm B the follower then there may be an advantage to A in making a move to change output having estimated the response by Firm B. What is crucial in this model is that the decision made by Firm A is seen as being serious and credible by Firm B.

Assume that Firm A sets its output level at Q_1, and thus is the first mover. Firm B, the follower, will observe this and make its output decision based on Firm A's decision. Firm A knows this and so will have to take into consideration what Firm B's reaction is going to be. It is in Firm A's interest to set output at a higher level to generate more profits but Firm B must also be sure that this is what Firm A is going to do, hence the importance of Firm A's announcement being serious and credible. If Firm A announces that it intends to build a new plant and production facility to enable it to produce 70 per cent of the market output then Firm B must set its output to produce 30 per cent. If Firm B knows that Firm A is serious (and the investment announcement is an indicator of this) then if it produced any more that 30 per cent of the market output price would be driven down due to excess supply and it would be worse off as a result.

In addition, moving first in the market could mean that Firm A is able to exploit the profits that accrue from its investment first and use these profits to reinvest in expanding the firm further in the future. The risk for Firm A is that in making the move first it might experience considerable costs in so doing – costs which Firm B will also have to pay but possibly at lower levels because it can learn from the mistakes of the first mover.

PUBLIC POLICIES TOWARD OLIGOPOLIES

Cooperation among oligopolists is undesirable from the standpoint of society as a whole, because it leads to production that is too low and prices that are too high. To move the allocation of resources closer to the social optimum, policy makers try to induce firms in an oligopoly to compete rather than cooperate. Let's consider how policy makers do this and then examine the controversies that arise in this area of public policy.

Restraint of Trade and Competition Law

One way that policy discourages cooperation is through the common law. Normally, freedom of contract is an essential part of a market economy. Businesses and households use contracts to arrange mutually advantageous trades. In doing this, they rely on the court system to enforce contracts. Yet, for many centuries, courts in Europe and North America have deemed agreements among competitors to reduce quantities and raise prices to be contrary to the public interest. They have therefore refused to enforce such agreements.

Given the long experience of many European countries in tackling abuses of market power, it is perhaps not surprising that competition law is one of the few areas in which the European Union has been able to agree on a common policy. The European Commission can refer directly to the Treaty of Rome to prohibit price-fixing and other restrictive practices such as production limitation, and is especially likely to do so where a restrictive practice affects trade between EU member countries. The EU Competition Commission sets out its role as follows:

> *The antitrust area covers two prohibition rules set out in the Treaty on the Functioning of the European Union.*
>
> * *First, agreements between two or more firms which restrict competition are prohibited by Article 101 of the Treaty, subject to some limited exceptions. This provision covers a wide variety of behaviours. The most obvious example of illegal conduct infringing [the Article] is a cartel between competitors (which may involve price-fixing or market sharing).*
> * *Second, firms in a dominant position may not abuse that position (Article 102 of the Treaty). This is for example the case for predatory pricing aiming at eliminating competitors from the market.*
>
> *The Commission is empowered by the Treaty to apply these prohibition rules and enjoys a number of investigative powers to that end (e.g. inspection in business and non-business premises, written requests for information, etc). It may also impose fines on undertakings which violate EU antitrust rules. Since 1 May 2004, all national competition authorities are also empowered to apply fully the provisions of the Treaty in order to ensure that competition is not distorted or restricted. National courts may also apply these prohibitions so as to protect the individual rights conferred to citizens by the Treaty.*
>
> *(Source: http://ec.europa.eu/competition/antitrust/overview_en.html)*

Controversies Over Competition Policy

Over time, much controversy has centred on the question of what kinds of behaviour competition law should prohibit. Most commentators agree that price-fixing agreements among competing firms should be illegal. Yet competition law has been used to condemn some business practices whose effects are not obvious. Here we consider three examples.

Resale Price Maintenance One example of a controversial business practice is *resale price maintenance,* also called *fair trade.* Imagine that Superduper Electronics sells DVD players to retail stores for €300. If Superduper requires the retailers to charge customers €350, it is said to engage in resale price maintenance. Any retailer that charged less than €350 would have violated its contract with Superduper.

At first, resale price maintenance might seem anti-competitive and, therefore, detrimental to society. Like an agreement among members of a cartel, it prevents the retailers from competing on price. For this reason, the courts have often viewed resale price maintenance as a violation of competition law.

Yet some economists defend resale price maintenance on two grounds. First, they deny that it is aimed at reducing competition. To the extent that Superduper Electronics has any market power, it can exert that power through the wholesale price, rather than through resale price maintenance. Moreover, Superduper has no incentive to discourage competition among its retailers. Indeed, because a cartel of retailers sells less than a group of competitive retailers, Superduper would be worse off if its retailers were a cartel.

Secondly, economists believe that resale price maintenance has a legitimate goal. Superduper may want its retailers to provide customers with a pleasant showroom and a knowledgeable salesforce. Yet, without resale price maintenance, some customers would take advantage of one store's service to learn about the DVD player's special features and then buy the item at a discount retailer that does not provide this service. To some extent, good service is a public good among the retailers that sell Superduper products. As we saw in Chapter 8, when one person provides a public good, others are able to enjoy it without paying for it. In this case, discount retailers would free ride on the service provided by other retailers, leading to less service than is desirable. Resale price maintenance is one way for Superduper to solve this free-rider problem.

The example of resale price maintenance illustrates an important principle: business practices that appear to reduce competition may in fact have legitimate purposes. This principle makes the application of competition law all the more difficult. The competition authorities in each EU nation under the European Competition Network are in charge of enforcing these laws and must determine what kinds of behaviour public policy should prohibit as impeding competition and reducing economic well-being. Often that job is not easy.

Predatory Pricing Firms with market power normally use that power to raise prices above the competitive level. But should policy makers ever be concerned that firms with market power might charge prices that are too low? This question is at the heart of a second debate over competition policy.

Imagine that a large airline, call it National Airlines, has a monopoly on some route. Then Fly Express enters and takes 20 per cent of the market, leaving National with 80 per cent. In response to this competition, National starts slashing its fares. Some anti-trust analysts argue that National's move could be anti-competitive: the price cuts may be intended to drive Fly out of the market so National can recapture its monopoly and raise prices again. Such behaviour is called *predatory pricing*.

Although it is common for companies to complain to the relevant authorities that a competitor is pursuing predatory pricing, some economists are sceptical of this argument and believe that predatory pricing is rarely, and perhaps never, a profitable business strategy. Why? For a price war to drive out a rival, prices have to be driven below cost. Yet if National starts selling cheap tickets at a loss, it had better be ready to fly more planes, because low fares will attract more customers. Fly Express, meanwhile, can respond to National's predatory move by cutting back on flights. As a result, National ends up bearing more than 80 per cent of the losses, putting Fly Express in a good position to survive the price war. In such cases, the predator can suffer more than the prey.

Economists continue to debate whether predatory pricing should be a concern for competition policy makers. Various questions remain unresolved. Is predatory pricing ever a profitable business strategy? If so, when? Are the authorities capable of telling which price cuts are competitive and thus good for consumers and which are predatory? There are no simple answers.

Tying A third example of a controversial business practice is *tying*. Suppose that Makemoney Movies produces two new films – *Spiderman* and *Hamlet*. If Makemoney offers cinemas the two films together at a single price, rather than separately, the studio is said to be tying its two products.

Some economists have argued that the practice of tying should be banned. Their reasoning is as follows: imagine that *Spiderman* is a blockbuster, whereas *Hamlet* is an unprofitable art film. Then the studio could use the high demand for *Spiderman* to force cinemas to buy *Hamlet*. It seemed that the studio could use tying as a mechanism for expanding its market power.

Other economists are sceptical of this argument. Imagine that cinemas are willing to pay €20 000 for *Spiderman* and nothing for *Hamlet*. Then the most that a cinema would pay for the two films together is €20 000 – the same as it would pay for *Spiderman* by itself. Forcing the cinema to accept a worthless film as part of the deal does not increase the cinema's willingness to pay. Makemoney cannot increase its market power simply by bundling the two films together.

Why, then, does tying exist? One possibility is that it is a form of price discrimination. Suppose there are two cinemas. City Cinema is willing to pay €15 000 for *Spiderman* and €5000 for *Hamlet*. Country Cinema is just the opposite: it is willing to pay €5000 for *Spiderman* and €15 000 for *Hamlet*. If Makemoney charges separate prices for the two films, its best strategy is to charge €15 000 for each film, and each cinema chooses to show only one film. Yet if Makemoney offers the two films as a bundle, it can charge each cinema €20 000 for the films. Thus, if different cinemas value the films differently, tying may allow the studio to increase profit by charging a combined price closer to the buyers' total willingness to pay.

Tying remains a controversial business practice. We saw in Chapter 12 how Microsoft had been investigated for 'tying' its internet browser and other software like its Windows Media Player with its Windows operating system and the arguments that the company had put forward in its defence. The argument that tying allows a firm to extend its market power to other goods is not well founded, at least in its simplest form. Yet economists have proposed more elaborate theories for how tying can impede competition. Given our current economic knowledge, it is unclear whether tying has adverse effects for society as a whole.

All the analysis is based on an assumption that rivals may have sufficient information to be able to make a decision and that the decision will be a rational one based on this information. In reality firms do not have perfect information and do not behave rationally. Most firms in oligopolistic markets work very hard to protect sensitive information and only give out what they have to by law. Some information may be given to deliberately obfuscate the situation and hide what their true motives/strategies/tactics are. Economists have tried to include these imperfections into theories. Behavioural economics has become more popular in recent years because it offers some greater insights into the observed behaviour of the real world which often does not conform to the assumptions implied by the assumption of rationality.

> **Quick Quiz** What kind of agreement is illegal for businesses to make?
> • Why is competition law controversial?

CONCLUSION

Oligopolies would like to act like monopolies, but self-interest drives them closer to competition. Thus, oligopolies can end up looking either more like monopolies or more like competitive markets, depending on the number of firms in the oligopoly and how cooperative the firms are. The story of the prisoners' dilemma shows why oligopolies can fail to maintain cooperation, even when cooperation is in their best interest.

Policy makers regulate the behaviour of oligopolists through competition law. The proper scope of these laws is the subject of ongoing controversy. Although price fixing among competing firms clearly reduces economic welfare and should be illegal, some business practices that appear to reduce competition may have legitimate if subtle purposes. As a result, policy makers need to be careful when they use the substantial powers of competition law to place limits on firm behaviour.

IN THE NEWS

Anti-Competitive Behaviour

One aspect of anti-trust or anti-competitive behaviour is price-fixing where a group of firms act together to set prices at a level which is above the market clearing price. The cement industry in a number of countries has been subject to investigation by competition authorities and in this article, the industry in Egypt has come under scrutiny.

Accusations of Price Fixing in Egypt's Cement Sector

The Egyptian Competition Authority (ECA) referred 11 cement companies – essentially every major producer in the sector – to the public prosecutor last month (October 2007). All the 11 companies were accused of violating antitrust laws after a 14-month investigation into the sector. The final report of the investigation alleged widespread anticompetitive practices, particularly related to price fixing efforts in the local market.

Allegations of price fixing in the cement industry have been made across the world – not just in Egypt.

In statements following the announcement, Minister of Trade and Industry Rachid Mohamed Rachid said that competing in a free market involves complying with laws and regulations, and that such laws exist to ensure that all competitors play on an even field. The minister stressed that antitrust investigations by the ECA (also known by its official title of the Authority for the Protection of Competition and the Prohibition of Monopolistic Practices) will

not be exclusive to the steel and cement sectors.

Samiha Fawzy, an assistant to the minister, said that fines will start at LE 30 000 and could go up to a crippling LE 10 million, and that Rachid only decided to act when it was demonstrated that the companies were making profits from illegal collusion.

Reactions from cement sector leaders were predictably hostile. Abdel Meguid Mahmoud, an exporter and investor in the sector, confirmed that there was a 'verbal' agreement between cement companies to raise prices from US$58 to US$75 per ton, noting that production was set to increase from the current 35 million tons to 49 million tons in 2008. Mahmoud justified such an agreement based on the fact that cement demand is not flexible, and that any shortage in supply will cause direct price hikes. According to Mahmoud, by informally agreeing to a price target, producers were attempting to keep demand and prices in check.

Medhat Stefano, commercial head of the Egyptian arm of France-based global cement company Lafarge, told local reporters that the decision will negatively impact the investment environment, and that there may have been political influence on the court's final decision.

In support of the charges, Ahmed El-Zieny, deputy of the construction material division in the Chamber of Trade, said that several cement companies tried to pressure the minister not to

go ahead with the charges, attributing recent price rises to increasing transportation costs.

Hassan Rateb, head of the Building Material Exporting Board and head of Sinai Cement Group, said that free market mechanisms must be respected and followed, but he criticized Rachid for indicting the entire sector, including state-owned companies, saying that the move will give the impression that the state can't control the actions of its own companies. Rateb defended the sector, claiming that given export market prices are significantly higher than local ones, there is little incentive to game the domestic market.

Accusations of price fixing in the construction materials sector have been made in countries throughout the world in recent years, after a 20-year wave of consolidation left the industry dominated by a small group of large global players. In 2003, the German Federal Cartel Office (a national competition watchdog) levied almost US$650 million in antitrust fines against the country's leading cement producers. Bertrand Collomb, then CEO of Lafarge, later acknowledged that his company had engaged in 'unacceptable practices' in the German market.

Antitrust investigations into the cement sector, most ending in charges being made, have recently taken place in France, Poland, Argentina, Hungary, Ukraine, Romania and Taiwan.

Richard Whish, an expert on cartels and Professor of Law at Kings College,

London, told a group of UK competition authority officials in 2001 that 'every system of competition law will deal with cartels and the first thing for any regulator to do is to go out and find the cement cartel. The only countries in which I have been unable to find the cement cartel is where there is a national state-owned monopoly,' he said.

Questions

1. Explain why price-fixing is seen as being 'anti-competitive'.
2. Outline the argument put forward by cement sector leaders to counter the accusations by the authorities. Do you agree with their argument?
3. Why might there be little incentive to 'game the domestic market' because of high export prices?
4. Does the article suggest that the authorities in countries around the world have been successful in preventing anti-competitive practices in the cement industry? Explain your answer.
5. Why is it difficult to prove that cartels actually exist in practice?

Source: **http://www.bi-me.com/main.php? id=15015&t=1** November 2007, accessed 11 March 2011.

SUMMARY

- A monopolistically competitive market is characterized by three attributes: many firms, differentiated products and free entry.

- The equilibrium in a monopolistically competitive market differs from that in a perfectly competitive market in two related ways. First, each firm in a monopolistically competitive market has excess capacity. That is, it operates on the downward sloping portion of the average total cost curve. Secondly, each firm charges a price above marginal cost.

- Monopolistic competition does not have all the desirable properties of perfect competition. There is the standard deadweight loss of monopoly caused by the mark-up of price over marginal cost. In addition, the number of firms (and thus the variety of products) can be too large or too small. In practice, the ability of policy makers to correct these inefficiencies is limited.

- Oligopolists maximize their total profits by forming a cartel and acting like a monopolist. Yet, if oligopolists make decisions about production levels individually, the result is a greater quantity and a lower price than under the monopoly outcome. The larger the number of firms in the oligopoly, the closer the quantity and price will be to the levels that would prevail under competition.

- The prisoners' dilemma shows that self-interest can prevent people from maintaining cooperation, even when cooperation is in their mutual interest.

- Policy makers use competition law to prevent oligopolies from engaging in behaviour that reduces competition. The application of these laws can be controversial, because some behaviour that may seem to reduce competition may in fact have legitimate business purposes.

KEY CONCEPTS

monopolistic competition, p. 302
oligopoly, p. 308
collusion, p. 310
cartel, p. 310

nash equilibrium, p. 312
game theory, p. 314
prisoners' dilemma, p. 314
dominant strategy, p. 315

residual demand, p. 320
reaction function, p. 321

QUESTIONS FOR REVIEW

1. Describe the three attributes of monopolistic competition. How is monopolistic competition like monopoly? How is it like perfect competition?

2. Draw a diagram depicting a firm in a monopolistically competitive market that is making profits in the short run.
   a. Now show what happens to this firm as new firms enter the industry.
   b. Now draw the diagram of the long-run equilibrium in a monopolistically competitive market. How is price related to average total cost? How is price related to marginal cost?

3. Does a monopolistic competitor produce too much or too little output compared to the most efficient level? What practical considerations make it difficult for policy makers to solve this problem?

4. If a group of sellers could form a cartel, what quantity and price would they try to set?

5. How does the number of firms in an oligopoly affect the outcome in its market?

6. What is the prisoners' dilemma, and what does it have to do with oligopoly?

7. Give two examples other than oligopoly to show how the prisoners' dilemma helps to explain behaviour.

PROBLEMS AND APPLICATIONS

1. Classify the following markets as perfectly competitive, monopolistic or monopolistically competitive, and explain your answers.
   a. wooden HB pencils
   b. bottled water
   c. copper
   d. local telephone service
   e. strawberry jam
   f. lipstick

2. Sparkle is one firm of many in the market for toothpaste, which is in long-run equilibrium.
   a. Draw a diagram showing Sparkle's demand curve, marginal revenue curve, average total cost curve, and marginal cost curve. Label Sparkle's profit-maximizing output and price.
   b. What is Sparkle's profit? Explain.
   c. On your diagram, show the consumer surplus derived from the purchase of Sparkle toothpaste. Also show the deadweight loss relative to the efficient level of output.
   d. If the government forced Sparkle to produce the efficient level of output, what would happen to the firm? What would happen to Sparkle's customers?

3. If you were thinking of entering the ice cream business, would you try to make ice cream that is just like one of the existing (successful) brands? Explain your decision using the ideas of this chapter.

4. *The Economist* (15 November 2001) reported that 'OPEC has failed to agree immediate production cuts to shore up oil prices. Afraid of losing market share, it wants nonmembers, who would also benefit from any price support, to cut output as well. So far, they have refused to agree. If oil prices continue to fall, that would provide relief to the beleaguered world economy, but it might wreak havoc on the finances of OPEC members.'
   a. Why do you suppose OPEC was unable to agree on cutting production?
   b. Why do you think oil-producing non-members refused to cut output?

5. A large share of the world supply of diamonds comes from Russia and South Africa. Suppose that the marginal cost of mining diamonds is constant at €1000 per diamond, and the demand for diamonds is described by the following schedule:

8. What kinds of behaviour do the competition laws prohibit?

9. What is resale price maintenance, and why is it controversial?

10. Why might predatory pricing not be a useful tactic for an oligopolistic firm to pursue?

Price (€)	Quantity
8000	5000
7000	6000
6000	7000
5000	8000
4000	9000
3000	10000
2000	11000
1000	12000

   a. If there were many suppliers of diamonds, what would be the price and quantity?
   b. If there was only one supplier of diamonds, what would be the price and quantity?
   c. If Russia and South Africa formed a cartel, what would be the price and quantity? If the countries split the market evenly, what would be South Africa's production and profit? What would happen to South Africa's profit if it increased its production by 1000 while Russia stuck to the cartel agreement?
   d. Use your answer to part (c) to explain why cartel agreements are often not successful.

6. This chapter discusses companies that are oligopolists in the market for the goods they sell. Many of the same ideas apply to companies that are oligopolists in the market for the inputs they buy. If sellers who are oligopolists try to increase the price of goods they sell, what is the goal of buyers who are oligopolists?

7. The chapter states that the ban on cigarette advertising on television which many countries imposed in the 1970s increased the profits of cigarette companies. Could the ban still be good public policy? Explain your answer.

8. Assume that two airline companies decide to engage in collusive behaviour.
   Let's analyze the game between two such companies. Suppose that each company can charge either a high price for tickets or a low price. If one company charges €100, it earns low profits if the other company charges €100 also, and high profits if the other company charges €200. On the other hand, if the company charges €200, it earns very low profits if the other company charges €100, and medium profits if the other company charges €200 also.
   a. Draw the decision box for this game.
   b. What is the Nash equilibrium in this game? Explain.

c. Is there an outcome that would be better than the Nash equilibrium for both airlines? How could it be achieved? Who would lose if it were achieved?

9. Farmer Jones and Farmer MacDonald graze their cattle on the same field. If there are 20 cows grazing in the field, each cow produces €4000 of milk over its lifetime. If there are more cows in the field, then each cow can eat less grass, and its milk production falls. With 30 cows on the field, each produces €3000 of milk; with 40 cows, each produces €2000 of milk. Cows are priced at €1000 apiece.

a. Assume that Farmer Jones and Farmer MacDonald can each purchase either 10 or 20 cows, but that neither knows how many the other is buying when he makes his purchase. Calculate the pay-offs of each outcome.

b. What is the likely outcome of this game? What would be the best outcome? Explain.

c. There used to be more common fields than there are today. Why?

10. Little Kona is a small coffee company that is considering entering a market dominated by Big Brew. Each company's profit depends on whether Little Kona enters and whether Big Brew sets a high price or a low price:
Big Brew threatens Little Kona by saying, 'If you enter, we're going to set a low price, so you had better stay out'. Do you think Little Kona should believe the threat? Why or why not? What do you think Little Kona should do?

Big brew

	High price	Low price
Enter	Brew makes €3 million Kona makes €2 million	Brew makes €1 million Kona loses €1 million
Don't enter	Brew makes €7 million Kona makes zero	Brew makes €2 million Kona makes zero

Little kona

PART 5

MICROECONOMICS – FACTOR MARKETS

14 LABOUR MARKETS

LEARNING OBJECTIVES

In this chapter you will:

- Analyze the labour demand of competitive, profit-maximizing firms

- Consider the household decisions that lie behind labour supply

- Learn why equilibrium wages equal the value of the marginal product of labour

- Consider how the other factors of production – land and capital – are compensated

- Examine how a change in the supply of one factor alters the earnings of all the factors

After reading this chapter you should be able to:

- Explain why the labour demand curve is the value of the marginal product curve for labour

- Explain why the labour supply curve is usually upward sloping

- Explain why a competitive firm maximizes profit when it hires labour to the point where the wage equals the value of the marginal product of labour

- Demonstrate the similarity between the labour market and the market for other factors of production

- Explain why the change in the supply of one factor alters the value of the marginal product of the other factors

THE MARKETS FOR THE FACTORS OF PRODUCTION

The factors of production of land, labour and capital have to be paid for. For many businesses one of the most significant costs they face is paying for labour. They also have to pay interest on loans and pay rent for the factor land.

Your income, of course, is a small piece of a larger economic picture. In 2013 the total income of all 27 EU countries as measured by gross domestic product (GDP) was about €12.96 trillion (€12 960 000 000 000). In South Africa in 2011, total income was 3.36 billion. This income is earned in various ways. Workers earned some of it in the form of wages, fringe benefits and from self-employment. The rest is accounted for by income to landowners and to the owners of capital – the economy's stock of equipment and structures – in the form of rent, profit and interest.

What prices businesses pay for labour, capital and land is determined in part by the supply and demand of factors of production. This chapter provides the basic theory for the analysis of factor markets. When a computer firm, for example, produces a new software program, it uses programmers' time (labour), the physical space on which its offices sit (land), and an office building and computer equipment (capital). Similarly, when a petrol station sells petrol, it uses attendants' time (labour), the physical space (land), and the petrol tanks and pumps (capital).

derived demand when demand for a factor of production is derived (determined) from its decision to supply a good in another market

Although in many ways factor markets resemble the goods markets we have analyzed in previous chapters, they are different in one important way: the demand for a factor of production is a **derived demand**. That is, a firm's demand for a factor of production is derived (determined) from its decision to supply a good in another market. The demand for computer programmers is inextricably tied to the supply of computer software, and the demand for petrol station attendants is inextricably tied to the supply of petrol.

The initial analysis will be based on firms operating in a competitive market – both for goods and labour. More will be said on this below but it is also worth remembering that the analysis assumes that labour is free to enter and exit the market and firms are equally free to employ and shed labour at will – in other words people can move into and out of work easily and employers can 'hire and fire' workers when they need to. In reality, of course, there are a number of imperfections in the labour market but our initial analysis serves to act as a benchmark for looking at how labour markets work in reality.

> **?** **what if…**labour markets were perfect markets – would there ever be any unemployment and would firms ever have problems accessing the labour market skills they need?

THE DEMAND FOR LABOUR

Labour markets, like other markets in the economy, are governed by the forces of supply and demand. This is illustrated in Figure 14.1. In panel (a) the supply and demand for apples determines the price of apples. In panel (b) the supply and demand for apple pickers determine the price, or wage, of apple pickers.

As we have already noted, labour markets are different from most other markets because labour demand is a derived demand. Most labour services, rather than being final goods ready to be enjoyed by consumers, are inputs into the production of other goods. To understand labour demand, we need to focus on the firms that hire the labour and use it to produce goods for sale. By examining the link between the production of goods and the demand for labour, we gain insight into the determination of equilibrium wages.

FIGURE 14.1

The Versatility of Supply and Demand

The basic tools of supply and demand apply to goods and to labour services. Panel (a) shows how the supply and demand for apples determine the price of apples. Panel (b) shows how the supply and demand for apple pickers determine the wage of apple pickers.

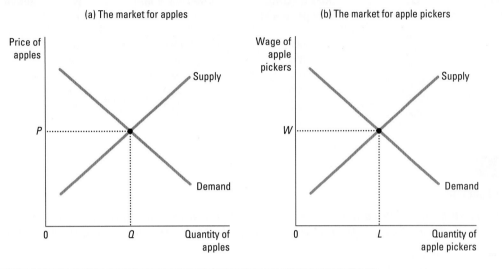

Pitfall Prevention Remember that the demand for factors of production, because of their very nature, are inextricably linked with the demand for the goods and services which they are associated with in production. This is one of the reasons why the workings of the economy as a whole is so interdependent.

The Competitive Profit-Maximizing Firm

Let's look at how a typical firm, such as an apple producer, decides the quantity of labour to demand. The firm owns an apple orchard and each week must decide how many apple pickers to hire to harvest its crop. After the firm makes its hiring decision, the workers pick as many apples as they can. The firm then sells the apples, pays the workers, and keeps what is left as profit.

We assume that our firm is *competitive* both in the market for apples (where the firm is a seller) and in the market for apple pickers (where the firm is a buyer). Because there are many other firms selling apples and hiring apple pickers, a single firm has little influence over the price it gets for apples or the wage it pays apple pickers. The firm takes the price and the wage as given by market conditions. It only has to decide how many workers to hire and how many apples to sell.

Secondly, we assume that the firm is *profit-maximizing*. Thus, the firm does not directly care about the number of workers it has or the number of apples it produces. It cares only about profit, which equals the total revenue from the sale of apples minus the total cost of producing them. The firm's supply of apples and its demand for workers are derived from its primary goal of maximizing profit.

The Production Function and the Marginal Product of Labour

To make its hiring decision, the firm must consider how the number of apple pickers affects the quantity of apples it can harvest and sell. Table 14.1 gives a numerical example. In the first column is the number of workers. In the second column is the quantity of apples the workers harvest each week.

TABLE 14.1

How the Competitive Firm Decides How Much Labour to Hire

Labour	Output	Marginal product of labour	Value of the marginal product of labour	Wage	Marginal profit
L (number of workers)	Q (kilos per week)	MPL = ΔQ/ΔL (kilos per week)	VMPL = P × MPL €	W €	ΔProfit = VMPL – W €
0	0				
		1000	1000	500	500
1	1000				
		800	800	500	300
2	1800				
		600	600	500	100
3	2400				
		400	400	500	–100
4	2800				
		200	200	500	–300
5	3000				

FIGURE 14.2

The Production Function

The production function is the relationship between the inputs into production (apple pickers) and the output from production (apples). As the quantity of the input increases, the production function gets flatter, reflecting the property of diminishing marginal product.

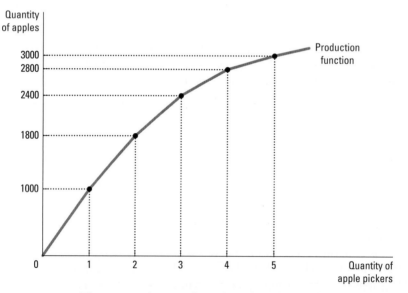

These two columns of numbers describe the firm's ability to produce. As we noted in Chapter 9, economists use the term production function to describe the relationship between the quantity of the inputs used in production and the quantity of output from production. Here the 'input' is the apple pickers and the 'output' is the apples. The other inputs – the trees themselves, the land, the firm's trucks and tractors, and so on – are held fixed for now. This firm's production function shows that if the firm hires 1 worker, that worker will pick 1000 kilos of apples per week. If the firm hires 2 workers, the two workers together will pick 1800 kilos per week, and so on.

Figure 14.2 graphs the data on labour and output presented in Table 14.1. The number of workers is on the horizontal axis, and the amount of output is on the vertical axis. This figure illustrates the production function.

One of the *Ten Principles of Economics* introduced in Chapter 1 is that rational people think at the margin. This idea is the key to understanding how firms decide what quantity of labour to hire. To take a step towards this decision, the third column in Table 14.1 gives the **marginal product of labour**, the increase in the amount of output from an additional unit of labour. When the firm increases the number of workers from

marginal product of labour the increase in the amount of output from an additional unit of labour

1 to 2, for example, the amount of apples produced rises from 1000 to 1800 kilos. Therefore, the marginal product of the second worker is 800 kilos.

Notice that as the number of workers increases, the marginal product of labour declines. This is because we are adding more units of a variable factor (labour) to a quantity of fixed factors (land and capital) – the firm is operating in the short run. This property is called diminishing marginal product. At first, when only a few workers are hired, they pick apples from the best trees in the orchard. As the number of workers increases, additional workers have to pick from the trees with fewer apples. Hence, as more and more workers are hired, each additional worker contributes less to the production of apples. For this reason, the production function in Figure 14.2 becomes flatter as the number of workers rises.

> **Pitfall Prevention** Calculating marginal product is not always easy especially when looking at service industries. In such cases firms will have to think of how they can measure the productivity of workers.

The Value of the Marginal Product and the Demand for Labour

Our profit-maximizing firm is concerned more with money than with apples. As a result, when deciding how many workers to hire, the firm considers how much profit each worker would bring in. Because profit is total revenue minus total cost, the profit from an additional worker is the worker's contribution to revenue minus the worker's wage.

To find the worker's contribution to revenue, we must convert the marginal product of labour (which is measured in kilos of apples) into the *value* of the marginal product (which is measured in euros). We do this using the price of apples. To continue our example, if a kilo of apples sells for €1 and if an additional worker produces 800 kilos of apples, then the worker produces €800 of revenue for the firm.

The **value of the marginal product** of any input is the marginal product of that input multiplied by the market price of the output. The fourth column in Table 14.1 shows the value of the marginal product of labour in our example, assuming the price of apples is €1 per kilo. Because the market price is constant for a competitive firm, the value of the marginal product (like the marginal product itself) diminishes as the number of workers rises. Economists sometimes call this column of numbers the firm's *marginal revenue product*: it is the extra revenue the firm gets from hiring an additional unit of a factor of production.

value of the marginal product the marginal product of an input times the price of the output

Now consider how many workers the firm will hire. Suppose that the market wage for apple pickers is €500 per week. In this case, as you see in Table 14.1, the first worker that the firm hires is profitable: the first worker yields €1000 in revenue, or €500 in profit. Similarly, the second worker yields €800 in additional revenue, or €300 in profit. The third worker produces €600 in additional revenue, or €100 in profit. After the third worker, however, hiring workers is unprofitable. The fourth worker would yield only €400 of additional revenue. Because the worker's wage is €500, hiring the fourth worker would mean a €100 reduction in profit. Thus, the firm hires only three workers.

It is instructive to consider the firm's decision graphically. Figure 14.3 graphs the value of the marginal product. This curve slopes downward because the marginal product of labour diminishes as the number of workers rises. The figure also includes a horizontal line at the market wage. To maximize profit, the firm hires workers up to the point where these two curves cross. Below this level of employment, the value of the marginal product exceeds the wage, so hiring another worker would increase profit. Above this level of employment, the value of the marginal product is less than the wage, so the marginal worker is unprofitable. Thus, a competitive, profit-maximizing firm hires workers up to the point where the value of the marginal product of labour equals the wage.

Having explained the profit-maximizing hiring strategy for a competitive firm, we can now offer a theory of labour demand. Recall that a firm's labour demand curve tells us

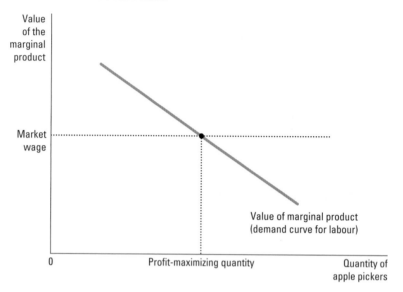

FIGURE 14.3

The Value of the Marginal Product of Labour

This figure shows how the value of the marginal product (the marginal product times the price of the output) depends on the number of workers. The curve slopes downward because of diminishing marginal product. For a competitive, profit-maximizing firm, this value of marginal product curve is also the firm's labour demand curve.

the quantity of labour that a firm demands at any given wage. We have just seen in Figure 14.3 that the firm makes the decision by choosing the quantity of labour at which the value of the marginal product equals the wage. As a result, the value of marginal product curve is the labour demand curve for a competitive, profit-maximizing firm.

What Causes the Labour Demand Curve to Shift?

The labour demand curve reflects the value of the marginal product of labour. With this insight in mind, let's consider a few of the things that might cause the labour demand curve to shift.

The Output Price   The value of the marginal product is marginal product times the price of the firm's output. Thus, when the output price changes, the value of the marginal product changes, and the labour demand curve shifts. An increase in the price of apples, for instance, raises the value of the marginal product of each worker who picks apples and, therefore, increases labour demand from the firms that supply apples. Conversely, a decrease in the price of apples reduces the value of the marginal product and decreases labour demand.

Technological Change   Increases in labour productivity can be attributed in part to technological progress: scientists and engineers are constantly figuring out new and better ways of doing things. This has profound implications for the labour market. Technological advance raises the marginal product of labour, which in turn increases the demand for labour. Such technological advances allow firms to increase wages and employment but still make profits providing productivity rises faster than labour costs.

The Supply of other Factors   The quantity available of one factor of production can affect the marginal product of other factors. A fall in the supply of ladders, for instance, will reduce the marginal product of apple pickers and thus the demand for apple pickers. We consider this linkage among the factors of production more fully later in the chapter.

ONCE WE'D PUT IN THE STAFF BUNK BEDS „IT JUST SEEMED THE NEXT LOGICAL STEP TO MAKE BUNK DESKS AS WELL... I MEAN, NOW PRODUCTIVITY IS WAY UP, & NO ONE IS EVER LATE.

P.J CURRIER/MEDIA SELECT INTERNATIONAL

FYI

Input Demand and Output Supply: Two Sides of the Same Coin

Remember that a competitive, profit-maximizing firm decides how much of its output to sell: it chooses the quantity of output at which the price of the good equals the marginal cost of production. We have just seen how such a firm decides how much labour to hire: it chooses the quantity of labour at which the wage equals the value of the marginal product. Because the production function links the quantity of inputs to the quantity of output, you should not be surprised to learn that the firm's decision about input demand is closely linked to its decision about output supply. In fact, these two decisions are two sides of the same coin.

To see this relationship more fully, let's consider how the marginal product of labour (MPL) and marginal cost (MC) are related. Suppose an additional worker costs €500 and has a marginal product of 50 kilos of apples. In this

case, producing 50 more kilos costs €500; the marginal cost of a kilo is €500/50, or €10. More generally, if W is the wage, and an extra unit of labour produces MPL units of output, then the marginal cost of a unit of output is $MC = W/MPL$.

This analysis shows that diminishing marginal product is closely related to increasing marginal cost. When our apple orchard grows crowded with workers, each additional worker adds less to the production of apples (MPL falls). Similarly, when the apple firm is producing a large quantity of apples, the orchard is already crowded with workers, so it is more costly to produce an additional kilo of apples (MC rises).

Now consider our criterion for profit maximization. We determined earlier that a profit-maximizing firm chooses the quantity of labour so that the value of the marginal product ($P \times$

MPL) equals the wage (W). We can write this mathematically as:

$$P \times MPL = W$$

If we divide both sides of this equation by MPL, we obtain:

$$P = W/MPL$$

We just noted that W/MPL equals marginal cost MC. Therefore, we can substitute to obtain:

$$P = MC$$

This equation states that the price of the firm's output is equal to the marginal cost of producing a unit of output. *Thus, when a competitive firm hires labour up to the point at which the value of the marginal product equals the wage, it also produces up to the point at which the price equals marginal cost.* Our analysis of labour demand in this chapter is just another way of looking at the production decision we first saw in Chapter 9.

> **Quick Quiz** Define *marginal product of labour* and *value of the marginal product of labour.* • Describe how a competitive, profit-maximizing firm decides how many workers to hire.

THE SUPPLY OF LABOUR

Having analyzed labour demand let's turn to the other side of the market and consider labour supply. Here we discuss briefly and informally the decisions that lie behind the labour supply curve.

The Trade-Off Between Work and Leisure

One of the *Ten Principles of Economics* in Chapter 1 is that people face trade-offs. Probably no trade-off is more obvious or more important in a person's life than the trade-off between work and leisure. The more hours you spend working, the fewer hours you have to watch TV, socialize with friends or pursue your favourite hobby. Firms are increasingly aware of the effect on productivity of the work–life balance and how employees view this trade-off. The development in technology has meant that many workers are in touch with their work more than ever before and the temptation to put in ever more hours is considerable. This is not always a good thing for productivity. The trade-off between labour and leisure lies behind the labour supply curve.

What do you give up to get an hour of leisure? You give up an hour of work, which in turn means an hour of wages. Thus, if your wage is €15 per hour, the opportunity cost of an hour of leisure is €15. And when you get a pay rise to €20 per hour, the opportunity cost of enjoying leisure goes up.

The labour supply curve reflects how workers' decisions about the labour–leisure trade-off respond to a change in that opportunity cost. An upward sloping labour supply curve means that an increase in the wage induces workers to increase the quantity of labour they supply. Because time is limited, more hours of work means that workers are enjoying less leisure. That is, workers respond to the increase in the opportunity cost of leisure by taking less of it.

It is worth noting that the labour supply curve need not be upward sloping. Imagine you got that raise from €15 to €20 per hour. The opportunity cost of leisure is now greater, but you are also richer than you were before. You might decide that with your extra wealth you can now afford to enjoy more leisure. That is, at the higher wage, you might choose to work fewer hours. If so, your labour supply curve would slope backwards.

What Causes the Labour Supply Curve to Shift?

The labour supply curve shifts whenever people change the amount they want to work at a given wage. Let's now consider some of the events that might cause such a shift.

Changes in Tastes The proportion of women in the workforce in many countries is growing and has been since the 1960s. There are many explanations for this development, but one of them is changing tastes, or attitudes toward work. A generation or two ago, it was the norm for women to stay at home while raising children. Today, family sizes are smaller and more mothers choose to work. The result is an increase in the supply of labour. In a number of countries governments are looking to provide incentives to people to get back to work; this, along with the difficult economic conditions which many countries have faced since the financial crisis in 2007–2009, has also led to more people coming into the workforce who were previously economically inactive – in other words they are of working age but for some reason have chosen not to be either in work or actively seeking employment.

Changes in Alternative Opportunities The supply of labour in any one labour market depends on the opportunities available in other labour markets. If the wage earned by pear pickers suddenly rises, some apple pickers may choose to switch occupations. The supply of labour in the market for apple pickers falls.

Immigration Movement of workers from region to region, or country to country, is an obvious and often important source of shifts in labour supply. When immigrants move from one European country to another – from Poland to the UK, for instance – the supply of labour in the United Kingdom increases and the supply of labour in Poland contracts. In fact, much of the policy debate about immigration centres on its effect on labour supply and, thereby, equilibrium in the labour market.

Quick Quiz Who has a greater opportunity cost of enjoying leisure – a petrol station attendant or a brain surgeon? Explain. Can this help explain why doctors work such long hours?

JEOPARDY PROBLEM

A manufacturing firm wants to increase productivity and thinks that increasing wages is the way to achieve this. It has a working system where workers have a basic working week of 35 hours and any additional hours are paid as overtime. The vast majority of its workers take advantage of the overtime opportunities whenever possible, especially when there are periods of high demand for the product. However, overtime pay, especially at weekends and during periods classed as 'unsociable hours' attracts a higher rate than the normal basic pay and the firm has noticed that productivity during these periods of overtime is higher than that recorded during the normal working week. The firm announces that all workers will receive a basic 20 per cent increase in pay for the normal working week but that overtime pay will remain at previous rates. It hopes this increase in pay will boost productivity during the week. Six months after the increase an internal review shows that productivity during the week has not changed but that the amount of overtime workers are prepared to do has also gone down. What could the explanation be for this situation?

EQUILIBRIUM IN THE LABOUR MARKET

So far we have established two facts about how wages are determined in competitive labour markets:

- The wage adjusts to balance the supply and demand for labour.
- The wage equals the value of the marginal product of labour.

At first, it might seem surprising that the wage can do both these things at once. In fact, there is no real puzzle here, but understanding why there is no puzzle is an important step to understanding wage determination.

FIGURE 14.4

Equilibrium in a Labour Market

Like all prices, the price of labour (the wage) depends on supply and demand. Because the demand curve reflects the value of the marginal product of labour, in equilibrium workers receive the value of their marginal contribution to the production of goods and services.

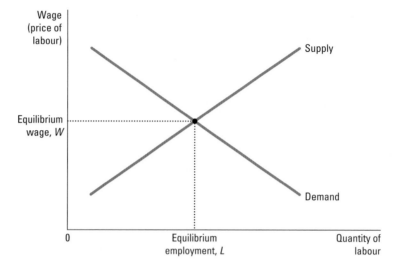

Figure 14.4 shows the labour market in equilibrium. The wage and the quantity of labour have adjusted to balance supply and demand. When the market is in this equilibrium, each firm has bought as much labour as it finds profitable at the equilibrium wage. That is, each firm has followed the rule for profit maximization: it has hired workers until the value of the marginal product equals the wage. Hence, the wage must equal the value of the marginal product of labour once it has brought supply and demand into equilibrium.

This brings us to an important lesson: any event that changes the supply or demand for labour must change the equilibrium wage and the value of the marginal product by the same amount, because these must always be equal. This can affect the costs of firms and influence their labour structures. To see how this works, let's consider some events that shift these curves.

Shifts in Labour Supply

Suppose that immigration increases the number of workers willing to pick apples. As Figure 14.5 shows, the supply of labour shifts to the right from S_1 to S_2. At the initial wage W_1, the quantity of labour supplied now exceeds the quantity demanded. This surplus of labour puts downward pressure on the wage of apple pickers, and the fall in the wage from W_1 to W_2 in turn makes it profitable for firms to hire more workers. As the number of workers employed in each apple orchard rises, the marginal product of a worker falls, and so does the value of the marginal product. In the new equilibrium, both the wage and the value of the marginal product of labour are lower than they were before the influx of new workers.

Shifts in Labour Demand

Now suppose that an increase in the popularity of apples causes their price to rise. This price increase does not change the marginal product of labour for any given number of

FIGURE 14.5

A Shift in Labour Supply

When labour supply increases from S_1 to S_2, perhaps because of immigration of new workers, the equilibrium wage falls from W_1 to W_2. At this lower wage, firms hire more labour, so employment rises from L_1 to L_2. The change in the wage reflects a change in the value of the marginal product of labour: with more workers, the added output from an extra worker is smaller.

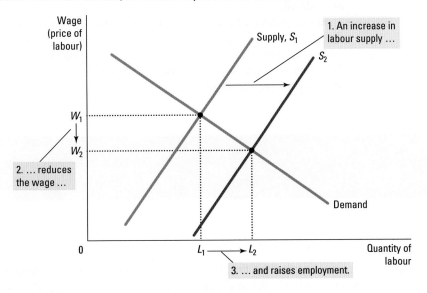

FIGURE 14.6

A Shift in Labour Demand

When labour demand increases from D_1 to D_2, perhaps because of an increase in the price of the firm's output, the equilibrium wage rises from W_1 to W_2, and employment rises from L_1 to L_2. Again, the change in the wage reflects a change in the value of the marginal product of labour: with a higher output price, the added output from an extra worker is more valuable.

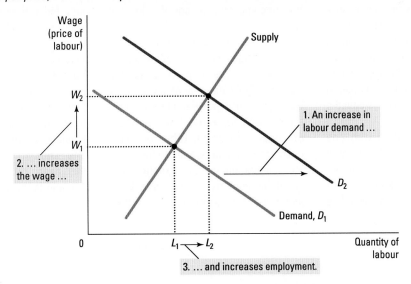

workers, but it does raise the *value* of the marginal product. With a higher price of apples, hiring more apple pickers is now profitable. As Figure 14.6 shows, when the demand for labour shifts to the right from D_1 to D_2, the equilibrium wage rises from W_1 to W_2, and equilibrium employment rises from L_1 to L_2. Once again, the wage and the value of the marginal product of labour move together.

This analysis shows that prosperity for firms in an industry is often linked to prosperity for workers in that industry. When the price of apples rises, apple producers make greater profit and apple pickers earn higher wages. When the price of apples falls, apple producers earn smaller profit and apple pickers earn lower wages. This lesson is well known to workers in industries with highly volatile prices. Workers in oil fields, for instance, know from experience that their earnings are closely linked to the world price of crude oil.

In competitive labour markets, therefore, labour supply and labour demand together determine the equilibrium wage, and shifts in the supply or demand curve for labour cause the equilibrium wage to change. At the same time, profit maximization by the firms that demand labour ensures that the equilibrium wage always equals the value of the marginal product of labour.

FYI

Monopsony

On the preceding pages, we built our analysis of the labour market with the tools of supply and demand. In doing so, we assumed that the labour market was competitive. That is, we assumed that there were many buyers of labour and many sellers of labour, so each buyer or seller had a negligible effect on the wage.

Yet imagine the labour market in a small town dominated by a single large employer. That employer can exert a large influence on the going wage, and it may well use that market power to alter the outcome. Such a market in which there is a single buyer is called a *monopsony*.

A monopsony (a market with one buyer) is in many ways similar to a monopoly (a market with one seller). A monopsony firm in a labour market hires fewer workers than would a competitive firm: by reducing the number of jobs available, the monopsony firm moves along the labour supply curve, reducing the wage it pays and raising its profits. Thus, both monopolists and monopsonists reduce economic activity in a market below the socially optimal level. In both cases, the existence of market power distorts the outcome and causes deadweight losses.

In the real world, monopsonies are rare although, on a small scale, a number of towns in parts of Europe may be highly dependent on a major employer – a motor vehicle manufacturer, a steel works or chocolate manufacturer, for example. Other examples have been cited in relation to the plans by multinationals to expand into emerging markets. There have been concerns expressed in the Indian press, for example, about US grocery firm Wal-Mart's plans to expand its operations into the Asian sub-continent. Wal-Mart faces critics in the USA who claim that it applies monopsony practices by squeezing suppliers and also using predatory pricing tactics to force out smaller competitors. If Wal-Mart does move into India then what protection can small firms and local markets expect, if any? In such situations, the analysis may have to be amended to take into consideration the effect that monopoly power of the employer has on the local labour market. In most labour markets, however, workers have many possible employers, and firms compete with one another to attract workers. In this case, the model of supply and demand is the best one to use.

Quick Quiz How does immigration of workers affect labour supply, labour demand, the marginal product of labour and the equilibrium wage?

CASE STUDY

The Minimum Wage

An important example of a price floor is the minimum wage. Minimum wage laws dictate the lowest price for labour that any employer may pay. The USA and 20 of the 27 European Union countries now have a statutory minimum wage.

To examine the effects of a minimum wage, we must consider the market for labour. Panel (a) of Figure 14.7 shows the labour market, which, like all markets, is subject to the forces of supply and demand. Workers determine the supply of labour, and firms determine the demand. If the government doesn't intervene, the wage normally adjusts to balance labour supply and labour demand.

FIGURE 14.7

How the Minimum Wage Affects the Labour Market

Panel (a) shows a labour market in which the wage adjusts to balance labour supply and demand. Panel (b) shows the impact of a binding minimum wage. Because the minimum wage is a price floor, it causes a surplus: the quantity of labour supplied exceeds the quantity demanded. The result is unemployment. Panel (c) shows that the more elastic labour demand is, the higher will be ensuing unemployment. In panel (d), because the minimum wage is binding across the whole industry, firms are able to pass a higher proportion of the wage costs onto higher prices without a drastic fall in demand for output, and so the labour demand curve for an individual firm actually shifts to the right at or above the minimum wage, so that the impact on employment is much less.

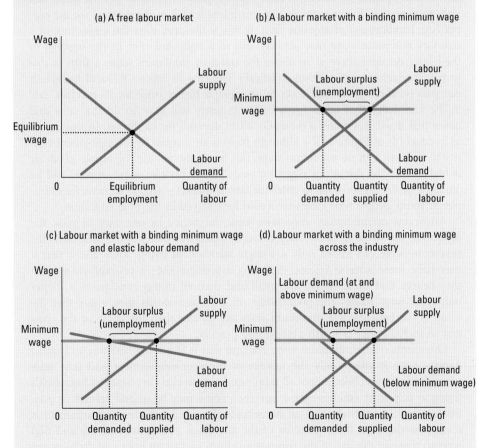

Panel (b) of Figure 14.7 shows the labour market with a minimum wage. If the minimum wage is above the equilibrium level, as it is here, the quantity of labour supplied exceeds the quantity demanded. The result is unemployment. Thus, the minimum wage raises the incomes of those workers who have jobs, but it lowers the incomes of those workers who cannot find jobs.

To understand fully the minimum wage, keep in mind that the economy contains not a single labour market, but many labour markets for different types of workers. The impact of the minimum wage depends on the skill and experience of the worker. Workers with high skills and much experience are not affected, because their equilibrium wages are well above the minimum. For these workers, the minimum wage is not binding. One would therefore expect a diagram such as that in panel (b) of Figure 14.7, where the minimum wage is above the equilibrium wage and unemployment results, to apply primarily to the market for low-skilled and teenage labour. Note, however, that the *extent* of the unemployment that results depends upon the elasticities of the supply and demand for labour. In panel (c) of Figure 14.7 we have redrawn the diagram with a more elastic demand curve for labour and we can see that this results in a higher level of unemployment. It is often argued that the demand for unskilled labour is in fact likely to be highly elastic with respect to the price of labour because employers of unskilled labour, such as fast food restaurants, usually face highly price-elastic demand curves for their own product and so cannot easily pass on wage rises in the form of higher prices without seeing their revenue fall.

This is only true, however, if one firm raises its price while others do not. If all fast food companies are forced to raise prices slightly in order to pay the minimum wage to their staff, this may result in a much smaller fall in the demand for the output (e.g. hamburgers) of any one firm. If this is the case, then the imposition of a statutory minimum wage may actually lead to a rightward shift in the segment of the labour demand curve at or above the statutory minimum wage: a firm is able to pay the higher wage without drastically reducing its labour demand because it can pass on the higher wage costs by charging a higher price for its product, safe in the knowledge that other firms in the industry will have to do the same and hence that it will not suffer a dramatic fall in demand for its output. In this case – as in panel (d) of Figure 14.7 – although there is an increase in unemployment relative to the case with no minimum wage, this is mainly because the supply of labour is higher with the minimum wage imposed. This is because some workers will be attracted by the higher wage to enter the labour market – second earners, for example, or young people who otherwise would have stayed in full-time education.

Advocates of minimum wage laws view the policy as one way to raise the income of the working poor. They correctly point out that workers who earn the minimum wage can afford only a meagre standard of living. They admit that it may have some adverse effects, including a possible rise in unemployment, but they believe that these effects are small and that, all things considered, a higher minimum wage makes the poor better off. In other words they argue that the value of the benefits of a minimum wage are greater than the value of the costs and so such a policy is worth putting into practice.

Opponents of the minimum wage contend that it is not the best way to combat poverty since it affects only the income of those in employment and may raise unemployment, and because not all minimum wage workers are heads of households trying to help their families escape poverty – some may be second earners or even third earners in relatively well-off households. To decide whether this argument is more powerful than the arguments of the advocates, economists will try and find ways to measure the size of the contrasting effects so that an informed decision can be made with regard to the value of the benefits versus the costs. This is often harder than it may at first appear but is a crucial part of an economist's work.

In short, the effects of the minimum wage on the labour market are complicated. It is one of those cases where there are no clear-cut answers: it all depends on what assumptions you make. At this point you may throw up your hands in despair and ask 'so what's the point of studying economics if it can't tell me one way or the other if introducing a minimum wage benefits the poor or not?' But all our brief economic analysis of the minimum wage has shown is that the issue is very complex: don't shoot the messenger for telling you so. The economist tries to shed light on this complexity so that the costs and benefits of such a policy can be better understood; this is partly why economics is so valuable and so fascinating!

THE OTHER FACTORS OF PRODUCTION: LAND AND CAPITAL

We have seen how firms decide how much labour to hire and how these decisions determine workers' wages. At the same time that firms are hiring workers, they are also deciding about other inputs to production. For example, our apple-producing firm might have to choose the size of its apple orchard and the number of ladders to make available to its apple pickers. We can think of the firm's factors of production as falling into three categories: labour, land and capital.

For our apple firm, the capital stock includes the ladders used to climb the trees, the baskets that are used to collect the picked apples, trucks used to transport the apples, the buildings used to store the apples, and even the trees themselves.

Equilibrium in the Markets for Land and Capital

What determines how much the owners of land and capital earn for their contribution to the production process? Before answering this question, we need to distinguish between two prices: the purchase price and the rental price. The *purchase price* of land or capital is the price a person pays to own that factor of production indefinitely. The *rental price* is the price a person pays to use that factor for a limited period of time. It is important to keep this distinction in mind because, as we will see, these prices are determined by somewhat different economic forces.

Having defined these terms, we can now apply the theory of factor demand that we developed for the labour market to the markets for land and capital. The wage is, after all, simply the rental price of labour. Therefore, much of what we have learned about wage determination applies also to the rental prices of land and capital. As Figure 14.8 illustrates, the rental price of land, shown in panel (a), and the rental price of capital, shown in panel (b), are determined by supply and demand. Moreover, the demand for land and capital is determined just like the demand for labour. That is, when our apple-producing firm is deciding how much land and how many ladders to rent, it follows the same logic as when deciding how many workers to hire. For both land and capital, the firm increases the quantity hired until the value of the factor's marginal product equals the factor's price. Thus, the demand curve for each factor reflects the marginal productivity of that factor.

We can now explain how much income goes to labour, how much goes to landowners and how much goes to the owners of capital. As long as the firms using the factors of production are competitive and profit-maximizing, each factor's rental price must equal the value of the marginal product for that factor: labour, land and capital each earn the value of their marginal contribution to the production process.

FIGURE 14.8

The Markets for Land and Capital

Supply and demand determine the compensation paid to the owners of land, as shown in panel (a), and the compensation paid to the owners of capital, as shown in panel (b). The demand for each factor, in turn, depends on the value of the marginal product of that factor.

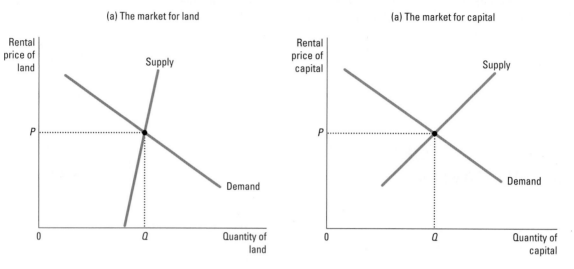

Now consider the purchase price of land and capital. The rental price and the purchase price are obviously related: buyers are willing to pay more for a piece of land or capital if it produces a valuable stream of rental income. And, as we have just seen, the equilibrium rental income at any point in time equals the value of that factor's marginal product. Therefore, the equilibrium purchase price of a piece of land or capital depends on both the current value of the marginal product and the value of the marginal product expected to prevail in the future.

Linkages Among the Factors of Production

We have seen that the price paid for any factor of production – labour, land, or capital – equals the value of the marginal product of that factor. The marginal product of any factor, in turn, depends on the quantity of that factor that is available. Because of diminishing marginal product, a factor in abundant supply has a low marginal product and thus a low price, and a factor in scarce supply has a high marginal product and a high price. As a result, when the supply of a factor falls, its equilibrium factor price rises and so firm's costs rise.

When the supply of any factor changes, however, the effects are not limited to the market for that factor. In most situations, factors of production are used together in a way that makes the productivity of each factor dependent on the quantities of the other factors available to be used in the production process. As a result, a change in the supply of any one factor alters the earnings of all the factors.

For example, suppose one night lightning strikes the storehouse in which are kept the ladders that the apple pickers use to pick apples from the orchards, and many of the ladders are destroyed in the ensuing fire. What happens to the earnings of the various factors of production? Most obviously, the supply of ladders falls and, therefore, the equilibrium rental price of ladders rises. Those owners who were lucky enough to avoid damage to their ladders now earn a higher return when they rent out their ladders to the firms that produce apples.

Yet the effects of this event do not stop at the ladder market. Because there are fewer ladders with which to work, the workers who pick apples have a smaller marginal product. Thus, the reduction in the supply of ladders reduces the demand for the labour of apple pickers, and this causes the equilibrium wage to fall.

This story shows a general lesson: an event that changes the supply of any factor of production can alter the earnings of all the factors. The change in earnings of any factor can be found by analyzing the impact of the event on the value of the marginal product of that factor.

FYI

What is Capital Income?

Labour income is an easy concept to understand: it is the wages and salaries that workers get from their employers. The income earned by capital, however, is less obvious.

In our analysis, we have been implicitly assuming that households own the economy's stock of capital – equipment, machinery, computers, warehouses and so forth – and rent it to the firms that use it. Capital income, in this case, is the rent that households receive for the use of their capital. This assumption simplified our analysis of how capital owners are compensated, but it is not entirely realistic. In fact, firms usually own the capital they use and, therefore, they receive the earnings from this capital.

These earnings from capital, however, eventually get paid to households. Some of the earnings are paid in the form of interest to those house-

holds who have lent money to firms (anyone who has savings in a financial institution, who pays into a pension fund or an insurance policy is indirectly actually lending money to businesses!). Bondholders and bank depositors are two examples of recipients of interest. Thus, when you receive interest on your bank account, that income is part of the economy's capital income.

In addition, some of the earnings from capital are paid to households in the form of dividends. Dividends are payments by a firm to the firm's shareholders. A shareholder is a person who has bought a share in the ownership of the firm and, therefore, is entitled to share in the firm's profits. (This is usually called an equity or, quite simply, a share.)

A firm does not have to pay out all of its earnings to households in the

form of interest and dividends. Instead, it can retain some earnings within the firm and use these earnings to buy additional capital. Although these retained earnings do not get paid to the firm's shareholders, the shareholders benefit from them nonetheless. Because retained earnings increase the amount of capital the firm owns, they tend to increase future earnings and, thereby, the value of the firm's equities.

These institutional details are interesting and important, but they do not alter our conclusion about the income earned by the owners of capital. Capital is paid according to the value of its marginal product, regardless of whether this income gets transmitted to households in the form of interest or dividends or whether it is kept within firms as retained earnings.

EARNINGS AND DISCRIMINATION

Our analysis of the labour market so far has largely been based on an assumption of a competitive market. Imperfections in the market will lead to anomalies in the way in which workers are paid and firms have to face the issues and consequences that arise as a result of these imperfections. Governments pass laws and regulations aiming to reduce the effects of imperfections in the market and firms are often the ones which pick up the bill in terms of the additional costs that have to be paid to meet legislation and regulation. In this section we consider how the characteristics of workers and jobs affect labour supply, labour demand and equilibrium wages.

Compensating Differentials

The sort of jobs firms offer varies. The wage is only one of many job attributes that have to be taken into account. Some jobs require few skills, and are 'easy' and safe; others might require considerable skill, experience and may be very dull, whilst others can be very dangerous. The 'better' the job as gauged by these non-monetary characteristics, the more people there are who are willing (and able) to do the job at any given wage. In other words, the supply of labour for jobs requiring few skills or no experience is greater than the supply of labour for highly skilled and dangerous jobs. As a result, 'good' jobs will tend to have lower equilibrium wages than 'bad' jobs. Economists use the term **compensating differential** to refer to a difference in wages that arises from non-monetary characteristics of different jobs.

compensating differential a difference in wages that arises to offset the non-monetary characteristics of different jobs

Human Capital

Human capital is the accumulation of investments in people. The most important type of human capital is education. Like all forms of capital, education represents an expenditure of resources at one point in time to raise productivity in the future. But, unlike an investment in other forms of capital, an investment in education is tied to a specific person, and this linkage is what makes it human capital.

human capital the accumulation of investments in people, such as education and on-the-job training

Not surprisingly, workers with more human capital on average earn more than those with less human capital. University graduates in Europe and North America, for example, earn almost twice as much as those workers who end their education after secondary school. This large difference tends to be even larger in less developed countries, where educated workers are in scarce supply.

It is easy to see why education raises wages from the perspective of supply and demand. Firms – the demanders of labour – are willing to pay more for the highly educated because highly educated workers have higher marginal products. Workers – the suppliers of labour – are willing to pay the cost of becoming educated only if there is a reward for doing so. In essence, the difference in wages between highly educated workers and less educated workers may be considered a compensating differential for the cost of becoming educated.

Ability, Effort and Chance

Natural ability is important for workers in all occupations. Because of heredity and upbringing, people differ in their physical and mental attributes. Some people have physical and mental strength whereas others have less of both. Some people are able to solve complex problems, others less so. Some people are outgoing, others awkward in social situations. These and many other personal characteristics determine how productive workers are and, therefore, play a role in determining the wages they earn.

Closely related to ability is effort. Some people are prepared to put long hours and considerable effort into their work whereas others are content to do what they are required to do and no more. We should not be surprised to find that those who put in more effort may be more productive and earn higher wages. To some extent, firms reward workers directly by paying people on the basis of what they produce. Salespeople, for instance, are often paid based on a percentage of the sales they make. At other times, greater effort is rewarded less directly in the form of a higher annual salary or a bonus.

Chance also plays a role in determining wages. If a person attended college to learn how to repair televisions with vacuum tubes and then found this skill made obsolete by the invention of solid-state electronics, he or she would end up earning a low wage compared to others with similar years of training. The low wage of this worker is due to chance – a phenomenon that economists recognize but do not shed much light on.

How important are ability, effort and chance in determining wages? It is hard to say, because ability, effort and chance are hard to measure. But indirect evidence suggests that they are very important. When labour economists study wages, they relate a worker's wage to those variables that can be measured – years of schooling, years of experience, age and job characteristics. Although all of these measured variables affect a worker's wage as theory predicts, they account for less than half of the variation in wages in our economy. Because so much of the variation in wages is left unexplained, omitted variables, including ability, effort and chance, must play an important role.

An Alternative View of Education: Signalling

Earlier we discussed the human capital view of education, according to which schooling raises workers' wages because it makes them more productive. Although this view is widely accepted, some economists have proposed an alternative theory, which emphasizes that firms use educational attainment as a way of sorting between high-ability and low-ability workers. According to this alternative view, when people earn a university degree, for instance, they do not become more productive (indeed there are often complaints that graduates leave university without the skills that business needs), but they do *signal* their high ability to prospective employers. Because it is easier for high-ability people to earn a university degree than it is for low-ability people, more high-ability people get college degrees. As a result, it is rational for firms to interpret a college degree as a signal of ability.

The signalling theory of education is similar to the signalling theory of advertising discussed in Chapter 7. In the signalling theory of education, schooling has no real productivity benefit, but the worker signals his innate productivity to employers by his willingness to spend years at school. In both cases, an action is being taken not for its intrinsic benefit but because the willingness to take that action conveys private information to someone observing it.

Thus, we now have two views of education: the human capital theory and the signalling theory. Both views can explain why more educated workers tend to earn more than less educated workers. According to the human capital view, education makes workers more productive; according to the signalling view, education is correlated with natural ability. But the two views have radically different predictions for the effects of policies that aim to increase educational attainment. According to the human capital view, increasing educational levels for all workers would raise all workers' productivity and thereby their wages. According to the signalling view, education does not enhance productivity, so raising all workers' educational levels would not affect wages.

Most likely, the truth lies somewhere between these two extremes. The benefits to education are probably a combination of the productivity enhancing effects of human capital and the productivity revealing effects of signalling. The open question is the relative size of these two effects.

Above-Equilibrium Wages: Minimum Wage Laws, Unions and Efficiency Wages

For some workers, wages are set above the level that brings supply and demand into equilibrium. Let's consider three reasons why this might be so.

One reason for above-equilibrium wages is minimum wage laws. Most workers in the economy are not affected by these laws because their equilibrium wages are well above the legal minimum. But for some workers, especially the least skilled and experienced, minimum wage laws raise wages above the level they would earn in an unregulated labour market.

A second reason that wages might rise above their equilibrium level is the market power of labour unions. A **union** is a worker association that bargains with employers over wages and working conditions. Unions often raise wages above the level that would prevail without a union, perhaps because they can threaten to withhold labour from the firm by calling a **strike**. Studies suggest that union workers earn about 10 to 20 per cent more than similar non-union workers.

A third reason for above-equilibrium wages is suggested by the theory of **efficiency wages**. This theory holds that a firm can find it profitable to pay high wages because doing so increases the productivity of its workers. In particular, high wages may reduce worker turnover (hiring and training new workers is an expensive business), increase worker effort, and raise the quality of workers who apply for jobs at the firm. In addition, a firm may feel it has to offer high wages in order to attract and keep the best people – this has been an argument put forward by the banking sector in response to plans by governments in Europe to

union a worker association that bargains with employers over wages and working conditions

strike the organized withdrawal of labour from a firm by a union

efficiency wages above-equilibrium wages paid by firms in order to increase worker productivity

tax bankers' earning in the wake of the financial crisis. If this theory is correct, then some firms may choose to pay their workers more than they would normally earn.

Above-equilibrium wages, whether caused by minimum wage laws, unions or efficiency wages, have similar effects on the labour market. In particular, pushing a wage above the equilibrium level raises the quantity of labour supplied and reduces the quantity of labour demanded. The result is a surplus of labour, or unemployment. The study of unemployment and the public policies aimed to deal with it is usually considered a topic within macroeconomics, so it goes beyond the scope of this chapter. But it would be a mistake to ignore these issues completely when analyzing earnings. Although most wage differences can be understood while maintaining the assumption of equilibrium in the labour market, above-equilibrium wages play a role in some cases.

> **Quick Quiz** Define *compensating differential* and give an example.
> • Give two reasons why more educated workers earn more than less educated workers.

THE ECONOMICS OF DISCRIMINATION

discrimination the offering of different opportunities to similar individuals who differ only by race, ethnic group, sex, age or other personal characteristics

Another source of differences in wages is discrimination. **Discrimination** occurs when the marketplace offers different opportunities to similar individuals who differ only by race, ethnic group, sex, age or other personal characteristics. Discrimination reflects some people's prejudice against certain groups in society. Although discrimination is an emotionally charged topic that often generates heated debate, economists try to study the topic objectively in order to separate myth from reality.

Measuring Labour Market Discrimination

How much does discrimination in labour markets affect the earnings of different groups of workers? This question is important, but answering it is not easy.

There is no doubt that different groups of workers earn substantially different wages. Different reports show that inequalities in incomes and earnings persist in many industrialized countries. Women, for example, often are reported to earn less in terms of median hourly pay for all employees and less than men for those working full time. Reports also note that people from different ethnic backgrounds are paid at different rates.

Taken at face value, such differentials appear to be evidence that there is widespread discrimination in countries against those from ethnic minorities and women. Yet there is a potential problem with this inference. Even in a labour market free of discrimination, different people have different wages. People differ in the amount of human capital they have and in the kinds of work they are able and willing to do. The wage differences we observe in the economy are, to some extent, attributable to the determinants of equilibrium wages we discussed in the preceding section. Simply observing differences in wages among broad groups – whites and blacks, men and women – does not prove that employers discriminate.

Consider, for example, the role of human capital. Whether an individual has a degree can account for some of these differences and, in addition, the type of degree can also have an impact, for example, a first class degree in economics or maths might have more 'value' in the labour market than a degree in media arts or theatre. Some of the difference between wages can be traced to differences in educational attainment. Moreover, human capital may be more important in explaining wage differentials than measures of years of schooling suggest. In many countries measures of the quality of education across regions of in terms of expenditure, class size and so on, vary considerably.

If we could measure the quality as well as the quantity of education, the differences in human capital among these groups would seem even larger. The Federal Bureau of Statistics in Germany points out that gender pay differences in Germany may be due to a number of factors including differences in educational attainment, a high proportion of women work in part-time occupations and the type of employment they go into; many of the jobs women enter tend to be low-skill, low-paid jobs.

Human capital acquired in the form of job experience can also help explain wage differences. In particular, women tend to have less job experience on average than men. One reason is that female labour force participation has increased in industrialized economies over the past several decades. Because of this historic change, in both Europe and North America, the average female worker today is younger than the average male worker. In addition, women are more likely to interrupt their careers to raise children. For both reasons, the experience of the average female worker is less than the experience of the average male worker.

Yet another source of wage differences is compensating differentials. Men and women do not always choose the same type of work, and this fact may help explain some of the earnings differential between men and women. For example, women are more likely to be personal assistants or receptionists and men are more likely to be lorry drivers. (Some people would argue that women get 'ushered' into these types of jobs because of stereotypes.) The relative wages of personal assistants, receptionists and lorry drivers depend in part on the working conditions of each job. Because these non-monetary aspects are hard to measure, it is difficult to gauge the practical importance of compensating differentials in explaining the wage differences that we observe.

In the end, the study of wage differences among groups does not establish any clear conclusion about the prevalence of discrimination in labour markets. Most economists believe that some of the observed wage differentials are attributable to discrimination, but there is no consensus about how much. The only conclusion about which economists are in consensus is a negative one: because the differences in average wages among groups in part reflect differences in human capital and job characteristics, they do not by themselves say anything about how much discrimination there is in the labour market.

Of course, differences in human capital among groups of workers may themselves reflect discrimination. The less rigorous curriculums historically offered to female students, for instance, can be considered a discriminatory practice. Similarly, schools which suffer from low quality may be traced to other underlying social problems. In this case, the disease is social and political, even if the symptom is economic.

Support groups exist to help those who believe they are suffering from discrimination.

Discrimination by Employers

Let's now turn from measurement to the economic forces that lie behind discrimination in labour markets. If one group in society receives a lower wage than another group, even after controlling for human capital and job characteristics, who is to blame for this differential?

The answer is not obvious. It might seem natural to blame employers for discriminatory wage differences. After all, employers make the hiring decisions that determine labour demand and wages. If some groups of workers earn lower wages than they should, then it seems that employers are responsible. Yet many economists are sceptical of this easy answer. They believe that competitive, market economies provide a natural antidote to employer discrimination. That antidote is called the profit motive.

Imagine an economy in which workers are differentiated by their hair colour. Blondes and brunettes have the same skills, experience and work ethic. Yet, because of discrimination, employers prefer not to hire workers with blonde hair. Thus, the demand for blondes is lower than it otherwise would be. As a result, blondes earn a lower wage than brunettes.

How long can this wage differential persist? In this economy, there is an easy way for a firm to beat out its competitors: it can hire blonde workers. By hiring blondes, a firm pays lower wages and thus has lower costs than firms that hire brunettes. Over time, more and more 'blonde' firms enter the market to take advantage of this cost advantage. The existing 'brunette' firms have higher costs and, therefore, begin to lose money when faced with the new competitors. These losses induce the brunette firms to go out of business. Eventually, the entry of blonde firms and the exit of brunette firms cause the demand for blonde workers to rise and the demand for brunette workers to fall. This process continues until the wage differential disappears.

Put simply, business owners who care only about making money are at an advantage when competing against those who also care about discriminating. As a result, firms that do not discriminate tend to replace those that do. In this way, competitive markets have a natural remedy for employer discrimination.

CASE STUDY

Becker's 'Employer Taste' Model

As you might expect by now, economists have spent some time looking at the economics of discrimination. One important piece of research into this area is from Nobel Prize winner Gary Becker from the University of Chicago, who in 1971 revised his earlier 1957 work on the economics of discrimination. The basis of the employer taste model is that (for whatever reason) some employees will resist working with other employees, possibly because of gender or race. People may, therefore, have a 'taste' for only working with certain groups of people. Those outside this accepted group may end up being disadvantaged as a result.

Assume that a UK firm, which grows asparagus, hires workers to cut the spears. It has a choice of employing locals or migrant workers. Local people have a prejudice against migrant workers for some reason. Our analysis of a competitive firm assumes that workers will be employed up to the point at which the wage equals the marginal revenue product of labour. Assume that both local and migrant workers have the same level of productivity. If the firm has to employ workers at a going wage (which is above the minimum wage) then it may choose not to employ workers from the disadvantaged group because of the preferences of its core workforce. If, however, the firm is able to pay workers from the disadvantaged group lower wages then it faces a trade-off. There is an incentive for it to increase profits by employing these 'disadvantaged' workers – the migrant workers from Europe. If migrant workers were prepared to work for the minimum wage then the firm could lower its costs and increase profit as a result.

A discriminatory firm might employ some migrant workers but would pay these workers a lower wage to avoid upsetting their local workers. This is the 'employer taste' model – discrimination will exist because employers do not employ labour from certain genders, race, etc. unless the workers are prepared to accept lower wages. This discrimination may continue whilst there is some limit to the competition in the labour market – in this case it might be that all firms are prepared to act in the same way.

However, if there were other asparagus farms in the area who were not discriminatory then they might choose to hire all workers at the minimum wage which would increase their overall profits. Such firms would also employ more workers (remember that the lower the wage rate the more workers a firm is willing to employ). There could be an influx of migrant workers to the area who are willing to take advantage of the jobs available. These non-discriminatory firms could not only produce more output but at a lower wage cost per unit and so make more profit, possibly driving out the discriminatory firm from the industry.

In the UK, such a situation has manifested itself in recent years. The extension of membership of the EU in 2004 led to an increase in the number of migrant workers from countries such as Poland, Lithuania and the Czech Republic coming to Britain to find work. Many of these workers appeared willing to take on jobs that paid relatively low wages, such as cutting asparagus spears. In Cambridgeshire in the south-east of England, a large number found work on the farms in the region picking and packing fruit and vegetables. In the town of Wisbech, for example, there are over 2000 'local' people who are unemployed but there have been around 9000 migrant workers who have secured jobs in the area – mostly in jobs where the wages are traditionally low.

The sensitivity of the situation in Wisbech with some of the local unemployed blaming migrant workers for their lack of work is difficult. Some employers have been accused of exploiting migrant labour by paying them low wages but some counter that they are paying at least the minimum wage and that they find migrant workers not only willing to work for lower pay but also that their productivity levels are relatively high compared with some 'local' labour. In this case not only are migrant workers prepared to work for lower wages but their marginal product is higher at each price (wage). Some farmers claim that 'local' workers are not prepared to do the sort of work that is available and believe that it is too low paid. It seems that regardless of discrimination, employers are more concerned with getting value for money from their employees and are prepared to put profit before discrimination.

Quick Quiz Why is it hard to establish whether a group of workers is being discriminated against? • Explain how profit-maximizing firms tend to eliminate discriminatory wage differentials. • How might a discriminatory wage differential persist?

? **what if…**a government decided to pass a law stating that every firm employing over 100 people had to have a proportion of male and female workers, able bodied and disabled workers and ethnic minorities which closely reflected the proportions found in society as a whole. Would this help reduce discrimination?

CONCLUSION

The theory developed in this chapter is called the *neoclassical theory of distribution*. According to the neoclassical theory, the amount paid to each factor of production depends on the supply and demand for that factor. The demand, in turn, depends on that particular factor's marginal productivity. In equilibrium, each factor of production earns the value of its marginal contribution to the production of goods and services.

The neoclassical theory of distribution is widely accepted. Most economists begin with the neoclassical theory when trying to explain how an economy's income is distributed among the economy's various members. In the later chapters, we consider the distribution of income in more detail. As you will see, the neoclassical theory provides the framework for this discussion.

Even at this point you can use the theory to answer the question that began this chapter: why are computer programmers paid more than petrol station attendants? It is because programmers can produce a good of greater market value than can a petrol station attendant. People are willing to pay dearly for a good computer game, but they are willing to pay little to have their petrol pumped and their windscreen washed. The wages of these workers reflect the market prices of the goods they produce. If people suddenly got tired of using computers and decided to spend more time driving, the prices of these goods would change, and so would the equilibrium wages of these two groups of workers.

In competitive markets, workers earn a wage equal to the value of their marginal contribution to the production of goods and services. There are, however, many things that affect the value of the marginal product. Firms pay more for workers who are more talented, more diligent, more experienced and more educated because these workers are more productive. Firms pay less to those workers against whom customers discriminate because these workers contribute less to revenue.

IN THE NEWS

The Labour Market and Wages

This article looks at a situation where intern workers at hi-tech firms in the United States can earn more for twelve weeks work than Chinese workers in factories earn in two years. Is this simply due to exploitation of workers in China or is it really down to supply and demand?

Karl Marx Tells Us About Chinese Manufacturing Wages and Silicon Valley Interns

There's a lot that old Karl Marx got wrong, most of the stuff he worked out for himself for example. There's a lot he got right too, mostly the stuff he cribbed from earlier writers. And in that stuff he got right we can see the answer to this little conundrum: why Silicon Valley interns are getting, for three months work, about what a Chinese manufacturing worker gets in two years. It's all about the reserve army of the unemployed.

Here's what's happening with those interns on the West Coast [of the USA]:

Bay Area tech companies, already in a fierce fight for full-time hires, are now also battling to woo summer interns. Technology giants like Google Inc. have been expanding their summer-intern programs, while smaller tech companies are ramping up theirs in response – sometimes even luring candidates away from college.

Dropbox Inc. plans to hire 30 engineering interns for next summer, up from nine this year, says engineering manager Rian Hunter, who adds the company wants interns to comprise one-third of its engineering team. ...

'More interns means more opportunities to bring people to the company,' Mr. Hunter says, noting Dropbox is seeking people as young as college freshmen.

'Interns allow you to "try before you buy",' says Bump Technologies Inc. Chief Executive Dave Lieb, who plans to hire as many as 10 for next summer.

Workers on an assembly line at a Foxconn plant in China.

He says the 30-person company pays intern engineers about $10 000 for a roughly 12-week stint, similar to what other tech start-ups say they pay.

And we went through the situation for Chinese manufacturing workers, like those who produce for Apple and others at Foxconn, back here. They're getting perhaps $4500 a year in general, maybe $6000 a year at Foxconn. So it's fair enough to say that those interns are getting 2 years' worth of Chinese wages for their 12 weeks during the summer vacation.

And what we'd like to know is, why? Sure, we could look to their being trained engineers, not mid-skill level line workers. We could argue about different levels of productivity but that's likely to end up with us arguing that the Chinese should be paid more than the interns: they're likely to produce something saleable after all. The interns are, in one way of looking at it, being paid to come along for an extended job interview.

So, this is where we turn to Karl Marx and his idea of the reserve army of the unemployed. As Marx, quite correctly, pointed out, capitalists make a profit out of the labour they employ (OK, they hope to, but let's not argue with the other parts of Karl's philosophy about exploitation and so on). If and when worker productivity rises then the amount of profit that can be made rises. Which means that, as long as there are competing capitalists, greedy for the profit that they can make by employing this newly more productive labour, then wages will get bid up.

This fails in two different scenarios. The first is when we have monopoly capitalism (what we would now call a monopsony, a word unknown in his time, a single purchaser of labour), and the second is when there is a reserve army of the unemployed-when there is no competition for the labour as there are vast armies of it sitting around twiddling their thumbs and looking for something to do. For why compete and bid up the price of labour when you can just grab some more off the street?

And it's that that explains a goodly portion of the wage difference. Yes, I know, there is unemployment in the US. But unemployment among trained engineers in Silicon Valley, among those able to do the work and in the place where the work is done, is near non-existent. Thus there is no relevant army of the unemployed and thus wages get bid up in the manner we see.

Compare and contrast that with interns in media businesses: there are an awful lot of journalism majors on the look out for that first break which is why media businesses rarely pay for an internship and there's even been one or two rumours of people charging for them.

Or, compare and contrast that with the situation in China. These are not highly skilled positions: most people could do most of the work with a couple of week's training. And there is a relevant army of the unemployed to consider as well: the hundreds of millions (some say 800 million but that's probably too high) of peasants still living out there in the countryside. We would need *hundreds* of companies the size of Foxconn to absorb this labour and thus get that competition for labour pushing up the wages to labour.

Fortunately, this is what has been happening in China: not hundreds of giant companies, but tens of thousands, hundreds of thousands, of smaller ones starting up and employing labour, thus making that labour scarcer and so more expensive. You know, those factories making nice things for us to buy: they're exactly the ones that, entirely unintentionally, are improving the lot of the average Chinese worker.

Just as Marx insisted, indeed predicted, would happen as competing capitalists fight for the profits that can be made from labour when the reserve army of the unemployed begins to run out.

One final note though: just because Marx was right at times does not mean that you want to go drink the whole barrel of Kool-Aid. As I said at the top, Marx was right when he was copying, not when he was thinking.

Questions

1. The demand for workers with hi-tech skills is high. Why do you think this is?
2. If there is a shortage of workers with hi-tech skills, what would you expect to happen to the wage rate and to the number of people entering this industry?
3. Why might there be a continuing shortage of hi-tech workers in this industry? What does this tell you about this labour market?
4. What is meant by the phrase 'the reserve army of the unemployed'?
5. Discuss the relevance of the development of new businesses in China to the improvement in the welfare of Chinese workers (note we have used the term welfare and not just wages).

Source: http://www.forbes.com/sites/ timworstall/2012/02/01/karl-marx-tells-us- about-chinese-manufacturing-wages-and- silicon-valley-interns/

SUMMARY

- The economy's income is distributed in the markets for the factors of production. The three most important factors of production are labour, land and capital.

- The demand for factors, such as labour, is a derived demand that comes from firms that use the factors to produce goods and services. Competitive, profit-maximizing firms hire each factor up to the point at which the value of the marginal product of the factor equals its price.

- The supply of labour arises from individuals' trade-off between work and leisure. An upward sloping labour supply curve means that people respond to an increase in the wage by enjoying less leisure and working more hours.

- The price paid to each factor adjusts to balance the supply and demand for that factor. Because factor demand reflects the value of the marginal product of that factor, in equilibrium each factor is compensated according to its marginal contribution to the production of goods and services.

- Because factors of production are used together, the marginal product of any one factor depends on the quantities of all factors that are available. As a result, a change in the supply of one factor alters the equilibrium earnings of all the factors.

- Workers earn different wages for many reasons. To some extent, wage differentials compensate workers for job attributes. Other things equal, workers in hard, unpleasant jobs get paid more than workers in easy, pleasant jobs.

- Workers with more human capital get paid more than workers with less human capital. The return to accumulating human capital is high and has increased over the past two decades.

- Although years of education, experience and job characteristics affect earnings as theory predicts, there is much variation in earnings that cannot be explained by things that economists can measure. The unexplained variation in earnings is largely attributable to natural ability, effort and chance.

- Some economists have suggested that more educated workers earn higher wages not because education raises productivity but because workers with high natural ability use education as a way to signal their high ability to employers. If this signalling theory is correct, then increasing the educational attainment of all workers would not raise the overall level of wages.

- Wages are sometimes pushed above the level that brings supply and demand into balance. Three reasons for above-equilibrium wages are minimum wage laws, unions and efficiency wages.

- Some differences in earnings are attributable to discrimination on the basis of race, sex or other factors. Measuring the amount of discrimination is difficult, however, because one must correct for differences in human capital and job characteristics.

- Competitive markets tend to limit the impact of discrimination on wages. If the wages of a group of workers are lower than those of another group for reasons not related to marginal productivity, then non-discriminatory firms will be more profitable than discriminatory firms. Profit-maximizing behaviour, therefore, can reduce discriminatory wage differentials. Discrimination persists in competitive markets, however, if customers are willing to pay more to discriminatory firms or if the government passes laws requiring firms to discriminate.

KEY CONCEPTS

derived demand, p. 334
marginal product of labour, p. 336
value of the marginal product, p. 337

compensating differential, p. 350
human capital, p. 350
union, p. 351

strike, p. 351
efficiency wages, p. 351
discrimination, p. 352

QUESTIONS FOR REVIEW

1. Explain how a firm's production function is related to its marginal product of labour, how a firm's marginal product of labour is related to the value of its marginal product and how a firm's value of marginal product is related to its demand for labour.

2. Give two examples of events that could shift the demand for labour.

3. Give two examples of events that could shift the supply of labour.

4. Explain how the wage can adjust to balance the supply and demand for labour while simultaneously equalling the value of the marginal product of labour.

5. If the population of Norway suddenly grew because of a large immigration, what would you expect to happen to wages? What would happen to the rents earned by the owners of land and capital?

6. Why do coal miners get paid more than other workers with similar amounts of education?

7. How might education raise a worker's wage without raising the worker's productivity?

8. Give three reasons why a worker's wage might be above the level that balances supply and demand.

9. What difficulties arise in deciding whether a group of workers has a lower wage because of discrimination?

10. Give an example of how discrimination might persist in a competitive market.

PROBLEMS AND APPLICATIONS

1. Suppose that the government proposes a new law aimed at reducing heath care costs: all citizens are to be required to eat one apple daily.
   a. How would this apple-a-day law affect the demand and equilibrium price of apples?
   b. How would the law affect the marginal product and the value of the marginal product of apple pickers?
   c. How would the law affect the demand and equilibrium wage for apple pickers?

2. Show the effect of each of the following events on the market for labour in the computer manufacturing industry.
   a. The government buys personal computers for all university students.
   b. More university students graduate in engineering and computer science.
   c. Computer firms build new manufacturing factories.

3. Your enterprising uncle opens a sandwich shop that employs 7 people. The employees are paid €6 per hour and a sandwich sells for €13. If your uncle is maximizing his profit, what is the value of the marginal product of the last worker he hired? What is that worker's marginal product?

4. Suppose a harsh winter in Normandy destroys part of the French apple crop.
   a. Explain what happens to the price of apples and the marginal product of apple pickers as a result of the freeze. Can you say what happens to the demand for apple pickers? Why or why not?
   b. Suppose the price of apples doubles and the marginal product falls by 30 per cent. What happens to the equilibrium wage of apple pickers?
   c. Suppose the price of apples rises by 30 per cent and the marginal product falls by 50 per cent. What happens to the equilibrium wage of apple pickers?

5. In recent years, the United Kingdom has experienced a significant inflow of capital in the form of direct investment, especially from the Far East. For example, both Honda and Nissan have built car plants in the United Kingdom.
   a. Using a diagram of the UK capital market, show the effect of this inflow on the rental price of capital in the United Kingdom and on the quantity of capital in use.
   b. Using a diagram of the UK labour market, show the effect of the capital inflow on the average wage paid to UK workers.

6. Suppose that labour is the only input used by a perfectly competitive firm that can hire workers for €150 per day. The firm's production function is as follows:

Days of labour	Units of output
0	0
1	7
2	13
3	19
4	25
5	28
6	29

Each unit of output sells for €110. Plot the firm's demand for labour. How many days of labour should the firm hire? Show this point on your graph.

7. This chapter has assumed that labour is supplied by individual workers acting competitively. In some markets, however, the supply of labour is determined by a union of workers.
   a. Explain why the situation faced by a labour union may resemble the situation faced by a monopoly firm.
   b. The goal of a monopoly firm is to maximize profits. Is there an analogous goal for labour unions?
   c. Now extend the analogy between monopoly firms and unions. How do you suppose that the wage set by a union compares to the wage in a competitive market? How do you suppose employment differs in the two cases?
   d. What other goals might unions have that make unions different from monopoly firms?

8. A minimum wage law distorts the market for low-wage labour. To reduce this distortion, some economists advocate a two-tiered minimum wage system, with a regular minimum wage for adult workers and a lower, 'subminimum' wage for teenage workers. Give two reasons why a single minimum wage might distort the labour market for teenage workers more than it would the market for adult workers.

9. Hannah works for Joachim, whom she hates because of his snobbish attitude. Yet when she looks for other jobs, the best she can do is find a job paying €15 000 less than her current salary. Should she take the job? Analyze Hannah's situation from an economic point of view.

10. Imagine that someone were to offer you a choice: you could spend four years studying at the world's best university, but you would have to keep your attendance there a secret. Or you could be awarded an official degree from the world's best university, but you couldn't actually attend (although no one need ever know this). Which choice do you think would enhance your future earnings more? What does your answer say about the debate over signalling versus human capital in the role of education?

15 FINANCIAL MARKETS

LEARNING OBJECTIVES

In this chapter you will:

- Learn the relationship between present value and future value

- Learn how risk-averse businesses reduce the risk they face

- Analyze how asset prices are determined

- Learn about some of the important financial institutions in the economy

- Develop a model of the supply and demand for loanable funds in financial markets

- Use the loanable funds model to analyze various government policies

- Consider how government budget deficits affect the economy

After reading this chapter you should be able to:

- Choose between receiving €100 now or €120 two years from now, given an interest rate of 8 per cent

- List and describe four important types of financial institutions

- Describe the relationship between saving, government deficits and investment

- Explain the slope of the supply and demand for loanable funds

- Shift supply and demand curves in a model of the loanable funds market in response to a change in taxes on interest or investment

- Shift supply and demand curves in a model of the loanable funds market in response to a change in the government's budget deficit

INTRODUCTION

Imagine that you have just graduated from university (with a degree in economics, of course) and you decide to start your own business – an economic forecasting firm. Before you make any money selling your forecasts, you have to incur substantial costs to set up your business. You have to buy computers with which to make your forecasts, as well as desks, chairs and filing cabinets to furnish your new office. Each of these items is a type of capital that your firm will use to produce and sell its services.

How do you obtain the funds to invest in these capital goods? Perhaps you are able to pay for them out of your past savings. More likely, however, like most entrepreneurs, you do not have enough money of your own to finance the start of your business. As a result, you have to get the money you need from other sources.

There are various ways for you to finance these capital investments. You could borrow the money, perhaps from a bank or from a friend or relative. In this case, you would promise not only to return the money at a later date but also to pay interest for the use of the money (assuming you were not raising the finance under Islamic principles in which case a different arrangement would exist). Alternatively, you could convince someone to provide the money you need for your business in exchange for a share of your future profits, whatever they might happen to be. In either case, your investment in computers and office equipment is being financed by someone else's saving.

financial markets financial institutions through which savers can directly provide funds to borrowers

Financial markets consists of those institutions in the economy that help to match one person's saving with another person's investment and how firms are able to access capital for initial development and for growth.

At any time, some people want to save some of their income for the future, and others want to borrow in order to finance investments in new and growing businesses. What brings these two groups of people together? (Not physically of course!) What ensures that the supply of funds from those who want to save, balances the demand for funds from those who want to invest? This chapter examines how the financial markets work and how firms can access capital.

FINANCIAL INSTITUTIONS IN THE ECONOMY

At the broadest level, the financial system moves the economy's scarce resources from savers (people who spend less than they earn) to borrowers (people who spend more than they earn). Savers could include individuals and businesses, and firms will want to borrow for various reasons, for example, to start a business, to invest in new equipment or machines, to take over another firm, to set up a new subsidiary or to expand into new markets. Savers supply their money to the financial system with the expectation that they will get it back with interest at a later date. Firms demand money from the financial system with the knowledge that they will be required to pay it back with interest at a later date.

Financial Markets

Financial markets are the institutions through which a person who wants to save can directly supply funds to a person who wants to borrow. Two of the most important financial markets in advanced economies are the bond market and the stock market.

The Bond Market   When BP, the oil company, wants to borrow to finance a major new oil exploration project, it can borrow directly from the public. It does this by selling bonds. A **bond** is a certificate of indebtedness that specifies the obligations of the borrower to the holder of the bond. Put simply, a bond is an IOU. It identifies the time at which the loan will be repaid, called the *date of maturity*, and the rate of interest that

bond a certificate of indebtedness

will be paid periodically (called the *coupon*) until the loan matures. The buyer of a bond gives his or her money to BP in exchange for this promise of interest and eventual repayment of the amount borrowed (called the *principal*). The buyer can hold the bond until maturity or can sell the bond at an earlier date to someone else.

An image of a bond certificate issued in 1913 for the North Butte Mining Company. The bond has a principal of $1000 and a coupon of 5 per cent.

There are literally millions of bonds traded in advanced economies. When large corporations or the national government, or even local governments, need to borrow in order to finance the purchase of a new factory, a new jet fighter or a new school, they often do so by issuing bonds. If you look at the business section of any national newspaper or online, you will find a listing of the prices and interest rates on some of the most important bond issues. Although these bonds differ in many ways, two characteristics of bonds are most important.

The first characteristic is a bond's *term* – the length of time until the bond matures. Some bonds have short terms, such as a few months, while others have terms as long as 30 years. (The British government has even issued a bond that never matures, called a *perpetuity*. This bond pays interest forever, but the principal is never repaid.) The interest rate on a bond depends, in part, on its term. Long-term bonds are riskier than short-term bonds because holders of long-term bonds have to wait longer for repayment of principal. If a holder of a long-term bond needs his money earlier than the distant date of maturity, he has no choice but to sell the bond to someone else, perhaps at a reduced price. To compensate for this risk, long-term bonds usually (but not always) pay higher interest rates than short-term bonds.

? what if... demand for a bond increased – what would happen to its price and the yield from the bond?

The second important characteristic of a bond is its *credit risk* – the probability that the borrower will fail to pay some of the interest or principal. Such a failure to pay is called a *default*. Borrowers can (and sometimes do) default on their loans by declaring bankruptcy. When bond buyers perceive that the probability of default is high, they demand a higher interest rate to compensate them for this risk. Some government bonds are considered a safe credit risk, such as those from Germany, for example, and tend to pay low interest rates. Others are much more risky and the interest rate attached to these bonds is high, for example, the government bonds issued by Greece, Portugal, Italy and Spain in 2011–2013. Financially shaky corporations raise money by issuing *junk bonds,* which pay very high interest rates; in recent years some countries' debt has been graded as 'junk'. Buyers of bonds can judge credit risk by checking with various private agencies, such as Standard & Poor's, which rate the credit risk of different bonds. Sometimes, these bonds are referred to euphemistically but less graphically as *below investment grade bonds.*

The Stock Market   Another way for BP to raise funds for its oil exploration project is to sell stock in the company. **Stock** represents ownership in a firm and is, therefore, a claim to the profits that the firm makes. For example, if BP sells a total of 1 000 000 shares of stock, then each share represents ownership of 1/1 000 000 of the business. A stock is also commonly referred to as a *share* or as an *equity,* which can be used with the term 'stock' more or less interchangeably.

> **stock (or share or equity)** a claim to partial ownership in a firm

The sale of stock to raise money is called *equity finance,* whereas the sale of bonds is called *debt finance.* Although businesses use both equity and debt finance to raise money for new investments, stocks and bonds are very different. The owner of BP shares is a part owner of BP; the owner of a BP bond is a creditor of the corporation. If BP is very profitable, the shareholders enjoy the benefits of these profits, whereas the bondholders get only the interest on their bonds. And if BP runs into financial difficulty, the bondholders are paid what they are due before shareholders receive anything at all. Compared to bonds, stocks offer the holder both higher risk and potentially higher return.

After a business issues stock by selling shares to the public, these shares trade among stockholders on organized stock exchanges. In these transactions, the business itself receives no money when its stock changes hands. Most of the world's countries have their own stock exchanges on which the shares of national companies trade.

The prices at which shares trade on stock exchanges are determined by the supply and demand for the stock in these companies. Because stock represents ownership in a business, the demand for a stock (and thus its price) reflects people's perception of the business's future profitability. When people become optimistic about a company's future, they raise their demand for its stock and thereby bid up the price of a share of stock. Conversely, when people come to expect a company to have little profit or even losses, the price of a share tends to fall.

Various stock indices are available to monitor the overall level of stock prices for any particular stock market. A *stock index* is computed as an average of a group of share prices. The Dow Jones Industrial Average has been computed regularly for the New York Stock Exchange since 1896. It is now based on the prices of the shares of 30 major US companies. The Financial Times Stock Exchange (FTSE) 100 Index is based on the top 100 companies (according to the total value of their shares) listed on the London Stock Exchange (LSE), while the FTSE All-Share Index is based on all companies listed on the LSE. Indices of prices on the Frankfurt stock market, based on 30 and 100 companies respectively, are the DAX 30 and DAX 100. The NIKKEI 225 (or just plain NIKKEI Index) is based on the largest 225 companies, in terms of market value of shares, traded on the Tokyo Stock Exchange.

Because share prices reflect expected profitability, stock indices are watched closely as possible indicators of future economic conditions.

Financial Intermediaries

Organized financial markets trade in a wide variety of financial and commodity products bringing together buyers and sellers from across the globe.

Financial intermediaries are financial institutions through which savers can indirectly provide funds to borrowers. The term *intermediary* reflects the role of these institutions in standing between savers and borrowers. Here we consider two of the most important financial intermediaries – banks and investment funds.

> **financial intermediaries** financial institutions through which savers can indirectly provide funds to borrowers

Banks   If the owner of a small restaurant wants to finance an expansion of his business, he probably takes a strategy quite different from BP. Unlike BP, a small businessman would find it difficult to raise funds in the bond and stock markets. Most buyers of stocks and bonds prefer to buy those issued by larger, more familiar companies. The small businessman, therefore, most likely finances his business expansion with a loan from a bank.

Banks are the financial intermediaries with which people are most familiar. A primary function of banks is to take in deposits from people who want to save and use these deposits to make loans to people who want to borrow. Banks pay depositors interest on their deposits and charge borrowers slightly higher interest on their loans. The difference between these rates of interest covers the banks' costs and returns some profit to the owners of the banks.

Besides being financial intermediaries, banks play a second important role in the economy: they facilitate purchases of goods and services by allowing people to transfer money from their account to the account of the person or corporation they are buying something from. In other words, banks help create a special asset that people can use as a *medium of exchange*. A medium of exchange is an item that people can easily use to engage in transactions. A bank's role in providing a medium of exchange distinguishes it from many other financial institutions. Stocks and bonds, like bank deposits, are a possible *store of value* for the wealth that people have accumulated in past saving.

Investment Funds   A financial intermediary of increasing importance is the investment fund. An **investment fund** is an institution that sells shares to the public and uses the proceeds to buy a selection, or *portfolio,* of various types of shares, bonds, or both shares and bonds. The shareholder of the investment fund accepts all the risk and return associated with the portfolio. If the value of the portfolio rises, the shareholder benefits; if the value of the portfolio falls, the shareholder suffers the loss. These intermediaries are important in providing the lifeblood of finance to businesses.

investment fund an institution that sells shares to the public and uses the proceeds to buy a portfolio of stocks and bonds

> **Quick Quiz**   What is stock? What is a bond? How are they different? How are they similar?

We know that firms will raise finance in different ways and through different intermediaries. The decision about what to borrow, how much to borrow, from whom, for how long and at what price are key decisions that businesses need to take at some point in their existence if not at the very outset. Invariably, a business will borrow money to finance an investment which will only begin to yield streams of income at some point in the future. For example, an oil company may raise finance to invest in exploration which may result in a successful discovery and supplies of oil flowing some years after the initial discovery. Those oil flows may then continue for the next 30 years generating income streams. A pharmaceutical company may spend many years researching and developing a new drug which may bring returns for a limited period of time depending on whether it is able to take out a patent to protect its discovery.

Businesses take decisions on such investments on the basis of whether the expected returns over a period of time are greater than the cost of the investment and, in many cases, on the size of the difference between the expected return and the cost. For example, if an investment only brought a return of 2 per cent over a ten-year period then a firm may decide that is not enough but would go ahead with the investment if the expected return was 8 per cent over the same period.

One important factor here is time – sums of money are not worth the same at different time periods and so a firm not only has to make a decision based on borrowing money at a rate of interest today to gain returns over a period of time in the future, but what the risk involved in making that decision might be. Such decisions might have a significant impact on the value of a company. We are now going to turn to these three topics. First, we discuss how to compare sums of money at different points in time. Secondly, we discuss how to manage risk. Thirdly, we build on our analysis of time and risk to examine what determines the value of an asset, such as a share of stock.

CASE STUDY

Financial Crises

In 2008 and 2009, the US economy and many other major economies around the world experienced a financial crisis, which in turn led to a deep downturn in global economic activity. Here we outline the key elements of financial crises.

The first element of a financial crisis is a large decline in some asset prices. In 2008 and 2009, that asset was real estate. The price of housing, after experiencing a boom earlier in the decade, fell by about 30 per cent over just a few years. Such a large decline in real estate prices had not been seen in the United States since the 1930s.

The second element of a financial crisis is insolvencies at financial institutions. In 2008 and 2009, many banks and other financial firms had in effect placed bets on real estate prices by holding mortgages backed by that real estate. When house prices fell, large numbers of homeowners stopped repaying their loans. These defaults pushed several financial institutions toward bankruptcy.

The third element of a financial crisis is a decline in confidence in financial institutions. While some deposits in banks are insured by government policies, not all are. As insolvencies mounted, every financial institution became a possible candidate for the next bankruptcy. Individuals and firms with uninsured deposits in those institutions pulled out their money. Facing a rash of withdrawals, banks started selling off assets (sometimes at reduced 'fire-sale' prices), and they cut back on new lending.

The fourth element of a financial crisis is a credit crunch. With many financial institutions facing difficulties, would-be borrowers had trouble getting loans, even if they had profitable investment projects. In essence, the financial system had trouble performing its normal function of directing the resources of savers into the hands of borrowers with the best investment opportunities.

The fifth element of a financial crisis is an economic downturn. With people unable to obtain financing for new investment projects, the overall demand for goods and services declined. As a result, for reasons we discuss more fully later in the book, national income fell and unemployment rose.

The sixth and final element of a financial crisis is a vicious circle. The economic downturn reduced the profitability of many companies and the value of many assets. Thus, we return to step one, and the problems in the financial system and the economic downturn reinforce each other.

Financial crises, such as that of 2008 and 2009, can have severe consequences. Fortunately, they do end. Financial institutions eventually get back on their feet, perhaps with some help from government policy, and they return to their normal function of financial intermediation but this can take many years.

MEASURING THE TIME VALUE OF MONEY

Imagine that someone offered to give you €100 today or €100 in ten years. Which would you choose? This is an easy question. Getting €100 today is better, because you can always deposit the money in a bank, still have it in ten years, and earn interest on the €100 along the way. The lesson: money today is more valuable than the same amount of money in the future.

Now consider a harder question: imagine that someone offered you €100 today or €200 in ten years. Which would you choose? To answer this question, you need some way to compare sums of money from different points in time. Economists do this with a concept called *present value*. The **present value** of any future sum of money is the amount today that would be needed, at current interest rates, to produce that future sum.

To learn how to use the concept of present value, let's work through a couple of simple examples.

Question: If a business put €100 in a bank account today, how much will it be worth in N years? That is, what will be the **future value** of this €100?

Answer: Let's use r to denote the interest rate expressed in decimal form (so an interest rate of 5 per cent means $r = 0.05$). Suppose that interest is paid annually and that the interest paid remains in the bank account to earn more interest – a process called **compounding**. Then the €100 will become:

$(1 + r)$ €100	after one year
$(1 + r)(1 + r)$ €100	after two years
$(1 + r)(1 + r)(1 + r)$ €100	after three years
$(1 + r)^N$ €100	after N years

For example, if we are investing at an interest rate of 5 per cent for 10 years, then the future value of the €100 will be $(1.05)^{10} \times$ €100, which is €163.

Question: Now suppose the business was going to earn €200 in N years. What is the *present value* of this future payment? That is, how much would the business have to deposit in a bank right now to yield €200 in N years?

Answer: To answer this question, just turn the previous answer on its head. In the first question, we computed a future value from a present value by *multiplying* by the factor $(1 + r)^N$. To compute a present value from a future value, we *divide* by the factor $(1 + r)^N$. Thus, the present value of €200 in N years is €200$/(1 + r)^N$. If that amount is deposited in a bank today, after N years it would become $(1 + r)^N \times$ [€200$/(1 + r)^N$], which is €200. For instance, if the interest rate is 5 per cent, the present value of €200 in ten years is €200$/(1.05)^{10}$, which is €123.

This illustrates the general formula: if r is the interest rate, then an amount X to be received in N years has present value of $X/(1 + r)^N$.

Let's now return to our earlier question: should a business choose €100 today or €200 in 10 years? We can infer from our calculation of present value that if the interest rate is 5 per cent, the business should prefer the €200 in ten years. The future €200 has a present value of €123, which is greater than €100. You are better off waiting for the future sum.

Notice that the answer to our question depends on the interest rate. If the interest rate were 8 per cent, then the €200 in ten years would have a present value of €200$/(1.08)^{10}$, which is only €93. In this case, the business should take the €100 today. Why should the interest rate matter for your choice? The answer is that the higher the interest rate, the more you can earn by depositing your money at the bank, so the more attractive getting €100 today becomes.

The concept of present value is useful in assessing the decisions that companies face when evaluating investment projects. For instance, imagine that Citroën is thinking about building a new car factory. Suppose that the factory will cost €100 million today and will

present value the amount of money today that would be needed to produce, using prevailing interest rates, a given future amount of money

future value the amount of money in the future that an amount of money today will yield, given prevailing interest rates

compounding the accumulation of a sum of money in, say, a bank account where the interest earned remains in the account to earn additional interest in the future

yield the company €200 million in ten years. Should Citroën undertake the project? You can see that this decision is exactly like the one we have been studying. To make its decision, the company will compare the present value of the €200 million return to the €100 million cost.

The company's decision, therefore, will depend on the interest rate. If the interest rate is 5 per cent, then the present value of the €200 million return from the factory is €123 million, and the company will choose to pay the €100 million cost. By contrast, if the interest rate is 8 per cent, then the present value of the return is only €93 million, and the company will decide to forgo the project. Thus, the concept of present value helps explain why investment declines when the interest rate rises.

Here is another application of present value: suppose a small business is the subject of a takeover. The business owners are given an option about the way the takeover will work. They could either remain as part of the business and take a guaranteed sum of money over a specified period or take an upfront payment and leave the company. Imagine the owner is given the choice between €20 000 a year for 50 years (totalling €1 000 000) or an immediate payment of €400 000. Which should the owner choose? To make the right choice, they need to calculate the present value of the stream of payments. After performing 50 calculations similar to those above (one calculation for each payment) and adding up the results, they would learn that the present value of this stream of income totalling €1 million at a 7 per cent interest rate is only €276 000. The owner would be better off picking the immediate payment of €400 000. The million euros may seem like more money, but the future cash flows, once discounted to the present, are worth far less.

> **Quick Quiz** The interest rate is 7 per cent. What is the present value of €150 to be received in ten years?

MANAGING RISK

Life is full of gambles. When you go skiing, you risk breaking your leg in a fall. When you cycle to work or university, you risk being knocked off your bike by a car. When a business makes an investment decision, it risks the decision failing and the value of the business falling as a result. The rational response to this risk is not necessarily to avoid it at any cost, but to take it into account in your decision making. Let's consider how a business might do that.

Risk Aversion

risk averse exhibiting a dislike of uncertainty

Many businesses are **risk averse**. This means more than simply businesses dislike bad things happening to them. It means that they dislike bad things more than they like comparable good things. (This is also reflected in *loss aversion* – research suggests that losing something makes people twice as miserable as gaining something makes them happy!)

For example, suppose a business colleague offers you the following opportunity. He will flip a coin. If it comes up heads, he will pay you €1000. But if it comes up tails, you will have to pay him €1000. Would you accept the bargain? You wouldn't if you were risk averse, even though the probability of winning is the same as the probability of losing. For a risk-averse person, the pain from losing the €1000 would exceed the gain from winning €1000.

Economists have developed models of risk aversion using the concept of *utility,* the subjective measure of a person's well-being or satisfaction. Every level of wealth provides a certain amount of utility, as shown by the utility function in Figure 15.1. But the function exhibits the property of diminishing marginal utility: the more wealth a person has, the less utility he gets from an additional euro. Thus, in the figure, the utility function gets flatter as wealth increases. Because of diminishing marginal utility, the utility lost from losing the €1000 bet is more than the utility gained from winning it. As a result, businesses can be risk averse.

Risk aversion provides the starting point for explaining various things we observe in relation to how businesses operate in the economy.

The Markets for Insurance

One way for a business to deal with risk is to buy insurance. The general feature of insurance contracts is that a business facing a risk pays a fee to an insurance company, which in return agrees to accept all or part of the risk. Firms have to take out different types of insurance. They can insure against the risk of their buildings catching fire, theft of goods, losses of revenue for various reasons, in case a customer has an accident whilst on the premises of the business or if workers have accidents and damage or loss to capital equipment.

In a sense, every insurance contract is a gamble. It is possible that none of these things will happen to a business. In most years, businesses pay the insurance company the premium and get nothing in return except peace of mind. Indeed, the insurance company is counting on the fact that most businesses will not make claims on their

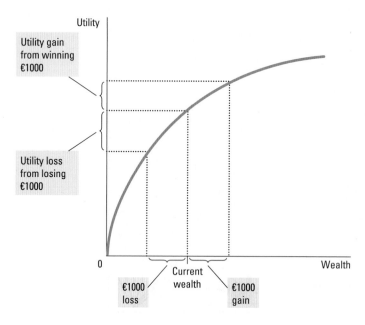

FIGURE 15.1

The Utility Function

This utility function shows how utility, a subjective measure of satisfaction, depends on wealth. As wealth rises, the utility function becomes flatter, reflecting the property of diminishing marginal utility. Because of diminishing marginal utility, a €1000 loss decreases utility by more than a €1000 gain increases it.

policies; otherwise, it couldn't pay out the large claims to those few who are unlucky and still stay in business.

From the standpoint of the economy as a whole, the role of insurance is not to eliminate the risks inherent in life but to spread them around more efficiently. Consider fire insurance on a business, for instance. Owning fire insurance does not reduce the risk of losing a business in a fire. But if that unlucky event occurs, the insurance company compensates the business owners. The risk, rather than being borne by that business alone, is shared among the thousands of insurance company shareholders. Because people are risk averse, it is easier for 10 000 businesses to bear 1/10 000 of the risk than for one business to bear the entire risk itself.

The markets for insurance suffer from two types of problems that impede their ability to spread risk. One problem is *adverse selection:* a high-risk business is more likely to apply for insurance than a low-risk business. A second problem is *moral hazard:* after businesses buy insurance, they have less incentive to be careful about their risky behaviour. Insurance companies are aware of these problems, and the price of insurance reflects the actual risks that the insurance company will face after the insurance is bought. The high price of insurance is why some businesses, especially those who know themselves to be low risk, decide against buying insurance if it is not a legal requirement and, instead, endure some of life's uncertainty on their own.

Quick Quiz Describe three ways by which a risk-averse business might reduce the risk they face.

FYI

Pricing Risk

We have seen how bond issues are a means by which firms can borrow money. The buyer has to have confidence that they will get their money back and also receive an appropriate reward for lending the money in the first place. There is a risk involved that the issuer will not be able to pay back the money and that risk is associated with a probability. If the issuer is very sound then the probability of default may be zero but if extremely weak then the probability is closer to 1. Financial markets now deal in pools of debt (collections of different types of loans sold to an investor). As debt is pooled the outcomes become more varied. In any given pool of business debt, for example, there will be some firms who will default and not be able to pay off their loans. Other firms may look to pay off their loans early or will increase monthly payments or pay lump sums to help reduce the repayment period of their loan and so on. Assessing probabilities with such a wide range of outcomes becomes difficult.

The risk involved with such debt is therefore difficult to assess with any certainty. However, investors, including businesses, want to price risk as part of their decision making so that they can judge the value of an asset. If an asset is very risky then the returns expected will be higher and vice versa. In order to have an efficient market, that risk has to be priced and the information on which the risk is based has to be reliable, accurate – and understood.

Let's consider an example. In your class there may be a number of students that you associate with every day. Take any one individual and we can identify a number of 'risks' for that person. For example, there is a risk that the individual:

- fails their exams and has to leave the course
- will be involved in a car crash
- will travel on an aircraft more than five times a year
- may get mugged
- may get swine flu.

What are the chances of these events happening? The analysis of such outcomes is what actuaries in the insurance industry have to do. An estimate of the probability of such events happening can be derived from analysis of data, specifically historical data. It is possible, therefore, to gather data on the average 19-year-old student coming from a particular area and with a particular background and use this data to arrive at the probability of the event occurring. Historical data tell us, for example, that young people aged between 18 and 24 are more likely to be mugged than the elderly, despite popular perception. If we are able to identify these probabilities then they can be priced. Securities can be issued based on the chances of these things happening – the more likely the event to occur, the higher the price and vice versa.

Whilst it may be possible to identify probabilities for an individual it may be more problematic when looking at relationships between individuals. For example, if person X fails their exams what is the probability that you will also fails your exams? If that individual gets swine flu what are the chances that you also get swine flu? In both cases the probability might depend on your relationship with that person. If you spend a lot of time with that person then it may be that you share similar distractions – going out every night instead of studying, skipping lectures

to play pool and so on. If this were the case then the probability of you also failing your exams and getting swine flu might be high but if you have no relationship at all then the chance of you sharing bad habits which lead you to also fail your exams are lower. However, given that you share some time with that person in a lecture hall or seminar room, for example, might mean that the probability of also getting swine flu is relatively high.

Looking at such relationships involves the concept of correlation. If person X is involved in a car crash (and you were not in the car with them) what is the chance of you also being involved in a car crash? The chances are the correlation is very low; the probability of you both getting mugged is higher regardless of the relationship between you and so there will be a stronger correlation in this instance. The correlation is likely to become more and more unstable the more variables are introduced (number of students in this example). In the case of pools of debt, the same problems arise and the efficiency of the information on which investors are basing their decision becomes ever more complex; probabilities become very difficult to assess and therefore to price.

Actuaries have been studying these types of correlations for some years. The job of the actuary is to provide information to the insurer on the chances of an outcome occurring under different situations. Where information becomes available which indicates risk factors change, actuaries have to incorporate these into models to help insurers price the risk adequately (i.e. set the premiums for the policy), which in turn influence the costs that firms have to pay to get insurance.

ASSET VALUATION

Now that we have developed a basic understanding of the two building blocks of finance – time and risk – let's apply this knowledge. Valuing assets is an important part of any business activity. For large businesses, asset valuation can make a big difference to the financial accounts of the business which it reports to its shareholders. This section considers a simple question which applies to a range of assets. What determines the price of an asset? Like most prices, the answer is supply and demand.

> **Pitfall Prevention** Always take into consideration the type of asset being analyzed and note its different characteristics – shares in a business, for example, may have to be treated slightly differently even if the same principles are applied to a decision to launch a takeover bid for a rival firm (the asset in this case) or investing in new plant.

Fundamental Analysis

Let's imagine that a business is deciding how to allocate cash holdings in investments. When buying any asset, it is natural to consider two things: the value of the asset and the price at which the asset being sold. If the price is less than the value, the asset is said to be *undervalued*. If the price is more than the value, the asset is said to be *overvalued*. If the price and the value are equal, the asset is said to be *fairly valued*. When buying assets, the business should prefer undervalued assets. In these cases, they are getting a bargain by paying less than the asset is worth.

This is easier said than done. Learning the price is easy but determining the value of the asset is the hard part. The term **fundamental analysis** refers to the detailed analysis of an asset to determine its value. Many firms, especially those in the financial sector, hire analysts to conduct such fundamental analysis and offer advice about which assets to buy.

fundamental analysis the study of an asset to determine its value

The value of an asset to a business is what they get out of owning it, which includes the present value of the stream of income and the possible final sale price or scrap value. The stream of income an asset can generate depends on a large number of factors: the demand for the product that the asset helps produce; how quickly technology renders the asset obsolete; how flexible the asset is and how easily it can be used for other purposes; and so on. The job of fundamental analysts is to take all these factors into account to determine how much an asset is worth.

JEOPARDY PROBLEM

A business does detailed analysis of a rival firm which it is thinking of taking over. It arrives at a value for the company based on fundamentals such as the current share price, profitability, earnings, the volume of shares traded in recent months, the ratio of its share price to its earnings and dividend payments. Having undertaken this analysis, the firm believes the takeover target is underpriced and that it would be beneficial to launch the takeover bid. When it announces its plans to do so, its own share price falls. What might be the reason, given the amount of analysis the firm has carried out?

SAVINGS AND INVESTMENTS IN THE NATIONAL INCOME ACCOUNTS

Access to funds for business development and growth is closely related to the rate of interest that firms have to pay to borrow money. Whether there are funds available for firms to borrow is dependent on the number of people who are willing to save money. There is a market in loanable funds and the financial institutions we looked at earlier in the chapter play a big part in this market.

The Market for Loanable Funds

We are going to build a model of financial markets. Our purpose in building this model is to explain how financial markets coordinate the economy's saving and investment and thus help channel finance to businesses that need it. The model also gives us a tool with which we can analyze various government policies that influence saving and investment which in turn can affect the amount of funds available to businesses. The supply and demand of loanable funds determines the price of loanable funds – the interest rate.

To keep things simple, we assume that the economy has only one financial market, called the **market for loanable funds**. All savers go to this market to deposit their savings, and all borrowers go to this market to get their loans. Thus, the term *loanable funds* refers to all income that people have chosen to save and lend out, rather than use for their own consumption. In the market for loanable funds, there is one interest rate, which is both the return to saving and the cost of borrowing.

We can identify two types of saving in the economy, *private saving* and *public saving*. **Private saving** is the amount of income that households have left after paying their taxes and paying for their consumption. In particular, because households receive income, which we denote as Y, pay taxes of T, and spend C on consumption, private saving is $Y - T - C$. **Public saving** is the amount of tax revenue that the government has left after paying for its spending. The government receives T in tax revenue and spends G on goods and services. If T exceeds G, the government runs a budget surplus because it receives more money than it spends. This surplus of $T - G$ represents public saving. If the government spends more than it receives in tax revenue, then G is larger than T. In this case, the government runs a budget deficit, and public saving $T - G$ is a negative number.

The assumption of a single financial market, of course, is not literally true. As we have seen, the economy has many types of financial institutions. But, as we have mentioned several times before, the art in building an economic model is simplifying the world in order to explain it. For our purposes here, we can ignore the diversity of financial institutions and assume that the economy has a single financial market.

> **market for loanable funds** the market in which those who want to save supply funds and those who want to borrow to invest demand funds

> **private saving** the income that households have left after paying for taxes and consumption

> **public saving** the tax revenue that the government has left after paying for its spending

Supply and Demand for Loanable Funds

The supply of loanable funds comes from those people who have some extra income they want to save and lend out. This lending can occur directly, such as when a household buys a bond from a firm, or it can occur indirectly, such as when a household makes a deposit in a bank, which in turn uses the funds to make loans. In both cases, saving is the source of the supply of loanable funds.

The demand for loanable funds comes from households and firms who wish to borrow to make investments. This demand includes families taking out mortgages to buy homes. It also includes firms borrowing to buy new equipment or build factories. In both cases, investment is the source of the demand for loanable funds.

FIGURE 15.2

The Market for Loanable Funds

The interest rate in the economy adjusts to balance the supply and demand for loanable funds. The supply of loanable funds comes from national saving, including both private saving and public saving. The demand for loanable funds comes from firms and households that want to borrow for purposes of investment. Here the equilibrium interest rate is 5 per cent, and €500 billion of loanable funds are supplied and demanded.

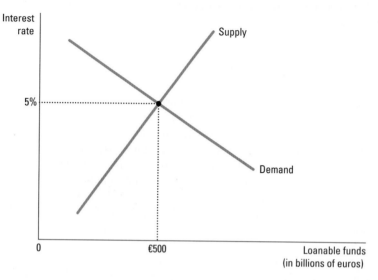

The interest rate is the price of a loan. It represents the amount that borrowers pay for loans and the amount that lenders receive on their saving. Because a high interest rate makes borrowing more expensive, the quantity of loanable funds demanded falls as the interest rate rises. Similarly, because a high interest rate makes saving more attractive, the quantity of loanable funds supplied rises as the interest rate rises. In other words, the demand curve for loanable funds slopes downward, and the supply curve for loanable funds slopes upward.

Figure 15.2 shows the interest rate that balances the supply and demand for loanable funds. In the equilibrium shown, the interest rate is 5 per cent, and the quantity of loanable funds demanded and the quantity of loanable funds supplied both equal €500 billion.

The adjustment of the interest rate to the equilibrium level occurs for the usual reasons. If the interest rate was lower than the equilibrium level, the quantity of loanable funds supplied would be less than the quantity of loanable funds demanded. The resulting shortage of loanable funds would encourage lenders to raise the interest rate they charge. A higher interest rate would encourage saving (thereby increasing the quantity of loanable funds supplied) and discourage borrowing for investment (thereby decreasing the quantity of loanable funds demanded). Conversely, if the interest rate was higher than the equilibrium level, the quantity of loanable funds supplied would exceed the quantity of loanable funds demanded. As lenders competed for the scarce borrowers, interest rates would be driven down. In this way, the interest rate approaches the equilibrium level at which the supply and demand for loanable funds exactly balance.

Recall that economists distinguish between the real interest rate and the nominal interest rate. The nominal interest rate is the interest rate as usually reported – the monetary return to saving and cost of borrowing. The real interest rate is the nominal interest rate corrected for inflation; it equals the nominal interest rate minus the inflation rate. Because inflation erodes the value of money over time, the real interest rate more accurately reflects the real return to saving and cost of borrowing. Therefore, the supply and demand for loanable funds depend on the real (rather than nominal) interest rate, and the equilibrium in Figure 15.2 should be interpreted as determining the real interest rate in the economy.

This model of the supply and demand for loanable funds shows that financial markets work much like other markets in the economy. Because saving represents the supply of loanable funds and investment represents the demand, we can see how the invisible hand coordinates saving and investment. When the interest rate adjusts to balance supply and demand in the market for loanable funds, it coordinates the behaviour of people who want to save (the suppliers of loanable funds) and the behaviour of people who want to invest (the demanders of loanable funds). When the interest rate changes it affects the risk involved in investment for a business and affects the value of the returns. We are likely to see firms reducing their investment plans when the interest rate rises but increasing them when the interest rate falls.

We can now use this analysis of the market for loanable funds to examine various government policies that affect the economy's saving and investment and in particular the ability of firms to borrow.

Policy 1: Saving Incentives   One of the *Ten Principles of Economics* in Chapter 1 is that a country's standard of living depends on its ability to produce goods and services. If a country can raise its saving rate, the interest rate (other things being equal) will fall and firms can invest more. This in turn leads to the growth rate of the economy to increase and, over time, the citizens of that country should enjoy a higher standard of living.

Another of the *Ten Principles of Economics* is that people respond to incentives. Many economists have used this principle to suggest that the savings rates in some countries are depressed because of tax laws that discourage saving. In response to this problem, many economists and some politicians have sometimes advocated replacing income taxes with a consumption tax. Under a consumption tax, income that is saved would not be taxed until the saving is later spent; in essence, a consumption tax is like the value-added tax (VAT) that European countries impose on many goods and services. VAT is an indirect tax, however, levied on a good or service at the time it is purchased, whereas a consumption tax could also be a direct tax levied on an individual by calculating how much consumer expenditure they carried out over the year and taxing them on that, perhaps at higher and higher rates as the level of consumer expenditure rises.

A more modest proposal is to expand eligibility for special savings accounts that allow people to shelter some of their saving from taxation. Let's consider the effect of such a saving incentive on the market for loanable funds, as illustrated in Figure 15.3.

First, which curve would this policy affect? Because the tax change would alter the incentive for households to save *at any given interest rate,* it would affect the quantity of loanable funds supplied at each interest rate. Thus, the supply of loanable funds would shift. The demand for loanable funds would remain the same, because the tax change would not directly affect the amount that borrowers want to borrow at any given interest rate.

Secondly, which way would the supply curve shift? Because saving would be taxed less heavily, households would increase their saving by consuming a smaller fraction of their income. Households would use this additional saving to increase their deposits in banks or to buy more bonds. The supply of loanable funds would increase, and the supply curve would shift to the right from S_1 to S_2, as shown in Figure 15.3.

Finally, we can compare the old and new equilibria. In the figure, the increased supply of loanable funds reduces the interest rate from 5 per cent to 4 per cent. The lower interest rate raises the quantity of loanable funds demanded from €500 billion to €600 billion. That is, the shift in the supply curve moves the market equilibrium along the demand curve. With a lower cost of borrowing, households and firms are motivated to borrow more to finance greater investment. Thus, if a reform of the tax laws encouraged greater saving, the result would be lower interest rates and greater investment.

FIGURE 15.3

An Increase in the Supply of Loanable Funds

A change in the tax laws to encourage more saving would shift the supply of loanable funds to the right from S_1 to S_2. As a result, the equilibrium interest rate would fall, and the lower interest rate would stimulate investment. Here the equilibrium interest rate falls from 5 per cent to 4 per cent, and the equilibrium quantity of loanable funds saved and invested rises from €500 billion to €600 billion.

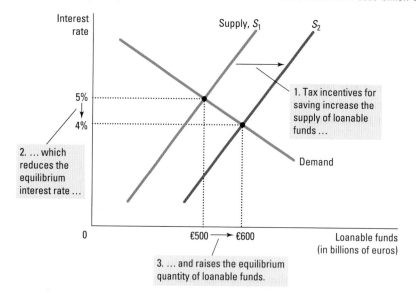

Although this analysis of the effects of increased saving is widely accepted among economists, there is less consensus about what kinds of tax changes should be enacted. Many economists endorse tax reform aimed at increasing saving in order to stimulate investment and growth. Yet others are sceptical that these tax changes would have much effect on national saving. These sceptics also doubt the equity of the proposed reforms. They argue that, in many cases, the benefits of the tax changes would accrue primarily to the wealthy, who are least in need of tax relief.

Policy 2: Investment Incentives   Suppose that the government passed a tax reform aimed at making investment more attractive. In essence, this is what the government does when it institutes an *investment tax credit*, which some governments put in place. An investment tax credit gives a tax advantage to any firm building a new factory or buying a new piece of equipment. Let's consider the effect of such a tax reform on the market for loanable funds, as illustrated in Figure 15.4.

Firstly, would the reform affect supply or demand? Because the tax credit would reward firms that borrow and invest in new capital, it would alter investment at any given interest rate and, thereby, change the demand for loanable funds. By contrast, because the tax credit would not affect the amount that households save at any given interest rate, it would not affect the supply of loanable funds.

Secondly, which way would the demand curve shift? Because firms would have an incentive to increase investment at any interest rate, the quantity of loanable funds demanded would be higher at any given interest rate. Thus, the demand curve for loanable funds would move to the right, as shown by the shift from D_1 to D_2 in the figure.

Thirdly, consider how the equilibrium would change. In Figure 15.4, the increased demand for loanable funds raises the interest rate from 5 per cent to 6 per cent, and the higher interest rate in turn increases the quantity of loanable funds supplied from €500 billion to €600 billion, as households respond by increasing the amount they save.

FIGURE 15.4

An Increase in the Demand for Loanable Funds

If the passage of an investment tax credit encouraged firms to invest more, the demand for loanable funds would increase. As a result, the equilibrium interest rate would rise, and the higher interest rate would stimulate saving. Here, when the demand curve shifts from D_1 to D_2, the equilibrium interest rate rises from 5 per cent to 6 per cent, and the equilibrium quantity of loanable funds saved and invested rises from €500 billion to €600 billion.

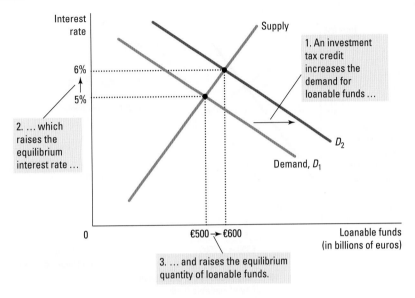

This change in household behaviour is represented here as a movement along the supply curve. Thus, if a reform of the tax system encouraged greater investment, the result would be higher interest rates and greater saving.

Policy 3: Government Budget Deficits and Surpluses   A *budget deficit* is an excess of government spending over tax revenue. Governments finance budget deficits by borrowing in the bond market, and the accumulation of past government borrowing is called the *government debt.* A *budget surplus,* an excess of tax revenue over government spending, can be used to repay some of the government debt. If government spending exactly equals tax revenue, the government is said to have a *balanced budget.*

Imagine that the government starts with a balanced budget and then, because of a tax cut or a spending increase, starts running a budget deficit. We can analyze the effects of the budget deficit by following our three steps in the market for loanable funds, as illustrated in Figure 15.5.

First, which curve shifts when the government starts running a budget deficit? Recall that national saving – the source of the supply of loanable funds – is composed of private saving and public saving. A change in the government budget balance represents a change in public saving and, thereby, in the supply of loanable funds. Because the budget deficit does not influence the amount that households and firms want to borrow to finance investment at any given interest rate, it does not alter the demand for loanable funds.

Secondly, which way does the supply curve shift? When the government runs a budget deficit, public saving is negative, and this reduces national saving. In other words, when the government borrows to finance its budget deficit, it reduces the supply of loanable funds available to finance investment by households and firms. Thus, a budget deficit shifts the supply curve for loanable funds to the left from S_1 to S_2, as shown in Figure 15.5.

The Effect of a Government Budget Deficit

When the government spends more than it receives in tax revenue, the resulting budget deficit lowers national saving. The supply of loanable funds decreases, and the equilibrium interest rate rises. Thus, when the government borrows to finance its budget deficit, it crowds out households and firms who otherwise would borrow to finance investment. Here, when the supply shifts from S_1 to S_2, the equilibrium interest rate rises from 5 per cent to 6 per cent, and the equilibrium quantity of loanable funds saved and invested falls from €500 billion to €300 billion.

DEPT of The Treasury
Deficit Spending division

Thirdly, we can compare the old and new equilibria. In the figure, when the budget deficit reduces the supply of loanable funds, the interest rate rises from 5 per cent to 6 per cent. This higher interest rate then alters the behaviour of the households and firms that participate in the loan market. In particular, many demanders of loanable funds are discouraged by the higher interest rate. Fewer families buy new homes, and fewer firms choose to build new factories. The fall in investment because of government borrowing is called **crowding out** and is represented in the figure by the movement along the demand curve from a quantity of €500 billion in loanable funds to a quantity of €300 billion. That is, when the government borrows to finance its budget deficit, it crowds out private borrowers who are trying to finance investment.

> **crowding out** a decrease in investment that results from government borrowing

Thus, the most basic lesson about budget deficits follows directly from their effects on the supply and demand for loanable funds: when the government reduces national saving by running a budget deficit, the interest rate rises and investment falls. Because investment is important for long-run economic growth, government budget deficits reduce the economy's growth rate.

Government budget surpluses work just the opposite way to budget deficits. When government collects more in tax revenue than it spends, it saves the difference by retiring some of the outstanding government debt. This budget surplus, or public saving, contributes to national saving. Thus, a budget surplus increases the supply of loanable funds, reduces the interest rate and stimulates investment. Higher investment, in turn, means greater capital accumulation and more rapid economic growth.

CONCLUSION

This chapter has developed some of the basic tools that businesses use as they make financial decisions. The concept of present value reminds us that a sum of money in the future is less valuable than a sum of money today, and it gives us a way to compare sums of money at different points in time. The theory of risk management reminds us that the future is uncertain and that risk-averse businesses can take precautions to guard against this uncertainty. The study of asset valuation tells us that the value of an asset should reflect its expected future profitability.

In most economies, people borrow and lend often, and usually for good reason. You may borrow one day to start your own business or to buy a home. And people may lend to you in the hope that the interest you pay will allow them to enjoy a more prosperous retirement. The financial system has the job of coordinating all this borrowing and lending activity.

In many ways, financial markets are like other markets in the economy. The price of loanable funds – the interest rate – is governed by the forces of supply and demand, just as other prices in the economy are. And we can analyze shifts in supply or demand in financial markets as we do in other markets. One of the *Ten Principles of Economics* introduced in Chapter 1 is that markets are usually a good way to organize economic activity. This principle applies to financial markets as well. When financial markets bring the supply and demand for loanable funds into balance, they help allocate the economy's scarce resources to their most efficient use.

In one way, however, financial markets are special. Financial markets, unlike most other markets, serve the important role of linking the present and the future. Those who supply loanable funds – savers – do so because they want to convert some of their current income into future purchasing power. Those who demand loanable funds – borrowers – do so because they want to invest today in order to have additional capital in the future to produce goods and services. Thus, well-functioning financial markets are important not only for current generations but also for future generations who will inherit many of the resulting benefits.

IN THE NEWS

The Market for Loanable Funds

This article looks at the effects of the growth in government-backed banks in Thailand and how their entry into the industry may be causing crowding out.

What's Keeping Thai Bankers Awake at Night?

If you think Thai banks have been competing fiercely in the past few years, you are absolutely correct. But no, their toughest competitors have not been the Association of Southeast Asian Nations (ASEAN) banks seeking dominance as the ASEAN Economic Community draws closer in 2015. Nor have they been Chinese banks looking to expand into this region. Surprisingly, the most unforeseen, yet aggravating, competitors are those that have shared home turf with Thai commercial banks for almost 100 years: the government-backed specialized financial institutions (SFIs).

These state-backed institutions have been growing at a breathtaking rate. Back in 2003, commercial banks' loans were 4.6 times those of the SFIs and deposits were 4.8 times. Eight years later, the same figures were 2.7 and 2.6 times, respectively. These figures translate to a 27 per cent share for SFIs in the loan and deposit market at the end of 2011 compared with 18 per cent back in 2003. That's a 50 per cent increase in their market share. So, it's not Malaysian, Singaporean or Chinese banks that keep Thai bankers up at night.

Among the six government banks, the Government Savings Bank (GSB) is in the forefront, with a phenomenal growth rate that puts the phrase 'eat my dust' into perspective. The GSB's average annual loan growth rate over the past three years was a whopping 28 per cent. In 2009 alone, when most banks slowed lending due to the subprime crisis, the GSB loan book grew by

A Thai Government Savings Bank branch in Chiang Mai.

almost 40 per cent, expanding in all directions.

GSB deposits, meanwhile, averaged 29.5 per cent annual growth in the past three years and 31 per cent in 2009. Compare those figures with 7.4 per cent, the best loan growth of a commercial bank in 2009 or 13 per cent, the maximum deposit growth in the same year. Even in the banner year of 2010, maximum loan and deposit growth rates for commercial banks were 32 per cent and 14 per cent, respectively.

The exceptional growth rates of the SFIs have redefined one fundamental economic concept, the crowding-out effect. Conventional wisdom holds that expansionary government policy, i.e. more spending and more deficits, will draw out loanable funds in the financial markets, causing market interest rates to be sticky, or at worst, to rise. Lately, more and more Thai government poli-

cies have been funded through 'off-budget' accounts, SFIs included. So looking at government deficits alone for evidence of the crowding-out effect is so 1980s. We must now take into account the competition SFIs pose in the loanable funds market.

In 2011, the GSB's deposits increased by 345 billion baht, while total SFI deposits increased by 535 billion. These numbers are equivalent to a full year of government bond issues. The planned budget deficit for fiscal 2012 is 400 billion baht and possibly another 300 billion in 2013. Even though the government is trying to reduce its deficit, GSB deposits could absorb more funds at an increasing rate. Assuming the average growth rate persists, we could be looking at 450 billion baht in 2011 and 580 billion in 2012 of fund absorption by the GSB. So during this downward interest rate cycle, do not expect market rates to automatically move with the policy rate. When funds are tough to find, interest rates must remain high. Simple as that.

Elsewhere on the financial front, new headaches have emerged in the form of a damning report by the Financial Action Task Force (FATF). Two weeks ago, the FATF put Thailand on its list of non-cooperative countries, citing our inability to enact substantiated anti-money laundering laws and to criminalize terrorist financing. We are now a member of an exclusive club with the likes of Myanmar, Pakistan and Cuba. This makes our policymakers' brave talk about financial liberalization and hoopla around the Asean Economic Community seem academic at best.

So what is all the fuss about? After all, we are a sovereign state, right? Unfortunately, being on the FATF watch list is a major blow to the Thai banking industry given the highly inter-twined nature of the world financial system. To put it in perspective, let's look at a real-life case. If a bank from a watch-list country wants to do any transaction with a US counterparty, that US bank is required to file a 'Sus-picious Activity Report' with regulators, regardless of any past transactional relationship and credit rating history. This means heaps more paperwork for all parties including the clients – even for mundane trade finance deals such as letter of credit or letter of guarantee. Imagine the incremental costs of these processes both in terms of time and money. It is indeed staggering.

Another setback for Thai banks is mounting regulatory costs. Banks previ-ously had to pay 0.4 per cent of their deposit amounts to the Deposit Protec-tion Agency. This fee is being raised to 0.47 per cent, with a large chunk to be used to settle the Financial Institutions Development Fund debt. The headache doesn't end here. In the past, banks seeking to save on deposit levies raised funds via bills of exchange (B/Es), which were not insured by the state deposit guarantee and hence exempted from any fee. This is about to change and banks will have to contribute 40 satang on every baht that they raise from B/Es. This will weigh hard, especially on some smaller banks where B/Es represent as much as 70 per cent of total book.

While things are getting tough for banks, they're actually not too bad for depositors. Some savers are concerned that the deposit guarantee will decline in August to 1 million baht per bank and per depositor, from 50 million, which in turn was a change from the unlimited guarantee that had prevailed for so long. But even one million baht in cov-erage is in fact generous vis-a-vis what our neighbours offer.

Our study reveals that Thailand's 1-million baht guarantee is tantamount to 5.8 times per capita GDP, the highest in ASEAN. Indonesia comes second at 3.3 times, followed by Malaysia at just 2 times.

All in all, commercial banks are fac-ing stiff competition both at home and abroad. The higher cost of funds will undermine their regional competitive-ness, while Thailand's dismal FATF standing will increase paperwork and related costs. As you can see, 2012 isn't really Thai commercial banks' year. And now you know what keeps bankers awake at night.

Questions

1. Explain how the market for loanable funds determines the interest rate.
2. Using appropriate diagrams, explain the possible effect of the increase in SFI growth on the market for loan-able funds in Thailand.
3. Explain why 'expansionary govern-ment policy, i.e. more spending and more deficits, will draw out loan-able funds in the financial markets, causing market interest rates to be sticky, or at worst, to rise'.
4. What is meant by the phrase: 'When funds are tough to find interest rates must remain high. Simple as that'.
5. Explain how the additional regulatory processes faced by Thai banks is likely to affect their competitiveness.

Source: http://www.bangkokpost.com/ business/economics/282449/what-s-keeping-thai-bankers-awake-at-night accessed 18 March 2012.

SUMMARY

- The financial system of an advanced economy is made up of many types of financial institutions, such as the bond market, the stock market, banks and investment funds. All of these institutions act to direct the resources of households who want to save some of their income into the hands of house-holds and firms who want to borrow.

- Because savings can earn interest, a sum of money today is more valuable than the same sum of money in the future. A person can compare sums from different times using the concept of present value. The present value of any future sum is the amount that would be needed today, given prevailing interest rates, to produce that future sum.

- Because of diminishing marginal utility, most people are risk averse. Risk-averse people can reduce risk using insurance.

- The value of an asset equals the present value of the income streams the owner of the asset will receive and the final sale price if appropriate.

- The interest rate is determined by the supply and demand for loanable funds. The supply of loanable funds comes from households who want to save some of their income and lend it out. The demand for loanable funds comes from households and firms who want to borrow for investment. To analyze how any policy or event affects the interest rate, one must consider how it affects the supply and demand for loanable funds.

- National saving equals private saving plus public saving. A government budget deficit represents negative public saving and, therefore, reduces national saving and the supply of loanable funds available to finance investment. When a government budget deficit crowds out investment, it reduces the growth of productivity and GDP.

KEY CONCEPTS

financial markets, p. 362
bond, p. 362
stock, p. 364
financial intermediaries, p. 364
investment fund, p. 365

present value, p. 367
future value, p. 367
compounding, p. 367
risk averse, p. 368
fundamental analysis, p. 372

market for loanable funds, p. 373
private saving, p. 373
public saving, p. 373
crowding out, p. 379

QUESTIONS FOR REVIEW

1. What is the role of the financial system? Name and describe two markets that are part of the financial system in our economy. Name and describe two financial intermediaries.

2. The interest rate is 7 per cent. Use the concept of present value to compare €200 to be received in 10 years and €300 to be received in 20 years.

3. What might be some of the advantages and disadvantages to a firm of issuing bonds or issuing shares as a source of finance?

4. A chemical processing manufacturer is considering investing in a new process to produce a constituent ingredient for an agricultural fertilizer. It expects the return on the investment to last for at least 10 years. How might it decide whether to proceed with the investment?

5. What benefit do people get from the market for insurance? What two problems impede the insurance company from working perfectly?

6. What is private saving? What is public saving? How are these two variables related?

7. What is investment? How is it related to national saving?

8. What factors should an analyst think about in determining the value of an asset?

9. Describe a change in the tax system that might increase private saving. If this policy were implemented, how would it affect the market for loanable funds?

10. What is a government budget deficit? How does it affect interest rates, investment and economic growth?

PROBLEMS AND APPLICATIONS

1. A company has an investment project that would cost €10 million today and yield a pay off of €15 million in four years.
   a. Should the firm undertake the project if the interest rate is 11 per cent? 10 per cent? 9 per cent? 8 per cent?
   b. Can you figure out the exact cut-off for the interest rate between profitability and non-profitability?

2. For each of the following pairs, which bond would you expect to pay a higher interest rate? Explain.
   a. A bond of the UK government or a bond of an east European government.
   b. A bond that repays the principal in year 2014 or a bond that repays the principal in year 2031.
   c. A bond from BP or a bond from a software company you run in your garage.
   d. A bond issued by the national government or a bond issued by a local authority.

3. For which kind of asset would you expect to pay the higher average return: stock in an industry that is very sensitive to economic conditions (such as a car manufacturer) or stock in an industry that is relatively insensitive to economic conditions (such as a water company). Why?

4. When the Greek government announced that it could default on its debt to foreigners in the latter part of 2011, interest rates rose on bonds issued by many other European countries but fell on German debt. Why do you suppose this happened?

5. Suppose that BP is considering exploring a new oil field.
   a. Assuming that BP needs to borrow money in the bond market to finance the purchase of new oil rigs and drilling machinery, why would an increase in interest rates affect BP's decision about whether to carry out the exploration?
   b. If BP has enough of its own funds to finance the development of the new oil field without borrowing, would an increase in interest rates still affect BP's decision about whether to undertake the new project? Explain.

6. Suppose the government borrows €5 billion more next year than this year.

a. Use a supply-and-demand diagram to analyze this policy. Does the interest rate rise or fall?

b. What happens to investment? To private saving? To public saving? Compare the size of the changes to the €5 billion of extra government borrowing.

c. How does the elasticity of supply of loanable funds affect the size of these changes?

d. How does the elasticity of demand for loanable funds affect the size of these changes?

e. Suppose households believe that greater government borrowing today implies higher taxes to pay off the government debt in the future. What does this belief do to private saving and the supply of loanable funds today? Does it increase or decrease the effects you discussed in parts (a) and (b)?

7. Over the past 20 years, new computer technology has enabled firms to reduce substantially the amount of inventories they hold for each unit of sales. Illustrate the effect of this change on the market for loanable funds. (Hint: expenditure on inventories is a type of investment.) What do you think has been the effect on investment in factories and equipment?

8. 'Some economists worry that the ageing populations of industrial countries are going to start running down their savings just when the investment appetite of emerging economies is growing' (*The Economist,* 6 May 1995). Illustrate the effect of these phenomena on the world market for loanable funds.

9. This chapter explains that investment can be increased both by reducing taxes on private saving and by reducing the government budget deficit.

a. Why is it difficult to implement both of these policies at the same time?

b. What would you need to know about private saving in order to judge which of these two policies would be a more effective way to raise investment?

10. Is it ever possible for fundamental analysis to tell an investor everything they need to know about the value of an asset? Explain your answer.

PART 6

INTRODUCTION TO
MACROECONOMICS

16 THE MACROECONOMIC ENVIRONMENT

LEARNING OBJECTIVES

In this chapter you will:

- Consider why an economy's total income equals its total expenditure

- Learn how gross domestic product (GDP) is defined and calculated

- See the breakdown of GDP into its four major components

- Learn the distinction between real GDP and nominal GDP

- Learn how the consumer prices index (CPI) is constructed

- Consider why the CPI is an imperfect measure of the cost of living

- Compare the CPI and the GDP deflator as measures of the overall price level

- Learn about the data used to measure the amount of unemployment

After reading this chapter you should be able to:

- Demonstrate why income equals expenditure equals output

- Explain the key words and phrases in the definition of GDP

- Define consumption, investment, government purchases and net exports

- Calculate real and nominal GDP using base year and current year prices

- List the five steps necessary to calculate the inflation rate

- Discuss three reasons why the CPI may be biased

- Describe two differences between the CPI and GDP deflator

- Explain the relationship between the real interest rate, the nominal interest rate, and the inflation rate

- Learn the distinction between real and nominal interest rates

- Learn the meaning of absolute advantage and comparative advantage

- See how comparative advantage explains the gains from trade

- See how saving, domestic investment, and net capital outflow are related

- Learn how net exports measure the international flow of goods and services

- Learn how net capital outflow measures the international flow of capital

- Consider why net exports must always equal net capital outflow

- Learn the meaning of the nominal exchange rate and the real exchange rate

- Examine purchasing power parity as a theory of how exchange rates are determined

- Use data on the number of employed, unemployed, and not in the labour force to calculate the unemployment rate and the labour force participation rate

- Explain why all businesses have a comparative advantage even if they have no absolute advantage

- Demonstrate the link between comparative advantage and opportunity cost

- Define net exports

- Define net capital outflow

- Explain why net exports and net capital outflow are two sides of the same coin

- Explain why a trade deficit and a negative net capital outflow can be beneficial to a country if that country has a small savings rate

- Show the relationship between the real and nominal exchange rate

- Show why the nominal exchange rate between two country's currencies should equal their relative price levels

INTRODUCTION

In Chapter 3 we looked at a framework for understanding the various influences on business activity. One of the external environments was the economic environment. All businesses have to operate within this economic environment and how the economy as a whole works is largely out of an individual firm's control. In some years, firms throughout the economy are expanding their production of goods and services. This helps create more business activity for other firms who act as suppliers, distributors, provide financial services or advice, act as wholesalers or suppliers and so many businesses benefit as a result. In other years, firms are cutting back on production; as employment declines spending gets cut back and firms throughout the economy find that business activity has slowed and operating becomes increasingly challenging.

Because the condition of the overall economy profoundly affects all of us, including businesses, changes in economic conditions are widely reported by the media. These reports cover the total income of everyone in the economy called gross domestic product (GDP), the rate at which average prices are rising (inflation), the percentage of the labour force that is out of work (unemployment), total spending in shops (retail sales), or the imbalance of trade between the domestic economy and the rest of the world (the trade deficit). All these statistics are *macroeconomic*. Rather than telling us about a particular household or firm, they tell us something about the entire economy.

Central to the study of macroeconomics is data. Firms pay close attention to macroeconomic data because it gives clues about the direction in which the economy, not only in the domestic country but around the world, is heading. This information can be factored into decision making so that the firm can try and anticipate events and be better prepared to be able to manage the changing macroeconomic environment as a result. For example, if data suggests the economy is slowing down, firms may put plans in place to cut back production and sell off inventory (stock). If the economy looks to be picking up firms may invest to ensure they have the capacity to meet anticipated demand.

In this chapter we will look at some key macroeconomic variables: gross domestic product, inflation, unemployment, savings and investment and exchange rates.

THE ECONOMY'S INCOME AND EXPENDITURE

When judging whether the economy is doing well or poorly, we look at how total incomes earned from overall production is changing. This is referred to as gross domestic product (GDP). GDP measures two things at once: the total income of everyone in the economy and the total expenditure on the economy's output of goods and services. An economy's income is the same as its expenditure because every transaction has two parties: a buyer and a seller. Every euro of spending by some buyer is a euro of income for some seller. Suppose, for instance, that John Watson, a local builder, is constructing an extension for a client and purchases €1000 worth of bricks, cement and timber from a local builder's merchants. The builder's merchant earns €1000 and John spends €1000. Thus, the transaction contributes equally to the economy's income and to its expenditure. GDP, whether measured as total income or total expenditure, rises by €1000.

Another way to see the equality of income and expenditure is with the circular-flow diagram in Figure 16.1. This is a model which describes all the transactions between households and firms in a simple economy. In this economy, households buy goods

FIGURE 16.1

The Circular-Flow Diagram

Households buy goods and services from firms, and firms use their revenue from sales to pay wages to workers, rent to landowners and profit to firm owners. GDP equals the total amount spent by households in the market for goods and services. It also equals the total wages, rent and profit paid by firms in the markets for the factors of production.

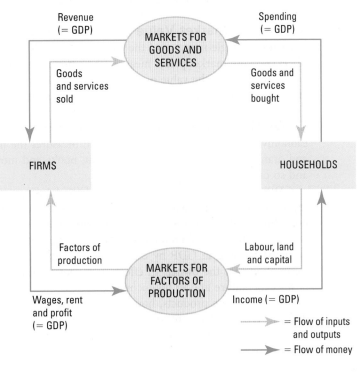

and services from firms; these expenditures flow through the markets for goods and services. The firms in turn use the money they receive from sales to pay workers' wages, landowners' rent and firm owners' profit; this income flows through the markets for the factors of production. In this economy, money flows from households to firms and then back to households.

We can compute GDP for this economy in one of two ways: by adding up the total expenditure by households or by adding up the total income (wages, rent and profit) paid by firms. Because all expenditure in the economy ends up as someone's income, GDP is the same regardless of how we compute it.

The actual economy is, of course, more complicated than the one illustrated in Figure 16.1. In particular, households do not spend all of their income. They pay some of it to the government in taxes, and they save some for use in the future. In addition, households do not buy all goods and services produced in the economy. Some goods and services are bought by governments, and some are bought by firms that plan to use them in the future to produce their own output. Some goods are bought from sellers in foreign countries and some domestic products are sold abroad. Yet, regardless of whether a household, government or firm buys a good or service, the transaction has a buyer and seller. Thus, for the economy as a whole, expenditure and income are always the same.

> **Quick Quiz** What two things does gross domestic product measure? How can it measure two things at once?

THE MEASUREMENT OF GROSS DOMESTIC PRODUCT

The following is a more detailed breakdown of how GDP is measured:

gross domestic product (GDP)
the market value of all final goods and services produced within a country in a given period of time

> ***Gross domestic product (GDP)*** *is the market value of all final goods and services produced within a country in a given period of time.*

Let's consider each phrase in this definition.

'GDP Is the Market Value ...'   GDP adds together many different kinds of products into a single measure of the value of economic activity. To do this, it uses market prices. Because market prices measure the amount people are willing to pay for different goods, they reflect the value of those goods. If the price of an apple is twice the price of an orange, then an apple contributes twice as much to GDP as does an orange.

'... Of All ...'   GDP tries to be comprehensive. It includes all items produced in the economy and sold legally in markets. GDP measures the market value of not just apples and oranges, but also pears and grapefruit, books and movies, haircuts and health care, and so on.

GDP also includes the market value of the housing services provided by the economy's stock of housing. For rental housing, this value is easy to calculate – the rent equals both the tenant's expenditure and the landlord's income. Yet many people own the place where they live and, therefore, do not pay rent. The government includes this owner-occupied housing in GDP by estimating its rental value. That is, GDP is based on the assumption that the owner, in effect, pays rent to himself, so the rent is included both in his expenditure and in his income.

There are some products, however, that GDP excludes because measuring them is so difficult. GDP excludes most items produced and sold illicitly, such as illegal drugs or when work is done on a cash-in-hand basis and is not declared as income by the receiver. It also excludes most items that are produced and consumed at home and, therefore, never enter the marketplace. Vegetables you buy at the greengrocer's shop or the supermarket are part of GDP; vegetables you grow in your garden are not.

'... Final ...' When a paper company sells paper to a greetings card company, the paper is called an *intermediate good,* and the card is called a *final good.* GDP includes only the value of final goods. The reason is that the value of intermediate goods is already included in the prices of the final goods. Adding the market value of the paper to the market value of the card would be double counting. That is, it would (incorrectly) count the paper twice.

An important exception to this principle arises when an intermediate good is produced and, rather than being used, is added to a firm's inventory of goods to be used or sold at a later date. In this case, the intermediate good is taken to be 'final' for the moment, and its value as inventory investment is added to GDP. When the inventory of the intermediate good is later used or sold, the firm's inventory investment is negative, and GDP for the later period is reduced accordingly.

'... Goods and Services ...' GDP includes both tangible goods (food, clothing, cars) and intangible services (haircuts, house cleaning, doctor visits). When you (legally) download an album by your favourite band, you are buying a good, and the purchase price is part of GDP. When you pay to hear a concert by the same band, you are buying a service, and the ticket price is also part of GDP.

'... Produced ...' GDP includes goods and services currently produced. It does not include transactions involving items produced in the past. When Aston Martin produces and sells a new car, the value of the car is included in the GDP of the country in which Aston Martin operates. When one person sells a used car to another person, the value of the used car is not included in GDP.

'... Within a Country ...' GDP measures the value of production within the geographic confines of a country. When an Australian citizen works temporarily in South Africa, his production is part of South African GDP. When a UK citizen owns a factory in Bulgaria, the production at his factory is not part of UK GDP (it's part of Bulgaria's GDP). Thus, items are included in a nation's GDP if they are produced domestically, regardless of the nationality of the producer.

'... in a Given Period of Time.' GDP measures the value of production that takes place within a specific interval of time. Usually that interval is a year or a quarter (three months). GDP measures the economy's flow of income and expenditure during that interval.

When the government reports the GDP for a quarter, it usually presents GDP 'at an annual rate'. This means that the figure reported for quarterly GDP is the amount of income and expenditure during the quarter multiplied by 4. The government uses this convention so that quarterly and annual figures on GDP can be compared more easily.

In addition, when the government reports quarterly GDP, it presents the data after they have been modified by a statistical procedure called *seasonal adjustment.* The unadjusted data show clearly that the economy produces more goods and services during some times of the year than during others. (As you might guess, December's holiday shopping season is a high point in many countries whilst the period before Ramadan is a high point for many Muslim countries.) When monitoring the condition of the economy, economists and policy makers often want to look beyond these regular seasonal changes. Therefore, government statisticians adjust the quarterly data to take out the seasonal cycle. The GDP data reported in the news are always seasonally adjusted.

FYI

Other Measures of Income

When the Office for National Statistics or Eurostat computes the GDP every three months for the UK and the EU respectively, they also compute various other measures of income to arrive at a more complete picture of what's happening in the economy. These other measures differ from GDP by excluding or including certain categories of income. What follows is a brief description of five of these income measures.

- *Gross national product* (GNP) is the total income earned by a nation's permanent residents (called nationals). It differs from GDP by including income that citizens earn abroad and excluding income that foreigners earn as we saw above. For most countries domestic residents are responsible for most domestic production, so GDP and GNP are quite close.
- *Net national product* (NNP) is the total income of a nation's residents (GNP) minus losses from deprecia-

tion. *Depreciation* is the wear and tear on the economy's stock of equipment and structures, such as lorries rusting and computers becoming obsolete.
- *National income* is the total income earned by a nation's residents in the production of goods and services. It differs from net national product by excluding indirect business taxes (such as sales taxes) and including business subsidies. NNP and national income also differ because of a 'statistical discrepancy' that arises from problems in data collection.
- *Personal income* is the income that households and non-corporate businesses receive. Unlike national income, it excludes *retained earnings*, which is income that corporations have earned but have not paid out to their owners. It also subtracts corporate income taxes and contributions for social insurance. In addition, personal income includes

the interest income that households receive from their holdings of government debt and the income that households receive from government transfer programmes, such as welfare and social security payments.
- *Disposable personal income* is the income that households and non-corporate businesses have left after satisfying all their obligations to the government. It equals personal income minus personal taxes and certain non-tax payments (such as parking tickets).

Although the various measures of income differ in detail, they almost always tell the same story about economic conditions. When GDP is growing rapidly, these other measures of income are usually growing rapidly. And when GDP is falling, these other measures are usually falling as well. For monitoring fluctuations in the overall economy, it does not matter much which measure of income we use.

? **what if...** a business receives a cash payment for a job – does the value of the work carried out contribute to GDP? What might your answer depend upon?

THE COMPONENTS OF GDP

Spending in the economy takes many forms. At any moment, the Müller family may be having lunch in a Munich restaurant; Honda may be building a car factory on the banks of the Rhine; the German Army may be procuring weapons from German arms manufacturers; and a New York investment company may be buying bonds from a German bank. German GDP includes all of these various forms of spending on domestically produced goods and services. Similarly, each country in Europe will monitor the forms of spending and income to arrive at the GDP for that country.

To understand how the economy is using its scarce resources and how this use affects business activity and planning, economists are often interested in studying the composition of GDP among various types of spending. To do this, GDP (which we denote as Y) is divided into four components: consumption (C), investment (I), government purchases (G) and net exports (NX):

$$Y \equiv C + I + G + NX$$

This equation is an *identity* – an equation that must be true by the way the variables in the equation are defined. (That's why we used the three-bar, 'identically equals' symbol, '$\equiv$', although for the most part we'll follow normal practice in dealing with identities and use the usual equals sign, '$=$'.) In this case, because each pound, dirham, rand or euro of expenditure included in GDP is placed into one of the four components of GDP, the total of the four components must be equal to GDP. Let's look at each of these four components more closely.

Consumption

Consumption is spending by households on goods and services. 'Goods' include household spending on durable goods, such as cars and appliances like washing machines and fridges, and non-durable goods, such as food and clothing.

'Services' include intangible items such as haircuts and medical care. Household spending on education is also included in consumption of services (although one might argue that it would fit better in the next component).

> **consumption** spending by households on goods and services, with the exception of purchases of new housing

Investment

Investment is the purchase of goods that will be used in the future to produce more goods and services. It is the sum of purchases of capital equipment, inventories and structures. Investment in structures includes expenditure on new housing. By convention, the purchase of a new house is the one form of household spending categorized as investment rather than consumption.

The treatment of inventory accumulation is noteworthy. When Honda produces a car and, instead of selling it, adds it to its inventory, Honda is assumed to have 'purchased' the car for itself. That is, the national income accountants treat the car as part of Honda's investment spending. (If Honda later sells the car out of inventory, Honda's inventory investment will then be negative, offsetting the positive expenditure of the buyer.) Inventories are treated this way because one aim of GDP is to measure the value of the economy's production, and goods added to inventory are part of that period's production.

Government Purchases

Government purchases include spending on goods and services by local and national governments. It includes the salaries of government workers and spending on public works.

The meaning of 'government purchases' requires a little clarification. When the government pays the salary of an army general, that salary is part of government purchases. But what happens when the government pays a social security benefit to one of the elderly? Such government spending is called a **transfer payment** because it is not made in exchange for a currently produced good or service. Transfer payments alter household income, but they do not reflect the economy's production. (From a macroeconomic standpoint, transfer payments are like negative taxes.) Because GDP is intended to measure income from, and expenditure on, the production of goods and services, transfer payments are not counted as part of government purchases.

> **government purchases** spending on goods and services by local, state and national governments

> **transfer payment** a payment for which no good or service is exchanged

Net Exports

Net exports equal the purchases of domestically produced goods by foreigners (exports) minus the domestic purchases of foreign goods (imports). A domestic firm's sale to a buyer in another country, such as the sale of Honda cars to customers in South Africa from the UK, increases UK net exports.

The 'net' in 'net exports' refers to the fact that the value of imports is subtracted from the value of exports. This subtraction is made because imports of goods and services are included in other components of GDP. For example, suppose that a UK household buys a £30 000 car from Volvo, the Swedish car maker. That transaction increases consumption in the UK by £30 000 because car purchases are part of consumer spending in the UK. It also reduces net exports by £30 000 because the car is an import (note it represents an export for Sweden). In other words, net exports include goods and services produced abroad (with a minus sign) because these goods and services are included in consumption, investment and government purchases (with a plus sign). Thus, when a domestic household, firm or government buys a good or service from abroad, the purchase reduces net exports – but because it also raises consumption, investment or government purchases, it does not affect GDP. The above example shows the importance of making sure that we focus on a particular country when discussing imports and exports because of the potential for confusion to arise.

Quick Quiz List the four components of expenditure. Which is the largest?

REAL VERSUS NOMINAL GDP

As we have seen, GDP measures the total spending on goods and services in all markets in the economy. If total spending rises from one year to the next, one of two things must be true (or a combination of the two): (1) the economy is producing a larger output of goods and services, or (2) goods and services are being sold at higher prices. When studying changes in the economy over time, economists want to separate these two effects and businesses need to be able to have an accurate and stable picture of what is happening on which to base decision making. In particular, they want a measure of the total quantity of goods and services the economy is producing that is not affected by changes in the prices of those goods and services.

The answer is *real GDP*. Real GDP answers a hypothetical question: what would be the value of the goods and services produced this year if we valued these goods and services at the prices that prevailed in some specific year in the past? By evaluating current production using prices that are fixed at past levels, real GDP shows how the economy's overall production of goods and services changes over time.

To see more precisely how real GDP is constructed, let's consider an example. Table 16.1 shows some data for an economy that produces only two goods – hot dogs and hamburgers. The table shows the quantities of the two goods produced and their prices in the years 2011, 2012 and 2013.

To compute total spending in this economy, we would multiply the quantities of hot dogs and hamburgers by their prices. In the year 2011, 100 hot dogs are sold at a price of €1 per hot dog, so expenditure on hot dogs equals €100. In the same year, 50 hamburgers are sold for €2 per hamburger, so expenditure on hamburgers also equals €100. Total expenditure in the economy – the sum of expenditure on hot dogs and expenditure on hamburgers – is €200. This amount, the production of goods and services valued at current prices, is called **nominal GDP**.

TABLE 16.1

Real and Nominal GDP

This table shows how to calculate nominal GDP, real GDP and the GDP deflator for a hypothetical economy that produces only hot dogs and hamburgers.

Prices and quantities

Year	Price of hot dogs €	Quantity of hot dogs	Price of hamburgers €	Quantity of hamburgers
2011	1	100	2	50
2012	2	150	3	100
2013	3	200	4	150

Year	Calculating nominal GDP
2011	(€1 per hot dog × 100 hot dogs) + (€2 per hamburger × 50 hamburgers) = €200
2012	(€2 per hot dog × 150 hot dogs) + (€3 per hamburger × 100 hamburgers) = €600
2013	(€3 per hot dog × 200 hot dogs) + (€4 per hamburger × 150 hamburgers) = €1200

Year	Calculating real GDP (base year 2011)
2011	(€1 per hot dog × 100 hot dogs) + (€2 per hamburger × 50 hamburgers) = €200
2012	(€1 per hot dog × 150 hot dogs) + (€2 per hamburger × 100 hamburgers) = €350
2013	(€1 per hot dog × 200 hot dogs) + (€2 per hamburger × 150 hamburgers) = €500

Year	Calculating the GDP deflator
2011	(€200/€200) × 100 = 100
2012	(€600/€350) × 100 = 171
2013	(€1200/€500) × 100 = 240

The table shows the calculation of nominal GDP for these three years. Total spending rises from €200 in 2011 to €600 in 2012 and then to €1200 in 2013. Part of this rise is attributable to the increase in the quantities of hot dogs and hamburgers, and part is attributable to the increase in the prices of hot dogs and hamburgers.

To obtain a measure of the amount produced that is not affected by changes in prices, we use **real GDP**, which is the production of goods and services valued at constant prices. We calculate real GDP by first choosing one year as a *base year*. We then use the prices of hot dogs and hamburgers in the base year to compute the value of goods and services in all of the years. In other words, the prices in the base year provide the basis for comparing quantities in different years.

Suppose that we choose 2011 to be the base year in our example. We can then use the prices of hot dogs and hamburgers in 2011 to compute the value of goods and services produced in 2011, 2012 and 2013. Table 16.1 shows these calculations. To compute real GDP for 2011 we use the prices of hot dogs and hamburgers in 2011 (the base year) and the quantities of hot dogs and hamburgers produced in 2011. (Thus, for the base year, real GDP always equals nominal GDP.) To compute real GDP for 2012, we use the prices of hot dogs and hamburgers in 2011 (the base year) and the quantities of hot dogs and hamburgers produced in 2012. Similarly, to compute real GDP for 2013, we use the prices in 2011 and the quantities in 2013. When we find that real GDP has risen from €200 in 2011 to €350 in 2012 and then to €500 in 2013, we know that the increase is attributable to an increase in the quantities produced, because the prices are being held fixed at base-year levels.

To sum up: nominal GDP uses current prices to place a value on the economy's production of goods and services, while real GDP uses constant base-year prices to place a value on the economy's production of goods and services. Because real GDP is not affected by

real GDP a measure of the amount produced that is not affected by changes in prices changes in prices, changes in real GDP reflect only changes in the amounts being produced. Thus, real GDP is a measure of the economy's production of goods and services.

Our goal in computing GDP is to gauge how well the overall economy is performing. Because real GDP measures the economy's production of goods and services, it reflects the economy's ability to satisfy people's needs and desires. Thus, real GDP is a better gauge of economic well-being than is nominal GDP. When economists talk about the economy's GDP, they usually mean real GDP rather than nominal GDP. And when they talk about growth in the economy, they measure that growth as the percentage change in real GDP from one period to another.

The GDP Deflator

Nominal GDP reflects both the prices of goods and services and the quantities of goods and services the economy is producing. In contrast, by holding prices constant at base-year levels, real GDP reflects only the quantities produced. From these two statistics we can compute a third, called the GDP deflator, which reflects the prices of goods and services but not the quantities produced.

The **GDP deflator** is calculated as follows:

$$\text{GDP deflator} = (\text{Nominal GDP}/\text{Real GDP}) \times 100$$

GDP deflator a measure of the price level calculated as the ratio of nominal GDP to real GDP times 100

Because nominal GDP and real GDP must be the same in the base year, the GDP deflator for the base year always equals 100. The GDP deflator for subsequent years measures the change in nominal GDP from the base year that cannot be attributable to a change in real GDP.

The GDP deflator measures the current level of prices relative to the level of prices in the base year. To see why this is true, consider a couple of simple examples. First, imagine that the quantities produced in the economy rise over time but prices remain the same. In this case, both nominal and real GDP rise together, so the GDP deflator is constant. Now suppose, instead, that prices rise over time but the quantities produced stay the same. In this second case, nominal GDP rises but real GDP remains the same, so the GDP deflator rises as well. Notice that, in both cases, the GDP deflator reflects what's happening to prices, not quantities.

Let's now return to our numerical example in Table 16.1. The GDP deflator is computed at the bottom of the table. For year 2011, nominal GDP is €200, and real GDP is €200, so the GDP deflator is 100. For the year 2012, nominal GDP is €600, and real GDP is €350, so the GDP deflator is 171. Because the GDP deflator rose in year 2012 from 100 to 171, we can say that the price level increased by 71 per cent.

Quick Quiz Define real and nominal GDP. Which is a better measure of economic well-being? Why?

MEASURING THE COST OF LIVING

Distinguishing between real and nominal GDP is important but this leads us to another question – how do we measure changes in prices over time and the change in prices of all goods and services produced in the economy as opposed to the bundle of goods bought by the average household? Changes in prices affect businesses as well as consumers. If firms face increases in the price of component parts, raw materials and other supplies then they will have to consider whether to increase prices of finished goods to the consumer or maintain their selling price and accept lower profit margins. If they do pass on these price increases to consumers, what will rivals do and how will consumers respond?

To measure these changes in prices we use a statistic called the *consumer prices index*. The consumer prices index is used to monitor changes in the cost of living over time. Economists use the term *inflation* to describe a situation in which the economy's overall price level is rising. The *inflation rate* is the percentage change in the price level from the previous period.

THE CONSUMER PRICES INDEX

The **consumer prices index (CPI)** is a measure of the overall prices of the goods and services bought by a typical consumer. It is a standard method of measuring changes in prices adopted in many countries.

consumer prices index (CPI) a measure of the overall prices of the goods and services bought by a typical consumer

How the Consumer Prices Index Is Calculated

To calculate the consumer prices index and the inflation rate, national statistics offices use data on the prices of thousands of goods and services. To see exactly how these statistics are constructed, let's revisit our simple economy in which consumers buy only two goods – hot dogs and hamburgers. Table 16.2 shows the five steps that national statistics offices follow.

1. *Fix the basket.* The first step in computing the consumer prices index is to determine which prices are most important to the typical consumer. If the typical consumer buys

---

TABLE 16.2

Calculating the Consumer Prices Index and the Inflation Rate: An Example

This table shows how to calculate the consumer prices index and the inflation rate for a hypothetical economy in which consumers buy only hot dogs and hamburgers.

Step 1: Survey consumers to determine a fixed basket of goods

4 hot dogs, 2 hamburgers

Step 2: Find the price of each good in each year

Year	Price of hot dogs €	Price of hamburgers €
2011	1	2
2012	2	3
2013	3	4

Step 3: Compute the cost of the basket of goods in each year

2011	(€1 per hot dog × 4 hot dogs) + (€2 per hamburger × 2 hamburgers) = €8
2012	(€2 per hot dog × 4 hot dogs) + (€3 per hamburger × 2 hamburgers) = €14
2013	(€3 per hot dog × 4 hot dogs) + (€4 per hamburger × 2 hamburgers) = €20

Step 4: Choose one year as a base year (2011) and compute the consumer prices index in each year

2011	(€8/€8) × 100 = 100
2012	(€14/€8) × 100 = 175
2013	(€20/€8) × 100 = 250

Step 5: Use the consumer prices index to compute the inflation rate from previous year

2012	(175 − 100)/100 × 100 = 75%
2013	(250 − 175)/175 × 100 = 43%

New products like tablet PCs have to be added to the basket and others removed in order to keep the representative sample of goods up to date and relevant to household spending decisions.

more hot dogs than hamburgers, then the price of hot dogs is more important than the price of hamburgers and, therefore, should be given greater weight in measuring the cost of living. The statistics office sets these weights by surveying consumers and finding the basket of goods and services that the typical consumer buys. In the example in the table, the typical consumer buys a basket of 4 hot dogs and 2 hamburgers.

2. *Find the prices.* The second step in computing the consumer prices index is to find the prices of each of the goods and services in the basket for each point in time. The table shows the prices of hot dogs and hamburgers for three different years.

3. *Compute the basket's cost.* The third step is to use the data on prices to calculate the cost of the basket of goods and services at different times. The table shows this calculation for each of the three years. Notice that only the prices in this calculation change. By keeping the basket of goods the same (4 hot dogs and 2 hamburgers), we are isolating the effects of price changes from the effect of any quantity changes that might be occurring at the same time.

4. *Choose a base year and compute the index.* The fourth step is to designate one year as the base year, which is the benchmark against which other years are compared. To calculate the index, the price of the basket of goods and services in each year is divided by the price of the basket in the base year, and this ratio is then multiplied by 100. The resulting number is the consumer prices index.

In the example in the table, the year 2011 is the base year. In this year, the basket of hot dogs and hamburgers costs €8. Therefore, the price of the basket in all years is divided by €8 and multiplied by 100. The consumer prices index is 100 in 2011. (The index is always 100 in the base year.) The consumer prices index is 175 in 2012. This means that the price of the basket in 2012 is 175 per cent of its price in the base year. Put differently, a basket of goods that costs €100 in the base year costs €175 in 2012. Similarly, the consumer prices index is 250 in 2013, indicating that the price level in 2013 is 250 per cent of the price level in the base year.

inflation rate the percentage change in the price index from the preceding period

1. *Compute the inflation rate.* The fifth and final step is to use the consumer prices
5. index to calculate the **inflation rate**, which is the percentage change in the price index from the preceding period. That is, the inflation rate between two consecutive years is computed as follows:

Inflation rate in year 2 = 100 × (CPI in year 2 − CPI in year 1)/CPI in year 1

In our example, the inflation rate is 75 per cent in 2012 and 43 per cent in 2013.

Although this example simplifies the real world by including only two goods, it shows how statistics offices compute the consumer prices index and the inflation rate. Statistics offices collect and process data on the prices of thousands of goods and services every month and, by following the five foregoing steps, determines how quickly the cost of living for the typical consumer is rising.

In addition to the consumer prices index for the overall economy, statistics offices may calculate price indices for the sub-categories of 'goods' and of 'services' separately, as well as the **producer price index**, which measures the change in prices of a basket of goods and services bought by firms rather than consumers. Because firms eventually pass on their costs to consumers in the form of higher consumer prices, changes in the producer price index are often thought to be useful in predicting changes in the consumer prices index.

producer price index a measure of the change in prices of a basket of goods and services bought by firms

Problems in Measuring the Cost of Living

The goal of the consumer prices index is to measure changes in the cost of living. In other words, the consumer prices index tries to gauge how much incomes must rise in order to maintain a constant standard of living. The consumer prices index, however, is not a perfect measure of the cost of living. Three problems with the index are widely acknowledged but difficult to solve.

Substitution Bias The first problem is called *substitution bias*. When prices change from one year to the next, they do not all change proportionately: some prices rise more than others and some prices fall. Consumers respond to these differing price changes by buying less of the goods whose prices have risen by large amounts and by buying more of the goods whose prices have risen less or perhaps even have fallen. That is, consumers substitute towards goods that have become relatively less expensive. If a price index is computed assuming a fixed basket of goods, it ignores the possibility of consumer substitution and, therefore, overstates the increase in the cost of living from one year to the next.

Let's consider a simple example. Imagine that in the base year apples are cheaper than pears, and so consumers buy more apples than pears. When the statistics office constructs the basket of goods, it will include more apples than pears. Suppose that next year pears are cheaper than apples. Consumers will naturally respond to the price changes by buying more pears and fewer apples. Yet, when computing the consumer prices index, the statistics office uses a fixed basket, which in essence assumes that consumers continue buying the now expensive apples in the same quantities as before. For this reason, the index will measure a much larger increase in the cost of living than consumers actually experience.

Introduction of New Goods The second problem with the consumer prices index is the *introduction of new goods*. When a new good is introduced, consumers have more variety from which to choose. Greater variety, in turn, makes each pound more valuable, so consumers need fewer euro to maintain any given standard of living. Yet because the consumer prices index is based on a fixed basket of goods and services, it does not reflect this change in the purchasing power of the pound.

Unmeasured Quality Change The third problem with the consumer prices index is *unmeasured quality change*. If the quality of a good deteriorates from one year to the next, the effective value of a pound falls, even if the price of the good stays the same. Similarly, if the quality rises from one year to the next, the effective value of a pound rises. The ONS does its best to account for quality change. When the quality of a good in the basket changes – for example, when a car model has more horsepower or gets better petrol mileage from one year to the next – the statistics office adjusts the price of the good to account for the quality change. It is, in essence, trying to compute the price of a basket of goods of constant quality.

To take another example, digital cameras were introduced into some baskets in around 2004 but are subject to very rapid technological progress – features such as zoom and the number of megapixels in the pictures taken keep on improving. Thus, while the average price of a digital camera might remain the same over a period, the average quality may have risen substantially. Statistics offices attempt to correct for this by a method known as hedonic quality adjustment. This involves working out the average characteristics (e.g. LCD screen size, number of megapixels, zoom features, etc.) of the average digital camera and adjusting the price when one of these average characteristics increases.

Despite these efforts, changes in quality remain a problem, because quality is so hard to measure.

Relevance A final problem with the index is that people may not see the reported CPI measure of inflation as relevant to their particular situation. This is because their spending patterns are individual and might not be typical of the representative pattern on which the official figures are based. For example, if an individual spent a high proportion of their income on fuel and their mortgage, the effect of price rises in gas, electricity, petrol and a rise in mortgage rates would have a disproportionate effect on their own experience of inflation.

The GDP Deflator versus the Consumer Prices Index

Earlier in this chapter, we introduced the GDP deflator. Economists and policy makers monitor both the GDP deflator and the consumer prices index to gauge how quickly prices are rising. Usually, these two statistics tell a similar story. Yet there are two important differences that can cause them to diverge.

The first difference is that the GDP deflator reflects the prices of all goods and services *produced domestically,* whereas the consumer prices index reflects the prices of all goods and services *bought by consumers.* For example, suppose that the price of an aeroplane produced by Dassault, a French aerospace firm and sold to the French Air Force, rises. Even though the aeroplane is part of GDP in France, it is not part of the basket of goods and services bought by a typical consumer. Thus, the price increase shows up in the GDP deflator for France but not in the consumer prices index.

This first difference between the consumer prices index and the GDP deflator is particularly important when the price of oil changes. Although the United Kingdom does produce some oil, as with all of Europe and also North America, much of the oil used in the UK is imported from the Middle East. As a result, oil and oil products such as petrol and heating oil comprise a much larger share of consumer spending than they do of GDP. When the price of oil rises, the consumer prices index rises by much more than does the GDP deflator.

The second and subtler difference between the GDP deflator and the consumer prices index concerns how various prices are weighted to yield a single number for the overall level of prices. The consumer prices index compares the price of a *fixed* basket of goods and services with the price of the basket in the base year. Whilst, as we have seen, statistics offices revise the basket of goods on a regular basis, in contrast, the GDP deflator compares the price of *currently produced* goods and services with the price of the same goods and services in the base year. Thus, the group of goods and services used to compute the GDP deflator changes automatically over time. This difference is not important when all prices are changing proportionately. But if the prices of different goods and services are changing by varying amounts, the way we weight the various prices matters for the overall inflation rate.

Comparing Inflation Over Time

The purpose of measuring the overall level of prices in the economy is to permit comparisons of monetary figures from different points in time. A business might want to compare what it is paying for raw materials in 2014 compared to 2000, for example. Now that we know how price indices are calculated, let's see how we might use such an index to compare a certain figure from the past to a figure in the present.

To do this we need to know the level of prices in 2000 and the level of prices in 2014. To compare prices we need to inflate the 2000 prices to turn 2000 euro into today's euro. A price index determines the size of this inflation correction.

The formula for turning euro figures from *year T* into today's euro is the following:

$$\text{Amount in today's euro} = \text{amount in year } T \text{ euro} \times \frac{\text{Price level today}}{\text{Price level in year } T}$$

A price index such as the CPI measures the price level and determines the size of the inflation correction.

Real and Nominal Interest Rates

Correcting economic variables for the effects of inflation is particularly important, and somewhat tricky, when we look at data on interest rates. Firms have cash deposits in bank accounts which may earn interest. Conversely, when firms borrow from a bank to buy capital equipment, they will pay interest on the loan. Interest represents a payment in the future for a transfer of money in the past. As a result, interest rates always involve comparing amounts of money at different points in time. To fully understand interest rates, we need to know how to correct for the effects of inflation.

Let's consider an example. Suppose that a firm has cash deposits of €10 000 in a bank account that pays an annual interest rate of 2 per cent. After a year passes, the firm has accumulated €200 in interest. The firm then withdraws the €10 200. Is the firm €200 richer than a year earlier?

The answer depends on what we mean by 'richer'. The firm does have €200 more than before. In other words, the number of euros has risen by 2 per cent. But if prices have risen at the same time, each euro now buys less than it did a year ago. Thus, the firm's purchasing power has not risen by 2 per cent. If the inflation rate was 1 per cent, then the amount of resources the firm can buy has increased by only 1 per cent. And if the inflation rate was 5 per cent, then the price of goods has increased proportionately more than the number of euros in the account. In that case, the firm's purchasing power has actually fallen by 3 per cent.

The interest rate that the bank pays is called the **nominal interest rate**, and the interest rate corrected for inflation is called the **real interest rate**. We can write the relationship between the nominal interest rate, the real interest rate and inflation as follows:

nominal interest rate the interest rate as usually reported without a correction for the effects of inflation

$$\text{Real interest rate} = \text{Nominal interest rate} - \text{Inflation rate}$$

The real interest rate is the difference between the nominal interest rate and the rate of inflation. The nominal interest rate tells you how fast the number of pounds or euros in your bank account rises over time. The real interest rate tells you how fast the purchasing power of your bank account rises over time.

real interest rate the interest rate corrected for the effects of inflation

PRODUCTION AND GROWTH

When you travel around the world, you see tremendous variation in the standard of living. The average person in a rich country, such as the countries of Western Europe, has an income more than ten times as high as the average person in a poor country, such as India, Indonesia or Nigeria. These large differences in income are reflected in large differences in the quality of life. Richer countries have more cars, more telephones, more televisions, better nutrition, safer housing, better health care and longer life expectancy.

Growth rates vary substantially from country to country. In some East Asian countries, such as Singapore, South Korea and Taiwan, average income has risen about 7 per cent per year in recent decades. At this rate, average income doubles about every ten years. These countries have, in the length of one generation, gone from being among the poorest in the world to being among the richest. In contrast, in some African countries, such as Chad, Ethiopia and Nigeria, average income has been stagnant for many years.

There have been a number of theories advanced by economists to explain how economies grow.

Productivity

Productivity is a key determinant of living standards and growth in productivity is the key determinant of growth in living standards. The more products are produced per time period the more are available for consumption. If more is produced in a given period of time this also can mean that workers, for example, can have more leisure time and this also improves living standards. In many developed countries the average working week in hours for many people has fallen in recent decades and this means that more leisure pursuits can be followed.

A nation can enjoy a high standard of living only if it can produce a large quantity of goods and services. Western Europeans live better than Nigerians because Western European workers are more productive than Nigerian workers. The Japanese have enjoyed more rapid growth in living standards than Argentineans because Japanese workers have experienced more rapidly growing productivity. Indeed, one of the *Ten Principles of Economics* in Chapter 1 is that a country's standard of living depends on its ability to produce goods and services.

ECONOMIC GROWTH AND PUBLIC POLICY

Let's now turn to a question faced by policy makers around the world: what can government policy do to raise productivity and living standards?

The Importance of Saving and Investment

Because capital is a produced factor of production, a society can change the amount of capital it has. If today the economy produces a large quantity of new capital goods, then tomorrow it will have a larger stock of capital and be able to produce more of all types of goods and services. Thus, one way to raise future productivity is to invest more current resources in the production of capital.

One of the *Ten Principles of Economics* presented in Chapter 1 is that people face trade-offs. This principle is especially important when considering the accumulation of capital. Because resources are scarce, devoting more resources to producing capital requires devoting fewer resources to producing goods and services for current consumption. That is, for society to invest more in capital, it must consume less and save more of its current income. The growth that arises from capital accumulation is not a free lunch: it requires that society sacrifice consumption of goods and services in the present in order to enjoy higher consumption in the future.

Investment From Abroad

Investment from abroad takes several forms. BMW might build a car factory in Portugal. A capital investment that is owned and operated by a foreign entity is called *foreign direct investment*. Alternatively, a German might buy equity in a Portuguese corporation (that is, buy a share in the ownership of the corporation); the Portuguese corporation can use the proceeds from the equity sale to build a new factory. An investment that is financed with foreign money but operated by domestic residents is called *foreign portfolio investment*. In both cases, Germans provide the resources necessary to increase the stock of capital in Portugal. That is, German saving is being used to finance Portuguese investment.

When foreigners invest in a country, they do so because they expect to earn a return on their investment. BMW's car factory increases the Portuguese capital stock and, therefore, increases Portuguese productivity and Portuguese GDP. Yet BMW takes some of this additional income back to Germany in the form of profit. Similarly, when a German investor buys Portuguese equity, the investor has a right to a portion of the profit that the Portuguese corporation earns.

Investment from abroad, therefore, does not have the same effect on all measures of economic prosperity. Recall that gross domestic product (GDP) is the income earned within a country by both residents and non-residents, whereas gross national product (GNP) is the income earned by residents of a country both at home and abroad. When BMW opens its car factory in Portugal, some of the income the factory generates accrues to people who do not live in Portugal. As a result, foreign investment in Portugal raises the income of the Portuguese (measured by GNP) by less than it raises the production in Portugal (measured by GDP).

Nevertheless, investment from abroad is one way for a country to grow. Even though some of the benefits from this investment flow back to the foreign owners, this investment does increase the economy's stock of capital, leading to higher productivity and higher wages. Moreover, investment from abroad is one way for poorer countries to learn the state-of-the-art technologies developed and used in richer countries. For these reasons, many economists who advise governments in less developed economies advocate policies that encourage investment from abroad. Often this means removing restrictions that governments have imposed on foreign ownership of domestic capital.

Education

Education – investment in human capital – is at least as important as investment in physical capital for a country's long-run economic success. In the developed economies of Western Europe and North America, each extra year of schooling raises a worker's income by about 10 per cent on average. In less developed countries, where human capital is especially scarce, the gap between the wages of educated and uneducated workers is even larger. Thus, one way in which government policy can enhance the standard of living is to provide good schools and to encourage the population to take advantage of them.

Health and Nutrition

The term *human capital* usually refers to education, but it can also be used to describe another type of investment in people: expenditures that lead to a healthier population. Other things equal, healthier workers are more productive. The right investments in the health of the population provide one way for a nation to increase productivity and raise living standards.

Poverty invariably means poor living conditions, inadequate nourishment, health problems and lower productivity as a result.

Today, malnutrition is fortunately rare in developed nations (obesity is a more widespread problem). But for people in developing nations, poor health and inadequate nutrition remain obstacles to higher productivity and improved living standards. The United Nations estimates that almost a third of the population in sub-Saharan Africa is undernourished.

The causal link between health and wealth runs in both directions. Poor countries are poor, in part, because their populations are not healthy, and their populations are not healthy, in part, because they are poor and cannot afford adequate health care and nutrition. It is a vicious circle. But this fact opens the possibility of a virtuous circle. Policies that lead to more rapid economic growth would naturally improve health outcomes, which in turn would further promote economic growth.

Property Rights, Political Stability and Good Governance

An important prerequisite for the price system to work is an economy-wide respect for *property rights*. A mining company will not make the effort to mine iron ore if it expects the ore to be stolen. The company mines the ore only if it is confident that it will benefit from the ore's subsequent sale. For this reason, courts serve an important role in a market economy: they enforce property rights. Through the criminal justice system, the courts discourage direct theft. In addition, through the civil justice system, the courts ensure that buyers and sellers live up to their contracts.

Although those of us in developed countries tend to take property rights for granted, those living in less developed countries understand that lack of property rights can be a major problem. In many countries, the system of justice does not work well. Contracts are hard to enforce, and fraud often goes unpunished. In more extreme cases, the government not only fails to enforce property rights but actually infringes upon them. To do business in some countries, firms are expected to bribe powerful government officials. Such corruption impedes the coordinating power of markets. It also discourages domestic saving and investment from abroad.

One threat to property rights is political instability. When revolutions and coups are common, there is doubt about whether property rights will be respected in the future. If a revolutionary government might confiscate the capital of some businesses domestic residents have less incentive to save, invest and start new businesses. At the same time, foreigners have less incentive to invest in the country. Even the threat of revolution can act to depress a nation's standard of living.

Free Trade

Trade is, in some ways, a type of technology. When a country exports wheat and imports steel, the country benefits in the same way as if it had invented a technology for turning wheat into steel. A country that eliminates trade restrictions will, therefore, experience the same kind of economic growth that would occur after a major technological advance.

However, some of the world's poorest countries have tried to achieve more rapid economic growth by pursuing *inward-oriented policies*. These policies are aimed at raising productivity and living standards within the country by avoiding interaction with the rest of the world. This approach gets support from some domestic firms, which claim that they need protection from foreign competition in order to compete and grow. This infant-industry argument, together with a general distrust of foreigners, has at times led policy makers in less developed countries to impose tariffs and other trade restrictions.

Research and Development

The primary reason that living standards are higher today than they were a century ago is that technological knowledge has advanced. The telephone, the transistor, the computer and the internal combustion engine are among the thousands of innovations that have improved the ability to produce goods and services.

Although most technological advance comes from private research by firms and individual inventors, there is also a public interest in promoting these efforts. To a large extent, knowledge is a *public good:* once one person discovers an idea, the idea enters society's pool of knowledge and other people can freely use it (subject to any legal restrictions such as those imposed by intellectual property rights). Just as government has a role in providing a public good such as national defence, it also has a role in encouraging the research and development of new technologies. The governments in most advanced countries do this in a number of ways, for example through science research laboratories owned and funded by the government, or through a system of research grants offered to promising researchers. It may also offer tax breaks and concessions for firms engaging in research and development.

Yet another way in which government policy encourages research is through the patent system. When a person or firm invents a new product, such as a new drug, the inventor can apply for a patent. If the product is deemed truly original, the government awards the patent, which gives the inventor the exclusive right to make the product for a specified number of years. In essence, the patent gives the inventor a property right over his invention, turning his new idea from a public good into a private good. By allowing inventors to profit from their inventions – even if only temporarily – the patent system enhances the incentive for individuals and firms to engage in research.

Population Growth

Economists and other social scientists have long debated how population growth affects a society. The most direct effect is on the size of the labour force: a large population means more workers to produce goods and services. At the same time, it means more people to consume those goods and services. Beyond these obvious effects, population growth interacts with the other factors of production in ways that are less obvious and more open to debate.

Promoting Technological Progress

Although rapid population growth may depress economic prosperity by reducing the amount of capital each worker has, it may also have some benefits. Some economists have suggested that world population growth has been an engine of technological progress and economic prosperity. The mechanism is simple: if there are more people, then the greater the probability that some of those people will come up with new ideas that will lead to technological progress, which benefits everyone.

UNEMPLOYMENT

What is Unemployment?

The answer to this question may seem obvious: an unemployed person is someone who does not have a job. But as business economists we need to be precise and careful in our definitions of economic categories. If you are in full-time education, for example, you do not have a full-time job in the usual sense of the word, i.e. you are not in full-time paid employment and not available for work. If you were suffering from some long-term illness that meant that you were unfit for work although you would not have a job, we would not say that you were unemployed because you would not be available for work. From these two examples, it seems clear that we need to qualify our original definition of an unemployed person as 'someone who does not have a job' to 'someone who does not have a job and who is available for work'.

But we still need to be clear as to what we mean by 'available for work'. Suppose you were not in full-time employment and were looking for a job and I offered you a job as my research assistant for €1 a day. Would you take it? You would probably not take the job because the wage rate offered is so low. At another extreme, suppose you won so much money on the Euro Millions Lottery that you decided you would leave university and live off your winnings for the rest of your life. Would you be unemployed? No, because you would still be unavailable for work, no matter what wage rate you were offered. Thus, being unemployed also depends upon whether you are willing to work (whether you are 'available for work') at going wage rates.

We are now in a position to give a more precise definition of what it means to be unemployed: the number unemployed in an economy is the number of people of working age who are able and available for work at current wage rates and who do not have a job.

Normally, economists find it more convenient to speak of the *unemployment rate*. This expresses the number unemployed as a percentage of the *labour force*, which in turn can be defined as the total number of people who could possibly be employed in the economy at any given point in time. If you think about it, this must be equal to the total number of people who are employed plus the total number of people who are unemployed.

How is Unemployment Measured?

How do government agencies go about measuring the unemployment rate in the economy? There are two basic ways.

The Claimant Count   One simple way is to count the number of people who, on any given day, are claiming unemployment benefit payments from the government – the so-called *claimant count*. Since a government agency is paying out the benefits, it will be easy to gather data on the number of claimants. The government also has a good idea of the total labour force in employment, since it is receiving income tax payments from them. Adding to this the number of unemployment benefit claimants is a measure of the total labour force, and expressing the claimant count as a proportion of the labour force is a measure of the unemployment rate.

Labour Force Surveys   The second, and probably more reliable method of measuring unemployment is through the use of surveys – in other words, going out and asking people questions – based on an accepted definition of unemployment. Questions then arise as to whom to speak to, how often (since surveys use up resources and are costly) and what definition of unemployment to use. Although the definition of unemployment that we developed earlier seems reasonable enough, the term 'available for work at current wage rates' may be too loose for this purpose. In many countries, the government carries out Labour Force Surveys based on the standardized definition of unemployment from the International Labour Office, or ILO. The ILO definition of an unemployed person is someone who is without a job and who is willing to start work within the next two weeks and either has been looking for work within the past four weeks or was waiting to start a job. The Labour Force Survey is carried out quarterly throughout Europe. The surveys are published in different languages but scrutinized by statisticians to ensure comparability between the surveys carried out in each member state.

Once the government has placed all the individuals covered by the survey in a category, it computes various statistics to summarize the state of the labour market. The **labour force** is defined as the sum of the employed and the unemployed:

labour force the total number of workers, including both the employed and the unemployed

$$\text{Labour force} = \text{Number of employed} + \text{Number of unemployed}$$

Then the **unemployment rate** can be measured as the percentage of the labour force that is unemployed:

unemployment rate the percentage of the labour force that is unemployed

$$\text{Unemployment rate} = (\text{Number of unemployed}/\text{Labour force}) \times 100$$

The government computes unemployment rates for the entire adult population and for more narrowly defined groups – men, women, youths and so on.

The same survey results are used to produce data on labour force participation. The **labour force participation rate** measures the percentage of the total adult population of the country that is in the labour force:

labour force participation rate (or economic activity rate) the percentage of the adult population that is in the labour force

$$\text{Labour force participation rate} = (\text{Labour force}/\text{Adult population}) \times 100$$

This statistic tells us the fraction of the population that has chosen to participate in the labour market. The labour force participation rate, like the unemployment rate, is computed both for the entire adult population and for more specific groups.

Data on the labour market also allow economists and policy makers to monitor changes in the economy over time. The normal rate of unemployment, around which the unemployment rate fluctuates, is called the **natural rate of unemployment** and the deviation of unemployment from its natural rate is called **cyclical unemployment**.

natural rate of unemployment the normal rate of unemployment around which the unemployment rate fluctuates

Unemployment figures represent an important statistic for businesses because they give an indication of the performance of the economy as a whole and thus helps put together parts of the jigsaw so that businesses can make more informed decisions about the state of the economy, whether to make investments, what the labour market is like and how this might impact on wage rates and costs and how they might fill skill shortages.

cyclical unemployment the deviation of unemployment from its natural rate

Quick Quiz How is the unemployment rate measured? • How might the unemployment rate overstate the amount of joblessness? How might it understate it?

CASE STUDY

Doing Business in South Africa

This case study presents a statement by Helen Zille, leader of the Democratic Alliance and premier of the Western Cape in South Africa and outlines some of the reasons why businesses need to be aware of the macroeconomy and why governments are interested in promoting policies to help boost business activity.

The week before the state of the nation address, I walked through some streets of Cape Town to find out from members of the public what they expected from the president's speech.

In St George's Mall, I stopped to speak to Mrs Priscilla Fischer, from Mitchells Plain. Mrs Fischer had found out that day that she was being retrenched from the company where she worked as a cleaner. The company had fallen on hard times,

Even simple business activity can be difficult to set up in some countries.

and was having to retrench a number of workers. She told me that all she wanted was a chance at getting another job, but she wasn't hopeful.

Her words, and her prospects, weighed on my mind as I sat in parliament on 9 February and listened to President Jacob Zuma deliver his state of the nation address, and later when Finance Minister Pravin Gordhan delivered his budget speech. Surely it must be possible for our economy to grow fast enough to give Priscilla Fischer the opportunity she is looking for to support her family, beyond the paltry unemployment insurance she will now collect while she tries to figure out what to do next?

This is not the South Africa we want for ourselves or for our children. Our country has the resources and the potential to develop the human capital we need to grow our economy at a sufficient rate to create millions more jobs and reduce inequality.

If our economy were to grow by 8 per cent a year, it would double in size in 10 years. That would mean that by 2022 we would have R2 trillion to spend on service delivery a year; and it would mean millions of people who were previously excluded from the economy would get the life-changing experience of stepping out of dire poverty and into employment.

At the heart of our approach to the economy is the concept of opportunity – recognizing the role of the state to give each person a fair chance to succeed. We believe that the only way to increase economic growth to 8 per cent is to ensure that every young person gets a decent education, enabling them as job seekers and entrepreneurs to have a real chance at 'making it' in an appropriately regulated market.

What are the tough decisions we need to make? I have welcomed the president's announcement of massive infrastructure investment over the next few years. This is one essential element in boosting competitiveness. However, it is not sufficient to unlock the 8 per cent economic growth we need. Poor infrastructure is listed only as number six on the list of 'most problematic factors for doing business in South Africa', by the World Economic Forum's Competitiveness Report for 2010/2011. At number one, the biggest obstacle to doing business in South Africa is an inefficient government bureaucracy. Next follow issues such as inflexible labour regulations, a poorly educated workforce, and corruption. According to the World Bank's 2010 *Doing Business* report, South Africa ranks 75th in the world for ease of starting a business.

We must make it easier to do business in South Africa.

We need to recognize the value of entrepreneurs and small businesses. Writing recently in the *Financial Mail*, Neren Rau of the South African Chamber of Commerce and Industry, revealed an instructive statistic: 68 per cent of private sector employment and 50 per cent of our GDP are contributed by businesses that employ fewer than 50 people. This statistic alone should make the value of entrepreneurs in creating jobs crystal clear. We also need a tax system that gives a fair chance to small businesses. Our current tax regime assists big businesses in making massive investments of hundreds of millions of rands. Our tax system should reward and support the risk takers and job creators – the entrepreneurs.

Next, we've got to give young unemployed South Africans a foot in the door. A full 72 per cent of South Africa's unemployed are below the age of 34. The centrepiece of the Democratic Alliance's job-creating growth strategy is a comprehensive youth wage subsidy programme to lower the barriers to entry in the labour market by providing firms with a financial incentive to employ more people.

I have written extensively about the crisis in education. There is no chance of achieving the sustained growth levels we need over the medium to longer term if we do not fix our schooling system. In a knowledge-based economy, the workers of the next 20 years will increasingly need scientific, financial or technological skills to get ahead. At the moment, many thousands of deserving young students are excluded from a higher education because of spiralling fees. That is not a fair chance.

The proposals above are only a few that could be offered. A full discussion on how to create jobs could fill volumes. However, these few proposals are all based on a simple conviction: we cannot succeed unless South Africa's economy is made accessible to all. If we can achieve sustained 8 per cent growth in South Africa, we will halve unemployment in under 10 years.

Source: Adapted from: **http://www.timeslive.co.za/local/2012/03/11/we-have-to-make-it-easier-to-do-business-in-sa** accessed 11 March 2012.

SPECIALIZATION AND TRADE

Consider your typical day. You wake up in the morning and you make yourself some coffee from beans grown by farmers in Brazil, processed by businesses from the United States, or tea from leaves grown in Sri Lanka processed and turned into tea bags made in Europe. Over breakfast, you might listen to a radio programme on a radio set made by businesses in Japan. You get dressed in clothes manufactured in Thailand and sold by retail outlets. You might drive to the university or take public transport in a vehicle made of parts manufactured in more than a dozen countries around the world. Then you open up your economics textbook written by three authors of whom one lives in the USA and the other two live in England, published by a company located in Hampshire and printed on paper made from trees grown in Finland.

Every day you rely on many businesses from around the world, most of whom you have never heard of, to provide you with the goods and services that you enjoy. Such interdependence is possible because people and businesses trade with one another. These people and businesses who provide you with goods and services are not totally acting out of generosity or concern for your welfare. Nor is some government or supra-governmental agency directing them to make products you want and to give them to you. Instead, businesses provide you and other consumers with the goods and services they produce because they get something in return.

One of the *Ten Principles of Economics* highlighted in Chapter 1 is that trade can make everyone better off. This principle explains why businesses trade with each other both within an economy and internationally. In this section we examine this principle more closely.

The Principle of Comparative Advantage

Access to resources can mean that some businesses are better at producing some goods and services than others. For example, in Spain the climate means that the production of soft fruit is much less costly in terms of resource use than would be the case in Sweden. The City of London houses a large number of banks and financial institutions and London is well known for its expertise in financial products. In the Cape, conditions allow for the growth and processing of grapes for wine and in Germany, manufacturing firms are widely recognized for their high levels of productivity and quality. We call this *specialization*. If businesses specialize and trade then everyone can be made better off.

Some countries house businesses where the cost of production is always lower, for example, a farmer in one country might be better at both rearing cattle and growing potatoes. Does that mean that a farmer in another country who also grows potatoes and rears cattle cannot gain from trade? The principle of comparative advantage suggests that specialization can still occur and benefits can be gained from trading.

A key to this principle is the relative costs of production. Economists use the term **absolute advantage** when comparing the productivity of one business to that of another. The producer that requires a smaller quantity of inputs to produce a good is said to have an absolute advantage in producing that good.

A farmer can have an absolute advantage both in producing meat and in producing potatoes if he requires less time than the other farmer to produce a unit of either good. If Farmer A needs to input only 2 hours in order to produce a kilogram of meat and 1 hour to produce a kilogram of potatoes, whereas Farmer B needs 6 hours to produce a kilogram of meat and 1.5 hours for a kilogram of potatoes, then based on this information, we can conclude that Farmer A has the lower cost of producing potatoes, if we measure cost in terms of the quantity of inputs.

Opportunity Cost and Comparative Advantage

There is another way to look at the cost of producing potatoes. Rather than comparing inputs required, we can compare the opportunity costs. Let us assume that both farmers each spend 48 hours a week working. Time spent producing potatoes, therefore, takes away from time available for producing meat. As both farmers reallocate time between producing the two goods, they give up units of one good to produce units of the other. The opportunity cost measures the trade-off between the two goods that each producer faces.

Economists use the term **comparative advantage** when describing the opportunity cost of two producers. The producer who gives up less of other goods to produce good X has the smaller opportunity cost of producing good X and is said to have a comparative advantage in producing it. Although it is possible for one person to have an absolute advantage in both goods (as the farmer does in our example), it is impossible for one business to have a comparative advantage in both goods. Because the opportunity cost of one good is the inverse of the opportunity cost of the other, if a business's opportunity cost of one good is relatively high, the opportunity cost of the other good must be relatively low. Comparative advantage reflects the relative opportunity cost. Unless two businesses have exactly the same opportunity cost, one business will have a comparative advantage in one good, and the other business will have a comparative advantage in the other good. If each business specializes in the product in which they have a comparative advantage and then engage in trade, both can be better off as a result and total world output can increase.

OPEN-ECONOMY MACROECONOMICS: BASIC CONCEPTS

When you next buy some fruit in the supermarket, the chances are that you will have a choice between a domestically produced fruit – perhaps apples – and fruit produced abroad, such as mangoes or bananas. When you take your next holiday, you may consider spending it in one of the cultural capitals of Europe or taking a trip to Dubai or Egypt. When you start saving for your retirement, you may choose between a unit trust that buys mainly shares in domestic companies or one that buys shares of US or Japanese companies instead. In all of these cases, you are participating not just in the economy of your own country but in economies around the world.

There are clear benefits to being open to international trade: trade allows people to produce what they produce best and to consume the great variety of goods and services produced around the world. International trade can raise living standards in all countries by allowing each country to specialize in producing those goods and services in which it has a comparative advantage.

The International Flows of Goods and Capital

Businesses in an economy buy and sell goods and services in world product markets and they buy and sell capital assets such as stocks and bonds in world financial markets. Here we discuss these two activities and the close relationship between them.

The Flow of Goods and Services: Exports, Imports and Net Exports

Exports are domestically produced goods and services that are sold abroad, and **imports** are foreign-produced goods and services that are sold domestically. When Lloyd's of London insures a building in New York, it is paid an insurance premium for this service by the owner of the building. The sale of the insurance service provided by Lloyd's is an export for the United Kingdom and an import for the United States. When Volvo, the Swedish car manufacturer, makes a car and sells it to a Swiss resident, the sale is an import for Switzerland and an export for Sweden.

exports goods produced domestically and sold abroad

imports goods produced abroad and purchased for use in the domestic economy

> **Pitfall Prevention** Students often get confused about imports and exports and focus on the physical movement of the good rather than the direction of payment. For example, if a Dutch family decide to take a holiday in Dubai they physically travel to Dubai. However, what they are actually doing is buying a service – tourism in this case – from Dubai and so their visit represents an import to the Netherlands and an export to Dubai.

The net exports of any country are the value of its exports minus the value of its imports. The sale of insurance services abroad by Lloyd's raises UK net exports, and the Volvo sale reduces Swiss net exports. Because net exports tell us whether a country is, in total, a seller or a buyer in world markets for goods and services, net exports are also called the **trade balance**. If net exports are positive, exports are greater than imports, indicating that the country sells more goods and services abroad than it buys from other countries. In this case, the country is said to run a **trade surplus**. If net exports are negative, exports are less than imports, indicating that the country sells fewer goods and services abroad than it buys from other countries. In this case, the country is said to run a **trade deficit**. If net exports are zero, its exports and imports are exactly equal, and the country is said to have **balanced trade**.

trade balance the value of a nation's exports minus the value of its imports; also called net exports

trade surplus an excess of exports over imports

Some of the factors that might influence a country's exports, imports and net exports include the following:

trade deficit an excess of imports over exports

- The tastes of consumers for domestic and foreign goods
- The prices of goods at home and abroad
- The exchange rates at which people can use domestic currency to buy foreign currencies
- The incomes of consumers at home and abroad
- The cost of transporting goods from country to country
- The policies of the government towards international trade

balanced trade a situation in which exports equal imports

As these variables change over time, so does the amount of international trade.

The Flow of Financial Resources: Net Capital Outflow

So far we have been discussing how residents of an open economy participate in world markets for goods and services. In addition, residents of an open economy participate in world financial markets. A UK resident with £20 000 could use that money to buy a car from BMW, but he could instead use that money to buy stock in the German BMW corporation. The first transaction would represent a flow of goods, whereas the second would represent a flow of capital.

The term **net capital outflow** refers to the purchase of foreign assets by domestic residents minus the purchase of domestic assets by foreigners. (It is sometimes called *net*

net capital outflow the purchase of foreign assets by domestic residents minus the purchase of domestic assets by foreigners

foreign investment.) When a UK resident buys shares in BMW, the purchase raises UK net capital outflow. When a Japanese resident buys a bond issued by the UK government, the purchase reduces UK net capital outflow.

Recall that the flow of capital abroad takes two forms. If the French car manufacturer Renault opens up a factory in Romania, that is an example of foreign *direct investment.* Alternatively, if a French citizen buys shares in a Romanian company that is an example of *foreign portfolio investment.* In the first case, the French owner is actively managing the investment, whereas in the second case the French owner has a more passive role. In both cases, French residents are buying assets located in another country, so both purchases increase French net capital outflow.

Let's consider briefly some of the more important variables that influence net capital outflow:

- The real interest rates being paid on foreign assets
- The real interest rates being paid on domestic assets
- The perceived economic and political risks of holding assets abroad
- The government policies that affect foreign ownership of domestic assets

For example, consider German investors deciding whether to buy Mexican government bonds or German government bonds. To make this decision, German investors compare the real interest rates offered on the two bonds. The higher a bond's real interest rate, the more attractive it is. While making this comparison, however, German investors must also take into account the risk that one of these governments might *default* on its debt (that is, not pay interest or principal when it is due), as well as any restrictions that the Mexican government has imposed, or might impose in the future, on foreign investors in Mexico.

The Equality of Net Exports and Net Capital Outflow

Net exports and net capital outflow each measure a type of imbalance in these markets. Net exports measure an imbalance between a country's exports and its imports. Net capital outflow measures an imbalance between the amount of foreign assets bought by domestic residents and the amount of domestic assets bought by foreigners.

An important but subtle fact of accounting states that, for an economy as a whole, these two imbalances must offset each other. That is, net capital outflow (*NCO*) always equals net exports (*NX*):

$$NCO = NX$$

This equation holds because every transaction that affects one side of this equation must also affect the other side by exactly the same amount. This equation is an *identity* – an equation that must hold because of the way the variables in the equation are defined and measured.

To see why this accounting identity is true, consider an example. Suppose that BP sells some aircraft fuel to a Japanese airline. In this sale, a UK company (BP) gives aircraft fuel to a Japanese company, and a Japanese company gives yen to a UK company. Notice that two things have occurred simultaneously. The United Kingdom has sold to a foreigner some of its output (the fuel), and this sale increases UK net exports. In addition, the United Kingdom has acquired some foreign assets (the yen), and this acquisition increases UK net capital outflow.

Although BP most probably will not hold on to the yen it has acquired in this sale, any subsequent transaction will preserve the equality of net exports and net capital outflow. For example, BP may exchange its yen for pounds with a UK investment fund that wants the yen to buy shares in Sony Corporation, the Japanese maker of consumer electronics. In this case, BP's net export of aircraft fuel equals the investment fund's net capital outflow in Sony shares. Hence, *NX* and *NCO* rise by an equal amount.

Alternatively, BP may exchange its yen for pounds with another UK company that wants to buy computers from Toshiba, the Japanese computer maker. In this case, UK imports (of computers) exactly offset UK exports (of aircraft fuel). The sales by BP and Toshiba together affect neither UK net exports nor UK net capital outflow. That is, *NX* and *NCO* are the same as they were before these transactions took place.

The equality of net exports and net capital outflow follows from the fact that every international transaction is an exchange. When a seller country transfers a good or service to a buyer country, the buyer country gives up some asset to pay for this good or service. The value of that asset equals the value of the good or service sold. When we add everything up, the net value of goods and services sold by a country (*NX*) must equal the net value of assets acquired (*NCO*). The international flow of goods and services and the international flow of capital are two sides of the same coin.

Saving and Investment, and Their Relationship to the International Flows

A nation's saving and investment is crucial to its long-run economic growth. Let's consider how these variables are related to the international flows of goods and capital as measured by net exports and net capital outflow. We can do this most easily with the help of some simple mathematics.

The economy's gross domestic product (*Y*) is divided among four components: consumption (*C*), investment (*I*), government purchases (*G*) and net exports (*NX*). We write this as:

$$Y = C + I + G + NX$$

Total expenditure on the economy's output of goods and services is the sum of expenditure on consumption, investment, government purchases and net exports. Because each pound or euro of expenditure is placed into one of these four components, this equation is an accounting identity: it must be true because of the way the variables are defined and measured.

Recall that national saving is the income of the nation that is left after paying for current consumption and government purchases. National saving (*S*) equals $Y - C - G$. If we rearrange the above equation to reflect this fact, we obtain:

$$Y = C + G + I + NX$$

$$S = I + NX$$

Because net exports (*NX*) also equal net capital outflow (*NCO*), we can write this equation as:

$$
\begin{array}{ccccc}
S & = & I & + & NCO \\
\text{Saving} & = & \text{Domestic investemt} & + & \text{Net capital outflow}
\end{array}
$$

This equation shows that a nation's saving must equal its domestic investment plus its net capital outflow. In other words, when Dutch citizens save a euro of their income for the future, that euro can be used to finance accumulation of domestic capital or it can be used to finance the purchase of capital abroad.

In a closed economy (with no external trade), net capital outflow is zero (*NCO* = 0), so saving equals investment (*S* = *I*). In an open economy with trade there are two uses for its saving: domestic investment and net capital outflow.

We can view the financial system as standing between the two sides of this identity. For example, suppose the Smith family decides to save some of its income for retirement. This decision contributes to national saving, the left-hand side of our equation. If the Smiths deposit their saving in an investment fund, the fund may use some of the deposit to buy shares issued by BP, which uses the proceeds to build an oil refinery in Aberdeen.

In addition, the investment fund may use some of the Smiths' deposit to buy shares issued by Toyota, which uses the proceeds to build a factory in Osaka. These transactions show up on the right-hand side of the equation. From the standpoint of UK accounting, the BP expenditure on a new oil refinery is domestic investment, and the purchase of Toyota stock by a UK resident is net capital outflow. Thus, all saving in the UK economy shows up as investment in the UK economy or as UK net capital outflow.

> **Quick Quiz** Define net exports and net capital outflow. • Explain how they are related.

THE PRICES FOR INTERNATIONAL TRANSACTIONS: REAL AND NOMINAL EXCHANGE RATES

nominal exchange rate the rate at which a person can trade the currency of one country for the currency of another

Just as the price in any market serves the important role of coordinating buyers and sellers in that market, international prices help coordinate the decisions of consumers and producers as they interact in world markets.

Nominal Exchange Rates

appreciation an increase in the value of a currency as measured by the amount of foreign currency it can buy

depreciation a decrease in the value of a currency as measured by the amount of foreign currency it can buy

The **nominal exchange rate** is the rate at which a person can trade the currency of one country for the currency of another. For example, a business in Belgium trading with one in Japan might be quoted an exchange rate of 125 yen per euro. If the business gives up one euro, they would get 125 Japanese yen in return and vice versa.

An exchange rate can always be expressed in two ways. If the exchange rate is 125 yen per euro, it is also 1/125 (= 0.008) euro per yen. If a euro is worth £0.88, a pound is worth 1/0.88 (= 1.136) euros. This can be source of confusion, and there is no real hard and fast convention that people use. For example, it is customary to quote the US dollar–pound exchange rate as dollars per pound, e.g. $1.50 if £1 exchanges for $1.50. On the other hand, the pound–euro exchange rate can be quoted either way, as pounds per euro or euros per pound. In this book we shall for the most part think of the exchange rate as being the quantity of foreign currency that exchanges for one unit of domestic currency, or the foreign price of a unit of domestic currency. For example, if we are thinking of the UK as the domestic economy and the USA as the foreign economy, then the exchange rate is $1.90 per pound. If we are thinking of, say, Germany as the domestic economy, then we could express the exchange rate as dollars per euro, e.g. $1.33 dollars per euro.

If the exchange rate changes so that a euro buys more of another currency, that change is called an **appreciation** of the euro. If the exchange rate changes so that a euro buys less of another currency, that change is called a **depreciation** of the euro. For example, when the exchange rate rises from 125 to 127 yen per euro, the euro is said to appreciate. At the same time, because a Japanese yen now buys less of the European currency, the yen is said to depreciate. When the exchange rate falls from 125 to 123 yen per euro, the euro is said to depreciate, and the yen is said to appreciate. (It is sometimes helpful to think how much of the domestic currency an individual has to give up to get the required amount of the foreign currency and vice versa.)

At times you may have heard the media report that the pound or the euro is either 'strong' or 'weak'. These descriptions usually refer to recent changes in the nominal exchange rate. When a currency appreciates, it is said to *strengthen* because it can then

Currency traders in a dealing room in Seoul, South Korea spend their day trading currencies on behalf of clients from around the world. Their decisions and those of thousands of other traders across the world help determine the price of currencies, the exchange rate.

buy more foreign currency. Similarly, when a currency depreciates, it is said to *weaken*. If the individual gets more of the foreign currency in exchange for the same amount of the domestic currency, the domestic currency is stronger. If the individual has to give up more of the domestic currency to get the same amount of the foreign currency then the domestic currency is weaker.

For any currency, there are many nominal exchange rates. The euro can be used to buy US dollars, UAE dirham, South African rand, British pounds, Mexican pesos and so on. When economists study changes in the exchange rate, they often use indices that average these many exchange rates. Just as the consumer price index turns the many prices in the economy into a single measure of the price level, an exchange rate index turns these many exchange rates into a single measure of the international value of the currency. So when economists talk about the euro or the pound appreciating or depreciating, they often are referring to an exchange rate index that takes into account many individual exchange rates.

Real Exchange Rates

The **real exchange rate** is the rate at which a person can trade the goods and services of one country for the goods and services of another. For example, suppose that you go shopping and find that a kilo of Swiss cheese is twice as expensive as a kilo of English Cheddar cheese. We would then say that the real exchange rate is a ½ kilo of Swiss cheese per kilo of English cheese. Notice that, like the nominal exchange rate, we express the real exchange rate as units of the foreign item per unit of the domestic item. But in this instance the item is a good rather than a currency.

real exchange rate the rate at which a person can trade the goods and services of one country for the goods and services of another

Real and nominal exchange rates are closely related. To see how, consider an example. Suppose that a kilo of British wheat sells for £1, and a kilo of European wheat sells for €3. What is the real exchange rate between British and European wheat? To answer this question, we must first use the nominal exchange rate to convert the prices into a common currency. If the nominal exchange rate is €2 per pound, then a price for British wheat of £1 per kilo is equivalent to €2 per kilo. European wheat, however, sells for €3 a kilo, so British wheat is only ⅔ as expensive as European wheat. The real exchange rate is ⅔ of a kilo of European wheat per kilo of British wheat.

We can summarize this calculation for the real exchange rate with the following formula, where we are measuring the exchange rate as the amount of foreign currency needed to buy 1 unit of domestic currency:

$$\text{Real exchange rate} = \frac{(\text{Nominal exchange rate} \times \text{Domestic price})}{(\text{Foreign price})}$$

Using the numbers in our example, the formula applies as follows:

$$\text{Real exchange rate} = \frac{(\text{€2 per pound}) \times (\text{£1 per kilo of UK wheat})}{(\text{€3 per kilo of European wheat})}$$

$$= \text{⅔ kilo of European wheat per kilo of UK wheat}$$

Thus, the real exchange rate depends on the nominal exchange rate and on the prices of goods in the two countries measured in the local currencies.

The real exchange rate is a key determinant of how much a country exports and imports. For example, when a British bread company is deciding whether to buy British or European wheat to make into flour and use in making its bread, it will ask which wheat is cheaper. The real exchange rate gives the answer.

When studying an economy as a whole, macroeconomists focus on overall prices rather than the prices of individual items. That is, to measure the real exchange rate, they use price indices, such as the consumer prices index, which measure the price of a basket of goods and services. By using a price index for a UK or European basket (P), a price index for a foreign basket (P^*) and the nominal exchange rate between the UK pound or euro and foreign currencies (e = foreign currency per pound), we can compute the overall real exchange rate between the United Kingdom or Europe and other countries as follows:

$$\text{Real exchange rate} = (e \times P)/P^*$$

This real exchange rate measures the price of a basket of goods and services available domestically relative to a basket of goods and services available abroad.

A country's real exchange rate is a key determinant of its net exports of goods and services. A depreciation (fall) in the real exchange rate of the euro means that EU goods have become cheaper relative to foreign goods. This change encourages consumers both at home and abroad to buy more EU goods and fewer goods from other countries. Businesses in the EU selling goods to South Africa, for example, will benefit from the depreciation whereas those buying goods and services from South Africa will find the depreciation has increased their costs. As a result, EU exports rise and EU imports fall, and both of these changes raise EU net exports. Conversely, an appreciation (rise) in the euro real exchange rate means that EU goods have become more expensive compared to foreign goods, so EU net exports fall. It is important to remember that whilst we are talking about the prices of exports and imports changing, the domestic price for these goods and services may not change. For example, a French wine producer may have wine for sale priced at €10 per bottle. If the exchange rate between the euro and the South African rand is €1 = R9.9 then a South African buyer of wine will have to give up R69 to buy a bottle of wine. If the euro exchange rate appreciates to €1 = 10.5 then the South African buyer now has to give up R105 to buy the bottle of wine. The euro price of the wine has not changed but to the South African buyer the price has risen. Equally, if the euro exchange rate depreciated from €1 = R9.9 to €1 = R9.00 then the South African buyer would now have to give up R90 to buy the wine. Again, the euro price of the wine has not changed but the price to the South African buyer has fallen because the exchange rate between the pound and the euro has changed.

Quick Quiz Define nominal exchange rate and real exchange rate, and explain how they are related. • If the nominal exchange rate goes from 100 to 120 yen per euro, has the euro appreciated or depreciated?

JEOPARDY PROBLEM

A firm based in the Netherlands buys raw materials from firms in South Africa and Saudi Arabia and sells its output to firms elsewhere in the EU and to the United States. The exchange rate between the euro and those other currencies in which it trades depreciates significantly over a period of a year. The Dutch firm finds that far from benefiting from the depreciation its profits are falling. Why might this happen?

A FIRST THEORY OF EXCHANGE RATE DETERMINATION: PURCHASING POWER PARITY

Exchange rates vary substantially over time. Economists have developed many models to explain how exchange rates are determined, each emphasizing just some of the many forces at work. Here we develop the simplest theory of exchange rates, called purchasing power parity. This theory states that a unit of any given currency should be able to buy the same quantity of goods in all countries. Many economists believe that **purchasing power parity** describes the forces that determine exchange rates in the long run. We now consider the logic on which this long-run theory of exchange rates is based, as well as the theory's implications and limitations.

purchasing power parity a theory of exchange rates whereby a unit of any given currency should be able to buy the same quantity of goods in all countries

The Basic Logic of Purchasing Power Parity

The theory of purchasing power parity is based on a principle called the *law of one price*. This law asserts that a good must sell for the same price in all locations. Otherwise, there would be opportunities for profit left unexploited. For example, suppose that coffee beans sold for less in Munich than in Frankfurt. A person could buy coffee in Munich for, say, €4 a kilo and then sell it in Frankfurt for €5 a kilo, making a profit of €1 per kilo from the difference in price. The process of taking advantage of differences in prices in different markets is called *arbitrage*. In our example, as people took advantage of this arbitrage opportunity, they would increase the demand for coffee in Munich and increase the supply in Frankfurt. The price of coffee would rise in Munich (in response to greater demand) and fall in Frankfurt (in response to greater supply). This process would continue until, eventually, the prices were the same in the two markets.

Now consider how the law of one price applies to the international marketplace. If a euro (or any other currency) could buy more coffee in Germany than in Japan, international traders could profit by buying coffee in Germany and selling it in Japan. This export of coffee from Germany to Japan would drive up the German price of coffee and drive down the Japanese price. Conversely, if a euro could buy more coffee in Japan than in Germany, traders could buy coffee in Japan and sell it in Germany. This import of coffee into Germany from Japan would drive down the German price of coffee and drive up the Japanese price. In the end, the law of one price tells us that a euro must buy the same amount of coffee in all countries.

This logic leads us to the theory of purchasing power parity. According to this theory, a currency must have the same purchasing power in all countries. That is, a euro must buy the same quantity of goods in Germany and Japan, and a Japanese yen must buy the same quantity of goods in Japan as in Germany. Indeed, the name of this theory describes it well. *Parity* means equality, and *purchasing power* refers to the value of money. *Purchasing power parity* states that a unit of all currencies must have the same real value in every country.

Implications of Purchasing Power Parity

What does the theory of purchasing power parity say about exchange rates? It tells us that the nominal exchange rate between the currencies of two countries depends on the price levels in those countries. If a euro buys the same quantity of goods in Germany (where prices are measured in euros) as in Japan (where prices are measured in yen), then the number of yen per euro must reflect the prices of goods in Germany and Japan. For example, if a kilo of coffee is priced at 500 yen in Japan and €5 in Germany, then the nominal exchange rate must be 100 yen per euro (500 yen/€5 = 100 yen per euro). Otherwise, the purchasing power of the euro would not be the same in the two countries.

To see more fully how this works, it is helpful to use just a little mathematics. Think of Germany as the home or domestic economy. Suppose that P is the price of a basket of goods in Germany (measured in euros), P^* is the price of a basket of goods in Japan (measured in yen), and e is the nominal exchange rate (the number of yen needed to buy one euro). Now consider the quantity of goods a euro can buy at home (in Germany) and abroad. At home, the price level is P, so the purchasing power of €1 at home is $1/P$. Abroad, a euro can be exchanged into e units of foreign currency, which in turn have purchasing power e/P^*. For the purchasing power of a euro to be the same in the two countries, it must be the case that:

$$1/P = e/P^*$$

With rearrangement, this equation becomes:

$$1 = eP/P^*$$

Notice that the left-hand side of this equation is a constant, and the right-hand side is the real exchange rate. Thus, if the purchasing power of the euro is always the same at home and abroad, then the real exchange rate – the relative price of domestic and foreign goods – cannot change.

To see the implication of this analysis for the nominal exchange rate, we can rearrange the last equation to solve for the nominal exchange rate:

$$e = P^*/P$$

That is, the nominal exchange rate equals the ratio of the foreign price level (measured in units of the foreign currency) to the domestic price level (measured in units of the domestic currency). According to the theory of purchasing power parity, the nominal exchange rate between the currencies of two countries must reflect the different price levels in those countries.

Limitations of Purchasing Power Parity

The theory of purchasing power parity is not completely accurate. That is, exchange rates do not always move to ensure that a euro has the same real value in all countries all the time. There are two reasons why the theory of purchasing power parity does not always hold in practice.

The first reason is that many goods are not easily traded. Imagine, for instance, that haircuts are more expensive in Paris than in New York. International travellers might avoid getting their haircuts in Paris, and some haircutters might move from New York to Paris. Yet such arbitrage would probably be too limited to eliminate the differences in prices. Thus, the deviation from purchasing power parity might persist, and a euro (or dollar) would continue to buy less of a haircut in Paris than in New York.

The second reason that purchasing power parity does not always hold is that even tradable goods are not always perfect substitutes when they are produced in different countries. For example, some consumers prefer German cars, and others prefer Japanese cars. Moreover, consumer tastes can change over time. If German cars suddenly become more popular, the increase in demand will drive up the price of German cars compared to Japanese cars. But despite this difference in prices in the two markets, there might be no opportunity for profitable arbitrage because consumers do not view the two cars as equivalent.

Thus, both because some goods are not tradable and because some tradable goods are not perfect substitutes with their foreign counterparts, purchasing power parity is not a perfect theory of exchange rate determination. For these reasons, real exchange rates fluctuate over time. Nonetheless, the theory of purchasing power parity does provide a useful first step in understanding exchange rates. The basic logic is persuasive: as the real exchange rate drifts from the level predicted by purchasing power parity, people have greater incentive to move goods across national borders. Even if the forces of purchasing power parity do not completely fix the real exchange rate, they provide a reason to expect that changes in the real exchange rate are most often small or temporary. As a result, large and persistent movements in nominal exchange rates typically reflect changes in price levels at home and abroad.

CONCLUSION

The purpose of this chapter has been to develop some basic concepts in macroeconomics that businesses need to be aware of and indeed monitor. GDP gives an indication of how the economy is performing and inflation and unemployment are closely linked to this. If economic activity is growing then businesses might be tempted to expand output and invest but how easily they can do this might depend on the level of savings in the economy which might in turn be dependent on the level of interest rates and inflation. During periods of a slowdown in economic activity firms may choose to cut production and lay off workers thus raising unemployment, but if the economy is growing then unemployment may be falling and firms might find it more difficult to attract new workers with the skills they need and may also find that they have to pay higher wages to attract these workers.

Many businesses will engage in some form of trade with the rest of the world. If they are buying goods and services from abroad or selling goods and services abroad then the rate of exchange will have an effect on relative prices and sales. Understanding the determinants of the exchange rate better, as well as how exchange rates might vary with the performance of the economy, might be important in making business decisions. The macroeconomic variables defined here offer a starting point for analyzing an economy's interactions with the rest of the world and how they have an effect on businesses.

IN THE NEWS

The effects of exchange rates on businesses

This article looks at how exchange rate movements can have effects on business performance by changing the costs and revenues that the business receives.

Tecan Group

Tecan is a Swiss firm with operations in Europe and North America and has sales interests in 52 different countries. Tecan manufactures laboratory instruments for the pharmaceutical, forensic and clinical diagnosis markets. In 2011 it generated sales of CHF377 million (€313 million). This represented an increase of 1.7 per cent on 2010's figures but sales had increased by over 11 per cent. It might be expected that such a growth is sales might have a more positive impact on its revenue figures but the business saw a number of negative impacts from exchange rate movements.

Because Tecan sells to so many countries and has operations across Europe and North America, movements in exchange rates against the Swiss franc

Tecan produce a wide range of technical products for different industries. Movements in the exchange rate can affect the business in major ways.

COURTESY OF TECAN

can be damaging to the overall performance of the business. If exchange rate movements are taken out of the equation, Tecan increased its profit margin by 15.9 per cent but whilst firms can report such figures, adjusting for exchange rate movements, the reality is that exchange rates do have an effect. During the course of 2011, the euro fell against the Swiss franc by 10.9 per cent and the US dollar fell by 14.4 per cent. What this meant for Tecan is that its sales revenues were depressed by the changes in the value of the Swiss franc against other currencies.

Companies like Tecan who know they are exposed to negative effects from exchange rate movements often try to protect themselves by using forward markets to hedge their exposure. In other words they may take out exchange rate contracts which are designed to even out exchange rate fluctuations, but this sort of activity is also fraught with risks and requires highly specialized operators to make it work.

Questions

1. Assume Tecan sells some instruments to a buyer in Europe that are priced in Swiss francs at CHF10 000. Assume the exchange rate between the Swiss franc and the euro is CHF1 = €0.95. What is the price of the transaction in euros?

2. Assume now that the exchange rate changes to CHF1 = €0.8, what is the euro price of the product now? What effect would you expect this change to have on Tecan's business with the European buyer?

3. Tecan imports metals for its instruments from the USA. Tecan buys a quantity of metal each month priced at $15 000. The exchange rate between the Swiss franc and the US dollar at the beginning of 2011 is CHF1 = $1.00. Six months later the value of the Swiss franc against the dollar changes to CHF1 = $1.40. What effect does this have on Tecan?

4. Tecan sells some of its products to customers in Europe and some to Japan. Assume the Swiss franc depreciates against the euro but appreciates against the yen, what would determine the overall outcome for Tecan of these different movements in the exchange rate?

5. How might Tecan protect itself from exchange rate movements by using forward exchange rate markets?

SUMMARY

- Economic prosperity, as measured by GDP per person, varies substantially around the world.

- Because every transaction has a buyer and a seller, the total expenditure in the economy must equal the total income in the economy.

- Gross domestic product (GDP) measures an economy's total expenditure on newly produced goods and services and the total income earned from the production of these goods and services. More precisely, GDP is the market value of all final goods and services produced within a country in a given period of time.

- The standard of living in an economy depends on the economy's ability to produce goods and services.

- Government policies can try to influence the economy's growth rate by encouraging saving and investment, encouraging investment from abroad, fostering education, maintaining property rights and political stability, allowing free trade, promoting the research and development of new technologies, and controlling population growth.

- Nominal GDP uses current prices to value the economy's production of goods and services. Real GDP uses constant base-year prices to value the economy's production of goods and services. The GDP deflator – calculated from the ratio of nominal to real GDP – measures the level of prices in the economy.

- The consumer prices index shows the changes in the prices of a basket of goods and services relative to the prices of the same basket in the base year. The index is used to measure the overall level of prices in the economy. The percentage change in the consumer prices index measures the inflation rate.

- The consumer prices index is an imperfect measure of the cost of living for three reasons. First, it does not take into account consumers' ability to substitute towards goods that become relatively cheaper over time. Secondly, it does not take into account increases in the purchasing power of money due to the introduction of new goods. Thirdly, it is distorted by unmeasured changes in the quality of goods and services. Because of these measurement problems, the CPI overstates true inflation.

- The nominal interest rate is the interest rate usually reported; it is the rate at which the amount of money in a savings account increases over time. In contrast, the real interest rate takes into account changes in the value of money over time. The real interest rate equals the nominal interest rate minus the rate of inflation.

- An economy's saving can be used either to finance investment at home or to buy assets abroad. Thus, national saving equals domestic investment plus net capital outflow.

- The unemployment rate is the percentage of those who would like to work who do not have jobs. The government calculates this statistic monthly based on a survey of thousands of households.

- The unemployment rate is an imperfect measure of joblessness. Some people who call themselves unemployed may actually not want to work, and some people who would like to work have left the labour force after an unsuccessful search.

- Net exports are the value of domestic goods and services sold abroad minus the value of foreign goods and services sold domestically. Net capital outflow is the acquisition of foreign assets by domestic residents minus the acquisition of domestic assets by foreigners. Because every international transaction involves an exchange of an asset for a good or service, an economy's net capital outflow always equals its net exports.

- The nominal exchange rate is the relative price of the currency of two countries, and the real exchange rate is the relative price of the goods and services of two countries. When the nominal exchange rate changes so that each unit of domestic currency buys more foreign currency, the domestic currency is said to *appreciate* or *strengthen*. When the nominal exchange rate changes so that each unit of domestic currency buys less foreign currency, the domestic currency is said to *depreciate* or *weaken*.

- According to the theory of purchasing power parity, a unit of currency should be able to buy the same quantity of goods in all countries. This theory implies that the nominal exchange rate between the currencies of two countries should reflect the price levels in those countries. As a result, countries with relatively high inflation should have depreciating currencies, and countries with relatively low inflation should have appreciating currencies.

KEY CONCEPTS

gross domestic product (GDP), p. 390
consumption, p. 393
government purchases, p. 393
transfer payment, p. 393
net exports, p. 394
nominal GDP, p. 394
real GDP, p. 395
GDP deflator, p. 396
consumer prices index (CPI), p. 397
inflation rate, p. 398
producer price index, p. 398

nominal interest rate, p. 401
real interest rate, p. 401
labour force, p. 406
unemployment rate, p. 406
labour force participation rate, p. 406
natural rate of unemployment, p. 407
cyclical unemployment, p. 407
absolute advantage, p. 410
comparative advantage, p. 410
exports, p. 411
imports, p. 411

trade balance, p. 411
trade surplus, p. 411
trade deficit, p. 411
balanced trade, p. 411
net capital outflow, p. 411
nominal exchange rate, p. 414
appreciation, p. 414
depreciation, p. 414
real exchange rate, p. 415
purchasing power parity, p. 417

QUESTIONS FOR REVIEW

1. Explain why an economy's income must equal its expenditure.

2. What does the level of a nation's GDP measure? What does the growth rate of GDP measure? Would you rather live in a nation with a high level of GDP and a low growth rate, or in a nation with a low level of GDP and a high growth rate?

3. A farmer sells wheat to a baker for €2. The baker uses the wheat to make bread, which is sold for €3. What is the total contribution of these transactions to GDP?

4. Which do you think has a greater effect on the consumer prices index: a 10 per cent increase in the price of chicken or a 10 per cent increase in the price of caviar? Why?

5. Over a long period of time, the price of a chocolate bar rose from €0.10 to €0.60. Over the same period, the consumer

prices index rose from 150 to 300. Adjusted for overall inflation, how much did the price of the chocolate bar change?

6. Why do economists use real GDP rather than nominal GDP to gauge economic well-being?

7. What is the GDP deflator and how does it differ to the consumer prices index?

8. Define net exports and net capital outflow. Explain how and why they are related.

9. If a Japanese car is priced at 500 000 yen, a similar German car is priced at €10 000, and a euro can buy 100 yen, what are the nominal and real exchange rates?

10. Describe the economic logic behind the theory of purchasing power parity.

PROBLEMS AND APPLICATIONS

1. Below are some data from the land of milk and honey.

Year	Price of milk €	Quantity of milk (litres)	Price of honey €	Quantity of honey (litres)
2012	1	100	2	50
2013	1	200	2	100
2014	2	200	4	100

a. Compute nominal GDP, real GDP and the GDP deflator for each year, using 2012 as the base year.
b. Compute the percentage change in nominal GDP, real GDP and the GDP deflator in 2013 and 2014 from the preceding year. For each year, identify the variable that does not change. Explain in words why your answer makes sense.
c. Did economic well-being rise more in 2013 or 2014? Explain.

2. One day Boris the Barber, plc, collects €400 for haircuts. Over this day, his equipment depreciates in value by €50. Of the remaining €350, Boris sends €30 to the government in sales taxes, takes home €220 in wages, and retains €100 in his business to add new equipment in the future. From the €220 that Boris takes home, he pays €70 in income taxes. Based on this information, compute Boris' contribution to the following measures of income:
   a. gross domestic product
   b. net national product
   c. national income
   d. personal income, i e. disposable personal income

3. Suppose that a borrower and a lender agree on the nominal interest rate to be paid on a loan. Then inflation turns out to be higher than they both expected:
   a. Is the real interest rate on this loan higher or lower than expected?
   b. Does the lender gain or lose from this unexpectedly high inflation? Does the borrower gain or lose?

4. Do you think that firms in small towns or in cities have more market power in hiring? Do you think that firms generally have more market power in hiring today than 50 years ago, or less? How do you think this change over time has affected the role of unions in the economy? Explain.

5. How would the following transactions affect UK net capital outflow? Also, state whether each involves direct investment or portfolio investment.
   a. A British mobile telephone company establishes an office in the Czech Republic
   b. A US company's pension fund buys shares in BP
   c. Toyota expands its factory in Derby, England
   d. A London-based investment trust sells its Volkswagen shares to a French investor

6. How would the following transactions affect UK exports, imports and net exports?
   a. A British art lecturer spends the summer touring museums in Italy
   b. Students in Paris flock to see the Royal Shakespeare Company perform *King Lear* on tour
   c. The British art lecturer buys a new Volvo
   d. A student in Munich buys a Manchester United official team shirt (in Munich)
   e. A British citizen goes to Calais for the day to stock up on cheap wine

7. International trade in each of the following products has increased over time. Suggest some reasons why this might be so.
   a. wheat
   b. banking services
   c. computer software
   d. automobiles

8. Would each of the following groups be happy or unhappy if the euro appreciated? Explain.
   a. US pension funds holding French government bonds
   b. German manufacturing industries
   c. Australian tourists planning a trip to Europe
   d. A British firm trying to purchase property overseas

9. Suppose that a car company owned entirely by South Korean citizens opens a new factory in the north of England.
   a. What sort of foreign investment would this represent?
   b. What would be the effect of this investment on UK GDP? Would the effect on UK GNP be larger or smaller?

10. What is happening to the Swiss real exchange rate in each of the following situations? Explain.
   a. The Swiss nominal exchange rate is unchanged, but prices rise faster in Switzerland than abroad
   b. The Swiss nominal exchange rate is unchanged, but prices rise faster abroad than in Switzerland
   c. The Swiss nominal exchange rate declines, and prices are unchanged in Switzerland and abroad
   d. The Swiss nominal exchange rate declines, and prices rise faster abroad than in Switzerland

17 AGGREGATE DEMAND AND AGGREGATE SUPPLY

LEARNING OBJECTIVES

In this chapter you will:

- Consider how the economy in the short run differs from the economy in the long run

- Use the model of aggregate demand and aggregate supply to explain economic fluctuations

- Examine the causes of shifts in aggregate demand and aggregate supply

- See how shifts in either aggregate demand or aggregate supply can cause changes in economic activity

- Examine why the aggregate supply curve is vertical in the long run and upward sloping in the short run

After reading this chapter you should be able to:

- Outline three key facts about economic fluctuations

- Explain the difference between the short run and the long run

- Analyse at least three reasons why the aggregate demand and aggregate supply curve can shift

- Assess the effect of a shift in either the aggregate demand curve or the aggregate supply curve

- Assess the effect of shifts in both the aggregate demand and aggregate supply curve

INTRODUCTION

economic activity the amount of buying and selling (transactions) that take place in an economy over a period of time

Economic activity fluctuates from year to year. In most years, the production of goods and services rises. Because of increases in the labour force, increases in the capital stock and advances in technological knowledge, the economy can produce more and more over time. This growth allows everyone to enjoy a higher standard of living.

In some years, however, this normal growth does not occur. Firms find themselves unable to sell all of the goods and services they have to offer, so they cut back on production. Workers are laid off, unemployment rises and factories are left idle. With the economy producing fewer goods and services, real GDP and other measures of income fall. Such a period of falling incomes and rising unemployment is called a **recession** if it is relatively mild and a **depression** if it is more severe.

recession a period of declining real incomes and rising unemployment. The technical definition gives recession occurring after two successive quarters of negative economic growth

What causes short-run fluctuations in economic activity? How are businesses affected by these fluctuations and how do they react? What, if anything, can public policy do to moderate swings in economic activity? These are the questions that we take up now.

depression a severe recession

The variables that we study are largely those we have already seen in the last chapter. They include GDP, unemployment and the price level. The main policy instruments include government spending, taxes, and the money supply and interest rates. Many of these policies are designed to influence how the economy works in the short run. Although there remains some debate among economists about how to analyze short-run fluctuations, most economists use the *model of aggregate demand and aggregate supply*. Learning how to use this model for analyzing the short-run effects of various events and policies is the primary task ahead. This chapter introduces the model's two key elements – the aggregate demand curve and the aggregate supply curve. But before turning to the model, let's look at the facts.

THREE KEY FACTS ABOUT ECONOMIC FLUCTUATIONS

Short-run fluctuations in economic activity occur in all countries and in all times throughout history. As a starting point for understanding these year-to-year fluctuations, let's discuss some of their most important properties.

Fact 1: Economic Fluctuations are Irregular and Unpredictable

Fluctuations in the economy are often called *the business cycle*. As this term suggests, economic fluctuations correspond to changes in business conditions. When real GDP grows rapidly, business is good. During such periods of economic expansion, firms find that customers are plentiful and that profits are growing. On the other hand, when real GDP falls during recessions, businesses have trouble. During such periods of economic contraction, many firms experience declining sales and dwindling profits.

The term *business cycle* is somewhat misleading, however, because it seems to suggest that economic fluctuations follow a regular, predictable pattern. In fact, economic fluctuations are not at all regular, and they are almost impossible to predict with much accuracy. Over a period of time, the general trend in real GDP is to rise steadily in many countries but the path of GDP is not always smooth. We can define a recession as occurring when real GDP falls for two successive quarters. From this definition we can identify recessions in almost every decade since the 1960s in Europe and across other parts of the world. The most recent global recession which began around 2008 has caused major uncertainty and many firms have either gone out of business or found carrying out business extremely difficult.

Fact 2: Most Macroeconomic Quantities Fluctuate Together

Real GDP is the variable that is most commonly used to monitor short-run changes in the economy because it is the most comprehensive measure of economic activity. Real GDP measures the value of all final goods and services produced within a given period of time. It also measures the total income (adjusted for inflation) of everyone in the economy.

It turns out, however, that for monitoring short-run fluctuations, it does not really matter which measure of economic activity one looks at. Most macroeconomic variables that measure some type of income, spending or production fluctuate closely together. When real GDP falls in a recession, so do personal income, corporate profits, consumer spending, investment spending, industrial production, retail sales, home sales, auto sales and so on. Because recessions are economy-wide phenomena, they show up in many sources of macroeconomic data.

Although many macroeconomic variables fluctuate together, they fluctuate by different amounts. In particular, investment spending varies greatly over the business cycle. Even though investment averages about one-seventh of GDP, declines in investment account for about two-thirds of the declines in GDP during recessions. In other words, when economic conditions deteriorate, much of the decline is attributable to reductions in spending on new factories, housing and inventories.

Fact 3: As Output Falls, Unemployment Rises

Changes in the economy's output of goods and services are strongly correlated with changes in the economy's utilization of its labour force. In other words, when real GDP declines the rate of unemployment rises. This fact is hardly surprising: when firms choose to produce a smaller quantity of goods and services, they lay off workers, expanding the pool of unemployed. However, there is generally a time-lag between any downturn in economic activity and a rise in unemployment and vice versa. Even when positive growth resumes, therefore, unemployment is likely to continue to rise for some time afterwards. Unemployment is referred to as a 'lagged indicator'.

Quick Quiz List and discuss three key facts about economic fluctuations.

EXPLAINING SHORT-RUN ECONOMIC FLUCTUATIONS

Describing the patterns that economies experience as they fluctuate over time is easy. Explaining what causes these fluctuations is more difficult. Indeed, compared to the topics we have studied in previous chapters, the theory of economic fluctuations remains controversial.

How the Short Run Differs From the Long Run

There are a number of theories to explain what determines most important macroeconomic variables in the long run. Much of this analysis is based on two related ideas – the classical dichotomy and monetary neutrality. The classical dichotomy is the separation of variables into real variables (those that measure quantities or relative prices) and nominal variables (those measured in terms of money). Monetary neutrality refers to the assumption that changes in the money supply affect nominal variables but not real variables.

The Classical Dichotomy and Monetary Neutrality

nominal variables variables measured in monetary units

real variables variables measured in physical units

classical dichotomy the theoretical separation of nominal and real variables

The political philosopher David Hume (1711–1776) suggested that all economic variables should be divided into two groups. The first group consists of **nominal variables** – variables measured in monetary units. The second group consists of **real variables** – variables measured in physical units. For example, the income of corn farmers is a nominal variable because it is measured in euros, whereas the quantity of corn they produce is a real variable because it is measured in kilos. Similarly, nominal GDP is a nominal variable because it measures the euro value of the economy's output of goods and services; real GDP is a real variable because it measures the total quantity of goods and services produced and is not influenced by the current prices of those goods and services. This separation of variables into these groups is now called the **classical dichotomy**. (A *dichotomy* is a division into two groups, and *classical* refers to the earlier economic thinkers or classical economists.)

Application of the classical dichotomy is somewhat tricky when we turn to prices. Prices in the economy are normally quoted in terms of money and, therefore, are nominal variables. For instance, when we say that the price of corn is €2 a kilo or that the price of wheat is €1 a kilo, both prices are nominal variables. But what about a *relative* price – the price of one thing compared to another? In our example, we could say that the price of a kilo of corn is two kilos of wheat. Notice that this relative price is no longer measured in terms of money. When comparing the prices of any two goods, the euro signs cancel, and the resulting number is measured in physical units. The lesson is that money prices (e.g. in pounds, euros or dollars) are nominal variables, whereas relative prices are real variables.

This lesson has several important applications. For instance, the real wage (the money wage adjusted for inflation) is a real variable because it measures the rate at which the economy exchanges goods and services for each unit of labour. Similarly, the real interest rate (the nominal interest rate adjusted for inflation) is a real variable because it measures the rate at which the economy exchanges goods and services produced today for goods and services produced in the future.

Why bother separating variables into these two groups? Hume suggested that the classical dichotomy is useful in analyzing the economy because different forces influence real and nominal variables. In particular, he argued, nominal variables are heavily influenced by developments in the economy's monetary system, whereas the monetary system is largely irrelevant for understanding the determinants of important real variables.

Hume's idea is implicit in discussions of the real economy in the long run. Real GDP, saving, investment, real interest rates and unemployment are determined without any mention of the existence of money. The economy's production of goods and services depends on productivity and factor supplies, the real interest rate adjusts to balance the supply and demand for loanable funds, the real wage adjusts to balance the supply and demand for labour, and unemployment results when the real wage is for some reason kept above its equilibrium level. These important conclusions have nothing to do with the quantity of money supplied.

monetary neutrality the proposition that changes in the money supply do not affect real variables

Changes in the supply of money, according to Hume, affect nominal variables but not real variables. When the central bank doubles the money supply, the price level doubles, the euro wage doubles, and all other euro values double. Real variables, such as production, employment, real wages and real interest rates, are unchanged. This irrelevance of monetary changes for real variables is called **monetary neutrality**.

An analogy sheds light on the meaning of monetary neutrality. Recall that, as the unit of account, money is the yardstick we use to measure economic transactions. When a central bank doubles the money supply, all prices double, and the value of the unit of account falls by half. A similar change would occur if a European Union directive reduced the definition of the metre from 100 to 50 centimetres: as a result of the new unit of measurement, all *measured* distances (nominal variables) would double, but the *actual* distances (real variables) would remain the same. The euro, like the metre, is merely a unit of measurement, so a change in its value should not have important real effects.

Is this conclusion of monetary neutrality a realistic description of the world in which we live? The answer is, not completely. A change in the length of the metre from 100 to 50 centimetres would not matter much in the long run, but in the short run it would certainly lead to confusion and various mistakes. Similarly, most economists today believe that over short periods of time – within the span of a year or two – there is reason to think that monetary changes do have important effects on real variables. Hume himself also doubted that monetary neutrality would apply in the short run. Most economists today accept Hume's conclusion as a description of the economy in the long run. Over the course of a decade, for instance, monetary changes have important effects on nominal variables (such as the price level) but only negligible effects on real variables (such as real GDP). When studying long-run changes in the economy, the neutrality of money offers a good description of how the world works.

Beyond a period of several years, changes in the money supply affect prices and other nominal variables but do not affect real GDP, unemployment or other real variables. When studying year-to-year changes in the economy, however, the assumption of monetary neutrality is no longer appropriate. Most economists believe that, in the short run, real and nominal variables are highly intertwined. In particular, changes in the money supply can temporarily push output away from its long-run trend.

To understand the economy in the short run, therefore, we need a different model. To build this new model, we rely on many of the tools we have developed in previous chapters, but we have to abandon the classical dichotomy and the neutrality of money.

The Basic Model of Economic Fluctuations

Our model of short-run economic fluctuations focuses on the behaviour of two variables. The first variable is the economy's output of goods and services, as measured by real GDP. The second variable is the overall price level, as measured by the CPI or the GDP deflator. Notice that output is a real variable, whereas the price level is a nominal variable. Hence, by focusing on the relationship between these two variables, we are highlighting the breakdown of the classical dichotomy.

We analyze fluctuations in the economy as a whole with the **model of aggregate demand and aggregate supply**, which is illustrated in Figure 17.1. On the vertical axis is the overall price level in the economy. On the horizontal axis is the overall quantity of goods and services. The **aggregate demand curve** shows the quantity of goods and services that households, firms and the government want to buy at each price level. The **aggregate supply curve** shows the quantity of goods and services that firms produce and sell at each price level. According to this model, the price level and the quantity of output adjust to bring aggregate demand and aggregate supply into balance.

It may be tempting to view the model of aggregate demand and aggregate supply as nothing more than a large version of the model of market demand and market supply, which we introduced in Chapter 4. Yet in fact this model is quite different. When we consider demand and supply in a particular market – wheat, for instance – the behaviour of buyers and sellers depends on the ability of resources to move from one market to another. When the price of wheat rises, the quantity demanded falls because buyers will use their incomes to buy products other than wheat. Similarly, a higher price of wheat raises the quantity supplied because firms that produce wheat can increase production by hiring

model of aggregate demand and aggregate supply the model that most economists use to explain short-run fluctuations in economic activity around its long-run trend

aggregate demand curve a curve that shows the quantity of goods and services that households, firms and the government want to buy at each price level

aggregate supply curve a curve that shows the quantity of goods and services that firms choose to produce and sell at each price level

FIGURE 17.1

Aggregate Demand and Aggregate Supply

Economists use the model of aggregate demand and aggregate supply to analyze economic fluctuations. On the vertical axis is the overall level of prices. On the horizontal axis is the economy's total output of goods and services. Output and the price level adjust to the point at which the aggregate supply and aggregate demand curves intersect.

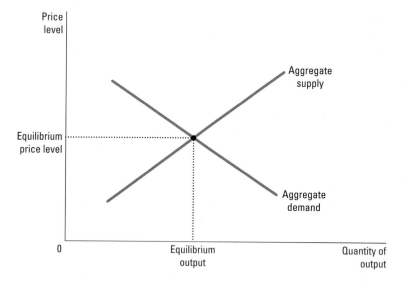

workers away from other parts of the economy. This *microeconomic* substitution from one market to another is impossible when we are analyzing the economy as a whole. After all, the quantity that our model is trying to explain – real GDP – measures the total quantity produced in all of the economy's markets. To understand why the aggregate demand curve is downward sloping and why the aggregate supply curve is upward sloping, we need a *macroeconomic* theory. Developing such a theory is our next task.

> **Quick Quiz** How does the economy's behaviour in the short run differ from its behaviour in the long run? • Draw the model of aggregate demand and aggregate supply. What variables are on the two axes?

THE AGGREGATE DEMAND CURVE

The aggregate demand curve tells us the quantity of all goods and services demanded in the economy at any given price level. As Figure 17.2 illustrates, the aggregate demand curve is downward sloping. This means that, other things equal, a fall in the economy's overall level of prices (from, say, P_1 to P_2) tends to raise the quantity of goods and services demanded (from Y_1 to Y_2).

Why the Aggregate Demand Curve Slopes Downward

Why does a fall in the price level raise the quantity of goods and services demanded? To answer this question, it is useful to recall that GDP (which we denote as Y) is the sum of consumption (C), investment (I), government purchases (G) and net exports (NX):

$$Y = C + I + G + NX$$

FIGURE 17.2

The Aggregate Demand Curve

A fall in the price level from P_1 to P_2 increases the quantity of goods and services demanded from Y_1 to Y_2. There are three reasons for this negative relationship. As the price level falls, real wealth rises, interest rates fall and the exchange rate depreciates. These effects stimulate spending on consumption, investment and net exports. Increased spending on these components of output means a larger quantity of goods and services demanded.

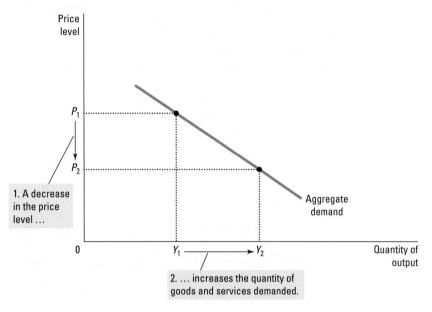

Each of these four components contributes to the aggregate demand for goods and services. For now, we assume that government spending is fixed by policy. The other three components of spending – consumption, investment and net exports – depend on economic conditions and, in particular, on the price level. To understand the downward slope of the aggregate demand curve, therefore, we must examine how the price level affects the quantity of goods and services demanded for consumption, investment and net exports.

The Price Level and Consumption: The Wealth Effect   Consider the money that you hold in your wallet and your bank account. The nominal value of this money is fixed, but its real value is not. When prices fall, this money is more valuable because then it can be used to buy more goods and services. Thus, a decrease in the price level makes consumers wealthier, which in turn encourages them to spend more. The increase in consumer spending means a larger quantity of goods and services demanded.

The Price Level and Investment: The Interest Rate Effect   The price level is one determinant of the quantity of money demanded. The lower the price level, the less money households need to hold to buy the goods and services they want. When the price level falls, therefore, households try to reduce their holdings of money by lending some of it out. For instance, a household might use its excess money to buy interest-bearing bonds. Or it might deposit its excess money in an interest-bearing savings account, and the bank would use these funds to make more loans. In either case, as households try to convert some of their money into interest-bearing assets, they drive down interest rates. Lower interest rates, in turn, encourage borrowing by firms that want to invest in new factories and equipment and by households who want to invest in new housing. Thus, a lower price level reduces the interest rate, encourages greater spending on investment goods, and thereby increases the quantity of goods and services demanded.

The Price Level and Net Exports: The Exchange Rate Effect   As we have just discussed, a lower price level lowers the interest rate. In response, some investors will seek higher returns by investing abroad. For instance, as the interest rate on European government bonds falls, an investment fund might sell European government bonds in order to buy US government bonds. As the investment fund tries to convert its euros into dollars in order to buy the US bonds, it increases the supply of euros in the market for foreign currency exchange. The increased supply of euros causes the euro to depreciate relative to other currencies. Because each euro buys fewer units of foreign currencies, non-European goods (i.e. imports) become more expensive to European residents but exporters find that foreign buyers get more euros for each unit of their currency. This change in the real exchange rate (the relative price of domestic and foreign goods) increases European exports of goods and services and decreases European imports of goods and services. Net exports, which equal exports minus imports, also increase. Thus, when a fall in the European price level causes European interest rates to fall, the real value of the euro falls, and this depreciation stimulates European net exports and thereby increases the quantity of goods and services demanded in the European economy.

Summary

There are, therefore, three distinct but related reasons why a fall in the price level increases the quantity of goods and services demanded: (1) Consumers are wealthier, which stimulates the demand for consumption goods. (2) Interest rates fall, which stimulates the demand for investment goods. (3) The exchange rate depreciates, which stimulates the demand for net exports. For all three reasons, the aggregate demand curve slopes downward.

It is important to keep in mind that the aggregate demand curve (like all demand curves) is drawn holding 'other things equal'. In particular, our three explanations of the downward sloping aggregate demand curve assume that the money supply is fixed. That is, we have been considering how a change in the price level affects the demand for goods and services, holding the amount of money in the economy constant. As we will see, a change in the quantity of money shifts the aggregate demand curve. At this point, just keep in mind that the aggregate demand curve is drawn for a given quantity of money.

Why the Aggregate Demand Curve Might Shift

The downward slope of the aggregate demand curve shows that a fall in the price level raises the overall quantity of goods and services demanded. Many other factors, however, affect the quantity of goods and services demanded at a given price level. When one of these other factors changes, the aggregate demand curve shifts.

Let's consider some examples of events that shift aggregate demand. We can categorize them according to which component of spending is most directly affected.

Shifts Arising From Consumption   Suppose people suddenly become more concerned about saving for retirement and, as a result, reduce their current consumption. Because the quantity of goods and services demanded at any price level is lower, the aggregate demand curve shifts to the left. Conversely, imagine that a stock market boom makes people wealthier and less concerned about saving. The resulting increase in consumer spending means a greater quantity of goods and services demanded at any given price level, so the aggregate demand curve shifts to the right.

Thus, any event that changes how much people want to consume at a given price level shifts the aggregate demand curve. One policy variable that has this effect is the level of taxation. When the government cuts taxes, it encourages people and businesses to spend more, so the aggregate demand curve shifts to the right. When the government raises taxes, people and businesses cut back on their spending and the aggregate demand curve shifts to the left.

Shifts Arising From Investment   Any event that changes how much firms want to invest at a given price level also shifts the aggregate demand curve. For instance, imagine that the telecommunications industry introduces faster broadband access, and many firms decide to invest in this new access. Because the quantity of goods and services demanded at any price level is higher, the aggregate demand curve shifts to the right. Conversely, if firms become pessimistic about future business conditions, they may cut back on investment spending, shifting the aggregate demand curve to the left.

Tax policy can also influence aggregate demand through investment. An investment tax credit (a tax rebate tied to a firm's investment spending) increases the quantity of investment goods that firms demand at any given interest rate. It therefore shifts the aggregate demand curve to the right. The repeal of an investment tax credit reduces investment and shifts the aggregate demand curve to the left.

Another policy variable that can influence investment and aggregate demand is the money supply. An increase in the money supply lowers the interest rate in the short run. This makes borrowing less costly, which stimulates investment spending and thereby shifts the aggregate demand curve to the right. Conversely, a decrease in the money supply raises the interest rate, discourages investment spending, and thereby shifts the aggregate demand curve to the left. Many economists believe that changes in monetary policy have been an important source of shifts in aggregate demand in most developed economies at some points in their history.

CASE STUDY

Investment and Economic Growth

Business investment is a driver of economic growth – we have seen that in our analysis of aggregate demand so far. Is there any evidence to support this relationship in real life? Absolutely. Let us take the UK economy in the last quarter of 2011 as an example. The country's Office for National Statistics (ONS) reported in February 2012 that fourth quarter growth in the UK fell by 0.2 per cent. One of the major reasons suggested by the ONS was the decline in business investment which fell by 5.6 per cent. The ONS also noted that such a fall in investment was equivalent to a fall in GDP of around 0.5 per cent. A number of reporters have noted that UK companies had been sitting on very large cash reserves built up in the aftermath of the financial crisis. The amount has been estimated at some £70 billion. The logical assumption would be that companies are saving cash and not spending it on investment. In the last quarter of 2011, business investment stood at £28.7 billion compared to £30.4 billion in the previous quarter, and since 2008 the average reduction in business investment spending has been around £5 billion less than pre-financial crisis levels. Why would this be the case?

The main reason is a lack of confidence in the economy, not only of the UK but its key trading partners the USA and the EU. The problems in the eurozone over the debt of countries like Greece, Spain, Italy, Portugal and Ireland and the prospects of Europe slipping back into recession have convinced many companies that investing at this time would be too risky. It would lead to increased capacity but if consumer or business spending is weak then businesses risk having unsold stock which merely adds to their costs and reduces profitability. As a result the temptation is to sit on the cash and wait until the economy picks up.

Shifts Arising From Government Purchases   The most direct way that policy makers shift the aggregate demand curve is through government purchases. For example, suppose the government decides to reduce purchases of new weapons systems. Because the quantity of goods and services demanded at any price level is lower, the aggregate demand curve shifts to the left. Conversely, if the government starts building more motorways, the result is a greater quantity of goods and services demanded at any price level, so the aggregate demand curve shifts to the right.

Shifts Arising From Net Exports   Any event that changes net exports for a given price level also shifts aggregate demand. For instance, when the USA experiences a recession, it buys fewer goods from Europe. This reduces European net exports and shifts the aggregate demand curve for the European economy to the left. When the USA recovers from its recession, it starts buying European goods again, shifting the aggregate demand curve to the right.

   Net exports sometimes change because of movements in the exchange rate. Suppose, for instance, that international speculators bid up the value of the euro in the market for foreign currency exchange. This appreciation of the euro would make goods produced in the eurozone more expensive compared to foreign goods, which would depress net exports and shift the aggregate demand curve to the left. Conversely, a depreciation of the euro stimulates net exports and shifts the eurozone aggregate demand curve to the right.

Summary

In this chapter we have looked at why the aggregate demand curve slopes downward and what kinds of events and policies can shift this curve. Table 17.1 summarizes what we have learned so far.

TABLE 17.1

The Aggregate Demand Curve: Summary

Why does the aggregate demand curve slope downward?
1. *The wealth effect*: A lower price level increases real wealth, which encourages spending on consumption.
2. *The interest-rate effect*: A lower price level reduces the interest rate, which encourages spending on investment.
3. *The exchange-rate effect*: A lower price level causes the real exchange rate to depreciate, which encourages spending on net exports.

Why might the aggregate demand curve shift?
1. *Shifts arising from consumption*: An event that makes consumers spend more at a given price level (a tax cut, a stock market boom) shifts the aggregate demand curve to the right. An event that makes consumers spend less at a given price level (a tax increase, a stock market decline) shifts the aggregate demand curve to the left.
2. *Shifts arising from investment*: An event that makes firms invest more at a given price level (optimism about the future, a fall in interest rates due to an increase in the money supply) shifts the aggregate demand curve to the right. An event that makes firms invest less at a given price level (pessimism about the future, a rise in interest rates due to a decrease in the money supply) shifts the aggregate demand curve to the left.
3. *Shifts arising from government purchases*: An increase in government purchases of goods and services (greater spending on defence or motorway construction) shifts the aggregate demand curve to the right. A decrease in government purchases on goods and services (a cutback in defence or motorway spending) shifts the aggregate demand curve to the left.
4. *Shifts arising from net exports*: An event that raises spending on net exports at a given price level (a boom overseas, an exchange rate depreciation) shifts the aggregate demand curve to the right. An event that reduces spending on net exports at a given price level (a recession overseas, an exchange rate appreciation) shifts the aggregate demand curve to the left.

> **Quick Quiz** Explain the three reasons why the aggregate demand curve slopes downward. • Give an example of an event that would shift the aggregate demand curve. Which way would this event shift the curve?

THE AGGREGATE SUPPLY CURVE

The aggregate supply curve tells us the total quantity of goods and services that firms produce and sell at any given price level. Unlike the aggregate demand curve, which is always downward sloping, the aggregate supply curve shows a relationship that depends crucially on the time horizon being examined. In the long run, the aggregate supply curve is vertical, whereas in the short run, the aggregate supply curve is upward sloping. To understand short-run economic fluctuations, and how the short-run behaviour of the economy deviates from its long-run behaviour, we need to examine both the long-run aggregate supply curve and the short-run aggregate supply curve.

Why the Aggregate Supply Curve is Vertical in the Long Run

What determines the quantity of goods and services supplied in the long run? We implicitly answered this question earlier in the book when we analyzed the process of economic growth. In the long run, an economy's production of goods and services (its real GDP) depends on its supplies of labour, capital and natural resources, and on the available technology used to turn these factors of production into goods and services. Because the price level does not affect these long-run determinants of real GDP, the long-run aggregate supply curve is vertical, as in Figure 17.3. In other words, in the long run, the economy's labour, capital, natural resources and technology determine the

FIGURE 17.3

The Long-Run Aggregate Supply Curve

In the long run, the quantity of output supplied depends on the economy's quantities of labour, capital and natural resources and on the technology for turning these inputs into output. The quantity supplied does not depend on the overall price level. As a result, the long-run aggregate supply curve is vertical at the natural rate of output.

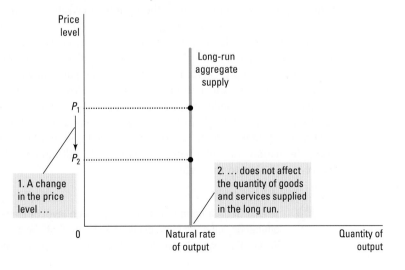

total quantity of goods and services supplied, and this quantity supplied is the same regardless of what the price level happens to be.

The vertical long-run aggregate supply curve is, in essence, just an application of the classical dichotomy and monetary neutrality. As we have already discussed, classical macroeconomic theory is based on the assumption that real variables do not depend on nominal variables. The long-run aggregate supply curve is consistent with this idea because it implies that the quantity of output (a real variable) does not depend on the level of prices (a nominal variable). As noted earlier, most economists believe that this principle works well when studying the economy over a period of many years, but not when studying year-to-year changes. Thus, the aggregate supply curve is vertical only in the long run.

One might wonder why supply curves for specific goods and services can be upward sloping if the long-run aggregate supply curve is vertical. The reason is that the supply of specific goods and services depends on *relative prices* – the prices of those goods and services compared to other prices in the economy. For example, when the price of ice cream rises, holding other prices in the economy constant, there is an incentive for suppliers of ice cream to increase their production by taking labour, milk, chocolate and other inputs away from the production of other goods, such as frozen yoghurt. By contrast, the economy's overall production of goods and services is limited by its labour, capital, natural resources and technology. Thus, when all prices in the economy rise together, there is no change in the overall quantity of goods and services supplied because relative prices and thus incentives have not changed.

Why the Long-Run Aggregate Supply Curve Might Shift

The position of the long-run aggregate supply curve shows the quantity of goods and services predicted by classical macroeconomic theory. This level of production is sometimes called *potential output* or *full-employment output*. To be more accurate, we call it the **natural rate of output** because it shows what the economy produces when unemployment is at its natural, or normal, rate. The natural rate of output is the level of production towards which the economy gravitates in the long run.

natural rate of output the output level in an economy when all existing factors of production (land, labour, capital and technology resources) are fully utilized and where unemployment is at its natural rate

Any change in the economy that alters the natural rate of output shifts the long-run aggregate supply curve. Because output in the classical model depends on labour, capital, natural resources and technological knowledge, we can categorize shifts in the long-run aggregate supply curve as arising from these sources.

Shifts Arising From Labour Imagine that an economy experiences an increase in immigration from abroad. Because there would be a greater number of workers, the quantity of goods and services supplied would increase. As a result, the long-run aggregate supply curve would shift to the right. Conversely, if many workers left the economy to go abroad, the long-run aggregate supply curve would shift to the left.

The position of the long-run aggregate supply curve also depends on the natural rate of unemployment, so any change in the natural rate of unemployment shifts the long-run aggregate supply curve. For example, if the government were to raise the minimum wage substantially, the natural rate of unemployment would rise, and the economy would produce a smaller quantity of goods and services. As a result, the long-run aggregate supply curve would shift to the left. Conversely, if a reform of the unemployment insurance system were to encourage unemployed workers to search harder for new jobs, the natural rate of unemployment would fall, and the long-run aggregate supply curve would shift to the right.

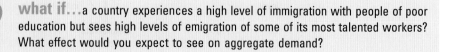

? **what if**...a country experiences a high level of immigration with people of poor education but sees high levels of emigration of some of its most talented workers? What effect would you expect to see on aggregate demand?

Shifts Arising From Capital   An increase in the economy's capital stock increases productivity and, thereby, the quantity of goods and services supplied. As a result, the long-run aggregate supply curve shifts to the right. Conversely, a decrease in the economy's capital stock decreases productivity and the quantity of goods and services supplied, shifting the long-run aggregate supply curve to the left.

Notice that the same logic applies regardless of whether we are discussing physical capital or human capital. An increase either in the number of machines or in the number of university degrees will raise the economy's ability to produce goods and services. Thus, either would shift the long-run aggregate supply curve to the right.

Shifts Arising From Natural Resources   An economy's production depends on its natural resources, including its land, minerals and weather. A discovery of a new mineral deposit shifts the long-run aggregate supply curve to the right. A change in weather patterns that makes farming more difficult shifts the long-run aggregate supply curve to the left.

In many countries, important natural resources are imported from abroad. A change in the availability of these resources can also shift the aggregate supply curve.

Shifts Arising From Technological Knowledge   Perhaps the most important reason that the economy today produces more than it did a generation ago is that our technological knowledge has advanced. The invention of the computer, for instance, has allowed us to produce more goods and services from any given amounts of labour, capital and natural resources. As a result, it has shifted the long-run aggregate supply curve to the right.

Although not literally technological, there are many other events that act like changes in technology. Opening up international trade has effects similar to inventing new production processes, so it also shifts the long-run aggregate supply curve to the right. Conversely, if the government passed new regulations preventing firms from using some production methods, perhaps because they were too dangerous for workers, the result would be a leftward shift in the long-run aggregate supply curve.

Summary

The long-run aggregate supply curve reflects the classical model of the economy we developed in previous chapters. Any policy or event that raise real GDP can now be viewed as increasing the quantity of goods and services supplied and shifting the long-run aggregate supply curve to the right. Any policy or event that lowers real GDP can now be viewed as decreasing the quantity of goods and services supplied and shifting the long-run aggregate supply curve to the left.

A New Way to Depict Long-Run Growth and Inflation

Having introduced the economy's aggregate demand curve and the long-run aggregate supply curve, we now have a new way to describe the economy's long-run trends. Figure 17.4 illustrates the changes that occur in the economy from decade to decade. Notice that both curves are shifting. Although there are many forces that govern the economy in the long run and can in principle cause such shifts, the two most important in practice are technology and monetary policy. Technological progress enhances the economy's ability to produce goods and services, and this continually shifts the long-run aggregate supply curve to the right. At the same time, because the central bank increases the money supply over time, the aggregate demand curve also shifts to the right. As the figure illustrates, the result is trend growth in output (as shown by increasing Y) and continuing inflation (as shown by increasing P).

FIGURE 17.4

Long-Run Growth and Inflation in the Model of Aggregate Demand and Aggregate Supply

As the economy becomes better able to produce goods and services over time, primarily because of technological progress, the long-run aggregate supply curve shifts to the right. At the same time, as the central bank increases the money supply, the aggregate demand curve also shifts to the right. In this figure, output grows from Y_{1990} to Y_{2000} and then to Y_{2010}, and the price level rises from P_{1990} to P_{2000} and then to P_{2010}. Thus, the model of aggregate demand and aggregate supply offers a new way to describe the classical analysis of growth and inflation.

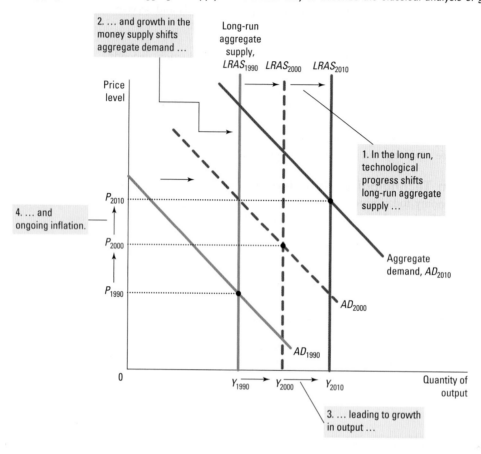

The purpose of developing the model of aggregate demand and aggregate supply, however, is not to dress our long-run conclusions in new clothing. Instead, it is to provide a framework for short-run analysis, as we will see in a moment. As we develop the short-run model, we keep the analysis simple by not showing the continuing growth and inflation depicted in Figure 17.4. But always remember that long-run trends provide the background for short-run fluctuations. Short-run fluctuations in output and the **price level** should be viewed as deviations from the continuing long-run trends.

price level the price of a basket of goods and services measured as the weighted arithmetic average of current prices

Why the Aggregate Supply Curve Slopes Upward in the Short Run

We now come to the key difference between the economy in the short run and in the long run: the behaviour of aggregate supply. As we have already discussed, the long-run aggregate supply curve is vertical. By contrast, in the short run, the aggregate supply curve is upward sloping, as shown in Figure 17.5. That is, over a period of a year or two, an increase in the overall level of prices in the economy tends to raise the quantity of goods and services supplied, and a decrease in the level of prices tends to reduce the quantity of goods and services supplied.

FIGURE 17.5

The Short-Run Aggregate Supply Curve

In the short run, a fall in the price level from P_1 to P_2 reduces the quantity of output supplied from Y_1 to Y_2. This positive relationship could be due to sticky wages, sticky prices or misperceptions. Over time, wages, prices and perceptions adjust, so this positive relationship is only temporary.

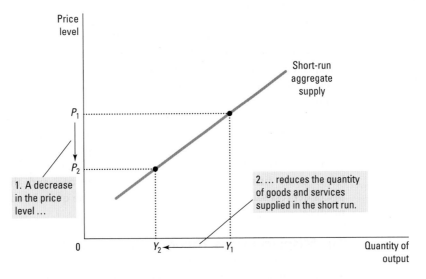

What causes this positive relationship between the price level and output? Macroeconomists have proposed three theories for the upward slope of the short-run aggregate supply curve. In each theory, a specific market imperfection causes the supply side of the economy to behave differently in the short run than it does in the long run. Although each of the following theories will differ in detail, they share a common theme: the quantity of output supplied deviates from its long-run, or 'natural' level when the price level deviates from the price level that people expected to prevail. When the price level rises above the expected level, output rises above its natural rate, and when the price level falls below the expected level, output falls below its natural rate.

The Sticky Wage Theory   The first and simplest explanation of the upward slope of the short-run aggregate supply curve is the sticky wage theory. According to this theory, the short-run aggregate supply curve slopes upward because nominal wages are slow to adjust, or are 'sticky', in the short run. To some extent, the slow adjustment of nominal wages is attributable to long-term contracts between workers and firms that fix nominal wages, sometimes for as long as three years. In addition, this slow adjustment may be attributable to social norms and notions of fairness that influence wage setting and that change only slowly over time.

To see what sticky nominal wages mean for aggregate supply, imagine that a firm has agreed in advance to pay its workers a certain nominal wage based on what it expected the price level to be. If the price level P falls below the level that was expected and the nominal wage remains stuck at W, then the real wage W/P rises above the level the firm planned to pay. Because wages are a large part of a firm's production costs, a higher real wage means that the firm's real costs have risen. The firm responds to these higher costs by hiring less labour and producing a smaller quantity of goods and services. In other words, because wages do not adjust immediately to the price level, a lower price level makes employment and production less profitable, so firms reduce the quantity of goods and services they supply.

The Sticky Price Theory   Some economists have advocated another approach to the short-run aggregate supply curve, called the sticky price theory. As we just discussed, the sticky wage theory emphasizes that nominal wages adjust slowly over time. The sticky price theory emphasizes that the prices of some goods and services also adjust sluggishly in response to changing economic conditions. This slow adjustment of prices occurs in part because there are costs to adjusting prices, called *menu costs*. These menu costs include the cost of printing and distributing price lists or mail-order catalogues and the time required to change price tags. As a result of these costs, prices as well as wages may be sticky in the short run.

To see the implications of sticky prices for aggregate supply, suppose that each firm in the economy announces its prices in advance based on the economic conditions it expects to prevail. Then, after prices are announced, the economy experiences an unexpected contraction in the money supply, which will reduce the overall price level in the long run. Although some firms reduce their prices immediately in response to changing economic conditions, other firms may not want to incur additional menu costs and, therefore, may temporarily lag behind. Because these lagging firms have prices that are too high, their sales decline. Declining sales, in turn, cause these firms to cut back on production and employment. In other words, because not all prices adjust instantly to changing conditions, an unexpected fall in the price level leaves some firms with higher-than-desired prices, and these higher-than-desired prices depress sales and induce firms to reduce the quantity of goods and services they produce.

The Misperceptions Theory   A third approach to the short-run aggregate supply curve is the misperceptions theory. According to this theory, changes in the overall price level can temporarily mislead suppliers about what is happening in the individual markets in which they sell their output. As a result of these short-run misperceptions, suppliers respond to changes in the level of prices, and this response leads to an upward sloping aggregate supply curve.

To see how this might work, suppose the overall price level falls below the level that people expected. When suppliers see the prices of their products fall, they may mistakenly believe that their *relative* prices have fallen. For example, wheat farmers may notice a fall in the price of wheat before they notice a fall in the prices of the many items they buy as consumers. They may infer from this observation that the reward to producing wheat is temporarily low, and they may respond by reducing the quantity of wheat they supply. Similarly, workers may notice a fall in their nominal wages before they notice a fall in the prices of the goods they buy. They may infer that the reward to working is temporarily low and respond by reducing the quantity of labour they supply. In both cases, a lower price level causes misperceptions about relative prices, and these misperceptions induce suppliers to respond to the lower price level by decreasing the quantity of goods and services supplied.

Pitfall Prevention Misperceptions on changes in prices is not only a mistake that businesses and consumers make but also economics students. There is a difference between changes in the overall price level and particular prices of goods and services and there is always the danger of generalizing one from the other too easily.

Summary

There are three alternative explanations for the upward slope of the short-run aggregate supply curve: (1) sticky wages, (2) sticky prices and (3) misperceptions. Economists debate which of these theories is correct, and it is very possible each contains an element of truth. For our purposes in this book, the similarities of the theories are more important than the differences. All three theories suggest that output deviates from its natural rate when the price level deviates from the price level that people expected. We can express this mathematically as follows:

$$\begin{array}{ccccc} \text{Quantity} & & \text{Natural} & & \left(\text{Actual} & & \text{Expected} \right) \\ \text{of output} & = & \text{rate of} & + & a \left(\text{price} & - & \text{price} \right) \\ \text{supplied} & & \text{output} & & \left(\text{level} & & \text{level} \right) \end{array}$$

where a is a number that determines how much output responds to unexpected changes in the price level.

Notice that each of the three theories of short-run aggregate supply emphasizes a problem that is likely to be only temporary. Whether the upward slope of the aggregate supply curve is attributable to sticky wages, sticky prices or misperceptions, these conditions will not persist forever. Eventually, as people adjust their expectations, nominal wages adjust, prices become unstuck and misperceptions are corrected. In other words, the expected and actual price levels are equal in the long run, and the aggregate supply curve is vertical rather than upward sloping.

Why the Short-Run Aggregate Supply Curve Might Shift

The short-run aggregate supply curve tells us the quantity of goods and services supplied in the short run for any given level of prices. We can think of this curve as similar to the long-run aggregate supply curve but made upward sloping by the presence of sticky wages, sticky prices and misperceptions. Thus, when thinking about what shifts the short-run aggregate supply curve, we have to consider all those variables that shift the long-run aggregate supply curve plus a new variable – the expected price level – that influences sticky wages, sticky prices and misperceptions.

Let's start with what we know about the long-run aggregate supply curve. As we discussed earlier, shifts in the long-run aggregate supply curve normally arise from changes in labour, capital, natural resources or technological knowledge. These same variables shift the short-run aggregate supply curve. For example, when an increase in the economy's capital stock increases productivity, both the long-run and short-run aggregate supply curves shift to the right. When an increase in the minimum wage raises the natural rate of unemployment, both the long-run and short-run aggregate supply curves shift to the left.

The important new variable that affects the position of the short-run aggregate supply curve is people's expectation of the price level. As we have discussed, the quantity of goods and services supplied depends, in the short run, on sticky wages, sticky prices and misperceptions. Yet wages, prices and perceptions are set on the basis of expectations of the price level. So when expectations change, the short-run aggregate supply curve shifts.

To make this idea more concrete, let's consider a specific theory of aggregate supply – the sticky wage theory. According to this theory, when workers and firms expect the price level to be high, they are more likely to negotiate high nominal wages. High wages raise firms' costs and, for any given actual price level, reduce the quantity of goods and services that firms supply. When the expected price level rises, wages are higher, costs increase, and firms supply a smaller quantity of goods and services at any given actual price level. Thus, the short-run aggregate supply curve shifts to the left. Conversely, when the expected price level falls, wages are lower, costs decline, firms increase production at any given price level, and the short-run aggregate supply curve shifts to the right.

A similar logic applies in each theory of aggregate supply. The general lesson is the following: an increase in the expected price level reduces the quantity of goods and services supplied and shifts the short-run aggregate supply curve to the left. A decrease in the expected price level raises the quantity of goods and services supplied and shifts the short-run aggregate supply curve to the right. As we will see in the next section, this influence of expectations on the position of the short-run aggregate supply curve plays

TABLE 17.2

The Short-Run Aggregate Supply Curve: Summary

Why does the short-run aggregate supply curve slope upward?

1. *The sticky wage theory*: An unexpectedly low price level raises the real wage, which causes firms to hire fewer workers and produce a smaller quantity of goods and services.
2. *The sticky price theory*: An unexpectedly low price level leaves some firms with higher-than-desired prices, which depresses their sales and leads them to cut back production.
3. *The misperceptions theory*: An unexpectedly low price level leads some suppliers to think their relative prices have fallen, which induces a fall in production.

Why might the short-run aggregate supply curve shift?

1. *Shifts arising from labour*: An increase in the quantity of labour available (perhaps due to a fall in the natural rate of unemployment) shifts the aggregate supply curve to the right. A decrease in the quantity of labour available (perhaps due to a rise in the natural rate of unemployment) shifts the aggregate supply curve to the left.
2. *Shifts arising from capital*: An increase in physical or human capital shifts the aggregate supply curve to the right. A decrease in physical or human capital shifts the aggregate supply curve to the left.
3. *Shifts arising from natural resources*: An increase in the availability of natural resources shifts the aggregate supply curve to the right. A decrease in the availability of natural resources shifts the aggregate supply curve to the left.
4. *Shifts arising from technology*: An advance in technological knowledge shifts the aggregate supply curve to the right. A decrease in the available technology (perhaps due to government regulation) shifts the aggregate supply curve to the left.
5. *Shifts arising from the expected price level*: A decrease in the expected price level shifts the short-run aggregate supply curve to the right. An increase in the expected price level shifts the short-run aggregate supply curve to the left.

a key role in reconciling the economy's behaviour in the short run with its behaviour in the long run. In the short run, expectations are fixed, and the economy finds itself at the intersection of the aggregate demand curve and the short-run aggregate supply curve. In the long run, expectations adjust, and the short-run aggregate supply curve shifts. This shift ensures that the economy eventually finds itself at the intersection of the aggregate demand curve and the long-run aggregate supply curve.

You should now have some understanding about why the short-run aggregate supply curve slopes upward and what events and policies can cause this curve to shift. Table 17.2 summarizes our discussion.

Quick Quiz Explain why the long-run aggregate supply curve is vertical.
• Explain three theories for why the short-run aggregate supply curve is upward sloping.

TWO CAUSES OF ECONOMIC FLUCTUATIONS

Now that we have introduced the model of aggregate demand and aggregate supply, we have the basic tools we need to analyze fluctuations in economic activity. In particular, we can use what we have learned about aggregate demand and aggregate supply to examine the two basic causes of short-run fluctuations.

To keep things simple, we assume the economy begins in long-run equilibrium, as shown in Figure 17.6. Equilibrium output and the price level are determined by the intersection of the aggregate demand curve and the long-run aggregate supply curve, shown as point A in the figure. At this point, output is at its natural rate. The short-run aggregate supply curve passes through this point as well, indicating that wages, prices and perceptions have fully adjusted to this long-run equilibrium. That is, when

FIGURE 17.6

The Long-Run Equilibrium

The long-run equilibrium of the economy is found where the aggregate demand curve crosses the long-run aggregate supply curve (point A). When the economy reaches this long-run equilibrium, wages, prices and perceptions will have adjusted so that the short-run aggregate supply curve crosses this point as well.

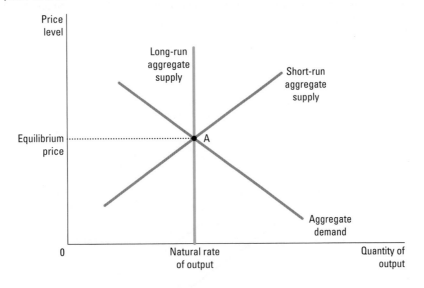

an economy is in its long-run equilibrium, wages, prices and perceptions must have adjusted so that the intersection of aggregate demand with short-run aggregate supply is the same as the intersection of aggregate demand with long-run aggregate supply.

The Effects of a Shift in Aggregate Demand

Suppose that for some reason a wave of pessimism suddenly overtakes the economy. The cause might be a government scandal, a crash in the stock market or the outbreak of war overseas. Because of this event, many people lose confidence in the future and alter their plans. Households cut back on their spending and delay major purchases, and firms put off buying new equipment.

What is the impact of such a wave of pessimism on the economy? Such an event reduces the aggregate demand for goods and services. That is, for any given price level, households and firms now want to buy a smaller quantity of goods and services. As Figure 17.7 shows, the aggregate demand curve shifts to the left from AD_1 to AD_2.

In this figure we can examine the effects of the fall in aggregate demand. In the short run, the economy moves along the initial short-run aggregate supply curve AS_1, going from point A to point B. As the economy moves from point A to point B, output falls from Y_1 to Y_2, and the price level falls from P_1 to P_2. The falling level of output indicates that the economy is in a recession. Although not shown in the figure, firms respond to lower sales and production by reducing employment. Thus, the pessimism that caused the shift in aggregate demand is, to some extent, self-fulfilling: pessimism about the future leads to falling incomes and rising unemployment.

What should policy makers do when faced with such a recession? One possibility is to take action to increase aggregate demand. As we noted earlier, an increase in government spending or an increase in the money supply would increase the quantity of goods and services demanded at any price and, therefore, would shift the aggregate demand curve to the right. If policy makers can act with sufficient speed and precision, they can offset the initial shift in aggregate demand, return the aggregate demand curve back to AD_1, and bring the economy back to point A.

A Contraction in Aggregate Demand

A fall in aggregate demand, which might be due to a wave of pessimism in the economy, is represented with a leftward shift in the aggregate demand curve from AD_1 to AD_2. The economy moves from point A to point B. Output falls from Y_1 to Y_2, and the price level falls from P_1 to P_2. Over time, as wages, prices and perceptions adjust, the short-run aggregate supply curve shifts to the right from AS_1 to AS_2, and the economy reaches point C, where the new aggregate demand curve crosses the long-run aggregate supply curve. The price level falls to P_3, and output returns to its natural rate, Y_1.

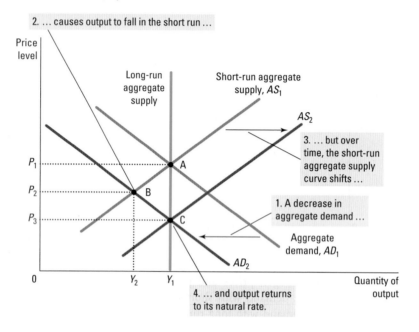

Even without action by policy makers, the recession will remedy itself over a period of time. Because of the reduction in aggregate demand, the price level falls. Eventually, expectations catch up with this new reality, and the expected price level falls as well. Because the fall in the expected price level alters wages, prices and perceptions, it shifts the short-run aggregate supply curve to the right from AS_1 to AS_2 in Figure 17.7. This adjustment of expectations allows the economy over time to approach point C, where the new aggregate demand curve (AD_2) crosses the long-run aggregate supply curve.

In the new long-run equilibrium, point C, output is back to its natural rate. Even though the wave of pessimism has reduced aggregate demand, the price level has fallen sufficiently (to P_3) to offset the shift in the aggregate demand curve. Thus, in the long run, the shift in aggregate demand is reflected fully in the price level and not at all in the level of output. In other words, the long-run effect of a shift in aggregate demand is a nominal change (the price level is lower) but not a real change (output is the same).

To sum up, this story about shifts in aggregate demand has two important lessons:

- In the short run, shifts in aggregate demand cause fluctuations in the economy's output of goods and services.
- In the long run, shifts in aggregate demand affect the overall price level but do not affect output.

The Effects of a Shift in Aggregate Supply

Imagine once again an economy in its long-run equilibrium. Now suppose that suddenly some firms experience an increase in their costs of production. For example, bad weather might destroy some agricultural crops, driving up the cost of producing food products.

FIGURE 17.8

An Adverse Shift in Aggregate Supply

When some event increases firms' costs, the short-run aggregate supply curve shifts to the left from AS_1 to AS_2. The economy moves from point A to point B. The result is stagflation: output falls from Y_1 to Y_2, and the price level rises from P_1 to P_2.

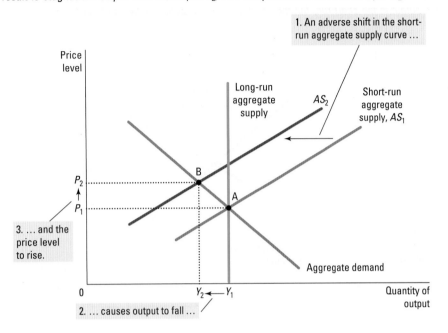

Or a dispute in the Middle East might interrupt the shipping of crude oil, driving up the cost of producing oil products.

What is the macroeconomic impact of such an increase in production costs? For any given price level, firms now want to supply a smaller quantity of goods and services. Thus, as Figure 17.8 shows, the short-run aggregate supply curve shifts to the left from AS_1 to AS_2. (Depending on the event, the long-run aggregate supply curve might also shift. To keep things simple, however, we will assume that it does not.)

In this figure we can trace the effects of the leftward shift in aggregate supply. In the short run, the economy moves along the existing aggregate demand curve, going from point A to point B. The output of the economy falls from Y_1 to Y_2, and the price level rises from P_1 to P_2. Because the economy is experiencing both *stagnation* (falling output) and *inflation* (rising prices), such an event is sometimes called **stagflation**.

What should policy makers do when faced with stagflation? There are no easy choices. One possibility is to do nothing. In this case, the output of goods and services remains depressed at Y_2 for a while. Eventually, however, the recession will remedy itself as wages, prices and perceptions adjust to the raise production costs. A period of low output and high unemployment, for instance, puts downward pressure on workers' wages. Lower wages, in turn, increase the quantity of output supplied. Over time, as the short-run aggregate supply curve shifts back toward AS_1, the price level falls, and the quantity of output approaches its natural rate. In the long run, the economy returns to point A, where the aggregate demand curve crosses the long-run aggregate supply curve. This is the view that believers of free markets might adopt.

Alternatively, policy makers who control monetary and fiscal policy might attempt to offset some of the effects of the shift in the short-run aggregate supply curve by shifting the aggregate demand curve. This possibility is shown in Figure 17.9. In this case, changes in policy shift the aggregate demand curve to the right from AD_1 to AD_2 – exactly enough to prevent the shift in aggregate supply from affecting output. The

stagflation a period of falling output and rising prices

FIGURE 17.9

Accommodating an Adverse Shift in Aggregate Supply

Faced with an adverse shift in aggregate supply from AS_1 to AS_2, policy makers who can influence aggregate demand might try to shift the aggregate demand curve to the right from AD_1 to AD_2. The economy would move from point A to point C. This policy would prevent the supply shift from reducing output in the short run, but the price level would permanently rise from P_1 to P_3.

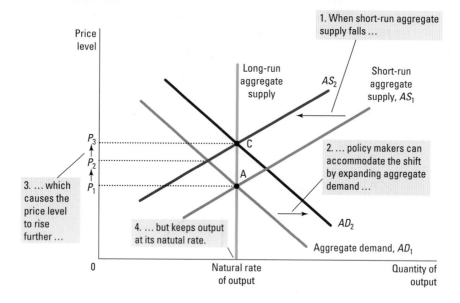

economy moves directly from point A to point C. Output remains at its natural rate, and the price level rises from P_1 to P_3. In this case, policy makers are said to *accommodate* the shift in aggregate supply because they allow the increase in costs to permanently affect the level of prices. This intervention by policy makers would be seen as being desirable by supporters of Keynes. These different views on policy action form a key aspect of the debate between economists about action in the face of short-run fluctuations in economic activity.

To sum up, this story about shifts in aggregate supply has two important lessons:

- Shifts in aggregate supply can cause stagflation – a combination of recession (falling output) and inflation (rising prices).
- Policy makers who can influence aggregate demand cannot offset both of these adverse effects simultaneously.

Quick Quiz Suppose that the election of a popular prime minister suddenly increases people's confidence in the future. Use the model of aggregate demand and aggregate supply to analyze the effect on the economy.

JEOPARDY PROBLEM

Over a period of 20 years an economy has found that despite periods of growth it has ended up with higher inflation rates and a level of unemployment no different to that it started with at the beginning of the time period. Explain, using aggregate demand and supply diagrams, why this may have occurred.

CONCLUSION

This chapter has achieved two goals. First, we have discussed some of the important facts about short-run fluctuations in economic activity. Secondly, we have introduced a basic model to explain those fluctuations, called the model of aggregate demand and aggregate supply. We will use this model in later chapters in order to understand more fully what causes fluctuations in the economy and how policy makers might respond to these fluctuations.

IN THE NEWS

Economic Growth in BRIC Countries

There has been much talk in recent years about the emerging economies and the so-called BRIC countries (Brazil, Russia, India and China). Much hope has been pinned on these countries providing investment opportunities and driving global growth. As this article shows, this optimism needs to be tempered.

March 2012 – Brazil's Economy Expands 2.7 Per Cent

Brazil's government promised aggressive new stimulus measures after data showed the economy expanded just 2.7 per cent in 2011, raising fears that one of the world's most dynamic emerging markets is slipping into a new era of mediocre growth. The sharp slowdown during President Dilma Rousseff's first year in office saw Brazil underperform its peers among big developing countries as local industries struggled with soaring business costs and an overvalued currency. A rebound in consumer spending and strong agricultural exports only barely allowed Brazil to avoid recession during the second half of the year, the data released last week showed.

Investors bet the weak performance would lead Brazil's central bank to slash interest rates more aggressively, with a cut of at least half a percentage point, and possibly 75 basis points, expected following the bank's meeting. Worries about a slowdown in Brazil and China, two of the biggest growth engines in an otherwise troubled

world economy in recent years, contributed to the largest declines in global equities in about three months on Tuesday. Brazil's Bovespa stock index fell 3 per cent, while its currency weakened 1.5 per cent.

Finance Minister Guido Mantega pointed to data showing a modest recovery in the fourth quarter that he said was likely to accelerate throughout 2012, while vowing that the government would offer tax incentives and other unspecified stimulus measures to spur manufacturing and investment in particular. 'We are better placed to give stimulus this year,' Mantega told reporters in Brasilia. 'We will implement all the necessary measures to stimulate the economy.'

Nonetheless, the data reinforced the biggest concern of Rousseff and many business leaders – that Brazil may be downshifting into a prolonged period of lacklustre 3 per cent annual growth as a tight labour market, woeful infrastructure and other barriers prevent the economy from expanding any faster. 'Things just aren't taking off,' said Senator Valdir Raupp, the head of the PMDB party, which is part of Rousseff's

coalition. 'Investments aren't happening. There are just a few sectors where things are going well.'

The slowdown has come as a shock for many Brazilians following 7.5 per cent growth in 2010. Even when factoring in the global crisis, growth averaged 4.2 per cent from 2005 to 2010. 'If this year continues at the same rhythm as last year, the (economy) could frustrate us again. Starting now, we're going to have to give it a boost,' Raupp said.

Yet, stimulus could backfire. Inflation reached a seven-year high of 6.5 per cent last year, and while it has slowed in recent months, there may not be much room for the government to jolt the economy without risking another bout of price rises. Economic activity expanded 0.3 per cent in the fourth quarter after a revised 0.1 per cent contraction in the previous quarter, government statistics agency Instituto Brasileiro de Geografia e Estatistica (IBGE) said. The biggest drag on Brazil's economy continues to be industry, which contracted 0.5 per cent in the fourth quarter compared with the previous quarter. Manufacturers have blamed most of their problems on Brazil's currency, which has strengthened about 40 per cent since the depths of the financial crisis in 2009 and 6 per cent this year. 'Worse than the gross domestic product (GDP) result is the proof that Brazil is becoming an uncompetitive country,' said Senator José Agripino, from the opposition DEM party.

Rousseff has already implemented targeted tax incentives in recent months to try to help sectors such as autos and consumer goods that have struggled. Her government also has raised the ire of some countries and multinational companies by threatening to raise tariffs on vehicle imports from Mexico, for example. Mantega said the government was still aiming for 4.5 per cent growth this year. However, many business leaders and politicians say that the core problems are more related to high taxes and other costs that will necessitate tough economic reforms to fix – something Rousseff has shown little interest in doing.

'The time has come for us to prioritize courageous structural reforms that really address the competitive problems of the Brazilian economy,' said Paulo Godoy, president of ABDIB, a prominent industry group. 'The country needs urgently to reduce the existing barriers to investment.' Despite the disappointing result of 2011, the residual glow of recent years means that Brazil still feels in many places like a country enjoying an economic boom. However, that boom is arguably responsible for the problems occurring now. The tight labour market has driven up costs and made it difficult for businesses to see through expansion plans. One high-profile example is the delayed construction of Brazil's stadiums to host the 2014 World Cup. Brazil may not be able to depend on its usual partners to spur its economy. A less bullish economic outlook for China and the continued threat of a crisis in the euro zone mean that it may have to continue to rely on its own consumers for growth.

Questions

1. Using an aggregate demand and aggregate supply diagram, explain how a 'rebound in consumer spending and strong agricultural exports only barely allowed Brazil to avoid recession during the second half of the year'.
2. Explain how a cut in interest rates might be expected to give a boost to Brazil's economy.
3. Should tax incentives be given to businesses primarily or to consumers in an effort to boost the economy? Explain your answer.
4. How might the appreciation of Brazil's currency lead to the country becoming 'less competitive'.
5. Explain the meaning of the phrase 'The tight labour market has driven up costs and made it difficult for businesses to see through expansion plans.'

Source: **http://www.iol.co.za/business/ international/brazil-s-economy-expands-2-7-1.1253555** accessed 11 March 2012.

SUMMARY

- All societies experience short-run economic fluctuations around long-run trends. These fluctuations are irregular and largely unpredictable. When recessions do occur, real GDP and other measures of income, spending and production fall, and unemployment rises.

- Economists analyze short-run economic fluctuations using the model of aggregate demand and aggregate supply. According to this model, the output of goods and services and the overall level of prices adjust to balance aggregate demand and aggregate supply.

- The aggregate demand curve slopes downward for three reasons. First, a lower price level raises the real value of households' money holdings, which stimulates consumer spending. Secondly, a lower price level reduces the quantity of money households' demand; as households try to convert money into interest-bearing assets, interest rates fall, which stimulates investment spending. Thirdly, as a lower price level reduces interest rates, the local currency depreciates

in the market for foreign currency exchange, which stimulates net exports.

- Any event or policy that raises consumption, investment, government purchases or net exports at a given price level increases aggregate demand. Any event or policy that reduces consumption, investment, government purchases or net exports at a given price level decreases aggregate demand.

- The long-run aggregate supply curve is vertical. In the long run, the quantity of goods and services supplied depends on the economy's labour, capital, natural resources and technology, but not on the overall level of prices.

- Three theories have been proposed to explain the upward slope of the short-run aggregate supply curve. According to the sticky wage theory, an unexpected fall in the price level temporarily raises real wages, which induces firms to reduce employment and production. According to the sticky price theory, an unexpected fall in the price level leaves some firms with prices that are temporarily too high, which reduces their sales and causes them to cut back production. According to the misperceptions theory, an unexpected fall in the price level leads suppliers to mistakenly believe that their relative prices have fallen, which induces them to reduce production. All three theories imply that output deviates from its natural rate when the price level deviates from the price level that people expected.

- Events that alter the economy's ability to produce output, such as changes in labour, capital, natural resources or technology, shift the short-run aggregate supply curve (and may shift the long-run aggregate supply curve as well). In addition, the position of the short-run aggregate supply curve depends on the expected price level.

- One possible cause of economic fluctuations is a shift in aggregate demand. When the aggregate demand curve shifts to the left, for instance, output and prices fall in the short run. Over time, as a change in the expected price level causes wages, prices and perceptions to adjust, the short-run aggregate supply curve shifts to the right, and the economy returns to its natural rate of output at a new, lower price level.

- A second possible cause of economic fluctuations is a shift in aggregate supply. When the aggregate supply curve shifts to the left, the short-run effect is falling output and rising prices – a combination called stagflation. Over time, as wages, prices and perceptions adjust, the price level falls back to its original level, and output recovers.

KEY CONCEPTS

economic activity, p. 424
recession, p. 424
depression, p. 424
nominal variables, p. 426
real variables, p. 426

classical dichotomy, p. 426
monetary neutrality, p. 426
model of aggregate demand and
aggregate supply, p. 427
aggregate demand curve, p. 427

aggregate supply curve, p. 427
natural rate of output, p. 434
price level, p. 436
stagflation, p. 443

QUESTIONS FOR REVIEW

1. Name two macroeconomic variables that decline when the economy goes into a recession. Name one macroeconomic variable that rises during a recession.

2. Draw a diagram with aggregate demand, short-run aggregate supply and long-run aggregate supply. Be careful to label the axes correctly.

3. List and explain the three reasons why the aggregate demand curve is downward sloping.

4. Explain why the long-run aggregate supply curve is vertical.

5. List and explain the three theories for why the short-run aggregate supply curve is upward sloping.

6. What might shift the aggregate demand curve to the left? Use the model of aggregate demand and aggregate supply to trace through the effects of such a shift.

7. What might shift the aggregate supply curve to the left? Use the model of aggregate demand and aggregate supply to trace through the effects of such a shift.

8. Use a supply and demand diagram to show how an economy can experience rising prices and falling growth (stagflation) at the same time.

9. Why do recessions ultimately come to an end?

10. What sort of policy do you think would be the most appropriate to bring about a reduction in a country's natural rate of unemployment?

PROBLEMS AND APPLICATIONS

1. Why do you think that investment is more variable over the business cycle than consumer spending? Which category of consumer spending do you think would be most volatile: durable goods (such as furniture and car purchases), non-durable goods (such as food and clothing) or services (such as haircuts and medical care)? Why?

2. Suppose that the economy is in a long-run equilibrium:
   a. Use a diagram to illustrate the state of the economy. Be sure to show aggregate demand, short-run aggregate supply and long-run aggregate supply.
   b. Now suppose that a financial crisis causes aggregate demand to fall. Use your diagram to show what happens

to output and the price level in the short run. What happens to the unemployment rate?
   c. Use the sticky wage theory of aggregate supply to explain what will happen to output and the price level in the long run (assuming there is no change in policy). What role does the expected price level play in this adjustment? Be sure to illustrate your analysis with a graph.

3. Explain whether each of the following events will increase, decrease or have no effect on long-run aggregate supply:
   a. The country experiences a wave of immigration.
   b. The government raises the minimum wage above the national average wage level.

c. A war leads to the destruction of a large number of factories.

4. In Figure 17.7, how does the unemployment rate at points B and C compare to the unemployment rate at point A? Under the sticky wage explanation of the short-run aggregate supply curve, how does the real wage at points B and C compare to the real wage at point A?

5. Explain why the following statements are false:
   a. 'The aggregate demand curve slopes downward because it is the horizontal sum of the demand curves for individual goods.'
   b. 'The long-run aggregate supply curve is vertical because economic forces do not affect long-run aggregate supply.'
   c. 'If firms adjusted their prices every day, then the short-run aggregate supply curve would be horizontal.'
   d. 'Whenever the economy enters a recession, its long-run aggregate supply curve shifts to the left.'

6. For each of the three theories for the upward slope of the short-run aggregate supply curve, carefully explain the following:
   a. How the economy recovers from a recession and returns to its long-run equilibrium without any policy intervention.
   b. What determines the speed of that recovery?

7. Suppose the central bank expands the money supply, but because the public expects this action, it simultaneously raises its expectation of the price level. What will happen to output and the price level in the short run? Compare this result to the outcome if the central bank expanded the money supply but the public didn't change its expectation of the price level.

8. Suppose that the economy is currently in a recession. If policy makers take no action, how will the economy evolve over time? Explain in words and using an aggregate demand/aggregate supply diagram.

9. Suppose workers and firms suddenly believe that inflation will be quite high over the coming year. Suppose also that the economy begins in long-run equilibrium, and the aggregate demand curve does not shift.
   a. What happens to nominal wages? What happens to real wages?
   b. Using an aggregate demand/aggregate supply diagram, show the effect of the change in expectations on both the short-run and long-run levels of prices and output.
   c. Were the expectations of high inflation accurate? Explain.

10. Explain whether each of the following events shifts the short-run aggregate supply curve, the aggregate demand curve, both, or neither. For each event that does shift a curve, use a diagram to illustrate the effect on the economy.
    a. Households decide to save a larger share of their income.
    b. Cattle farmers suffer a prolonged period of foot-and-mouth disease which cuts average cattle herd sizes by 80 per cent.
    c. Increased job opportunities overseas cause many people to leave the country.

18 MACROECONOMICS – EMPLOYMENT AND UNEMPLOYMENT

LEARNING OBJECTIVES

In this chapter you will:

- Learn about the data used to measure the amount of unemployment

- Consider how unemployment can result from minimum wage laws

- See how unemployment can arise from bargaining between firms and unions

- Examine how unemployment results when firms choose to pay efficiency wages

After reading this chapter you should be able to:

- Explain why some unemployment is inevitable

- Illustrate in a diagram the impact of the minimum wage on high wage and low wage sectors

- List the reasons why unions cause unemployment and, alternatively, why unions might increase efficiency in some cases

- Describe the four reasons why firms may choose to pay wages in excess of the competitive wage

INTRODUCTION

Businesses rely on people – workers who provide labour services in return for payment. This payment allows the individual to provide for themselves and their families. For the business, the payment represents an investment in that individual in terms of the returns that the individual can help generate for the business. We have seen in Chapter 14 how marginal revenue product (MRP) for labour is related to the wage rate. Sadly, when the MRP falls below the wage rate for whatever reason, there is a risk that the worker will have to be released.

Losing a job can be the most distressing economic event in a person's life. Most people rely on their labour earnings to maintain their standard of living, and many people get from their work not only income but also a sense of personal accomplishment. A job loss means a lower living standard in the present, anxiety about the future and reduced self-esteem. It is not surprising, therefore, that politicians campaigning for office often speak about how their proposed policies will help create jobs.

Businesses have a considerable impact on the number of people employed in a society and to a certain extent the number of people who are out of work. The level of unemployment provides an indicator to the state of the labour market. If the demand for labour is higher than the available supply we say the labour market is 'tight'. If labour supply exceeds labour demand then there is likely to be a high level of unemployment and the labour market could be described as being 'loose'.

In previous chapters we have seen some of the forces that determine the level and growth of a country's standard of living. A country that saves and invests a high fraction of its income, for instance, enjoys more rapid growth in its capital stock and its GDP than a similar country that saves and invests less. An even more obvious determinant of a country's standard of living is the amount of unemployment it typically experiences. People who would like to work but cannot find a job are not contributing to the economy's production of goods and services. Although some degree of unemployment is inevitable in a complex economy with thousands of firms and millions of workers, the amount of unemployment varies substantially over time and across countries. When a country keeps its workers as fully employed as possible, it achieves a higher level of GDP than it would if it left many of its workers standing idle.

In Chapter 16 we provided an outline of unemployment from a macroeconomic perspective. In this chapter we are going to look into unemployment in more detail. The problem of unemployment is usefully divided into two categories – the long-run problem and the short-run problem. The economy's *natural rate of unemployment* refers to the amount of unemployment that the economy normally experiences. *Cyclical unemployment* refers to the year-to-year fluctuations in unemployment around its natural rate, and it is closely associated with the short-run ups and downs of economic activity. In this chapter we discuss the determinants of an economy's natural rate of unemployment. As we will see, the designation *natural* does not imply that this rate of unemployment is desirable. Nor does it imply that it is constant over time or impervious to economic policy. It merely means that this unemployment does not go away on its own, even in the long run.

IDENTIFYING UNEMPLOYMENT

In Chapter 16 we looked at some core definitions of unemployment and how unemployment is measured. We are going to take these definitions one step further in this section to look at how unemployment can be calculated. Remember that the labour force is defined as the sum of the employed and the unemployed, that the unemployment rate is measured as the percentage of the labour force that is unemployed and that labour force participation rate measures the percentage of the total adult population of the country that is in the labour force as noted on page 406.

Labour force participation rate = (Labour force/Adult population) × 100

To see how these data are computed, consider the figures for Germany in spring 2011. According to data from the Federal Statistical Office, 41.04 million people were employed and 2.50 million people were unemployed. The labour force was:

$$\text{Labour force} = 41.04 + 2.50 = 43.54 \text{ million}$$

The unemployment rate was:

$$\text{Unemployment rate} = (2.50/43.54) \times 100 = 5.7 \text{ per cent}$$

Because the adult population (the number of people aged between 16 and 65) was around 54.6 million, the labour force participation rate was:

$$\text{Labour force participation rate} = (43.54/54.6) \times 100 = 79.7 \text{ per cent}$$

Hence, in spring 2011, just over three-quarters of the German adult population were participating in the labour market, and 5.7 per cent of those labour market participants were without work.

We know that the economy will always have some unemployment. Looking at figures for Europe we can see that there are different levels of unemployment across the EU. Figure 18.1 shows a snapshot of unemployment in the EU at the end of 2011. In this chapter we examine why there is always some unemployment in market economies.

FIGURE 18.1

Unemployment in Europe

The chart shows unemployment across the EU. Note the high levels of unemployment in Spain and Greece largely due to the debt crisis being experienced by those two countries.

**Harmonized unemployment rate by gender
% (seasonally adjusted)**

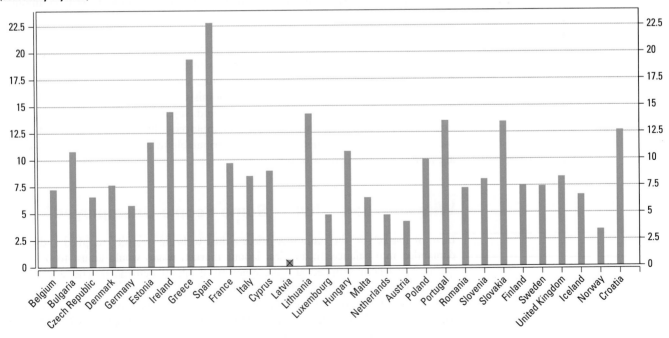

■ 2011M10 ✕ No data

Source: **http://epp.eurostat.ec.europa.eu/tgm/graph.do?tab=graph&plugin=1&pcode=teilm020&language=en&toolbox=data**

How Long are the Unemployed Without Work?

In judging how serious the problem of unemployment is, one question to consider is whether unemployment is typically a short-term or long-term condition. If unemployment is short term, one might conclude that it is not a big problem. Workers may require a few weeks between jobs to find the openings that best suit their tastes and skills. Yet if unemployment is long term, one might conclude that it is a serious problem. Workers unemployed for many months are more likely to suffer economic and psychological hardship.

Because the duration of unemployment can affect our view about how big a problem it is, economists have devoted much energy to studying data on the duration of unemployment spells. In this work, they have uncovered a result that is important, subtle and seemingly contradictory: most spells of unemployment are short, and most unemployment observed at any given time is long term.

To see how this statement can be true, consider an example. Suppose that you visited the government's unemployment office every week for a year to survey the unemployed. Each week you find that there are four unemployed workers. Three of these workers are the same individuals for the whole year, while the fourth person changes every week. Based on this experience, would you say that unemployment is typically short term or long term?

Some simple calculations help answer this question. In this example, you meet a total of 55 unemployed people; 52 of them are unemployed for 1 week, and 3 are unemployed for the full year. This means that 52/55, or 95 per cent, of unemployment spells end in 1 week. Thus, most spells of unemployment are short. Yet consider the total amount of unemployment. The 3 people unemployed for 1 year (52 weeks) make up a total of 156 weeks of unemployment. Together with the 52 people unemployed for 1 week, this makes 208 weeks of unemployment. In this example, 156/208, or 75 per cent, of unemployment is attributable to those individuals who are unemployed for a full year. Thus, most unemployment observed at any given time is long term.

This subtle conclusion implies that economists and policy makers must be careful when interpreting data on unemployment and when designing policies to help the unemployed. Most people who become unemployed will soon find jobs. Yet most of the economy's unemployment problem is attributable to the relatively few workers who are jobless for long periods of time.

Why are There Always Some People Unemployed?

In most markets in the economy, prices adjust to bring quantity supplied and quantity demanded into balance. In an ideal labour market, wages would adjust to balance the quantity of labour supplied and the quantity of labour demanded. This adjustment of wages would ensure that all workers are always fully employed.

Of course, reality does not resemble this ideal. There are always some workers without jobs, even when the overall economy is doing well. In other words, the unemployment rate never falls to zero; instead, it fluctuates around the natural rate of unemployment. To understand this natural rate, the remaining sections in the chapter examine the reasons why actual labour markets depart from the ideal of full employment.

To preview our conclusions, we will find that there are four ways to explain unemployment in the long run. The first explanation is that it takes time for workers to search for the jobs that are best suited for them. The unemployment that results from the process of matching workers and jobs is sometimes called **frictional unemployment**, and it is often thought to explain relatively short spells of unemployment.

The next three explanations for unemployment suggest that the number of jobs available in some labour markets may be insufficient to give a job to everyone who wants one. This occurs when the quantity of labour supplied exceeds the quantity demanded. Unemployment of this sort is sometimes called **structural unemployment**, and it is often thought to explain longer spells of unemployment. As we will see, this kind of unemployment results when wages are, for some reason, set above the level that brings supply and demand into equilibrium. We will later examine three possible reasons for an above-equilibrium wage: minimum wage laws, unions and efficiency wages.

frictional unemployment
unemployment that results because it takes time for workers to search for the jobs that best suit their tastes and skills

structural unemployment
unemployment that results because the number of jobs available in some labour markets is insufficient to provide a job for everyone who wants one

> **Quick Quiz** How is the unemployment rate measured? • How might the unemployment rate overstate the amount of joblessness? How might it understate it?

Since the 1930s there has been an ongoing debate in economics about the principal causes of unemployment and the extent to which these causes stem from the supply side of the economy or the demand side. That debate has continued and has been brought into sharper focus with the rise in unemployment in many European countries and the United States in the post-financial crisis world. Policies designed to improve the workings of the supply side of the economy which includes cutting taxes, investing in training an education, changing the benefits system and improving incentives to get work have to be viewed alongside those which affect the level of aggregate demand in the economy. In essence, the debate centres on the extent to which unemployment is cyclical or structural – the latter accounting for the level of unemployment not due to changes in the economic cycle. As we build the theoretical building blocks of macroeconomics it must be remembered that policies to cut unemployment still deeply divide opinion in the economics profession.

JOB SEARCH

One reason why economies always experience some unemployment is job search. **Job search** is the process of matching workers with appropriate jobs. If all workers and all jobs were the same, so that all workers were equally well suited for all jobs, job search would not be a problem. Laid-off workers would quickly find new jobs that were well suited for them. But, in fact, workers differ in their tastes and skills, jobs differ in their attributes, and information about job candidates and job vacancies is disseminated slowly among the many firms and households in the economy.

job search the process by which workers find appropriate jobs given their tastes and skills

Why Some Frictional Unemployment is Inevitable

Frictional unemployment is often the result of changes in the demand for labour among different firms. When consumers decide that they prefer Brand X to Brand Y, the company producing Brand X increases employment, and the other firm lays off workers. The former Brand Y workers must now search for new jobs, and the Brand X producer must decide which new workers to hire for the various jobs that have opened up. The result of this transition is a period of unemployment.

Similarly, because different regions of the country produce different goods, employment can rise in one region while it falls in another. Consider, for instance, what happens when the world price of oil falls. Firms extracting oil from the fields below the North Sea, off the coast of Scotland, respond to the lower price by cutting back on production and employment. At the same time, cheaper petrol stimulates car sales, so car manufacturing firms in northern and central England raise production and employment. Changes in the composition of demand among industries or regions are called *sectoral shifts*. Because it takes time for workers to search for jobs in the new sectors, sectoral shifts temporarily cause unemployment.

Frictional unemployment is inevitable simply because the economy is always changing. In 1960, manufacturing as a percentage of GDP was 38 per cent in the UK; it now accounts for around 15 per cent. The number of people employed in manufacturing in 1960 was around 9 million compared to about 3 million today. The gross value added by industry (where gross value added is defined as the value of newly generated goods and services) in the EU 27 (which includes manufacturing) fell from 23.1 per cent in 1998 to 18.1 per cent in 2009. Even Germany, traditionally heavily reliant on industry for its export earnings, has seen the value added by industry fall from 25.3 per cent in 1998 to 22 per cent in 2009. On the other hand, business services and finance contributed only about 3 per cent of UK GDP in the mid-1950s but contribute more than a quarter today. The EU 27 has seen gross value added by business activities and financial services increasing from 25.1 per cent of GDP in 1998 to 29.1 per cent in 2009. In Latvia the transition has been significant with an increase from 15.1 per cent in 1998 to 26.7 per cent by 2009. As these transitions take place, jobs are created in some firms and destroyed in others. The end result of this process has been higher productivity and higher living standards. But, along the way, workers in declining industries found themselves out of work and searching for new jobs.

In addition to the effects of sectoral shifts on unemployment, workers will leave their jobs sometimes because they realize that the jobs are not a good match for their tastes and skills and they wish to look for a better job. Many of these workers, especially younger ones, find new jobs at higher wages, although given the vast improvements in information technology in recent years (especially the internet) it is likely that many people search for new jobs without actually quitting their current job. Nevertheless, this churning of the labour force is normal in a well functioning and dynamic market economy, and the result is some amount of frictional unemployment.

Public Policy and Job Search

Even if some frictional unemployment is inevitable, the precise amount is not. The faster information spreads about job openings and worker availability, the more rapidly the economy can match workers and firms. The internet, for instance, may help facilitate job search and reduce frictional unemployment. In addition, public policy may play a role. If policy can reduce the time it takes unemployed workers to find new jobs, it can reduce the economy's natural rate of unemployment.

Government policies try to facilitate job search in various ways. One way is through government-run employment agencies or job centres, which give out information about job vacancies. Another way is through public training schemes, which aim to ease the transition of workers from declining to growing industries and to help disadvantaged groups escape poverty. Advocates of these policies believe that they make the economy operate more efficiently by keeping the labour force more fully employed, and that they reduce the inequities inherent in a constantly changing market economy.

Critics of these policies question whether the government should get involved with the process of job search. They argue that it is better to let the private market match workers and jobs. In fact, most job search in the economy takes place without intervention by the government. Newspaper advertisements, internet job sites, head-hunters and word of mouth all help spread information about job openings and job candidates. Similarly, much worker education is done privately, either through schools or through on-the-job training. These critics contend that the government is no better – and most likely worse – at disseminating the right information to the right workers and deciding what kinds of worker training would be most valuable. They claim that these decisions are best made privately by workers and employers.

Unemployment Insurance

One government policy that increases the amount of frictional unemployment, without intending to do so, is **unemployment insurance** (or, as it is called in the UK, national insurance). This policy is designed to offer workers partial protection against job loss. The unemployed who quit their jobs, were fired for just cause or who have just entered the labour force are not eligible. Benefits are paid only to the unemployed who were laid off because their previous employers no longer needed their skills.

> **unemployment insurance** a government programme that partially protects workers' incomes when they become unemployed

While unemployment insurance reduces the hardship of unemployment, it is argued that it can also increase the amount of unemployment. This explanation is based on one of the *Ten Principles of Economics* in Chapter 1: people respond to incentives. Because unemployment benefits stop when a worker takes a new job, the unemployed, it is argued, devote less effort to job search and are more likely to turn down unattractive job offers. In addition, because unemployment insurance makes unemployment less onerous, workers are less likely to seek guarantees of job security when they negotiate with employers over the terms of employment. However, research on unemployment insurance in Europe gives a different perspective. In a paper by Konstantinos Tatsiramos the benefits to workers searching for jobs and receiving unemployment insurance is greater than the costs:

> *This paper provides evidence on the effect of unemployment benefits on unemployment and employment duration in Europe, using individual data from the European Community Household Panel for eight countries. Even if receiving benefits has a direct negative effect increasing the duration of unemployment spells, there is also a positive indirect effect of benefits on subsequent employment duration. This indirect effect is pronounced in countries with relatively generous benefit systems, and for recipients who have remained unemployed for at least six months. In terms of the magnitude of the effect, recipients remain employed on average two to four months longer than non-recipients. This represents a ten to twenty per cent increase relative to the average employment duration, compensating for the additional time spent in unemployment.*
>
> *Source:* Tatsiramos, K. (2006) *Unemployment Insurance in Europe: Unemployment Duration and Subsequent Employment Stability.* Institute for the Study of Labor Discussion Paper no. 2280.

The effect of unemployment insurance is likely to be related to the way the scheme is designed and operated. In one US study, when unemployed workers applied to collect unemployment insurance benefits, some of them were randomly selected and each offered a $500 bonus if they found new jobs within 11 weeks. This group was then compared with a control group not offered the incentive. The average spell of unemployment for the group offered the bonus was 7 per cent shorter than the average spell for the control group. This experiment shows that the design of the unemployment insurance system influences the effort that the unemployed devote to job search.

Several other studies examined search effort by following a group of workers over time. Unemployment insurance benefits, rather than lasting forever, usually run out after six months or a year. These studies found that when the unemployed become ineligible for benefits, the probability of their finding a new job rises markedly. Thus, receiving unemployment insurance benefits does reduce the search effort of the unemployed.

Even though unemployment insurance reduces search effort and raises unemployment, we should not necessarily conclude that the policy is a bad one. The policy does achieve its primary goal of reducing the income uncertainty that workers face. In addition, when workers turn down unattractive job offers, they have the opportunity to look for jobs that better suit their tastes and skills. Some economists have argued that unemployment insurance improves the ability of the economy to match each worker with the most appropriate job.

The study of unemployment insurance shows that the unemployment rate is an imperfect measure of a nation's overall level of economic well-being. Most economists agree that eliminating unemployment insurance would reduce the amount of unemployment in the economy. Yet economists disagree on whether economic well-being would be enhanced or diminished by this change in policy.

Quick Quiz How would an increase in the world price of oil affect the amount of frictional unemployment? Is this unemployment undesirable? What public policies might affect the amount of unemployment caused by this price change?

CASE STUDY

Rethinking Unemployment Insurance

With millions more people across Europe and North America unemployed compared with the start of the year [2009], unemployment insurance has returned to the forefront as a public policy issue. Most of the talk has been about extending unemployment benefits. It may be time, though, for lawmakers to engage in a more comprehensive reform debate – one that includes a proposal by Jeff Kling [Senior Fellow and Deputy Director of the Centre on Children and families at the Brookings Institution in Washington DC] to alter the structure of unemployment insurance in such a way that recognizes the psychology of losing a job and strengthens the incentives for returning to work.

Kling's revenue-neutral proposal would reform unemployment insurance by shifting government resources toward protection against especially damaging long stretches of unemployment or permanent effects of job loss, such as lifetime wage reductions. Laid-off workers can remain unemployed for long stretches for two major reasons, one economic and one psychological. 1) They simply cannot find work; 2) They refuse to take lower paying jobs thinking they can find a new one that pays as much as their last.

To create an incentive for workers to clear the psychological hurdle, Kling proposes setting up temporary earnings replacement accounts (TERAs) to improve the protection against the effects of long-term unemployment and permanent wage-reduction. The account would be funded by the workers themselves during more prosperous times, and drawn from during periods of distress. Workers could also borrow against the account from future earnings. During periods of unemployment or lower-wage jobs, workers would draw funds from both their unemployment account and more traditional unemployment insurance (UI), which would result in a broader safety net from a similar government budget. While the unemployment accounts would be funded by workers, the unemployment insurance would be funded by firms, as it is currently.

In comparison with UI, use of TERAs should reduce the average amount of time that people spend out of work. Use of TERAs instead of UI increases the price for additional unemployment (at least among those who do not expect to retire with an unpaid loan), because TERA withdrawals would need to be repaid from future income. As a result, the introduction of TERAs may reduce the overall duration of unemployment by 5 to 10 per cent.

The duration of unemployment would also be affected by the availability of wage-loss insurance. Individuals considering a job offering a wage below their insured wage level would be more likely to accept it, since the hourly rate of pay would be augmented by wage loss insurance payments. Making work more rewarding should reduce the tendency of some people to become discouraged and to remain unemployed or even stop looking for work. This reduced duration of unemployment is unlikely to be associated with workers taking jobs too rapidly, rather than waiting more patiently for a more productive job match.

Kling makes the argument that his proposal will actually reduce temporary lay-offs by 10–15 per cent and permanent layoffs by an unspecified amount. How? By forcing firms to bear the costs of unemployment. Under the current unemployment insurance system, firms make payments to the government to cover payments. Kling proposes that firms contribute to government coffers for wage-loss insurance, repayment insurance, assistance on earnings and replacement accounts for those with lower wages. Since the proposal is revenue neutral, the total costs to these forms of insurance would be the same as they are now. But Kling proposes raising the taxable earnings base to a real value of $90 000 (in some states in the USA it is currently below $10 000), cutting the overall unemployment insurance payroll tax rate and lowering the minimum amounts that firms must pay. The result, Kling says, would be a tighter linkage between layoffs and direct firm costs. Intra-firm subsidies for unemployment insurance would thus be reduced.

In addition, since most employees who become unemployed would bear the costs of unemployment benefits directly, they would be much more likely to voice strong opposition to temporary layoffs than they are under UI when they receive payments with no corresponding future obligations. Firms in industries with frequent temporary layoffs would be pressured by the labour market to raise wages in order to continue to attract workers who, under the proposal, would be self-insuring income loss during layoff through savings and borrowing.

Here is one more reason why individuals might be more likely to return to work faster under Kling's plan. Recent research by economist Raj Chetty argues unemployment insurance raises some problems of moral hazard, but that equally serious effects come from something he calls the 'liquidity effect'. In essence, unemployment benefits allow an individual to remain out of work longer since they have enough cash-on-hand to survive. But if workers have to use the money they saved themselves through their earnings replacement accounts to fund their short-term unemployment, they could be more motivated to find a job. Certainly more motivated than if the entire insurance check was coming out of some other taxpayer's pocket.

Source: Adapted from: **http://nudges.wordpress.com/2008/12/10/rethinkingunemployment-insurance-part-i/** and **http://nudges.wordpress.com/2008/12/16/rethinking-unemployment-insurance-part-ii/** accessed 9 April 2009.

MINIMUM WAGE LAWS

Having seen how frictional unemployment results from the process of matching workers and jobs, let's now examine how structural unemployment results when the number of jobs is insufficient for the number of workers.

To understand structural unemployment, we begin by reviewing how unemployment arises from minimum wage laws. We saw the basis of why a minimum wage can lead to unemployment in a case study Chapter 14. Although minimum wages are not the predominant reason for unemployment in an economy, they have an important effect on certain groups with particularly high unemployment rates. An analysis of minimum wages is a natural place to start because, as we will see, it can be used to understand some of the other reasons for structural unemployment.

Minimum wage laws dictate the lowest price for labour that any employer may pay. The USA and 20 of the 27 European Union countries now have a statutory minimum wage.

As noted in Chapter 14, there is an argument that minimum wage laws can lead to unemployment, the extent of which may be dependent on the relative elasticity of demand for labour and the nature of the industry. It is important to note, however, why minimum wage laws are not a predominant reason for structural unemployment: most workers in the economy have wages well above the legal minimum. Minimum wage laws are binding most often for the least skilled and least experienced members of the labour force, such as teenagers. It is only among these workers that minimum wage laws explain the existence of unemployment.

Our brief analysis of minimum wage laws allows us to draw a more general lesson: if the wage is kept above the equilibrium level for any reason, the result is unemployment. Minimum wage laws are just one reason why wages may be 'too high'. In the remaining two sections of this chapter, we consider two other reasons why wages may be kept above the equilibrium level – unions and efficiency wages.

At this point, however, we should stop and notice that the structural unemployment that arises from an above-equilibrium wage is, in an important sense, different from the frictional unemployment that arises from the process of job search. The need for job search is not due to the failure of wages to balance labour supply and labour demand. When job search is the explanation for unemployment, workers are *searching* for the jobs that best suit their tastes and skills. By contrast, when the wage is above the equilibrium level, the quantity of labour supplied exceeds the quantity of labour demanded, and workers are unemployed because they are *waiting* for jobs to open up.

Pitfall Prevention The logic is for the minimum wage to be set at a level above market equilibrium. Assuming this is the case then a minimum wage is an example of a price floor – a legal minimum imposed by a government which is above the market equilibrium. It should not be confused with a price ceiling which is a legal maximum price that can be charged.

Quick Quiz Draw the supply curve and the demand curve for a labour market in which the wage is fixed above the equilibrium level. Show the quantity of labour supplied, the quantity demanded and the amount of unemployment.

UNIONS AND COLLECTIVE BARGAINING

Remember a union is a worker association that bargains with employers over wages and working conditions. Union density measures the proportion of the workforce that is unionized, excluding people who cannot, for legal or other reasons, be members of a union – for example, members of the armed forces. Broadly speaking, this amounts to expressing the number of union members as a proportion of civilian employees plus the unemployed. In the UK in 2010, union density was 26.5 per cent, and has been steadily falling since 1995 when it stood at around 32.4 per cent and an even greater marked fall from the beginning of the 1980s, when it was over 50 per cent. In other European countries there is a similar trend of falling union density. In Germany density has fallen from 25.3 per cent in 1999 to 18.6 per cent in 2010, in Austria the fall has been from 37.4 per cent to 28.1 per cent and in Poland from 26.0 per cent to 15.0 per cent in the same period. However, there are exceptions with countries like Finland, Denmark and Sweden having stable densities between 68 per cent and 70 per cent. In the United States, by comparison, density is 11.4 per cent and in Australia 18.0 per cent (figures for 2010).

The Economics of Unions

A union is a type of cartel. Like any cartel, a union is a group of sellers acting together in the hope of exerting their joint market power. Businesses have had conflict with unions for hundreds of years and relations can often be strained. The basis of union activity is that individually a worker cannot bargain for improvements in pay and conditions in the face of the might of the business but as a group they have more 'power'. Workers in a union, therefore, act as a group when discussing their wages, benefits and working conditions with their employers. The process by which unions and firms agree on the terms of employment is called **collective bargaining**.

collective bargaining the process by which unions and firms agree on the terms of employment

When a union bargains with a firm, it asks for higher wages, better benefits and better working conditions than the firm would offer in the absence of a union. If the union and the firm do not reach agreement, the union can take various steps to put pressure on employers to come to an agreement including working to rule (doing only what is agreed in the contract of employment) and as a last resort organizing a withdrawal of labour from the firm, called a strike. Because a strike reduces production, sales and profit, a firm facing a strike threat is likely to agree to pay higher wages than it otherwise would. Economists who study the effects of unions typically find that union workers earn significantly more than similar workers who do not belong to unions.

When a union raises the wage above the equilibrium level, it raises the quantity of labour supplied and reduces the quantity of labour demanded, resulting in unemployment. Those workers who remain employed are better off, but those who were previously employed and are now unemployed are worse off. Indeed, unions are often thought to cause conflict between different groups of workers – between the *insiders* who benefit from high union wages and the *outsiders* who do not get the union jobs.

The outsiders can respond to their status in one of two ways. Some of them remain unemployed and wait for the chance to become insiders and earn the high union wage. Others take jobs in firms that are not unionized. Thus, when unions raise wages in one part of the economy, the supply of labour increases in other parts of the economy. This increase in labour supply, in turn, reduces wages in industries that are not unionized. In other words, workers in unions reap the benefit of collective bargaining, while workers not in unions bear some of the cost.

The role of unions in the economy depends in part on the laws that govern union organization and collective bargaining. Normally, explicit agreements among members of a cartel are illegal. If firms that sell a common product were to agree to set a high price for that product, they would generally be held to be in breach of competition law and the government would prosecute these firms in the civil and criminal courts. In contrast, unions are given exemption from these laws in the belief that workers need greater market power as they bargain with employers.

Legislation affecting the market power of unions is a perennial topic of political debate. Members of parliament sometimes debate *right-to-work laws,* which give workers in a unionized firm the right to choose whether to join the union. In the absence of such laws, unions can insist during collective bargaining that firms make union membership a requirement for employment.

JEOPARDY PROBLEM

A firm has been in dispute with workers represented by a trade union for a number of months. The union was pushing for a pay rise 5 per cent above inflation and the firm was only prepared to initially offer an inflation-related rise. In the end, the dispute was resolved with workers getting a 4 per cent pay rise in return for specified productivity increases linked to the length of the working week and changes to working practices. Why might the firm have been prepared to agree fairly closely to the demands of the union?

Are Unions Good or Bad for the Economy?

Economists disagree about whether unions are good or bad for the economy as a whole. Let's consider both sides of the debate.

Critics of unions argue that unions are merely a type of cartel. When unions raise wages above the level that would prevail in competitive markets, they reduce the quantity of labour demanded, cause some workers to be unemployed and reduce the wages in the rest of the economy. The resulting allocation of labour is, critics argue, both inefficient and inequitable. It is inefficient because high union wages reduce employment in unionized firms below the efficient, competitive level. It is inequitable because some workers benefit at the expense of other workers.

Advocates of unions contend that unions are a necessary antidote to the market power of the firms that hire workers. In some regions where one particular company is the dominant employer, if workers do not accept the wages and working conditions that the firm offers, they may have little choice but to move or stop working. In the absence of a union, therefore, the firm could use its market power to pay lower wages and offer worse working conditions than would prevail if it had to compete with other firms for the same workers. In this case, a union may balance the firm's market power and protect the workers from being at the mercy of the firm owners.

Advocates of unions also claim that unions are important for helping firms respond efficiently to workers' concerns. Whenever a worker takes a job, the worker and the firm must agree on many attributes of the job in addition to the wage: hours of work, overtime, holidays, sick leave, health benefits, promotion schedules, job security and so on. By representing workers' views on these issues, unions allow firms to provide the right mix of job attributes. In many countries unions have now taken on additional roles in supporting workers with respect to offering legal support in the event of an individual dispute at work, advice on pensions, financial services such as insurance and support for those who have been injured or disabled at work and have to retire early. Even if unions have the adverse effect of pushing wages above the equilibrium level and causing unemployment, they have the benefit of helping firms keep a happy and productive workforce.

In the end, there is no consensus among economists about whether unions are good or bad for the economy. Like many institutions, their influence is probably beneficial in some circumstances and adverse in others.

THE THEORY OF EFFICIENCY WAGES

A fourth reason why economies always experience some unemployment – in addition to job search, minimum wage laws and unions – is suggested by the theory of efficiency wages. According to this theory, firms operate more efficiently if wages are above the equilibrium level. Therefore, it may be profitable for firms to keep wages high even in the presence of a surplus of labour.

In some ways, the unemployment that arises from efficiency wages is similar to the unemployment that arises from minimum wage laws and unions. In all three cases, unemployment is the result of wages above the level that balances the quantity of labour supplied and the quantity of labour demanded. Yet there is also an important difference. Minimum wage laws and unions prevent firms from lowering wages in the presence of a surplus of workers. Efficiency wage theory states that such a constraint on firms is unnecessary in many cases because firms may be better off keeping wages above the equilibrium level.

Why should firms want to keep wages high? This decision may seem odd at first, for wages are a large part of firms' costs. Normally, we expect profit-maximizing firms to want to keep costs – and therefore wages – as low as possible. The novel insight of efficiency wage theory is that paying high wages might be profitable because they might raise the efficiency of a firm's workers.

There are several types of efficiency wage theory. Each type suggests a different explanation for why firms may want to pay high wages. Let's now consider four of these types.

Worker Health

The first and simplest type of efficiency wage theory emphasizes the link between wages and worker health. Better paid workers eat a more nutritious diet, and workers who eat a better diet are healthier and more productive. A firm may find it more profitable to pay high wages and have healthy, productive workers than to pay lower wages and have less healthy, less productive workers.

This type of efficiency wage theory is not relevant for firms in rich countries such as many of those in the EU. In these countries, the equilibrium wages for most workers are well above the level needed for an adequate diet. Firms are not concerned that paying equilibrium wages would place their workers' health in jeopardy.

This type of efficiency wage theory is more relevant for firms in less developed countries where inadequate nutrition is a more common problem. Unemployment is high in the cities of many poor African countries, for example. In these countries, firms may fear that cutting wages would, in fact, adversely influence their workers' health and productivity. In other words, concern over nutrition may explain why firms do not cut wages despite a surplus of labour.

Worker Turnover

A second type of efficiency wage theory emphasizes the link between wages and worker turnover. Workers quit jobs for many reasons – to take jobs in other firms, to move to other parts of the country, to leave the labour force and so on. The frequency with which they quit depends on the entire set of incentives they face, including the benefits of leaving and the benefits of staying. The more a firm pays its workers, the less often its workers will choose to leave. Thus, a firm can reduce turnover among its workers by paying them a high wage.

Why do firms care about turnover? The reason is that it is costly for firms to hire and train new workers. Moreover, even after they are trained, newly hired workers are not as productive as experienced workers. Firms with higher turnover, therefore, will tend to have higher production costs. Firms may find it profitable to pay wages above the equilibrium level in order to reduce worker turnover.

Worker Effort

A third type of efficiency wage theory emphasizes the link between wages and worker effort. In many jobs, workers have some discretion over how hard to work. As a result, firms monitor the efforts of their workers, and workers caught shirking their responsibilities can be disciplined and possibly dismissed. But not all shirkers are caught immediately because monitoring workers is costly and imperfect. A firm can respond to this problem by paying wages above the equilibrium level. High wages make workers more eager to keep their jobs and, thereby, give workers an incentive to put forward their best effort.

This particular type of efficiency wage theory is similar to the old Marxist idea of the 'reserve army of the unemployed'. Marx thought that employers benefited from unemployment because the threat of unemployment helped to discipline those workers who had jobs. In the worker effort variant of efficiency wage theory, unemployment fills a similar role. If the wage were at the level that balanced supply and demand, workers would have less reason to work hard because if they were fired, they could quickly find new jobs at the same wage. Therefore, firms raise wages above the equilibrium level, causing unemployment and providing an incentive for workers not to shirk their responsibilities.

Worker Quality

A fourth and final type of efficiency wage theory emphasizes the link between wages and worker quality. When a firm hires new workers, it cannot perfectly gauge the quality of the applicants. By paying a high wage, the firm attracts a better pool of workers to apply for its jobs.

To see how this might work, consider a simple example. Waterwell Company owns one well and needs one worker to pump water from the well. Two workers, Singh and Patel, are interested in the job. Singh, a proficient worker, is willing to work for €10 per hour. Below that wage, he would rather start his own car washing business. Patel, a complete incompetent, is willing to work for anything above €2 per hour. Below that wage, he would rather sit on the beach. Economists say that Singh's *reservation wage* – the lowest wage he would accept – is €10, and Patel's reservation wage is €2.

What wage should the firm set? If the firm were interested in minimizing labour costs, it would set the wage at €2 per hour. At this wage, the quantity of workers supplied (one) would balance the quantity demanded. Patel would take the job, and Singh would not apply for it. Yet suppose Waterwell knows that only one of these two applicants is competent, but it does not know whether it is Singh or Patel. If the firm hires the incompetent worker, he may damage the well, causing the firm huge losses. In this case, the firm has a better strategy than paying the equilibrium wage of €2 and hiring Patel. It can offer €10 per hour, inducing both Singh and Patel to apply for the job. By choosing randomly between these two applicants and turning the other away, the firm has a 50:50 chance of hiring the competent one. By contrast, if the firm offers any lower wage, it is sure to hire the incompetent worker.

This story illustrates a general phenomenon. When a firm faces a surplus of workers, it might seem profitable to reduce the wage it is offering. But by reducing the wage, the firm induces an adverse change in the mix of workers. In this case, at a wage of €10, Waterwell has two workers applying for one job. But if Waterwell responds to this labour surplus by reducing the wage, the competent worker (who has better alternative opportunities) will not apply. Thus, it is profitable for the firm to pay a wage above the level that balances supply and demand.

Quick Quiz Give four explanations for why firms might find it profitable to pay wages above the level that balances quantity of labour supplied and quantity of labour demanded.

CONCLUSION

In this chapter we discussed the reasons why economies always experience some degree of unemployment. We have seen how job search, minimum wage laws, unions and efficiency wages can all help explain why some workers do not have jobs. Which of these four explanations for the natural rate of unemployment are the most important? Unfortunately, there is no easy way to tell. Economists differ in which of these explanations of unemployment they consider most important.

The analysis of this chapter yields an important lesson: although the economy will always have some unemployment, its natural rate is not immutable. Many events and policies can change the amount of unemployment the economy typically experiences. As the information revolution changes the process of job search, as government adjusts the minimum wage, as workers form or quit unions, and as firms alter their reliance on efficiency wages, the natural rate of unemployment evolves. Unemployment is not a simple problem with a simple solution. But how we choose to organize our society can profoundly influence how prevalent a problem it is.

IN THE NEWS

Directing Employment

In a number of countries around the world, there are laws passed designed to achieve some specific policy objective. This can include increasing the number of women in senior positions in the workforce or directing firms to employ domestic nationals before filling posts with foreign nationals. This article looks at the effects of a policy in the Gulf region to increase the number of nationals hired by firms across the region.

Gulf Companies Under Pressure to Meet Nationalization Quota

Private sector companies in the Gulf Cooperation Council (GCC), under a great pressure to meet their government quota by nationalizing its workforce, are choosing to pay fines rather than meet government targets for hiring nationals.

Companies have been changing their policies to absorb more nationals into their businesses, but the pressure on labor markets to reduce the number of unemployed has created dual assumption among companies to be able to attract the workers they need while meeting quotas for their sector.

The UAE Ministry of Labor requires employers in some sectors to increase the number of nationals they employ by a set percentage each year. 'There is a quota for the banking sector, for the trade sector and for the insurance sector,' said Essa Al Mulla, executive director of the Emirates Nationals Development Program (ENDP) to *The National* [newspaper on Sunday March 11th]. 'The quota system has worked very well with the banking sector, but it failed big-time with the trade and insurance sectors,' he added.

The ENDP was set up in 2005 to help UAE nationals find jobs in the private sector. Emiratis are said to prefer careers in the government, and reportedly avoid careers in hospitality and retail.

Insurance companies inexplicably began refusing to hire Emiratis. Employees of companies were quoted in *The National* as saying, 'In the insurance sector, we have to pay approximately 0.01 per cent of our net profit if we have not achieved the minimum quota required. "OK, we'll pay the amount the government is asking us for, and we will not recruit Emiratis".'

The Emirates is not the only Gulf country trying to address the hiring of nationals.

Meanwhile, a report by Saudi Fransi Bank in June 2011 said that plans to refuse expatriate work permits to companies that do not have enough local employees could force smaller firms out of business and could stall the recovery of the private sector in the kingdom.

'The initial shock of Nitaqat Color system (Company Category) [the name of the quota system] if enforced with vigor, could lead numerous smaller businesses to shut down, shake already feeble foreign investor confidence in the economy, and further stall the private sector's recovery,' the report claims.

Kristian Ulrichsen, a Gulf specialist at the London School of Economics, said it might not be possible for the UAE and other Gulf states to continue operating nationalization programs in the private sector.

'In the modern era of global governance and multiple jurisdictions it may become harder to achieve outright nationalization measures outside the purely public sector, as private companies and multilateral corporations become bound by international frameworks of governance,' he said. 'This could be a clash that grows sharper in the years ahead.'

The Middle East region has the world's highest rate of youth unemployment, estimated at more than 25 per cent – the rate in North Africa is around 24 per cent. Unemployment among female youth is much worse, surpassing 30 per cent in the Arab region, according to a McKinsey report on April 19, 2011.

The issue is even more acute in the Gulf, where unemployment rates among young nationals exceed 35 per cent – ranging from 40 per cent in Saudi Arabia (2009) to 11 per cent in Qatar (2010), according to Silatech research report.

Questions

1. If a government imposes a quota specifying that 60 per cent of a firm's employees must be domestic nationals, what would you expect to happen to the domestic wage rate and the number of nationals employed as a result?

2. What barriers might exist to a firm in meeting such quotas set by governments?

3. If the Nitaqat system is enforced, why would it mean 'smaller businesses shutting down'?

4. To what extent do you think that the increasing globalization of business will mean that Nitaqat systems will be difficult to enforce?

5. Despite the problems inherent in such a system, are the high levels of youth unemployment in the GCC region a justification for a policy which seeks to focus on domestic employment?

SUMMARY

- The unemployment rate is an imperfect measure of joblessness. Some people who call themselves unemployed may actually not want to work, and some people who would like to work have left the labour force after an unsuccessful search.

- In many advanced economies, most people who become unemployed find work within a short period of time. Nevertheless, most unemployment observed at any given time is attributable to the few people who are unemployed for long periods of time.

- One reason for unemployment is the time it takes for workers to search for jobs that best suit their tastes and skills. Unemployment insurance is a government policy that, while protecting workers' incomes, increases the amount of frictional unemployment.

- A second reason why an economy may always have some unemployment is if there is a minimum wage that exceeds the wage that would balance supply and demand for the workers who are eligible for the minimum wage. By raising the wage of unskilled and inexperienced workers above the equilibrium level, minimum wage laws raise the quantity of labour supplied and reduce the quantity demanded. The resulting surplus of labour represents unemployment.

- A third reason for unemployment is the market power of unions. When unions push the wages in unionized industries above the equilibrium level, they create a surplus of labour.

- A fourth reason for unemployment is suggested by the theory of efficiency wages. According to this theory, firms find it profitable to pay wages above the equilibrium level. High wages can improve worker health, lower worker turnover, increase worker effort and raise worker quality.

KEY CONCEPTS

frictional unemployment, p. 453
structural unemployment, p. 453

job search, p. 453
unemployment insurance, p. 455

collective bargaining, p. 459

QUESTIONS FOR REVIEW

1. What is the difference between the labour force and the population of working age?

2. Explain how the number of people employed and the number of people unemployed can both rise at the same time.

3. Why is there an apparent contradiction between short spells of unemployment and unemployment being long term?

4. Why is frictional unemployment inevitable? How might the government reduce the amount of frictional unemployment?

5. Explain how minimum wage laws can lead to an increase in unemployment.

6. Are minimum wage laws a better explanation for structural unemployment among teenagers or among university graduates? Why?

7. How do unions affect the natural rate of unemployment?

8. How does the existence of unions add to a firm's costs?

9. What claims do advocates of unions make to argue that unions are good for the economy?

10. Explain four ways in which a firm might increase its profits by raising the wages it pays.

PROBLEMS AND APPLICATIONS

1. If the unemployment rate is rising in a country, does this mean that firms will find it easier to be able to hire new workers? What might your answer depend on?

2. Should firms be forced to contribute to the costs of improving job search? Explain your answer.

3. Assume that there is an increase in the labour participation rate in a country with a growing number of females entering the workforce. What would you expect to happen to the average wage rate and how firms would respond to such a trend?

4. Are the following workers more likely to experience short-term or long-term unemployment? Explain.
   a. A construction worker laid off because of bad weather.
   b. A manufacturing worker who loses her job at a plant in an isolated area.
   c. A bus industry worker laid off because of competition from the railway.
   d. A short-order cook who loses his job when a new restaurant opens across the street.
   e. An expert welder with little formal education who loses her job when the company installs automatic welding machinery.

5. Using a diagram of the labour market, show the effect of an increase in the minimum wage on the wage paid to workers, the number of workers supplied, the number of workers demanded and the amount of unemployment.

6. Consider the minimum wage law.
   a. Suppose the minimum wage is above the equilibrium wage in the market for unskilled labour. Using a supply-and-demand diagram of the market for unskilled labour, show the market wage, the number of workers who are employed and the number of workers who are unemployed. Also show the total wage payments to unskilled workers.
   b. Now suppose the minister for employment proposes an increase in the minimum wage. What effect would this increase have on employment? Does the change in employment depend on the elasticity of demand, the elasticity of supply, both elasticities, or neither?
   c. What effect would this increase in the minimum wage have on unemployment? Does the change in unemployment depend on the elasticity of demand, the elasticity of supply, both elasticities, or neither?
   d. If the demand for unskilled labour were inelastic, would the proposed increase in the minimum wage raise or lower total wage payments to unskilled workers?

Would your answer change if the demand for unskilled labour were elastic?

7. Do you think that firms in small towns or in cities have more market power in hiring? Do you think that firms generally have more market power in hiring today than 50 years ago, or less? How do you think this change over time has affected the role of unions in the economy? Explain.

8. Consider an economy with two labour markets, neither of which is unionized. Now suppose a union is established in one market.
   a. Show the effect of the union on the market in which it is formed. In what sense is the quantity of labour employed in this market an inefficient quantity?
   b. Show the effect of the union on the non-unionized market. What happens to the equilibrium wage in this market?

9. Some workers in the economy are paid a flat salary and some are paid by commission. Which compensation scheme would require more monitoring by supervisors? In which case do firms have an incentive to pay more than the equilibrium level (as in the worker effort variant of efficiency wage theory)? What factors do you think determine the type of compensation firms choose?

10. Suppose that the government passes a law requiring employers to provide employees some benefit (such as a guaranteed pension) that raises the cost of an employee by €4 per hour.
   a. What effect does this new law have on the demand for labour? (In answering this and the following questions, be quantitative when you can.)
   b. If employees place a value on this benefit exactly equal to its cost, what effect does the new law have on the supply of labour?
   c. If the wage is free to balance supply and demand, how does this law affect the wage and the level of employment? Are employers better or worse off? Are employees better or worse off?
   d. If a minimum wage law prevents the wage from balancing supply and demand, how does the new law affect the wage, the level of employment and the level of unemployment? Are employers better or worse off? Are employees better or worse off?
   e. Now suppose that workers do not value the benefit arising from the new law at all. How does this alternative assumption change your answers to parts (b), (c) and (d) above?

19 MACROECONOMICS – INFLATION AND PRICE STABILITY

LEARNING OBJECTIVES

In this chapter you will:

- Consider the various costs that inflation imposes on society

- Learn why policy makers face a short-run trade-off between inflation and unemployment

- Consider why the inflation-unemployment trade-off disappears in the long run

- See how supply shocks can shift the inflation-unemployment trade-off

- Consider the short-run cost of reducing the rate of inflation

- See how policy makers' credibility affects the cost of reducing inflation

After reading this chapter you should be able to:

- Explain why money has no impact on real variables in the long run

- Explain the concept of an inflation tax

- Explain who gains and who loses on a loan contract when inflation rises unexpectedly

- Draw a graph of a short-run Phillips curve

- Draw a graph of a long-run Phillips curve

- Show the relationship between a shift in the short-run aggregate supply curve and a shift in the short-run Phillips curve

- Explain the sacrifice ratio

- Explain why more than rational expectations are needed to reduce inflation costlessly

MONEY GROWTH AND INFLATION

In advanced economies, most prices tend to rise over time. This increase in the overall level of prices is called *inflation*. Although inflation has been the norm in more recent history, there has been substantial variation in the rate at which prices rise. Inflation in the UK during the late 1990s and the first half of the 2000s was low and stable at round 2 per cent or so. However, in the mid-1970s, annual UK inflation, as measured by increases in the retail prices index, exceeded 20 per cent.

International data show an even broader range of inflation experiences. In recent times there have been episodes of hyperinflation in the former Yugoslavia and in Zimbabwe. Inflation in Yugoslavia ran at 5 quadrillion per cent (5 with 15 zeros after it) between October 1993 and January 1995. In January 2009, the Zimbabwean authorities announced that inflation had reached 231 million per cent in June 2008. What that means is that a product (say a loaf of bread) priced at Z$1 in June 2007 would have a price tag of Z$2.31 million in June 2008. The Zimbabwean central bank reported that some goods on the black market had risen by 70 million per cent. Laundry soap was one of the goods that had risen by this much, but cooking oil also rose by 60 million per cent and sugar by 36 million per cent. Inflation made almost every Zimbabwean a billionaire. Unskilled workers earned around Z$200 billion a month – at the time, equivalent to about US$10. In July 2008 the government issued a Z$100 billion note. If you had one it would just about have got you a loaf of bread.

This theory of inflation can explain both moderate inflations, such as those experienced in many countries in Europe, the Middle East and parts of Africa, and hyperinflations, such as those outlined above.

THE CLASSICAL THEORY OF INFLATION

We begin our study of inflation by developing the quantity theory of money. This theory is often called 'classical' because it was developed by some of the earliest thinkers about economic issues back in the 18th century such as David Hume, who are often referred to as the 'classical economists'. Most economists today rely on this theory to explain the long-run determinants of the price level and the inflation rate.

The Level of Prices and the Value of Money

Our first insight about inflation is that it is more about the value of money (the goods and services any given amount of money can be exchanged for) than about the value of goods. Inflation is an economy-wide phenomenon that concerns, first and foremost, the value of the economy's medium of exchange and so affects businesses and their customers.

The economy's overall price level can be viewed in two ways. We can view the price level as the price of a basket of goods and services as we saw when looking at how to measure inflation in Chapter 16. When the price level rises, businesses and people have to pay more for the goods and services they buy. Alternatively, we can view the price level as a measure of the value of money. A rise in the price level means a lower value of money because each unit of money now buys a smaller quantity of goods and services.

It may help to express these ideas mathematically. Suppose P is the price level as measured, for instance, by the consumer prices index or the GDP deflator. Then P measures the number of euros needed to buy a basket of goods and services. Now turn this idea around: the quantity of goods and services that can be bought with €1 equals $1/P$. In other words, if P is the price of goods and services measured in terms of money, $1/P$ is the value of money measured in terms of goods and services. Thus, when the overall price level rises, the value of money falls.

Pitfall Prevention Remember to link the increase in the price level to that for incomes/wages so that the distinction can be made between real incomes and nominal incomes.

Money Supply, Money Demand and Monetary Equilibrium

Supply and demand determines the value of money. First consider money supply. The central bank, together with the banking system, determines the supply of money. In this chapter, we take the quantity of money supplied as a policy variable that the central bank controls. The demand for money reflects how much wealth people want to hold in liquid form. Many factors influence the quantity of money demanded. The amount of currency that businesses and people hold at any one time, depends in part on their view of the future, how much they rely on credit to make purchases and the ease with which cash can be accessed. For consumers this might depend on whether an automatic cash dispenser is easy to find. The quantity of money demanded depends on the interest rate that businesses and consumers could earn by using the money to buy an interest-bearing security rather than leaving it in a wallet or low-interest bank account.

Although many variables affect the demand for money, one variable stands out in importance: the average level of prices in the economy. Businesses and people hold money because it is the medium of exchange. Unlike other assets, such as bonds or stocks, money can be used to buy the raw materials, equipment and goods and services to operate and to live. How much money they choose to hold for this purpose depends on the prices of those goods and services. The higher prices are, the more money the typical transaction requires, and the more money businesses and people will choose to hold in their wallets and bank accounts. That is, a higher price level (a lower value of money) increases the quantity of money demanded.

What ensures that the quantity of money the central bank supplies balances the quantity of money people demand? The answer, it turns out, depends on the time horizon being considered. *In the long run, the overall level of prices adjusts to the level at which the demand for money equals the supply.* Figure 19.1 illustrates this idea. The horizontal axis of this graph shows the quantity of money. The left-hand vertical axis shows the value of money $1/P$, and the right-hand vertical axis shows the price level P. Notice that the price level axis on the right is inverted: a low price level is shown near the top of this axis, and a high price level is shown near the bottom. This inverted axis illustrates that when the value of money is high (as shown near the top of the left axis), the price level is low (as shown near the top of the right axis).

The two curves in this figure are the supply and demand curves for money. The supply curve is vertical because the central bank has fixed the quantity of money available. The demand curve for money is downward sloping, indicating that when the value of money is low (and the price level is high), people demand a larger quantity of it to buy goods and services. At the equilibrium, shown in the figure as point A, the quantity of money demanded balances the quantity of money supplied. This equilibrium of money supply and money demand determines the value of money and the price level.

To summarize, if the price level is above the equilibrium level, businesses and people will want to hold more money than the central bank has created, so the price level must fall to balance supply and demand. If the price level is below the equilibrium level, people will want to hold less money than the central bank has created, and the price level must rise to balance supply and demand. At the equilibrium price level, the quantity of money that people want to hold exactly balances the quantity of money supplied by the central bank.

FIGURE 19.1

How the Supply and Demand for Money Determine the Equilibrium Price Level

The horizontal axis shows the quantity of money. The left vertical axis shows the value of money, and the right vertical axis shows the price level. The supply curve for money is vertical because the quantity of money supplied is fixed by the central bank. The demand curve for money is downward sloping because people want to hold a larger quantity of money when each euro buys less. At the equilibrium, point A, the value of money (on the left axis) and the price level (on the right axis) have adjusted to bring the quantity of money supplied and the quantity of money demanded into balance.

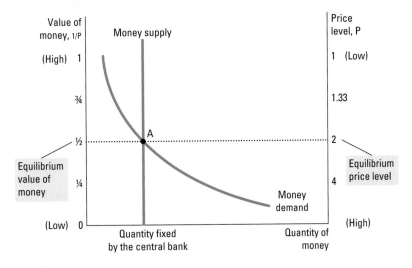

? what if…the assumption that the central bank can control the money supply was dropped and instead the supply of money was positively related to the interest rate. What effect would a rise in the demand for money have on interest rates in comparison to that when the supply of money is assumed to be fixed?

The Effects of a Monetary Injection

Let's now consider the effects of a change in monetary policy. Assume that the economy is in equilibrium and then, suddenly, the central bank doubles the supply of money by printing large amounts of money. This may be done through the central bank injecting money into the economy by buying some government bonds from the public in open-market operations (this is what quantitative easing has done in recent years in the UK and the USA). What happens after such a monetary injection? How does the new equilibrium compare to the old one?

Figure 19.2 shows what happens. The monetary injection shifts the supply curve to the right from MS_1 to MS_2, and the equilibrium moves from point A to point B. As a result, the value of money (shown on the left axis) decreases from ½ to ¼, and the equilibrium price level (shown on the right axis) increases from 2 to 4. In other words, when an increase in the money supply makes euros more plentiful, the result is an increase in the price level that makes each euro less valuable.

This explanation of how the price level is determined and why it might change over time is called the **quantity theory of money**. According to the quantity theory, the quantity of money available in the economy determines the value of money, and growth in the quantity of money is the primary cause of inflation.

quantity theory of money a theory asserting that the quantity of money available determines the price level and that the growth rate in the quantity of money available determines the inflation rate

FIGURE 19.2

An Increase in the Money Supply

When the central bank increases the supply of money, the money supply curve shifts from MS₁ to MS₂. The value of money (on the left axis) and the price level (on the right axis) adjust to bring supply and demand back into balance. The equilibrium moves from point A to point B. Thus, when an increase in the money supply makes euros more plentiful, the price level increases, making each euro less valuable.

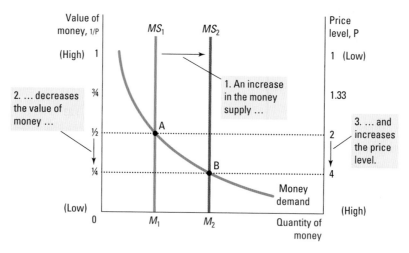

A Brief Look at the Adjustment Process

The immediate effect of a monetary injection is to create an excess supply of money. Before the injection, the economy was in equilibrium (point A in Figure 19.2). At the prevailing price level, people had exactly as much money as they wanted. But after the increase in the money supply, businesses and people have more euros in their wallets than they need to buy goods and services. At the prevailing price level, the quantity of money supplied now exceeds the quantity demanded.

This excess supply of money is used in various ways. It might be used to buy more raw materials or goods and services. Or it might be used to make loans to others by buying bonds or by depositing the money in a bank savings account. These loans allow other businesses and people to buy goods and services. In either case, the injection of money increases the demand for goods and services.

The economy's ability to supply goods and services, however, has not changed. As we saw in Chapter 17, the economy's output of goods and services is determined by the available labour, physical capital, human capital, natural resources and technological knowledge. None of these is altered by the injection of money.

Thus, the greater demand for goods and services causes the prices of goods and services to increase. The increase in the price level, in turn, increases the quantity of money demanded because people are using more euros for every transaction. Eventually, the economy reaches a new equilibrium (point B in Figure 19.2) at which the quantity of money demanded again equals the quantity of money supplied. In this way, the overall price level for goods and services adjusts to bring money supply and money demand into balance.

THE COSTS OF INFLATION

Inflation is closely watched and widely discussed because it is thought to be a serious economic problem. Many business leaders rank inflation as a serious problem that must be kept under control although many would agree that some inflation is desirable. In this next section we will look at some of the costs of inflation to businesses and people in general.

A Fall in Purchasing Power? The Inflation Fallacy

If you ask the typical person or business why inflation is bad, they will tell you that the answer is obvious: inflation robs them of the purchasing power of hard-earned money. When prices rise, each euro of income buys fewer goods and services. Thus, it might seem that inflation directly lowers living standards and affects the ability of businesses to buy.

Yet further thought reveals a fallacy in this answer. When prices rise, buyers of goods and services pay more for what they buy. At the same time, however, businesses get more for what they sell. Because most people earn their incomes by selling their services, such as their labour, inflation in incomes goes hand in hand with inflation in prices. *Thus, inflation does not in itself reduce people's real purchasing power.*

The inflation fallacy is an issue because of the principle of monetary neutrality. A worker who receives an annual rise of 10 per cent in her salary, for example, tends to view that rise as a reward for her own talent and effort. When an inflation rate of 6 per cent reduces the real value of that pay rise to only 4 per cent, the worker might feel that she has been cheated of what is rightfully her due. In fact, real incomes are determined by real variables, such as physical capital, human capital, natural resources, and the available production technology. Nominal incomes are determined by those factors and the overall price level. If the central bank were to succeed in lowering the inflation rate from 6 per cent to zero, our worker's annual rise might only be 4 per cent rather than 10 per cent. She might feel less robbed by inflation, but her real income would not rise more quickly.

If nominal incomes tend to keep pace with rising prices, why then is inflation a problem? It turns out that there is no single answer to this question. Instead, economists have identified several costs of inflation. Each of these costs shows some way in which persistent growth in the money supply does, in fact, have some effect on real variables.

Shoe Leather Costs

As we have discussed, inflation is like a tax on the holders of money. The tax itself is not a cost to society: it is only a transfer of resources from households to the government. Yet most taxes give people an incentive to alter their behaviour to avoid paying the tax, and this distortion of incentives causes deadweight losses for society as a whole. Like other taxes, the **inflation tax** also causes deadweight losses because businesses and people waste scarce resources trying to avoid it.

inflation tax the revenue the government raises by creating money

How can a business or person avoid paying the inflation tax? Because inflation erodes the real value of the money held, you can avoid the inflation tax by holding less money. One way to do this is to manage cash flow more carefully. For example, if a business can keep more cash in interest-bearing accounts the effect of inflation is reduced. Active management of cash flow in all businesses, but especially in large businesses where the amounts of cash reserves being held can be significant, is a vital part of overall financial management of the business.

The cost of reducing money holdings is called the **shoe leather cost** of inflation because such active cash management involves the time and convenience that must be sacrificed to keep less money on hand than you would if there were no inflation – it is in effect a *transaction cost*.

shoe leather costs the resources wasted when inflation encourages people to reduce their money holdings

Menu Costs

Most firms do not change the prices of their products every day. Instead, firms often announce prices and leave them unchanged for weeks, months or even years. Firms change prices infrequently because there are costs involved in changing prices. Costs of price adjustment are called **menu costs**, a term derived from a restaurant's cost of printing a new menu. Menu costs include the cost of deciding on new prices, the cost of printing

menu costs the costs of changing prices

new price lists and catalogues, the cost of sending these new price lists and catalogues to dealers and customers, amending prices on websites, the cost of advertising the new prices, and even the cost of dealing with customer annoyance over price changes.

Inflation increases the menu costs that firms must bear. In an economy with low inflation of just a few percentage points a year, annual price adjustment is an appropriate business strategy for many firms. But when high inflation makes firms' costs rise rapidly, annual price adjustment is impractical. If inflation is rising strongly then firms may have to adjust prices more regularly and this can not only be expensive but disruptive.

Relative Price Variability and the Misallocation of Resources

Suppose that the Eatabit Eatery prints a new menu with new prices every January and then leaves its prices unchanged for the rest of the year. If there is no inflation, Eatabit's relative prices – the prices of its meals compared with other prices in the economy – would be constant over the course of the year. By contrast, if the inflation rate is 12 per cent per year, Eatabit's relative prices will automatically fall by 1 per cent each month. The restaurant's relative prices (that is, its prices compared with others in the economy) will be high in the early months of the year, just after it has printed a new menu, and low in the later months. And the higher the inflation rate, the greater is this automatic variability. Thus, because prices change only once in a while, inflation causes relative prices to vary more than they otherwise would.

Why does this matter? The reason is that market economies rely on relative prices to allocate scarce resources. Consumers decide what to buy by comparing the quality and prices of various goods and services. Through these decisions, they determine how the scarce factors of production are allocated among industries and firms. When inflation distorts relative prices, consumer decisions are distorted, and markets are less able to allocate resources to their best use.

Inflation-Induced Tax Distortions

Almost all taxes distort incentives, cause businesses and people to alter their behaviour, and lead to a less efficient allocation of the economy's resources. Many taxes, however, become even more problematic in the presence of inflation. The reason is that politicians often fail to take inflation into account when writing the tax laws. Economists who have studied the tax system conclude that inflation tends to raise the tax burden on income earned from savings.

The taxes on nominal capital gains and on nominal interest income are two examples of how the tax system interacts with inflation. There are many others. Because of these inflation-induced tax changes, higher inflation tends to discourage people from saving. If a business has cash reserves that are attracting interest of 5 per cent, for example, and the inflation rate is 7 per cent, the cash reserves are effectively diminishing in value at a rate of 2 per cent. This provides a disincentive for holding cash reserves. Recall that the economy's saving provides the resources for investment, which in turn is a key ingredient to long-run economic growth. Thus, when inflation raises the tax burden on saving, it tends to depress the economy's long-run growth rate. There is, however, no consensus among economists about the size of this effect.

Confusion and Inconvenience

Imagine that we took a poll and asked people the following question: 'This year the metre is 100 centimetres. How long do you think it should be next year?' Assuming we could get people to take us seriously, they would tell us that the metre should stay the same length – 100 centimetres. Anything else would just complicate life needlessly.

What does this finding have to do with inflation? Money, as the economy's unit of account, is what we use to quote prices and record debts. In other words, money is the yardstick with which we measure economic transactions. The job of the central bank is to ensure the reliability of a commonly used unit of measurement. When the central bank increases the money supply and creates inflation, it erodes the real value of the unit of account.

It is difficult to judge the costs of the confusion and inconvenience that arise from inflation. Accountants can incorrectly measure firms' earnings when prices are rising over time. Because inflation causes money at different times to have different real values, computing a firm's profit – the difference between its revenue and costs – is more complicated in an economy with inflation. Therefore, to some extent, inflation makes investors less able to sort out successful from unsuccessful firms, which in turn impedes financial markets in their role of allocating the economy's saving to alternative types of investment.

A Special Cost of Unexpected Inflation: Arbitrary Redistributions of Wealth

So far, the costs of inflation we have discussed occur even if inflation is steady and predictable. Inflation has an additional cost, however, when it comes as a surprise. Unexpected inflation redistributes wealth among the population in a way that has nothing to do with either merit or need. These redistributions occur because many loans in the economy are specified in terms of the unit of account – money.

Consider an example. Suppose that a small business takes out a €20 000 loan from a bank at a 7 per cent interest rate to expand the business. In ten years the loan will have to be repaid. After the debt has compounded for ten years at 7 per cent, the business will owe the bank €39 343. The real value of this debt will depend on inflation over the decade. If the business is lucky, the economy will have hyperinflation. In this case, wages and prices will rise so high that it will be able to pay the €39 343 debt out of pocket change. In contrast, if the economy goes through a major deflation, then wages and prices will fall, and the business will find the €39 343 debt a greater burden than anticipated.

This example shows that unexpected changes in prices redistribute wealth among debtors and creditors. A hyperinflation enriches the business at the expense of the bank because it diminishes the real value of the debt; the business can repay the loan in less valuable euros than anticipated. Deflation enriches the bank at the business' expense because it increases the real value of the debt; in this case, the business has to repay the loan in more valuable euros than anticipated. If inflation were predictable, then the bank and the business could take inflation into account when setting the nominal interest rate. But if inflation is hard to predict, it imposes risk on the business and the bank that both would prefer to avoid.

This cost of unexpected inflation is important to consider together with another fact: inflation is especially volatile and uncertain when the average rate of inflation is high. This is seen most simply by examining the experience of different countries. Countries with low average inflation, such as Germany in the late 20th century, tend to have stable inflation. Countries with high average inflation, such as many countries in Latin America, tend also to have unstable inflation. There are no known examples of economies with high, stable inflation. This relationship between the level and volatility of inflation points to another cost of inflation. If a country pursues a high-inflation monetary policy, it will have to bear not only the costs of high expected inflation but also the arbitrary redistributions of wealth associated with unexpected inflation.

JEOPARDY PROBLEM

In ten successive years, the rate of inflation in a country increases, rising from 3 per cent in year one to 35 per cent in year 10. However, at the same time, incomes rise in line with inflation. A poll of workers suggests that few have a problem with the rate of inflation in the country. Explain why this might be and whether, as a result, the government should not worry about the rising inflation rate.

INFLATION AND UNEMPLOYMENT

Having looked at unemployment in Chapter 18 and inflation in this chapter we now look at the extent to which these two key variables are related. The natural rate of unemployment depends on various features of the labour market, such as minimum wage laws, the market power of unions, the role of efficiency wages and the effectiveness of job search. The inflation rate depends primarily on growth in the money supply, which a nation's central bank controls. In the long run, therefore, inflation and unemployment are largely unrelated problems.

In the short run, just the opposite is true. One of the *Ten Principles of Economics* discussed in Chapter 1 is that society faces a short-run trade-off between inflation and unemployment. If monetary and fiscal policy makers expand aggregate demand and move the economy up along the short-run aggregate supply curve, they can lower unemployment for a while, but only at the cost of higher inflation. If policy makers contract aggregate demand and move the economy down the short-run aggregate supply curve, they can lower inflation, but only at the cost of temporarily higher unemployment. The best way to understand this relationship is to see how thinking about it has evolved over time.

THE PHILLIPS CURVE

'Probably the single most important macroeconomic relationship is the Phillips curve.' These are the words of economist George Akerlof from the lecture he gave when he received the Nobel Prize for Economics in 2001. The Phillips curve is the short-run relationship between inflation and unemployment.

Origins of the Phillips Curve

In 1958, a New Zealand economist working at the London School of Economics, A.W. Phillips, published an article in the British journal *Economica* that would make him famous. The article was entitled 'The Relationship Between Unemployment and the Rate of Change of Money Wages in the United Kingdom, 1861–1957'. In it, Phillips showed a negative correlation between the rate of unemployment and the rate of inflation. That is, Phillips showed that years with low unemployment tend to have high inflation, and years with high unemployment tend to have low inflation. (Phillips examined inflation in nominal wages rather than inflation in prices, but for our purposes that distinction is not important. These two measures of inflation usually move together.) Phillips concluded that two important macroeconomic variables – inflation and unemployment – were linked in a way that economists had not previously appreciated.

Although Phillips's discovery was based on data for the United Kingdom, researchers quickly extended his finding to other countries. Two years after Phillips published his article, economists Paul Samuelson and Robert Solow published an article in the

American Economic Review called 'Analytics of Anti-inflation Policy' in which they showed a similar negative correlation between inflation and unemployment in data for the United States. They reasoned that this correlation arose because low unemployment was associated with high aggregate demand, which in turn puts upward pressure on wages and prices throughout the economy. Samuelson and Solow dubbed the negative association between inflation and unemployment the Phillips curve. Figure 19.3 shows an example of a Phillips curve like the one found by Samuelson and Solow.

FIGURE 19.3

The Phillips Curve

The Phillips curve illustrates a negative association between the inflation rate and the unemployment rate. At point A, inflation is low and unemployment is high. At point B, inflation is high and unemployment is low.

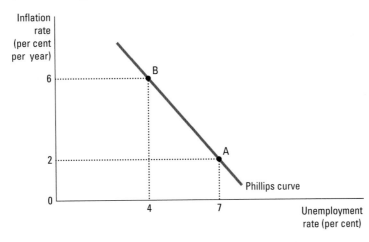

As the title of their paper suggests, Samuelson and Solow were interested in the Phillips curve because they believed that it held important lessons for policy makers. In particular, they suggested that the Phillips curve offers policy makers a menu of possible economic outcomes. By altering monetary and fiscal policy to influence aggregate demand, policy makers could choose any point on this curve. Point A offers high unemployment and low inflation. Point B offers low unemployment and high inflation. Policy makers might prefer both low inflation and low unemployment, but the historical data as summarized by the Phillips curve indicate that this combination is impossible. According to Samuelson and Solow, policy makers face a trade-off between inflation and unemployment, and the Phillips curve illustrates that trade-off.

Aggregate Demand, Aggregate Supply and the Phillips Curve

The model of aggregate demand and aggregate supply provides an easy explanation for the menu of possible outcomes described by the Phillips curve. The Phillips curve simply shows the combinations of inflation and unemployment that arise in the short run as shifts in the aggregate demand curve move the economy along the short-run aggregate supply curve. As we saw in Chapter 17, an increase in the aggregate demand for goods and services leads, in the short run, to a larger output of goods and services and a higher price level. Larger output means greater employment and, thus, a lower rate of unemployment. In addition, whatever the previous year's price level happens to be, the higher the price level in the current year, the higher the rate of inflation. Thus, shifts in aggregate demand push inflation and unemployment in opposite directions in the short run – a relationship illustrated by the Phillips curve.

FIGURE 19.4

How the Phillips Curve Is Related to the Model of Aggregate Demand and Aggregate Supply

This figure assumes a price level of 100 for the year 2013 and charts possible outcomes for the year 2014. Panel (a) shows the model of aggregate demand and aggregate supply. If aggregate demand is low, the economy is at point A; output is low (7500), and the price level is low (102). If aggregate demand is high, the economy is at point B; output is high (8000), and the price level is high (106). Panel (b) shows the implications for the Phillips curve. Point A, which arises when aggregate demand is low, has high unemployment (7 per cent) and low inflation (2 per cent). Point B, which arises when aggregate demand is high, has low unemployment (4 per cent) and high inflation (6 per cent).

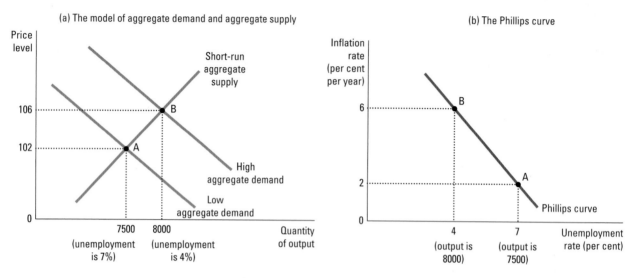

To see more fully how this works, let's consider an example. To keep the numbers simple, imagine that the price level (as measured, for instance, by the consumer price index) equals 100 in the year 2013. Figure 19.4 shows two possible outcomes that might occur in year 2014. Panel (a) shows the two outcomes using the model of aggregate demand and aggregate supply. Panel (b) illustrates the same two outcomes using the Phillips curve.

In panel (a) of the figure, we can see the implications for output and the price level in the year 2014. If the aggregate demand for goods and services is relatively low, the economy experiences outcome A. The economy produces output of 7500, and the price level is 102. By contrast, if aggregate demand is relatively high, the economy experiences outcome B. Output is 8000, and the price level is 106. Thus, higher aggregate demand moves the economy to an equilibrium with higher output and a higher price level.

In panel (b) of the figure, we can see what these two possible outcomes mean for unemployment and inflation. Because firms need more workers when they produce a greater output of goods and services, unemployment is lower in outcome B than in outcome A. In this example, when output rises from 7500 to 8000, unemployment falls from 7 per cent to 4 per cent. Moreover, because the price level is higher at outcome B than at outcome A, the inflation rate (the percentage change in the price level from the previous year) is also higher. In particular, since the price level was 100 in year 2013, outcome A has an inflation rate of 2 per cent, and outcome B has an inflation rate of 6 per cent. Thus, we can compare the two possible outcomes for the economy either in terms of output and the price level (using the model of aggregate demand and aggregate supply), or in terms of unemployment and inflation (using the Phillips curve).

We will see in Chapter 20 how monetary and fiscal policy can shift the aggregate demand curve. Monetary and fiscal policy can move the economy along the Phillips curve. Increases in the money supply, increases in government spending, or cuts in taxes expand aggregate demand and move the economy to a point on the Phillips curve with lower unemployment and higher inflation. Decreases in the money supply, cuts in government spending, or increases in taxes contract aggregate demand and move the economy to a point on the Phillips curve with lower inflation and higher unemployment. In this sense, the Phillips curve offers policy makers a menu of combinations of inflation and unemployment.

> **Quick Quiz** Draw the Phillips curve. Use the model of aggregate demand and aggregate supply to show how policy can move the economy from a point on this curve with high inflation to a point with low inflation.

THE ROLE OF EXPECTATIONS

The Phillips curve seems to offer policy makers a menu of possible inflation–unemployment outcomes. But does this menu remain stable over time? Is the Phillips curve a relationship on which policy makers can rely? Economists took up these questions in the late 1960s, shortly after Samuelson and Solow had introduced the Phillips curve into the macroeconomic policy debate.

The Long-Run Phillips Curve

In 1968 economist Milton Friedman published a paper in the *American Economic Review*, based on an address he had recently given as president of the American Economic Association. The paper, entitled 'The Role of Monetary Policy', contained sections on 'What Monetary Policy Can Do' and 'What Monetary Policy Cannot Do'. Friedman argued that one thing monetary policy cannot do, other than for only a short time, is pick a combination of inflation and unemployment on the Phillips curve. At about the same time, another economist, Edmund Phelps, also published a paper denying the existence of a long-run trade-off between inflation and unemployment.

Friedman and Phelps based their conclusions on classical principles of macroeconomics. Classical theory points to growth in the money supply as the primary determinant of inflation. But classical theory also states that monetary growth does not have real effects – it merely alters all prices and nominal incomes proportionately. In particular, monetary growth does not influence those factors that determine the economy's unemployment rate, such as the market power of unions, the role of efficiency wages, or the process of job search. Friedman and Phelps concluded that there is no reason to think the rate of inflation would, *in the long run*, be related to the rate of unemployment.

Here, in his own words, is Friedman's view about what the central bank can hope to accomplish in the long run:

> *The monetary authority controls nominal quantities – directly, the quantity of its own liabilities [currency plus bank reserves]. In principle, it can use this control to peg a nominal quantity – an exchange rate, the price level, the nominal level of national income, the quantity of money by one definition or another – or to peg the change in a nominal quantity – the rate of inflation or deflation, the rate of growth or decline in nominal national income, the rate of growth of the quantity of money. It cannot use its control over nominal quantities to peg a real quantity – the real rate of interest, the rate of unemployment, the level of real national income, the real quantity of money, the rate of growth of real national income, or the rate of growth of the real quantity of money.*

These views have important implications for the Phillips curve. In particular, they imply that monetary policy makers face a long-run Phillips curve that is vertical, as in Figure 19.5. If the central bank increases the money supply slowly, the inflation rate is low, and the economy finds itself at point A. If the central bank increases the money supply quickly, the inflation rate is high, and the economy finds itself at point B. In either case, the unemployment rate tends towards its normal level, called the *natural rate of unemployment*. The vertical long-run Phillips curve illustrates the conclusion that unemployment does not depend on money growth and inflation in the long run.

FIGURE 19.5

The Long-Run Phillips Curve

According to Friedman and Phelps, there is no trade-off between inflation and unemployment in the long run. Growth in the money supply determines the inflation rate. Regardless of the inflation rate, the unemployment rate gravitates towards its natural rate. As a result, the long-run Phillips curve is vertical.

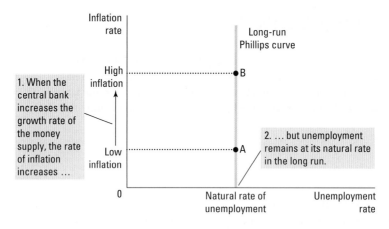

FIGURE 19.6

How the Long-Run Phillips Curve is Related to the Model of Aggregate Demand and Aggregate Supply

Panel (a) shows the model of aggregate demand and aggregate supply with a vertical aggregate supply curve. When expansionary monetary policy shifts the aggregate demand curve to the right from AD_1 to AD_2, the equilibrium moves from point A to point B. The price level rises from P_1 to P_2, while output remains the same. Panel (b) shows the long-run Phillips curve, which is vertical at the natural rate of unemployment. Expansionary monetary policy moves the economy from lower inflation (point A) to higher inflation (point B) without changing the rate of unemployment.

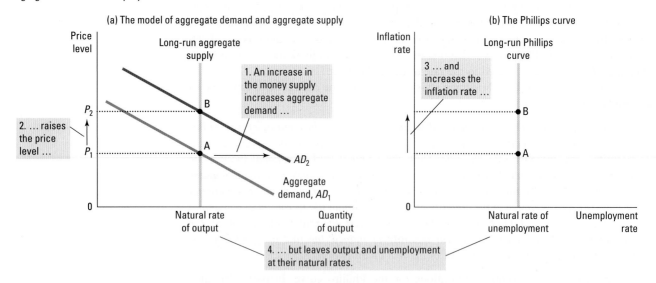

The vertical long-run Phillips curve is, in essence, one expression of the classical idea of monetary neutrality. As you may recall, we expressed this idea in Chapter 17 with a vertical long-run aggregate supply curve. Indeed, as Figure 19.6 illustrates, the vertical long-run

Phillips curve and the vertical long-run aggregate supply curve are two sides of the same coin. In panel (a) of this figure, an increase in the money supply shifts the aggregate demand curve to the right from AD_1 to AD_2. As a result of this shift, the long-run equilibrium moves from point A to point B.

The price level rises from P_1 to P_2, but because the aggregate supply curve is vertical, output remains the same. In panel (b), more rapid growth in the money supply raises the inflation rate by moving the economy from point A to point B. But because the Phillips curve is vertical, the rate of unemployment is the same at these two points. Thus, the vertical long-run aggregate supply curve and the vertical long-run Phillips curve both imply that monetary policy influences nominal variables (the price level and the inflation rate) but not real variables (output and unemployment). Regardless of the monetary policy pursued by the central bank, output and unemployment are, in the long run, at their natural rates.

What is so 'natural' about the natural rate of unemployment? Friedman and Phelps used this adjective to describe the unemployment rate towards which the economy tends to gravitate in the long run. Yet the natural rate of unemployment is not necessarily the socially desirable rate of unemployment. Nor is the natural rate of unemployment constant over time. For example, suppose that a newly formed union uses its market power to raise the real wages of some workers above the equilibrium level. The result is an excess supply of workers and, therefore, a higher natural rate of unemployment. This unemployment is 'natural' not because it is good but because it is beyond the influence of monetary policy. More rapid money growth would not reduce the market power of the union or the level of unemployment; it would lead only to more inflation.

Although monetary policy cannot influence the natural rate of unemployment, other types of policy can. To reduce the natural rate of unemployment, policy makers should look to policies that improve the functioning of the labour market. Earlier in the book we discussed how various labour market policies, such as minimum wage laws, collective bargaining laws, unemployment insurance, and job-training schemes, affect the natural rate of unemployment. A policy change that reduced the natural rate of unemployment would shift the long-run Phillips curve to the left. In addition, because lower unemployment means more workers are producing goods and services, the quantity of goods and services supplied would be larger at any given price level, and the long-run aggregate supply curve would shift to the right. The economy could then enjoy lower unemployment and higher output for any given rate of money growth and inflation.

Reconciling Theory and Evidence

At first, the conclusion of Friedman and Phelps of a long-run trade-off between inflation and unemployment might not seem persuasive. Their argument was based on an appeal to *theory*. In contrast, the negative correlation between inflation and unemployment documented by Phillips, Samuelson and Solow was based on *data*. Why should anyone believe that policy makers faced a vertical Phillips curve when the world seemed to offer a downward sloping one? Shouldn't the findings of Phillips, Samuelson and Solow lead us to reject the classical conclusion of monetary neutrality?

Friedman and Phelps were well aware of these questions, and they offered a way to reconcile classical macroeconomic theory with the finding of a downward sloping Phillips curve in data from the United Kingdom and the United States. They claimed that a negative relationship between inflation and unemployment holds in the short run but that it cannot be used by policy makers in the long run. In other words, policy makers can pursue expansionary monetary policy to achieve lower unemployment for a while, but eventually unemployment returns to its natural rate, and more expansionary monetary policy leads only to higher inflation.

Friedman and Phelps reasoned as we did in Chapter 17 when we explained the difference between the short-run and long-run aggregate supply curves. (In fact, the discussion in that chapter drew heavily on the legacy of Friedman and Phelps.) As you may recall, the short-run aggregate supply curve is upward sloping, indicating that an increase in the price level raises the quantity of goods and services that firms supply. In contrast, the long-run aggregate supply curve is vertical, indicating that the price level does not influence quantity supplied in the long run. Chapter 17 presented three theories to explain the upward slope of the short-run aggregate supply curve: sticky wages, sticky prices and misperceptions about relative prices. Because wages, prices and perceptions adjust to changing economic conditions over time, the positive relationship between the price level and quantity supplied applies in the short run but not in the long run. Friedman and Phelps applied this same logic to the Phillips curve. Just as the aggregate supply curve slopes upward only in the short run, the trade-off between inflation and unemployment holds only in the short run. And just as the long-run aggregate supply curve is vertical, the long-run Phillips curve is also vertical.

To help explain the short-run and long-run relationship between inflation and unemployment, Friedman and Phelps introduced a new variable into the analysis: *expected inflation*. Expected inflation measures how much people expect the overall price level to change. The expected price level affects the wages and prices that people set and the perceptions of relative prices that they form. As a result, expected inflation is one factor that determines the position of the short-run aggregate supply curve. In the short run, the central bank can take expected inflation (and thus the short-run aggregate supply curve) as already determined. When the money supply changes, the aggregate demand curve shifts, and the economy moves along a given short-run aggregate supply curve. In the short run, therefore, monetary changes lead to unexpected fluctuations in output, prices, unemployment and inflation. In this way, Friedman and Phelps explained the Phillips curve that Phillips, Samuelson and Solow had documented.

Yet the central bank's ability to create unexpected inflation by increasing the money supply exists only in the short run. In the long run, people come to expect whatever inflation rate the central bank chooses to produce. Because wages, prices and perceptions will eventually adjust to the inflation rate, the long-run aggregate supply curve is vertical. In this case, changes in aggregate demand, such as those due to changes in the money supply, do not affect the economy's output of goods and services. Thus, Friedman and Phelps concluded that unemployment returns to its natural rate in the long run.

The Short-Run Phillips Curve

The analysis of Friedman and Phelps can be summarized in the following equation (which is, in essence, another expression of the aggregate supply equation we saw in Chapter 17):

$$\begin{pmatrix} \text{Unemployment} \\ \text{rate} \end{pmatrix} = \begin{pmatrix} \text{Natural rate} \\ \text{of unemployment} \end{pmatrix} - a\begin{pmatrix} \text{Actual} \\ \text{inflation} - \frac{\text{Expected}}{\text{inflation}} \end{pmatrix}$$

This equation relates the unemployment rate to the natural rate of unemployment, actual inflation and expected inflation. In the short run, expected inflation is given. As a result, higher actual inflation is associated with lower unemployment. (How much unemployment responds to unexpected inflation is determined by the size of *a*, a number that in turn depends on the slope of the short-run aggregate supply curve.) In the long run, however, people come to expect whatever inflation the central bank produces. Thus, actual inflation equals expected inflation, and unemployment is at its natural rate.

This equation implies there is no stable short-run Phillips curve. Each short run Phillips curve reflects a particular expected rate of inflation. (To be precise, if you graph the equation, you'll find that the short-run Phillips curve intersects the long-run Phillips curve at the expected rate of inflation.) Whenever expected inflation changes, the short-run Phillips curve shifts.

FIGURE 19.7

How Expected Inflation Shifts the Short-Run Phillips Curve

The higher the expected rate of inflation, the higher the short-run trade-off between inflation and unemployment. At point A, expected inflation and actual inflation are both low, and unemployment is at its natural rate. If the central bank pursues an expansionary monetary policy, the economy moves from point A to point B in the short run. At point B, expected inflation is still low, but actual inflation is high. Unemployment is below its natural rate. In the long run, expected inflation rises, and the economy moves to point C. At point C, expected inflation and actual inflation are both high, and unemployment is back to its natural rate.

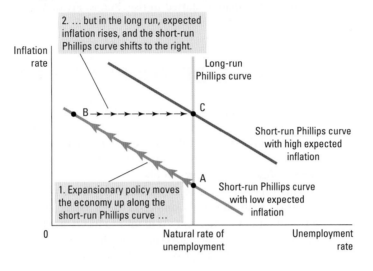

According to Friedman and Phelps, it is dangerous to view the Phillips curve as a menu of options available to policy makers. To see why, imagine an economy at its natural rate of unemployment with low inflation and low expected inflation, shown in Figure 19.7 as point A. Now suppose that policy makers try to take advantage of the trade-off between inflation and unemployment by using monetary or fiscal policy to expand aggregate demand. In the short run when expected inflation is given, the economy goes from point A to point B. Unemployment falls below its natural rate, and inflation rises above expected inflation. Over time, people get used to this higher inflation rate, and they raise their expectations of inflation. When expected inflation rises, firms and workers start taking higher inflation into account when setting wages and prices. The short-run Phillips curve then shifts to the right, as shown in the figure. The economy ends up at point C, with higher inflation than at point A but with the same level of unemployment.

Thus, Friedman and Phelps concluded that policy makers do face a trade-off between inflation and unemployment, but only a temporary one. If policy makers use this trade-off, they lose it.

The Unemployment–Inflation Trade-off

Friedman and Phelps had made a bold prediction in 1968: if policy makers try to take advantage of the Phillips curve by choosing higher inflation in order to reduce unemployment, they will succeed at reducing unemployment only temporarily. This view – that unemployment eventually returns to its natural rate, regardless of the rate of inflation – is called the **natural-rate hypothesis**.

To some economists at the time, it seemed ridiculous to claim that the Phillips curve would break down once policy makers tried to use it. But, in fact, that is exactly what happened in both the UK and the United States. Beginning in the late 1960s, the UK government, for example, followed policies that expanded the aggregate demand for

natural-rate hypothesis the claim that unemployment eventually returns to its normal, or natural, rate, regardless of the rate of inflation

goods and services. On top of this, the UK and many other developed economies in the late 1960s and early 1970s experienced an increase in aggregate demand due to American involvement in the Vietnam War, which increased US government spending (on the military), which boosted US aggregate demand and so boosted net exports from other countries to the USA. In addition, in 1971, as a result of the relaxation of certain controls on bank lending, the UK experienced a major expansion in the money supply. In the following year, the government announced an extraordinarily expansionary fiscal policy, in terms of extra spending and tax reduction, and the economy began seriously to overheat and inflation started to rise. But, as Friedman and Phelps had predicted, unemployment did not stay low.

THE ROLE OF SUPPLY SHOCKS

Friedman and Phelps had suggested in 1968 that changes in expected inflation shift the short-run Phillips curve, and the experience of the early 1970s convinced most economists that Friedman and Phelps were right. Within a few years, however, the economics profession would turn its attention to a different source of shifts in the short-run Phillips curve: shocks to aggregate supply.

This time, the shift in focus came not from two economics professors but from a group of Arab sheikhs. Conflict between Israel and its Arab neighbours triggered a series of oil price shocks as Arab oil producers used their market power to exert political pressure on western governments who supported Israel. In 1974, the Organization of Petroleum Exporting Countries (OPEC) also began to exert its power as a cartel in order to increase its members' profits. The countries of OPEC, such as Saudi Arabia, Kuwait and Iraq, restricted the amount of crude oil they pumped and sold on world markets. This reduction in supply caused the price of oil to almost double over a few years in the 1970s.

supply shock an event that directly alters firms' costs and prices, shifting the economy's aggregate supply curve and thus the Phillips curve

A large increase in the world price of oil is an example of a supply shock. A **supply shock** is an event that directly affects firms' costs of production and thus the prices they charge; it shifts the economy's aggregate supply curve and, as a result, the Phillips curve. Oil is a constituent part of so many production processes that increases in its price have far reaching effects. For example, when an oil price increase raises the cost of producing petrol, heating oil, tyres, plastic products, distribution and many other products, it reduces the quantity of goods and services supplied at any given price level. As panel (a) of Figure 19.8 shows, this reduction in supply is represented by the leftward shift in the aggregate supply curve from AS_1 to AS_2. The price level rises from P_1 to P_2, and output falls from Y_1 to Y_2. The combination of rising prices and falling output is sometimes called *stagflation*.

This shift in aggregate supply is associated with a similar shift in the short-run Phillips curve, shown in panel (b). Because firms need fewer workers to produce the smaller output, employment falls and unemployment rises. Because the price level is higher, the inflation rate – the percentage change in the price level from the previous year – is also higher. Thus, the shift in aggregate supply leads to higher unemployment and higher inflation. The short-run trade-off between inflation and unemployment shifts to the right from PC_1 to PC_2.

Confronted with an adverse shift in aggregate supply, policy makers face a difficult choice between fighting inflation and fighting unemployment. If they contract aggregate demand to fight inflation, they will raise unemployment further. If they expand aggregate demand to fight unemployment, they will raise inflation further. In other words, policy makers face a less favourable trade-off between inflation and unemployment than they did before the shift in aggregate supply: they have to live with a higher rate of inflation for a given rate of unemployment, a higher rate of unemployment for a given rate of inflation, or some combination of higher unemployment and higher inflation.

FIGURE 19.8

An Adverse Shock to Aggregate Supply

Panel (a) shows the model of aggregate demand and aggregate supply. When the aggregate supply curve shifts to the left from AS₁ to AS₂, the equilibrium moves from point A to point B. Output falls from Y₁ to Y₂, and the price level rises from P₁ to P₂. Panel (b) shows the short-run trade-off between inflation and unemployment. The adverse shift in aggregate supply moves the economy from a point with lower unemployment and lower inflation (point A) to a point with higher unemployment and higher inflation (point B) The short-run Phillips curve shifts to the right from PC₁ to PC₂. Policy makers now face a worse trade-off between inflation and unemployment.

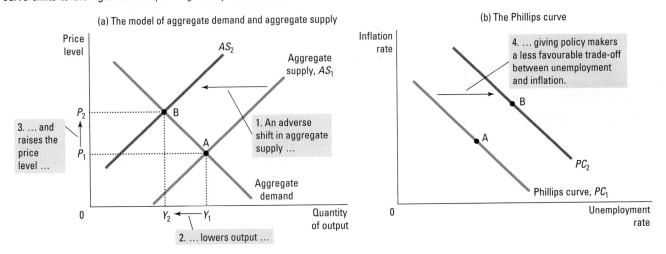

An important question is whether this adverse shift in the Phillips curve is temporary or permanent. The answer depends on how businesses and people adjust their expectations of inflation. If both view the rise in inflation due to the supply shock as a temporary aberration, expected inflation does not change, and the Phillips curve will soon revert to its former position. But if it is believed the shock will lead to a new era of higher inflation, then expected inflation rises, and the Phillips curve remains at its new, less desirable position.

Quick Quiz Give an example of a favourable shock to aggregate supply. Use the model of aggregate demand and aggregate supply to explain the effects of such a shock. How does it affect the Phillips curve?

THE COST OF REDUCING INFLATION

Economic theory suggests that controlling the money supply is a way of reducing inflation. But what is the short-run cost of disinflation?

The Sacrifice Ratio

To reduce the inflation rate, the central bank has to pursue contractionary monetary policy. Figure 19.9 shows some of the effects of such a decision. When the central bank slows the rate at which the money supply is growing, it contracts aggregate demand. The fall in aggregate demand, in turn, reduces the quantity of goods and services that firm's produce, and this fall in production leads to a fall in employment. The economy begins at point A in the figure and moves along the short-run Phillips curve to point B, which has lower inflation and higher unemployment. Over time, as people come to understand that prices are rising more slowly, expected inflation falls, and the short-run Phillips curve shifts downward. The economy moves from point B to point C. Inflation is lower, and unemployment is back at its natural rate.

Thus, if a nation wants to reduce inflation, it must endure a period of high unemployment and low output. In Figure 19.9, this cost is represented by the movement of the economy through point B as it travels from point A to point C. The size of this cost depends on the slope of the Phillips curve and how quickly expectations of inflation adjust to the new monetary policy.

FIGURE 19.9

Disinflationary Monetary Policy in the Short Run and Long Run

When the central bank pursues contractionary monetary policy to reduce inflation, the economy moves along a short-run Phillips curve from point A to point B. Over time, expected inflation falls, and the short-run Phillips curve shifts downward. When the economy reaches point C, unemployment is back at its natural rate.

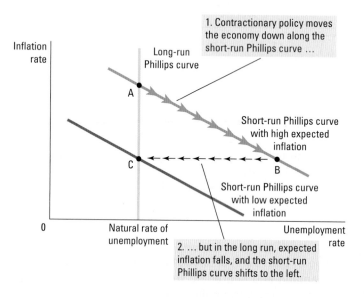

Many studies have examined the data on inflation and unemployment in order to estimate the cost of reducing inflation. The findings of these studies are often summarized in a statistic called the **sacrifice ratio**. The sacrifice ratio is the number of percentage points of annual output lost in the process of reducing inflation by 1 percentage point. A typical estimate of the sacrifice ratio is around 3 to 5. That is, for each percentage point that inflation is reduced, 3 to 5 per cent of annual output must be sacrificed in the transition.

sacrifice ratio the number of percentage points of annual output lost in the process of reducing inflation by 1 percentage point

According to studies of the Phillips curve and the cost of disinflation, this sacrifice could be paid in various ways. An immediate reduction in inflation by a significant amount would depress output for a single year, but the cost in terms of lost output would be extremely harsh even for the most hard-line inflation hawks. It would be better, many argued, to spread out the cost over several years. If the reduction in inflation took place over 5 years, for instance, then the cost would be lower each year. An even more gradual approach would be to reduce inflation slowly over a decade. Whatever path was chosen, however, it seemed that reducing inflation would not be easy.

Rational Expectations and the Possibility of Costless Disinflation

Just as policy makers were pondering how costly reducing inflation might be, a group of economics professors were leading an intellectual revolution that would challenge the conventional wisdom on the sacrifice ratio. This group included such prominent economists as Robert Lucas, Thomas Sargent and Robert Barro. Their revolution was based on a new approach to economic theory and policy called **rational expectations**. According to the theory of rational expectations, people optimally use all the information they have, including information about government policies, when forecasting the future.

This new approach has had profound implications for many areas of macroeconomics, but none is more important than its application to the trade-off between inflation and unemployment. As Friedman and Phelps had first emphasized, expected inflation is an important variable that explains why there is a trade-off between inflation and unemployment in the short run but not in the long run. How quickly the short-run trade-off disappears depends on how quickly expectations adjust. Proponents of rational expectations built on the Friedman-Phelps analysis argue that when economic policies change, people adjust their expectations of inflation accordingly. Studies of inflation and unemployment that tried to estimate the sacrifice ratio had failed to take account of the direct effect of the policy regime on expectations. As a result, estimates of the sacrifice ratio were, according to the rational expectations theorists, unreliable guides for policy.

In a 1982 paper entitled 'The End of Four Big Inflations' (one of which was the UK inflation of the late 1970s and early 1980s), Thomas Sargent described this new view as follows:

> An alternative 'rational expectations' view denies that there is any inherent momentum to the present process of inflation. This view maintains that firms and workers have now come to expect high rates of inflation in the future and that they strike inflationary bargains in light of these expectations. However, it is held that people expect high rates of inflation in the future precisely because the government's current and prospective monetary and fiscal policies warrant those expectations. ... An implication of this view is that inflation can be stopped much more quickly than advocates of the 'momentum' view have indicated and that their estimates of the length of time and the costs of stopping inflation in terms of forgone output are erroneous. This is not to say that it would be easy to eradicate inflation. On the contrary, it would require more than a few temporary restrictive fiscal and monetary actions. It would require a change in the policy regime. ... How costly such a move would be in terms of forgone output and how long it would be in taking effect would depend partly on how resolute and evident the government's commitment was.

According to Sargent, the sacrifice ratio could be much smaller than suggested by previous estimates. Indeed, in the most extreme case, it could be zero. If the government made a credible commitment to a policy of low inflation, people would be rational enough to lower their expectations of inflation immediately. The short-run Phillips curve would shift downward, and the economy would reach low inflation quickly without the cost of temporarily high unemployment and low output. The credibility of government policy is thus of prime importance.

Does this experience refute the possibility of costless disinflation as suggested by the rational expectations theorists? Some economists have argued that the answer to this question is a resounding yes.

Yet perhaps there is good reason not to reject the conclusions of the rational expectations theorists so quickly. Even though disinflation can impose a cost of temporarily high unemployment, the cost may not be as large as many economists had initially predicted.

rational expectations the theory according to which people optimally use all the information they have, including information about government policies, when forecasting the future

Most estimates of the sacrifice ratio based on UK disinflation policies in the 1980s are smaller than estimates that had been obtained from previous data. One explanation is that a tough stand on inflation does have some direct effect on expectations, as the rational expectations theorists claimed.

> **Quick Quiz** What is the sacrifice ratio? How might the credibility of the government's commitment to reduce inflation affect the sacrifice ratio?

CONCLUSION

This chapter discussed the causes and costs of inflation. The primary cause of inflation is simply growth in the quantity of money. When the central bank creates money in large quantities, the value of money falls quickly. To maintain stable prices, the central bank must maintain strict control over the money supply.

The costs of inflation are more subtle. They include shoe leather costs, menu costs, increased variability of relative prices, unintended changes in tax liabilities, confusion and inconvenience, and arbitrary redistributions of wealth. Are these costs, in total, large or small? All economists agree that they become huge during hyperinflation. But their size for moderate inflation – when prices rise by less than 10 per cent per year – is more open to debate.

When the central bank reduces the rate of money growth, prices rise less rapidly, as the quantity theory suggests. Yet as the economy makes the transition to this lower inflation rate, the change in monetary policy will have disruptive effects on production and employment. That is, even though monetary policy is neutral in the long run, it has profound effects on real variables in the short run.

We also examined how economists' thinking about inflation and unemployment has evolved over time. We have discussed the ideas of many of the best economists of the 20th century: from the Phillips curve of Phillips, Samuelson and Solow, to the natural-rate hypothesis of Friedman and Phelps, to the rational expectations theory of Lucas, Sargent and Barro.

Although the trade-off between inflation and unemployment has generated much intellectual turmoil over the past 40 years, certain principles have developed that today command consensus. Here is how Milton Friedman expressed the relationship between inflation and unemployment in 1968 (in an *American Economic Review* paper entitled 'The Role of Monetary Policy'):

> *There is always a temporary trade-off between inflation and unemployment; there is no permanent trade-off. The temporary trade-off comes not from inflation per se, but from unanticipated inflation, which generally means, from a rising rate of inflation. The widespread belief that there is a permanent trade-off is a sophisticated version of the confusion between 'high' and 'rising' that we all recognize in simpler forms. A rising rate of inflation may reduce unemployment, a high rate will not.*

> *But how long, you will say, is 'temporary'? ... We can at most venture a personal judgment, based on some examination of the historical evidence, that the initial effects of a higher and unanticipated rate of inflation last for something like two to five years.*

Today, nearly 40 years later, this statement still summarizes the view of most macroeconomists.

IN THE NEWS

Help Economy

Central Bank Decision Making

Much of this chapter has considered economic theory and it may be that theory would work in practice if other things remained equal. Unfortunately in most cases, economics has to operate within a political context and this can compromise attempts by policy makers to achieve macroeconomic goals.

India's Central Bank Faces a Dilemma

India is one of the emerging economies, a country with a population of around 1.2 billion people and a GDP or around $4.46 trillion, making GDP per capita around $3700. Economic growth has been around 7–10 per cent in recent years with latest estimates putting 2011 growth at 7.8 per cent.

Despite these impressive-sounding figures there are problems within the country. Inflation in particular is proving difficult to get under control. The CPI has been in double digits at times since 2005 and although rates in 2011 were around 7 per cent it seems that attempts by the central bank to reduce inflation below this level to targets of around 4–5 per cent is proving difficult.

The central bank, the Reserve Bank of India (RBI) increased base rates 13 times between 2010 and 2012 to try and curtail inflation. Part of the reason why its attempts are proving difficult is because of the approach of the government which some argue is borrowing too much and not spending the money wisely on things that would help boost aggregate supply in the economy. Rather than spending money on infrastructure and helping Indian businesses to boost invest-

ment, the government has borrowed heavily to fund so-called 'populist measures' which have included subsidies on food and fuel. The former is necessary because it impedes the flow of goods from producers to the consumer. Some reports, for example, suggest that around two-fifths of food produced does not reach consumers.

The government is in a predicament of its own because it survives on the basis of a coalition and getting agreement to push through much needed but tough reforms would be difficult. As a result, critics argue that it has borrowed money to fund its subsidies programme and this has led to crowding out of private investment and a credit squeeze which has led to growth slowing below the 9 per cent predicted a few years ago. There is a concern, therefore, that India might face stubborn inflation and sluggish growth (in comparison to expectations).

The response of the RBI has been to try to increase liquidity in the banking system. It has cut the amount of cash reserves that banks need to keep to cover withdrawals in an attempt to encourage banks to lend more. Observers are suggesting that this might signal a change of emphasis from the RBI from trying to maintain price stability and instead focusing on

encouraging growth. In addition to reducing cash reserves it was also expected at the beginning of March 2012 that the RBI would begin to cut interest rates. How the banking sector would respond to such a cut (or cuts) was being debated by economists in India. Some suggested that the cut in rates would not lead to banks lending that much more because of structural problems in the banking system while others suggested that lower rates would simply make it even easier for the government to borrow more and crowd out private investment further.

Questions

1. What is meant by the term 'crowding out' (see Chapter 15).
2. Explain how a rise in interest rates would be expected to feed through to a fall in the rate of growth of prices.
3. Why might the government be spending money on subsidizing food and fuel?
4. What is the importance of improving infrastructure and promoting investment to businesses and the growth of the Indian economy as a whole?
5. Should the RBI focus its policy on controlling inflation or boosting economic growth in India? Explain your answer.

SUMMARY

- The overall level of prices in an economy adjusts to bring money supply and money demand into balance. When the central bank increases the supply of money, it causes the price level to rise. Persistent growth in the quantity of money supplied leads to continuing inflation.

- A government can pay for some of its spending simply by printing money. When countries rely heavily on this 'inflation tax', the result is hyperinflation.

- Many people think that inflation makes them poorer because it raises the cost of what they buy. This view is a fallacy, however, because inflation also raises nominal incomes.

- Economists have identified six costs of inflation: shoe leather costs associated with reduced money holdings; menu costs associated with more frequent adjustment of prices; increased variability of relative prices; unintended changes in tax liabilities due to non-indexation of the tax system; confusion and inconvenience resulting from a changing unit of account; and arbitrary redistributions of wealth between debtors and creditors. Many of these costs are large during hyperinflation, but the size of these costs for moderate inflation is less clear.

- The Phillips curve describes a negative relationship between inflation and unemployment. By expanding aggregate demand, policy makers can choose a point on the Phillips curve with higher inflation and lower unemployment. By con-

tracting aggregate demand, policy makers can choose a point on the Phillips curve with lower inflation and higher unemployment.

- The trade-off between inflation and unemployment described by the Phillips curve holds only in the short run. In the long run, expected inflation adjusts to changes in actual inflation, and the short-run Phillips curve shifts. As a result, the long-run Phillips curve is vertical at the natural rate of unemployment.

- The short-run Phillips curve also shifts because of shocks to aggregate supply. An adverse supply shock, such as the increase in world oil prices during the 1970s, gives policy makers a less favourable trade-off between inflation and unemployment. That is, after an adverse supply shock, policy makers have to accept a higher rate of inflation for any given rate of unemployment, or a higher rate of unemployment for any given rate of inflation.

- When the central bank contracts growth in the money supply to reduce inflation, it moves the economy along the short-run Phillips curve, which results in temporarily high unemployment. The cost of disinflation depends on how quickly expectations of inflation fall. Some economists argue that a credible commitment to low inflation can reduce the cost of disinflation by inducing a quick adjustment of expectations.

KEY CONCEPTS

quantity theory of money, p. 469

inflation tax, p. 471

shoe leather cost, p. 471

menu costs, p. 471

natural-rate hypothesis, p. 481

supply shock, p. 482

sacrifice ratio, p. 484

rational expectations, p. 485

QUESTIONS FOR REVIEW

1. Explain how an increase in the price level affects the real value of money.

2. In what sense is inflation like a tax? How does thinking about inflation as a tax help explain hyperinflation?

3. What are the costs of inflation? Which of these costs do you think are most important for your economy?

4. If inflation is less than expected, who benefits – debtors or creditors? Explain.

5. Explain how business planning can be affected by inflation rising at rates deemed to be 'too fast'.

6. Draw the short-run trade-off between inflation and unemployment. How might the central bank move the economy from one point on this curve to another?

7. Draw the long-run trade-off between inflation and unemployment. Explain how the short-run and long-run trade-offs are related.

8. What's so natural about the natural rate of unemployment? Why might the natural rate of unemployment differ across countries?

9. Suppose a drought destroys farm crops and drives up the price of food. What is the effect on the short-run trade-off between inflation and unemployment?

10. The central bank decides to reduce inflation. Use the Phillips curve to show the short-run and long-run effects of this policy. How might the short-run costs be reduced?

PROBLEMS AND APPLICATIONS

1. Suppose that changes in bank regulations expand the availability of credit cards, so that people need to hold less cash.
   a. How does this event affect the demand for money?
   b. If the central bank does not respond to this event, what will happen to the price level?
   c. If the central bank wants to keep the price level stable, what should it do?

2. The economist John Maynard Keynes wrote: 'Lenin is said to have declared that the best way to destroy the capitalist system was to debauch the currency. By a continuing process of inflation, governments can confiscate, secretly and unobserved, an important part of the wealth of their citizens.' Justify Lenin's assertion.

3. Suppose that a country's inflation rate increases sharply. What happens to the inflation tax on the holders of money? Why is wealth that is held in savings accounts not subject to a change in the inflation tax? Can you think of any way in which holders of savings accounts are hurt by the increase in the inflation rate?

4. What are your shoe leather costs of going to the bank? How might you measure these costs in euros? How do you think the shoe leather costs of the head of your university or college differ from your own?

5. Explain whether the following statements are true, false or uncertain.
   a. 'Inflation hurts borrowers and helps lenders, because borrowers must pay a higher rate of interest.'
   b. 'If prices change in a way that leaves the overall price level unchanged, then no one is made better or worse off.'
   c. 'Inflation does not reduce the purchasing power of most workers.'

6. Suppose the natural rate of unemployment is 6 per cent. On one graph, draw two Phillips curves that can be used to describe the four situations listed here. Label the point that shows the position of the economy in each case.
   a. Actual inflation is 5 per cent and expected inflation is 3 per cent.
   b. Actual inflation is 3 per cent and expected inflation is 5 per cent.
   c. Actual inflation is 5 per cent and expected inflation is 5 per cent.
   d. Actual inflation is 3 per cent and expected inflation is 3 per cent.

7. Illustrate the effects of the following developments on both the short-run and long-run Phillips curves. Give the economic reasoning underlying your answers.
   a. A rise in the natural rate of unemployment.
   b. A decline in the price of imported oil.
   c. A rise in government spending.
   d. A decline in expected inflation.

8. Suppose that a fall in consumer spending causes a recession.
   a. Illustrate the changes in the economy using both an aggregate supply/aggregate demand diagram and a Phillips curve diagram. What happens to inflation and unemployment in the short run?
   b. Now suppose that over time expected inflation changes in the same direction that actual inflation changes. What happens to the position of the short-run Phillips curve? After the recession is over, does the economy face a better or worse set of inflation–unemployment combinations?

9. Suppose the central bank announced that it would pursue contractionary monetary policy in order to reduce the inflation rate. Would the following conditions make the ensuing recession more or less severe? Explain.
   a. Wage contracts have short durations.
   b. There is little confidence in the central bank's determination to reduce inflation.
   c. Expectations of inflation adjust quickly to actual inflation.

10. Imagine an economy in which all wages are set in three-year contracts. In this world, the central bank announces a disinflationary change in monetary policy to begin immediately. Everyone in the economy believes the central bank's announcement. Would this disinflation be costless? Why or why not? What might the central bank do to reduce the cost of disinflation?

20

MACROECONOMICS – FISCAL, MONETARY AND SUPPLY-SIDE POLICY

LEARNING OBJECTIVES

In this chapter you will:

- Learn the difference between monetary, fiscal and supply-side policies

- Learn the difference between planned and actual spending, saving and investment

- Consider why deflationary and inflationary gaps occur

- Examine the concept of the marginal propensity to withdraw

- Learn how governments can influence aggregate demand to bring about desired macroeconomic outcomes in the short run

- Learn the theory of liquidity preference as a short-run theory of the interest rate

- Analyze how monetary policy affects interest rates and aggregate demand

After reading this chapter you should be able to:

- Give a clear definition to outline the differences between monetary, fiscal and supply-side policies

- Explain the difference between planned and actual spending, saving and investment

- Draw a diagram of the Keynesian cross and use it to show both an inflationary and deflationary gap

- Be able to calculate the value of the multiplier given data on the marginal propensities to withdraw

- Draw a diagram to explain the relevance of the slope of the expenditure line in relation to changes in autonomous expenditure

- Show what an increase in the money supply does to the interest rate in the short run

- Illustrate what an increase in the money supply does to aggregate demand

- Analyze how fiscal policy affects interest rates and aggregate demand

- Discuss the debate over whether policy makers should try to stabilize the economy

- Describe how a change in the money supply (both increase and decrease) feeds through to the interest rate in the short run.

- Explain crowding out

- Describe the lags in fiscal and monetary policy

MONETARY POLICY, FISCAL POLICY AND SUPPLY-SIDE POLICY

In this chapter we are going to examine three main policies used to control the economy. These policies are *monetary policy, fiscal policy* and *supply-side policy*. In each case policy is designed to influence economic activity but in different ways. The effects on business and consumer behaviour in each case can be very different and the consequences for the economy will also vary.

Thus, a change in monetary and fiscal policy can lead to short-run fluctuations in output and prices; changes to supply-side policy tend to be longer term. Fiscal and monetary policy tends to have an impact on aggregate demand whereas supply-side policies are focused on the aggregate supply curve.

Many factors influence aggregate demand besides monetary and fiscal policy. In particular, desired spending by households and firms determines the overall demand for goods and services. When desired spending changes, aggregate demand shifts. If policy makers do not respond, such shifts in aggregate demand cause short-run fluctuations in output and employment. As a result, monetary and fiscal policy makers sometimes use the policy levers at their disposal to try to offset these shifts in aggregate demand and thereby stabilize the economy. Here we discuss the theory behind these policy actions and some of the difficulties that arise in using this theory in practice.

We are going to introduce each policy in turn.

MONETARY POLICY

Monetary policy refers to attempts to influence the level of economic activity (the amount of buying and selling in the economy) through changes to the amount of money in circulation and the price of money – short-term interest rates. The basis of the relationship between the money supply and inflation is set out in the classical quantity theory of money encapsulated in the formula:

monetary policy the set of actions taken by the central bank in order to affect the money supply

MV = PY where M = the money stock, V = velocity of circulation, P = price level and Y = level of national income. This can be stated more formally as $M_d = kPY$ where P is the price level, Y is the level of real national income, M_d is demand for money for transactions purposes, k = proportion of national income held as transactions balances

In equilibrium $M_d = M_s$, so: P = (1/kY) × M_s. It follows that a rise in Ms will lead to a proportional rise in P.

The main weapon used to control the money supply is interest rates set by the central bank. Changes in the rate at which the central bank lends to the banking system helps determine the structure of interest rates throughout the financial system. The structure of interest rates then feeds through to different parts of the economy through the *interest rate transmission mechanism*. This transmission mechanism is summarized in Figure 20.1.

FIGURE 20.1

The Interest Rate Transmission Mechanism

The three panels (a), (b) and (c) show the effect of changes in interest rates on different parts of the economy. In panel (a), the effect is traced through changes to borrowing by individuals and firms on consumption and investment. In panel (b) the effect is traced through mortgage holders and savers and in panel (c) the effect in exchange rates, import and export prices and the demand for imports and exports is shown which together have an impact on net exports.

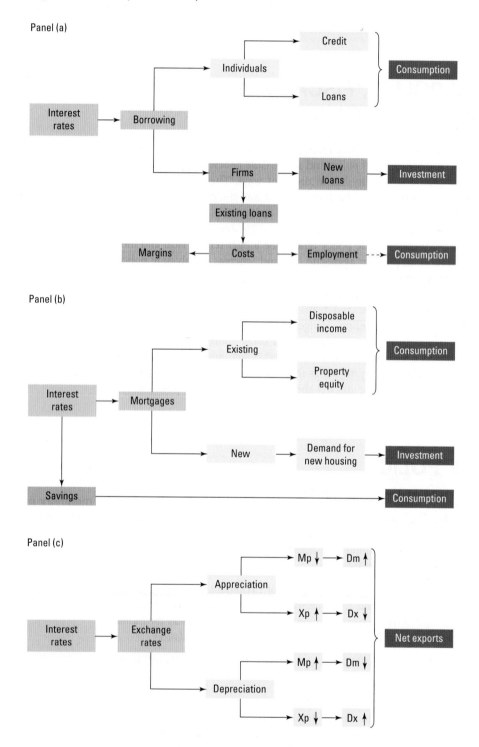

In panel (a), changes in interest rates affect the amount of borrowing by businesses and individuals which in turn affect levels of consumption and investment. At the same time, businesses which have existing loans may find that the cost of servicing the loan changes if interest rates rise, which affects their costs and margins and may cause them to cut back production or find other ways to reduce costs such as shed employment which will then affect consumption if workers lose their jobs and their incomes fall.

In panel (b), the effect occurs through mortgages and savings. Changes to interest rates affect those with mortgages and can impact on disposable income thus affecting consumption. It will also affect the demand for new mortgages and can feed through to investment in new housing stock. There might also be changes to property prices which can affect homeowners' equity. For example, if interest rates rise significantly the demand for mortgages might fall, which in turn slows down the housing market causing a fall in house prices. The fall in house prices can leave some homeowners in a position where the value of their mortgage is greater than the value of the property. If they have to sell they end up saddled with debt and this may lead to them cutting their consumption. There will also be effects from changes in interest rates on savings. Between 2009 and 2013, interest rates across the developed world have remained very low and savers have found that returns have been very low as a result. This affects their consumption. Low interest rates also tend to discourage saving and this can not only lead to increased consumption (remember, $Y = C + S$) but also have an effect on funds available for investment through the financial system.

Panel (c) shows how changes in interest rates feed through to exchange rates. If the central bank changes interest rates and other countries interest rates remain constant, then the difference in relative interest rates affects the demand and supply of currencies as traders look to move funds to higher interest rate countries to improve returns. This affects the demand and supply of currencies causing an appreciation or depreciation which in turn affects import and export prices denoted by M_p and X_p respectively and the demand for imports and exports. There will be a resulting effect on net exports.

The Central Bank's Tools of Monetary Control

The central bank is responsible for controlling the supply of money in the economy. When the central bank decides to change the money supply, it must consider how its actions will work through the banking system.

In general, a central bank has three main tools in its monetary toolbox: open-market operations, the refinancing rate and reserve requirements.

Open-Market Operations   If the central bank wants to increase the money supply, it can create currency and use it to buy bonds from the public in the bond market. After the purchase, the extra currency is in the hands of the public. Thus, an open-market purchase of bonds by the central bank increases the money supply. If, on the other hand, the central bank wants to decrease the money supply, it can sell bonds from its portfolio to the public. After the sale, the currency it receives for the bonds is out of the hands of the public. Thus an open-market sale of bonds by the central bank decreases the money supply. To be precise, the open-market operations discussed in these simple examples are called outright open-market operations, because they each involve an outright sale or purchase of non-monetary assets to or from the banking sector without a corresponding agreement to reverse the transaction at a later date.

The Refinancing Rate   The central bank of an economy will set an interest rate at which it is willing to lend to commercial banks on a short-term basis.

The way in which the central bank lends to the banking sector is through a special form of open-market operations. In the previous paragraph we discussed the use of outright open-market operations. Although outright open-market operations have traditionally been used by central banks to regulate the money supply, central banks nowadays more often use a slightly more sophisticated form of open-market operations that involves buying bonds or other assets from banks and at the same time agreeing to sell them back later. When it does this, the central bank has effectively made a loan and taken the bonds or other assets as collateral or security on the loan. The central bank will have a list of eligible assets that it will accept as collateral – 'safe' assets such as government bonds or assets issued by large corporations, on which the risk of default by the issuer is negligible. The interest rate that the central bank charges on the loan is the refinancing rate. Because the central bank has bought the assets but the seller has agreed to buy them back later at an agreed price, this kind of open-market operation is often called a repurchase agreement or 'repo' for short. To see how central bank's use repos as a means of controlling the money supply and how this is affected by the refinancing rate, we need to look a little more closely at the way commercial banks lend money to one another and borrow from the central bank.

Banks need to carry enough reserves to cover their lending and will generally aim for a certain ratio of reserves to deposits, known as the reserve ratio. The minimum reserve ratio may be set by the central bank, but even if it isn't, banks will still have a reserve ratio that they consider prudent. Now, because deposits and withdrawals at banks can fluctuate randomly, some banks may find that they have an excess of reserves one day (i.e. their reserve ratio is above the level the bank considers prudent or above the minimum reserve ratio, or both), while other banks may find that they are short of reserves and their reserve ratio is too low. Therefore, the commercial banks in an economy will generally lend money to one another on a short-term basis – overnight to a couple of weeks – so that banks with excess reserves can lend them to banks who have inadequate reserves to cover their lending. This market for short-term reserves is called the money market. If there is a general shortage of liquidity in the money market (because the banks together have done a lot of lending), then the short-term interest rate at which they lend to one another will begin to rise, while it will begin to fall if there is excess liquidity among banks. The central bank closely monitors the money market and may intervene in it in order to affect the supply of liquidity to banks, which in turn affects their lending and hence affects the money supply.

Suppose, for example, that there is a shortage of liquidity in the market because the banks have been increasing their lending and they need to increase their reserves. A commercial bank may then attempt to obtain liquidity from the central bank by selling assets to the central bank and at the same time agreeing to purchase them back a short time later. As we said before, in this type of open-market operation the central bank effectively lends money to the bank and takes the assets as collateral on the loan. Because the commercial bank is legally bound to repurchase the assets at a set price, this is called a 'repurchase agreement' and the difference between the price the bank sells the assets to the central bank and the price at which it agrees to buy them back, expressed as an annualized percentage of the selling price, is called the repurchase or repo rate by the Bank of England and the refinancing rate by the European Central Bank. The ECB's refinancing rate is thus the rate at which it will lend to the banking sector of the euro area, while the repo rate is the rate at which the Bank of England lends short term to the UK banking sector.

In the example given, the central bank added liquidity to the banking system by lending reserves to banks. This would have the effect of increasing the money supply. Because the loans made through open-market operations are typically very short term, with a maturity of at most two weeks, the banks are constantly having to repay the loans and borrow again, or 'refinance' the loans. If the central bank wants to mop up liquidity it can simply decide not to renew some of the loans. In practice, however, the central bank will set a reference rate of interest – the Bank of England's repo rate or the

ECB's refinancing rate – and will conduct open-market operations, adding to or mopping up liquidity, close to this reference rate.

In the USA the interest rate at which the Federal Reserve lends to the banking sector (corresponding to the ECB's refinancing rate or the Bank of England's repo rate) is called the discount rate.

Now we can see why the setting of the central bank's refinancing rate is the key instrument of monetary policy. If the central bank raises the refinancing rate, commercial banks will try and rein in their lending rather than borrow reserves from the central bank, and so the money supply will fall. If the central bank lowers the refinancing rate, banks will feel freer to lend, knowing that they will be able to borrow more cheaply from the central bank in order to meet their reserve requirements, and so the money supply will tend to rise.

Reserve Requirements   The central bank may also influence the money supply with reserve requirements, which are regulations on the minimum amount of reserves that banks must hold against deposits. Reserve requirements influence how much money the banking system can create with each euro of reserves.

The amount of money the banking system generates with each euro of reserves is called the **money multiplier**. It is important to remember that when banks make loans no new 'cash' (actual notes and coins) is created. Most transactions in modern economies are simply 'book entries'; when you get a bank statement telling you that there is a balance of €1500 in your current account there is not a box with this sum of money stored somewhere in the bank's vault. The banking system is such that we have trust that if we did wish to withdraw all that money in cash the bank would have sufficient funds to be able to meet our demand. The size of the money multiplier is the reciprocal of the reserve ratio. If R is the reserve ratio for all banks in the economy, then each euro of reserves generates 1/R euros of money. If the reserve ratio is set at R = 1/10, the money multiplier is 10.

This reciprocal formula for the money multiplier makes sense. If a bank holds €1000 in deposits, then a reserve ratio of 1/10 (10 per cent) means that the bank must hold €100 in reserves. The money multiplier just turns this idea around: if the banking system as a whole holds a total of €100 in reserves, it can have only €1000 in deposits. In other words, if R is the ratio of reserves to deposits at each bank (that is, the reserve ratio), then the ratio of deposits to reserves in the banking system (that is, the money multiplier) must be 1/R.

If the reserve ratio is changed by the central bank then the money multiplier changes. If the reserve ratio were only 1/20 (5 per cent), then the banking system would have 20 times as much in deposits as in reserves, implying a money multiplier of 20. Each euro of reserves would generate €20 of money. Similarly, if the reserve ratio were 1/5 (20 per cent), deposits would be 5 times reserves, the money multiplier would be 5, and each euro of reserves would generate €5 of money. Thus, the higher the reserve ratio, the less of each deposit banks lend out and the smaller the money multiplier.

Central banks have traditionally tended to use changes in reserve requirements only rarely because frequent changes would disrupt the business of banking. When the central bank increases reserve requirements, for instance, some banks find themselves short of reserves, even though they have seen no change in deposits. As a result, they have to curtail lending until they build their level of reserves to the new required level.

Following the financial crisis, negotiations have taken place on improving banks' reserves to avoid the problems faced during the crisis. The so-called Basel III negotiations between 27 countries set new reserve requirements in September 2010. The new rules will come into force in 2013 and then be phased in over a period of six years. The regulations mean that banks will have to have higher reserves to support lending; for every €50 of lending banks will have to have €3.50 of reserves compared to €1 prior to the Basel III agreement. This obviously more than triples the amount of reserves that banks will have to keep. If banks do not adhere to the new regulations then they risk seeing the authorities placing restrictions on their activities, including paying out dividends to shareholders and bonuses to staff.

money multiplier the amount of money the banking system generates with each unit of reserves

Problems in Controlling the Money Supply

Through the setting of its refinancing rate and the associated open-market operations, the central bank can exert an important degree of control over the money supply. Yet the central bank's control of the money supply is not precise. The central bank must wrestle with two problems, each of which arises because much of the money supply is created by the system of fractional-reserve banking.

The first problem is that the central bank does not control the amount of money that households choose to hold as deposits in banks. The more money households deposit, the more reserves banks have, and the more money the banking system can create. And the less money households deposit, the less reserves banks have, and the less money the banking system can create. To see why this is a problem, suppose that one day people begin to lose confidence in the banking system and, therefore, decide to withdraw deposits and hold more currency. When this happens, the banking system loses reserves and creates less money. The money supply falls, even without any central bank action.

The second problem of monetary control is that the central bank does not control the amount that bankers choose to lend. When money is deposited in a bank, it creates more money only when the bank lends it out. Because banks can choose to hold excess reserves instead, the central bank cannot be sure how much money the banking system will create. For instance, suppose that one day bankers become more cautious about economic conditions and decide to make fewer loans and hold greater reserves. In this case, the banking system creates less money than it otherwise would. This is a situation which has arisen following the financial crisis and the consequences are that many businesses have found it harder to secure vital loans for managing their business or for expansion or that the price of securing a loan is prohibitively high. Because of the bankers' decision, the money supply falls.

Quick Quiz Describe how banks create money. • If the ECB wanted to use all three of its policy tools to decrease the money supply, what would it do?

FISCAL POLICY

fiscal policy influencing the level of economic activity through manipulation of government income and expenditure

Fiscal policy involves Influencing the level of economic activity though manipulation of government income and expenditure. It works through affecting key variables in aggregate demand, consumption, investment and government spending. In most developed countries, government spending accounts for around 40 per cent of total spending. This fact alone suggests that governments can have a significant effect on economic activity.

In 1936, economist John Maynard Keynes published a book entitled *The General Theory of Employment, Interest and Money*, which attempted to explain short-run economic fluctuations in general and the Great Depression in particular. Keynes' primary message was that recessions and depressions can occur because of inadequate aggregate demand for goods and services. Keynes had long been a critic of classical economic theory because it could explain only the long-run effects of policies.

When he published *The General Theory*, the world's economies were suffering very high levels of unemployment. Keynes advocated policies to increase aggregate demand through the government manipulating its own income and expenditure through changing taxes and government spending on public works. Keynes argued that short-run interventions in the economy could lead to improvements in the economy that would be beneficial rather than waiting for the long-run equilibrium to establish itself.

The Keynesian Cross

Classical economics placed a fundamental reliance on the efficiency of markets and the assumption that they would clear. At a macro level, this meant that if the economy was in disequilibrium and unemployment existed, wages and prices would adjust to bring the economy back into equilibrium at full employment. **Full employment** is defined as a point where those people who want to work at the going market wage level are able to find a job. Any unemployment that did exist would be classed as voluntary unemployment. The experience of the Great Depression of the 1930s brought the classical assumptions under closer scrutiny; the many millions suffering from unemployment could not all be volunteering to not take jobs at the going wage rates so some must, therefore, be involuntarily unemployed.

Fundamental to Keynesian analysis is the distinction between planned and actual decisions by households and firms. **Planned spending, saving or investment** refers to the desired or intended actions of firms and households. A publisher may plan to sell 1000 copies of a textbook in the first three months of the year, an individual may plan to go on holiday to Turkey in the summer and to save up to finance the trip, a person may intend to save €1000 over the year to pay for a wedding next year.

Actual spending, saving or investment refers to the realized, ex post (after the event) outcome. The publisher may only sell 800 copies in the first three months and so has a build-up of stock of 200 more than planned; the holidaymaker may fall ill and so is unable to go on holiday and so actual consumption is lower than planned (whereas actual saving is more than planned) and the plans for saving for the wedding may be compromised by the need to spend the money on repairing a house damaged by a flood.

Planned and actual outcomes might be very different as briefly outlined above. As a result Keynes argued that there was no reason why equilibrium national income would coincide with full employment output. Wages and prices might not adjust in the short run (so called sticky wages and prices) and so the economy could be at a position where the level of demand in the economy was insufficient to bring about full employment. It is useful at this point to refer back to the circular flow of income described in Chapter 16. Households and firms interact in the market for goods and services and in the factor market. Recall also the identity given in Chapter 16 which described how a country's gross domestic product (national income, Y) is divided among four components, i.e. consumption spending, investment spending, spending by government and net exports – the difference between the funds received from selling exports minus the expenditure on imports. Figure 20.2 summarizes this analysis.

In panels (a) and (b), the 45° line connects all points where consumption spending would be equal to national income. This line can be thought of as the equivalent of the capacity of the economy – the aggregate supply (AS) curve. The economy is in equilibrium where the $C + I + G + (X - M)$ line cuts the 45° line at Y_1. In panel (a) the equilibrium is less than that required to give full employment output (Y_f). At this equilibrium there is spare capacity in the economy and unemployment will rise. The difference between full employment output and the expenditure required to meet it is termed the **deflationary gap**. In panel (b) equilibrium is above full employment output and in this case the economy does not have the capacity to meet the demand. This will trigger inflationary pressures in the economy. The difference between full employment output and the expenditure line here is called the inflationary gap. To eradicate these gaps governments can influence the components of aggregate demand through both fiscal and monetary policy to bring about an equilibrium that is closer to the desired full employment output.

The Multiplier Effect

When a government makes a purchase, say a contract for €10 billion to build three new nuclear power generating stations, that purchase has repercussions. The immediate impact of the higher demand from the government is to raise employment and profits at the construction company (which we shall call Nucelec). Nucelec, in turn, has to buy resources

full employment a point where those people who want to work at the going market wage level are able to find a job

planned spending, saving or investment the desired or intended actions of households and firms

actual spending, saving or investment the realized or ex post outcome resulting from actions of households and firms

deflationary gap the difference between full employment output and the expenditure required to meet it

FIGURE 20.2

Deflationary and Inflationary Gaps

The 45° line shows all the points where consumption spending equals income. The vertical intercept of the expenditure line shows autonomous expenditure. The economy is in equilibrium where the expenditure line, $C + I + G + (X - M)$, cuts the 45° line. In panel (a) this equilibrium is lower than full employment output (Y_f) at Y_1 – there is insufficient demand to maintain full employment output. The government would need to shift the expenditure line up to $C + I + G + (X - M)_1$ to eliminate the deflationary gap as shown. In panel (b) the equilibrium is higher than full employment output – the economy does not have the capacity to meet demand. In this case the government needs to shift the $C + I + G + (X - M)$ line down to $C + I + G + (X - M)_2$ to eliminate the inflationary gap.

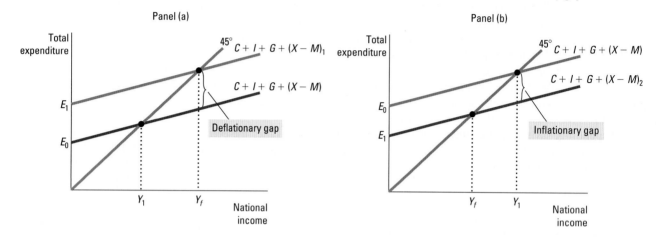

from other contractors to carry out the job and so these suppliers also experience an increase in orders. Then, as the workers see higher earnings and the firm owners see higher profits, they respond to this increase in income by raising their own spending on consumer goods. As a result, the government purchase from Nucelec raises the demand for the products of many other firms and consumers in the economy. Because each euro spent by the government can raise the aggregate demand for goods and services by more than a euro, government purchases are said to have a **multiplier effect** on aggregate demand.

This multiplier effect continues even after this first round. When consumer spending rises, the firms that produce these consumer goods hire more people and experience higher profits. Higher earnings and profits stimulate consumer spending once again, and so on. Thus, there is positive feedback as higher demand leads to higher income, which in turn leads to even higher demand. Once all these effects are added together, the total impact on the quantity of goods and services demanded can be much larger than the initial impulse from higher government spending.

This multiplier effect arising from the response of consumer spending can be strengthened by the response of investment to higher levels of demand. For instance, Nucelec might respond to the higher demand for building services by buying more cranes and other mechanized building equipment. In this case, higher government demand spurs higher demand for investment goods. This positive feedback from demand to investment is sometimes called the investment accelerator.

multiplier effect the additional shifts in aggregate demand that result when expansionary fiscal policy increases income and thereby increases consumer spending

CASE STUDY

The Accelerator Principle

The accelerator principle relates the rate of change of aggregate demand to the rate of change in investment. To produce goods, a firm needs equipment. Imagine that a machine is capable of producing 1000 DVDs per week. Demand for DVDs is currently 800. A rise in demand for DVDs of up to 200 is capable of being met without any further investment in new machinery. However, if the rate of growth of demand continues to rise, it may be necessary to invest in a new machine.

Imagine that in year 1, demand for DVDs rises by 10 per cent to 880. The business can meet this demand through existing equipment. In year 2, demand increases by 20 per cent and is now 1056. The existing capacity of the machine means that this demand cannot be met but the shortage is only 56 units so the firm decides that it might increase price rather than invest in a new machine. In year 3, demand rises by a further 25 per cent. Demand is now 1320 but the machine is only capable of producing a maximum of 1000 DVDs. The firm decides to invest in a new machine. The manufacturers of the new machine will therefore see a rise in their order books as a result of the increase in demand. An increase in demand of 25 per cent has led to an 'accelerated' rise in investment of 100 per cent. Investment is a component of aggregate demand and so economists are interested in the way investment adjusts to changes in demand in the economy. As this brief example shows, the relationship between an increase in demand and an increase in investment is not a simple one.

A Formula for the Spending Multiplier

A little algebra permits us to derive a formula for the size of the multiplier effect that arises from consumer spending. An important number in this formula is the **marginal propensity to consume** (MPC) – the fraction of extra income that a household spends rather than saves. For example, suppose that the marginal propensity to consume is ¾. This means that for every extra pound or euro that a household earns, the household spends ¾ of it and saves ¼. The **marginal propensity to save** is the fraction of extra income that a household saves rather than consumes. With an MPC of ¾, when the workers and owners of Nucelec earn €10 billion from the government contract, they increase their consumer spending by ¾ × €10 billion, or €7.5 billion. (You should see from the above that the MPC + MPS = 1. The formula below can also be expressed in terms of the MPS as a result.)

To gauge the impact on aggregate demand of a change in government purchases, we follow the effects step-by-step. The process begins when the government spends €10 billion, which implies that national income (earnings and profits) also rises by this amount. This increase in income in turn raises consumer spending by MPC × €10 billion, which in turn raises the income for the workers and owners of the firms that produce the consumption goods. This second increase in income again raises consumer spending, this time by MPC × (MPC × €10 billion). These feedback effects go on and on.

To find the total impact on the demand for goods and services, we add up all these effects:

Change in government purchases	= €10 billion
First change in consumption	= MPC × €10 billion
Second change in consumption	= MPC² × €10 billion
Third change in consumption	= MPC³ × €10 billion
•	•
•	•
•	•
Total change in demand	= (1 + MPC + MPC² + MPC³ = ...) × €10 billion

Here, '...' represents an infinite number of similar terms. Thus, we can write the multiplier as follows:

$$\text{Multiplier} = 1 + MPC + MPC^2 + MPC^3 + ...$$

marginal propensity to consume the fraction of extra income that a household spends rather than saves

marginal propensity to save the fraction of extra income that a household saves rather than consumes

This multiplier tells us the demand for goods and services that each euro of government purchases generates.

To simplify this equation for the multiplier, recall from your school algebra that this expression is an infinite geometric series. For x between -1 and $+1$:

$$1 + x + x^2 + x^3 + \ldots = 1/(1 - x)$$

The sum of this series, as the number of terms tends to infinity, is given by the expression:

$$\frac{1}{1 - x}$$

In our case, $x = MPC$. Thus:

$$\text{Multiplier} = 1/(1 - MPC)$$

We have said that the $MPC + MPS = 1$ so the multiplier can also be expressed as:

$$\text{Multiplier} = 1/MPS$$

For example, if MPC is ¾, the multiplier is $1/(1 - ¾)$, which is 4. In this case, the €10 billion of government spending generates €40 billion of demand for goods and services.

This formula for the multiplier shows an important conclusion: the size of the multiplier depends on the marginal propensity to consume. While an MPC of ¾ leads to a multiplier of 4, an MPC of ½ leads to a multiplier of only 2. Thus, a larger MPC means a larger multiplier. To see why this is true, remember that the multiplier arises because higher income induces greater spending on consumption. The larger the MPC is, the greater is this induced effect on consumption, and the larger is the multiplier.

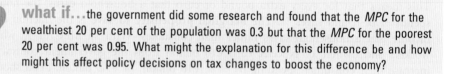

? **what if**…the government did some research and found that the *MPC* for the wealthiest 20 per cent of the population was 0.3 but that the *MPC* for the poorest 20 per cent was 0.95. What might the explanation for this difference be and how might this affect policy decisions on tax changes to boost the economy?

Other Applications of the Multiplier Effect

Because of the multiplier effect, a euro of government purchases can generate more than a euro of aggregate demand. The logic of the multiplier effect, however, is not restricted to changes in government purchases. Instead, it applies to any event that alters spending on any component of GDP – consumption, investment, government purchases or net exports.

For example, suppose that a recession overseas reduces the demand for German net exports by €1 billion. This reduced spending on German goods and services depresses German national income, which reduces spending by German consumers. If the marginal propensity to consume is ¾ and the multiplier is 4, then the €1 billion fall in net exports means a €4 billion contraction in aggregate demand.

As another example, suppose that a stock market boom increases households' wealth and stimulates their spending on goods and services by €2 billion. This extra consumer spending increases national income, which in turn generates even more consumer spending. If the marginal propensity to consume is ¾ and the multiplier is 4, then the initial impulse of €2 billion in consumer spending translates into an €8 billion increase in aggregate demand.

The multiplier is an important concept in macroeconomics because it shows how the economy can amplify the impact of changes in spending. A small initial change in consumption, investment, government purchases or net exports can end up having a large effect on aggregate demand and, therefore, on the economy's production of goods and services.

Another important concept in this analysis is that of **autonomous expenditure** – spending which does not depend on income – government spending being a key element of this expenditure. The amount spent in each successive 'round' of spending is termed induced expenditure. The multiplier showed how the eventual change in income would be determined by the size of the *MPC* and the *MPS* – the proportion of an extra €1 spent or saved by consumers. The higher the *MPC* the greater the multiplier effect.

However, in an open economy with government, any extra €1 is not simply either spent or saved, some of the extra income may be spent on imported goods and services or go to the government in taxation. These are all classed as withdrawals from the circular flow of income. Withdrawals (W) from the circular flow are classed as endogenous as they are directly related to changes in income. There are also injections to the circular flow of income. Governments receive tax revenue but use it to spend on the goods and services they provide for citizens, firms earn revenue from selling goods abroad (exports) and firms, as we have seen, use savings as a source of funds to borrow for investment. Injections into the circular flow are exogenous – they are not related to the level of output or income – and are investment (I), government spending (G) and export earnings (X).

The slope of the expenditure line, therefore, will be dependent on how much of each extra €1 is withdrawn. There will be a marginal propensity to taxation (*MPT*), a marginal propensity to import (*MPM*) in addition to the *MPS*. Collectively these are referred to as the marginal propensity to withdraw (*MPW*). The multiplier (k) would be expressed as:

$$k = \frac{1}{MPS + MPT + MPM}$$

Or:

$$k = \frac{1}{MPW}$$

A higher *MPW* will reduce the value of the multiplier and thus the impact on national income. In equilibrium, planned withdrawals would equal planned injections:

Planned S + T + M = Planned I + G + X

At this point all the output being produced by the economy would be 'bought' by households and firms. However, if actual withdrawals are greater than planned injections then the economy would be experiencing a deficiency in demand. For example, assume that equilibrium output is €100 billion. Planned withdrawals amount to €60 billion. If this planned withdrawal level is not 'bought' by governments, firms and foreigners (i.e. planned injections) then firms will build up stocks and plan to cut back on output in the next period. This leads to a fall in income and as withdrawals are endogenous, planned withdrawals for the next period will fall. The process will continue until planned withdrawals equal planned injections once again and the economy is in equilibrium.

In situations where the economy is experiencing such demand deficiency, the government can budget for a deficit (i.e., spend more than it receives in tax revenue by borrowing or cutting taxes) to boost spending in the economy. It could also influence monetary policy to cut the cost of borrowing and so boost investment; there may also have been an incentive to find ways of boosting exports or cutting imports through imposing various trade barriers and offering export subsidies. However, the emphasis was primarily on fiscal policy which was something that the government could have a direct influence over and whose effect was more immediate. The multiplier process meant that the increase in government spending did not need to be as high as the size of the inflationary or deflationary gap. The steeper the slope of the expenditure line the greater the size of the multiplier, as shown in Figure 20.3.

The Keynesian cross as it is known, gives us a picture of the economy in short-run equilibrium. (Note, if you access a copy of Keynes' *General Theory* you might be surprised to see a complete absence of Keynesian cross diagrams. The use of these diagrams to explain Keynesian ideas was developed by later economists to help portray Keynes' ideas.) In equilibrium, planned expenditure (*E*), (*C* + *I* + *G* + (*X* − *M*) equals actual

autonomous expenditure
spending which is not dependent on income

real money balances what money can actually buy given the ratio of the money supply to the price level M/P

income (GDP or national income (Y)), ($E = Y$). This equilibrium is referred to as equilibrium in the goods market. Equilibrium in the money market is given by the intersection of the demand for money and the supply of **real money balances**. The goods market and the money market are both interrelated with the linking factor being the interest rate.

FIGURE 20.3

The Slope of the Expenditure Line and Changes in Autonomous Expenditure

Panel (a) shows a relatively shallow expenditure line which would mean that the marginal propensity to withdraw would be high and the value of the multiplier was relatively low. The impact on national income (ΔY) of a change in government spending (ΔG) would be more limited in comparison to the effect as shown in panel (b) where the expenditure line is much steeper reflecting a higher value of the multiplier where the MPW was relatively low. In this case it takes a smaller rise in government spending to achieve the same increase in national income.

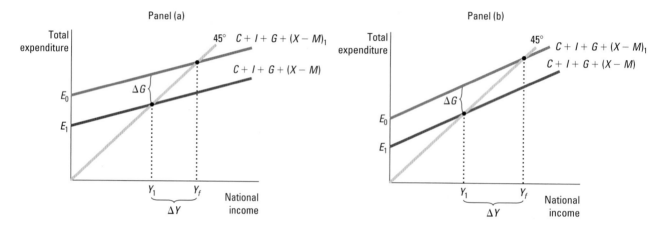

JEOPARDY PROBLEM

Over a 30-year period a government adopts demand management policies as its primary weapon in managing its economy. After 20 years, politicians are congratulating themselves on maintaining low levels of inflation, consistent growth of around 2 per cent a year and unemployment below 5 per cent. However, in the next few years things seem to go wrong. Unemployment starts to rise and inflation accelerates to over 9 per cent. What might have gone wrong?

SUPPLY-SIDE POLICIES

supply-side policy policy aimed at influencing the level of aggregate supply in the economy

Supply-side policy is a macroeconomic policy that seeks to improve the efficiency of the operation of markets in an economy to increase the capacity of the economy. The aim of such a policy is to shift the aggregate supply curve to the right and in so doing generate economic growth (and thus reduce unemployment) but without creating inflationary pressures.

This is illustrated in Figure 20.4. The aggregate supply curve is shown as a curve which gets steeper as it approaches full employment output Y_f, where the long-run aggregate supply would be vertical. Assume equilibrium output is initially at a price level of 2.3 per cent and an output level of Y_0 where the AD curve cuts the AS curve. If the capacity of the economy was increased by policies which shift the AS curve to

FIGURE 20.4

Shifting Aggregate Supply

Successful supply-side policies could increase the capacity of the economy by shifting the AS curve to the right to AS₁. Given aggregate demand (AD), the economy could now support an increased level of capacity from Y_f to Y_{f2} and lower inflation from 2.3 per cent to 2.0 per cent.

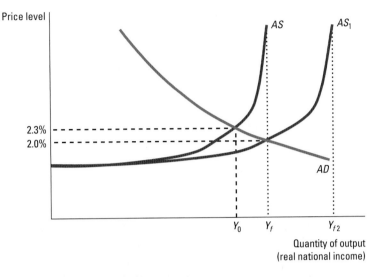

the right to AS_1, then the economy could not only support a higher level of output (and hence reduce unemployment) but also reduce the price level to 2.0 per cent.

Supply-side policies are characterized by a number of features detailed in the following subsections.

Deregulation   Deregulation refers to the removal of controls, laws or rules governing a particular market aimed at improving the economic efficiency of that market and therefore the performance of the economy at the microeconomic level. An example would be the abandonment of a licencing system for taxis or reducing the processes, procedures and paperwork that entrepreneurs need to go through in order to set up a new business. **Deregulation** aims to help promote enterprise, risk and incentives and create a climate where private businesses can go about their activities unencumbered by bureaucracy and distractions.

deregulation the removal of controls, laws or rules governing a particular market aimed at improving the economic efficiency of that market and therefore the performance of the economy at the microeconomic level

Tax Laws   Reducing the tax burden on individuals and companies is seen as a key part of supply-side policy with the aim of promoting incentives which may include incentives to work rather than claim benefits, to be entrepreneurial, to invest and to expand. Part of such tax changes might include reductions in business taxes on profits and payroll and reductions in income taxes. The emphasis may instead be switched from direct to indirect taxes so that people have choices as to whether they spent money on items that attracted indirect taxes such as value added tax (VAT) but did not have such choices with regard to their income. Part of the basis for reducing income taxes is linked to the Laffer Curve.

So the story goes, in 1974, the American economist Arthur Laffer sat in a Washington restaurant with some prominent journalists and politicians. He took out a napkin and drew a figure on it to show how tax rates affect tax revenue. It looked much like Figure 20.5. Laffer then suggested that the United States was on the downward sloping side of this curve. Tax rates were so high, he argued, that reducing them would actually raise tax revenue. Economists have, however, found it hard to trace any strong incentive effects of these tax cuts leading to increases in total tax revenue, as the Laffer curve would suggest. A study by the UK Institute for Fiscal Studies (IFS), for example, concluded that at most about 3 per

FIGURE 20.5

The Laffer Curve

The Laffer curve is the name given to the relationship between tax and revenue which shows that tax revenue rises at first but then falls.

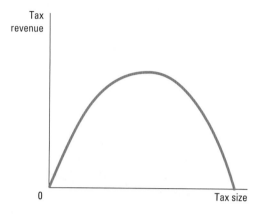

cent of the increase in tax revenue between 1980 and 1986 in the UK could be attributed to income tax cuts in 1980. Evidence from the US was less convincing.

Laffer's argument is not completely without merit, however. Although an overall cut in tax rates normally reduces revenue, some taxpayers at some times may be on the wrong side of the Laffer curve. The idea that cutting taxes can raise revenue may be correct if applied to those taxpayers facing the highest tax rates, but most people face lower marginal rates. Where the typical worker is on the top end of the Laffer curve, it may be more appropriate. In Sweden in the early 1980s, for instance, the typical worker faced a marginal tax rate of about 80 per cent. Such a high tax rate provides a substantial disincentive to work. Studies have suggested that Sweden would indeed have raised more tax revenue if it had lowered its tax rates.

Part of the disagreement over the Laffer curve is about the size of the relevant elasticities. The more elastic that supply and demand are in any market, the more taxes in that market distort behaviour, and the more likely it is that a tax cut will raise tax revenue. There is no debate, however, about the general lesson: how much revenue the government gains or loses from a tax change cannot be computed just by looking at tax rates. It also depends on how the tax change affects people's behaviour.

Welfare Reform The welfare policies adopted by countries are designed to help support those in society who are most vulnerable. Welfare benefits may include some sort of health insurance, unemployment insurance, disability and housing benefits and so on. However, whilst the system is designed to support the most vulnerable, it is invariably also open to abuse and accusations that some individuals in society come to rely on state benefits rather than helping themselves. When this happens, long-term unemployment becomes more likely and not only is the opportunity cost of lost output a factor in reducing the efficiency of the economy, but government spending increases.

Adjustments to welfare policy, therefore, aim to reverse these incentives and to encourage those out of work to try to find employment rather than rely on the state. This might include amendments to the tax and benefits system that make the hoops people have to go through to claim benefit harder as well as making the financial incentive of getting work more significant. Such a policy is fraught with problems because every individual who feels they have a need which society should help them with might expect some support, but the definition of what those needs are and what level of support is required, vary tremendously. There is also the problem of the poverty trap — the problems people face when moving from state support to work whereby tax systems may mean an individual can be worse off by having a job because they become liable for paying tax. Every government is very aware of the potential for damaging news headlines about how policies have left families 'in need' hungry, destitute and worse off as a result.

Flexible Labour Markets

Flexible labour markets focus on the ease with which the demand and supply of labour responds to changing wage conditions. This determines the extent to which unemployment or underemployment will exist in the economy. **Underemployment** is a situation where a worker has a job but may not be working to full capacity or does not have all their skills utilized or is working for a lower income than their qualifications, training or experience might suggest.

Elements of reforming the labour market to make it more flexible might include new employment regulations or legislation relating to the hiring, firing and dealing with employees. A firm with a very seasonal operation, for example, may need large numbers of workers at certain times of the year but very few at others. If the market mechanism is working effectively then, in theory, the firm will be able to do this but if there are restrictions to the working of the labour market then this may not be possible and as such, workers may be left without jobs that technically are available; or where a firm has labour which is underutilized because they have to be retained and paid even if there is insufficient work for them.

The more flexibility firms have to match the workforce to their output needs, the more efficient they can be but this can mean that workers' rights can be compromised. Measures may be taken to help improve job search as mentioned in Chapter 19 through helping both **geographical mobility**, the ease with which people can move to different parts of the country where jobs may be available, and **occupational mobility**, the ease with which people are able to move from occupation to occupation including the degree to which skills and qualifications are transferable between occupations.

Education and Training

Investment in human capital to help improve productivity, innovation and creativity are factors we have mentioned earlier in the book. However, important questions emerge about whom should pay for training – the state or the employer – and what type of qualifications structure should a country put in place? Should science and engineering courses be prioritized at the expense of arts and humanities courses? Should education and training be aimed at preparing people for work or is education more than that? Should students in higher education pay for their studies or should the state subsidize it?

Whatever the answers to these questions, the importance of having a well-educated workforce is crucial to the economic well-being of a country and it is generally agreed that the link between high standards and levels of education in a country and productive capacity (aggregate supply in other words) is clear.

Infrastructure

Investment in infrastructure can take on many forms but ultimately the aim is to help the economy operate more efficiently. Whether this be through improved transport links which help speed up delivery and distribution, reducing congestion, providing better schools and medical facilities (including keeping the population healthy and thus reducing days missed at work through ill-health), promoting entrepreneurship, reliable energy supplies, technology solutions and communications. The latter is particularly important in an economy that is based around knowledge and information exchange, which many service industry economies are. Having fast broadband access, good telephone links, mobile and cell phone signals is almost essential for knowledge-based economies and service industries.

Investment in new technologies for information exchange, for example, can also help job search by providing help to both employers and employees seeking information about vacancies and skills available as well as helping improve geographical mobility.

---

underemployment a situation where a worker has a job but may not be working to full capacity or does not have all their skills utilized or is working for a lower income than their qualifications, training or experience might suggest

geographical mobility the ease with which people can move to different parts of the country where jobs may be available

occupational mobility the ease with which people are able to move from occupation to occupation including the degree to which skills and qualifications are transferable between occupations

Trade Unions We saw in Chapter 14 how trade union activity can distort the working of the labour market. Partly because of the belief by some politicians that trade unions had become too powerful and that the distorting effects too significant, and partly because of changed working practices, the role of trade unions in many countries has changed in the last 20 years. The number of days lost to industrial action has fallen and unions now tend to take on roles that help support workers in legal disputes, with certain types of welfare and financial advice as well as representing the views of workers in national policy debates.

Summary

The three main policies outlined above are not used independently of each other nor exclusively. The extent to which a country has control over fiscal and monetary policy does depend on particular circumstances. In Europe, for example, governments in the eurozone have surrendered control of monetary policy to the European Central Bank and discussions in the latter part of 2011 and into 2012 have been ongoing regarding greater fiscal unity within the eurozone as a result of the debt problems faced by some countries. In the UK, South Africa and parts of the Middle East, governments have control over fiscal policy but have handed over control of monetary policy to the country's central bank.

Where countries do have some control over fiscal policy, decisions made are not simply designed to influence macroeconomic variables like growth, unemployment or inflation but also to focus on specific microeconomic goals which may be associated with a broader supply-side policy. Examples include increasing funds available for research into science and technology or improving transport and communication networks which are publicly funded.

> **Pitfall Prevention** Remember that monetary, fiscal and supply-side policies tend to be used together in order to target not only macroeconomic objectives but also microeconomic objectives which may help boost the overall efficiency of the economy. Given the prevailing economic orthodoxy of the day, one policy might take more prominence than another but the reality is that the three have to work in harmony.

HOW MONETARY POLICY INFLUENCES AGGREGATE DEMAND

In this next section we are going to look at how monetary and fiscal policy affect aggregate demand. To understand how policy influences aggregate demand, we need to examine the interest rate effect in more detail. Here we develop a theory of how the interest rate is determined, called the **theory of liquidity preference**, which was originally developed by John Maynard Keynes in the 1930s.

theory of liquidity preference
Keynes' theory that the interest rate adjusts to bring money supply and money demand into balance

The Theory of Liquidity Preference

The theory is, in essence, just an application of supply and demand. According to Keynes, the interest rate adjusts to balance the supply and demand for money. In the analysis that follows, we hold constant the expected rate of inflation. (This assumption is reasonable for studying the economy in the short run.) Thus, when the nominal interest rate rises or falls, the real interest rate that people expect to earn rises or falls as well. For the rest of this chapter, when we refer to changes in the interest rate, you should envision the real and nominal interest rates moving in the same direction.

Money Supply   The first element of the theory of liquidity preference is the supply of money. The money supply is controlled by the central bank which can alter the money supply by changing the quantity of reserves in the banking system through the purchase and sale of government bonds in outright open-market operations. In addition to these open-market operations, the central bank can alter the money supply by changing reserve requirements (the amount of reserves banks must hold against deposits) or the refinancing rate (the interest rate at which banks can borrow reserves from the central bank). For the purpose of our analysis we are going to assume that the quantity of money supplied in the economy is fixed at whatever level the central bank decides to set it.

Because the quantity of money supplied is fixed by central bank policy, it does not depend on other economic variables. In particular, it does not depend on the interest rate. Once the central bank has made its policy decision, the quantity of money supplied is the same, regardless of the prevailing interest rate. We represent a fixed money supply with a vertical supply curve in Figure 20.6.

FIGURE 20.6

Equilibrium in the Money Market

According to the theory of liquidity preference, the interest rate adjusts to bring the quantity of money supplied and the quantity of money demanded into balance. If the interest rate is above the equilibrium level (such as at r_1), the quantity of money people want to hold (M_1^d) is less than the quantity the central bank has created, and this surplus of money puts downward pressure on the interest rate. Conversely, if the interest rate is below the equilibrium level (such as at r_2), the quantity of money people want to hold (M_2^d) is greater than the quantity the central bank has created, and this shortage of money puts upward pressure on the interest rate. Thus, the forces of supply and demand in the market for money push the interest rate towards the equilibrium interest rate, at which people are content holding the quantity of money the central bank has created.

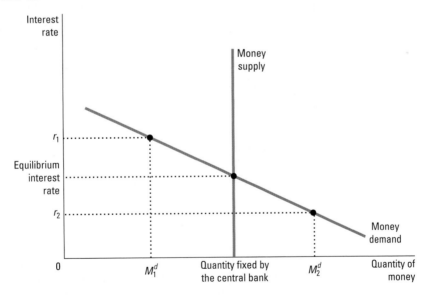

Money Demand   The second element of the theory of liquidity preference is the demand for money. Any asset's *liquidity* refers to the ease with which that asset is converted into the economy's medium of exchange. Money is the economy's medium of exchange, so it is by definition the most liquid asset available. The liquidity of money explains the demand for it: businesses and people choose to hold money instead of other assets that offer higher rates of return because money can be used to buy raw materials, equipment and goods and services.

Although many factors determine the quantity of money demanded, the one emphasized by the theory of liquidity preference is the interest rate. The reason is that the interest rate is the opportunity cost of holding money. That is, when wealth is held as cash, instead of as an interest-bearing bond or bank account, the benefits of the interest which could have been earned (the opportunity cost) are foregone. An increase in the interest rate raises the opportunity cost of holding money. Figure 20.6 shows the money demand curve sloping downward. At higher interest rates the opportunity cost in terms of foregone interest is higher and so demand for money as cash is lower than at lower interest rates.

Equilibrium in the Money Market   According to the theory of liquidity preference, the interest rate adjusts to balance the supply and demand for money. There is one interest rate, called the *equilibrium interest rate,* at which the quantity of money demanded exactly balances the quantity of money supplied. If the interest rate is at any other level, businesses and people will try to adjust their portfolios of assets and, as a result, drive the interest rate toward the equilibrium.

For example, suppose that the interest rate is above the equilibrium level, such as r_1 in Figure 20.6. In this case, the quantity of money that businesses and people want to hold, M_t^d, is less than the quantity of money that the central bank has supplied. Those who are holding the surplus of money will try to get rid of it by buying interest-bearing bonds or by depositing it in an interest-bearing bank account. Because bond issuers and banks prefer to pay lower interest rates, they respond to this surplus of money by lowering the interest rates they offer. As the interest rate falls, people become more willing to hold money until, at the equilibrium interest rate, businesses and people are happy to hold exactly the amount of money the central bank has supplied.

Conversely, at interest rates below the equilibrium level, such as r_2 in Figure 20.6, the quantity of money that people want to hold, M_2^d, is greater than the quantity of money that the central bank has supplied. As a result, businesses and people try to increase their holdings of money by reducing their holdings of bonds and other interest-bearing assets. As holdings of bonds are reduced, bond issuers find that they have to offer higher interest rates to attract buyers. Thus, the interest rate rises and approaches the equilibrium level.

The Downward Slope of the Aggregate Demand Curve   Suppose that the overall level of prices in the economy rises. What happens to the interest rate that balances the supply and demand for money, and how does that change affect the quantity of goods and services demanded?

The price level is one determinant of the quantity of money demanded. At higher prices, more money is exchanged every time a good or service is sold. As a result, businesses and people will choose to hold a larger quantity of money. That is, a higher price level increases the quantity of money demanded for any given interest rate. Thus, an increase in the price level from P_1 to P_2 shifts the money demand curve to the right from MD_1 to MD_2, as shown in panel (a) of Figure 20.7.

Notice how this shift in money demand affects the equilibrium in the money market. For a fixed money supply, the interest rate must rise to balance money supply and money demand. The higher price level has increased the amount of money businesses and people want to hold, and has shifted the money demand curve to the right. Yet the quantity of money supplied is unchanged, so the interest rate must rise from r_1 to r_2 to discourage the additional demand.

This increase in the interest rate has ramifications not only for the money market but also for the quantity of goods and services demanded, as shown in panel (b). At a higher interest rate, the cost of borrowing and the return to saving are greater. Fewer households choose to borrow to buy a new house, and those who do buy smaller houses, so the demand for residential investment falls. Fewer firms choose to borrow to build new factories and buy new equipment, so business investment falls. Thus, when the price level rises from P_1 to P_2, increasing money demand from MD_1 to MD_2 and raising the interest rate from r_1 to r_2, the quantity of goods and services demanded falls from Y_1 to Y_2.

Of course, the same logic works in reverse as well: a lower price level reduces money demand, which leads to a lower interest rate, and this in turn increases the quantity of goods and services demanded. The end result of this analysis is a negative relationship between the price level and the quantity of goods and services demanded, which is illustrated with a downward sloping aggregate demand curve.

FIGURE 20.7

The Money Market and the Slope of the Aggregate Demand Curve

An increase in the price level from P_1 to P_2 shifts the money demand curve to the right, as in panel (a). This increase in money demand causes the interest rate to rise from r_1 to r_2. Because the interest rate is the cost of borrowing, the increase in the interest rate reduces the quantity of goods and services demanded from Y_1 to Y_2. This negative relationship between the price level and quantity demanded is represented with a downward sloping aggregate demand curve, as in panel (b).

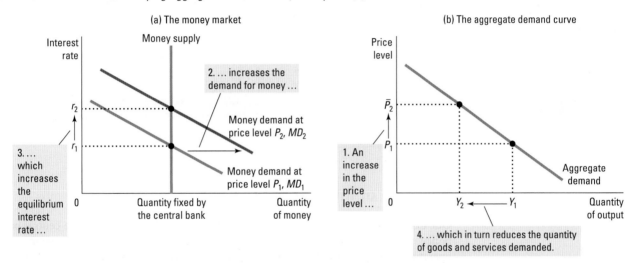

Changes in the Money Supply

Whenever the quantity of goods and services demanded changes *for a given price level,* the aggregate demand curve shifts. Suppose that the central bank increases the money supply by buying government bonds in open-market operations. Let's consider how this monetary injection influences the equilibrium interest rate for a given price level. This will tell us what the injection does to the position of the aggregate demand curve.

As panel (a) of Figure 20.8 shows, an increase in the money supply shifts the money-supply curve to the right from MS_1 to MS_2. Because the money demand curve has not changed, the interest rate falls from r_1 to r_2 to balance money supply and money demand. That is, the interest rate must fall to induce people to hold the additional money that the central bank has created.

Once again, the interest rate influences the quantity of goods and services demanded, as shown in panel (b) of Figure 20.8. The lower interest rate reduces the cost of borrowing and the return to saving. Households buy more and larger houses, stimulating the demand for residential investment. Firms spend more on new factories and new equipment, stimulating business investment. As a result, the quantity of goods and services demanded at a given price level $\bar{P}$, rises from Y_1 to Y_2. Of course, there is nothing special about $\bar{P}$: the monetary injection raises the quantity of goods and services demanded at every price level. Thus, the entire aggregate demand curve shifts to the right. Conversely, when the central bank contracts the money supply, the interest rate rises to bring the money market into equilibrium and reduces the quantity of goods and services demanded for any given price level, shifting the aggregate demand curve to the left.

FIGURE 20.8

A Monetary Injection

In panel (a), an increase in the money supply from MS₁ to MS₂ reduces the equilibrium interest rate from r₁ to r₂. Because the interest rate is the cost of borrowing, the fall in the interest rate raises the quantity of goods and services demanded at a given price level from Y₁ to Y₂. Thus, in panel (b), the aggregate demand curve shifts to the right from AD₁ to AD₂.

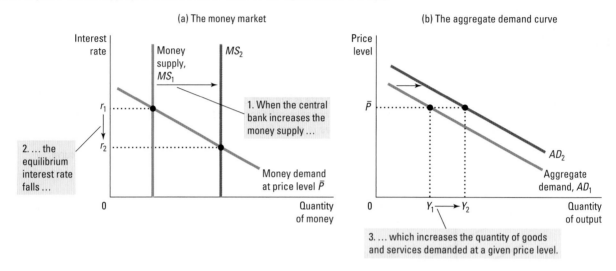

The Role of Interest Rates

Our discussion so far in this chapter has treated the money supply as the central bank's policy instrument. When the central bank buys government bonds in open-market operations, it increases the money supply and expands aggregate demand. When the central bank sells government bonds in open-market operations, it decreases the money supply and contracts aggregate demand.

Often, however, discussions of central bank policy treat the interest rate, rather than the money supply, as the central bank's policy instrument. Some central banks conduct policy by setting the interest rate at which they will lend to the banking sector – the refinancing rate for the European Central Bank, the repurchase or 'repo' rate for the Bank of England, and the discount rate for the Federal Reserve.

The central bank's decision to set interest rates rather than target a certain level (or rate of growth) of the money supply does not fundamentally alter our analysis of monetary policy. The theory of liquidity preference illustrates an important principle: monetary policy can be described either in terms of the money supply or in terms of the interest rate. When the central bank sets a target for the refinancing rate of, say, *x* per cent, the central bank's bond traders are told: 'Conduct whatever open-market operations are necessary to ensure that the equilibrium interest rate equals *x* per cent.' In other words, when the central bank sets a target for the interest rate, it commits itself to adjusting the money supply in order to make the equilibrium in the money market hit that target.

As a result, changes in monetary policy can be viewed either in terms of a changing target for the interest rate or in terms of a change in the money supply.

Quick Quiz Use the theory of liquidity preference to explain how a decrease in the money supply affects the equilibrium interest rate. How does this change in monetary policy affect the demand curve?

HOW FISCAL POLICY INFLUENCES AGGREGATE DEMAND

In the short run, the primary effect of fiscal policy is on the aggregate demand for goods and services.

Changes in Government Purchases

We have seen that changes in autonomous spending can have an effect on the level of spending in the economy which is greater than the initial injection. The multiplier effect means that aggregate demand will shift by a larger amount than the increase in government spending. However, the **crowding-out effect** suggests that the shift in aggregate demand could be *smaller* than the initial injection.

crowding-out effect the offset in aggregate demand that results when expansionary fiscal policy raises the interest rate and thereby reduces investment spending

The Crowding-Out Effect

In Chapter 15 we introduced the concept of 'crowding out'. To see why crowding out occurs, let's consider what happens in the money market when the government invests in nuclear power stations from Nucelec. As we have discussed, this increase in demand raises the incomes of the workers and owners of this firm (and, because of the multiplier effect, of other firms as well). As incomes rise, households plan to buy more goods and services and, as a result, choose to hold more of their wealth in liquid form. That is, the increase in income caused by the fiscal expansion raises the demand for money.

The effect of the increase in money demand is shown in panel (a) of Figure 20.9. Because the central bank has not changed the money supply, the vertical supply curve

---

FIGURE 20.9

The Crowding-Out Effect

Panel (a) shows the money market. When the government increases its purchases of goods and services, the resulting increase in income raises the demand for money from MD_1 to MD_2, and this causes the equilibrium interest rate to rise from r_1 to r_2. Panel (b) shows the effects on aggregate demand. The initial impact of the increase in government purchases shifts the aggregate demand curve from AD_1 to AD_2. Yet, because the interest rate is the cost of borrowing, the increase in the interest rate tends to reduce the quantity of goods and services demanded, particularly for investment goods. This crowding out of investment partially offsets the impact of the fiscal expansion on aggregate demand. In the end, the aggregate demand curve shifts only to AD_3

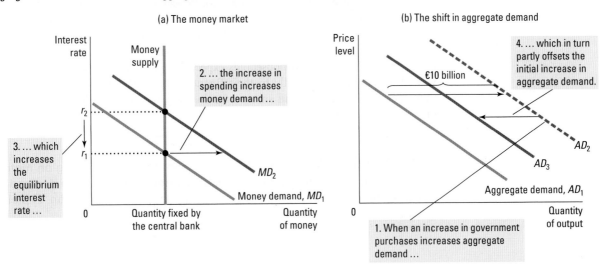

remains the same. When the higher level of income shifts the money demand curve to the right from MD_1 to MD_2, the interest rate must rise from r_1 to r_2 to keep supply and demand in balance.

The increase in the interest rate, in turn, reduces the quantity of goods and services demanded. In particular, because borrowing is more expensive, the demand for residential and business investment goods declines. That is, as the increase in government purchases increases the demand for goods and services, it may also crowd out investment. This crowding-out effect partially offsets the impact of government purchases on aggregate demand, as illustrated in panel (b) of Figure 20.9. The initial impact of the increase in government purchases is to shift the aggregate demand curve from AD_1 to AD_2, but once crowding out takes place, the aggregate demand curve drops back to AD_3.

To sum up: when the government increases its purchases by €10 billion, the aggregate demand for goods and services could rise by more or less than €10 billion, depending on whether the multiplier effect or the crowding-out effect is larger.

Changes in Taxes

The other important instrument of fiscal policy, besides the level of government purchases, is the level of taxation. When the government cuts personal income taxes, for instance, it increases households' take-home pay. Households will save some of this additional income, but they will also spend some of it on consumer goods. Because it increases consumer spending, the tax cut shifts the aggregate demand curve to the right. Similarly, a tax increase depresses consumer spending and shifts the aggregate demand curve to the left.

The size of the shift in aggregate demand resulting from a tax change is also affected by the multiplier and crowding-out effects. When the government cuts taxes and stimulates consumer spending, earnings and profits rise, which further stimulates consumer spending. This is the multiplier effect. At the same time, higher income leads to higher money demand, which tends to raise interest rates. Higher interest rates make borrowing more costly, which reduces investment spending. This is the crowding-out effect. Depending on the size of the multiplier and crowding-out effects, the shift in aggregate demand could be larger or smaller than the tax change that causes it.

In addition to the multiplier and crowding-out effects, there is another important determinant of the size of the shift in aggregate demand that results from a tax change: households' perceptions about whether the tax change is permanent or temporary. For example, suppose that the government announces a tax cut of €1000 per household. In deciding how much of this €1000 to spend, households must ask themselves how long this extra income will last. If households expect the tax cut to be permanent, they will view it as adding substantially to their financial resources and, therefore, increase their spending by a large amount. In this case, the tax cut will have a large impact on aggregate demand. By contrast, if households expect the tax change to be temporary, they will view it as adding only slightly to their financial resources and, therefore, will increase their spending by only a small amount. In this case, the tax cut will have a small impact on aggregate demand.

Quick Quiz Suppose that the government reduces spending on motorway construction by €1 billion. Which way does the aggregate demand curve shift? Explain why the shift might be larger than €1 billion. Explain why the shift might be smaller than €1 billion.

CONCLUSION

Before policy makers make any change in policy, they need to consider all the effects of their decisions. In this chapter we looked at three main policies that can be adopted to influence the economy. We then examined the short-run effects of monetary and fiscal policy. We saw how these policy instruments can change the aggregate demand for goods and services and, thereby, alter the economy's production and employment in the short run. When the government reduces spending in order to balance the budget, it needs to consider both the long-run effects on saving and growth and the short-run effects on aggregate demand and employment. When the central bank reduces the growth rate of the money supply, it must take into account the long-run effect on inflation as well as the short-run effect on production.

IN THE NEWS

Supply-Side Policies

This article looks at a perspective on adopting supply-side policies in India.

India needs a dose of supply-side economics

One useful way to understand the economic situation right now is through a motoring analogy: Has the Indian economy hit a speed bump or is it suffering from engine trouble? A lot depends on the answer. A speed bump leads to a temporary loss of momentum. Engine trouble leads to a stuttering journey that could even end in an unexpected halt. The nature of the economic strategy that finance minister Pranab Mukherjee unveils on Friday [16 March 2012] will be critically dependent on how he reads the economic situation: is it a speed bump or engine trouble?

It increasingly looks like the latter. The economy has been losing momentum for several quarters. The Reserve Bank of India has already indicated that the rate of economic growth that can be sustained without sparking off an inflationary fire is now 7 per cent, a full 1.5 percentage points lower than the years before the financial crisis. India seems to have moved to a

lower growth trajectory. And India is likely in a structural rather than cyclical slowdown.

The problem has its roots in two policy failures: the lack of any significant economic reforms since 2004 and the callous disregard of the growing fiscal deficit after 2008. The reforms inertia has generated serious constraints in important sectors such as agriculture, energy, logistics and infrastructure that could eventually compromise the long-term growth trajectory. Fiscal profligacy has led to a perverse inflationary stimulus to consumption at a time when India needs more investments in new production capacity.

Both policy failures are intimately linked to the politics of the United Progressive Alliance. Both have combined to lead India down a path marked by declining growth and rising inflation. Both have put future prosperity at risk. What India needs right now is a healthy dose of supply-side economics – a set of policies that will help raise the national investment rate as well as address serious structural constraints such as energy.

So the implicit economic strategy in the finance minister's speech on Friday will be as important as the actual budget arithmetic. To be sure, the wide gap between government revenue and spending is the most immediate source of worry. India has traditionally been more successful in closing this gap through increasing tax revenues rather than spending cuts. The politics of austerity can be a death warrant in India. Raising tax revenue in a slowing economy is a tough task. What needs to be watched is whether the cycle of tax cuts that began in 1985 will now be replaced by a regime of rising tax rates. There is ample speculation about the revival of the wealth tax, a special tax for the super-rich, higher taxes on stock market profits, a tax on personal wealth held abroad. The other option is to move ahead with overdue tax reforms, especially the direct taxes code and the goods and services tax.

There are challenges on the spending side as well. The ruling alliance is committed to ambitious entitlement programmes that are supposed to help the poor. The regime led by Sonia Gandhi and Manmohan Singh has front-loaded a lot of these spending commitments, perhaps in the belief that guaranteed 9 per cent-plus growth would generate ample tax revenue to fund these commitments. The recent loss of economic momentum has torn that assumption to shreds, hopefully forcing the government to take a hard look at its spending bill. One obvious, though politically challenging, target would be subsidies, especially the fuel and fertilizer subsidies that are cornered by the middle class and large farmers.

Budget 2012 will be unveiled at a time when there are momentous changes in the Chinese economy. Its labour force is peaking. Wage costs are going up. There is continuous international pressure on its government to let the yuan appreciate even further. These developments have encouraged the Chinese leadership to accept a lower growth target as well as to begin moving its economy up the value chain. The changes in the Chinese economic model open up a tremendous opportunity for India to move in as the low-cost workshop of the world, generating millions of jobs that will allow people to escape the overcrowded farming sector.

However, the process will not be an automatic one. India needs huge investments in infrastructure, energy and skills before it can step into the void. It needs more efficient markets for factors of production such as capital, land and labour. It needs a single domestic market that allows companies to plan their manufacturing facilities in an efficient manner.

The new budget needs to be understood against this wider backdrop. A fiscal correction will raise national savings. Economic reforms will boost investment activity. These will help shift the aggregate supply curve to the right. India can neither create enough jobs nor fund an ambitious welfare state without faster economic growth. It is no coincidence that the rate of poverty reduction in India picked up between 2005 and 2010, a five-year period when economic growth averaged 8.6 per cent, and when 67 million Indians were pulled above the international poverty line of $1.25 a day, according to World Bank data. Supply-side policies are the best bet if India has to steer clear of the new normal of 7 per cent growth, some 2.5 percentage points below its peak in 2006–07.

Niranjan Rajadhyaksha

Questions

1. What do you think is the difference between a 'structural slowdown' and a 'cyclical slowdown'?
2. The author suggests that 'Fiscal profligacy has led to a perverse inflationary stimulus to consumption at a time when India needs more investments in new production capacity'. Using appropriate diagrams, explain how this situation could have arisen and how investment in production capacity could help alleviate the problem.
3. Why is 'raising tax revenue in a slowing economy' a 'tough task'?
4. Analyze how supply-side policies might help the Indian economy to 'steer clear of the new normal of 7 per cent growth'.
5. The author notes changes in the Chinese economy and suggests that these changes represent an opportunity for India to 'move in as the low-cost workshop of the world'. What do you think the author means by this and how might supply-side policies help achieve such a goal?

Source: http://www.livemint.com/2012/03/14235531/India-needs-a-dose-of-supplys.html accessed 16 March 2012.

SUMMARY

- The three main policies used to affect economic activity are monetary policy, fiscal policy and supply-side policy.
- Keynes developed The General Theory as a response to the mass unemployment which existed in the 1930s.
- He advocated governments intervene to boost demand through influencing aggregate demand.
- The Keynesian cross diagram shows how the economy can be in equilibrium when E = Y.
- This equilibrium may not be sufficient to deliver full employment output and so the government can attempt to boost demand to help achieve full employment.
- Supply-side policies aim to improve the efficiency of the economy and increase the capacity of the economy by shifting the aggregate supply curve to the right.

- Key elements of a supply-side policy include tax and welfare reforms, improving the flexibility of labour markets including trade union reform, education and training, and investing in improved infrastructure.
- In developing a theory of short-run economic fluctuations, Keynes proposed the theory of liquidity preference to explain the determinants of the interest rate. According to this theory, the interest rate adjusts to balance the supply and demand for money.
- An increase in the price level raises money demand and increases the interest rate that brings the money market into equilibrium. Because the interest rate represents the cost of borrowing, a higher interest rate reduces investment and, thereby, the quantity of goods and services demanded.

The downward sloping aggregate demand curve expresses this negative relationship between the price level and the quantity demanded.

- Policy makers can influence aggregate demand with monetary policy. An increase in the money supply reduces the equilibrium interest rate for any given price level. Because a lower interest rate stimulates investment spending, the aggregate demand curve shifts to the right. Conversely, a decrease in the money supply raises the equilibrium interest rate for any given price level and shifts the aggregate demand curve to the left.

- Policy makers can also influence aggregate demand with fiscal policy. An increase in government purchases or a cut in taxes shifts the aggregate demand curve to the right. A decrease in government purchases or an increase in taxes shifts the aggregate demand curve to the left.

- When the government alters spending or taxes, the resulting shift in aggregate demand can be larger or smaller than the fiscal change. The multiplier effect tends to amplify the effects of fiscal policy on aggregate demand. The crowding-out effect tends to dampen the effects of fiscal policy on aggregate demand.

KEY CONCEPTS

monetary policy, p. 491
money multiplier, p. 495
fiscal policy, p. 496
full employment, p. 497
planned spending, saving or investment, p. 497
actual spending, saving or investment, p. 497

deflationary gap, p. 497
multiplier effect, p. 498
marginal propensity to consume, p. 499
marginal propensity to save, p. 499
autonomous expenditure, p. 501
real money balances, p. 502
supply-side policy, p. 502
deregulation, p. 503

underemployment, p. 505
geographical mobility, p. 505
occupational mobility, p. 505
theory of liquidity preference, p. 506
crowding-out effect, p. 511

QUESTIONS FOR REVIEW

1. Define monetary policy, fiscal policy and supply-side policy.

2. Explain how the interest rate transmission mechanism works to bring about changes in the components of aggregate demand and help to boost growth.

3. Distinguish between planned expenditure and actual expenditure.

4. Draw a Keynesian cross diagram to show the effects of a rise in autonomous expenditure on an economy operating below full employment output.

5. Explain how the marginal propensity to withdraw affects the outcome of a rise in autonomous expenditure.

6. How can supply-side policies help an economy to produce greater output, reduce unemployment but reduce the price level at the same time?

7. Why are flexible labour markets such an important element in supply-side policies.

8. What is the theory of liquidity preference? How does it help explain the downward slope of the aggregate demand curve?

9. Use the theory of liquidity preference to explain how a decrease in the money supply affects the aggregate demand curve.

10. The government spends €500 million to buy police cars. Explain why aggregate demand might increase by more than €500 million. Explain why aggregate demand might increase by less than €500 million.

PROBLEMS AND APPLICATIONS

1. Prior to national elections, the existing government says that if elected again it wants to focus on delivering the following:
   a. a reduction in child poverty
   b. improvements in productivity in manufacturing industries
   c. increases in investment by businesses
   d. a reduction in the rate of inflation.
   What policy options would you suggest the government use to deliver these objectives?

2. Explain, using an appropriate diagram, how a deflationary gap can occur and how this gap can be eliminated.

3. Suppose economists observe that an increase in government spending of €10 billion raises the total demand for goods and services by €30 billion.
   a. If these economists ignore the possibility of crowding out, what would they estimate the marginal propensity to consume (MPC) to be?
   b. Now suppose the economists allow for crowding out. Would their new estimate of the MPC be larger or smaller than their initial one? Explain your answer.

4. Suppose the government reduces taxes by €2 billion, that there is no crowding out, and that the marginal propensity to consume is 0.75:
   a. What is the initial effect of the tax reduction on aggregate demand?
   b. What additional effects follow this initial effect? What is the total effect of the tax cut on aggregate demand?
   c. How does the total effect of this €2 billion tax cut compare to the total effect of a €2 billion increase in government purchases? Why?

5. Explain how each of the following developments would affect the supply of money, the demand for money and the interest rate. Illustrate your answers with diagrams.
   a. The central bank's bond traders buy bonds in open-market operations.
   b. An increase in credit card availability reduces the cash people hold.
   c. The central bank reduces banks' reserve requirements.
   d. Households decide to hold more money to use for holiday shopping.
   e. A wave of optimism boosts business investment and expands aggregate demand.
   f. An increase in oil prices shifts the short-run aggregate supply curve to the left.

6. Suppose banks install automatic teller machines on every street corner and, by making cash readily available, reduce the amount of money people want to hold.
   a. Assume the central bank does not change the money supply. According to the theory of liquidity preference, what happens to the interest rate? What happens to aggregate demand?
   b. If the central bank wants to stabilize aggregate demand, how should it respond?

7. Consider two policies – a tax cut that will last for only one year, and a tax cut that is expected to be permanent. Which policy will stimulate greater spending by consumers? Which policy will have the greater impact on aggregate demand? Explain.

8. The economy is in a recession with high unemployment and low output.
   a. Use a graph of aggregate demand and aggregate supply to illustrate the current situation. Be sure to include the aggregate demand curve, the short-run aggregate supply curve and the long-run aggregate supply curve.
   b. Identify an open-market operation that would restore the economy to its natural rate.
   c. Use a graph of the money market to illustrate the effect of this open-market operation. Show the resulting change in the interest rate.
   d. Use a graph similar to the one in part (a) to show the effect of the open-market operation on output and the price level. Explain in words why the policy has the effect that you have shown in the graph.

9. In which of the following circumstances is expansionary fiscal policy more likely to lead to a short-run increase in investment? Explain.
   a. When the investment accelerator is large, or when it is small?
   b. When the interest sensitivity of investment is large, or when it is small?

10. Assume the economy is in a recession. Explain how each of the following policies would affect consumption and investment. In each case, indicate any direct effects, any effects resulting from changes in total output, any effects resulting from changes in the interest rate and the overall effect. If there are conflicting effects making the answer ambiguous, say so.
    a. an increase in government spending
    b. a reduction in taxes
    c. an expansion of the money supply.

PART 7

GLOBAL BUSINESS
AND ECONOMICS

21 THE GLOBAL ECONOMY

LEARNING OBJECTIVES

In this chapter you will:

- Examine the nature of emerging markets and look at some of the costs and benefits to firms of doing business in emerging markets

- Cover an outline of European monetary union and the single market

- Consider the benefits and costs that might be expected to arise from a country joining a currency union

- Consider fiscal policy in common currency areas

- Examine the practice of outsourcing and consider some of the costs and benefits of outsourcing

- Look at an outline of issues facing business in conducting operations in a global context

After reading this chapter you should be able to:

- Give a definition of an emerging market

- Outline at least three key characteristics of an emerging market

- Be able to present an argument outlining the costs and benefits of doing business in an emerging market.

- Explain the key features of a currency area and a single market

- Explain and illustrate with diagrams the macroeconomic effects of asymmetric shocks in a common currency area, wherein exchange rate adjustment is not possible

- Explain and illustrate with diagrams how fiscal policy could be used for macroeconomic stabilization in the absence of exchange rate adjustment and independent monetary policy

- Present an argument on the costs and benefits of outsourcing

- Outline key issues facing businesses in a global environment

BUSINESS IN EMERGING MARKETS

The economies of the developed world tend to dominate textbooks and the global news media. However, in the last 20 years political and economic changes have meant that increasing focus is now centred on economies in other countries termed 'emerging economies' or 'emerging markets'. An **emerging market economy** is one where the per capita income of the population is in the middle to low range compared to the rest of the global economies. Given the dominance of the developed economies it might be obvious to state that emerging economies account for a very large proportion of all global economies. The United Nations puts the number of emerging economies at 120 out of the 160 it recognizes. That is a lot of countries.

emerging market economy a country where the per capita income of the population is in the middle to low range compared to the rest of the global economies

Each country differs in its state of development but major attention has been focused in recent years on the so-called BRIC countries, Brazil, Russia, India and China. These are countries with huge productive potential due in part to their respective size, population and resource endowment. However, there are a growing number of countries which deserve to be classed in a similar category to these countries in terms of their increasing GDP per capita. These countries include Turkey, South Africa, Mexico, Malaysia, Taiwan, Hungary, Poland and the Czech Republic. Together these countries could be referred to as advanced emerging economies.

Below this a secondary tier of emerging economies likely to include Chile, Indonesia, Philippines, Thailand, the United Arab Emirates, Saudi Arabia, Egypt, Colombia, Peru and Morocco.

Characteristics of Emerging Markets

One of the reasons why these countries are categorized in the terms outlined above is because of their state of economic development. It is not just size that matters but the internal economic structures that are important. Countries like China, Russia, Saudi Arabia and Poland, for example, have been under different types of political regime which have shaped their economic development over the last 100 years. Russia and Poland were former states within the Union of Soviet Socialist Republics (USSR) where a planned market economy was the economic system which determined resource allocation. China was similarly governed by a communist regime although would claim to be following a different brand of communism. In a planned economy, state planning authorities sought to answer the three basic questions of any economic system: what is to be produced, how is it going to be produced and who gets what is produced?

In the former USSR, the state central planning authority was called Gosplan. Its function was to identify what goods and services were needed by the people, how these goods and services would be produced and how the state output would be distributed. Agencies were also given the resources that the planners had worked out would be necessary for producing that output. Most factories and farms were given output targets to reach; once produced, it might be the job of another body to ensure that goods were distributed. In return for the labour expended in producing this output, a wage was given. This wage, however, bore no relation to the value of the output being produced. The wage was planned to allow workers to be able to buy the things the planners had worked out they needed to live on. To enable this to happen, prices were also set by the planning authorities.

In theory, everyone had enough to live on. Wage differentials were minimal – whether you were a highly qualified university professor or a street cleaner, wages only varied by a small amount. Most people had a job if they wanted one, regardless of the type of job; unemployment was therefore zero. Inflation did not exist as we know it because of the system of price fixing and there were very few homeless people – the state provided housing.

State planning, however, was inefficient in comparison to the way in which economies which relied on the price mechanism allocated resources. The assumption that people would work hard for the common good was not always realized. Factories found that if they met their targets or even exceeded them, they were given higher targets next year but not necessarily the resources to achieve them, nor any extra wages – so what was the point? Targets soon appeared to become subject to what has been called 'Goodhart's Law', where targets used to manage something become corrupted to the extent that they cease to be able to be used to measure what you want them to measure!

The communication between the different sectors of the economy was not always good. It was estimated that something of the order of 40 per cent of all agricultural produce rotted before it could be processed or reach its intended markets. Price-fixing meant that the pressure of supply and demand was contained, shortages and surpluses developed and were not eliminated. Product quality fell, negative externalities like pollution increased and inefficiency was endemic.

In Saudi Arabia the situation was somewhat different given the key resource endowment of oil. The country has been able to generate massive wealth as a result of its reserves of oil but its political system is dominated by the Al Saud family. The King fulfils the role of commander-in-chief of the military, prime minister, head of government and chief of state. Saudi Arabia is an Islamic state and justice is governed by Islamic law. There are no political parties in Saudi. This different political and judicial system meant that for many years Saudi was almost a closed economy and indeed this is a key characteristic of emerging economies.

All the countries mentioned above are changing and economic reforms, the establishment of institutions and bodies which reflect broader international standards and regulations are being developed. Economies are taking on more and more characteristics of market economies and the willingness of these countries to engage in trade and open up their economies to outside investment is a major feature of the changes that have taken place. In order for these countries to take a growing part in the global economy it is essential that they have institutions and governance which reflect those of the developed world – why would a business risk investing in setting up operations in these countries if it believed there was not the same or at least similar rules of governance that existed in their home country? Having an economy based on the price mechanism with private property open to trade with the outside world is a characteristic of emerging economies.

It is accepted that there are still, in some cases, major obstacles to the integration of many emerging countries into the global economic system. Not least problems with corruption, questions over human rights and issues over corporate governance and the rule of law, particularly in relation to intellectual property. However, it is also recognized that no country can move from being an essentially closed economy to a fully integrated market economy overnight. This is part of the reason why these economies are referred to as emerging.

Many emerging economies will also have specific advantages which their respective governments are recognizing have some economic value. It might be something to do with resource endowment such as the reserves of oil and gas that exist in Russia, discoveries of oil on the Brazilian coast, copper in Zambia and minerals in other parts of Africa. Or it might be something to do with the huge human resources at the disposal of many emerging economies: China and India both have populations in excess of one billion and this provides huge reserves of cheap labour.

Some of the changes which have brought emerging economies into the global business environment have included a greater degree of political stability. Western governments may disagree fundamentally with the political systems in place in the likes of China and Saudi Arabia, but these countries are stable and as such provide the incentive for investment by businesses. The development of banking and financial sectors, systems and institutions to settle commercial disputes, having more harmonized business law as well as stock markets have also helped accelerate investment into emerging economies.

Why are Emerging Markets So Important?

There is a simple answer to this question – opportunity. Businesses in the developed world are finding that many of the 'traditional' markets they are operating in are mature. The opportunities for growth in these markets are limited; growth is likely to occur in some but only at low rates. Take mobile or cell phones, for example. In the UK, USA, Canada and countries of northern Europe and Scandinavia, penetration into the market is almost total. Virtually every person who wants a cell phone has now got (at least) one so why should they want to buy another? Opportunities exist if new more sophisticated models are brought out, but unless they do something very different the incentive for an individual to give up their existing phone and buy a new one is limited.

© JULIA BLOCH (2012)

However, in a country like Vietnam, for example, cell phone ownership has been growing at a rapid rate. Its 86 million people, therefore, represent a huge market for mobile phone manufacturers and service operators. This is a crucial reason for businesses seeking to do business in emerging markets – there are billions of potential customers. Equally important, many of these people are becoming wealthier and entering the middle classes where spending on the sort of consumer goods which could be classed as luxuries is likely to rise dramatically in the next 50 years.

The links between the increasing development of these economies and the rise in wages of workers in the countries has not been lost on businesses in the developed world. As they continue to industrialize and expand, workers will add more value, get paid more and will have more disposable income. The process may not be rapid but businesses have to look ahead to the next 10 to 20 years for sustained revenue and sales growth rather than the next 5 years.

It is not only businesses selling consumer goods that see the opportunities for securing new markets and growth in sales. Business-to-business (B2B) operations are also recognizing that part of the continued development of emerging economies rests on improved infrastructure. We saw in Chapter 20 how investment in infrastructure was an important feature in improving efficiency and the supply-side of the economy. Investment in energy supplies, telecommunications, internet supplies, construction plant, distribution networks, road and transport networks, and water and sewerage systems are all vital to the continued growth of emerging economies, and firms in the developed world have looked to invest heavily in such opportunities.

Firms that see and seize first mover opportunities may find that there are numerous problems in setting up and doing business in emerging economies but despite these challenges if they are in a position to become established the medium and longer-term benefits in terms of growth opportunities can be extensive. Mistakes will be made but the experience they gain and the scale opportunities that exist mean most want to be involved sooner rather than later for fear of missing the chances that exist. *The Economist* estimates that around 20 000 multinationals are operating in emerging economies and that almost three-quarters of anticipated future growth is expected in these economies.

Problems Facing Business in Emerging Markets

The opportunities for future growth may be large but there are many challenges. One of the biggest is the fact that businesses need to understand the markets they are getting into. Typical of the early forays into emerging markets have been attempts to replicate successful business models in Western developed economy markets in emerging economies. New offices are set up in the country chosen and senior staff installed to set up and run operations. However, many businesses have found that this replication model has not worked and that major changes to the way in which the business operates in these countries is required. Part of the reason may be the different political, cultural and religious systems and norms in place in some emerging economies. Part of the reason may be that assumptions about the markets and consumers within that market are flawed. Selling hi-tech gadgets in a country where there are very few people who own these may present a huge potential opportunity. This opportunity may only exist if there are enough people who are (a) wealthy enough to have the disposable income to be able to afford (and want) these gadgets; (b) that there are not other products which are deemed more important or valuable to these consumers; and (c) that the way consumers in developed economies see the products may not be the same as those in emerging economies.

The needs of customers in these markets may not be the same as those in developed economies and so the business may find that its model is fundamentally flawed because it assumes the needs of consumers everywhere to be the same. Focusing on reducing price or changing the features of the phone may not be sufficient to target the opportunities that exist if the fact remains that mobile phones tend to be used by those in the higher income brackets primarily.

Sales as a result may be disappointing. This sort of problem was noted by C.K. Prahalad, the noted management thinker who died in April 2010. In his book, *The Fortune at the Bottom of the Pyramid: Eradicating Poverty Through Profits*, Prahalad sought to show how poverty could be tackled by focusing products on the world's poorest people – around 5 billion of them. Not only could firms make a real difference to the world's poor but they could also secure new profits and growth in the process. Simple, but effective business ideas stemmed from this book such as the provision of data services to farmers which help to increase crop yields and reduce dependency. The key questions businesses need to ask in this regard are whether a market exists and if it does what sort of scale exists? Does the market and the scale enable profits to be made? If the answers to these questions are 'yes' then there are opportunities to be exploited. This meant that firms could now look at generating revenue from people who may only be earning very small incomes. One example is the market for shampoo. Do consumers in emerging markets want to buy shampoo in the same way as those in the Netherlands, for example? Prahalad suggested that these consumers may have a lot in common, not least their desire to purchase well-respected branded items such as Pantene shampoo produced by Procter & Gamble. However, whilst consumers in the Netherlands may want to purchase their shampoo in 500ml bottles for around €5, for consumers in India this may represent a week's wages. The solution might be to supply the same product in single-serve sachets so that the shampoo market in India (which in terms of tonnes is as large as in the USA) can be served.

Business Strategies in Emerging Markets

Finding new business models to satisfy different customer needs is key to succeeding in emerging markets, therefore. There are a number of different but often complementary strategies that have been identified as being appropriate for conducting business in emerging markets.

Hit and Run Strategies Firms might enter a market with the intention of 'creaming off' the value in the market and then getting out. They sell their products to those that can afford them, take the profits and then leave the market. The advantage is a boost to short-term profits but the disadvantage is that long-term growth prospects and business relationships are sacrificed and these relationships may be more profitable in the long run.

Enclave Strategies   This is often associated with firms doing business in emerging economies exploiting natural resources. The intention is to set up operations which do not depend on local supply networks and where local businesses and people have minimal involvement in the operation. This may be because the firm believes the local business environment is less than efficient and reliable but might also be because of concerns over security. Firms may engage with the local military to help provide that security. One of the problems of this is that such involvement can raise ethical questions about how the firm operates and the extent to which the payment to the local military is transparent. In addition it can also attract attention to the business, especially in more politically volatile areas where local conflicts and terrorism might be problematic. It also alienates the firm from the local stakeholders.

Learn to Earn   Committing to investing in emerging markets for the long term may involve the firm having to accept that in the short run profits will be slim if non-existent. By being involved in the economy, however, the firm will learn and as it does it develops longer term relationships and a better understanding of the market. In the long term it is hoped that this improved understanding and experience will lead to higher and more consistent profits.

Summary

There are many emerging markets – some more advanced than others, but the opportunities for business facing limited growth in domestic, mature markets are significant. However, firms have to be prepared to be flexible in their approach to doing business in emerging markets and be prepared to make mistakes, learn from experience and invest in time and new business models to succeed. Building relationships with governments, local suppliers, regional government and understanding cultural, political and religious differences are part of the process of developing sustainable platforms for future growth.

© ANDREW ASHWIN

European Union a family of democratic European countries, committed to working together for peace and prosperity

THE SINGLE EUROPEAN MARKET AND THE EURO

Following the devastation of two world wars in the first half of the 20th century, each of which had initially centred on European conflicts, some of the major European countries (in particular France and Germany) expressed a desire to make further wars impossible between them through a process of strong economic integration that, it was hoped, would lead to greater social and political harmony. This led to the development of the European Economic Community (EEC) – now referred to as the **European Union**, or EU. Initially the EU consisted of just six countries: Belgium, Germany, France, Italy, Luxembourg and the Netherlands. In 1973, Denmark, Ireland and the United Kingdom joined. Greece joined in 1981, Spain and Portugal in 1986, and Austria, Finland and Sweden in 1995. In 2004 the biggest ever enlargement took place with 10 new countries joining. At the time of writing there is one acceding country (Croatia) which has signed a treaty to become a full member, five 'candidate countries' seeking membership (Turkey, the Former Yugoslav Republic of Macedonia, Montenegro, Iceland and Serbia) and three potential candidates (Albania, Bosnia and Herzegovina, and Kosovo). The official website of the European Union defines the EU as 'a family of democratic European countries, committed to working together for peace and prosperity'.

The EU has certainly been successful in its original central aim of ensuring European peace: countries such as France, England, Germany, Italy and Spain who have been at war with each other on and off for centuries now work together for mutual benefit. This has led to greater emphasis being given to the EU's second objective – namely prosperity – and, to this end, a desire to create a **Single European Market** (SEM) throughout which labour, capital, goods and services can move freely. As member states got rid of obstacles to trade between themselves, it was argued, companies would start to enjoy economies of scale as they expanded their market across Europe. At the same time, inefficient firms would be exposed to more cross-border competition, either forcing them out of business or forcing them to improve their efficiency. The aim was therefore to provide businesses with an environment of fair competition in which economies of scale could be reaped and a strong consumer base developed from which they could expand into global markets. Households, on the other hand, would benefit from lower prices, greater choice of goods and services, and work opportunities across a wide area, while the economy in general would benefit from the enhanced economic growth that would result.

> **Single European Market** a (still-not-complete) EU-wide market throughout which labour, capital, goods and services can move freely

Early steps towards the creation of the SEM included the abolition of internal EU tariff and quota barriers in 1968 and a movement towards greater harmonization in areas such as indirect taxation, industrial regulation, and in common EU-wide policies towards agriculture and fisheries.

Nevertheless, it proved difficult to make progress on the more intangible barriers to free movement of goods, services, capital and labour. For example, even though internal tariffs and quotas had been abolished in the EU, local tax systems and technical regulations on goods and services still differed from country to country so that it was in practice often difficult to export from one country to another. Thus, a car produced in the UK might have to satisfy a certain set of emission and safety requirements in one European country and another set of requirements in another EU country. Or a qualified engineer might find that their qualifications, obtained in Italy, were not recognized in Germany. The result was that during the 1970s and early 1980s, growth in the EU member states began to lag seriously behind that of international competitors – especially the United States and Japan. Therefore, in 1985 a discussion document (in the jargon, a 'White Paper') was produced by the European Commission that subsequently led to a European Act of Parliament – the 1986 Single European Act. This identified some 300 measures that would have to be addressed in order to complete the Single European Market and set 31 December 1992 as the deadline for completion. The creation of the SEM was to be brought about by EU Directives telling the governments of member states what changes needed to be put into effect in order to achieve four goals:

- The free movement of goods, services, labour and capital between EU member states.
- The approximation of relevant laws, regulations and administrative provisions between member states.
- A common, EU-wide competition policy, administered by the European Commission.
- A system of common external tariffs implemented against countries who are not members of the EU.

Over 20 years on from the Single European Act, the SEM is still far from complete. In particular, there still exist between EU members strong differences in national fiscal systems which have come sharply into focus during the debt crisis, while academic and professional qualifications are not easily transferable and labour mobility across EU countries is generally low. Some of the reasons for this are hard to overcome: language barriers and relative levels of economic development hamper the movement of factors and member states continue to compete with one another economically, at times seeking their own national interest rather than the greater good of the EU.

Nevertheless, the years between 1985 and 1992 did see some important steps in the development of the SEM and the resulting achievements of the SEM project were not negligible: the European Commission estimates that the SEM helped create 2.5 million new jobs and generated €800 billion in additional wealth in the ten years or so following 1993.

In the context of the Single European Market project, therefore, the creation of a single European currency was seen as a final step towards 'completing the market', by which was meant two things: (a) getting rid of the transaction costs from intra-EU trade that result from different national currencies (and which act much as a tariff); and (b) removing the uncertainty and swings in national competitiveness among members that result from exchange rate movements. Before European Economic and Monetary Union (EMU), Union (EMU), most EU countries participated in the Exchange Rate Mechanism (ERM), which was a system designed to limit the variability of exchange rates between members' currencies. However, the ERM turned out not to be a viable way of reducing volatility in the exchange rate and, in any case, had no effect on the transaction costs arising from bank charges associated with changing currencies when engaging in intra-EU trade.

It is clearly important, therefore, to see EMU within a broader European framework and, in particular, the Single European Market project. Nevertheless, the benefits of adopting a single currency across a geographical area can be analyzed more generally using macroeconomic theory. Moreover, these benefits must be weighed against the costs of joining a common currency area.

COMMON CURRENCY AREAS AND EUROPEAN MONETARY UNION

During the 1990s, a number of European nations decided to give up their national currencies and use a new, common currency called the *euro*.

common currency area (or currency union or monetary union) a geographical area throughout which a single currency circulates as the medium of exchange

A **common currency area** is a geographical area throughout which a single currency circulates as the medium of exchange. Another term for a common currency area is a *currency union*, and a closely related phenomenon is a *monetary union*: a monetary union is, strictly speaking, a group of countries that have adopted permanently and irrevocably fixed exchange rates among their various currencies. Nevertheless, the terms common currency area, currency union and monetary union are often used more or less interchangeably, and in this chapter we'll follow this practice.

Usually we speak of common currency areas when the people of a number of economies, generally corresponding to different nation states, have taken a decision to adopt a common currency as their medium of exchange, as was the case with the European monetary union.

The Euro

European Economic and Monetary Union (EMU) the European currency union that has adopted the euro as its common currency

There are currently 17 countries that have joined **European Economic and Monetary Union**, or EMU. (Note that 'EMU' stands for 'Economic and Monetary Union', not European Monetary Union, as is often supposed.) The countries that currently form the Euro Area are Belgium, Germany, Estonia, Spain, France, Ireland, Italy, Luxembourg, the Netherlands, Austria, Portugal, Finland, Greece, Slovenia, Cyprus, Malta and Slovakia (informally known as 'Euroland' but more correctly as the Euro Area). The move towards a single European currency has a very long history but we can set out the main landmarks in its formation, starting in 1992 with the Maastricht Treaty (formally known as the Treaty on European Union), which laid down (among other things) various criteria for being eligible to join the proposed currency union. In order to participate in the new currency, member states had to meet strict criteria such as a government budget deficit of less than 3 per cent of GDP, a government debt-to-GDP ratio of less than 60 per cent, combined with low inflation and interest rates close to the EU average. The Maastricht Treaty also laid down a timetable for the introduction of the new single currency and rules concerning the setting up of a European Central Bank (ECB). The ECB actually came into existence in June 1998 and forms, together with the national central banks of the countries making up the common currency area, the European System of Central Banks (ESCB), which is given responsibility for ensuring price stability and implementing the single European monetary policy.

The single European currency – the euro – officially came into existence on 1 January 1999 when 12 countries adopted it (although Greece did not join EMU until 1 January 2001). On this date, exchange rates between the old national currencies of Euro Area countries were irrevocably locked and a few days later the financial markets began to trade the euro against other currencies such as the US dollar, as well as to trade securities denominated in euros.

The period from the beginning of 1999 until the beginning of 2002 was a transitional phase, with national currencies still circulating within the Euro Area countries and prices in shops displayed in both euros and local currency. On 1 January 2002 the first euro notes and coins came into circulation and, within a few months, the switch to the euro as the single medium of exchange was complete throughout the Euro Area.

There was a belief that having a common European currency would help 'complete the market' for European goods, services and factors of production that had been an ongoing project for much of the post-war period.

? **what if…**a country joins a single currency but is at a different stage in the business cycle to other countries in the single currency area. Is it still possible for the country to successfully embrace the single currency?

Benefits of a Single Currency

Elimination of Transaction Costs   One obvious and direct benefit of a common currency is that it makes trade easier between members and, in particular, there is a reduction in the transaction costs involved in trade between members of the common currency area. When a German company imports French wine, it no longer has to pay a charge to a bank for converting German marks into French francs with which to pay the wine producer, it can just pay in euros. Of course, the banking sector loses out on the commission it used to charge for converting currencies, but this does not affect the fact that the reduction in transaction costs is a net gain. This is because paying a cost to convert currencies is in fact a deadweight loss in the sense that companies pay the transaction cost but get nothing tangible in return. OK, so the banks were getting commission before and this was used to employ people who worked on currency transactions, but these people can now be used more productively in the economy, making everyone better off.

Reduction in Price Discrimination   It is sometimes argued that a second, albeit indirect gain, to the members of common currency area results from the reduction in price discrimination that should ensue when there is a single currency. If goods are priced in a single currency it should be much harder to disguise price differences across countries. This argument assumes that the transparency in prices that results from a common currency will lead to arbitrage in goods across the common currency area: people will buy goods where they are cheaper (tending to raise their price in that location) and reduce their demand for goods where they are more expensive (tending to reduce the price in that location).

Overall, however, EMU seems unlikely to bring an end to price discrimination across Euro Area countries. For items like groceries, having a single currency is unlikely to be much of an impetus to price convergence across the common currency area because of the large transaction costs (mainly related to travelling) involved in arbitraging, relative to the prices of the goods themselves.

Reduction in Foreign Exchange Rate Variability   A third argument relates to the reduction in exchange rate variability and the consequent reduction in uncertainty that results from having a single currency. Exchange rates can fluctuate substantially on a day-to-day basis. Before EMU, when a German supermarket imported wine from France to be delivered, say, three months later, it had to worry about how much a French franc would be worth in terms of German marks in three months time and therefore what the total cost of the wine would be in marks. This uncertainty might deter the supermarket company from importing wine at all, and instead lead them to concentrate on selling German wines, thereby foregoing gains from trade and reducing economic welfare. The supermarket could have eliminated the uncertainty by getting a bank to agree to sell the francs at an agreed rate against marks to be delivered three months later (an example of a forward foreign exchange contract). But the bank would charge for this service, and this charge would be equivalent to a tariff on the imported wine and so would represent a deadweight loss to society.

The reduction in uncertainty arising from the removal of exchange rate fluctuations may also affect investment in the economy. This would clearly be the case for companies that export a large amount of their output to other Euro Area countries, since less uncertainty concerning the receipts from its exports means that it is able to plan for the future with less risk, so that investment projects such as building new factories appear less risky. An increase in investment will benefit the whole economy because it is likely to lead to higher economic growth.

Costs of a Single Currency

The major cost to an economy in joining a common currency area relates to the fact that it gives up its national currency and thereby gives up its freedom to set its own monetary policy and the possibility of macroeconomic adjustment coming about through movements in the external value of its currency. Clearly, if the nations of the Euro Area have only one money, they can have only one monetary policy, which is set and implemented by the European Central Bank. This must be the case because, since there is only one currency, it's not possible to have a different set of interest rates in different countries. Why is this a potential problem?

Suppose, for example, that there is a shift in consumer preferences across the common currency area away from goods and services produced in one country (Germany, say) and towards goods and services produced in another country (France, say). This situation is depicted in Figure 21.1, which shows a leftward shift in the German short-run aggregate demand curve and a rightward shift in the French short-run aggregate demand curve. What should policy makers in France and Germany do about this? One answer to this is, nothing: in the long run, each economy will return to its natural rate of output. In Germany, this will occur as the price level falls and wages, prices and perceptions adjust. In particular, as unemployment rises in Germany, wages eventually begin to fall. Lower wages reduce firms' costs and so, for any given price level, the amount supplied will be higher. In other words, the German short-run aggregate supply curve will shift to the right, until eventually it intersects with the new short-run aggregate demand curve at the natural rate of output. The opposite happens in France, with the short-run aggregate supply curve shifting to the left. The adjustment to the new equilibrium levels of output are also shown in Figure 21.1.

Note that, if Germany and France had maintained their own currencies and a flexible foreign exchange rate, then the short-term fluctuations in aggregate demand would be alleviated by a movement in the exchange rate: as the demand for French goods rises and for German goods falls, this would increase the demand for French francs and depress the demand for German marks, making the value of francs rise in terms of marks in the foreign currency exchange market. This would make French goods more expensive to German residents since they now have to pay more marks for a given number of French francs. Similarly, German goods become less expensive to French residents. Therefore, French net exports would fall, leading to a fall in aggregate demand. This is shown in Figure 21.2, where the French aggregate demand schedule shifts back to the left until equilibrium is again established at the natural rate of output. Conversely – and also

FIGURE 21.1

A Shift in Consumer Preferences Away from German Goods Towards French Goods

The German fall in aggregate demand leads to a fall in output from Y_1^G to Y_2^G, and a fall in the price level from P_1^G to P_2^G. The increase in French aggregate demand raises output from Y_1^F to Y_2^F. Over time, however, wages and prices will adjust, so that German and French output return to their natural levels, Y_1^G and Y_1^F, with lower prices in Germany, at P_3^G, and higher prices in France, at P_3^F.

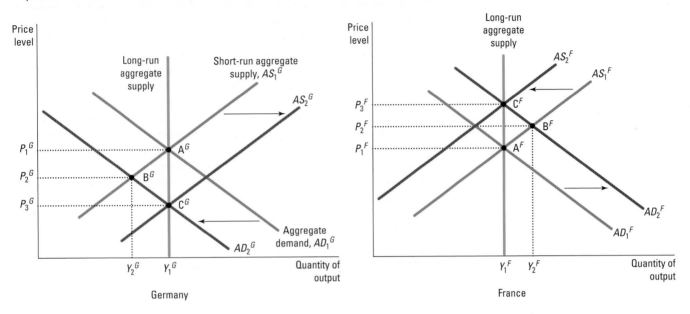

FIGURE 21.2

A Shift in Consumer Preferences with Flexible Exchange Rates

The fall in German aggregate demand leads, before prices have had time to adjust, to a fall in output from Y_1^G to Y_3^G. However, because this is due to a fall in net foreign demand, the value of the German currency falls, making German goods cheaper abroad. This raises net exports and restores aggregate demand. The converse happens in France: the increase in net foreign demand raises the external value of the French currency, making French goods more expensive abroad and choking off aggregate demand to its former level.

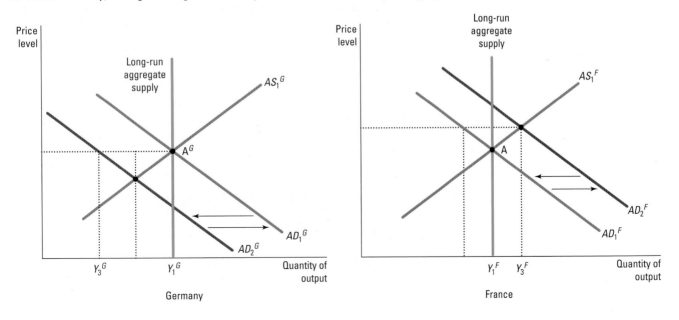

shown in Figure 21.2 – German net exports rise and the German aggregate demand schedule shifts to the right until equilibrium is again achieved in Germany.

In a currency union, however, this automatic adjustment mechanism is not available, since, of course, France and Germany have the same currency (the euro). The best that can be done is to wait for wages and prices to adjust in France and Germany so that the aggregate supply shifts in each country, as in Figure 21.1. The resulting fluctuations in output and unemployment in each country will tend to create tensions within the monetary union, as unemployment rises in Germany and inflation rises in France. German policy makers, dismayed at the rise in unemployment, will favour a cut in interest rates in order to boost aggregate demand in their country, while their French counterparts, worried about rising inflation, will be calling for an increase in interest rates in order to curtail French aggregate demand. The ECB will not be able to keep both countries happy. Most likely, it will set interest rates higher than the German desired level and lower than the French desired level. The ECB pursues an inflation targeting strategy, and the inflation rate it targets is based upon a consumer prices index constructed as an average across the Euro Area. If a country's inflation rate (or expected inflation rate) is below the Euro Area average, the ECB's monetary policy will be too tight for that country; if it is above the average, the ECB's monetary policy will be too loose for it. All that is possible is a 'one size fits all' monetary policy. It is for this reason that entry to the eurozone is restricted to those countries that can meet the criteria outlined above where inflation and interest rates are close to the EU average.

> **Quick Quiz**   List and discuss the key costs and benefits of joining a currency union.

Characteristics That Increase the Benefits of a Single Currency

High Degree of Trade Integration   The greater the amount of trade that takes place between a group of countries – i.e. the greater the degree of trade integration – the more they will benefit from adopting a common currency. One of the principal benefits of a currency union, and the most direct benefit, is the reduction in transaction costs that are incurred in trade transactions between the various countries when there is a constant need to switch one national currency into another on the foreign currency exchange market. Clearly, therefore, the greater the amount of international trade that is carried out between member countries – and therefore the greater the amount of foreign currency transactions – the greater the reduction in transaction costs that having a common currency entails.

The reduction in exchange rate volatility – another benefit of a currency union – will also clearly be larger, the greater is the degree of intra-union trade, since more firms will benefit from knowing with certainty exactly the revenue generated from their sales to other currency union members, rather than having to bear the uncertainty associated with exchange rate fluctuations.

FISCAL POLICY AND COMMON CURRENCY AREAS

Our discussion so far has tended to centre on the loss of autonomy in monetary policy that is entailed in adopting a single currency among a group of countries. However, it is obvious that there is nothing in the adoption of a common currency that implies that members of the currency union should not still retain independence in fiscal policy. For instance, in our example of an asymmetric demand shock that expands demand in France and contracts aggregate demand in Germany, the French government could reduce government spending in order to offset the demand shock, while the German government could expand government spending. In fact, even if France and Germany did not make up an optimal currency because wages were sticky and labour mobility was low between the countries, national fiscal policy could, in principle, still be used to ameliorate the loss of monetary policy autonomy.

Fiscal Federalism

Suppose that a currency union had a common fiscal policy in the sense of having a single, common fiscal budget covering tax and spending decisions across the common currency area. This means that fiscal policy in the currency union would work much as fiscal policy in a single national economy works, with a surplus of government tax revenue over government spending in one region used to pay for a budget deficit in another region. Return again to our example of an asymmetric demand shock that expands aggregate demand in France and contracts aggregate demand in Germany, as in Figure 21.1. Since almost all taxes are closely related to the level of economic activity in the economy, tax revenue will automatically decline in Germany as a result of the aggregate demand shock that shifts it into recession. At the same time, transfer payments in the form of unemployment benefit and other social security benefits will also rise in Germany. These effects are referred to as automatic stabilizers built into the fiscal policy of an economy that automatically stimulate aggregate demand when the economy goes into recession without policy makers having to take any deliberate action. The opposite will be true in France, where the automatic stabilizers will be operating in reverse as transfer payments fall and tax receipts rise with the level of economic activity. These changes will tend to expand aggregate demand in Germany and contract it in France, to some extent offsetting the asymmetric demand shock.

Now, if the governments of France and Germany have a common budget, then the increased net government revenue in France can be used to offset the reduction in net government revenue in Germany. If the resulting movements in aggregate are not enough to offset the demand shock, then the French and German governments may even go further and decide to increase government expenditure further in Germany and pay for it by reducing spending and perhaps raising taxes in France.

This kind of arrangement – a fiscal system for a group of countries involving a common fiscal budget and a system of taxes and fiscal transfers across countries – is known as **fiscal federalism**. The problem with it is that the taxpayers of one country (here France) may not be happy in paying for government spending and transfer payments in another country (in this example, Germany).

fiscal federalism a fiscal system for a group of countries involving a common fiscal budget and a system of taxes and fiscal transfers across countries

> **Pitfall Prevention** Being a member of a single currency does not mean that control over fiscal policy has to be surrendered. In a country like the USA, for example, although all states use the dollar, each has control over its own fiscal policy. The drive to a greater degree of fiscal coordination in Europe in some critics eyes, is an attempt to move to a European super-state and is primarily political rather than economic.

National Fiscal Policies in a Currency Union: The Free-Rider Problem

During 2010 and 2011, difficulties in Greece, Ireland, Portugal, Spain and Italy led to EU leaders having to negotiate successive bailouts because of problems arising from the sovereign debt crisis. There was (and remains at the time of writing) a high chance that

Greece could default on its debt liabilities. The Greek government borrowed heavily during the first decade of the 20th century but the financial crisis and subsequent recession has hit the country hard. The government simply does not have sufficient funds to pay off loans as they become due and the chances of it being able to borrow to help manage these debts is reduced because the interest on any loans it tries to secure would be too high. Similar problems have been experienced by Portugal, Italy and Spain. The European Central Bank can control short-term interest rates but not those on long-term 10–20-year bonds. As the stresses inside the Euro Area build, interest rates will generally be pushed up and at a time of fragile economic activity this is not good news for longer-term economic recovery. If the economy stalls then tax revenues go down, government spending on benefits increases and the debt problem intensifies.

Why has this debt problem arisen? One explanation is the *free-rider problem*. Given that there is a single currency in the EU but there is no fiscal federalism, there is the possibility of individual members of the currency union using fiscal policy in order to offset asymmetric macroeconomic shocks that cannot be dealt with by the common monetary policy. For example, what is wrong with Spain running a big government budget deficit in order to counteract a fall in aggregate demand and borrowing heavily in order to finance the deficit? One answer may lie in the effect on other members of the currency union of a rise in the debt of a member country.

Whenever a government raises its levels of debt to very high levels, there is an increased risk that the government may default on the debt. In general, this can be done in one of two ways. Where a country is not a member of a currency union and controls its own monetary policy, it can engineer a surprise inflation by a sudden increase in the money supply, so that the real value of the debt shrinks. In addition when there is a sharp rise in the price level, this will usually be accompanied by a sharp fall in the foreign currency value of the domestic currency. This means that, valued in foreign currency, the stock of government debt will now be worth far less. Thus, the government has in effect defaulted on a large portion of its debt by reducing its value both internally and externally.

If the markets believe in this possibility then the debt will not be seen as risky as it otherwise would be and so the interest rates charged to the debtor country on its debt will not be as high as they otherwise might be. The net effect is for that government to pay interest rates on its large stock of debt that are lower because of the implicit belief that it will be bailed out if it has problems servicing the debt, and for all other members of the currency union to pay higher interest rates on their government debt because the government has flooded the financial markets with euro-denominated government bonds. This is the free-rider problem; the government is enjoying the benefits of a fiscal expansion without paying the full costs.

In addition, if that government is using the proceeds of its borrowing to fund a strong fiscal expansion, this may undo or work against the anti-inflationary monetary policy of the ECB by stoking up aggregate demand throughout the whole of the Euro Area.

In order to circumvent some of these problems, the currency union members can enter into a 'no bailout' agreement which states that member countries cannot expect other members to come to their rescue if their debt levels become unsustainable, as an attempt to convince the markets to charge profligate spend-and-borrow countries higher interest rates on their debt. In fact, exactly such a no bailout agreement exists among members of EMU. Unfortunately, however, it seems clear that the no bailout clause is not credible.

At the outset of EMU, a set of fiscal rules was indeed drawn up and agreed to by EMU members. This set of rules was known as the **Stability and Growth Pact** (SGP). The Stability and Growth Pact was a set of formal rules by which members of EMU were supposed to be bound in their conduct of national fiscal policy. Its main components were as follows:

Stability and Growth Pact a set of formal rules by which members of EMU were supposed to be bound in their conduct of national fiscal policy

- Members should aim to achieve balanced budgets.
- Members with a budget deficit of more than 3 per cent of GDP will be subject to fines that may reach as high as 0.5 per cent of GDP unless the country experiences

exceptional circumstances (such as a natural disaster) or a very sharp recession in which GDP declines by 2 per cent or more in a single year.

Clearly, however, if EMU members adhered to the SGP, then it would rule out any free-rider problems associated with excessive spending and borrowing in any one member country by forcing members to put a limit on the national government budget. The choice of a maximum budget deficit of no more than 3 per cent of GDP was related to a clause in the 1992 Maastricht Treaty which suggested that a 'prudent' debt-to-GDP ratio should be no more than 60 per cent. This itself was perhaps somewhat arbitrary – although it was very close to the actual debt-to-GDP ratio of Germany in 1992. To see, however, that a 60 per cent ratio of debt to GDP could entail 'prudent' budget deficits of no more than 3 per cent a year, let's do some simple budgetary arithmetic.

Suppose a country is enjoying real GDP growth of 3 per cent a year and inflation of 2 per cent a year, so that nominal GDP is growing at the rate of 5 per cent a year. This means that the nominal value of its government debt can grow at a rate of 5 per cent a year and still be sustainable. But if the debt-to-GDP ratio is 60 per cent, this means that debt can increase by 5 per cent of 60 per cent, or 3 per cent of GDP a year while keeping the debt-to-GDP ratio constant. In other, words, it can run a budget deficit of 3 per cent of GDP a year.

While, however, there was some logic in setting a maximum budget deficit of 3 per cent a year (given a maximum prudent debt-to-GDP ratio of 60 per cent), it is not clear why the SGP suggested that members should aim for a balanced budget. It is clear from the budgetary arithmetic just discussed that it is not imprudent for countries to run small budget deficits so long as they are enjoying sustained long-term growth in GDP. The effective straitjacketing of national fiscal policy that the SGP implied may have reflected a desire among the architects of EMU for the ECB to maintain an effective monopoly on demand management, so that its policies could not be countered by national fiscal policies.

The crucial question for the SGP, however, was whether or not the maximum allowable budget deficit would be enough for a country to let its automatic fiscal stabilizers come into play when it goes into recession. This is crucial in a monetary union because member countries will have already given up their right to pursue an independent monetary policy and they cannot use the exchange rate as an instrument of policy.

In practice, the SGP proved to be something of a toothless watchdog. As the Euro Area experienced sluggish growth in the early years of EMU, several member countries – and in particular France and Germany, two of the largest member countries – found themselves in breach of the SGP excessive deficit criteria. However, both France and Germany managed to persuade other EMU members not to impose fines and, in 2004, the European Commission drew up guidelines for softening the SGP. These guidelines included considering more widely the sustainability of countries' public finances on an individual basis, paying more attention to overall debt burdens and to long-term liabilities such as pensions, rather than to a single year's deficit.

The Sovereign Debt Crisis

The SGP was effectively rendered redundant by the sovereign debt crisis. The debt crisis developed because countries like Portugal, Greece and Ireland were able to access funds at low interest rates. Greece, for example, borrowed extensively to finance the 2004 Olympic Games and the expansion of public debt built to around 115 per cent of GDP and its deficit stood at 14 per cent of GDP. Remember that the recommended maximum was 3 per cent of GDP.

The financial crisis of 2007–2008, which led to the credit crunch, resulted in access to funds for countries like Greece drying up. The cost of acquiring new debt rose and banks, investors and financial institutions across Europe and elsewhere faced massive losses if Greece and the others were allowed to default. This would almost certainly plunge the world into another deep and damaging recession.

As the crisis developed and the political will to keep the euro intact was being challenged, rates on Greek debt began to rise beyond affordable levels for the country. That, coupled with a deep and lasting recession, meant that the prospects for any growth-led recovery looked bleak. The markets seemed convinced that Greece would have to default and that any bailout plan would not solve its problems. EU finance minsters, EU leaders and the International Monetary Fund (IMF) conducted extensive negotiations to try and find a resolution to the crisis. A series of austerity measures aimed at drastically cutting public spending announced by and imposed on the Greek government caused widespread anger amongst the population with a series of strikes, civil protest and riots testing the resolve of all concerned.

Moves to find a way of preventing sovereign debt default led to the establishment of the European Financial Stability Fund (EFSF) to provide support for countries that faced default. €750 billion was initially set aside along with help from the International Monetary Fund. The initial bailout of Greece accounted for €110 billion of these funds; Ireland's €85 billion and Portugal around €80 billion. The establishment of the EFSF may have resolved some of the more immediate problems that existed in 2010 but merely led to the markets turning their attention to other states deemed to be in danger of default, notably Spain and Italy. The latter was of significance because it accounted for a much larger proportion of total EU GDP than Greece. If Italy were to default the consequences for the Euro Area and the global economy would be dire.

The bailout terms include implementation of significant measures to reduce public spending. We have already seen how such measures led to violence and protest in Greece. Another, perhaps more serious consequence for Europe as a whole and for the global economy was the prospect of such cuts leading to a further slowdown in economic activity. If a country like Greece is experiencing GDP growth rates of −7 per cent, then the chances of generating tax revenue to pay off debt and invest in improving the economy are slim.

By March 2012, the negotiations had led to an agreement to set aside €529 billion for long-term refinancing operations (LTRO) which meant that the total funds allocated to the bailouts broke the €1 trillion level. In addition, the negotiations led to the setting up of what has been termed the Fiscal Compact. The Treaty is due to come into force on 1 January 2013 (assuming it is ratified) and is designed to place a greater degree of fiscal discipline on EU members. Strict rules on government spending and borrowing will be imposed, designed to ensure that government budgets are either balanced or in surplus. To see the relevance of this we need to identify two types of deficit. A **cyclical deficit** occurs when government spending and income is disrupted by the 'normal' economic cycle. In times of strong economic growth government revenue from taxes will rise and spending on welfare and benefits will fall and so public finances will move into surplus (or the deficit shrinks appreciably). In times of economic slowdown the opposite occurs and the size of the budget deficit will rise (or the surplus shrinks). A **structural deficit** refers to a situation where the deficit is not dependent on movements in the economic cycle but where a government is 'living beyond its means' – spending what it has not got. The Fiscal Compact states that structural deficits must not exceed 0.5 per cent of GDP at market prices although this can rise to 1 per cent provided government debt as a whole is 'significantly' less than 60 per cent of GDP at market prices. If country's breach this limit fines will be imposed of up to 0.1 per cent of GDP and 'a correction mechanism' designed to correct any imbalance will be automatically triggered. If the Treaty is ratified then it will become law and as such have more 'teeth' than the SGP, so advocates suggest. Enshrining the balanced budget rule in law is a major step. In addition, the Treaty requires countries to report in advance plans for major bond sales and economic reforms to EU institutions and for Euro Area summits to be held at least twice a year.

There are many who believe that the debt crisis is far from over and that the demands made of Greece and other countries are simply too great. Without the prospect for economic growth and with considerable pressure on the population to accommodate the austerity measures, the challenges are set to continue for many years. Even if the funds

cyclical deficit a situation when government spending and income is disrupted by the 'normal' economic cycle

structural deficit a situation where the deficit is not dependent on movements in the economic cycle

set aside prove to be enough to bail out those countries that need it, the damage to confidence in the markets may be such that the future of the euro is still very uncertain.

JEOPARDY PROBLEM

A country with very high levels of sovereign debt announces that it is aiming to raise funds by borrowing on the bond market. It needs to raise €7 billion. As the time nears for the auction, the price of its existing debt starts to fall and yields rise. At the same time, the price of sovereign debt bonds of a country with a low level of debt starts to rise and yields fall.

Why might this be happening?

OUTSOURCING

The existence of emerging economies with large labour resources which often have high literacy levels but low wage costs, has encouraged a number of companies to look to move parts of their operations to these countries. The contracting out of a part of the business' operations to another organization is referred to as **outsourcing**. Whilst the focus has been on outsourcing labour operations to low-wage economies, outsourcing also refers to any operation. This might include accountancy activities, IT, various human resources activities such as payroll management and recruitment and training. Outsourcing does not have to mean the operation goes abroad – many businesses will outsource operations to other organizations within the domestic country.

outsourcing contracting out of a part of the business' operations to another organization

The main reason for outsourcing is to reduce costs and to improve efficiency. Taking advantage of the expertise of other organizations that may specialize in particular operations is a major factor in decision making. By outsourcing production and obtaining supplies from low-cost manufacturers, companies are able to focus their attention on their core competencies – the key strengths that they have. This leads to a more efficient operation whilst allowing the business concerned to benefit from economies of scale.

The benefit to the consumer is that they get good quality products – and more of them – at lower prices. The clothing industry is an excellent example of where these changes have been happening. Primark is one business that has adopted this business model. Owned by Associated British Foods, Primark has placed itself as a 'value retailer' offering low-priced but good quality clothing, and along with other value retailers like Matalan now account for around a quarter of total fashion spending in the UK.

The benefits of outsourcing have to be weighed against the possible disadvantages. There are costs associated with outsourcing not least of which involve the setting up of the agreement with the contractor but also the cost of closing down operations which the outsourced activity is replacing. Outsourcing call centre operations has been a high profile news story in the UK with, sometimes, thousands, of domestic workers losing their jobs to outsourced operations in countries like India where labour costs are significantly lower. The ethics of the decision of firms to outsource have been questioned and the firm has to consider the effect on its reputation.

In addition to this, some firms have found that the expected benefits have not been as large as they anticipated; there are complex issues that have arisen which may not have been foreseen. Customers, for example, have complained about the service they are receiving from outsourced services. Outsourced workers may not have the 'local' knowledge and understanding necessary to meet customer needs. Training of outsourced workers has also been a problem for some firms which has led companies like Newcastle Building Society and Lloyds TSB to move some operations back to the UK. In other cases, firms in financial services have found that security is an issue. Handling and protecting customer data is an important part of the business of financial services and something which is highly regulated. The UK insurance and financial services firm Aviva has encountered such problems of maintaining security, which have cost it an estimated £10 million in efforts to ensure that its outsourced operations meet regulatory requirements.

There are also problems associated with how some outsourced operations do business. The development of social networking sites and the ease with which individuals can post information and videos onto the internet have meant that firms are acutely aware of the damage to their reputation from stories about abuse of workers in outsourced operations. A number of firms have been attempting to counter stories that workers in plants in China are working long hours for low wages. A series of apparent suicides in a factory in Shenzhen in China which make products for Apple, Nokia, Dell, Sony and Nintendo were linked to the stresses imposed as a result of the conditions that workers have to operate in. For these types of companies which have a main demographic of young, socially aware individuals, when reports such as these filter through a balance has to be drawn between the benefits of the low cost of using outsourced manufacture, and the potential for the image of the company to be damaged. Similar reports have been released about worker abuse in clothing factories supplying big-name Western retailers which can be equally as damaging and the speed with which many of these firms react to the claims is perhaps testament to the potential for damage to the firm.

GLOBAL BUSINESS, CULTURE AND ETHICS

globalization the growth of inter-dependence amongst world economies usually seen as resulting from the removal of many international regulations affecting financial flows

The ethical issues outlined above are one aspect of doing business in a global market. The term **globalization** refers to the growth of interdependence amongst world economies usually seen as resulting from the removal of many international regulations affecting financial flows. In one respect this means that it is becoming easier for firms to conduct business across national boundaries and to engage in trade around the world. This clearly opens up major opportunities but also presents difficulties and challenges that have to be recognized and managed, not least the ethical and cultural issues of carrying out business in a global market.

Doing business globally means that a firm can get its product and brand positioned anywhere in the world. It is highly likely that regardless of where you are in the world you will be able to find a store that sells Coca-Cola, for example. Multinationals are characterized by having operations in a number of countries although their main headquarters will be in one country – normally the country in which the firm originally developed.

The benefits of a larger market and higher sales and profitability, along with the opportunities to exploit economies of scale, lower production costs and increased efficiencies, has to be balanced against some of the potential costs. These can include accusations of labour exploitation, the problems that can arise from firms having global monopoly power, damage to eco-systems, the use of non-renewable resources and damage to indigenous cultures. These problems can also have a wider social and political impact. Global trade can exacerbate the gap between rich and poor and when there is poverty there is unrest and the potential for terrorism, when impoverished people see no other option but to resort to violence to advance their cause or simply to exist. The problems of piracy off the coast of Somalia and the continued supply of heroin from Afghanistan exist in part because those involved have few alternatives to make a living. Despite the risks involved, the alternative is not sufficiently rewarding to encourage them to do anything else.

Firms are increasingly aware of these potential difficulties and make considerable attempts to demonstrate transparency in their actions and accountability. Many large firms produce social and environmental accountability reports which aim to highlight how they are managing their operations to limit the negative effects of their activities on stakeholders.

Cultural and religious differences are also challenges which face business. There are many examples of different cultural sensitivities which need to be taken into account such as how to greet people, how the use of colour has different meanings in different parts of the world, how certain gestures and body language can be interpreted very differently throughout the world (for example showing the soles of the feet is considered highly offensive in many Muslim countries). Touching has different interpretations in different parts of the world. Touching the head in parts of Asia is not polite because the head houses the soul, in Islamic and Hindu cultures the use of the left hand for social interaction is considered insulting. Having hands in pockets or sitting cross-legged is considered disrespectful in Turkey, while making eye contact is expected in the West and in some Arabic cultures but not in Japan, parts of Africa, the Caribbean and parts of Latin America.

CASE STUDY

Doing Business Abroad

Let's begin with a joke.

The United Nations sent out a worldwide survey. The request: please give your honest opinion about possible solutions to end the food shortage in the rest of the world. That survey has been a disaster:

- In Africa, nobody understood the meaning of food.
- In Eastern Europe, nobody understood the meaning of honest.
- In Western Europe, nobody understood the meaning of shortage.
- In China, nobody understood the meaning of give your opinion.
- In the Middle East, nobody understood the meaning of solution.
- And in the United States, nobody understood the rest of the world.

The joke presents a number of intercultural stereotypes and dangerous preconceived ideas. ... But where there's smoke there's fire.

A recent bitter clash between French giant Danone (which makes Evian bottled water, among other products) and its Chinese joint-venture partner showed once again that even world-leading companies underestimate the importance of studying foreign cultures before implementing business development plans abroad.

Very often, the corporate culture, self-confidence and pride of the company's stockholders or executives are so strong that they believe that it is just enough to know the do's and don'ts of foreign business practices to be able to grow and succeed in foreign markets, that it is just enough to have a good product with a good price.

This is a very risky and exclusively rational approach to business-making that underestimates the impact of unconscious emotional reactions in business relationships and management. And that costs a tremendous amount to money (expensive legal conflicts, strikes, lays-offs, recruitment errors, delays in research and production, wasted marketing and promotion budgets).

The only way to avoid frustration and disappointment is to study deeply the cultural habits of these countries to reach the point where one can:

- Understand if there is a good compatibility potential between one's own personality, the corporate culture of the company and the culture and values of the foreign counterparts. It is sometimes no use sending a technical expert or sales person into a country that is absolutely opposite to his own mind structure. It's better to send him to another country where his innate mind structure will be at ease and result in better performance.
- Be trained enough to sense when the other does not feel at ease, to avoid reaching the point of no return.

- Organize things so that the foreign staff/partners will feel at ease with you, the project and your company, meaning you must develop adaptation skills and policy.
- Know when and how to let go and accept giving control away.
- Know how to make people laugh.

These skills can provide the right clues, abilities and command over the key factors of fear/distrust and fun/interest that can be the difference between blocking or fostering projects in a professional environment. They can provide a way to lessen unpredictable reactions that would put the best business plans into danger.

Source: adapted from: **http://www.advancedimagingpro.com/publication/article. jsp?pubId=1&id=4637&pageNum=1** accessed 18 March 2012.

Doing business in countries where Islam is the religion may necessitate carrying out financial transactions in a different way. Islamic finance is governed by Shari'ah law which forbids certain types of activity which is perfectly acceptable in Christian cultures. Charging of interest (usury or *riba*) is not allowed and the principle of profit and loss sharing means that all parties to a transaction share in the profits as well as any potential loss. Transactions are based on ownership of real, tangible goods or property and as such trade in derivative products which has been common in financial services industries in the West as a means of hedging against risk is not allowed.

CONCLUSION

This chapter has examined business in the wider context of trading across the world. Emerging markets provide the potential for existing companies to be able to exploit growth opportunities that increasingly do exist in the developed world. We also developed some of the main issues around common currency areas, focusing in particular on European monetary union. Where there is a high degree of trade among a group of countries, there are benefits to be had from forming a currency union, largely arising from the reduction of transaction costs in international trade and reductions in exchange rate uncertainty. However, there are also costs associated with joining a monetary union, mainly associated with the loss of monetary autonomy (member countries are no longer free to set their own interest rates) and the loss of exchange rate movements as a means of achieving macroeconomic adjustment. Any decision to form a currency union must weigh these costs and benefits against one another to see if there is an overall net benefit. Although, in the long run, the loss of exchange rate adjustment and monetary autonomy may have little effect on the equilibrium levels of output and unemployment in the economies involved, there may be substantial short-term economic fluctuations in these macroeconomic variables as a result of joining the currency union. This is particularly the case if there are asymmetric demand shocks impacting on the currency union so that it is impossible to design a 'one-size-fits-all' monetary policy to suit every country. Short-run adjustment will also be long and painful when wages do not adjust very quickly, although this problem may be overcome by labour mobility across the member countries. The sovereign debt crisis in Europe has brought the whole single currency project into question and there are considerable challenges that still exist if the crisis is to be solved.

Firms doing business abroad and using outsourced operations have to weigh up the costs and benefits of doing so. Some of the costs, including being alert to cultural, religious and social sensitivities along with the effects on the environment and the potential for such operations to be questioned on ethical grounds, can mean that decisions to carry out business abroad in some form can be challenging.

IN THE NEWS

The Debt Crisis in Europe

The sovereign debt crisis has been labelled as one of the most serious facing the global economy in the past 200 years. Attempts by European leaders and finance ministers in conjunction with the International Monetary Fund to find a resolution to the crisis have brought criticism from all sides with some accusing European politicians of dithering and others of acting without carefully considering the future problems that may be stored up as a result of decisions being taken. This article by Jeremy Warner of the Daily Telegraph is symptomatic of the latter view.

Euroland Will Pay For This Monetary Madness

The flood of cheap money from the European Central Bank is storing up grave trouble for the future.

When something looks dangerous, it generally is. And few things look quite so high-wire right now as the European Central Bank's efforts to hold the euro together by flooding the banking system with free money.

This week [1 March 2012], the ECB injected a further 529.5 billion euros via 'long-term refinancing operations', or LTROs, bringing the tally to more than 1 trillion euros. When Mario Draghi, the new ECB president, embarked on the programme shortly before Christmas, it was hailed as a masterstroke which had saved the eurozone from financial and economic calamity. Even the Jeremiahs of Germany's Bundesbank, proud keepers of the sacred flame of monetary conservatism, were stunned into grudging acquiescence by the evident seriousness of the crisis. But now the doubts are beginning to set in, and with good reason.

The measures adopted are so extreme that it is no longer possible to know where they might lead, or what their eventual consequences might be. There is no precedent or road map for this kind of thing. All we do know is that they fail to provide any kind of lasting solution to the single currency's underlying difficulties, which are still largely unrecognized and unaddressed. If Dra-

ghi's intention was to buy time, it's not being well used.

It might be argued, of course, that a sticking-plaster solution is better than no solution. And isn't the ECB only following – if belatedly – the trail blazed by the Bank of England and the US Federal Reserve with their quantitative easing? If our monetary activism can be justified, it's hard to argue that the ECB's cannot.

Up to a point, this is correct. What all these programmes try to do is stop the contraction of the money supply threatened by very rapid deleveraging in the banking sector. As banks shrink their balance sheets, by writing off bad debts or refusing credit, the supply of money also shrinks. If unaddressed, this will cause economic collapse, as during the Great Depression.

Yet the particular constraints within the eurozone make the ECB's efforts somewhat different from those of Britain or America. Much of the Mediterranean rim is already in a depression, with disastrous levels of unemployment, contracting output, and a collapsing money supply. What was going on prior to the first tranche of LTROs was a banking run similar to that which culminated in the collapse of Lehman Brothers, as money was withdrawn from the troubled periphery and redeposited in the more solvent core.

The ECB's actions have succeeded in easing these difficulties, and removing the immediate threat of cascading insolvency throughout the European

banking system. But they have also stored up big problems for the future. To get the cheap funding, banks must lodge their better-quality collateral with the ECB. The effect is to dilute the quality of their remaining balance sheet, making it even more difficult to get funding from the markets as normal. As a result, European banking is becoming ever more dependent on ECB life-support, with no obvious way off it.

The rules prevent the ECB from the direct buying of government bonds that the Bank of England practises via quantitative easing. To get money into the system, it is therefore obliged to resort to this roundabout, backdoor approach. Its cheap funding is in part used by the banks to buy high-yield sovereign bonds issued in the periphery, which in turn eases the immediate fiscal crisis. Yet it's hard to see how getting European banks to buy bonds from potentially insolvent countries is going to restore confidence in the system as a whole.

The ECB's activities also create huge potential liabilities for the more solvent countries that ultimately – through their national central banks – provide the funding for all this. What is in essence happening is that the banking risks of the European periphery are being progressively foisted onto the taxpayers of the more solvent core. Once people in those countries actually realize what's going on, they're going to hit the roof.

Taken as a whole, the sophistry [superficial plausibility] of the process is breathtaking. The ECB is in effect being used as a mechanism for making fiscal transfers between countries, which can only legitimately be agreed by elected governments. To save the politicians' blushes, the transfers are being executed via an unelected monetary authority. It's another example of how legal and democratic niceties seem to have been abandoned in the scramble to save the euro. The fiscal compact, almost certainly illegal within the wider framework of the European Union, is not the paving stone to fiscal federalism it pretends to be, but a form of economic dictatorship which seems to condemn much of the periphery to permanent depression.

The more policy-makers dig, the deeper into the mire they sink. In despair, one of the most famous names in British finance, the Prudential, is threatening to redomicile to Asia to escape the latest madcap piece of insurance regulation to come out of Brussels: it would wipe 20 per cent off the value of many pensions, stop insurers investing in banks and infrastructure, and would have resulted in the entire sector being declared insolvent if it had been in place at the height of the financial crisis.

Europe has no strategy for growth, no strategy for jobs, and in truth, no strategy for saving the euro. The project is broken beyond repair.

Questions

1. What is the purpose of LTROs?
2. How does quantitative easing help bank balance sheets and how does it affect the money supply?
3. Why is the action of European banks in writing off bad debts caused by the sovereign debt crisis leading to a contraction in the money supply?
4. How does the ECB's action of supplying cheap money to European banks supposedly help ease the fiscal crisis?
5. 'The fiscal compact ... is not the paving stone to fiscal federalism it pretends to be, but a form of economic dictatorship which seems to condemn much of the periphery to permanent depression.' What do you think is meant by this statement? Do you agree with it – if so why? If not, why not?

Source: **http://www.telegraph.co.uk/finance/ financialcrisis/9115590/Euroland-will-pay-for- this-monetary-madness.html** Accessed 18 March 2012.

SUMMARY

- Emerging markets refer to countries which are between developed and developing status and have low to medium GDP per capita.

- Limited growth opportunities in developed countries mean that more businesses are turning to investing in emerging economies as the source of future growth.

- Existing business models often cannot be replicated in emerging markets and as a result more creative and innovative ways of doing business may have to be thought of which meet the needs of populations which have very limited incomes.

- A common currency area (currency union or monetary union) is a geographical area through which one currency circulates and is accepted as the medium of exchange.

- The formation of a common currency area can bring significant benefits to the members of the currency union, particularly if there is already a high degree of international trade among them (i.e. a high level of trade integration). This is primarily because of the reductions in transaction costs in trade and the reduction in exchange rate uncertainty.

- There are, however, costs of joining a currency union, namely the loss of independent monetary policy and also of the exchange rate as a means of macroeconomic adjustment. Given a long-run vertical supply curve, the loss of monetary policy and the lack of exchange rate adjustment affect mainly short-run macroeconomic adjustment, however.

- These adjustment costs will be lower the greater is the degree of real wage flexibility, labour mobility and capital market integration across the currency union, and also the less the members of the currency union suffer from asymmetric demand shocks.

- The problems of adjustment within a currency union may be alleviated by fiscal federalism – a common fiscal budget and a system of taxes and fiscal transfers across member countries. In practice, however, fiscal federalism may be difficult to implement for political reasons.

- The national fiscal policies of the countries making up a currency union may be subject to a free-rider problem, whereby one country issues a large amount of government debt and pays a lower interest rate on it than it might otherwise have paid, but also leads to other member countries having to pay higher interest rates. It is for this reason that a currency union may wish to impose rules on the national fiscal policies of its members.

- Businesses have used outsourcing as a means of cutting costs and increasing efficiency but there can be problems which have to be taken into consideration in making any decision to outsource.

- There are cultural, religious and social issues that are involved in carrying out business abroad. The reduction in global boundaries means that more and more businesses operate in a global business environment and so these factors have to be taken into consideration.

KEY CONCEPTS

emerging market economy, p. 520
European Union, p. 524
Single European Market, p. 525
common currency area, p. 526

European Economic and Monetary Union, p. 526
fiscal federalism, p. 531
Stability and Growth Pact, p. 532

cyclical deficit, p. 534
structural deficit, p. 534
outsourcing, p. 535
globalization, p. 536

QUESTIONS FOR REVIEW

1. Define the term 'emerging economies' and outline the main characteristics of an emerging economy.

2. Why do an increasing number of firms believe that investment in emerging economies represents their future?

3. What are the main costs and benefits of doing business in emerging economies?

4. What are the main advantages of forming a currency union? What are the main disadvantages?

5. Are the advantages and disadvantages you have listed in answer to Question 4 long run or short run in nature?

6. What is fiscal federalism? How might the problems of macroeconomic adjustment in a currency union be alleviated by fiscal federalism?

7. Why might the members of a currency union wish to impose rules on the conduct of national fiscal policies?

8. What is 'outsourcing'?

9. Outline the main costs and benefits to a firm of outsourcing.

10. What are the main challenges to firms doing business in a global environment?

PROBLEMS AND APPLICATIONS

1. A firm is planning to invest in setting up a new manufacturing facility in an emerging economy. It aims to use some of its existing highly skilled workforce to help in the setting up of the new facility. Examine some of the challenges that the firm might typically face in executing its plans.

2. In order to be able to get permission to obtain a licence to do business in an emerging economy, senior managers have been left in no doubt that a private payment to local administrative officials will be necessary. The opportunity to do business in this country is seen as being essential to the survival of the business in the medium term and to the security of 2000 jobs in the home country. How should the senior managers handle this situation? Explain your answer.

3. Consider two countries that trade heavily with one another – Cornsylvania and Techoland. The national currency of Cornsylvania is the cob, while the Techoland national currency is the byte. The output of Cornsylvania is mainly agricultural, while the output of Techoland is mainly high-technology electronic goods. Suppose that each economy is in a long-run macroeconomic equilibrium.

   a. Use diagrams to illustrate the state of each economy. Be sure to show aggregate demand, short-run aggregate supply and long-run aggregate supply.

   b. Now suppose that there is an increase in demand for electronic goods in both countries, and a simultaneous decline in demand for agricultural goods. Use your diagrams to show what happens to output and the price level in the short run in each country. What happens to the unemployment rate in each country?

   c. Show, using your diagrams, how each country could use monetary policy to reduce the short-run fluctuation in output.

   d. Show, using your diagrams, how movements in the cob-byte exchange rate could reduce short-run fluctuations in output in each country.

4. Suppose Techoland and Cornsylvania form a currency union and adopt the electrocarrot as their common currency. Now suppose again that there is an increase in demand for electronic goods in both countries, and a simultaneous decline in demand for agricultural goods. As president of the central bank for the currency union, would you raise or lower the electrocarrot interest rate, or keep it the same? Explain. (Hint: you are charged with maintaining low and stable inflation across the electrocarrot area.)

5. Suppose that Techoland and Cornsylvania decide to engage in fiscal federalism and adopt a common fiscal budget.

   a. Show, again using aggregate demand/aggregate supply diagrams, how fiscal policy can be used to alleviate the short-run fluctuations generated by the asymmetric demand shock.

b. Given the typical lags in the implementation of fiscal policy, would you advise the use of federal fiscal policy to alleviate short-run macroeconomic fluctuations?

6. The United States can be thought of as a non-trivial currency union since, although it is a single country, it encompasses many states that have economies comparable in size to those of some European countries. Given that the USA has had a single currency for 200 years, it may be thought of as a successful currency union. Yet many of the American states produce very different products and services, so that they are likely to be impacted by different kinds of macroeconomic shocks (expansionary and recessionary) over time. For example, Texas produces oil, while Kansas produces agricultural goods. How do you explain the long-term success of the US currency union given this diversity? Are there any lessons or predictions for Europe that can be drawn from the US experience?

7. Explain, giving reasons, whether the following statements are true or false.

a. 'A high degree of trade among a group of countries implies that there would be benefits from them adopting a common currency and forming a currency union.'

b. 'A high degree of trade among a group of countries implies that they should definitely adopt a common currency and form a currency union.'

8. Do you think that the free-rider problem associated with national fiscal polices in a currency union, as we discussed in the text, is likely to be a problem in actual practice? Justify your answer.

9. Put yourself in the position of a European finance minister in March 2012 negotiating with your fellow ministers on the sovereign debt crisis. To what extent do you think the setting up of the EFSF and the Fiscal Compact will solve the sovereign debt crisis? (Your answer to this question may be helped with the benefit of hindsight!)

10. A firm closes its call centre operations in Belgium with the loss of 3000 jobs which has a significant impact on the local economy where the call centre was located. It outsources the operation to Malaysia and its press release says that it will reduce costs as a result by €1 million a year. After the first six months the firm begins to receive complaints from customers that they are not happy with the level of service which they receive from the new call centre operation. What should the firm do in this situation? (Hint – you might want to consider as part of your answer why customers use the call centre in the first place.)

GLOSSARY

abnormal profit the profit over and above normal profit

absolute advantage the ability to produce a good using fewer inputs than another producer

accounting profit total revenue minus total explicit cost

actual spending, saving or investment the realized or ex post outcome resulting from actions of households and firms

added value the difference between the cost of factor inputs into production and the amount consumers are prepared to pay (the value placed on the product by consumers)

adverse selection the tendency for the mix of unobserved attributes to become undesirable from the standpoint of an uninformed party

agency theory where managers act as the agents of shareholders and as a result there may be a divorce between ownership and control such that managers pursue their own self-interests rather than the interests of shareholders

agent a person who is performing an act for another person, called the principal

aggregate demand curve a curve that shows the quantity of goods and services that households, firms and the government want to buy at each price level

aggregate supply curve a curve that shows the quantity of goods and services that firms choose to produce and sell at each price level

aims the long-term goals of a business

appreciation an increase in the value of a currency as measured by the amount of foreign currency it can buy

autonomous expenditure spending which is not dependent on income

average fixed cost fixed costs divided by the quantity of output

average revenue total revenue divided by the quantity sold

average total cost total cost divided by the quantity of output

average variable cost variable costs divided by the quantity of output

B2B business business activity where the business sells goods and services to another business

B2C business business activity where the business sells goods and services to a final consumer

balanced trade a situation in which exports equal imports

bond a certificate of indebtedness

bounded rationality the idea that humans make decisions under the constraints of limited, and sometimes unreliable, information, that they face limits to the amount of information they can process and that they face time constraints in making decisions

branding the means by which a business creates an identity for itself and highlights the way in which it differs from its rivals

break-even the level of output/sales at which total cost equals total revenue found by dividing the fixed costs by the contribution (selling price minus variable costs per unit)

budget constraint the limit on the consumption bundles that a consumer can afford

business cycle fluctuations in economic activity, such as employment and production

C2C business business activity where consumers exchange goods and services often facilitated by a third party such as an online auction site

capital any item used in production which is not used for its own sake but for what it contributes to production

cartel a group of firms acting in unison

classical dichotomy the theoretical separation of nominal and real variables

collective bargaining the process by which unions and firms agree on the terms of employment

collusion an agreement among firms in a market about quantities to produce or prices to charge

common currency area (or currency union or monetary union) a geographical area throughout which a single currency circulates as the medium of exchange

common resources goods that are rival but not excludable

comparative advantage the comparison among producers of a good according to their opportunity cost

compensating differential a difference in wages that arises to offset the non-monetary characteristics of different jobs

competition a situation when two or more firms are rivals for customers. Each firm strives to gain the attention and custom of buyers in the market

competitive market a market in which there are many buyers and many sellers so that each has a negligible impact on the market price

complements two goods for which an increase in the price of one leads to a decrease in the demand for the other (and vice versa).

compounding the accumulation of a sum of money in, say, a bank account where the interest earned remains in the account to earn additional interest in the future

constant returns to scale the property whereby long-run average total cost stays the same as the quantity of output changes

consumer prices index (CPI) a measure of the overall prices of the goods and services bought by a typical consumer

consumer surplus the amount a buyer is willing to pay for a good minus the amount the buyer actually pays for it

consumption spending by households on goods and services, with the exception of purchases of new housing

contribution the difference between the selling price and the variable cost per unit

core competencies the things a business does which are the source of competitive advantage over its rivals

cost refers to the payment to factor inputs in production.

cost leadership a strategy to gain competitive advantage through reducing costs below competitors

cross-price elasticity of demand a measure of how much the quantity demanded of one good responds to a change in the price of another good, computed as the percentage change in quantity demanded of the first good divided by the percentage change in the price of the second good

crowding out a decrease in investment that results from government borrowing

crowding-out effect the offset in aggregate demand that results when expansionary fiscal policy raises the interest rate and thereby reduces investment spending

cyclical deficit a situation when government spending and income is disrupted by the 'normal' economic cycle

cyclical unemployment the deviation of unemployment from its natural rate

deadweight loss the fall in total surplus that results from a market distortion, such as a tax

deflationary gap the difference between full employment output and the expenditure required to meet it

demand curve a graph of the relationship between the price of a good and the quantity demanded

demand schedule a table that shows the relationship between the price of a good and the quantity demanded

depreciation a decrease in the value of a currency as measured by the amount of foreign currency it can buy

depression a severe recession

deregulation the removal of controls, laws or rules governing a particular market aimed at improving the economic efficiency of that market and therefore the performance of the economy at the microeconomic level

derived demand when demand for a factor of production is derived (determined) from its decision to supply a good in another market

differentiation the way in which a firm seeks to portray or present itself as being different or unique in some way

diminishing marginal product the property whereby the marginal product of an input declines as the quantity of the input increases

diminishing marginal utility a 'law' that states that marginal utility will fall as consumption increases

discrimination the offering of different opportunities to similar individuals who differ only by race, ethnic group, sex, age or other personal characteristics

diseconomies of scale the property whereby long-run average total cost rises as the quantity of output increases

dominant strategy a strategy that is best for a player in a game regardless of the strategies chosen by the other players

economic activity the amount of buying and selling (transactions) that take place in an economy over a period of time

economic growth the increase in the amount of goods and services in an economy over a period of time

economic profit total revenue minus total cost, including both explicit and implicit costs

economics the study of how society manages its scarce resources

economies of scale the property whereby long-run average total cost falls as the quantity of output increases

efficiency the property of society getting the most it can from its scarce resources

efficiency wages above-equilibrium wages paid by firms in order to increase worker productivity

efficient scale the quantity of output that minimizes average total cost

elasticity a measure of the responsiveness of quantity demanded or quantity supplied to a change in one of its determinants

emerging market economy a country where the per capita income of the population is in the middle to low range compared to the rest of the global economies

enterprise the act of taking risks in the organization of factors of production to generate business activity

equilibrium a situation in which the price has reached the level where quantity supplied equals quantity demanded

equilibrium price the price that balances quantity supplied and quantity demanded

equilibrium quantity the quantity supplied and the quantity demanded at the equilibrium price

equity the property of distributing economic prosperity fairly among the members of society

ethical responsibility the moral basis for business activity and whether what the business does is 'right' and is underpinned by some moral purpose — doing what is 'right'.

European Economic and Monetary Union (EMU) the European currency union that has adopted the euro as its common currency

European Union a family of democratic European countries, committed to working together for peace and prosperity

excludable the property of a good whereby a person can be prevented from using it when they do not pay for it

expected utility theory the idea that buyers can rank preferences from best to worst (or vice versa)

explicit costs input costs that require an outlay of money by the firm

exports goods produced domestically and sold abroad

externality the uncompensated impact of one person's actions on the well-being of a bystander or third party

factors of production a classification of inputs used in business activity which includes land, labour, capital and enterprise

financial intermediaries financial institutions through which savers can indirectly provide funds to borrowers

financial markets financial institutions through which savers can directly provide funds to borrowers

fiscal federalism a fiscal system for a group of countries involving a common fiscal budget and a system of taxes and fiscal transfers across countries

fiscal policy influencing the level of economic activity though manipulation of government income and expenditure

fixed costs costs that are not determined by the quantity of output produced

free cash flow the cash generated from the firm's operations minus that spent on capital assets

frictional unemployment unemployment that results because it takes time for workers to search for the jobs that best suit their tastes and skills

full employment a point where those people who want to work at the going market wage level are able to find a job

fundamental analysis the study of an asset to determine its value

future value the amount of money in the future that an amount of money today will yield, given prevailing interest rates

game theory the study of how people behave in strategic situations

GDP deflator a measure of the price level calculated as the ratio of nominal GDP to real GDP times 100

geographical mobility the ease with which people can move to different parts of the country where jobs may be available

globalization the growth of inter-dependence amongst world economies usually seen as resulting from the removal of many international regulations affecting financial flows

government purchases spending on goods and services by local, state and national governments

gross domestic product (GDP) the market value of all final goods and services produced within a country in a given period of time

gross domestic product per head the market value of all final goods and services produced within a country in a given period of time divided by the population of a country to give a per capita figure

heuristics rules of thumb or shortcuts used in decision making

human capital the accumulation of investments in people, such as education and on-the-job training

implicit costs input costs that do not require an outlay of money by the firm

imports goods produced abroad and purchased for use in the domestic economy

income effect that part of the increase in quantity demanded which can be attributed to a rise in real income as a result of a fall in the price of a good meaning the consumer can now afford to purchase more of the good

income elasticity of demand a measure of how much the quantity demanded of a good responds to a change in consumers' income, computed as the percentage change in quantity demanded divided by the percentage change in income

indifference curve a curve that shows consumption bundles that give the consumer the same level of satisfaction

inferior good a good for which, other things equal, an increase in income leads to a decrease in demand (and vice versa)

inflation an increase in the overall level of prices in the economy

inflation rate the percentage change in the price index from the preceding period

inflation tax the revenue the government raises by creating money

internalizing an externality altering incentives so that people take account of the external effects of their actions

investment making money available to develop a project which will generate future returns including increasing future productive capacity

investment fund an institution that sells shares to the public and uses the proceeds to buy a portfolio of stocks and bonds

isocost line the different combination of factor inputs which can be purchased with a given budget

job search the process by which workers find appropriate jobs given their tastes and skills

labour all the human effort, mental and physical, which is used in production

labour force the total number of workers, including both the employed and the unemployed

labour force participation rate (or economic activity rate) the percentage of the adult population that is in the labour force

land all the natural resources of the earth which can be used in production

law of demand the claim that, other things equal, the quantity demanded of a good falls when the price of the good rises

law of supply the claim that, other things equal, the quantity supplied of a good rises when the price of the good rises

law of supply and demand the claim that the price of any good adjusts to bring the quantity supplied and the quantity demanded for that good into balance

long run the period of time in which all factors of production can be altered

macroeconomic environment the national or global economy within which the business operates

margin the amount of profit a firm makes on each sale

margin of safety the distance between the break-even output and current production where total revenue is greater than total cost

marginal changes small incremental adjustments to a plan of action

marginal cost the increase in total cost that arises from an extra unit of production

marginal product the increase in output that arises from an additional unit of input

marginal product of labour the increase in the amount of output from an additional unit of labour

marginal propensity to consume the fraction of extra income that a household spends rather than saves

marginal propensity to save the fraction of extra income that a household saves rather than consumes

marginal rate of substitution the rate at which a consumer is willing to trade one good for another

marginal rate of technical substitution the rate at which one factor input can be substituted for another at a given level of output

marginal revenue the change in total revenue from an additional unit sold

marginal utility the addition to total utility as a result of one extra unit of consumption

market a group of buyers and sellers of a particular good or service

market economy an economy that allocates resources through the decentralized decisions of many firms and households as they interact in markets for goods and services

market failure a situation in which a market left on its own fails to allocate resources efficiently

market for loanable funds the market in which those who want to save supply funds and those who want to borrow to invest demand funds

market niche a small segment of an existing market with specific wants and needs which are not currently being met by the market

market power the ability of a single economic agent (or small group of agents) to have a substantial influence on market prices

market share the proportion of total sales accounted for by a product/business in a market

menu costs the costs of changing prices

merit good a good which could be provided by the private sector but which may also be offered by the public sector because it is believed that a less than optimal amount would be available to the public if resource allocation was left entirely to the private sector

microeconomic environment factors and issues that affect an individual firm operating in a particular market or industry

model of aggregate demand and aggregate supply the model that most economists use to explain short-run fluctuations in economic activity around its long-run trend

monetary neutrality the proposition that changes in the money supply do not affect real variables

monetary policy the set of actions taken by the central bank in order to affect the money supply

money multiplier the amount of money the banking system generates with each unit of reserves

monopolistic competition a market structure in which many firms sell products that are similar but not identical

monopoly a firm that is the sole seller of a product without close substitutes

moral hazard the tendency of a person who is imperfectly monitored to engage in dishonest or otherwise undesirable behaviour

multiplier effect the additional shifts in aggregate demand that result when expansionary fiscal policy increases income and thereby increases consumer spending

Nash equilibrium a situation in which economic actors interacting with one another each choose their best strategy given the strategies that all the other actors have chosen

natural monopoly a monopoly that arises because a single firm can supply a good or service to an entire market at a smaller cost than could two or more firms

natural rate of output the output level in an economy when all existing factors of production (land, labour, capital and technology resources) are fully utilized and where unemployment is at its natural rate

natural rate of unemployment the normal rate of unemployment around which the unemployment rate fluctuates

natural-rate hypothesis the claim that unemployment eventually returns to its normal, or natural, rate, regardless of the rate of inflation

needs the essentials of life such as food, water, clothing and shelter, without which it would be difficult to survive

net capital outflow the purchase of foreign assets by domestic residents minus the purchase of domestic assets by foreigners

net exports spending on domestically produced goods by foreigners (exports) minus spending on foreign goods by domestic residents (imports)

nominal exchange rate the rate at which a person can trade the currency of one country for the currency of another

nominal GDP the production of goods and services valued at current prices

nominal interest rate the interest rate as usually reported without a correction for the effects of inflation

nominal variables variables measured in monetary units

normal good a good for which, other things equal, an increase in income leads to an increase in demand (and vice versa)

normal profit the minimum amount required to keep factors of production in their current use

objectives the means by which a business will be able to achieve its aims

occupational mobility the ease with which people are able to move from occupation to occupation including the degree to which skills and qualifications are transferable between occupations

oligopoly competition amongst the few – a market structure in which only a few sellers offer similar or identical products and dominate the market

opportunity cost whatever must be given up to obtain some item — the value of the benefits foregone (sacrificed)

outsourcing contracting out of a part of the business' operations to another organization

Phillips curve a curve that shows the short-run trade-off between inflation and unemployment

Pigovian tax a tax enacted to correct the effects of a negative externality

planned spending, saving or investment the desired or intended actions of households and firms

present value the amount of money today that would be needed to produce, using prevailing interest rates, a given future amount of money

price the amount of money a buyer (a business or a consumer) has to give up in order to acquire something.

price discrimination the business practice of selling the same good at different prices to different customers

price elasticity of demand a measure of how much the quantity demanded of a good responds to a change in the price of that good, computed as the percentage change in quantity demanded divided by the percentage change in price

price elasticity of supply a measure of how much the quantity supplied of a good responds to a change in the price of that good, computed as the percentage change in quantity supplied divided by the percentage change in price

price level the price of a basket of goods and services measured as the weighted arithmetic average of current prices

principal a person for whom another person, called the agent, is performing some act

prisoners' dilemma a particular 'game' between two captured prisoners that illustrates why cooperation is difficult to maintain even when it is mutually beneficial

private goods goods that are both excludable and rival

private saving the income that households have left after paying for taxes and consumption

private sector that part of the economy where business activity is owned, controlled and financed by private individuals

producer price index a measure of the change in prices of a basket of goods and services bought by firms

producer surplus the amount a seller is paid minus the cost of production

product life cycle a diagram representing the life cycle of a product from launch through to growth, maturity and decline

production function the relationship between quantity of inputs used to make a good and the quantity of output of that good

production isoquant a function which represents all the possible combinations of factor inputs that can be used to produce a given level of output

productivity the quantity of goods and services produced from each hour of a worker's time

profit total revenue minus total cost

property rights the exclusive right of an individual, group or organization to determine how a resource is used

public goods goods that are neither excludable nor rival

public saving the tax revenue that the government has left after paying for its spending

public sector that part of the economy where business activity is owned, financed and controlled by the government or its agencies on behalf of the public as a whole

purchasing power parity a theory of exchange rates whereby a unit of any given currency should be able to buy the same quantity of goods in all countries

quantity demanded the amount of a good that buyers are willing and able to purchase

quantity supplied the amount of a good that sellers are willing and able to sell

quantity theory of money a theory asserting that the quantity of money available determines the price level and that the growth rate in the quantity of money available determines the inflation rate

rational expectations the theory according to which people optimally use all the information they have, including information about government policies, when forecasting the future

reaction function the profit-maximizing output for a firm given the simultaneous output decisions of its rivals

real exchange rate the rate at which a person can trade the goods and services of one country for the goods and services of another

real GDP a measure of the amount produced that is not affected by changes in prices

real interest rate the interest rate corrected for the effects of inflation

real money balances what money can actually buy given the ratio of the money supply to the price level M/P

real variables variables measured in physical units

recession a period of declining real incomes and rising unemployment. The technical definition gives recession occurring after two successive quarters of negative economic growth

residual demand the difference between the market demand curve and the amount supplied by other firms in the market

risk the extent to which a decision leading to a course of action will result in some loss, damage, adverse effect or otherwise undesirable outcome to the decision maker

risk averse exhibiting a dislike of uncertainty

rival the property of a good whereby one person's use diminishes other people's use

sacrifice ratio the number of percentage points of annual output lost in the process of reducing inflation by 1 percentage point

scarce resources resources that are insufficient in quantity relative to the demand for them

scarcity the limited nature of society's resources

screening an action taken by an uninformed party to induce an informed party to reveal information

shareholder value the overall value delivered to the owners of business in the form of cash generated and the reputation and potential of the business to continue growing over time

shoe leather costs the resources wasted when inflation encourages people to reduce their money holdings

short run the period of time in which some factors of production cannot be changed

shortage a situation in which quantity demanded is greater than quantity supplied

signalling an action taken by an informed party to reveal private information to an uninformed party

Single European Market a (still-not-complete) EU-wide market throughout which labour, capital, goods and services can move freely

social responsibility the responsibility a firm has for the impact of their product and activities on society.

Stability and Growth Pact a set of formal rules by which members of EMU were supposed to be bound in their conduct of national fiscal policy

stagflation a period of falling output and rising prices

stakeholder any group or individual with an interest in a business such as workers, managers, suppliers, the local community, customers and owners

standard of living a measure of welfare based on the amount of goods and services a person's income can buy

stock (or share or equity) a claim to partial ownership in a firm

strategic intent a framework for establishing and sharing a vision of where a business wants to be at some point in the future and encouraging all those involved in the business to understand and work towards achieving this vision

strategy a series of actions, decisions and obligations which lead to the firm gaining a competitive advantage and exploiting the firm's core competencies

strike the organized withdrawal of labour from a firm by a union

structural deficit a situation where the deficit is not dependent on movements in the economic cycle

structural unemployment unemployment that results because the number of jobs available in some labour markets is insufficient to provide a job for everyone who wants one

subsidy a payment to buyers and sellers to supplement income or lower costs and which thus encourages consumption or provides an advantage to the recipient

substitutes two goods for which an increase in the price of one leads to an increase in the demand for the other

substitution effect that part of the increase in quantity demanded for a good which can be attributed to consumers switching from other goods which now appear more expensive

sunk cost a cost that has already been committed and cannot be recovered

supply chain the various processes, activities, organizations and resources used in moving a product from business to business or business to consumer

supply curve a graph of the relationship between the price of a good and the quantity supplied

supply schedule a table that shows the relationship between the price of a good and the quantity supplied

supply shock an event that directly alters firms' costs and prices, shifting the economy's aggregate supply curve and thus the Phillips curve

supply-side policy policy aimed at influencing the level of aggregate supply in the economy

surplus a situation in which quantity supplied is greater than quantity demanded

SWOT analysis an analysis of the firm's strengths, weaknesses, opportunities and threats

synergy situation where the combination of two or more businesses or business operations brings total benefits which are greater than those which would arise from the separate business entities

tactic short-term framework for decision making

tax incidence the manner in which the burden of a tax is shared among participants in a market

technology the application or use of knowledge in some way which enables individuals or businesses to have greater control over their environment

theory of liquidity preference Keynes' theory that the interest rate adjusts to bring money supply and money demand into balance

total cost the market value of the inputs a firm uses in production

total expenditure the amount paid by buyers, computed as the price of the good times the quantity purchased

total revenue the amount received by sellers of a good, computed as the price of the good times the quantity sold

trade balance the value of a nation's exports minus the value of its imports; also called net exports

trade deficit an excess of imports over exports

trade surplus an excess of exports over imports

transfer payment a payment for which no good or service is exchanged

transformation process the process in which businesses take factor inputs and process them to produce outputs which are then sold

underemployment a situation where a worker has a job but may not be working to full capacity or does not have all their skills utilised or is working for a lower income than their qualifications, training or experience might suggest

unemployment insurance a government programme that partially protects workers' incomes when they become unemployed

unemployment rate the percentage of the labour force that is unemployed

union a worker association that bargains with employers over wages and working conditions

utility the satisfaction derived from consumption

value the worth to an individual of owning an item represented by the satisfaction derived from its consumption

value chain the activities and operations which a firm carries out and how value is added at each of these stages

value for money a situation (mostly subjective) where the satisfaction gained from purchasing and consuming a product is greater than the amount of money the individual had to hand over to acquire it (the price)

value of the marginal product the marginal product of an input times the price of the output

variable costs costs that are dependent on the quantity of output produced

wants all the things we would like to have which we believe make our lives more comfortable and happy

willingness to pay a measure of how much a buyer values a good by the amount they are prepared to pay to acquire the good